Para Bráulio do Nascimento,
amigo sem par e ilustre pioneiro
no estudo do Conde Claros

CONTENTS

Judeo-Spanish Ballads
from Oral Tradition

FOLK LITERATURE OF THE SEPHARDIC JEWS
IV

Judeo-Spanish Ballads from Oral Tradition
III. Carolingian Ballads (2):
Conde Claros

collected by
SAMUEL G. ARMISTEAD
JOSEPH H. SILVERMAN
and
ISRAEL J. KATZ

Edition and study by
SAMUEL G. ARMISTEAD
With musical transcriptions and studies by
ISRAEL J. KATZ

Technical Editor
KAREN L. OLSON

Juan de la Cuesta
Newark, Delaware

The publication of this book was made possible by a generous grant from the Program for Cultural Cooperation between Spain's Ministry of Education and Culture and United States Universities.

MANUFACTURED IN THE UNITED STATES OF AMERICA

ISBN: 978-1-58871-058-1

PLATES

INTRODUCTION

In *Folk Literature of the Sephardic Jews*, Vol. IV, we continue the multivolume edition and study of our extensive collection of Eastern Mediterranean and North African Judeo-Spanish ballads brought together in the United States, Spain, Morocco, and Israel, between 1957 and 1980.[1] As in previous volumes, chapter divisions are determined by traditional combinations of narrative themes. The present volume consists of just two chapters devoted primarily to *romances* concerned with Count Claros de Montalbán:

Chapter 10: *Conde Claros y el esmperador + Conde Claros insomne + La jactancia del conde Vélez*

Chapter 11: *El nacimiento de Bernardo del Carpio + Conde Claros y la infanta + Conde Claros vestido de fraile*

We maintain the format and the critical objectives which inform previous volumes: to place each ballad within the modern Judeo-Spanish subtraditions and to define its relationship to the 16h-century Spanish tradition, to other modern Hispanic subtraditions, and, where analogues exist in other European linguistic domains, to study these as well; to document the presence of traditional motifs and topoi shared with other genres of medieval literature and modern international folk-narrative; and to study each ballad as an oral poem, a work of oral literature, elaborated over centuries of collective authorship by the uncounted and uncountable individuals who make up the *autor legión*.[2] The

---

1. Concerning our fieldwork, the localities represented, and the ballad narratives comprising our collection, see *Epic Ballads* (= FLSJ, II, pp. 4–16. The collection consists of approximately 1,485 texts (720 from the Eastern and 765 from the North African tradition). Some 183 different text-types are represented. In the chapter headings, each title is followed by a reference to the ballad's assonance (e.g. *á-e*) and to pertinent theme numbers in Menéndez Pidal's "Catálogo" (MP) and in my *Catálogo-índice* (CMP) (e.g. 23/B9 = MP 23 and CMP B9). For works cited by short titles or abbreviations, see the general bibliography at the end of the volume.

2. Concerning the concept of the *autor-legión*—all singers of a given ballad, in all its multiple variations, in whatever geographic subtraditions it may be sung and throughout

edition and study of the ballad texts is complemented by transcriptions of the music and each chapter includes a detailed synchronic and diachronic study of the ballads' musicological component.[3]

In approaching the ballads of Conde Claros, we temporarily set aside our concern with epic-balladic relationships to study in detail the four intricately entwined Claros narratives that have survived in Sephardic tradition, together with two other narrative themes which have come to be associated with them in the North African tradition: *La jactancia del conde Vélez* and *El nacimiento de Bernardo del Carpio*. As an indispensable prerequisite to such a complex task, we propose our own classification of the seven different Claros narratives that can be documented in the early tradition.

Despite sundry—and strategic—allusions to Francia, Montalbán, Carlos "el emperante," Roldán, Oliveros, Reinaldos, Montesinos, Urgel, and Beltrán, which seek to suggest the Claros narratives' Carolingian ambience, these gallant, amorous stories have essentially nothing to do with the medieval French epic. Claros de Montalbán may suggest some distant connection with the French hero, Renaud de Montauban, but the ballads of Conde Claros have no epic antecedents that we know of and must be characterized as Pseudo-Carolingian. The Conde Vélez ballad's Carolingian connections are even more tenuous: Here, though we are again at a royal court, with its attendant counts and dukes—one of whom is even identified in some of the Eastern versions as the Emperor's son—there is no substantive indication that this poem has anything at all to do with Charlemagne.[4] As to *Bernardo del Carpio*, the epic story evolves in a Carolingian context, but this particular ballad derives from a *romance viejo* which cannot be shown to relate in direct oral tradition to any epic antecedent.[5] In the present volume, we will, then, address concerns other than epic ancestry,

---

the centuries of its existence, are its collective authors—see RoH, I, 49–50, 233–234, 258–259.

3. For other features and criteria, see the introductions to FLSJ, II and III.

4. By contrast, one of the early versions of *La jactancia del conde Vélez* places the scene "en las cortes de León" and the other ballad referring to Vélez—*La prisión del conde Vélez*—also reflects a Spanish ambience: "Alterada esta Castilla / por vn caso desastrado // . . . con vna prima carnal / del rey Sancho el desseado" (*Silva* [1550], p. 453; Catalán, *Por campos*, p. 169).

5. See RT, I, 176–184. On the other hand, *Con cartas y mensajeros* (= *Primav.* 13a) and its early congeners do ultimately derive from a lost **Gesta de Bernardo*, but its only modern survivals—among Andalusian Gypsies—represent a traditionalization of late written versions (RT, I, 153–175; particularly pp. 164 and 175).

which are nonetheless of vital importance to the study of the *Romancero* as an oral-traditional genre.

The Conde Claros ballads offer a particularly complex example of the creative uses of contamination and of the modern tradition's consistent independence vis-à-vis the 16th-century printings, which, at best, offer a very partial and gravely deficient reflection of the realities of the early ballad tradition.[6]

In Chapter 10, after identifying the diverse narrative components concerned with Conde Claros in the 16th-century *Romancero*, we go on to study the complex juxtaposition of *Conde Claros y el Emperador* and *Conde Claros insomne* in the Sephardic subtraditions. *La jactancia del conde Vélez*, for its part, has suggested other crucially important perspectives on the intricate relationship between verse and prose narratives in oral tradition. Each of the ballad's three modern geographic modalities—León-Zamora, Morocco, and the Sephardic East—turns out to embody distinctive narrative features present also in local variants of a Pan-Hispanic (and Pan-European) folktale, likewise concerned with the chastity wager motif. *La jactancia del conde Vélez* thus throws new light on the complex traditional interaction of ballads and folktales, while stressing once again the futility of attempting to reduce oral literature to conventional stemmas and stable textual antecedents.[7] In studying *Conde Vélez*, we also explore the Hispanic ballad's distant analogues in the Scottish, German, Danish, and Modern Greek traditions: *The Twa Knights* and *Redesdale and Wise William*; *Die Wette*; *Vædemaalet*; and *Mavrianós and his Sister*.

In Chapter 11, we study *Conde Claros y la infanta* and *Conde Claros fraile*. While the Claros ballads studied in Chapter 10 survive only tenuously in the modern Peninsular tradition, both *Infanta* and very especially *Fraile* have richly documented modern avatars—*Fraile* being without doubt the most widely known Carolingian (or Pseudo-Carolingian) narrative in the modern repertoire. We study in detail these two ballads' symbiosis with a number of other balladic text-types in all the various subtraditions where they occur and thus, hopefully, we may help to clarify one of the most intricate thematic problems in Hispanic

---

6. On contamination, see Joseph H. Silverman, "La contaminación como arte," and concerning the incomplete character of the early evidence, S. G. Armistead, "Neo-Individualism and the *Romancero*," pp. 174–177.

7. See Diego Catalán, "El romancero medieval," pp. 482–484, and now *Arte poética*, I, 240–241. Joseph Duggan reaches identical conclusions concerning the French epic, in "Oral Performance," p. 89.

ballad scholarship.[8] Our approach to Conde Claros fraile also includes a comparative study of the ballad's extra-Hispanic congeners: the Scottish and Anglo-American *Lady Maisry*, the German *König von Mailand*, and the Hungarian *Dishonored Maiden*. Chapter 11 concludes with an analysis of *El nacimiento de Bernardo del Carpio*, which, as in numerous other cases, exemplifies the dynamic, poetic creativity of the modern oral tradition. The North African Sephardic tradition breaks with earlier tradition to invent an entirely new, novelesque dénouement, exemplifying the esteemed traditional and Biblical figure of the valiant woman (*ešeth ḥayil*) who appears in so many other ballads in the Moroccan tradition.[9]

If the ballads of Conde Claros have been enormously popular and have achieved vast diffusion in the Hispanic tradition, they have also justifiably attracted the attention of several contemporary ballad scholars. In her recent book, Judith Seeger has made a fundamental contribution to scholarship, suggesting, however, an approach to the problem of classification quite different from our own.[10] In his monumental two-volume study on Carolingian ballads in the Portuguese tradition, João David Pinto Correia proposes a semiotic approach to the analysis of ballad narratives and also provides a massive and enormously useful anthology of Count Claros narratives (Vol. I, 137–233).[11] The problems involved in analyzing the *Conde Claros* ballads are enormously complex. The present pages were written, at least in preliminary form (1989–1990), before either Judith Seeger's or João David Pinto Correia's eminently learned publications appeared in print (1990 and 1993–1994 respectively). What is suggested in the present study is one possible proposal for sorting out the narrative types in which Count Claros appears. It would not be productive to debate here the relative merits of our various approaches to classifying the ballads in question. It is encouraging to note, however, that such distinguished

---

8. Such contaminations include *La infanta parida, Aliarda y el alabancioso, Conde Claros insomne, Conde Claros preso, La canción del huérfano, El caballero burlado, Don Bueso, La fuente fecundante, La mala hierba*, and *La apuesta ganada*, to say nothing here of other sporadic associations. Note Braulio do Nascimento's fine study on "*Conde Claros* na Tradição Portuguesa."

9. On the Moroccan ballad's break with tradition, see RT, I, 184; for the valiant woman motif, see Rosalía Guzofsky's pathfinding study (*Mujeres valientes*).

10. See also her ancillary articles, "The Curious Case of *Conde Claros*"; "El «Conde Claros de Montalbán» en el siglo XVI"; "Can a Traditional Ballad be Myth?" and also her thought-provoking discussion of "Genre and the Ballad" (preliminary version: "Just How Bounded is the Ballad?").

11. Note also his earlier article, "Le cycle des romances du *Conde Claros*."

ballad scholars as Braulio do Nascimento, Manuel da Costa Fontes, and Pere Ferré da Ponte have chosen to follow the classification system proposed in the *Catálogo-Indice* of Judeo-Spanish ballads at the Archivo Menéndez Pidal (CMP) and refined, with reference to the *Conde Claros* ballads, on the present pages.[12]

A final note concerning some indispensable recent pubications: Lamentable circumstances, now, thankfully, of no more than anecdotal interest, made it necessary for S.G.A. to become co-chair of the Department of Spanish and Classics during the academic years 2001–2002 and 2002–2003. Before that time, FLSJ, IV, V, VI and VII had already been prepared in final form and, except for a good part of the general bibliographies, the various indices, and the glossaries, the full text of each volume had already been input on the computer. Further concerted work toward bringing these volumes to press during 2001–2003 came to be out of the question. So in each case, these four volumes of FLSJ will reflect a certain, hopefully almost imperceptible, time lag. We have done our very best to bridge it, but in certain cases it may still be evident. During those years, a number of crucially important contributions to our field were to appear in print or, at least, become available to us. They are Manuel Alvar, *El judeo español* (2003); Margit Frenk, *Nuevo Corpus de la antigua lírica* (2003); José Labrador (et al.), *Cancionero sevillano de Lisboa* (2003); José M. Pedrosa (et al.), *Héroes, santos, moros y brujas* (2001); Hilary S. Pomeroy, *The Sephardic Ballad Notebook of Halia Isaac Cohen* (2001); and Josep Romeu i Figueras, *Corpus d'antiga poesia popular* (2000). Where possible, we have tried to cite in vols. IV–VII these splendid and enormously useful sources, but it has, as yet, been impossible to make the full use of them that they indubitably deserve. It goes without saying, that, in subsequent volumes, *Deo volente*, they will inevitably occupy a plenary situation, as part of our scholarly apparatus.

———— · ————

Many friends and colleagues have given indispensable help with the multiple problems involved in the present study. First and foremost, we acknowledge here the magnificent editorial contribution of Karen L. Olson, our technical

---

12. See B. do Nascimento, "*Conde Claros* na Tradição Portuguesa," espec. pp. 140–147, and "Conde Claros Confessor," p. 549; M. da Costa Fontes, *O Romanceiro Português e Brasileiro* (= RPI); Pere Ferré and Cristina Carinhas, *Bibliografia do Romanceiro Português* (= BRP). The discrete narrative types presented in CMP were first suggested in *Yoná*, pp. 74–86 (FLSJ, I).

editor, who has consistently—and with great patience—captured and emended many a *gazapo* and whose sensitivity, not only to technical problems, but to philological and literary ones as well, has in every sense made possible the creation of this volume.

Diego Catalán, with the help of Ana Valenciano and Mariano de la Campa, has made available innumerable unedited texts and musical transcriptions from the Menéndez Pidal Archive, thus incalculably broadening and enriching our comparative perspectives. We also wish to thank very especially our friends Manuel da Costa Fontes, Pere Ferré da Ponte, and José Manuel Pedrosa for their unfailing generosity and their philological and bibliographic expertise. Arthur L.-F. Askins, with the characteristic generosity all of us working in this field have come to take for granted, has answered many a question and solved many a problem. James T. Monroe and Bruce Rosenstock have generously helped, respectively, with Arabic and Hebrew problems and David Traill has graciously checked some of the Latin translations. Thanks go also to Oro Anahory Librowicz and Rosalía Guzofsky for generously making available still unedited texts and offering invaluable advice. The following friends and colleagues have offered invaluable help in regard to the book's musicological component: María Amparo Amat Tuduri, Eduardo Anglada, Joana Crespi, Joaquín Díaz, Genoveva Galvez, John Griffiths, María José Rucio Zamorano, John M. Ward, and Rodrigo de Zayas.

Preliminary transcriptions of many of the Moroccan ballads were prepared many years ago by Jacqueline Thompson Elpers and they continue to be enormously useful as our work goes forward. At an early stage in proofreading, Kathryn Robinson's expert help was invaluable, as was that of Janet Casaverde during the later stages of this work. During the final countdown of going to press, Esther Fernández's and David Jerez Gómez's intrepid and infallibly accurate help was also crucial. The Interlibrary Loan Department at Shields Library, at the University of California, Davis, under the direction of Mary Helen Moreno, accomplished marvels in obtaining numerous works of difficult access.

Very special thanks go also to Carolyn Jamison, of the Department of Spanish and Classics at U.C. Davis, for her infallible administrative help and generous encouragement of our ongoing work, as also to Katherine Perrone, who, at a later date, expertly took over from Carolyn. Unlimited thanks and appreciation, as always, go also to Nancy Loeb, of California State University, Sacramento, for her vast knowledge of grantsmanship and her kind and expert advice so often and so generously offered.

Robert Blake's brilliant chairmanship of the Department of Spanish and Classics at U.C. Davis provided ideal conditions for the advancement of this work. His ongoing support is most gratefully acknowledged. This same tradition of devoted concern for scholarship has been flawlessly and brilliantly nurtured by Emilio Bejel, who, as of 2003, took charge of the departmental chairmanship. During early stages of our work, Dr. Robert Shelton (as Vice Chancellor for Research and Professor of Physics at U.C. Davis) was as enthusiastic as any Hispano-Medievalist in his generous support of our work. In 1989, S.G.A. was awarded a University of California President's Research Fellowship in the Humanities in support of the preliminary stages in the preparation of the present volume. From 1981 through to the present, the National Endowment for the Humanities generously supported this project through a series of Fellowships involving release time and electronic equipment. Their invaluable support is gratefully acknowledged, with very special thanks going to Margot Backas, for her expert and generously offered advice. The Lucius N. Littauer Foundation also continued generously to support our work through a series of grants. To all concerned go our heartfelt thanks and appreciation.

S.G.A. - I.J.K.

THE BALLADS

10

Conde Claros y el emperador (á-e) +
Conde Claros insomne (á) + La jactancia
del conde Vélez (ó)
(Count Claros and the Emperor + Sleepless Count
Claros + Count Vélez's Boast)
(23/B9 + B11 + B22)

10*A*

Fragment from Salonika (Greece), recited by Flor Tevet, 85 years, collected by I. J. K., at the old age home, Beth Avoth León Recanati, in Kiryat Matalón (Petah Tikva, Israel), August 25, 1971.

Se pa - se - an tí - o sov - ri - no, ǵun tos, van de un ba - ra - bar.

Por ca - yes que ha - ví - a gen- te hav -la - van de̦a va - gar.

1

Por ca - yes que no ha-ví- a   gen- te,   lo que le - sim - por- ta   más.

-- U- na mer-sed le   ro - go,   tí - o,   si me la pue-da a tor - gar.

Que me dé a Blan - ca-   ni - ña, por mu - jer y por i - gual.

-- Ca - za- da la   ten - goel   Fran-sia por sien do -ble-sy al - go   más.

Gue-rre- ro sox, el   mi   so - vri - no, la po - déis muy bien ga - nar.

Se pasean tío y sovrino,   ǧuntos van d'un barabar.
2 Por cayes que havía ǧente,   havlavan de avagar.
   Por cayes que no havía ǧente,   lo que les importa más.
4 —Una mersed le rogo, tío,   si me la pueda atorgar:
   Que me dé a Blancaniña,   por mujer y por igual.
6 —Cazada la tengo'n Fransia,   por sien dobles y algo más.
   Guerrero sox, el mi sovrino,   la podéis muy bien ganar.

10B

Version from Tetuán (Morocco), recited by Luna Farache, 78 years, collected by S. G. A. and I. J. K., in Tetuán, August 13, 1962.

♩= 132

Ya se sa - le el buen re - ye a sus pa - la - sios re - al.

Por de - trás sa - lió su so - bri - no, con- de Ni - ño Mon-teal - bar:

--¿Que me di - tes, di-joel mi tí - o, cas - ti - yo de Mon-te-al - bar?

Me lo di - tes por re - ga - lo; sa - lió- me po- rhe - re - dar.

Mi- sar-mas ten-go em-pe- ña - das, sien mar-cos de o - ro y más;

mis cri - a - dos se me fue -ron, por no te - ner qué pa - gar;

mis don - ze yas se mar - cha -ron, por no te - ner-las qu'en-do - ñar;

mis bar-co's - tán pa - ra - do, por que no tra - ta - ne - nel - mar.

Ya se sale el buen reye　a sus palasios real.

2　Por detrás salió su sobrino,　conde Niño Montealbar:
　　—¿Qué me dites, dijo, el mi tío,　castiyo de Montealbar?

4　Me lo dites por regalo;　salióme por heredar.
　　Mis armas tengo empeñadas,　sien marcos de oro y más;

6　mis criados se me fueron,　por no tener qué pagar;

     mis donẓeyas se marcharon,   por no tenerlas qu'endoñar;

8   mis barcọ están paradọ,   porque no tratan en el mar;

     mis mujeres no me quieren,   por no tener qué folgar.

10   —Dalde marcos de oro al conde,   dalde marcos de oro y mạ́;

     dalde marcọ de oro al conde,   para sus armas tomar;

12   dalde marcọ de oro al conde,   para sus mosas tomar;

     dalde marcos de oro al conde,   para sus navíos sacar;

14   dalde marcos de oro al conde,   para con damas folgar;

     dalde marcos de oro al conde,   para comprar y vistir.—

16   Ahi s'alḥadró un pajeθito,   que solía darle del vestir.

     Dióle camiẓa de holanda,   que en el agua se ha de beber;

18   dióle sapatito de charol,   que sólo se ha de andar.

     —De todo esto, mi tío,   nada puedo resibir.

20   [Claraniña, la tu hija],   por mujer la he de yevar.

     —Sobrino, eso no puede ser.   [. . . . .]

22   Comprometida la tengo   con el conde de Montealbar.

     —Mañanita sal te al campo   [. . . . .].

24   Quien de voẓotrọ la gane,   con Claraniña se ha de caẓar.—

     Como es'oyera el buen conde,   se fuera a cayar.

26   Le dieran camiẓa del holanda,   que de agua ha de beber;

     le dieran sapatos de charol,   que de suyo se ha de andar;

28   tomara un cavayo blanco,   que rey no la cabalga, no;

     con sientos de cascabelẹ,   que le puẓo en su coyar.

30   ¿Por dónde le fuera pasar?   Por la caye de Claraniña.

     Al son de los cascabelẹ,   Claraniña se asomó.

32   —¿Qué tal te paresco, prima?   ¿Qué tal te paresco yo?

     —Bien me pareses, conde;   conde Albar mucho mejor.—

34   Como es'oyera el conde Niño,   caigó desmayado.

     —No desmayes tú, conde Niño,   ni te quieraɗ haẓer mal.

36   Bueno me pareses, conde;   contigo me he de caẓar.

6a   mis muj . . . mis donẓeyas.

12a   al niño . . . al conde.

20a   *originally*: Claraniña . . . la . . . la . . . de tomar Clara, tu hija.

23a   *originally:* Mañanita entre . . . sal te [?] al campo.

28a   Caballó . . . Tomara un cabayo blanco.

28b   la *sic*.

Summaries:

Conde Claros y el emperador + *Conde Claros insomne*

E: The light of day and clarity, which provide sunlight, moonlight, and the light of stars at dawn, are invoked. Uncle and nephew go out riding together; they race their valuable horses to see which can run faster, but both are of equal worth. The riders talk together about what concerns them most. The nephew asks his uncle to give him Blancaniña (Claraniña) as his wife. The uncle answers that it is impossible: When he offered her to him, he did not want her and the uncle has betrothed her in France to the Count of Livorno (Aligornar; Alionar; Aligornás; Aligorná, Aligornal; Alimar; the king of Portugal). He suggests that, since the nephew is a warrior, he may be able to win her back. The nephew answers that he has pledged his weapons for a hundred doubloons and a bit more. The uncle calls the knights who are at his command: "Give the count a hundred doubloons to redeem his arms and I'll give him another hundred to spend along the way; give him a fine shirt, with golden thread and pearls on the collar, embroidered by three ladies, on the morning of St. John; give him a gold embroidered jacket, lined with fine red taffeta; give him a war horse, so he can rescue the girl." The knight quickly asks for clothing and shoes and departs. Through streets where there were people, he rode slowly; through streets where there was no one, he made sparks fly. Ladies and maidens appear at the windows to watch: "Who is this knight who is trying to destroy the city?" The knight answers: "I am not trying to destroy the city. I am only searching for Blancaniña (Claraniña)."

M: <Why not sing of my fortune? Why not sing of my grief? Exiled from my land, the kingdom of Portugal.> The king, accompanied by his nephew (Count Niño), goes out. He weeps because of what his nephew tells him: "Why did you give me the castle of Montalbán (Montalvar, Montealbán, Montealvar)? You gave it to me as an inheritance, but it turned out as if I had been disinherited. I have had to pledge my weapons for a hundred marks and more; my ships are idle and no longer trade on the sea; my knights (my horses) have departed, since I had nothing to give them; my friends scorn me, because I am not their equal; my servants have left me, since I could not pay them; my maidens have forgotten me, since I had nothing to give them; I have lost the ladies with whom I once took pleasure. I have neither silver nor gold to buy clothing or shoes!" The king answers: "Come here my loyal treasurers (scribes, knights): Give marks of gold and even more to the count, so he can redeem his weapons (his horses), fight with Moors, trade on the sea, take back his servant girls, take pleasure with ladies, and buy clothing and shoes." The nephew answers: "Thanks, many thanks, for this and for much more, but I spend even more just on the servants (wildmen) in my house (my garden). What I want is to take your daughter, Claraniña, as my wife." The king answers: "Pardon me, but I cannot give her to you. I have promised her to the Count of Montalbán." The nephew insists: "I will have her as my wife or as my mistress." The king answers: "Despite all this, you should not give up hope. Tomorrow you will both go out to joust on my royal fields. Whoever wins will have Claraniña." Count Niño (Claro(s); Flore(s); Vélez) goes to take an afternoon nap, having been unable to rest the night before, because he was dying of love for (his niece) Claraniña. He jumps out of bed as fast as a sparrow hawk and calls immediately for his clothing, shoes, and horse. A page (maiden), who usually serves him, appears and gives him a shirt of holland cloth, that surpasses what a king might wear; a hundred ladies had prepared it by the shores of the sea; another hundred washed it in water scented with orange blossoms; others carded it with metal carding combs; others spun it on crystal spindles; others wove it on walnut looms; others cut it with metal scissors; others sewed it with needles and thimbles; still others embroidered it by the light of the moon, decorating it with sprigs of rue, which had just begun to grow; with three hundred precious stones all around the collar; a hundred made him cool and a hundred made him warm and a hundred gave him charm to take pleasure with ladies. The page gave him such a fine undershirt that it could have been absorbed in water; he gave him a scarlet doublet all lined with cordovan leather; he gave him (red) openwork stockings all lined with taffeta frills; he gave him openwork shoes, with buckles made of coral; he gave him a white horse even better than a king would ride, with three hundred little bells around its breast strap; and there were three hundred thousand black servants to accompany him on his way. On the streets where he rode, he made sparks fly. <Now they go into the field and now they begin to fight. In the very first battle, Count Niño won the day.> He went riding by, through Claraniña's street. <She hears the bells on his horse's harness and appears at the window. Count Niño asks her what she thinks of him. She thinks well of him, but prefers "Count Albar." He faints, but she then assures him that she really likes Niño better. They are married the next day. (Or: Three days later, she marries Count Albar; or: On hearing her preference, Count Niño gives up and rides away or drops dead; Claraniña jumps from the window.)>

La jactancia del conde Vélez

E: Count Belo (Velo; Bello) boasts at court: "No woman, unmarried or married, can resist having a love affair and, no matter how chaste she may be, I can seduce her." The grand duke (great Cides), son of the emperor, answers: "If you seduce the princess, I'll give you seven cities; but if you don't seduce her, I'll cut out your heart." Belo answers: "I don't want your cities; I have better ones myself, but, if I seduce the princess, I'll cut your heart out." They draw up a written agreement. Count Belo departs, taking a sorrel horse that can run faster than a ray of sunlight (?), and makes a fifteen-day journey in seven days. Along the way, he meets one of the princess' slave girls. After he bribes her with a large sum, she describes the princess' house: "Parizi has three halls, one better than the other; Parizi sleeps in one, the emperor in another, and in the other the princess sleeps with a great lord. A watchman keeps vigil at the head of her bed and a nightingale sings at her right ear; it sings at dawn and at midday, at the hour when God should be praised." [Belo goes to the princess' castle.] He rides all around it, but cannot find the entrance. He looks up and sees another of her slave girls. After bribing her with a large sum, she tells him that the princess has a mole below her left breast. [Belo manages to gain access to the castle.] He meets yet another slave girl, who tells him: "If you're looking for the princess, I have her ring." Belo pays her a large sum for it and returns to the court. The grand duke says: "I'm going to cut out your heart." Belo describes the princess' palace, adding for further proof the detail of the mole [and, as final proof, he produces the ring]. The grand duke writes a furious letter to the "whorish princess." She disguises herself as a man. [. . .] She speaks to a talking parrot, asking it why it has not sung and mentioning the difficult situation of the grand duke. It advises her to sell all her possessions and obtain a golden slipper [which she will wear when she goes to court]. [. . .] As she is going into the city, she meets Count Belo and reproaches him: Even though he entered her court, she has committed no sin. She accuses him of stealing one of her golden slippers. Belo swears that he never entered her court. [. . .] The grand duke regrets the seven peerless cities he would have to give up. He orders Count Belo's heart to be cut out.

M: Count Vélez (Velo) boasts at court: No lady nor maiden can resist having a love affair (with him), except for the princess and he had not asked her about it, for if he had, she would not have denied him. All the gallants at court are furious about his boast and especially Don Güeso (Count Niño), who had recently fallen in love: "I know of a girl, Vélez, who is no older than fifteen. If you can seduce

her, you can cut out my heart; and if you can't seduce her, I'll cut out yours."
They post papers at court (in the square; on the corners) concerning their bet.
Everyone backs Don Güeso against the traitor Vélez, except for a renegade (a
little page), of evil birth (or who had eaten bread at his table): "I will support
Vélez; I will vouch for him." On subsequent days, Vélez decorates the streets
with fine silk, brocade, velvet, and taffeta; sets up rich tents of various colors
made of luxurious cloth and covered with pearls (jewels); organizes noisy
festivities, with musical instruments, drums, and different types of music; paves
the streets with pearls, precious stones, and emeralds; jousts with a hundred
Moors, killing fifty and wounding the others; duels with lances (swords), killing
a hundred opponents and wounding a hundred more; releases a hundred bulls; and
parades his black servants, dressed in (colorful) Turkish garb and covered with
fine jewels (looking like rays of sunlight). In spite of all this, the girl never
even comes to the window. They seize Vélez and carry him off to cut out his
heart. As they go through the princess' street, Vélez cries out: "Because of you,
they're going to cut out my heart!" On hearing this (his cries), the girl comes to
the window. Vélez asks her what she thinks of him. She answers that she thinks
well of him, but prefers Count Albar (Don Güeso). They take Vélez off to cut
out his heart. Moral: That's what they do to gallants who boast at court.

Motifs:

Conde Claros y el emperador + Conde Claros insomne:

P297. *Nephew.*
F567. *Wildman.*
V70.3.1. *Feast of Saint John the Baptist.*
D965.16. *Magic Rue.*
Cf. D1385.2.2. *Rue, when burned, keeps evil spirits at a distance.*
D1071. *Magic jewel (jewels).*
F826. *Extraordinary jewels.*
H217.2. *Decision by single combat of who is to marry girl.*
T80. *Tragic love.*
T81. *Death from love.*
Cf. N343.1. *Mistress kills self, believing lover dead.*

La jactancia del conde Vélez :

N15. *Chastity wager.*

N2. *Extraordinary stakes at gambling.*
Cf. N2.5.2. *Half kingdom as wager.*
K2252. *Treacherous maid-servant.*
K2112.1. *False tokens of woman's unfaithfulness.*
H51.1. *Recognition by birthmark.*
H94. *Recognition by ring.*
K2112. *Woman slandered as adulteress (prostitute).*
Cf. K442. *False claim of reward.*
K1837. *Disguise of woman in man's clothes.*
K1210. *Humiliated or baffled lovers.*
Q243.2.1. *Attempted seduction punished.*
Cf. S139.6. *Murder by tearing out heart.*
Cf. Q469.6. *Heart and liver of murderer torn out.*

Textual Commentary

The ballads concerning Count Claros of Montalbán must be characterized as Pseudo-Carolingian: Narratives which, in essence, have nothing to do with Charlemagne or the *chansons de geste* have been accomodated to a Carolingian milieu simply by designating the king as "Carlos el emperante" and by making a few strategic references to "París esa ciudad," to "Francia la natural," and to famous Carolingian heroes such as Oliveros, Roldán, Montesinos, Urgel de las Marchas, and "el honrado don Beltrán." More specifically, Count Claros is connected with the castle of Montalbán and is identified as the son of the famous Reinaldos, who, as the *infanta* reminds her father, "murió en las batallas, / por tu corona ensalzar"—even though, incongruously, Roland and Olivier, his partners in the fatal disaster at Roncevaux, are now also present to plead for Claros' life.[1] The Conde Claros ballads embody a complex interweaving of semi-autonomous narrative components, which, during the theme's multisecular traditional life, have been continuously rearranged and reassociated, in an ever-changing, dynamic process that can be seen as paradigmatic of the oral tradition

---

1. The allusions to Oliveros, Roldán, and Reinaldos are in *Media noche era por filo* (*Primav.* 190); to Oliveros and Roldán, are added Montesinos, Urgel (= Ogier), and Beltrán in *A misa va el emperador* (*Primav.* 192). For the Carolingian adaptation of non-Carolingian material and the allusions to "Francia" and "Carlos el emperante" in *A caza va el emperador* (*Primav.* 191), see RoH, I, 273. For Reinaldos' presence in the epic and ballad tradition, see the Appendix.

as a whole. In approaching the various Judeo-Spanish manifestations of the Conde Claros theme, it will be convenient to distinguish seven different narrative segments which figure in the 16th-century documentation:

(1)   *Conde Claros y el emperador:* Claros complains to the Emperor that he needs money; the Emperor offers him substantial sums; but what he really wants is to marry the princess, Claraniña; the Emperor refuses; he has already promised her to Don Beltrán (*A caza va el emperador* [*Primav.* 191.1–16]; *A misa va el emperador* [*Primav.* 192.1–43]).

(2)   *Conde Claros insomne:* Claros cannot sleep because of his love for Claraniña; he jumps out of bed and orders his servant to bring him his clothing; the servant brings him an array of luxurious clothes; he goes off to the palace to see Claraniña (*Media noche era por filo* [*Primav.* 190.1–20]; *A misa va el emperador* [*Primav.* 192.44–88]; *Dormiendo está el conde Claros* [ASW, p. 73, no. 56.1–31]).

(3)   *Conde Claros y la infanta:* Claros meets and seduces Claraniña; a hunter surprises them "under a rose bush" and goes to inform the king, who has the hunter killed and imprisons Claros (*Media noche era por filo* [*Primav.* 190.21–75]).

(4)   *Conde Claros preso:* Claros is imprisoned for seducing the princess; she rushes to the scaffold where he is to be beheaded, orders the execution stopped, and begs the king to spare his life; they are married and: "Los enojos y pesares / en placer hubieron de tornar" (*Media noche era por filo* [*Primav.* 190.76 ff.]).

(5)   *Conde Claros degollado:* The king surprises Claros conversing with the princess and orders him thrown into prison; a royal tribunal condemns him to be beheaded and the sentence is carried out; the king has his heart cut out and sent to the princess on a platter; she dies of grief and the lovers are buried together in a rich sepulcher (*Dormiendo está el conde Claros* [ASW, pp. 73–75, no. 56.32 ff.]).

(6)   *Conde Claros y la infanta huyen a Montalbán:* Claros persuades the princess to take refuge at Montalbán; he goes to the king and tells him that, despite his opposition, he intends to marry the princess and that she will soon bear his child; the king orders Claros seized, but he flees on

horseback through the streets of Paris; Oliveros and Roldán delay pursuing him long enough to allow him to escape; they intercede with the king, who pardons Claros; the lovers are married: "Ricas bodas le hicieran / en París esa ciudad" (*A misa va el emperador* [*Primav.* 192.89 ff.]).

(7) *Conde Claros fraile*: Claros tells the king that the *infanta* is pregnant and that, despite his opposition, he intends to marry her; the king has her imprisoned in water up to her waist; she is to be burned at the stake; she sends a page with a letter to Claros; he disguises himself as a friar and hears her confession: The only man she has been with is Don Claros de Montalbán; Claros carries her off on his horse (*A caza va el emperador* [*Primav.* 191.17 ff.]).

These seven narrative segments were combined in a variety of ways in the 16th-century tradition:

— *Media noche era por filo* (*Primav.* 190) = *Insomne* + *Infanta* + *Preso*.

— *A caza va el emperador* (*Primav.* 191) = *Emperador* + *Fraile*.

— *A misa va el emperador* (*Primav.* 192) = *Emperador* + *Insomne* + *Montalbán*.

— *Dormiendo está el conde Claros* (ASW 56) = *Insomne* + *Degollado*.

In addition, two brief fragments of *Conde Claros preso* achieved independent status as separate poems: *Pésame de vos, el conde* and *Más envidia he de vos, conde*.[2]

The modern tradition has continued to rearrange these early narrative components in patterns that vary from one geographic sub-tradition to another and which, in combination with additional narrative types originally extraneous to the Conde Claros cycle, attest to a complexity of thematic associations that is probably unrivalled in the entire *Romancero*. (1) *Conde Claros y el emperador* continues in oral tradition in both Morocco and Eastern Sephardic communities. In both areas, it is associated with elements pertaining to *Conde Claros*

---

2. Compare *Primav.* 190, pp. 438–439 and n. 3, 441–442, n. 3, with ASW, p. 72. For the excerpts, *Pésame de vos, el conde* and *Más envidia he de vos, conde*, which became enormously popular ballads in their own right, see the Appendix.

insomne. Components characteristic of *Conde Claros y el emperador* have also survived, as a prologue to *Conde Claros fraile*, in a limited number of versions from Upper Aragon (Alto Aragón), though these, to my knowledge, are, with one exception, not available in published sources.[3] These Aragonese texts are notable in having preserved (and perhaps elaborated upon) the *í-a* assonance characteristic of the initial verses of "A caza va el emperador / a Sant Juan de Montiña" and "A misa va el emperador / a San Juan de la Montiña" (*Primav.* 191–192), while the corresponding material in both Sephardic traditions is in *á* (as is the balance of the narrative). (2) *Conde Claros insomne* has continued to be sung in Morocco, in Castilian-speaking areas of the Peninsula, in Asturias, in Portugal, and in Catalonia. In Morocco, as we shall see, it is associated with *Conde Claros y el emperador*, though neither of the associated texts derive directly from those which were juxtaposed in the 16th century (*Media noche: Primav.* 190). In Castilian areas, *Insomne* survives vestigially as a prologue to *Conde Claros y la infanta + Conde Claros fraile*.[4] In Portugal and Catalonia, *Insomne*, in more ample form, introduces *Conde Claros y la infanta + Conde Claros preso*.[5] (3) *Conde Claros y la infanta* has also survived in both Sephardic traditions, in Castilian areas, in Portugal, in Catalonia, and fragmentarily among Andalusian Gypsies. In the Moroccan and Castilian traditions, it can be followed by *Conde Claros fraile*.[6] In the Portuguese versions, it can occur with *Conde Claros insomne* as a prologue and/or in association with *Conde Claros preso* or *Conde Claros fraile*.[7] In Catalonia, it can be preceded by *Insomne* and followed by *Preso*.[8] (4) *Conde Claros preso* has, to our knowledge, not survived in the modern Sephardic subtraditions, but is sung as an autonomous ballad in León and as a continuation of *Conde Claros*

---

3. For a text from Esposa (Huesca), see CGR, IA, 44. It is reproduced further on in the present chapter.

4. See, for example, CGR, IA, 45–46; *Voces nuevas*, I, 291, 292–293, 297; RPM 58; and the bibliography at the end of the present chapter.

5. See, for example, Braga, I, 306–307, 324, 329–330, 334, 405; VRP 50–51; Pinto-Correia, pp. 176–177 (= VRP); AFC 2973; Aguiló, pp. 307–308; and the bibliography at the end of the present chapter.

6. See, for example, RPM 58. For an extensive bibliography, see Chap. 11 below.

7. Preceded by *Insomne*: Braga, I, 306–309, 324–337, 405–407; VRP 50–51; and/or followed by *Preso*: Braga, I, 314–315, 324–341, 351–355; followed by *Fraile*: Braga, I, 309–313, 364–368. See also *Yoná*, p. 83, n. 7; extensive documentation in Chap. 11 below.

8. AFC 2973; Aguiló, pp. 307–314 and Chap. 11 below.

y la infanta in the Asturian, Portuguese, Brazilian, Catalan, and Argentine traditions.[9] (5) *Conde Claros degollado* and (6) *Conde Claros y la infanta huyen a Montalbán* have not, as far as I know, come over into the modern tradition.[10] The first has the appearance of an overly tragic, courtly contrivance, which would not have set well with the oral tradition—generally sympathetic toward the gallant *Conde Claros* and his beloved. The escape to Montalbán and the secret, collegial conspiracy of other Carolingian characters in the hero's flight to safety were, it would seem, not sufficiently distinctive to warrant their survival over against the more striking features of the other narrative segments: Claros' bold demands (*Emperador*); his overwhelming display of sartorial luxury (*Insomne*); a scene charged with piquant gallantry (*Infanta*); the princess' bold intervention on the hero's behalf (*Preso*); and, above all, the international motifs of friar disguise and mock confession (*Fraile*). (7) *Conde Claros fraile* is by far the most widely diffused of the themes current in the modern tradition: Though it has not been documented in the Sephardic East, it is well known in Morocco, in Castilian areas, in the Canaries, and, in Continental Portugal, Madeira, Azores, Brazil, and Catalonia.[11]

In addition to the intertwining of the various episodes directly pertaining to *Conde Claros*, the cycle has experienced an astounding number of contaminations from other, "extraneous" ballad types: In Morocco *Conde Claros y el emperador* + *Conde Claros insomne* is, as we shall see, preceded by *¿Por qué no cantáis fortuna?* and adapts elements of *La jactancia del conde Vélez* to contrive a distinctive dénouement. In Madeira, *Conde Claros y la infanta* has been contaminated by *Bodas de sangre, La canción del huérfano*, and *El prisionero*.[12] *Conde Claros fraile*'s associations are notable in their complexity: Verses from *Aliarda y el alabancioso* and *La infanta deshonrada* (or *parida*) function as a prologue in various Castilian-speaking Peninsular areas. In Asturias and in Portugal, *La apuesta ganada* serves the same purpose, while other Portuguese versions attest to contaminations with *La mala hierba*

---

9. For examples, see *Yoná*, p. 83, n. 7; CGR, IA, 47; Chap. 11 below. Moya's Argentine version (II, 23–24), which begins with *Insomne*, continues with *Princesa*, and ends with *Preso*, is certainly semi-learned in origin. But compare NCR 13A.1, vv. 47–101. For the autonomous Leonese form see, now, RGL 18.1 (and vol. I, ci–cii).

10. See, however, CGR, IA, 44, 55.

11. "El romance más difundido hoy es *Conde Claros en hábito de fraile*" (CGR, IA, 44). For examples from the various subtraditions, see *Yoná*, pp. 82–83, n. 7; FM 8 (II, 233); and the extensive documentation in Chap. 11 below and in B. do Nascimento, "Conde Claros Confessor."

12. Rodrigues de Azevedo, pp. 72–81.

(*á-a*) (CMP R6), *La fuente fecundante* (*á-a*) (= *El mal encanto*) (CMP R4; MP 108*bis*), *Blancaniña* (*La adúltera* [*ó*]), and *Aliarda y el alabancioso* (CMP R1). The Catalan tradition also documents the intervention of *La fuente fecundante* (*á-a*) (for example, AFC 3263).[13]

The 16th-century ballad of *Conde Claros y el emperador* + *Conde Claros insomne* has survived in both branches of the Sephardic tradition. In the East, only vestiges of the ballad have been recorded in relatively recent times (e.g.: CMP B9.23 [collected in 1946]; our 10*A* [both from the same informant]; LSO, p. 77, vv. 13–21) and the song can now probably be considered essentially extinct. Oro A. Librowicz's ample Moroccan versions, recorded in 1970 and 1972, possibly point to a somewhat more optimistic situation in the North African tradition. On the following pages, we offer synthetic texts of the ballad's Eastern and Moroccan forms.[14] Here is a synthetic version representing the Eastern tradition:

   Luz del día y luz del día,   luz del día y claridad,
2   el día me dax el sole,   la noche'l claro lunar;
   la mañanica las estreyas,   cuando quiere alvorear.
4   Se pasean tío y sovrino,   ǧuntos van a un barabar,
   havlando y platicando   lo que les importa más.
6   Cavayos yevan d'un presio,   por ver cuál corría más:
   Corre'l uno, corre'l otro;   ǧuntos van a un barabar.
8   Por en medio del camino,   s'empesan a preguntar:
   —Una mersed le rogo, tío,   cual me havéx d'atorgar,
10   que me dex a Blancaniña,   por mujer y por igual.
   —Esta mersed, el mi sovrino,   no vola puedo atorgar.
12   Cuando yo la había dado,   no la quijitex tomar.

---

13. For documentation, see *Yoná*, pp. 82–83, n. 7; and B. do Nascimento's splendid articles, "*Conde Claros* na Tradição Portuguesa" and "Conde Claros Confessor"; note also the indispensable discussion in CGR, IA, 44–51. For additional examples of *Aliarda + Fraile*, see *Voces Nuevas*, I, 286–289, 295–296, 298–300, 302–306. Exceptionally, text 17 (pp. 308–309) uses verses from *La mala suegra* as a prologue. For bibliography of these and other (sporadic) contaminations, see Chap. 11.

14. Crucial in preparing these texts have been the synthetic versions published by Diego Catalán (CGR, IA, 47–49), which, thanks to his characteristic generosity, we had also been able to consult in manuscript form, together with pertinent unedited materials at the Menéndez Pidal Archive.

Despozada la tengo en Fransia, con el conde Aligornar.
14 Guerrero sox, el mi sovrino; sepalda muy bien ganar.
—Las armas tengo empeñadas, por sien doblas y algo más.
16 —Aquí, aquí, mis cavayeros, los que en mi comando estáx:
Dexle sien doblas al conde, para las armas quitar;
18 otras sien yo le daría, para el camino gastar;
dexle camiza delgada, sirma y perla en su coyar;
20 tres damas se la lavraron, mañanica de San Genar;
dexle ǧaqueta de sirma, enforrada con ǧanfés al;
22 dexle cavayo de guerra, para la niña ir a quitar.—
Presto demandó el vistido, presto demandó el calsare.
24 Ya se parte el cavayero, ya se parte, ya se va.
Por cayes qu'havía ǧente, caminava de avagar;
26 por cayes que non hay ǧente, senteyas hazía saltar.
S'aparan damas y donzeyas a las ventanas mirar:
28 —¿Quién es este cavayero, que fundir quiere la sivdad?
—Yo no so el cavayero, que fundir quiere la sivdad.
30 Sólo quiero la Blancaniña, que la vo ir a buxcar.[15]

Sources

Sofia: *a* = CMP B9.1   *c* = CMP B9.2
Salonika: *b* = Attias 31   *d* = CMP B9.3

---

15. CMP B9.4, from the MS collection of Rabbi Isaac Bohor Amaradji, of Salonika, is so aberrant and garbled that it is almost totally useless for the purposes of our synthetic text. The singer has attempted to make something out of a poorly remembered and gravely jumbled rendition of vv. 25–30: Instead of a single knight, there are several, who ride through "las calles de París"; the blows of their horses' hoofs make holes (?) (foyones) in the earth and their cries (yemidos) strike sparks (centellas hazen saltar); special attention is given to a "caballo castaño" (cf. Attias 31.38); the women ask who the knights are; they have come to get Claraniña, "la meǰor de la ciudad, // que mora en altas torres, / en las más altas de la ciudad" (cf. aberrant conclusions at v. 30+). The fragment ends with an adaptation of v. 14. "En las salas de París" (v. 1*a*) is probably taken from *Las bodas en París*. (See FLSJ, III, Chap. 7.) The words *ǧanfés al* (v. 21*b*) represent T. *canfes al* 'red taffeta.' For the synonymic formula, *luz y claridad*, used with a different connotation (radiant feminine beauty), compare the wedding song from Istanbul collected by Alberto Hemsi in Alexandria (1930): "que la luz y la claridad, dama, con vos vino; / pedrí mi seso y mi tino" (Hemsi II, no. 131*A*, variant 2, p. 311).

e	= CMP B9.5	*l*	= LSO, p. 77, vv. 13-21
f	= CMP B9.6	*m*	= Onís B9
g	= CMP B9.7	*n*	= *Yoná* 4A
h	= CMP B9.8	*o*	= *Yoná* 4B
i	= CMP B9.9	*p*	= our 10A
j	= CMP B9.23	Larissa: *q*	= CMP B9.10
k	= Crews 12.15–19	Jerusalem: *r*	= CMP B9.11

Variants

1   *bcefghimnoq*

    1*a-b* Luz del día y claridad *cfhimnoq*.

    1*a*   y *omitted eg*.

2   *abcfghimnoq*

    2*a*   el día mos da el sol *a;* que el día le diera el sole *c;* que el día me dax el sol *fghn;* que el día me das el sol *m;* ke 'el dí'a le diera 'el sol *o;* sol *bq;* sole *n*.

    2*b*   y la noche *bchi;* y *omitted afgq;* el *omitted nq*.

3   *abcefghijmnoq*

    3*a*   que la mañana *c;* la noche *f;* la manyyana *n*.

    3*b*   que cuando *c;* la noche el lindo lunar *e;* i quoando *i;* y cuando *mo;* cuando quiere (empeza a) alborear *q;* quieren *h;* kere *in*.

4   *abcdfghijmnopqr*

    4*a*   Se pase'a *o*.

    4*b*   conversando barabar *a;* y djountos *h;* y ǧuntos *m;* yuntos en un barabar *q;* van un barabbar *bcm;* van baraba *h;* van de en barabar *j;* van d'un barabar *p*.

5   *bcdfgijnor*

    5*a*   Que hablando iban hablando *cf;* Que hablando van y platicando *d;* Están hablando y platicando *g;* caminando (?) ian avlando *i;* van havlando y platicando *j;* hablando ían, hablando *r*.

    5*b*   de qualo les emporta más *i*.

6   *abcdghijnoq*

    6*a*   que caballos *cdno;* sus cavallos *j*.

    6*b*   por ver cuál valía más *a;* a una van un barabar *c;* por ver el que corría más *d;* juntos van de en barabar *j*.

7   *abcdhimnoq*

    7*a*   corre uno *b;* que corre uno y corre otro *cmno;* corre uno, corre otro *i*.

7*b*   y juntos van un barabbar *b;* djountos van baraba *h;* (y) por ver cual corría más *cm;* gintos (?) van a un barabar *i.*

8   *b*

9   *abcdfghijnopqr*

9*a*   ¡Ah! Una merced *d;* Una demanda vos demando *g;* mercé *hi;* le digo *a;* vos rogo *cdfij;* le arogo *h;* el tío *i;* Tío mío, el mi querido *q.*

9*b*   cuala me la hadex de atorgar *d;* la cual *f;* cual me debéx de atorgar *g;* quoual mé la dévé dé atorgar *h;* qual me la deved accettar *i;* cuala me la devéš de atorgar *j;* y cual me la avéš de atorgar *no;* si me la pueda atorgar *p;* una merced le vo a demandar *q;* cual me la debe de otorgar *r;* habedes *a;* hubiera *b;* hubierais *c;* otorgar *acf.*

9+   Esta merced, mi señor tío, / ya se la tengo que pagar *q.*

10   *abcdfghijnopqr*

10*a*   diera *abhr;* dierais *c;* dierax *d;* dé *pq;* Claraniña *aor;* Clara nigna *h.*

10*b*   por esposa *bq;* o por *a.*

11   *cdfhinoqr*

11*a*   Una mersed, mi sobrino *c;* Esta merced, mi sobrino *fi;* Esta mercé, mi souvrino *h.*

11*b*   yo no la pudiera atorgar *d;* non la pu'edo ačetar *n;* no vola pu'edo ačetar *o;* no es coṣa en (?) vola dar *q;* que yo no vola puedo atorgar *r;* otorgar *cf;* accettar *i.*

12   *bdgn*

12*a*   Cuando te la di, subrino *b;* que cuando te la di, sobrino *d;* Cuando vola estaba dando *g.*

12*b*   non *dgn.*

12+   Ke dada la tengo 'en Fransyya / por syen doblas (rublas) 'i algo más *n.*

13   *bcdfghij(a)nopqr*

13*a*   Ya la desposí en Francia *b;* Esposada *ciq;* que desposada está en Francia *df;* Casada la tengo en Francia *j;* Ke despozada la tengo 'en Fransyya *n;* Cazada la tengo'n Fransia *p.*

13*b*   'i kon *n;* por sien dobles y algo más *p;* con el rey de Portugal *q;* Alionar *bh;* Aligornás *c;* Aligorná *d;* Alimar *f;* Aligornal *gir.*

14   *bcdfhijnopr*

14*a*   Sois guerrero *b;* Que guerrero sois, mi sobrino *c;* Si vos plazía, el mi sobrino *d;* Si guerrero sox, el mi sobrino *f;* Garrero sos, mi souvrino *h.*

14*b*   sepáišla y bien ganar *b;* Se la puedéis bien ganar *c;* vos lo fuerax a matar *d;* la pudierax bien ganar *f;* Sépaldo bien ganar *h;* sepach vos la bien ganar *i;* y la podéš muy bien ganar *j;* i la puedéš muyy byen ganar *n;* sepášlas byen ganar *o;* la podéis muy bien ganar *p;* sepalda muy bien guerrear *r.*

15   *bcdfghikoqr*

16   *bdhr*
    15*a*   bien empégnadas *h;* peñadas *k;* emprendadas *q.*
    15*b*   por sien doblas algo i más *i;* y no más *f;* y valen más *g.*
    15+   Si vos plazía, mi tío, / vos la iré a rescatar *g.*

16   *bdhr*
    16*a*   Venid aquí *b.*
    16*b*   a mi comando *dr;* al mi comando *h.*

17   *bcdfhkor*
    17*a*   Dalde *cdfo;* Dech *h.*
    17*b*   por las sus armas quitar *d;* para sus armas quitar *f;* para el camino gastar *r.*

18   *bdghior*
    18*a*   le(s) dierais otras unas cuantas *b;* Dalde otras cien al conde *g;* otras tantas io lé diéra *h;* otras tantas io vos diere *i;* 'otras tantas yyo le dyera *or.*
    18*b*   por *d;* para en camino *g;* qu'à Clara nigna va ganar *h;* para las armas quitar *r.*

19   *bfhnor*
    19*a*   Se viste (Dalde) camiṣa d'oro *f;* Desle *h;* Dešme *n;* Daldeš kamiza de seda *o.*
    19*b*   sirma, perla *b;* sirma y perla al su collar *fr.*

20   *r*
    20*b*   Yenar *r.*

21   *bhor*
    21*a*   deišle jaqueta de sirma *b;* deslé djaquéta dé séda *h;* daldeš ǧaketa de sirma *o;* dexle chaqueta de sirma *r.*
    21*b*   y el mi caballo alcastá *b;* enforada con sandá *h;* ke la lavró al bel lunar *o;* enforrada con yanfés al *r.*

22   *fr*
    22*a*   Dalde un buen caballo *f.*
    22*b*   que se vaya a guerrear *f.*

23   *k*

24   *bdghjnor*

24*a*   Ya se esparte el caballero *dgno;* ya se esparte el moro franco *j.*

24*b*   ya se esparte, ya se va *dg;* ya sé parte y ia sé va *h;* ya se esparte y ya se va *j;* yya se 'esparte 'i yya se va *n;* yya se 'esparte 'i se va *o.*

25   *bdfghijklnpqr*

25*a*   Por la calle que no hay gente *br;* Por las calles que hay yente *dhq;* Por las calles que había yente *fgil;* y ande havía gente *j;* Por kayes k'avía ŷente *kp.*

25*b*   caminaba d'avagar *b;* caminava a avagar *j;* kaminava avagar(e) *kl;* havlavan de avagar *p* (*referring to* tío y sobrino: v. 4)*;* caminan muy de avagar *q* (*referring to* caballos: v. 6)*.*

26   *bdfghijklnpqr*

26*a*   por la calle que hay gente *br;* por las calles que non hay yente *d;* por las calles que no había yente *f;* por las calles que no había *gl;* por las quayes qué no ay djenté *h;* por las caies ke eran solas *i;* por calles ande non havía gente *j;* por kayes ke no ai ŷente *k;* por las ka'es ke non aví'a gente *n;* por cayes que no havía gente *p;* por las calles que no hay yente *q.*

26*b*   cintellas hace saltar *b;* centellas hace saltar *dgjr;* sentéas fasé saltar *h;* sinteas azen saltar *i;* sinteyas aze saltare *k;* lo que les importa más *p* (*referring to* tío y sobrino: v. 4)*;* centellas hazen saltar *q* (*referring to* caballos: v. 6)*.*

27   *bhlr*

27*b*   a ver qué hay en la ciudad *l.*

28   *bdfghlnr*

28*a*   ¿Quién era este caballero *b;* ¿Quién es este perro moro *fg;* ¿Kén 'es 'este moro franko *n.*

28*b*   que la cibdad quiere quemar *bg;* que la ciudad quiere tomar *df;* que la civdad nos quiere quemar *l;* ke la sivdad va derokar *n.*

29   *bdfghlr*

29*a*   Yo era el caballero *b;* Yo no vine a guerrear *f;* Yo non so perro ni moro *g;* Yo no éra péro moro *h;* Yo no quiero a ninguno *l;* Yo no era el caballero *r.*

29*b*   que la cibdad no va quemar *b;* que la ciudad quiero tomar *d;* ni quería la ciudad *f;* ni la ciudad quiero quemar *g;* ni foundir kiéro la sivdad *h;* que me vo a ir a mi lugar *l.*

30   *bdfghlr*

30*a* Yo quiero a Blancanina *d;* Que me den a la mi esposa *f;* Toman a
Blancaniña *g;* Viné a tomar Clara nigna *h;* Vine a buxcar a mi espoza
l; Buxco yo a Claraniña *r.*

30*b* que la vine a tomar *b;* que me la vinieron a robar *f;* la toman y se la
dan *g;* Por moujer i por égual *h;* que es la mi mujer real *l;* que me la
mostréx onde está *r.*

30+ Esta niña tanto linda / por mujer la va tomar. // Beata a blanca niña,
/ que tal mansevo va tomar *b;* "Tu espoza está en altas torres, / que
no la puedéx topar." // Esto sintió el cavallero / y se tornó atrás *l;*
Claraniña está en altas torres, / más altas de una ciudad, // comiendo
está en una meṣa / con el conde Aligornal. // Caminaba otro poco
[. . .] *r.*

Our synthetic text from the Moroccan tradition reads as follows:

Ya se salía el buen reye,   ya se sale, ya se va.
2   Tras d'él salió su sobrino,   por compañía leal.
Palabras le iba diziendo,   qu'al buen rey hazen yorar:
4   —¿Qué me dites, el mi tío,   castiyo de Montalbán?
Me lo dites por herensia,   salióme por desheredar.
6   Mis armas tengo empeñadas,   en sien marcos de oro y más;
mis navíos se pararon,   porque no tratan en el mar;
8   mis cabayeros se fueron,   por no tenerles que dar;
mis amigos me despresian,   por no andar de su igual;
10   mis criados se me fueron,   por no tener que pagar;
mis donzeyas me olvidaron,   por no tener que endonar;
12   mis damas tengo perdidas,   con quien solía folgar.
¡Ya no tengo oro ni plata,   con que vestir y calsar!
14   —Vení acá, mis tesoreros,   mis tesoreros leal:
Dadle marcos de oro al conde,   dadle marcos de oro y más;
16   dadle marcos de oro al conde,   para sus armas tomar;
dadle marcos de oro al conde,   para con moros lidiar;
18   dadle marcos de oro al conde,   para tratar por la mar;
dadle marcos de oro al conde,   para sus mosas tomar;
20   dadle marcos de oro al conde,   para con damas folgar;
dadle marcos de oro al conde,   para vestir y calsar.
22   —Mercedes, dixo, mercedes,   por esto y mucho más;

qu'en criados de mi casa,   se me va esto y demás.
24   Vuestra hija, Claraniña,   por mujer la he de tomar.—
—Perdón, perdón, mi sobrino,   que no te la puedo dar;
26   apalabrada la tengo   con el conde de Montalbán.
—Por mujer o por amiga,   Claraniña he de yevar.
28   —Con todo esto, mi sobrino,   no te cortaré el ayás.
Mañana saldréis al juego   a los mis campos reales.
30   Quien de vosotros ganare   Claraniña ha de yevar.—
Durmiendo está el conde Niño   la siesta por descansar,
32   porque la noche pasada   no la pudo asosegar;
de amores de Claraniña,   que se quería finar.
34   Salto diera de su cama,   que parese un gavilán.
Presto demandó el vestido,   presto demandó el calsar;
36   presto demandó el cabayo,   donde solía montar.
Ahí se alḥadró un pajesito,   que se lo solía dar:
38   Diérale camiza de holanda,   que el rey no vestía tal.
Las sien damas la han curado,   a la orilla de la mar;
40   [las sien damas la han lavado],   con el agua de azahar;
las sien damas la han cardado,   en carditas de metal;
42   las sien damas la han filado,   en fusitos de cristal;
las sien damas la han tejido,   en maromas de nogal;
44   las sien damas la han cortado,   con tijeras de metal;
las sien damas la han cosido,   con agujita y dedal;
46   las sien damas la han bordado,   a la sombra del lunar,
con el labre de la ruda,   cuando empiesa a apuntar;
48   trezientas piedras presiozas   alderredor del coyar;
las siento le daban frío,   las siento calor le dan;
50   las siento le daban grasia,   para con damas folgar;
diérale camisón de holanda,   que en agua se beberá;
52   diérale jugón de grana,   enforrado en cordobán;
diérale medias caladas,   forradas en tafetán;
54   diérale sapato picado,   con abroches de coral;
diérale cabayo blanco,   que el rey no cabalga tal;
56   con trezientos cascabeles,   alderredor del frontal;
trezientos mil negritos,   que le van a acompañar.
58   Ya se sale el buen conde,   ya se sale y ya se va.

Cayes por donde pasaba,   senteyas haze saltar.
60   Por cayes de Claraniña,   ya se fuera a pasear.[16]

Sources

Tangier: *a* = CMP B9.12   *l* = CMP B9.21
            b = CMP B9.13   *m* = Larrea 27
            c = CMP B9.14   *n* = Larrea 28
            d = CMP B9.15   *o* = Larrea 29 + 31
            e = CMP B9.16   *p* = Larrea 30
            f = Nahón 5   *q* = Librowicz (II) B9
Tangier-   *r* = our 10*B*
Tetuán: *g* = Librowicz 2   Tetuán-Xauen: *s* = Castro MS
Tetuán: *h* = CMP B9.17   Larache-Tetuán: *t* = Amselem MS
           i = CMP B9.18   Alcázar: *u* = MRuiz 35
           j = CMP B9.19   Morocco (unloc.): *v* = CMP B9.22
           k = CMP B9.20

Variants

1   *acdefhijklmnprstuv*
  1a   Allá salía el buen rey *a*; salió *m*; sale *prstu*; el conde Niño *st*; conde *cjv*.
  1b   allá sale a pasear *a*; ya se salió, ya se va *d*; ya se sale o ya se va *ejnpv*; ya se sale u ya se va *h*; ya se sale a pasear *i*; ya se sale y ya se va *k*; de su palacio real *m*; a sus palasios real *r*.
2   *acdefghijklmnprstuv*
  2a   Con el salió su sobrino *a*; Detrás salió su sobrino *f*; Por allí pasara su tío *g*; Por encuentro se le puso *m*; Tras él sale *pt*; Por detrás *r*; cuñado *s*.
  2b   en compañía real *g*; por compañía le va *h*; el conde de Montealbar *m*; conde Niño Montealbar *r*; su sobrino natural *t*; ayá una legua y más *u*; real *als*; llevar *efkmp*.
3   *acdefghijklnst*

---

16. From a point corresponding to vv. 34 ff., CMP B9.12 (collected by José Benoliel) includes a series of aberrant verses, of dubious traditionality, which have not been taken into account in our synthetic text. For lexical items requiring comment, see the Appendix.

3*a* Palabra *hs*.

3*b* que le hacían llorar *ag*; que al conde haẓe llorar *cs*; que al buen rey le hace llorar *ft*; que al conde hizo llorar *j*; que el buen reye *n*; (le) hace llorar *fhknt*.

4 *abcdefghijklmnprst*

4*a* Aquí me diera mi tío *b* ; Que me dijís (*sic*) vos, mi tío *n*; Me dates vos, mi tío *p*; disteis *ac*; diteis *deik*; dates *fhs*; ditis *g*; dateis *jl*; distes *m*; daste tú *t*.

4*b* Monte Alvar *dh*; Montalbar *es*; Montalvar *f*; Montealbán *gnp*; Montalvá *i*; Montealvar *k*; Montealbar *lmr*.

5 *abcefghijklmnprs*

5*a* lo *omitted a;* le *bcghijl;* disteis *ac;* diera *b;* dates *fhns;* ditis *g;* dateis *ijl;* diteis *k;* distes *m;* en herencia *a;* en convite *cefgijklnps;* en convide *m;* por regalo *r*.

5*b* me salió *es;* desherdar *b;* heredar *ehlrs;* enredar *f;* heredad *gijkmnp*.

6 *abdefghiklmnprtu*

6*b* por *e;* en *omitted r;* por no tener yo qué pagar *u*.

7 *mr*

7*a* mis barcos están paradọ *r*.

7*b* por no tratar con el mar *m*.

8 *abcdefghijklnptu*

8*a* Mis caballos *af;* s'irían *u*.

8*b* tenerlos *abefhiknt;* teneryos *u*.

9 *fmq*

9*a* me dejaron *m;* se me fueron *q*.

9*b* por no tener qué tratar *m;* por no tener que gastar *q*.

10 *qr*

10*b* endonar *q*.

11 *cdefgijklmnpqrt*

11*a* mis damas *gjk;* se marcharon *r;* dejaron *m;* abandonaron *t*.

11*b* tenerlas *efr;* con qué entrar *g;* dar *ef;* llevar *ijl;* mandar *k;* endonar *npr;* gastar *t*.

12 *abqr*

12*a* las mujeres me olvidaron *q;* mis mujeres no me quieren *r*.

12*b* por no tenerlas que dar *q;* por no tener qué folgar *r*.

13 *b*

13+ Oído lo había su tío / desde la sala onde está *b*.

14 *abcdefghijklnpt*

14*a* Ven acá *abhi;* Venía y cá *c;* Ven acá, mis escribanos *d;* Ven aquí, mi escribano *f;* Pronto, pronto, mis criados *g;* Venid acá *jk;* Aína, mis caballeros *np;* Llamísme a mis tesoreros *t;* mis escribanos *k.*

14*b* mi tesorero *ch;* de mi palacio real *g;* daos, mi tesorero leal *n;* reales *at;* real *b.*

15 *adefgijklmnpqrtu*

15*a* Dais de marcos *f;* Daile *g;* Dailde *j;* Daisle *mn;* Daidle *p;* Darle *t;* Dalde *u;* d'oro *u.*

15*b* daile *ag;* dais de marcos *f;* dailde *j;* dadle *omitted n;* daidle *p;* dadle marcos y dalle más *q;* darle *t;* dalde *u;* d'oro *u;* y muchos más *e;* y mucho más *m.*

15+ dalde marcos d'oro al conde / para sus cabayos traer *u.*

16 *abdeghijklmprstu*

16*a* daisle *m;* daidle *p;* dailde *s;* darle *t;* dalde *u;* d'oro *u;* al Niño *t.*

16*b* quitar *u.*

17 *chijkl*

17*a* dailde *j;* marco *h.*

17*b* brillar *h;* tratar *j.*

18 *efhiklmrs*

18*a* dais de marcos *f;* daisle *m;* dailde *s;* marco *h.*

18*b* para sus navíos sacar *r;* lidiar *m;* por el mar *e.*

18+ dais de marcos de oro al conde, / para sus caballos traer *f;* daisle camisas de holanda, / que en agua se beberán *m.*

19 *r*

20 *bcdeghijklmqrs*

20*a* daile *g;* dailde *js;* dale *q;* marco *h.*

20*b* para sus damas tomar *c (var.);* para con doncellas folgar *m;* tratar *g.*

20+ ¿Para qué me abonda esto, / para qué me ha de abondar? *q.*

21 *bcdfghiklrst*

21*a* daisle de marcos *f;* daile *g;* dailde *s;* darle *t.*

21*b* para comprar y vestir *r;* vister *s;* carzar *h.*

21+ La hazienda mal lo cartaron; / la hazienda mal lo cuzieron *s.*

22 *abcdefghiklmp(a)qt*

22*a* Perdón, perdones, mi tío *a;* Perdón, perdón, el mi tío *egim;* Perdón, perdón, y el mi tío *f;* Perdón, perdón, mi señor rey *l.*

22*b* por esto mucho y demás *bdfikl;* con esto mucho y demás *c;* por esto mucho y que más *e;* de compañía real *g;* por esto y mucho y demás *h;* por ese mucho y demás *m;* por tanto y dijo más *q;* por esto y hay más que dar *t.*

23 *acdeghijklqu*

23*a* en salvajes *c;* que en afrechos *d;* con salvado *e;* que en salvajes *gijklu;* en criadas *h;* si en salvajes *q;* de mi huerta *g.*

23*b* gasto yo mucho más *a;* esto y más *eu;* eso y demás *gi;* esto y tres más *k.*

24 *abcdefghijklmnpqr(b)tu*

24*a* Claraniña, vuestra hija *a;* A vuestra hiſa, Claraniña *em;* A tu hija, Claraniña *q;* Claraniña es tu hija *u.*

24*b* por novia *cu;* quiero tomar *a;* la he de llevar *cdeghklnr;* la *omitted fp;* hei *p;* me la has de dar *t;* y de levar *u.*

25 *bcdefghijklmnpqr(a)t*

25*a* A mi hija Claraniña *q;* Sobrino, eso no puede ser *r.*

25*b* por esto que os voy a hablar *c;* por esto cuanto y demás *j;* yo no *m;* que *omitted q;* puedo y dar *g.*

26 *abcdefghijklmnpqrtu*

26*a* Apalabrada me la tengo *a;* Palabrada me la tengo *bcdhikl;* Palabra la tengoy dado *f;* Comprometida la tengo *gmr;* Palabrada ya la tengo *np;* Que la tengo apalabrada *q;* Me la tengo apalabrada *u.*

26*b* al conde *b;* con conde *cdehijkln;* de *omitted gq;* Monte Albar *cdh;* Montalbar *e;* Montalvar *f;* Montealbán *gnpq;* Montalvá *i;* Montealvar *kl;* Montealbar *mr.*

27 *abcefjklmnptu*

27*a* Que la tenga o no la tenga *c;* querida *u.*

27*b* a Claraniña *elm;* m'hais de dar *l (var.);* hei de llevar *n;* tomar *m;* hei de tomar *p;* tengo que llevar *t;* es de levar *u.*

28 *efghijkl*

28*a* A todo *ehijkl;* Con todo eso *fg.*

28*b* la halláz ('esperanza') *i;* la yas *hl;* la yaz *jk;* hallás ('esperanza') *e;* hallar *f;* hayás *g.*

29 *abcdefhijklmopqr(a)tu*

29*a* Sal mañana a la pelea *q;* Mañana sal te al campo *r;* Mañana por la mañana *u;* saldrís *f;* saldré *i;* saldrán *p;* fuego *a;* campo *d.*

29*b* (y) a los mis campos leal *cdefhijkp;* y en mis campos lear *m;* quien gane la llevará *q;* a mis campos reales *t;* juegos al campo real *u;* leales *o.*

30 *abcdefhijklmnprtu*

30*a* El que de vosotros ganare *a;* Cual de vosotros ganare *cefhijkmn;* Cual de vosotros ganareis *d;* Cual de vosotros ganara *l;* Quien de voẓotrọ la gane *r;* Quien de ustedes ganare *t;* Y el que de vosotros gane *u.*

30*b* a Claraniña *dhjkm;* con Claraniña se ha de caẓar *r;* hay *h;* hei *p;* es de *u;* levar *ku;* llevará *m.*

30+ Por mujer o por amiga, / Claraniña has de llevar *d;* Como es'oyera el buen conde, / se fuera a cayar *r.*

31 *abdefghijklot*

31*a* Levantóse el conde Niño *a;* Toda la noche durmiendo *de;* Ya descansa el conde Niño *t;* Flores *e;* Flore *g;* Claro *hi;* Vélez *j;* Claros *lo.*

31*b* las penas por descansar *a;* las mesas por escanciar *b;* la fiesta por descansar *d;* las siestas por descansar *ek;* las mesas por descanciar *il;* durmiendo por descansar *j;* y las bodas se han de hacer *t.*

32 *abdefghiklo*

32*b* sosegar *abego.*

33 *abdefghiklo*

33*a* amor *h.*

33*b* su sobrina natural *abdefhiklo.*

33+ Vueltas daba en la cama (Salto diera de la cama) / como un pece vivo en mar *e.*

34 *be*

34*a* de la *e.*

35 *bdehkopqu*

35*a* Presto le mandó el vestir *d;* Pronto *ek;* Presto demandó el conde *q;* Pronto mandó haẓer el vestido *u;* le mandó *ko;* demanda *p;* un vestido *h.*

35*b* presto le mandó el calzar *do;* pronto *e;* mejor le mandó el carzar *h;* pronto le mandó *k;* el vestido y el calsar *u;* demanda *p.*

36 *bq*

36*b* para poder cabalgar *q.*

37 *ehopr*

37*a* Ahí estaba el pagecito *e;* Allí se alhadre *h;* Presto estaba el pajecito *o;* una doncella *p.*

37*b* que solía darle del vestir *r.*

38 *bdefghijklopqr*

38a   Diéronle *b;* Diérale *del;* Hízole *fj;* Dio a hacer *g;* Diole *ir;* Mandóle *k;* Diera *o;* Daile *p;* Mandó hacer un camisoncito *q;* camisón *dfghijkp;* camisón picado *e.*

38b   que el agua se beberá *djop;* enforrado en tafetal *e;* que en aguas se beberá *fil;* que en agua se beberá *gk;* que en el agua se beberá *h;* que en agua se bebe *q;* que del agua s'ha de beber *r.*

39   *bhkq*

39a   le curaron *hk;* le sembraron *q.*

39b   las cien damas le cogieron *q.*

40   *a*

40a   Los cien pages la lavaban *a.*

41   *hil*

41a   otras tantas *h;* le cardaron *hil.*

41b   con carditas *h.*

42   *bhijklq(a)*

42a   otras tantas le filaron *ik;* le *hjlq;* filaron *hq.*

42b   con *b;* en fusito de fustar *h;* a la sombra del lunar *j;* metal *il.*

43   *bdhikl*

43a   otras tantas *hil;* le tex(i)eron *dik;* le tegieron *h;* le hurdieron *l.*

43b   cristal *dhikl.*

44   *bdefghijkloqu*

44a   otras tantas *ilo;* y otras tantas *k;* le *hijkloq;* lo *u;* cortaron *defhijklq;* cortaban *qu.*

44b   tiĵera *df;* tijereta *o;* cristal *q (var.);* coral *u.*

45   *bdefghijkloqu*

45a   (y) otras tantas *hiklo;* le *defhijkloq;* lo *u;* cusieron *defhijklo;* cosían *gu;* labraron *q.*

45b   agujas *h;* abujitas *u.*

45+   las sien damas le acababan, / cuando el sol empesó apuntar *u.*

46   *bdefghiklop*

46a   otras tantas *kl;* y otras tantas *o;* le *hiklo;* labraron *dehiklo;* bordaron *f;* bordaban *g;* tejieron *l (repetition) p.*

46b   a la luna del lunar *g.*

47   *bdeghiklopq*

47a   con una ruda menuda *b;* con el lambre *h;* como el labre *il;* con el lagre de la rueca *o;* luna *p.*

47*b*   al derredor del collar *b;* y cien perlas y ciento más *g;* alrededor del collar *p;* empezaba *dekq;* empeza *hi;* se empieza *l;* empieza a puntar *o*.

48   *bdehikloq*

48*a*   con doscientas perlas finas *q;* perlas *dh*.

48*b*   frontal *i*.

49   *bghikl*

49*a*   aire *hik;* gracia *l*.

49*b*   las cien le dan calor *g*.

50   *bhik*

51   *ilr*

51*a*   Le dieron camiẓa de holanda *r*.

51*b*   que de agua ha de beber *r;* en aguas *l*.

52   *bdhiklo*

52*a*   Diéronle *b;* Mandóle *k;* jubón *dikl;* jugor *h*.

52*b*   gorgorán *b;* tafetán *dil;* gorgorá *h;* gorgomán *k;* cordobá *o*.

53   *bhikl*

53*a*   diéronle *bl;* mandóle *k;* media calada *bhl;* media encarnada *k*.

53*b*   con zapato(s) de abrochar *il;* enforrada *k*.

54   *behkor*

54*a*   diéronle *b;* diole sapatito de charol *r;* le dieron sapatos de charol *r* *(repetition)*.

54*b*   que el agua se beberá *o;* que sólo se ha de andar *r;* que de suyo se ha de andar *r (repetition);* abroche *h;* metal *e*.

54+   De todo esto, mi tío, / nada puedo recibir *r*.

55   *abcdehiklopr*

55*a*   cabalga *a;* cabalgó en *c;* mandóle *k;* monta en un *p;* tomara un *r*.

55*b*   que el rey nunca tuvo igual *a;* saliérase a pasear *c;* acabalgó *dl;* cabalgó *ehik;* la cabalga, no *r;* en tal *dehiklop*.

56   *bdehiklopqr*

56*a*   doscientos *q;* sientos de *r;* caxcabeles *d;* cascabelitos *o*.

56*b*   alrededor *p;* que le puẓo en su coyar *r;* collar *ip*.

57   *e*

58   *j*

59   *bdhklop*

59*a*   Entre paso y paso que da *b;* Que por la calle que passa *dl;* Por las calles que pasaba *k;* Por la . . . pasa *o;* Por la calle donde pasa *p*.

59*b*   deja saltar *b*.

60 *abcdeghklpqr*
    60*a*   Por calle *abdk;* Por la calle de su dama *c;* ¿Por dónde vino a pasare?
         g; Por la calle *lp;* ¿Por dónde le fuera pasar? *r.*
    60*b* por ahí le vino a pasar *cklp;* por allí le vino a pasar *h;* por ahí fuera
         a passar *de;* por calle de Claraniña *g;* por allí le tocó el pasar *q;* Por
         la caye de Claraniña *r.*

Both *Conde Claros y el emperador* and *Conde Claros insomne* have survived in the Peninsular tradition. The former is very rare and we can cite no published examples other than the text in *í-a* assonance from Upper Aragon recently published in CGR, IA, 44:

> Paseándose estaba [el rey],   el buen rey de la Mantilla,
> contándole al conde Alarcos   cosas que en la corte había.
> —No me cuente usted, buen rey,   cosas que en la corte había,
> que una hija que tenéis   ella ha de ser mujer mía.
> —No lo creas tú, buen conde,   que la tengo prometida
> para un señor muy rico   que ha venido de las Indias.
> —Tengáis que no la tengáis,   ella ha de ser mujer mía,
> porque ya la tengo encinta   de seis meses y algún día.

Conde Claros insomne is, relatively speaking, much more widely known, at least in conservative lateral areas, where the most complete texts have been collected. A thorough analysis of all known evidence would involve numerous currently unavailable unedited versions and would take us beyond the limits of the present study. Here are a few of the more ample versions available in published sources: In León and Zamora, the *Insomne* verses presumably led into the narrative of *Conde Claros y la infanta*, as they also do in the case of the Ribatejo text. In the Penafiel, Madeiran, and Ibizan versions, *Insomne* precedes the combined narrative of *Infanta + Preso:*

>   Media noche va por hilo,   los gallos quieren cantar
> 2   y don Carlos por amores   no podía sosegar.
>   Ya manda ensillar la mula,   también la mandó alcotrar
> 4   y con doscientos cascabeles   ponérselos al petral.
>   Por donde lo ve la gente,   corre como un gavilán;
> 6   por donde nadie lo ve,   echa fuego de alquitrán.

Todas damas y doncellas,   todas salen a mirar;
8   también salió Galanzuca,   hija del Conde Galán. . . .
(Nocedo de Gordón, León: CGR, IA, 45–46)

Eso de la media noche,   antes del gallo cantar,
2   porque don Carlos de amor   no podía sosegar,
aprisa pide el vestido,   aprisa pide el calza[r].
4   Si muy aprisa lo pide,   más aprisa se lo dan.
Ya viste pantaloncino,   zapato de cordobán
6   y un sombrero con tres plumas   que parecía un galán.
—Aparejadme el caballo   de los siete el mejor que hay,
8   las herraduras de bronce,   los cravos de pedernal.—
Cien mil cascabeles lleva   colgados de su potral.
10   Las calles por donde él iba   parece trescientos van.
Muchas damas y doncellas   se salían a asomar;
12   también salió Galanzuca   cubierta con su bidrial. . . .
(Nuez, Zamora: CGR, IA, 45)

Conde Montalvar não dorme,   não pára no cabeçal;
2   salta pinotes na cama,   que nem galeão real.
E brada por seus creados,   a' pressa não devagar;
4   que lhe deem de vestir,   ginete p'ra cavalgar.
Fina camisa lhe trazem   de se fechar n'esta mão,
6   cozida por tres donzellas   na manhã de San João;
tambem lhe deram vestido,   recamado a primor,
8   que nem el-rei, com ser rei,   não lo vestia melhor.
No seu ginete puzeram,   a' roda do peitor[a]l,
10   sete estrellas de oiro fino,   sete do branco metal;
e meteu duas nos pés,   além das do pietoral;
12   tres ourives las lavraram   n'uma noite de natal.
E cavalgou no ginete,   depressa, não devagar,
14   que la infante já estava   na janella a viagiar. . . .
(Senhora do Monte, [Penafiel?]: Braga, I, 324)

Meia noite já é dada,   os gallos querem cantar,
2   o conde Claros na cama   não podia repousar;
chamou pagens e escudeiros,   que se quer já levantar;
4   que lhe tragam de vestir,   que lhe tragam de calçar.
Deram-lhe uma alva camisa,   que el-rei a não tinha tal;

6   deram-lhe saia de seda,   cintura de oiro o firmal.
Trazem-lhe esporas douradas   para com ellas montar;
8   cavalgou no seu cavallo,   poz-se logo a caminhar.
—Deus te salve, Claralinda,   tam cedo está a bordar? . . .

(Ribatejo: Braga, I, 307)

Conde Claros, com amores,   não podia descançar,
2   e dava pulos na cama,   nem gavião a pular.
Chamava pelo seu môço,   depressa, não de vagar:
4   que lhe désse de vestir,   de vestir e de calçar.
Vestiu camisa tão fina   que se fechava na mão,
6   lavrada por tres donzellas   na manhã de São João.
Mandou sellar seu cavallo,   que lo não houvesse egual;
8   duzentas e mil campanas,   a' roda do peitoral:
las duzentas eram de oiro,   las mil do branco metal;
10   seu vestido de brocado   luzia que nem cristal.
La infanta, da janella,   todo lo estava a mirar. . . .

(Madeira: Braga, I, 334)

Mitja nit era y passava,   els galls ja havian cantat,
2   comte Claros no dormia   ni podia reposar;
l'amor que té á Claranina   no 'l dexava sossegar.
4   Passejantse per la cambra   esperá que clarejás
y axí que trencava 'l dia   va cridar los seus criats:
6   —Treys me los vestits mellors,   treys me lo mellor calçat.—
Li duen calces de seda,   çabates d' un cordová
8   y lo gipó de setí   tot forrat de tafetá.
També promptament los mana   que li ormetgen lo cavall.
10   Lo cavall que li ensellaren   be valia una ciutat;
duya trescents cascavells   de part á part del pitrall;
12   n' hi havia cent de plata,   altres cent com un coral
y 'ls altres cent eran d'or   per mes el sò concordar.
14   Ja se 'n va lo Comte Claros   cap á 'n el palau reyal
á cercar la Claranina,   que Deu la vulla guardar. . . .

(Ibiza etc.: Aguiló, pp. 307–308)

Una nochu de porfedi   que eren los gallus cantar
2   Condi Flori està a l'amor,   no podia reposar.
Va manar an els seus criadus: —Dui-me de vestir i calçar,

4   dugueu-me calces de seda,   sabates de cordovà;
       enllestiu-me el meu cavallu   a punt d'anar a peleiar,
6   amb quatre-cents cascavells   per la redó del pitrall:
       cent de or i cent de plata   i altres dos-cents de metall.
8   [. . . . .]   Dret a la horta reial
       varen trobar Claranyina   que es deixava de regar. . . .
                                        (Ibiza: Macabich, p. 21)

Though the sampling presented here is limited and consequently far from
definitive, it is sufficient to provide, beyond all doubt, yet another example of
the autocthonous character of the modern tradition in relation to its 16th-century
antecedents. The texts which we have just read agree, sometimes with the early
versions, sometimes with the Moroccan, and sometimes with the Eastern
tradition. If we segregate various stages of the narrative, the following
correlations emerge: (*E* = Eastern; *M* = Morocco): Allusion to midnight (León,
Zamora, Ribatejo, Ibiza; *Media noche*); roosters crowing (León, Zam., Ribat.;
Media); comparison with sparrow hawk (Penafiel, Madeira; *M*; *Media*); Claros
calls servant(s) (Zam., Penaf., Ribat., Mad., Ib.; *E, M*; *Misa, Media,
Dormiendo*); "aprisa pide el vestido, / aprisa pide el calzar" (Zam.; *E, M*; Vélez
de Guevara); description of clothing: fine shirt (Penaf., Mad.; *M*); maidens
working on St. John's morning (Penaf., Mad.; *E*); "que el-rey a não tinha tal"
(Ribat.; *M* [vv. 38*b*, 55*b*]); Claros asks for horse (León, Zam., Mad.; *M*); horse
decorated with bells (León, Zam., Mad., Ib.; *M; Misa, Media, Dorm.*); "por
donde le ve la gente . . ." (León; *E, M*); ladies appear, to watch Claros ride by
(León, Zam.; *E*). It is, then, abundantly clear, in view of their shared features,
that the modern traditions do not depend directly on the early printings, but rather
that each goes back to other early subtypes, whose precise characteristics and
intermediate stages defy reduction to the fixed stemmata of conventional textual
criticism.

The early documentation of both *Conde Claros y el emperador* and *Conde
Claros insomne* is exceptional in that we are fortunate in having multiple
testimonies to their 16th-century modalities. For *Conde Claros y el emperador*,
we have two quite different versions: *A misa va el emperador* (*Primav.* 192) and
A caza va el emperador (*Primav.* 191). For *Conde Claros insomne*, there are
no less than three extensive and radically different treatments: A lengthy version,
already joined to *Conde Claros y el emperador*, which is embodied in *A misa
va el emperador* (*Primav.* 192.43–88); a briefer form represented by the first
part of *Media noche era por filo* (*Primav.* 190.1–20), which will continue with

Conde Claros y la infanta + *Conde Claros preso*; and an ample, contrived, and courtly reworking represented by *Dormiendo está el conde Claros* (ASW, no. 56), which continues with *Conde Claros degollado*. On the following pages, we offer transcriptions of each of these early texts, based on contemporary sources (rather than on *Primavera*, to which we have referred previously for the sake of clarity and easy reference). To the right of each text, the numbers corresponding to verses in our Eastern (*E*) and Moroccan (*M*) synthetic versions are indicated in parentheses. First, here is *A misa va el emperador* (= *Primav.* 192), which, just as in the modern Sephardic tradition, joins *Conde Claros y el emperador* (vv. 1–43) to *Conde Claros insomne* (vv. 44–91). We use, as our base text, a *pliego suelto* from the British Library and list significant variants from two other *pliegos* belonging to the Biblioteca Nacional and the Prague Library. As we have noted above, following v. 91, the ballad will continue with *Conde Claros y la infanta huyen a Montalbán*:

	A Missa va el emperador	a san juan dela montiña	
2	conel yua el conde claros	por le tener compañia	(*M*2)
	contando le yua contando	el menester que tenia	
4	dize le desta manera	desta manera le dezia	
	vos me lo distes emperador	castillo de Montaluan	(*M*4)
6	distes me lo por bien	yo tomelo por mi mal	(*M*5)
	los moros melo hā cercado	la mañana de san Juan	
8	tienen lo tambien cercado	q̃ no lo basto yo a descercar	
	por mi grande desuentura	y mi gran necessidad	
10	mis armas tēgo empeñadas	por mil doblas de oro y mas	(*E*15; *M*6)
	otras tantas deuo en Francia	sobre mi buena verdad	
12	mis caualleros el rey	no he con que los gouernar	(*M*8)
	y vna hermana que tengo	no he con que la casar	
14	que en todos mis palacios	no entiendo aya vn pan	
	si yo melo como rey	los otros que comeran	
16	si vuestra alteza no socorre	yo me yre moro a tornar	
	de questo piensa mi alma	mira que podra pensar	
18	alli hablo el emperador	mouido de piedad	
	esforçad vos el buen conde	no querades desmayar	
20	que para esto son los hombres	para passar bien y mal	
	mas dios voslo p̃done conde	que deuierades antes hablar	
22	mando llamar su thesorero	de su thesoro real	(*E*16; *M*14)
	dize le desta manera	empeçole demandar	

24	da mil doblas al conde para su verdad guardar	(*E*17; *M*16)
	y dale otras mil para sus armas quitar	(*E*17; *M*16)
26	dale tambien otras mil para con damas holgar	(*M*20)
	a Oliueros y Montesinos mandara luego llamar	
28	y tambien al esforçado esse paladin Roldan	
	y a Urgel delas marchas y al fuerte merian	
30	y que tomassen la gente y fuesse luego a montaluan	
	questa cercado de moros que lo ayan de descercar	
32	de que esto oyera el buẽ conde tal respuesta le fue a dar	
	muchas gracias el buen rey de vuestra buena voluntad	(*M*22)
34	que yo tengo tantos tesoros que puedo bien emprestar	
	mas vna merced vos pido esto me aueys de otorgar	(*E*9)
36	que me caseys conla infanta vuestra hija natural	(*E*10; *M*24)
	respondiera el buen rey tal respuesta le fue a dar	
38	ya no es tiempo el cõde claros de aquesso vos hablar	
	que la tengo prometida al honrrado don Beltran	(*E*13; *M*26)
40	y por esto el buen conde avos no lapuedo dar	(*E*11; *M*25)
	que vos soys niño y mochacho para tal muger tomar	
42	yo hos beso las manos rey pues me quereys desonrrar	
	y fuerase para su casa para auer de reposar	
44	ya se retrae el buen conde la siesta por descansar	(*M*31)
	porque la noche passada no la pudo reposar	(*M*32)
46	por amores dela infanta su señora natural	(*M*33)
	congoxas le congoxauan sospiros no dan lugar	
48	viendose en tal agonia comença de hablar	
	o maldito seas cupido y venus otro que tal	
50	porque assi me aueys metido eneste fuego infernal	
	que de noche yo no duermo ni de dia puedo holgar	
52	que si la causa tal no fuesse me yria a desesperar	
	mass en ser quien es la causa es dicha poder penar	
54	si dello ha de ser seruida essa pues no tiene par	
	que avn que mil vezes muriesse es nada por alcançar	
56	de conoscer ser querido por obras o por pensar	
	porque solo tu fauor es mas que quede dar	
58	dio bozes al camarero que se quiere leuantar	
	vistese vn jubon chapado que no se puede estimar	(*M*52)
60	y de oro de martillo vn mote bien de notar	
	en su braço que dezia gran dolor es dessear	

62	y vnas calças bigarradas de perlas ricas sin par	
	con vn mote que dezia no tiene nombre mi mal	
64	y vnos çapatos franceses de vn carmesi singular	(*M*54)
	con vnas llamas de oro relumbran como cristal	
66	el mote que tienen escrito es este que oyres nombrar	
	avnque de contino arden no se acaban de quemar	
68	y vna ropa roçegante sobre ella vn rico collar	
	el mote della dezia es vn dolor desigual	
70	y vna gorra enla cabeça que no se puede estimar	
	con tres letras coronadas el moto muy singular	
72	es tan alto mi desseo que no ay mas que dessear	
	caualgo en vna hacanea la qual hizo atauiar	(*M*55)
74	de vna guarnicion muy rica y las riendas y el petral	
	lleno de vnas campanillas que de oro era el metal	(*M*56)
76	y vnas lagrimas sembradas el mote no de oluidar	
	sin doleros vos señora no se puede acabar	
78	con doze moços despuelas para le acompañar	(*M*57)
	vestidos dela librea de aquella dama sin par	
80	los jubones de morado sayos de desesperar	
	todas las mãgas derechas les hizo el conde bordar	
82	de vnas matas de ruda que querian ya granar	(*M*47)
	el mote dellas dezia mas amargo es esperar	
84	embia delante vn paje por su alteza auisar	
	quel conde la quiere ver por las manos le besar	
86	antes quel paje no salga el conde fuera llegar	
	los porteros que lo veen abren le de par en par	
88	porque tienen mandamiento que le dexassen entrar	
	la princessa esta sola retrayda por rezar	
90	entrara el conde con ella y empeçarale de contar	
	lo que al rey auia dicho y la respuesta que le va dar . . .	

Sources

A   =   *Pliegos BL*, III, 977–982 (no. 54*a*)
B   =   *Pliegos BN*, II, 293–297
C   =   *Pliegos de Praga*, I, 41–45

Variants

3*b*	auia *B.*
4*b*	le *omitted BC.*
5*a*	distes me el emperador *C*; lo *omitted B.*
5*b*	el castillo *BC.*
6*a*	por mi bien *BC.*
7*b*	yo *omitted C.*
14*b*	no entiendo que ay un pan *BC.*
15*a*	si yo me le como el rey *BC.*
15*b*	los mios *BC.*
17	q̃ mas quiero perder la vida / que yo tal vida pasar *BC.*
18*a*	respondio *BC.*
19*a*	no desmayeys *BC.*
21*a*	os *BC.*
21*b*	que antes deuierades hablar *BC*; bablar (*sic*) *A.*
22*b*	su thesorero real *BC.*
24*a*	doblas de oro al conde *BC.*
25*a*	y dar le has otras mil *BC.*
27*a*	y a Montesinos *B.*
31	*omitted BC.*
32*a*	desque esto oyera el conde *BC.*
32*b*	fuera a dar *B.*
33*b*	por la buena voluntad *BC.*
35*a*	os *B.*
35*b*	esta no me aueys de negar *BC.*
42*a*	querays *B.*
43*a*	y fue se *B.*
49*a*	seas tu *B.*
53*a*	mass (*sic*) *A;* mas *BC.*
53*b*	dicho *C.*
54*b*	essa que no *B*; ella pues no *C.*
55*a*	mil jvezes (?) *B.*
57*a*	su *BC.*
57*b*	es mas que se puede dar *BC.*
60*a*	*omitted BC.*
60*b*	y vn mote *BC.*
65*a*	de fuego *BC.*

65*b*   como vn christal *BC*.
66*a*   tiene escripto *BC*.
66*b*   oyreys *BC*.
68*a*   roçagante *B*; rozagante *C*.
71*a*   coronada *BC*.
71*b*   mote *BC*.
75*a*   llenos *B*.
77*b*   pueden *BC*.
78*a*   de espuelas *B*.
80*a*   del morado *C*.
82*b*   geanar (*sic*) *B*.
83*a*   della *B*.
83*b*   amago (*sic*) *B*.
84*b*   para *B;* por a *C*.
85*a*   que el *B*.
86*a*   antes que el (quel *C*) page tornasse *BC*.
86*b*   fuerra (*sic*) *B*.
87*b*   las puertas abierto le han *BC*.
88   *omitted B*.
89*a*   estaua *BC*.
90*b*   y empieçale *BC*.
91   lo que el rey (le *C*) auia dicho / sin vn punto le faltar *BC*.

A caza va el emperador (= *Primav.* 191), which also represents *Conde Claros y el emperador*, has been preserved in a series of *cancioneros*, starting with the *Cancionero de romances* (1550). Various later printings, which we have not seen, are listed in MCR, II, 289*a*. Here is the text according to C1550. Following v. 20, *A caza* continues with the only known early version of *Conde Claros fraile*:

A caça va el emperador   a sant Iuan de Montiña
2   con el yua el conde Claros   por le tener compañia   (*M2*)
    contando le yua contando   el gran menester que tenia
4   no me lo digays el conde   hasta despues a la venida
    mis armas tengo empeñadas   por mil marcos de oro y mas   (*E15; M6*)
6   otros tantos deuo en Francia   sobre mi buena verdad
    llamen me mi camarero   de mi camara real   (*E16; M14*)

8	dad mil marcos de oro al conde para sus armas quitar	
	dad mil marcos de oro al conde para mantener verdad	
10	dalde otros tantos al conde para vestir y calçar	(*M*21)
	dalde otros tantos al conde para las tablas jugar	
12	dalde otros tantos al conde para torneos armar	
	dalde otros tantos al conde para con damas folgar.	(*M*20)
14	Muchas mercedes señor por esto y por mucho mas	(*E*9; *M*22)
	a la infanta Clara niña vos por muger me la dad:	(*E*10; *M*24)
16	Tarde acordastes el conde que mandada la tengo ya	(*E*13; *M*26)
	vos me la dareys señor acabo que no querays	(*M*27)
18	porque preñada la tengo de los seys meses o mas.	
	El emperador que esto oyera tomo dello gran pesar	
20	buelue riendas al cauallo y torno se a la ciudad. . . .	

Source

C1550, pp. 319–321.

Variant

1*a*   ACa ca *C1550*.

Media noche era por filo (= *Primav.* 190) begins with a relatively short version of *Conde Claros insomne* (vv. 1–20) and then continues with *Conde Claros y la infanta* (vv. 21–75), followed by *Conde Claros preso* (vv. 76 ff.). The ballad was abundantly printed in both *pliegos sueltos* and *cancioneros* (MCR, II, 584*a*; IV, 166*b*). Because both *pliegos* (Prague; Biblioteca Nacional) omit vv. 6*b* and 7*a*, we have chosen the *Cancionero sin año* as our base text, with variants listed from the two *pliegos* and from four other *cancioneros*:

	Media noche era por filo los gallos querian cantar	
2	conde claros con amores no podia reposar	(*M*32)
	dando muy grandes sospiros que el amor le hazia dar	
4	por amor de clara niña no le dexa sossegar	(*M*33)
	quando vino la mañana que queria alborear	
6	salto diera dela cama que parece vn gauilan	(*M*34)
	bozes da por el palacio y empeçara de llamar	

8	leuanta mi camarero dame vestir y calçar	(M35?)
	presto estaua el camarero para auer selo de dar	(M37)
10	dierale calças de grana borzeguis de cordouan	
	dieronle jubon de seda aforrado en zarzahan	(E21; M52)
12	dierale vn manto rico que no se puede apreciar	
	trezientas piedras preciosas al derredor del collar	(M48)
14	traele vn rico cauallo quen la corte no ay su par	(E22; M55)
	que la silla con el freno bien valia vna ciudad	
16	con trezientos cascaueles alrededor del petral	(M56)
	los ciento eran de oro 7 los ciento de metal	
18	7 los ciento son de plata por los sones concordar	
	7 vase para el palacio para el palacio real	(M60)
20	ala infanta clara niña alli la fuera hallar. . . .	

Sources (Base text: *C*)

A	=	*Pliegos de Praga*, I, 33–39.
B	=	*Pliegos BN*, II, 144–151.
C	=	CSA, fols. 83 ro.–90 ro.
D	=	C1550, pp. 168–173.
E	=	*Silva* (1550), pp. 390–396.
F	=	*Silva* (1561), fols. 80 vo.–87 vo.
G	=	Tortajada (1652), pp. 198–209.

Variants

1*b*   quierẽ *A*; quieren *B*.
3*a*   grandes sospiros va dando *AB*; Muy grandes suspiros dando *G*.
3*b*   que amor le haze penar *ABG*.
4*a*   que el amor *AB*; que amores *G*.
4*b*   dexo *B*; dexan *G*.
6*b*-7*a*   *omitted ABG*.
7*b*   y *omitted AB*.
8*a*   leuantad *AB*; levantaos *G*.
8*b*   dadme *ABG*.
9*a*   Camar (*sic*) *B*.
10*a*   calça *G*.
10*b*   borzeguies *BF*; borceguin *G*; de vn *B*.
11*a*   dierale vn jubon *G*.

11*b*   gorgueran *G.*
12*a*   manto muy rico *G.*
12*b*   podia preciar *G.*
13*b*   al deredor *A;* al rededor *BG.*
14*b*   que en *G.*
16*b*   al deredor *A;* alderredor *BFG.*
18*a*   los otros eran de plata *G.*
18*b*   concertar *B.*
19*a*   yuase *AB;* Ibase G.
20*b*   alla *ABG.*

Luis Vélez de Guevara's play, *Los hijos de la Barbuda*, written between 1608 and 1610, includes a brief parody of *Media noche era por filo*. Vélez's text is notably important, because, like so many ballads cited in *comedias*, it gives us a glimpse of a tradition quite different from that which was consecrated in the 16th-century *pliego* and *cancionero* printings. In this particular case, Vélez's version shares with the modern Sephardic and Zamoran versions a verse (vv. 398–399) which is otherwise undocumented in the early versions:

396	Conde Claros con amores	
	non podiera reposare,	(*M*32)
398	aprisa pide el vestido,	
	aprisa pide el calzare	(*E*23; *M*35)
400	cedo está su camarero	
	para habérselo de dare,	(*M*37)
402	que quien adama non duerme,	
	y más cuando celos haye.	
404	Salto diera de la cama	
	que parece un gavilane,	(*M*34)
406	que es, con amores, el lecho	
	mármol duro y lid campale. . . .	
412	Las calzas se pone el Conde	
	aprisa, y non de vagare,	
414	que amores de Blanca Niña	
	llamándole aprisa estane.	(*M*33?)[17]

---

17. Luis Vélez de Guevara, *Los hijos de la Barbuda*, ed. M.G. Profeti, pp. 106–107. Concerning the date, Profeti cites Bruerton ("Eight Plays," p. 253) for the

Much later (1650–1660?), Agustín Moreto would base his *Baile de Conde Claros* on another such variant text:

	media noche era por filo	
2	los gallos quieren cantar	(*Media* 1)
	conde claros con amores	
4	no podia reposar	(*M*32)
	aprisa pide el bestir	
6	aprisa pide el calçar	(*E*23; *M*35)
	dieronle una rica manga	
8	que la ynfanta fue a bordar	
	dieronle vn Rico caballo	(*E*22a; *M*55a)
10	Rucio rodado alaçan	
	que con el freno y la silla	
12	bien balia vna çiudad	(*Media* 15)
	fuerase açia los palaçios	(*M*60a)
14	de paris esa çiudad	
	donde esta la ynfanta clara	(*M*60b)
16	causa de todo su mal. . . .	

                                    (ed. Balbín, p. 97)

Here vv. 1–4, except for *quieren* (v. 2; but *queria* in a variant reading), are indistinguishable from *Media noche* (*Primav.* 190) and vv. 11–12 are also similar: "que la silla con el freno / bien valia vna ciudad" (v. 15). But it is clear that Moreto, like Vélez de Guevara, knew an early variant that shared an otherwise unknown verse with the modern tradition:

aprisa pide el vestido,   aprisa pide el calzare.
                    (Vélez, vv. 398–399)

---

proposed date of "1608–10," but suggests "acaso acercando la época de redacción más hacia 1608 que hacia 1610" (p. 65). Cf. ASW, p. 96. For agreements between *comedia* citations and the modern tradition (over against early *pliegos* and *cancioneros*), note, for example, Lope's text of *Blancaniña* (in *La locura por la honra*: RoH, II, 177; Yoná, p. 212, n. 12); Lope's version of *Las almenas de Toro* (in *Las almenas de Toro: Epic Ballads*, pp. 166–167); or the variants of *Búcar sobre Valencia* (in the anonymous *Comedia de las haçañas del Cid* and in Gil Vicente's *Auto da Lusitânia: Epic Ballads*, p. 277).

aprisa pide el bestir,　　aprisa pide el calçar.

(Moreto, vv. 4–5)

Si muy aprisa se lo pide,　　más aprisa se lo dan.

(Nuez, Zamora: CGR, IIA, 45)

Presto demandó el vistido,　　presto demandó el calsare.

(East, v. 23)

Presto demandó el vestido,　　presto demandó el calsar.

(Morocco, v. 35)

As Balbín correctly observes, Moreto's version "no parece literalmente inspirada en ninguna de las [otras versions antiguas] citadas" (p. 85). Moreto and Vélez—once again—thus attest to the importance of 16th- and 17th-century drama as an indispensable source of early variant readings.

Dormiendo está el conde Claros, preserved in a *pliego suelto* belonging to the Biblioteca Nacional (*Pliegos BN*, III, 277–280; DPS, no. 423; ASW, p. 73) represents a courtly reworking of the narrative also embodied in *A misa* (*Primav.* 192.43–88) and *Media noche* (*Primav.* 190.1–20). *Dormiendo* will continue with the tragic—if not mawkish—*Conde Claros degollado:*

	Dormiendo esta el conde claros　la siesta por descansar	(*M*31)
2	por que la noche passada　no la pudo reposar	(*M*32)
	dando bueltas en la cama　del secreto dessear	
4	sospiros no le dexauan　congoxa no le da lugar	
	por amores de la infanta　su señora natural	(*M*33)
6	da vozes al camarero　ya se quiere leuantar	
	viste se vn jubon chapado　que no se puede estimar	(*E*21; *M*52)
8	y de oro de martillo　vn mote muy de notar	
	enel braço que dezia　gran dolor es dessear	
10	vnas calças vigarradas　con perlas ricas sin par	
	el mote dellas dezia　no tiene precio mi mal	
12	vnos çapatos franceses　de vn carmesi singular	(*M*54)
	con vnas letras de oro　relumbran co mo cristal	
14	el mote dellas dezia　estas arden sin quemar	
	vna ropa roçagante　encima vn rico collar	

16 con vn mote que dezia   es mi dolor desigual
    vna gorra en la cabeça   que bien vale vna ciudad
18 con tres .yyy. coronadas   dize el mote ami pensar
    es tan alto mi desseo   que no ay mas que dessear
20 y doze moços despuelas   para le acompañar   (*M*57)
    vestidos delas colores   de aquella dama real
22 los jubones de morado   sayos de desesperar
    todas las mangas derechas   las hizo el conde broslar
24 con vnas matas de ruda   que querien ya granar   (*M*47)
    el mote dellas dezia   mas amarga el esperar
26 caualga en vn hacanea   la qual hizo atauiar   (*E*22; *M*55)
    de una guarnicion muy rica   y las riendas y el pretal
28 lleno de vnas campanillas   de oro y no de metal   (*M*56)
    y vnas lagrimas senbradas   y el mote para notar
30 sin doleros vos señora   no se puede nada acabar
    vase para los palacios   donde la infanta esta . . .   (*M*60)

Conde Claros insomne was enormously popular in the 16th century. There are various *ensalada* citations of the first verse, as well as of internal verses, of *Media noche era por filo*. Several of its verses were to enter folk-speech and become proverbial. The ballad is also documented in a pen trial and its music was annotated by Francisco Salinas in his *De Musica* and adapted by numerous *vihuelistas*.[18] Menéndez Pidal characterized the popularity of *Media noche era por filo* and its fragmentary derivatives: "El que más favor gozaba entre los músicos es el del *Conde Claros*, y lo merecía sin duda esa larga historia caballeresca de amor, llena de pasión, desenvoltura y tumulto de vida" (RoH, II, 84). *A misa* and *A caza* both clearly represent traditional variants of the *Emperador* narrative. *Dormiendo* would seem to be a learned, courtly reelaboration of the *Insomne* text which is joined to *A misa*, while *Media noche* gives us a different, more primitive, more traditional modality of *Insomne*. Vélez de Guevara's brief parody and Moreto's *Baile* both include, as we have seen, a verse which is paralleled in the Judeo-Spanish and Zamoran versions, but is present nowhere else in the early tradition (Vélez, vv. 398–399; Moreto, vv. 5–6 = *E*23; *M*35). Whether coincidental or not, it is also worthy of note that Vélez's text, like most Eastern Sephardic versions, prefers to call the princess

---

18. Concerning the early popularity of *Media noche era por filo*, see the Appendix.

Blancaniña. (Note, however, that the Eastern tradition, like most Moroccan versions, also knows *Claraniña* as a minority reading [vv. 10, 30, 30+].) The relationship of the early forms of *Emperador* and *Insomne* to their modern Sephardic counterparts (*E* = Eastern; *M* = Morocco) can be summarized in the following scheme. Since the order in which elements occur varies greatly from version to version, we arbitrarily follow the verse order of our Moroccan synthetic text:

— conel yua el conde claros por le tener compañia	(*Misa* 2)
con el yua el conde Claros por le tener compañia	(*Caza* 2)
Tras d'él salió su sobrino, por compañía leal.	(*M*2)
— vos me lo distes emperador castillo de Montaluan	(*Misa* 5)
¿Qué me dites, el mi tío, castiyo de Montalbán?	(*M*4)
— distes me lo por bien yo tomelo por mi mal	(*Misa* 6)
Me lo dites por herensia, salióme por desheredar;	(*M*5)
— mis armas tẽgo empeñadas por mil doblas de oro y mas	(*Misa* 10)
mis armas tengo empeñadas por mil marcos de oro y mas	(*Caza* 5)
Las armas tengo empeñadas por sien doblas y algo más.	(*E*15)
Mis armas tengo empeñadas en cien marcos de oro y más;	(*M*6)
— mis caualleros el rey no he con que los gouernar	(*Misa* 12)
mis caballeros se fueron, por no tenerles que dar;	(*M*8)
— mando llamar su thesorero de su thesoro real	(*Misa* 22)
llamen me mi camarero de mi camara real	(*Caza* 7)
Aquí, aquí, mis cavayeros, los que en mi comando estáx:	(*E*16)
Vení acá, mis tesoreros, mis tesoreros leal:	(*M*14)
— da mil doblas al conde [. . .] para sus armas quitar	(*Misa* 24a-25b)
dad mil marcos de oro al conde para sus armas quitar	(*Caza* 8)
Dexle sien doblas al conde para las armas quitar.	(*E*17)
dadle marcos de oro al conde para sus armas tomar;	(*M*16)
— dale tambien otras mil para con damas holgar	(*Misa* 26)
dalde otros tantos al conde para con damas folgar	(*Caza* 13)
dadle marcos de oro al conde para con damas folgar,	(*M*20)
— dalde otros tantos al conde para vestir y calçar	(*Caza* 10)
dadle marcos de oro al conde, para vestir y calsar;	(*M*21)
— muchas gracias el buen rey de vuestra buena voluntad	(*Misa* 33)
Muchas mercedes señor por esto y por mucho mas	(*Caza* 14)
Mersedes, dixo, mersedes, por esto y mucho más;	(*M*22)
— mas vna merced vos pido esto me aueys de otorgar	(*Misa* 35)

Una mersed le rogo, tío,   cual me havéx d'atorgar,   *(E9)*

— que me caseis conla infanta   vuestra hija natural   *(Misa 36)*

a la infanta Clara niña   vos por mujer me la dad   *(Caza 15)*

que me dex a Blancaniña,   por mujer y por igual.   *(E10)*

Vuestra hija, Claraniña,   por mujer la he de tomar.   *(M24)*

— 7 por esto el buen conde   avos no lapuedo dar   *(Misa 40)*

Esta mersed, el mi sovrino,   no vola puedo atorgar.   *(E11)*

Perdón, perdón, mi sobrino,   que no te la puedo dar;   *(M25)*

— que la tengo prometida   al honrrado don Beltran   *(Misa 39)*

Tarde acordastes el conde   que mandada la tengo ya   *(Caza 16)*

Despozada la tengo en Fransia,   con el conde Aligornar.   *(E13)*

apalabrada la tengo   con el conde de Montalbán.   *(M26)*

— vos me la dareys señor   acabo que no querays   *(Caza 17)*

Por mujer o por amiga,   Claraniña he de yevar.   *(M27)*

— ya se retrae el buen conde   la siesta por descansar   *(Misa 44)*

Dormiendo esta el conde claros   la siesta por descansar   *(Dorm. 1)*

Durmiendo está el conde Claros   la siesta por descansar,   *(M31 var.)*

— porque la noche passada   no la pudo reposar   *(Misa 45)*

conde claros con amores   no podia reposar   *(Media 2)*

Conde Claros con amores   non podiera reposare   (Vélez 396f.)

conde claros con amores   non podia reposar   (Moreto 3f.)

por que la noche passada   no la pudo reposar   *(Dorm. 2)*

porque la noche pasada   no la pudo asosegar   *(M32)*

— por amores dela infanta   su señora natural   *(Misa 46)*

por amor de clara niña   no le dexa sossegar   *(Media 4)*

que amores de Blanca Niña   llamándole aprisa estane   (Vélez 414f.)

por amores de la infanta   su señora natural   *(Dorm. 5)*

de amores de Claraniña   su sobrina natural;   *(M33 var.)*

— salto diera dela cama   que parece vn gauilan   *(Media 6)*

Salto diera de la cama   que parece un gavilane   (Vélez 404f.)

Salto diera de la cama,   que parese un gavilan.   *(M34)*

— leuanta mi camarero   dame vestir y calçar   *(Media 8)*

aprisa pide el vestido,   aprisa pide el calzare   (Vélez 398f.)

aprisa pide el bestir   aprisa pide el calçar   (Moreto 5f.)

Presto demandó el vistido,   presto demandó el calsare.   *(E23)*

Presto demandó el vestido,   presto demandó el calsar;   *(M35)*

— presto estaua el camarero   para auer selo de dar   *(Media 9)*

cedo está su camarero   para habérselo de dare   (Vélez 400f.)

Ahí se alḥadró un pajesito, que se lo solía dar:	(*M*37)
— de vnas matas de ruda que querian ya granar	(*Misa* 82)
con vnas matas de ruda que querien ya granar	(*Dorm.* 24)
con el labre de la ruda, cuando empiesa a apuntar;	(*M*47)
— trezientas piedras preciosas al derredor del collar	(*Media* 13)
trezientas piedras presiozas al derredor del coyar;	(*M*48)
— vistese vn jubon chapado que no se puede estimar	(*Misa* 59)
dierale jubon de seda aforrado en zarzahan	(*Media* 11)
viste se vn jubon chapado que no se puede estimar	(*Dorm.* 7)
dexle ǧaqueta de sirma, enforrada con ǧanfés al;	(*E*21)
diérale jugón de grana, enforrado en cordobán;	(*M*52)
— 7 vnos çapatos franceses de vn carmesi singular	(*Misa* 64)
vnos çapatos Franceses de vn carmesi singular	(*Dorm.* 12)
diérale sapato picado, con abroches de coral;	(*M*54)
— caualgo en vna hacanea la qual hizo atauiar	(*Misa* 73)
traele vn rico cauallo quen la corte no ay su par	(*Media* 14)
caualga en vn hacanea la qual hizo atauiar	(*Dorm.* 26)
dieronle vn Rico caballo Rucio rodado alaçan	(Moreto 9–10)
dexle cavayo de guerra, para la niña ir a quitar.	(*E*22)
diérale cabayo blanco, que el rey no cabalga tal;	(*M*35)
— lleno de vnas campanillas que de oro era el metal	(*Misa* 75)
con trezientos cascaueles alrededor del petral	(*Media* 16)
lleno de vnas campanillas de oro y no de metal	(*Dorm.* 28)
con trezientos cascabeles, alderredor del frontal;	(*M*56)
— con doze moços despuelas para le acompañar	(*Misa* 78)
y doze moços despuelas para le acompañar	(*Dorm.* 20)
trezientos mil negritos, que le van a acompañar.	(*M*57)
— 7 vase para el palacio para el palacio real	(*Media* 19)
vase para los palacios donde la infanta esta	(*Dorm.* 31)
fuerase açia los palaçios . . . donde esta la ynfanta clara	(Moreto 13, 15)
Por cayes de Claraniña, ya se fuera a pasear.	(*M*60)

Synoptically, the relationships between our texts can be summed up in the following table. The first column includes verse numbers from our Eastern and Moroccan synthetic texts, followed by a key word (or words); wherever an analogous verse is attested in the early texts, its presence is indicated by the pertinent verse number in the corresponding column(s):

E/M	Misa	Caza	Media	Vélez	Moreto	Dorm.
M2: compañía	2	2				
M4: castillo	5					
M5: herencia	6					
E15/M6: empeñadas	10	5				
M8: caballeros	12					
E16/M14: tesorero	22	7				
E17/M16: armas quitar	24a-25b	8				
M20: holgar	26	13				
M21: vestir-calzar		10				
M22: mercedes	33	14				
E9: otorgar	35					
E10/M24: Claraniña	36	15				
E11/M25: no puedo	40					
M27: he de llevar		17				
M31: Durmiendo	44					1
M32: reposar	45		2	396	4	2
M33: amores	46		4	414	3	5
M34: gavilán			6	404		
E13/M35: pedir			(8)	398	5	
M37: paje			9	400		
M47: ruda	82					24
M48: piedras			13			
E21/M52: jubón	59		11			7
M54: zapato	64					12
E22/M55: caballo	73		14		9	26
M56: cascabeles	75		16			28
M57: mozos	78					20
M61: palacios			19		13	31

It is abundantly clear from these comparisons that, as is the case with so many ballads in the modern tradition, neither the Eastern nor the Moroccan versions of *Emperador* + *Insomne* derive directly from any one of the early texts. In general, the Sephardic narratives of *Emperador* are closer to *A misa* than to *A caza*, but the Moroccan texts, at least, also embody elements present in *A caza,* but lacking in *A misa*, as is the case with *A caza*'s reading "dalde otros tantos al conde / para vestir y calçar" (v. 10 = *M*21) and Claros' arrogant persistence: "Vos me la dareys, señor . . ." (v. 17), probably echoed in the Moroccan tradition: "Por mujer o por amiga, / Claraniña he de yevar" (*M*27). Elsewhere, *A caza*'s wording is sometimes closer to the Sephardic texts than is *A misa*. Compare: "Muchas mercedes señor / por esto y por mucho mas" (*A caza*, v. 14) with the Moroccan: "Mersedes, dixo, mersedes, / por esto y mucho más" (v. 22), over against the only distantly similar reading of *A misa*: "muchas gracias el buen rey / de vuestra buena voluntad" (v. 33). It is worth noting too that many Eastern versions (v. 9: Una mersed le rogo, tío, / cual me havéx d'atorgar) have preserved a verse of *A misa* which seems to have died out in the Moroccan tradition: "mas vna merced vos pido / esto me aueys de otorgar" (*A misa*, v. 35). While the Sephardic traditions are more closely related to *A misa* than to *A caza*, that relationship is obviously indirect. There is no vestige in the Sephardic versions (nor in *A caza* for that matter) of an important contamination which is unique to *A misa*: The excuse that Claros' indigence is due to his castle's being besieged by the Moors and the Emperor's response in ordering the Carolingian heroes to go to Montalbán and help lift the siege.[19] Neither of the Sephardic forms attests to the prologue in *í-a*—extensively developed in the modern Aragonese tradition —which is characteristic of both *A misa* and *A caza*.

The relationship of the Sephardic *Conde Claros insomne* to its early counterparts is similarly complex. The Eastern tradition has preserved only a small vestige of *Insomne*, by combining the king's orders to his *caballeros* (= *camareros, tesoreros*) to provide the hero with money, as in *Emperador*, with the clothing and horse brought to Claros by his page (*E*19–23), as in *Insomne*. It is worth noting that some of these elements—the marvelous shirt embroidered

---

19. The Count's demands would seem unjustifiable, since, in reality, he turns out to have "tantos tesoros / que puedo bien emprestar" (v. 33). His invented problems appear to be simply a means of testing the Emperor's good will. Whoever introduced the motif of the siege of Montalbán was very probably thinking of the ballad of *Don García de Urueña* (Atal anda don García / por una sala adelante [*Primav.* 133]). For details, see the Appendix.

under special circumstances—are shared by the Eastern and Moroccan traditions (*E*19–20; *M*38–46), but are lacking in the early texts. The Moroccan modality continues *Emperador* with a fully developed—and indeed greatly amplified—rendition of *Insomne*. After an initial verse which is clearly related to *Dormiendo* (*M*31), the Moroccan tradition will agree more closely with *Media noche*—the most traditional in character of the three extensive early *Insomne* texts—than with the more courtly and elaborate *A misa* and *Dormiendo*, yet it also includes elements present in these latter texts, but absent from *Media noche*: Such is the case with the bitter rue (*ruda*) which adorns Claros' shirt (*M*47), the fancy shoes brought to him by his page (*M*54), and the servants who accompany the hero (*M*57). Again, in one case, the modern tradition will agree more closely with Vélez de Guevara's *comedia* and Moreto's *baile,* than with any other early testimony: The verse "Presto demandó el vestido, / presto demandó el calsar(e)" (*M*35; *E*23) has obvious counterparts in Vélez's "aprisa pide el vestido, / aprisa pide el calzare" (vv. 398–399) and Moreto's "aprisa pide el bestir / aprisa pide el calçar" (vv. 5–6), in contrast to the only distantly similar: "leuanta mi camarero / dame vestir y calçar" (*Media noche*, v. 8). Both *A misa* and *Dormiendo*, with their elaborate series of amorous devices (*motes*) embroidered on the hero's clothing, attest to the effects of courtly *remaniement* and, to judge by its close verbal agreement, *Dormiendo* would seem to have been based directly on *A misa*. For all the obvious gallantry and elaborate detail evoked by the Sephardic versions, there is no vestige in them of these contrived courtly mottoes. Just as in the case of *Conde Claros y el emperador*, we must conclude that the Sephardic forms of *Conde Claros insomne*—which agree sometimes with *Media noche*, sometimes with *A misa-Dormiendo*, sometimes with Vélez de Guevara and Moreto, and sometimes with each other against all the early witnesses—must derive, through the unknowable complexities of oral tradition, from some form or forms of the ballad which are otherwise unattested (except, of course, partially in other branches of the modern tradition). We can only agree with Bráulio do Nascimento's incisive characterization of the Conde Claros tradition as a whole: "Constitui-se num texto-mosaico, com grande dificultade e creio mesmo que impossibilidade de identificar-se um possível arquetipo."[20]

---

20. B. do Nascimento, "*Conde Claros* na Tradição Portuguesa," p. 145. On the non-existence of a "text" for oral balladry, see D. Catalán, "El romancero medieval"; *Arte poética*, I, 213–241. Joseph Duggan has reached similar conclusions for the *chansons de geste*: "Oral Performance," p. 89.

Let us now characterize the development of the Sephardic versions of *Conde Claros y el emperador* and *Conde Claros insomne* in relation to their 16th-century antecedents. The Eastern texts of *Conde Claros y el emperador* attest to a completely divergent initial segment. Most versions begin with an introductory invocation, indicating that it is at dawn when the king and his nephew go riding out together:

> Luz del día y luz del día,   luz del día y claridad,
> 2   el día me dax el sole,   la noche'l claro lunar;
>   la mañanica las estreyas,   cuando quiere alvorear.
> 4   Se pasean tío y sovrino,   ǧuntos van a un barabar. . . .

These initial verses combine a well known type of iterative invocation (in v. 1)—*Abenámar, Abenámar; Rey don Sancho, rey don Sancho; Blancaniña, Blancaniña*[21]—with a very frequent tripartite pattern (in vv. 2–3), having elements $A+B$ in the first verse and a third element, C, occupying the entire second verse.[22] Verse 1 recalls various Peninsular and Judeo-Spanish incipits, many of which allude, as here, to the ballad's temporal context:

> Días de mayo, días de mayo,   días de la rica calor. . . .
>   (*Prisionero:* San Ciprián de Sanabria)

> Mes de mayo, mes de mayo,   mes de mayo, primavera. . . .
>   (*Quintado:* Extremadura, CPE, II, 96)

> Nochebuena y nochebuena,   noche de la Navidad. . . .
>   (*Conde Sol:* Soria, *RH:Fronteras*, p. 262)

> Noches buenas, noches buenas,   noches son de enamorar. . . .
>   (*Melisenda insomne:* Sarajevo, CMP 17.3)

> ¡Ay Valensia y ay Valensia,   Valensia la bien sercada! . . .
>   (*Búcar:* Tetuán, *Epic Ballads*, no. 6*B*)

---

21. Also *Juan Lorenzo, Juan Lorenzo; Moro alcaide, moro alcaide; Reina Elena, Reina Elena.* On the pattern, see Monroe, "Hispano-Arabic Poetry during the Almoravid Period."

22. Concerning triadic patterns in the *Romancero*, see the Appendix.

Arbolero, arbolero,   arbolero atan yentil. . . .
(*Vuelta del marido [í]:* Rhodes, CMP I1.20)

Mañanita, mañanita,   mañanita de San Juan. . . .
(*Conde Niño:* Tetuán, CMP J1.30)

Más arriba y más arriba,   más arriba de Sofía. . . .
(*Fuente fecundante:* Istanbul, CMP R5.2)

Mañanita, mañanita,   mañanita de oración. . . .
(*Bella en misa:* Tetuán, CMP S7.22)

De día era, de día,   de día y no de noche. . . .
(*Prisionero:* Salonika, Attias 8)

That the protagonists ride out to race their horses seems distantly more similar to the hunting expedition in *A caza* (*Primav.* 191) than to the conversation on the way to mass (*A misa: Primav.* 192).[23] There is no trace here, nor in Morocco, of the initial verses in *í-a* assonance characteristic of the early forms, which can, as we have seen, be documented in Upper Aragon, where they function as a prologue to *Conde Claros fraile.* Here the *í-a* assonance extends to portions of the *Emperador* narrative that in all other areas are in *á.*[24] The Eastern forms are distinctive in placing Claros' demand of marriage to Blancaniña (or Claraniña) before his complaint (here reduced to a minimum) about having pawned his weapons (v. 15). Claros' feigned poverty and the emperor's generous offers usually serve as a prelude to the count's demand for Claraniña: He seems to be testing the emperor's intentions toward him and, when they turn out to be so overwhelmingly favorable, Claros confidently reveals his real purpose. The Eastern and Moroccan traditions share a singular

---

23. Compare *CMC*, vv. 3507 ff. The horse races that conclude the *Iliad* (Book 23) or *The Wedding of Smailagić Meho* (ed. Lord and Bynum, *SCHS*, III, 246, 321, 323; also I, 134 et alibi) are communal affairs and quite different from what is going on here. On the topic of ballad action taking place on the way to or from mass, see *En torno*, pp. 136, 141, 147; add also *Conde Alemán y la reina* (*Yoná* 7A.16, 7B.15).

24. See the version from Esposa, p.j. Jaca, Huesca, edited in CGR, IA, 44, and reproduced earlier in the present chapter. The influence of *Conde Alarcos* (which also involves discussion with a king about marriage to the king's daughter) may possibly help explain the preference for *í-a* assonance in the Aragonese form of *Conde Claros y el emperador.*

departure from the early texts in the king's suggestion that Claros may still be able to win Claraniña by force of arms (*E*, v. 14; *M*, vv. 29–30, 59–60). The motif may, as we have suggested elsewhere, reflect an early intrusion of *Gaiferos y Melisenda*.[25] As we have seen, the Eastern texts, having already stated Claros' demand before the king's offers, then combine the offers with the rich raiment brought to the count by his page, according to *Conde Claros insomne* (*E*, vv. 16–18 + 19–22). Only one of the Eastern versions preserves an additional verse from *Insomne*, which normally precedes the page's bringing the clothing: "Presto demandó el vistido, / presto demandó el calsare" (*E*, v. 23). Count Claros then departs, in the formulaic verse: "Ya se parte el cavayero, / ya se parte, ya se va" (*E*, v. 24).[26] The ballad continues with a pair of interrelated formulas, indicating that Claros rides slowly where he may be seen, but, along deserted streets, his horse's hoofs strike sparks. These verses are characteristic of the Peninsular versions of *Conde Claros insomne* and *Conde Claros fraile*, but similar ones are known in numerous other Sephardic and Peninsular ballads as well.[27] The Eastern versions end with a scene, shared with some Peninsular texts, in which ladies and maidens gather at the windows to watch the knight as he rides by. In the Eastern tradition, they ask him about his intentions and he answers that he is determined to search for Blancaniña (or Claraniña).[28] The Eastern *Conde Claros y el emperador* is characteristically brief and unelaborated,

---

25. See *Yoná*, pp. 81–82.

26. On this formula, see *Yoná*, pp. 29, n. 1, 44, n. 14, 84, 238, n. 30; *Tres calas*, pp. 74–75, n. 77.

27. For numerous examples, see *Yoná*, pp. 84–85 and nn. 8–10, 174 (vv. 14–15), 183, n. 15. Only the second formula, in which sparks are struck by the horse's hoofs, is present in the Moroccan *Emperador* (v. 58). In the *Chanson de Roland*, the pagan Valdabrun's horse Gramimund is "plus . . . isnels que nen est uns falcuns" (ed. Whitehead, v. 1572), just as, in Castilian forms of *Conde Claros fraile* (and other ballads), the hero's horse "corre como un gavilán" (RPM 58; *Yoná*, pp. 84, 85, n. 10).

28. The situation is distantly reminiscent of *El forzador*, where the luxuriously dressed knight, passing by, looks up to behold the brilliant beauty of "damas y donzeas," apparently standing at a window (*Tres calas*, A3.3–5). But, needless to say, there is nothing distinctive about the topic of beautiful women looking out of windows in folk narrative. For the situation's proverbial implications, note: *Mujer en la ventana, parra en el camino real* (O'Kane, p. 166*b*); *Mujer ventanera, uva de calle* (Sacristán, II, 28); *Mujer ventanera, ni para dentro ni para fuera* (Rodríguez Marín, *Los 6.666 refranes*, p. 112*b*); *Mujer en la ventana, más pierde que gana* (Rodríguez Marín, *10.700 Refranes*, p. 203); *Mujer en ventana, o puta o enamorada* (Burgos, oral tradition).

in contrast to its Moroccan counterpart: Claros' complaints are kept to a minimum, the king's offers include a total of only two hundred doubloons to redeem the count's weapons and to spend along the road, and there is merely a succinct allusion to the hero's richly decorated shirt and jacket. Only the three ladies, ritualistically embroidering on St. John's morning, hint at the fantastic amplifications which will characterize our ballad in its Moroccan modality.[29]

The intricately mixed version of *El sueño de doña Alda + Melisenda insomne,* collected by M. J. Benardete from a Salonikan singer in New York (Benardete 3), ends with three verses taken from *Conde Claros insome,* which supplement the testimony of our Eastern synthetic text:

>   Ya se hue la Merizelda,   para la caxa d'anxugare,
> 22   a meterse camisa de seda,   sirma y perla y cavesale.
>   Cien damas se la lavraron   a la oriya de la mare;
> 24   y otras cien se la cuzieron   mañanica de San Juare;
>   y las otras cien iban con eya,   la iyan acompañare.

Verses 22, 23*a,* 24*b* correspond to our synthetic vv. 19–20, but the contamination adds three details which are lacking in our synthetic text and agree with the Moroccan tradition: One hundred (rather than just three) ladies are embroidering by the seashore (v. 23*b* = Moroccan synthetic v. 39*b*) and, in addition to their embroidering, another one hundred are sewing (v. 24*a* = Moroccan v. 45*a*). These details suggest that, at some earlier stage, the Eastern tradition, like its Moroccan counterpart, must have embodied a more elaborate description of the shirt's manufacture.

The Moroccan texts, in their present state, keep the initial scene of *Conde Claros y el emperador,* in which the king and his nephew appear, to a minimum. There is no horse race: Both characters simply go out (Ya se salía el buen reye . . . Tras d'él salió su sobrino . . .) and Claros immediately launches into his bitter complaint, though no circumstantial details are provided. Many Moroccan versions do begin with a two-verse prologue of extraneous origin: *¿Por que no cantáis, fortuna?* (to be discussed below). These verses just possibly may have replaced some earlier prologue, on the order of the Eastern *Luz del día* verses, but we can now do nothing more than surmise what might

---

29. For the St. John's morning motif and some minor contaminations in the Eastern versions, see the Appendix.

have happened earlier on.[30] What is most striking about the Moroccan versions is their extensive elaboration of elements inherited from, but generally less developed in, the early tradition. The ballad embodies four lengthy and interrelated catalogues: Claros' complaint (vv. 4–13); the king's response (15–21); the fabulous shirt and its preparation (38–50); and the list of the count's other appurtenances: clothing, horse, servants (51–57). In regard to the hero's complaint, the 16th-century *A misa* (vv. 10–13) mentions only the pawning of his arms, his having borrowed another thousand doubloons against his "good word," the departure of his knights, and the fact that he has no money to marry off his sister (all occasioned here by the siege of Montalbán castle, perhaps, suggested, as we have seen, by the ballad of *Don García de Urueña*). *A caza* (vv. 5–6) is even more succinct and mentions only the pawned arms and the money borrowed against Claros' "good word." In *A misa* (vv. 24–26), the emperor answers by offering a thousand doubloons to redeem the hero's weapons, another thousand to redeem the hero's word, and another thousand so he can take pleasure with ladies. The offers are more elaborate in *A caza* (vv. 8–13), where one thousand marks are offered, in each case, for the weapons, for the count's word, for clothing and shoes, for playing at tables, for tourneys, and for taking pleasure with women. These early enumerations have been strikingly expanded in the Moroccan texts, which mention weapons, ships, knights, friends, servants, maidens, ladies, clothing and shoes—all lost to Claros because of his supposed indigence—and all of which the king offers to restore (vv. 6–13 and 15–21). According to *A misa* and *Dormiendo*, the page gives the count a doublet (*jubón*), breeches (*calças*), shoes, showy clothing (*ropa roçegante*), and a cap (*gorra*), all richly decorated, he mounts a small horse (*hacanea*), with bells around its breast-strap (*petral*) and is accompanied by twelve attendants (*moços despuelas*). In both *A misa* and its derivative, *Dormiendo*, the enumeration is encumbered by descriptions of elaborate courtly *motes* (devices) embroidered on the various articles of clothing. *Media noche* embodies a different list: *calças*, boots (*borzeguís*), *jubón*, cloak (*manto*), a horse with no equal at the court, equipped with a splendid saddle and reins, and with three hundred bells around its breast-strap.[31] Again, the Moroccan enumeration has been vastly expanded by the addition of a second catalogue-within-a-catalogue:

---

30. For similar instances of contaminations which may indicate—indirectly—the existence of now lost narrative components at an earlier stage in the tradition, see *Conde Antores, Almenas de Toro*, and *Búcar sobre Valencia* (Nahón, p. 95; *Epic Ballads*, pp. 175, n. 8, 250 at n. 35).

31. For the motif of the three hundred bells, see the Appendix.

the lengthy list of operations necessary for creating Claros' exquisite shirt (vv. 39–46), all of which would seem to be an exclusive creation of the Moroccan tradition. This stupendous article of clothing has been fabricated by the consecutive intervention of groups of one hundred ladies, who prepare, wash, card, spin, weave, cut, sew, and embroider it—by moonlight—and decorate it with sprigs of newly sprouted rue and with three hundred magical precious stones, a hundred of which cool the hero, a hundred warm him, and a hundred give him charm to take pleasure with women. The rue, probably now endowed with magical protective associations, corresponds to the lover's bitter rue embroidered on the servants' sleeves in *A misa* (v. 82) and *Dormiendo* (v. 24).[32] The three hundred precious stones may somehow have been suggested by the three hundred little bells and their properties, as envisioned in *Media noche:*

16   con trezientos cascaueles   alrededor del petral
       los ciento eran de oro   7 los ciento de metal
18   7 los ciento son de plata   por los sones concordar

It will be noted that both groups of attributes embody the same traditional tripartite pattern, but the verses' similarity is distant at best. In any case, the catalogue of activities centered around the marvelous shirt would seem to be an exclusively Judeo-Spanish feature. Such an enumeration of consecutive tasks may perhaps have been suggested by another traditional Judeo-Spanish song, *Vivardueña*, which probably originated as an agricultural work-song in the Peninsular tradition, but in the urban milieu of the North African and Eastern Sephardic communities, became a dance-game traditional to wedding festivities:

1   Vivardueña lo siembra'n su arenal
     y así lo siembra Vivardueña.
2   Vivardueña lo corta'n su arenal
     y así lo corta Vivardueña.
3   Vivardueña lo cría'n su arenal
     y así lo cría Vivardueña.
4   Vivardueña lo monda'n su arenal
     y así lo monda Vivardueña.
5   Vivardueña lo afrecha'n su arenal

---

32. For some of the motifs present in *A misa* and *Dormiendo*, see the Appendix.

y así lo afrecha Vivardueña.
6 Vivardueña lo muele'n su arenal
y así lo muele Vivardueña.
7 Vivardueña lo cuese en su arenal
y así lo cuese Vivardueña.
8 Vivardueña lo come'n su arenal
y así lo come Vivardueña.[33]

Certain Moroccan versions (CMP B9.17, 18, 20, 21; Larrea 31) have preferred to relieve the monotonous consecutive repetitions of *las sien damas* by using the formula *otras tantas* throughout, as in Larrea 31, or more effectively, in alternate verses, as in Eugenio Silvela's version (CMP B9.17):

28 Las sien damas le curaron,   a la orilla de la mar;
 otras tantas le cardaron,   con carditas de metal;
30 las sien damas le filaron,   en fusito[s] de fustar;
 otras tantas le tegieron,   en maromas de cristal;
32 las sien damas le cortaron,   con tijeras de metal;
 otras tantas le cosieron,   con agujas y dedal;
34 las sien damas le labraron,   a la sombra del lunar;
 con el lambre de la ruda   cuando empeza apuntar;
36 tresientas perlas presiosas,   al derredor del collar;
 las siento le daban aire,   las siento calor le dan;
38 las siento le daban gracia   para con damas folgar.[34]

After the verses pertaining to the fabulous shirt, the Moroccan texts take up the enumeration of other articles of clothing and appurtenances, following—and

---

33. *En torno*, p. 110. Concerning the song, its Peninsular and Romance congeners, and its possible significance for the history of rural Jewish commmunities in Spain, see pp. 111–117. Add to these references, Gauthier-Villars, *Villard-de-Lans*, p. 140; Libiez, *Hainaut*, II, 158–159 (no. 77); Senny and Pinon, *Ardenne*, I, 12–13; II, 126–132, where Pinon provides important comparative references concerning the French *Aveine*. Hemsi (*Coplas*, no. 26) collected an Eastern version from Istanbul.

34. For examples of the use of *otras tantas*, compare: "I lyyo malanyya tal chuflete, / las doblas ke di por ti. // I otras tantas lyyo les dyera / ke me lo kiten de akí. // . . . I otras tantas le dyera, / ke me lo trayygan akí" (*Chuflete: Yoná* 27.7–8, 12); "Siete veces fue templado / en la sangre de un dragón // y otras tantas fue afilado / porque cortase mejor" (*Infante vengador: Primav.* 150).

perhaps elaborating upon—some earlier form of *Conde Claros y el emperador*. The list —different from any known 16th-century text—includes a fine undershirt, a doublet, stockings, shoes, a white horse with three hundred bells, and, to cap everything off, three hundred thousand black servants. More than a narrative in its own right, the Moroccan *Conde Claros y el emperador* would seem to have become a mere pretext for dwelling and expatiating, in exquisite and delightful detail, upon the difficulties attending the gallant count's chivalrous life, the king's excessive generosity, and Claros' fabulously luxurious raiment. The winning of Claraniña, by force of arms, for which all of this stupendous effort has been expended, has come to be of strictly secondary importance—if indeed it can even be considered an authentic part of the narrative. It has become a mere afterthought and only two versions (CMP B9.13; Larrea 27.40–43) actually mention it at all. What is important here, in accord with the aristocratizing criteria of Sephardic balladry, is the song's brilliant, dazzling display of power, wealth, and luxury—evoking a fantastic medieval world, so different, one might add, from the dreadfully constrained everyday realities of the North African *mellaḥs*.[35]

The order in which the various components of these four interrelated catalogues are arranged varies greatly from version to version and the ordering of our synthetic text has consequently had to involve certain arbitrary decisions. The arrangement of one of José Benoliel's Tangier versions (CMP B9.13) suggests a reasonable pattern: That the king's offers should follow the same sequence as the count's complaints:

6	Mis armas tengo empeñadas, en cien marcos de oro y más;
	mis damas tengo perdidas, con quien solía folgar.
8	¡Ya no tengo oro ni plata, con que vestir y calzar!—
	Oído lo había su tío, desde su sala onde está:
10	—Ven acá, mis tesoreros, mis tesoreros leal:
	Dadle marcos de oro al conde, para sus armas tomar;
12	dadle marcos de oro al conde, para con damas folgar;
	dadle marcos de oro al conde, para vestir y calzar.[36]

---

35. On the aristocratizing character of Sephardic balladry, see *En torno*, pp. 145–147 and n. 36. On the poverty of Moroccan *mellaḥs*, see, for example, Chouraqui, *Les juifs*, pp. 176–177; Id., *L'Alliance*, p. 110; Deshen, p. 65; Orwell, "Marrakesh."

36. Needless to say, v. 9 is an impertinent contamination. The king and Claros are walking and talking together, yet now the king, in his hall, overhears what his nephew is saying! The verse could have originated in any one of several ballads:

Benoliel's text is also significant in that the count's complaint ends with the unique v. 8, stressing the hero's inability to buy clothing and footwear. By ending both the complaint and the king's response with such an allusion to *vestir y calzar*, the culmination of the first two catalogues thus anticipates the sartorial subject matter of the two other substantial enumerations in *Conde Claros insomne*.[37]

We must stress, however, that a synthetic text such as the one presented here is a philological creation, which could never have existed, in all its component parts, in oral tradition. All the same, Benoliel's version attests, if indeed its verse order is authentic, to just such an ending for both the complaint and the offers. Again, there is a certain thematic coherence in the beginning of the first catalogue and the ending of the last one. The count starts by alluding to the loss of his weapons (Mis armas tengo empeñadas . . . [v. 6]) and, at the end of the fourth catalogue, he rides off, in knightly fashion, on a horse that surpasses that of the king. The catalogues thus begin and end by evoking heroic images, but what really matters in this ballad is not chivalric prowess, but the fabulous display of Count Claros' luxurious wardrobe. The catalogues have here acquired a life of their own. They are important in and of themselves, in evoking the noble, medieval world of the Sephardic *Romancero*. All the same, the count's attire obviously functions within the narrative as a means of winning over Claraniña, at whose door Claros finally puts in an appearance: "Por calles de Claraniña, / ya se fuera a pasear" (v. 62).[38]

"Oyido lo había ese Sidi, / desde su sala'nde'stare" (*Búcar sobre Valencia*: *Epic Ballads*, no. 6A.14); "Oyéndolo está el buen reye, / desde su sala ande estare" (*Buena hija*: Larrea 179.36–37); "Oyéndolo está el buen rey, / desde su sala reale" (*Hijo vengador*: Larrea 182.15–16); "Oído lo había el buen reye, / desde su rico altar" (*Lavandera*: Ortega, p. 229).

In appraising Benoliel's text—and indeed any text collected by the great Tangier polymath—we must take into account his unfortunate tendency to rewrite and edit his *romances*. We cannot be completely sure that he has not done so in this case, though here the version looks authentic. See CMP, I, 51.

37. Note that v. 21 of our synthetic text (Dadle marcos de oro al conde, / para vestir y calsar), which corresponds to *A caza*, v. 10, is amply attested (in a total of 11 versions). Our text 10*B*, though defective, likewise supports such an arrangement by ending the king's offers with "para comprar y vestir" (v. 15).

38. Concerning the rhetorical question embodied in Librowicz 2.28 and our text 10*B*.30 (¿Por dónde vino (le fuera) a pasar(e)? / Por (la) calle de Claraniña), see S. G. Armistead, "Schoolmen or Minstrels?: Rhetorical Questions in Epic and Balladry," *La Corónica* (1987).

The Sephardic *Conde Claros y el emperador* + *Conde Claros insomne* has experienced a number of contaminations, both great and small, while in the Eastern tradition, our ballad has, in general, been less affected by "extraneous" narratives than in Morocco. The Eastern modality has tended occasionally to be associated with two other ballads also concerning the winning (or rescue) of a lady by force of arms: *Gaiferos jugador* and *La esposa de don García*. In a Salonikan version copied by Manrique de Lara from the mid-19th-century MS collection of Rabbi Isaac Bohor Amaradjí (CMP B9.3), the king curses his nephew: "Maldición te echo, sobrino, / a que la vayáx a buxcar" (before v. 15 of our synthetic text). This curse has its immediate origin in *Gaiferos jugador*, where Carlo (Charlemagne) curses Gaiferos because he has not gone in search of Melisenda: "Maldición t'echo, subrino, / si no la irás a buxcare."[39] Cynthia Crews' five verses pertaining to *Conde Claros y el emperador* (Crews 12.15– 19) are attached to a substantial version of *Gaiferos jugador*, but following the *Conde Claros* fragment the narrative continues with verses from *La esposa de don García*.[40] Michael Molho's text (LSO, p. 77, vv. 13–21), on the other hand, attaches *Conde Claros* verses (corresponding to vv. 25 ff. of our synthetic text) to the end of a version of *La esposa de don García*. Indeed, the verses in which Claros varies his pace on crowded or empty streets have, as we have seen, come to be a "normal" part of the *Don García* narrative. The same ballad has probably influenced one of the texts in the Menéndez Pidal Archive, in that, in the final verse (= our synthetic v. 30), the knight claims that he is riding to rescue his abducted wife: "Que me den a la mi esposa, / que me la vinieron a robar" (CMP B9.6), all of which squares perfectly with *Don García*, but contradicts *Emperador*, where Claros is, of course, searching for Blancaniña so he can marry her. As we shall see, in our four Salonikan versions of *Gaiferos jugador* (FLSJ, V, Chap. 12), all sung by Esther Varsano, which exemplify the tradition in its final stages of dissolution, *Gaiferos jugador* has become inextricably entwined with both *Conde Claros y el emperador* and *La esposa de don García*.

Our combined ballad, *Emperador* + *Insomne*, attests to various minor contaminations in Morocco. We have already seen how one of Benoliel's texts (CMP B9.13), under the possible influence of a variety of ballads, ineptly

---

39. Attias 26.21–22. Compare *Yoná* 5.13 and p. 95. As Costa Fontes has correctly shown, this curse points to the influence of an otherwise unattested Eastern Sephardic form of *Floresvento*. See Costa Fontes, "A Sephardic Vestige," and FLSJ, V, Chap. 12.

40. See our analysis in "Sobre los romances y canciones," pp. 23–24 (no. 12).

introduced the formulaic verse: "Oído lo había su tío, / desde la sala onde está" (at synthetic v. 13). After synthetic v. 20, Claros responds to the king's offers by asking: "¿Para qué me abonda esto, / para qué me ha de abondar?" (Librowicz [II] B9). The reading is typical of the Moroccan modalities of *La partida del esposo:* "¿Para qué me abonda esto, / para vino y para pan?" (Larrea 193.11–12).[41] Apropos of Count Claros' sleeplessness and the shared hemistich: "Salto diera de la cama . . .,"[42] one of Manrique de Lara's Tangier versions brings in the following verse: "Vueltas daba en la cama / como un pece vivo en mar" (CMP B9.16; after synthetic v. 33). Its origin is explained by the similar situation in *Melisenda insomne,* where the passionate girl, suffering for "amores del conde Niño," spends a similarly restless night, "dando vueltas en la cama, / como el pexe vivo en mare" (Bénichou, p. 69). In these instances, we have isolated sporadic contaminations, which, in each case, affect only one of the many versions recorded to date. However, our ballad's Moroccan modality also embodies two extensive contaminations which characterize a good number of the known versions and clearly have become an established part of the tradition. Both Sephardic subtraditions have been preoccupied with the ballad's beginning and ending. The poem's insubstantial narrative and its attention to description rather than action seem to have left some singers dissatisfied and have led to a variety of experiments. In the Eastern tradition, such concerns are manifested in the otherwise undocumented prologue, "Luz del día, luz del día, / luz del día y claridad. . . ." Eastern singers have likewise been uncomfortable with the dénouement. How can the protagonist simply be left in the middle of things, still searching for Blancaniña? Various idiosyncratic and quite feeble attempts by Eastern singers to bring the narrative to a more satisfactory conclusion—or at least to some conclusion—are reflected (following synthetic v. 30) in versions collected by Attias, Molho, and Manrique de Lara:

---

41. We modify Larrea's punctuation. For similar verses, all with *abondar,* see RT, III, nos. III.62–78 (with the exception of the Tangier version, no. 70: *abasta*). Eastern versions usually read: "¿Para qué me abasta esto, / para vino y para pan?" (RT, III, nos. III.9, 25, 32, 38; and other readings with *abasta:* nos. 1–61).

42. *Conde Claros insomne,* in agreement with the traditional suitor/bridegroom = hawk metaphor, reads: "Salto diera de su cama / que parece un gavilán" (synthetic v. 34)—as in *Media noche*: "salto diera dela cama / que parece vn gavilán" (v. 6). The amorous Melisenda is described in a more sensual verse: "Salto diera de la cama / como la parió su madre" (Bénichou, p. 69); note the identical reading in the early *Todas la aves dormían* (*Primav.* 198.4). Other Moroccan texts of *Melisenda* read: ". . . que parece un gaviláne" (Larrea 41.10). On the suitor = hawk image, see *Yoná,* pp. 249–250; *En torno,* pp. 204–205, n. 3; *Epic Ballads,* pp. 97–98 and n. 25.

Esta niña tanto linda,   por mujer la va tomar.
Beata a Blancaniña,   que tal mancebo va tomar.
                (Salonika: Attias 31.53–56)

—Tu espoza está en altas torres,   que no la puedéx topar.—
Esto sintió el cavallero   y se tornó atrás.
                (Salonika: LSO, no. 10.20–21)

—Claraniña está en altas torres,   más altas de una ciudad.
Comiendo está en una mesa,   con el conde Aligornal.
Caminaba otro poco [. . . .]
                (Jerusalem: CMP B9.11)

The *altas torres* verses, attested in two texts (as well as in the chaotic fragment, CMP B9.4), embody a traditional motif and seem to have gained at least an incipient traditionality in these Eastern versions of *Conde Claros y el emperador,* but basically these are individual, non-traditional attempts to fill out the ballad's unsatisfying conclusion.[43]

The Moroccan tradition attests to similar preoccupations. Numerous versions point to an attempt to fill out *Emperador*'s rather abrupt and uninformative beginning by adapting the first two verses of a brief courtly ballad dating at least from the final years of the 15th century. *Maldita seas ventura* was first printed in Hernando del Castillo's *Cancionero general* (1511) and subsequently appeared in a single *pliego suelto* printing (*Praga*, I, 54) and in numerous other *cancioneros* (MCR, I, 578). Earlier on, in a briefer form, it had figured in the *Cancionero del British Museum.* Here, first, is Hernando del Castillo's text:

    Maldita seas vẽtura   q̃ assi me hazes andar
2   desterrado de mis tierras   de donde soy natural
    por amar vna señora   la qual no deuiera amar
4   adamela por mi biẽ   y saliome por mi mal
    por q̃ ame donde nospero   galardones alcãçar
6   por hazer plazer amor   amor me hizo pesar

---

43. Concerning the *altas torres* motif, see the Appendix.

Sources (Base text: *A*):

A   =   *Cancionero general* (1511), fol. cxxxiij vo.*a*.
B   =   *Pliegos de Praga*, I, 54*b*.
C   =   *Pliegos de Praga*, I, 55 (*glosa*).
D   =   CSA, fol. 248 vo.
E   =   C1550, p. 298.
F   =   *Silva* (1550), p. 229.

Variants

2*b*   de donsoy natural *B*.
3*a*   amar a vna *BDEF*.
3*b*   deuia *DEF*.
5*a*   no espero *BCDEF*.
6*a*   plazer a amor *DEF*.

The late 15th-century manuscript version glossed in the *Cancionero del British Museum* consists of only three verses. We cite from the ed. of Hugo A. Rennert:

maldita seas, ventura,   que ansi me hazes andar.
2   desterrado de mis tierras,   donde yo soy natural.
adamar a una señora,   que no deuiera amar.[44]

The Judeo-Spanish adaptation of this courtly poem consists of only two verses and, with the exception of a single fragment from Alcazarquivir (*w* = CMP K11.1), is known only as a prologue to *Conde Claros y el emperador*. Martínez Ruiz's Alcazarquivir text (no. 35) interpolates the verses following v. 2

---

44. Rennert, *Der spanische Cancionero*, p. 34*a* (nos. 60–61). We have not seen the text included in the *Cancionero manuscrito de Pedro del Pozo* (1547), but according to Rodríguez-Moñino (p. 478, no. 40), the same text appears "sin variantes" in the *Cancionero general*. The *Segunda Parte del Lazarillo* (1555) cites an unknown poem concerning Conde Claros: "A esta hora me acordé y dixe entre mí aquel dicho del conde Claros antiguo, que dice: «¿Cuándo acabarás, ventura? / ¿Cuándo tienes de acabar? / En la tierra, mil desastres, / y en las mares, mucho más»" (ed. Piñero, pp. 176–177, n. 2). These verses, with their invocation of fortune (*ventura*), suggest perhaps some distant relationship to *Maldita seas, ventura.*

of our synthetic text.[45] The various Moroccan versions of *¿Por qué no cantáis, ventura?* embody only minimal variations:

> ¿Por qué no cantáis, fortuna? ¿Por qué no cantáis mi mal?
> 2   Desterrado de mis tierras,   del reino de Portugal.
> Ya se salía el buen reye,   ya se sale, ya se va. . . .

Sources

Tangier:	b	=	CMP B9.13		p	= Larrea 30
	f	=	Nahón 5		q	= Librowicz (II) B9
Tetuán:	i	=	CMP B9.18	Alcázar:	u	= CMP K11.1
	k	=	CMP B9.20		w	= MRuiz 35.3–4
	l	=	CMP B9.21			

Variants

1   *bfiklpuw*
2   *bfiklpquw*
   2a   Desterrada *p;* Desderrado (*sic*) *w.*
   2b   el reino *f;* de mis tierras *p;* de Francia y de Portugal *q.*

These verses have clearly been given a very Sephardic reinterpretation. The initial curse, probably for euphemistic reasons, has been replaced by a construction borrowed from *¿Por qué no cantáis, la bella?*: "¿Por qué no cantáis, la flor? / ¿Por qué no cantáis, la bella?" (Larrea 72.15–16).[46] The allusion to exile in *Maldita seas, ventura* must obviously have appealed to

---

45. Martínez Ruiz's Alcazarquivir version (*u*) places the *¿Por qué no cantáis, fortuna?* verses within the narrative and, presumably, they are directly associated with Conde Claros' troubles: "Ya se sale el buen reye, / ya se sale, ya se iba, // tras dél salió su sobrino / ayá una legua y más. // ¿Por qué no cantáis, fortuna, / por qué no cantáis, mi mal, // desderrado (*sic*) de mis tierras / del reino de Portugal. // Mis armas tengo empeñadas / por no tener yo qué pagar . . ." (MRuiz 35.1–5). (We maintain the original punctuation.)

46. For instances of the avoidance of curses (*maldiziendo > bendiziendo*) in Eastern Sephardic ballads (*Celinos; Doncella guerrera*), see *Yoná*, pp. 233–234; *Tres calas*, pp. 68–69 and n. 69. On the possible relationship to *¿Por qué no cantáis, la bella?*, see our comments in Nahón, p. 42.

Sephardic singers. Concerning the brief poem's Moroccan adaptation, we have elsewhere observed: "No es difícil imaginar el peculiar y triste atractivo que ejercían estos versos, en un principio meramente cortesanos y amatorios, sobre hispano-hebreos recién exilados de su patria. ... La alusión a Portugal especifica el refugio interino de incontables expulsos de finales del siglo XV y principios del siglo XVI, refugio que para muchos llegó a ser otra patria querida."[47] Despite their obvious attraction for Sephardic singers, in their present contest, our verses have little if any coherence with the narrative that follows, unless we assume that Claros' financial difficulties in regard to the castle of Montalbán somehow also involved his banishment.

Yet another experiment in providing our ballad with a more interesting beginning is reflected in the unique reading of a Tangier-Tetuán version collected by Oro A. Librowicz (*g* = Librowicz 2). Here the first three verses of *Conde Claros insomne* have been shifted to provide a new introduction for *Conde Claros y el emperador:*

	Durmiendo está el conde Flore la siesta por descansar,
2	porque la noche pasada no la pudo sosegar,
	de amores de Claraniña, que se quería finar.
4	Por allí pasara su tío, en compañía real;
	palabras le iba diziendo, que le hacían llorar:
6	—¿Qué me ditis, el mi tío, castillo de Montealbán?
	Me le ditis en convite, salióme por heredad.
8	Mis armas tengo empeñadas, en cien marcos de oro y más. ...

---

47. See Nahón, p. 42. José Benoliel records an example of the survival of a Portuguese expression in Moroccan Judeo-Spanish: "*Como quien se mea en la arena*: Denota lo inútil e improficuo que resulta un hecho, tentativa o esfuerzo." The Spanish expression only becomes clear in the light of its Portuguese model: *Como quem semea na area* (Benoliel, "Hakitía," p. 212, no. 2). Likewise, the word *janela* is sometimes used as a synonym for *ventana* in the Moroccan Sephardic *Romancero*. In the 16th century, some Moroccan Jews spoke Spanish with a significant admixture of Portuguese (for an example: Armistead, "Romancero e historia," p. 284, n. 36)—a mixed language which reminds us of similar, somewhat later developments in Amsterdam, London, Bayonne and elsewhere (Adams, "Castellano"; Davids, "Bijdrage"; Lévi, *Vestiges*). On the importance of Portugal in the Sephardic diaspora, see Nahón, p. 42, n. 2, and our articles "El Romancero entre los sefardíes de Holanda" and "Three Hispano-Jewish *romances*."

We do not know, of course, what the ending or endings of the ancestor form (or forms) of our Sephardic ballads were like. The early tradition varies from version to version: *A caza* continues with *Fraile; A misa*, with *Insomne*, followed by the flight to Montalbán; *Media noche* combines *Insomne* + *Infanta* + *Preso*; and *Dormiendo* completes the *Insomne* narrative with the tragic *Conde Claros degollado*. The modern Aragonese forms of *Emperador* (in *í-a* assonance) serve to introduce *Fraile* (CGR, IA, 44), while modern versions of *Insomne* from various regions can continue with *Infanta, Infanta* + *Preso*, and *Fraile*. The ending of the Moroccan versions of *Conde Claros y el emperador* + *Conde Claros insomne* has also remained enigmatic. Only two texts actually mention the hero's winning Claraniña by force of arms (*b* = CMP B9.13; *m* = Larrea 27) and only in Larrea does this feature function as the dénouement of a version which does not include *Conde Claros insomne:*

18   Mañana saldréis al juego   y en mis campos lear.
     —Por mujer o por amiga,   a Claraniña he de tomar.
20   —Cual de vosotros ganare,   a Claraniña llevará.—
     Mañana por la mañana,   salió el conde de Montealbar;
22   a las primeras batallas,   Montealbar la ganará.

(Larrea 27)

Since, in this version, as in most others, both the protagonist and his rival are called "conde de Montealbar," such an ending is, to say the very least, hardly enlightening. One of Benoliel's Tangier versions of *Conde Claros y el emperador* + *Conde Claros insomne* (*b* = CMP B9.13) also includes the single combat between the hero and the other count at a point corresponding to our synthetic v. 59:

42   Entre paso y paso que da,   centellas deja saltar.
     Ya se van al campo,   ya se van a guerrear.
44   A la primera batalla,   el conde Niño fue a ganar.
     Por calle de Claraniña,   ya se fuera a pasear.

There is, indeed, a non sequitur in introducing such a heroic motif into the narrative: It would, as Librowicz has pointed out (p. 24), be inappropriate for Claros to don such exquisitely elaborate finery if he were about to enter the lists in defense of his claim to Claraniña. It seems quite possible, then, that the dénouement in which Claros wins Claraniña in single combat, rather than by his courtly elegance and charm (*gracia*), may be a late development generated to fulfill the emperor's suggestion of just such a possibility: "Mañana saldréis al juego . . ." (synthetic vv. 29–30). In yet another version that omits the material corresponding to *Conde Claros insomne*, a minimal allusion to the latter ballad has been used to provide *Conde Claros y el emperador* with a new and happy ending heralding the count's marriage to Claraniña:

> —Mañana saldréis al juego,   a mis campos reales.
> Quien de ustedes ganare   Claraniña ha de llevar.—
> Ya descansa el conde Niño   y las bodas se han de hacer.
> (Larache-Tetuán: *t* = Amsélem MS)

Another of Larrea's texts, which likewise does not include material from *Conde Claros insomne*, ends in fragmentary fashion, after the king's rejection of Claros, with the expression of the hero's determination to win Claraniña: "—Por mujer o por amiga, / Claraniña hei de llevar" (*n* = Larrea 28.26–27). Essentially all the "complete" Moroccan versions of *Conde Claros y el emperador* + *Conde Claros insomne* embody an originally extraneous dénouement in *ó* assonance. Like many other *romances*, this one also admits of various quite contradictory outcomes.[48] Several versions end happily: Claros (= Niño) appears on Claraniña's street; when she hears the bells on his horse's harness, she comes to the window; he asks her what she thinks of him; she claims to like "Count Albar" better; Claros faints, but then she assures him that she really prefers Claros.[49] According to the typical happy ending formula, they are married the next day:[50]

---

48. For variability and traditional experimentation with ballad endings, note, for example, *El forzador* (*Tres calas*, pp. 33–41) and *Robo de Elena* (Nahón, pp. 66–68). In a crucially important study, Bénichou has pointed out various esthetically successful experiments that developed in the oral tradition of *El cautivo del renegado* (*Creación poética*, pp. 160–184). Another case in point is embodied in the regional differences in the dénouement of *Búcar sobre Valencia*. See Bénichou, *Creación*, pp. 153–154; Catalán, *Siete siglos*, pp. 195, 213–214; *Epic Ballads*, pp. 270–273.

49. In ballad tradition, only the beloved can resuscitate the fainted protagonist. For details, see the Appendix.

50. For happy ending formulas, see *Epic Ballads*, pp. 96, n. 21, 145, n. 28 (and references provided).

Por calle de Claraniña,   por ahí fuera a passar.
Al son de los casxcabeles,   Claraniña se asomó.
—¿Qué tal os parezco, prima?   ¿Qué tal os parezco yo?
—Bueno me pareces, primo;   conde Albar mucho mejor.—
Como eso oyó el conde Niño,   en un desmayo quedó.
—No vos desmayéis, mi alma,   no vos desmayéis vos.
Bueno me parecéis, primo,   bueno me parecéis vos.—
Otro día a la mañana,   la rica boda se armó.

(Tangier: *d* = CMP B9.15)

Por calle de Claraniña,   por allí le vino a pasar.
Al son de los cascabeles,   Claraniña se asomó.
—¿Qué tal le parezco, prima?   ¿Qué tal le parezco yo?
—Bueno me pareces, primo;   conde Albar mejor que vos.—
Como eso oyó el conde Niño,   en un desmayo quedó.
—No desmayéis vos, mi vida,   no desmayéis vos, mi bien.
Tiraos de ese caballo;   subíos a mi vergel.
Otra novia te doy mejor que mí   y no te sales de mi corazón.—
Otro dia en la mañana,   las ricas bodas se arman.

(Tetuán: *h* = CMP B9.17)

. . . . Claraniña,   por . . . . a pasar.
al son de los cascabeles,   Claraniña se asomó.
—¿Qué tal os parezco, mi prima?   ¿Qué tal os parezco y yo?
—Bueno me parecéis, primo;   conde de Alba mucho mejor.—
Como eso oyera el buen conde,   en un desmayo cayó.
—No te desmayís, mi alma,   mejor me pareces tú.—
Otros días en la mañana,   las ricas bodas se armaron.

(Tetuán: *o* = Larrea 31)

Por calle de Claraniña,   por ahí le vino a pasar.
Al son de los cascabeles,   Claraniña se asomó.
—¿Qué tal os parezco, prima?   ¿Qué tal os parezco yo?
—Bueno me parecéis, primo;   conde Albar mucho mejor.—
Como eso oyera el conde,   en un desmayo cayó.
—No vos desmayéis, mi primo;   no vos desmayéis, mi amor.
Bueno me parecéis, primo,   bueno me parecéis vos.—
Otro día en la mañana,   las ricas bodas se armó.

(Tetuán: *p* = Larrea 30)

¿Por dónde le fuera pasar?   Por la caye de Claraniña.
Al son de los cascabele̦,   Claraniña se asomó.
—¿Qué tal te paresco, prima?   ¿Qué tal te paresco yo?
—Bien me pareses, conde;   conde Albar mucho mejor.—
Como es'oyera el conde Niño,   caigó desmayado.
—No desmayes tú, conde Niño,   ni te quierad̦ hazer mal.
Bueno me pareses, conde;   contigo me he de cazar.
(Tetuán: r = our 10B)

In one of Benoliel's Tangier texts, the -*ó* assonant ending has been reworked
in *á* and the content has become altogether aberrant: When Claros asks the girl
what she thinks of him and she prefers "Count Montalbán," he threatens her
with a knife, after which everything ends happily with the usual *ricas bodas:*

Por calle de Claraniña,   ya se fuera a pasear:
—¿Qué tal te parezco, niña?   Dime, sobrina, ¿qué tal?
—Bueno me pareces, conde;   mejor conde Montalbán.
—Si tal me dices, sobrina,   te mato con mi puñal.
—Que me mates, que me dejes,   a mí poco se me da.—
Otro día de mañana,   ricas bodas hizo armar.
(Tangier: b = CMP B9.13)

Yet other versions end ambivalently: Claraniña consoles the count, but there
is no marriage (*e*); or the text ends with her stated preference for Count Albar (*i*);
or, again, there is a marriage (presumably to Albar), but we are not told
specifically (*jl*):

Por calles de Claraniña,   por ahí fuera a passar.
Al son de los cascabeles,   Claraniña se assomó.
—¿Qué tal te parezco, Clara?   ¿Qué tal te parezco yo?
—Bueno me pareces, primo;   conde Albar es mejor.—
Como eso oyó el conde Niño,   en un desmayo cayó.
—No vos desmayéis, mi vida,   no vos desmayéis vos.
(Tangier: e = CMP B9.16)

Al son de los cascabeles,   Claraniña se asoma.
—¿Qué tal os parezco, prima?   ¿Qué tal os parezco yo?
—Bueno me pareces, primo;   conde Albar mucho mejor.
(Tetuán: *i* = CMP B9.18)

Al son de los cascabeles,   Claraniña se asomó.
—¿Qué tal vos parezco, niña?   ¿Qué tal vos parezco yo?
—Bueno me parecéis, primo;   conde Albar mucho mejor.—
Otro día a la mañana,   las ricas bodas se harían.
(Tetuán: *j* = CMP B9.19)

Por calle de Claraniña,   por ahí le vino a passar.
Al son de los cascabeles,   Claraniña se asomó.
—¿Qué tal vos parezco, prima?   ¿Qué tal vos parezco yo?
—Bueno me pareces, primo;   conde Albar mucho mejor.—
Otro día en la mañana,   las ricas bodas se armó.
(Tetuán: *l* = CMP B9.21)

One version clearly states that Claraniña marries Albar (*c*), while in another, after she voices her preference for Albar, Count Niño gives up and rides away (*q*):

Por calle de su dama,   por ahí le vino a pasar:
—¿Qué tal vos parezco, prima?   ¿Qué tal vos parezco yo?
—Bueno me pareces, primo;   conde Albar mucho mejor.—
No son tres días pasados,   con conde Albar se casó.
(Tangier: *c* = CMP B9.14)

Por calles de Claraniña,   por allí le tocó pasar.
Al son de los cascabeles,   Claraniña se asomó.
—¿Qué tal vos parezco, prima?   ¿Qué tal vos parezco yo?
—Bueno me parecís, primo;   conde Alvar mucho mejor.—
. . . .
Dio vuelta a su caballo   y por donde vino se fuera.
(Tetuán: *q* = Librowicz [II] B9)

In still other texts, the ending is unequivocally tragic: After Claraniña prefers Albar, Count Niño (Flores) drops dead and, in one case (*u*), he is followed by Clara, who jumps from the window:

Por calle de Claraniña,   ya se fuera a pasear:
—¿Qué tal os parezco, prima?   ¿Qué tal os parezco yo?
—Bien me parecéis, mi primo;   conde Alván mucho mejor.—
Como eso oyó el conde Flores,   muerto al suelo cayó.
(Tangier: a = CMP B9.12)

Pues al sonar los cascabeles,   [. . . . .].
Siete veces echan suerte,   por ver quién la ha de llevar.
Las siete veces cayeron   en conde de Montalvar.
Al sonar los cascabeles,   Clara Niña se asomó.
—¿Qué tal os parezco, prima?   ¿Qué tal os parezco yo?
—Bueno me parecéis, primo;   conde Alvar mucho mejor.—
Como esto oyera el buen conde,   muerto y al suelo cayó.
La cabeza entre los hombros   encima del caballo cayó.
(Tangier: f = Nahón 5)

¿Por dónde vino a pasare?   Por calle de Claraniña.
—¿Qué tal vos parezco, y prima?   ¿Qué tal vos parezco yo?
Bueno me parecís, primo;   Montealbán mucho mejor.—
Como eso oyó el conde Flore,   de su caballo cayó;
de su caballo al suelo   y allí muerto quedó.
(Tangier-Tetuán: g = Librowicz 2)

Por calle de Claraniña,   por ahí le vino a passar.
Al son de los cascabeles,   Claraniña se asomó.
—¿Qué tal vos parezco, prima?   ¿Qué tal vos parezco yo?
—Bueno me parecéis, tío;   conde Albar mucho mejor.—
Como eso oyó el caballero,   muerto y al suelo cayó.
(Tetuán: k = CMP B9.20)

Pronto puzo el vestido,   que paresía un galán.
Con el ruido de los cascabeles,   Claraniña salió a mirar.
—¿Qué tal vos parese, y Clara?   ¿Qué tal vos paresco yo?
—Si bien me paresís, conde;   pero Montalbán mejor.—

Como eso oyera el conde,   muerto al suelo cayó.
Como eso viera la niña,   por la ventana cayó.
Las sinco no habían pasado   cuando l'intierro pasó.

(Alcazarquivir: *u* = MRuiz 35)[51]

All of these -*ó* assonant endings have been adapted from another Moroccan ballad, of venerable origins, which tells a very different story, but also attests to a series of thematic parallels, which easily explain why part of its dénouement was chosen and refashioned to provide an ending for *Conde Claros y el emperador* + *Conde Claros insomne*. The verses in question originate in *La jactancia del conde Vélez*, a ballad already documented in the 16th century, which has survived in two very different forms in the Judeo-Spanish subtraditions, as well as in the Spanish provinces of León and Zamora. Our Conde Claros ballad clearly reflects the dénouement of the Moroccan text-type, but here again we can only guess how the ballad might have ended in the early tradition and which of the Sephardic forms—if either—may represent its "authentic" early ending. Here is the text of *La jactancia del conde Vélez*, as it was printed in the third part (1551) of the *Silva de romances* (1550):

```
     Alabose el conde velez   en las cortes de Leon
2    que no ay dueña ni donzella   que le negasse su amor
     sino fuera el de la infanta   que no se le demando
4    que si se le demandara   no le dixera de no
     Mucho peso a los hidalgos   quantos en la corte son
6    mucho mas peso a don Bueso   que adamaua nueuo amor
     Una amiga tengo el conde   de quinze años que mas non
8    que si me la engañasses   sacassesme al coraçon
     y si no me la engañasses   quedarias por traydor
10   todos fian a don Bueso   y al conde ninguno non
     sino fuera vn infante   ques hijo de vn gran traydor
12   este fio al conde velez   en dos quentos que mas no.
```

(*Silva* [1550], p. 443)

---

51. For various motifs present in the Moroccan dénouement of *Conde Claros y el emperador* + *Conde Claros insomne*, see the Appendix.

La jactancia is also known in an early 16th-century manuscript copy (Bibl. Nac. [Madrid], MS 1317, fol. 454), which represents essentially the same version recorded in the *Silva*, but which elaborates upon the motif of the *fiador* (vv. 10–12) and which attests to a number of minor variants whose significance we will presently discuss:

> Romançe del conde velez

> alabose el conde velez   en las cortes sealabo
> 2   q̃ no aydama ni donzella   q̃ le negase su amor
> sino fuerael dela ynfanta   q̃ no selo demando
> 4   q̃ siselo demandara   no le dixeradeno
> mucho peso alos galanes   quantos ẽ la corteson
> 6   mucho mas peso adõbueso   q̃ adamava nuevo amor
> vna amiga tengo el cõde   de quinze años q̃ mas nõ
> 8   q̃ si tu mela engañares   sacases me el coraçõ
> ysi no mela engañases   q̃ quedases por traydor
> 10   paraeso q̃ dizes bueso   menester has fiador
> todos fian adõ bueso   quantos ẽla corte son
> 12   yel traydor del cõde velez   no hallava fiador
> sino fuera vn ynfante   hijo de vnpadre traydor
> 14   ese fio al conde velez   endos quẽtos q̃ mas nõ

Our ballad has developed two quite different forms in the Eastern and in the North African Sephardic traditions. Here is a synthetic text, that we have just barely been able to piece together from the gravely flawed evidence available in the subtraditions of Salonika, Larissa, and Jerusalem:

> Alavóse el conde Belo,   en sus cortes s'alavó:
> 2   —Que non hay ni mosa ni cazada   que s'encubra del amor;
> aunque fuera la más honesta,   venser la vensía yo.—
> 4   Ahí se topó el Gran Duque,   el hijo del emperador:
> —Si tú venses a la infanta,   siete sivdades te do;
> 6   y si non la venserías,   te quitaba el corasón.
> —Yo no quiero tus sivdades,   que mejor las tengo yo.
> 8   Si yo venso a la tu infanta,   el tuyo te quito yo.—
> Ya se hizieron los contratos;   en cansiyería se pozerón.
> 10   Ya se parte el conde Belo,   ya se parte, ya s'andó.

Tomó cavayo alazare,   que bola a la raya del sol.
12 Camino de quinze días,   en siete los ayegó.
Por en medio del camino,   una de sus esclavas topó.
14 A poder de muchos dineros,   señal de su caza le dio:
—Tres salas tiene Parizi,   una y otra más mejor:
16 La una durme Parizi,   la otra el emperador,
la otra durme la infanta,   durme con un gran señor.
18 En su cabesera tiene,   que le vela un velador;
en su oído derecho,   le canta un rosiñol;
20 le canta de prima noche   y a la mañana al alvor;
le canta y la mediodía,   la hora d'alavar al Dio.—[. . .]
22 Rodeó todo'l castiyo,   por ande entrar no topó.
Echó sus ojos en alto,   una de sus esclavas topó.
24 A poder de muchos dineros,   señal de su puerpo le dio:
—Debaxo del pecho estiedro,   tiene un lunar d'amor.—[. . .]
26 Por en medio d'aquel castiyo,   una de sus esclavas fayó.
—Si tú vienes por la infanta,   el aniyo tengo yo.—
28 A poder de muchos dineros,   el aniyo le tomó.
Ya se parte el conde Belo,   ya se parte, ya se andó.[. . .]
30 —Ven aquí tú, conde Belo,   te quitaré tu corasón.
—Tres salas tiene Parizi,   una y otra más mefor:
32 La una durme Parizi,   la otra el emperador;
[la otra la infanta   durme con un gran señor.]
34 Si quieres más pruebas d'éstas,   [aquí las traigo yo]:
Debaxo del pecho estiedro,   tiene un lunar d'amor.
36 [Y si quieres más pruebas d'éstas,   el aniyo lo traigo yo].
—Aspérate, conde Belo,   [. . . . .]
38 cuando escribo una carta   a esta puta infanta:
—Ven aquí, puta infanta,   mujer salida de razón;
40 por tenerte por honesta,   mira en qué vine yo.—
Tomando esta carta la infanta,   se vistió de varón.[. . .]
42 Estas palavras diziendo,   papagayo no cantó.
—¿De qué no cantas, papagayo?   En gran apreto está el señor.
44 —Vended todos vuestros bienes   y chapín de oro meted vos.— [. . .]
En entrando en la sivdad,   con el conde se encontró:
46 —Ven aquí tú, conde Belo,   hombre salido de razón:
Por entrar en la mi corte,   ¿qué pecado te hize yo?—
48 Me arrobatex un chapín de oro.   [. . . . .]

—Me mate el Dio del sielo,   si en tu corte entré yo.[. . .]
50   —Siete sivdades me cuesta   y su par no topo yo.
Ven aquí tú, conde Belo,   te quitaré tu corasón.

Sources

Salonika: *a* = Attias 34   *e* = Coello 10
            b = CMP B22.1   *f* = Crews 33
            c = CMP B22.2   Larissa: *g* = CMP B22.4
            d = CMP B22.3   Jerusalem: *h* = CMP B22.5

Variants

1   *abcdefgh*
    1*a*   Aquel conde y aquel conde *c;* en conde *b;* Belo *afgh;* Bello *bd.*
    1*b*   y en *bdf;* su corte *c.*
2   *abcefgh*
    2*a*   No hay *ag;* Ni moza ni casada *cg;* Que no hay ni moza *e;* ke no ai
           mosa *f.*
    2*b*   no se encubre del amor *c;* que s'enconara d'amor *e;* kjen se kuvra *f;*
           quien se cubra *g;* se encubra *b;* de amor *abef;* en el amor *h*(*var.*).
3   *abch(a)*
    3*a*   que si era *a;* aunque sea *ch;* honrada *a.*
    3*b*   vencerla sabía yo *b;* vencerla sabría yo *c.*
4   *abeg*
    4*a*   Ahí se topara el duque *b;* De allí saltó el gran Cides *g;* Allí *e.*
    4*b*   hijo *ab;* del gran señor *b.*
5   *abcefg*
    5*a*   Si tú vencéx a la mi infante *b;* Quien vence *c;* Si tú vensez a la
           infalta *f;* Si tú vences a la infante *g;* enfanta *e.*
    5*b*   sien *e;* le *c.*
6   *abceg*
    6*a*   si tú no la venceríais *a;* si non la vencerás *e.*
    6*b*   te quito *ag;* otras siete tomo yo *b;* te arranco tu corazón *c;* vos
           quitaba *e;* el tu corazón *g.*
7   *bc(a)e(a)*
    7*a*   Malaño a tus siodades *e.*

8 *abc(b)e(b)*

    8*a*   Y si yo la vencería *a.*

    8*b*   y el tuyo *a;* te quito tu corazón *b;* te arranco tu corazón *c;* volo quito yo a vos *e.*

9 *b*

    9*b*   poseron *b.*

10 *abeg*

    10*a*   Ya s'esparte *a;* Belo *ag;* Bello *b.*

    10*b*   ya s'esparte, ya se andó *a.*

11 *cf*

    11*a*   Se subiera en mula preta *c.*

    11*b*   que avola a la raya del sol *c.*

12 *abcefg*

    12*b*   en cinco *a;* en ocho *c;* los alcanzó *b.*

13 *abce*

    13*a*   Echó los ojos en lejos *a;* A poder de mucho dinero *b.*

    13*b*   con una dama encontró *a;* con una de sus esclavas habló *b;* con la esclavica topó *c.*

    13+   ¿Dónde durme la infanta? / Con ella quiero topar yo *c.*

14 *efg*

    14*a*   muĉa moneda *f;* mucho dinero *g.*

    14*b*   señas de su vergel le dio *e;* siñal *f;* señal del palacio le dio *g.*

15 *abefg*

    15*a*   Parizis *f;* el palacio *g.*

    15*b*   una y una más mejor *a;* uno y otro más meĵor *b.*

16 *abefg*

    16*a*   Una durme la infanta *b;* duerme *g;* el Parisi *ag.*

17 *ab(b)efg*

    17*a*   la otra durme la infalta *f;* la más chiquitica de ellas *g.*

    17*b*   durme con el gran señor (senor *f) bef;* dormià (?) un gran señor *g.*

    17+   Xwe él, djo estas siñales / i las sjete sivdadez ganó *f.*

18 *a*

19 *af(. . . b)*

    19*b*   . . . rušiñó *f* (*text includes only this word*).

20 *af*

    20*a*   le kantava día i noĉe *f.*

    20*b*   de prima fin al alvor *f.*

21 *a*

22 *abefg*
  22*a* Rodeó todo el palacio *a;* Arrodeó *b;* Arrodeó por el castillo entero *e;* Kaminó *f;* Rodió *g.*
  22*b* por onde entrar no(n) topó *bg;* una de sus esklavos fayó *f.*
23 *eg*
  23*a* Echó sus ojos en lexos *g.*
  23*b* y una esclava se aparó *g.*
24 *bef*
  24*a* Llorando y exclamando *b;* muĉa moneda *f.*
  24*b* señas de su cuerpo le dio *be.*
25 *bef*
  25*a* de su *f;* ezquierdo *b;* estiedro *ef.*
  25*b* lunar tiene de amor *b.*
26 *f*
  26*b* una de suz esklavos (*sic*) fayó *f.*
27 *f*
  27*a* infalta *f.*
28 *ag*
  28*a* muchas palabras *a;* mucho dinero *g.*
29 *bg*
  29*a* Estas palabras diziendo *g;* Bello *b.*
  29*b* conde Belo ya partió *g.*
30 *b*
  30*a* Bello *b.*
31 *b*
  31*b* una otra más mejor *b.*
32 *b* (*We repeat the reading of v. 16.*)
  32*a* La una duerme la infanta *b.*
33 *b(b)* (*We repeat the reading of v. 17.*)
  33*b* la otra durme el gran señor *b.*
34 *b(a)*
35 *b*
  35*a* izquierdo *b*
36 (*Compare vv. 27–28 and 34.*)
37 *b*
  37*a* Bello *b.*
38–41 *b*
42–44 *g*

45 *b*
46 *b*

  46*a* Bello *b*.

47–51 *b*

The above text is highly tentative—even more so than most such synthetic versions—and we cannot be quite sure that we have gotten either the content or the verse order even approximately correct. Each of the known texts attests to a very different order and combination of the ballad's possible constituent elements and, furthermore, we cannot even be certain that all of these are actually "original" features of the narrative. Does the sequence concerning the "salas de Parize" belong to *La jactancia* at all or is it a contamination from some different and otherwise unknown narrative?[52] Again, if the *infanta* is, in fact, "honorable," as the story must inevitably turn out, how then can she be sleeping with "un gran señor" (synthetic v. 17)? Here are three examples of how the latter part of the Eastern ballad is formulated in individual versions:

Ya se parte el conde Velo,   ya se parte, ya s'andó.

8 Camino de quinse días,   en siete los allegó.
  Por enmedio del camino,   una de sus esclavas topó.

10 A poder de muchos dineros,   señas de su vergel le dió:
  —Tres salas tiene Parisi,   una y otra más mejor:

12 La una durme Parisi,   la otra el emperador;
  la otra durme la enfanta,   durme con el gran Siñor.—

14 Arrodeó por el castillo entero,   por ande entrar no topó.
  Echó sus ojos en alto,   una de sus esclavas topó.

16 A poder de muchos dineros,   señas de su cuerpo le dió:
  —Debajo del pecho estiedro,   tiene un lunar d'amor.

18 En la su cabesera tiene,   que la canta un ruscón.

                         (Salonika: *e* = Coello 11)

4 Tomó kabayo alazare,   ke bola a la raya del sol.
  Kamino de kinze días,   en sjete loz ayegó.

6 Kaminó todo el kastiyo,   por ond'entrar no topó.
  Por em medjo d'akel kastiyo,   una de suz esklav[a]s fayó:

---

52. For traditional motifs present in Eastern versions of *La jactancia del Conde Vélez*, see the Appendix.

8   —Si tú vjenes por la infalta,   el aniyo tengo yo.—
     A poder de muĉa moneda,   señal de su pwerpo le djo:
10   —Debašo de su peĉo estjedro,   tjene un lunar d'amor.
     . . . . rušiñó,
12   le kantava día y noĉe,   de prima fin al alvor.—
     A poder de muĉa moneda,   siñal de su kaza le djo:
14   —Tres salas tjene Parizis,   una i otra máz mižor:
     la una durme Parizis,   la otra el imperador;
16   la otra durme la infalta,   durme don el gran se[ñ]or.—
     Xwe él, djo estas siñales   i las sjete sivdadez ganó.
                              (Salonika: *f* = Crews 33)

6   Ya se parte el conde Belo,   ya se parte, ya se andó.
     Camino de quince días   en siete los allegó.
8   Rodió todo el castillo,   por onde entrar no topó.
     Echó sus oĵos en lexos   y una esclava se aparó.
10   A poder de mucho dinero,   señal del palacio le dio:
     —Tres salas tiene el palacio,   una y otra más meĵor:
12   La una duerme el Pariṣi,   la otra el emperador;
     la más chiquitica de ellas,   dormía un gran señor.—
14   A poder de mucho dinero,   el anillo le tomó.
     Estas palabras diżiendo,   conde Belo ya partió.
16   Estas palabras diziendo,   papagayo no cantó.
     —¿De qué no cantas, papagayo?   En gran apreto está el señor.
18   —Vended todos vuestros bienes   y chapín de oro meted vos.
     . . . .
                              (Larissa: *g* = CMP B22.4)[53]

Attias' version embodies still other features, which cannot be reconciled with
the narrative as we have attempted to reconstruct it. Here, Vélez, apparently
unrecognized, incongruously would seem to meet the princess herself (hija d'un
gran duque, / ermuera de un emperador) and receive the ring from her in person,
rather than from a slave girl. Note that Attias has separated the verses about

---

53. We have simplified Crews' phonetic notation and have adjusted the
punctuation of the three texts to that of our synthetic version. Note that Crews' text
proposes an apocryphal dénouement, in which Vélez successfully passes off the false
tokens and wins seven cities.

Parizi's halls from the rest of the narrative, thus suggesting that it may constitute an independent ballad:

8   Ya s'esparte el conde Belo,   ya s'esparte, ya se andó.
     Camino de quince días,   en cinco los allegó.
10   Rodeó todo el palacio,   por ande entrar no topó.
     Echó los ojos en lejos,   con una dama escontró:
12   —¿Digáišme, la linda dama,   de quién hija éreis vos?
     —Yo so hija d'un gran duque,   ermuera de un emperador.
14   Si no vo lo creeríais,   el anillo llevo yo.—
     A poder de muchas palabras,   el anillo le tomó.
     . . . .
16   Tres salas tiene el Parisi,   una y una más mijor:
     La una durme el Parisi,   la otra el emperador;
18   en la otra la infanta   durme con un gran siñor.
     En su cabecera tiene,   que le vela, un velador;
20   en su oído derecho,   le canta un rosiñol;
     le canta de prima noche   y a la mañana al albor;
22   le canta y la mediodía,   la hora d'alabar al Dio.
                          (Salonika: *a* = Attias 34)

In Morocco, our ballad, though now rare, has been much better preserved than in the East. Here is a synthetic text—or perhaps synoptic would be a better term—in which we have attempted to combine all the protagonist's different ostentatious activities as attested in the various versions. It should be borne in mind, however, that, in most versions, Vélez's performances are limited to three, in a trinary pattern typical of balladic style—the silk adorned streets, the luxurious tents, and black servants on parade being the preferred items:[54]

    Alabóse el conde Veles,   en las cortes se alabó:
2   Que no hay dama ni donzeya   que reñegue el nuevo amor,
     si non fuera la infanta,   qu'él no se lo demandó;

---

54. Note that texts *d* (Alvar, *Textos*) and *o* (Amsélem MS) are ultimately based on *k* (Ortega, p. 213). Texts *glmnt* are brief fragments. Our synthetic v. 27 suggests a contamination from *Conde Claros y la infanta*: "La guerra de los cien moros / yo te la supe guerrear; // a los cincuenta matara / y cincuenta heridos van" (Larrea 33.15–18). For further details, see the Appendix.

4   que si él se lo demandara,   no le dixiera que no.
      Mucho pezó a los galanes,   cuantos en la corte son.

6   Más y más lo sintió don Güezo,   que adoraba nuevo amor:
      —Una niña tengo, Veles,   de quinse años, más no,

8   que si tú me la vensieras,   me sacas el corasón;
      y si no me la vensieras,   te lo sacaría yo.—

10   Papeles puzo en las cortes   del aposte que apostó.
      Todos fían a don Güezo   y al traidor de Veles, no,

12   si no fuera un renegado,   malo y de mala traisión:
      —Yo fiaré al conde Veles;   yo seré el fiador.—

14   Otro día en la mañana,   Veles sus cayes vistió
      de sedas y de brocados,   colores de gran valor.

16   A todo esto, el conde Veles,   la niña no se asomó.
      Otro día en la mañana,   Veles sus tiendas armó

18   de sedas y de brocados   y perlas de gran valor.
      A todo esto, el conde Veles,   la niña no se asomó.

20   Otro día en la mañana,   los sien torneos soltó,
      atabal y catablena   y música de color.

22   A todo esto, el conde Veles,   la niña no se asomó.
      Otro día en la mañana,   las cayes empedriscó

24   de ažofar y piedras finas,   esmeraldas de color.
      A todo esto, el conde Veles,   la niña no se asomó.

26   Otro día en la mañana,   con los sien moros jugó:
      A los sincuenta matara,   a los sincuenta hirió.

28   A todo esto, el conde Veles,   la niña no se asomó.
      Otro día en la mañana   y a las cañas ya jugó:

30   Sien almas matara Veles   y a las sien otras firió.
      A todo esto, el conde Veles,   la niña no se asomó.

32   Otro día en la mañana,   a los sien toros soltó. [. . .]
      A todo esto, el conde Veles,   la niña no se asomó.

34   Otro día en la mañana,   negros y negras vistió,
      vestidos a la Turquía,   paresen rayos de sol.

36   Y a todo eso, el conde Veles,   la niña no se asomó.
      Ya yevan al conde Veles   a sacarle el corasón.

38   Por caye de la infanta,   por ayí Veles pasó:
      —Por causa tuya, la infanta,   me sacan el corasón.—

40   A los gritos que él daba,   la niña ya se asomó.
      —¿Qué tal vos paresco, niña?   ¿Qué tal vos paresco yo?

42   —Bueno me pareses, Veles; conde Albar, mucho mejor.—
      Ya yevan al conde Veles a sacarle el corasón.
44   Y eso hazen a los galanes que a la corte se alabó.

Sources

Tangier:	a	= CMP B22.6		k	= Ortega, p. 213
	b	= CMP B22.7	Ceuta:	l	= Hassán B22*A*
	c	= CMP B22.8		m	= Hassán B22*B*
Tetuán:	d	= Alvar, *Textos*,		n	= Hassán B22*C*
		II, 760	Larache-Tetuán:	o	= Amsélem MS B22
	e	= CMP B22.9	Larache:	p	= CMP B22.14
	f	= CMP B22.10		q	= CMP B22.15
	g	= CMP B22.11	Alcázar:	r	= CMP B22.16
	h	= CMP B22.12		s	= CMP B22.17
	i	= CMP B22.13	Morocco (unloc.):	t	= CMP B22.18
	j	= Boaknín MS, pp. 5–7			

Variants

1   *abcdefghijkm(b)oqrst*
    1*a*   Velo *djk*; Bele *e*; Beles *t*.
    1*b*   y a la corte *s*; de alabó (*sic*) *t*.
2   *abcdefghijklmnoqrst*
    2*a*   No hay *e*; damas ni doncellas *fg*.
    2*b*   que le niegue nuevo amor *as*; que le reniegue su amor *b*; que no le
            trató en amor *b* (*var.*); que le niegue el nuevo amor *cr*; que reniega
            e; que renieguen nuevo amor *f*; que se nieguen al nuevo amor *g*; que
            le nieguen el amor *h*; que reniegue nuevo amor *i*; que le resista su
            amor *l*; que (no) se doblegue a su amor *m*; que le niegue el amor *n*;
            que no trató con él en amor *q*; que le niegue su nuevo amor *t*.
3   *abcdefhijkoqrs*
    3*a*   si no era *most texts*; si no fuera *a*; si no fuere *s*; sólo que lo de la
            infanta *b*; sólo la infanta *o*; una infanta *s*; ifanta *d*.
    3*b*   que no *bcehoqrs*; que ya *djk*; que ella se lo demandó *fi*.
4   *acdhijkoqs*
    4*a*   si no se lo demandara *dijk*; si él se lo *s*.

4*b*   no lo negaría, no *a*; no la dijera que no *djk*; no la dijera de no *i*; no le dijera de no *qs*.

5   *beos*

5*a*   Mucho miró a los galanes *e*; Tanto sintieron los galanes *o*.

5*b*   que esto en las cortes se oyó *b*; a don Güeso más mejor *e*; que a la corte se alabó *s*.

6   *aboq*

6*a*   Hi se alhadró el conde Niño *a*; Allí estaba el conde Güeṣo *b*; Allí está don Güeso *q*.

6*b*   que en el buen día nació *b*; que la trataba de amor *o*; en la corte asentado *q*.

7   *abcdefhijkopqrs*

7*a*   Y esa moza, Vélez *q*; Yo tengo una moza, Vélez *s*; hija *bc*; tengo y Vélez *cf*; tengo en casa *r*; Velo *djk*; Bele *e*.

7*b*   una niña tengo yo *o*; de más no *a*; y más no *bcehq*; más que no *d*; que más no *fikprs*.

8   *abcdefhijkopqrs*

8*a*   Si tú me la vences, Vélez *b*; Que si tú me la ganas *c*; Y si *e*; si te lo demandara *q*; me *omitted s*; vencieres *aefhiprs*; llevares *o*.

8*b*   sácasme mi corazón *b*; sácasme el corazón *c*; saquéisme mi corasón *dfijk*; sacarme mi corazón *e*; te daré mi corazón *h*; me sacarás el corazón *o*; sáquesme el corazón *p*; me quites el corazón *q*; saquéisme el corazón *r*; me quitas mi corazón *s*.

9   *abcdefhijkopqrs*

9*a*   que si tú no la vencieres *a*; que si no me la vencieras *b*; y si tú no me la ganas *c*; y si tú no la llevares *o*; y si no te lo demanda *q*; si la niña no se asoma *r*; y si tú no me la vences *s*; venciere *e*; vencieres *fhip*.

9*b*   sacarte he el tuyo yo *b*; te le sacaré yo a ti *o*; sacaré yo a ti *p*; te quito yo el corazón *q*; te quito y el corazón *s*; le *afhir*.

9+   Tocóse mano con mano, / en las cortes se citó *e*.

10   *defijk*

10*a*   la plaza *e*; la esquinas (*sic*) *fi*.

10*b*   de la posta que apostó *dk*.

11   *adeijks*

11*a*   Todas fían de don Güezo *d*; al conde Niño *a*; a don Bueso *s*.

11*b*   y al perro de Vélez no *a*; y al malo de Bele no *e*; y al malo de Vélez no *s*; Velo *djk*.

12 *aeqs*

  12*a* era *eq*; pajecito *qs*.

  12*b* que en su mesa pan comió *qs*; traición *a*; nación *e*.

13 *aeqs*

  13*a* Yo le fio al conde Bele *e*; a don Vélez *q*.

  13*b* su fiador *qs*.

14 *abdfhijk*

  14*a* de mañana *ab*; a la mañana *dh*.

  14*b* todas las calles vistió *a*; Velo *djk*; Las ricas calles vistió *h*; la calle *b*; las calles *f*.

15 *abdfhijk*

  15*a* que de sedas *a*; de terciopelo y brocado *b*.

  15*b* tafetanes de valor *a*; alhajas de gran valor *b*; y perlas de gran valor *f*; veludos de gran valor *h*.

16 *abdfhijk*

  16*a* Y a todo esto el conde *j*; el *omitted a*; Belo *b*; Velo *djk*; Veles *omitted jk*.

17 *cdefijkopqrs*

  17*a* Otro día siguiente *c*; Ya jugaba el conde Vélez *o*; (Y) otro día a la mañana *ps*.

  17*b* a las cien tiendas vistió *cp*; Velo sus tiendas vistió *djk*; las sien tiendas él armó *e*; en las tiendas de brocado *o*; a las cien tiendas llenó *q*; ya las cien tiendas vistió *r*; ya las cien tiendas llenó *s*; vistió *fi*.

18 *c(a)defijkopqrs*

  18*a* que de sedas *c*; en tersiopelo y brocados *e*; ¡qué de sedas y telas *o*; (que) de sedas y brocado(s) *pqs*; de colores y maneras *r*.

  18*b* y de seda de color *e*; y joyas de gran valor *f*; y colores de gran valor *i*; tafetanes de color! *o*; (y) tapetes de color *pqs*; ya las cien tiendas vistió *r*.

19 *cdefijkopqs*

  19*a* A *omitted p*; Y eso todo *s*; Velo *djk*; Bele *e*.

20 *a e*

  20*a* de mañana *a*; en *omitted e*.

  20*b* a los torneos jugó *a*; torneo *e*.

21 *e*

  21*b* mosica *e*.

22 *a e*

  22*a* el *omitted a*; Bele *e*.

23 *be*
    23*a* a la mañana *b*; en *omitted e*.
    23*b* dibujó *e*.
24 *be*
    24*a* aljófar *b*; achófar *e*.
    24*b* alhajas de gran valor *b*.
25 *be*
    25*a* Bele *e*.
26 *eop*
    26*a* Ya jugaba el conde Vélez *o*; a la mañana *p*.
    26*b* en los juegos de la China *o*; a los cien moros yugó *p*.
27 *ep*
    27*a* a cincuenta dejó muertos *p*.
    27*b* y a cincuenta los hirió *p*.
28 *eop*
    28*a* Bele *e*.
29 *ehs*
    29*a* Mañana por la mañana *s*; en *omitted e*; a la mañana *h*.
    29*b* ya las *es*; a las espadas *h*; cien lanzas jugó *s*.
30 *s*
    30*b* y a las otras (otras *deleted*) cien otras firió *s*.
31 *es*
    31*a* ya todo eso el conde Bele *e*; y eso todo el conde Vélez *s*.
32 *hpqrs*
    32*a* A otro *p*; L'otro día *q*; Y otro día *s*; a la mañana *hpqrs*.
    32*b* a los toreros *pqs*; a los toritos jugó *qr*; yugó *ps*.
    32+ Al son de los cascabeles, / la niña ya se asomó *h*.
33 *rs*
    33*a* A todo eso *r*; Y eso todo *s*.
34 *abdfijkr*
    34*a* de mañana *a*; a la mañana *bd*.
    34*b* los cien negritos vistió *ar*; Vélez con turcos juegó *b*.
35 *bdfijkr*
    35*a* de colores y maneras *r*; de la Turquía *j*.
    35*b* y joyas de gran valor *dfijk*; los cien colores pusió *r*.
36 *abdfijkr*
    36*a* Y a todo *j*; A *omitted r*; esto *djk (among others)*; el *omitted a*; Velo
        djk.

37 *abcdefijkr*
    37*a*   Ya sacan *r*; Velo *djk*; Bele *e*.
    37*b*   a quitarle *o*.
38 *be*
    38*a*   Por calle de la esa niña *e*.
    38*b*   le vino a pasar *e*.
39 *b*
40 *abcdefijkopqrs*
    40*a*   A los gritos que va dando *a*; A los gritos que da Vélez *b*; A los gritos que dio Vélez *c*; A los gritos que él daba *dfijk*; Al son de los sus bramidos *e*; De gritos que (que *deleted*) da el conde Vélez *o*; Y al alzar de los toreros *p*; En meatad de aquel jugo *q*; De los gritos que iba dando *r*; Y al alzar de los manteles *s*.
    40*b*   ya *omitted p*; que se asomó *q*.
41 *cdefhijkmoqs*
    41*a*   os *dfhjkmq*; te *os*; parezco y dama *q*; prima *hi*; bella *m*.
    41*b*   os *dfhjkmq*; te *os*.
42 *cdefhijkmoqs*
    42*a*   Muy bien *m*; Bueno me pareces, bueno *s*; parecéis *cejmq*; conde *c*; Velo *djk*; Bele *e*; Veli *m(var.)*.
    42*b*   conde Albas (*emended to* Albar) mejor que vos *e*; conde Aba *j*; conde Albán *k*; más mi marido (siempre) es mejor *m*; pero don Güeso mejor *oq*; mejor es el don Güeso *s*.
    42+   Como eso oyó el conde Vélez , / en un desmayo quedó *c*.
43 *dfhijkpqs*
    43*a*   Y yeva a conde Velo *d*; Ya traen *p*; a don Vélez *q*; Velo *jk*.
    43*b*   le sacan el corazón *fi*; a sacar y el corazón *h*; a quitar y el corazón *qs*.
44 *rs*
    44*a*   Eso se hace a los hombres *r*.
    44*b*   que en las cortes se alaban *r*.
    44+   que no hay dama ni doncella / que te niegue nuevo amor, // si no era la infanta / que si se lo demandó *r*.

La jactancia del conde Vélez is extremely rare in the modern Peninsular tradition. We know of only five versions and all form part of the monumental collection of the Menéndez Pidal Archive. One, still unedited, was collected at Ribadelago (Zamora); three (RGL 33.2–4) in the area around Astorga (León); and

one (RGL 33.1) in a Galician-speaking region near Ponferrada (León). All the
versions are quite similar. Here is a synthetic text:

	Alabóse conde Félix, alabóse el gran traidor,
2	que no hay dama ni doncella que a él le niegue el amor.
3A	Oído le había Carlos y muy mal le pareció:
3B	Saltó un chico de Mombuey, con una linda razón:
4	—Esposita tengo en Francia, de quince años, que más no,
	que si tú me la engañases, me sacas el corazón
6	y si no me la engañases, te lo tengo sacar yo.—
	'Sotro día a la mañana, el mal Félix madrugó
8	y a las puertas de la niña, una rica tienda plantó;
	en medio de la tienda, un cordón de oro colgó.
10	Todas damas y doncellas iban a ver el cordón.
	También salió la de don Carlos, más hermosita que un sol.
12	Pone saya sobre saya, por de fuera un tornasol:
	—¿Qué cuesta el cordón, don Félix? ¿Félix, qué cuesta el cordón?
14	—A mí me costó cien doblas, en el reino de Aragón;
	por ser para ti, la niña, de balde te lo doy yo,
16	por un beso de tu cara y un ramito de su amor.
	—Cuelgue usted el cordón, don Félix; Félix, cuelgue el cordón.
18	Tengo yo un novio en Francia; me lo ha de comprar mejor
	y si no me lo comprara, sin él tengo de andar mejor.
20	—¡Malhaya en ti, la niña, y en quien tanto te enseñó!
	Por l'amor de ti, la niña, me sacan el corazón.
22	—¿Qué culpa te tengo, Félix? ¿Qué culpa te tengo yo?
	Lo apostares en dinero y en perder la vida no.

Sources

a =   Ribadelago (p.j. Puebla de Sanabria, Zamora), informant: "María," 1949
(uned.).
b =   Truchillas (p.j. Astorga, León), informant: María Peregrina Carbajo, 70
years, July 23, 1982 (= RGL 33.4).
c =   Bustos (p.j. Astorga, León), informant: Rosa del Palacio del Río, 73
years, July 14, 1985 (= RGL 33.3).

d = San Martín de Agostedo (p.j. Astorga, León), informant: Francisca Rebaque, 73 years, June 29 and July 11, 1985 (= RGL 33.2).

e = Tejeira (p.j. Villafranco del Bierzo, León), informant: Bárbara Poncelas, 69 years, July 16, 1985 (= RGL 33.1).

Variants

1 *abde*

    1a   Alabárase don Félix *a;* Alabábase don Félix *b;* Alabándose anda Félix *d;* Alabouse conde Félix *e.*

    1b   alabárase el traidor *a;* alabábase el traidor *b;* Félix, como gran traidor *d;* e alabouse o gran traidor *e.*

2 *abde*

    2a   que no hay doncella ni dama *e.*

    2b   que no rindiese su amor *a;* que le negara el honor *e.*

3A *d*

3B *a*

4 *abcd*

    4a   Tengo yo una novia en Francia *a;* Tengo yo mi esposa en Francia *c.*

    4b   non *a.*

5 *abcd*

    5a   y si tú *c;* donde tú *d;* robaras *a;* llevaras *b.*

    5b   saque *b;* saques *c;* saquen *d.*

6 *abcd*

    6a   donde tú me la engañes *d;* robaras *a;* llevaras *b.*

    6b   te lo tengo'e sacar yo *ac;* el tuyo te saco yo *d.*

7 *abcd*

    7a   Ese otro día *b;* Al otro día *d;* por la mañana *ad;* de mañana *c.*

    7b   muy temprano madrugó *a;* para Francia caminó *b;* una media tienda plantó *c.*

8 *abde(a)*

    8a   y a la puerta de la dama *a;* a la puerta' la infantina *d;* Pone tienda sobre tienda *e.*

    8b   muy ricas tiendas plantó *b;* y una rica tienda armó *d.*

9 *abcde(b)*

    9a   en el medio *b;* por encima de la tienda *d.*

    9b   puso un lindo bordón *b;* un gordón de oro tendió *d;* por riba un rico cordón *e;* gordón *ac.*

10 *bcde*

    10*a* Toas las damas *bd*.

    10*b* salían a ver *d;* iban tratar ao cordón *e;* bordón *b;* gordón *cd*.

11 *bcde*

    11*a* Sal la niña por la tarde *b;* Iban un día a la tarde *c;* También la hija del rey *e*.

    11*b* porque no la queme el sol *b;* cuando no quemara el sol *c;* fue tratar al cordón *e*.

12 *abc*

    12*a* llevan saya sobre saya *c*.

    12*b* por cima un quitasol *b;* por encima un quitasol *c*.

13 *abcde*

    13*a* Cuánto cuesta *c;* Cuánto vale *d;* Cuánto vale o cordón *e;* gordón *acd;* bordón *b;* don *omitted cde*.

    13*b* y cuánto cuesta *c;* vale *de;* o cordón *e;* gordón *acd;* bordón *b*.

14 *abc*

    14*a* En el reino de Aragón *b*.

    14*b* cien doblones me costó *b*.

15 *abcde*

    15*a* pero por ser para usted *a;* pero para ti, la niña *b;* para usted, la señorita *d;* Nin se paga con diñeiro *e*.

    15*b* no cuesta dinero, no *b;* no tiene precio el gordón *d;* nin tampoco con doblón *e;* se *a*.

16 *abde*

    16*a* yo a usted se lo daría *d;* pagase co teu honor *e;* su *a*.

    16*b* el bordón te lo diera yo *b;* por un poquito de amor *d;* drento de meu corazón *e;* su *a*.

17 *acde*

    17*a* No quiero *c;* Guárdate *d;* Non che quero o cordón *e;* gordón *acd;* don *omitted cde*.

    17*b* ya no te quiero *c;* Félix, no quero o cordón *e;* guárdate *d;* gordón *acd*.

18 *abcde*

    18*a* Esposito tengo en Francia *bd;* Tengo yo mi esposo en Francia *c;* que meu padre vai en Francia *e;* Mombuey *a*.

    18*b* quien me lo ha traer mejor *b;* que me lo ha traer mejor *c;* que me ha dar otro mejor *d;* outro me traerá tan bon *e*.

19 *ae*

   19*a*   que si no me lo trouguera *e*.

   19*b*   que me lo traiga que no *e*.

20 *abcd*

   20*a*   Oh malhayas tú por dama *a;* Arreviente la infantina *d*.

   20*b*   y a quien *a;* por telas del corazón *d*.

21 *abcd*

   21*a*   que por mor de ti *c;* por causa de la infantina *d;* de ti, niña *a*.

   21*b*   saquen *b;* saques *c*.

22 *abcd*

   22*a*   Arrevientes tú, el mal Félix *d*.

23 *abcd*

   23*a*   Apostara a dinero *b;* Pa otra vez apuesta dinero *c;* Otro día apuesta dinero *d*.

   23*b*   y a perder *bc;* y no apuestes el corazón *d*.

In the case of vv. 3*A* and 3*B* it is impossible to choose between the readings: Both reflect elements present in the early texts and also in the Moroccan versions. 3*A* echoes "mucho mas peso a don Bueso" (*Silva*) or "Más y más lo sintió don Güezo" (Morocco), but, at the same time, the "chico de Mombuey" (3*B*) must also go back to a popular etymological interpretation of the protagonist's title and name: *don Bueso*. The ballad has experienced two notable contaminations: Verse 12 is taken from *La bella en misa:* "Lleva saya sobre saya / y jubón sobre jubón" (RPE, p. 90), but, with a more archaic reading in the second hemistich, which is closer to the early printing: "Saya lleva sobre saya, / mantillo de un tornasol" (*Primav.* 143.4) and reflects, in text *a*, the meaning recorded by Covarrubias: "Ay cierta tela de seda y lana deste nombre, por tener diversos visos puesta al sol" (ed. Riquer, p. 968*a*); texts *b* and *c* have rationalized the reading as "quitasol." The relation with *La bella en misa* is already suggested in the previous verse, as the girl appears: ". . . más hermosita que un sol." Compare, in *La bella en misa:* "a la entrada de la hermita / relumbrando como el sol" (*Primav.* 143.8). The imprecation: "¡Arreviente la infanta / por telas del corazón!" (text *d*) echoes *La doncella guerrera:* "¡No revientes, Catalina, / por telas del corazón!" (Castro, *Lengua*, p. 273). Verse 21 of the Peninsular versions is remarkable in that it corresponds to a verse documented in only a few Moroccan texts: "que por l'amor de ti, niña, / me sacan el corazón" (*a*; cf. *bc*) or "por causa de la infantina, / me sacan el corazón" (*d*). Compare CMP B22.7 (Moroccan text *b*): "Por causa tuya, la infanta, / me sacan el corazón."[55]

Let us now look briefly at how the three branches of the modern tradition (Eastern, Moroccan, and Peninsular) relate to the early texts, those of the *Silva* and the Biblioteca Nacional MS. Apart from the motif of the *fiador*, what is particularly striking about the MS version is that, in several of the relatively few instances in which it does not agree with the *Silva*, it offers readings (in italics below) which will reappear in the modern tradition (*E* = Eastern versions; *M* = Morocco; *L-Z* = León-Zamora; *L* = León):

—   Alabose el conde velez   en las cortes de Leon   (*Silva*)
      alabose el conde velez   en las cortes *se alabo*   (MS)
      Alavóse el conde Belo,   en sus cortes *s'alavó*   (*E*)
      Alabóse el conde Veles,   en las cortes *se alabó*   (*M*)
      Alabóse conde Félix,   *alabóse* el gran traidor   (*L-Z*)

—   que no hay dueña ni donzella   que le negasse su amor   (*Silva*)
      que no ay *dama* ni donzella   que le negase su amor   (MS)
      que no hay *dama* ni donzeya,   que reñegue el nuevo amor.   (*M*)
      que no hay *dama* ni doncella,   que a él le niegue el amor.   (*L-Z*)

—   Mucho peso a los hidalgos   quantos en la corte son   (*Silva*)
      Mucho peso a los *galanes*   quantos en la corte son   (MS)
      Mucho pezó a los *galanes*,   cuantos en la corte son.   (*M*)

—   todos fian a don Bueso   y al conde ninguno non   (*Silva*)
      todos fian a don Bueso   quantos en la corte son   (MS)
      y *el traidor del conde Velez*   no hallava fiador   (MS)
      Todos fían a don Güezo   y *al traidor de Veles*, no.   (*M*)

---

55. The ballad also embodies formulas familiar to Sephardic balladry: Verse 14 recalls the Eastern Judeo-Spanish *Chuflete:* "Sien dublones más me kosta / de las féridas de Budim" (*Yoná*, p. 356; *Bosnia* C20). Compare v. 20 with the Moroccan *Sancho y Urraca:* "Malhaya seáis, las mujeres, / que se las prometa un don; // malhaya sean las razones / y quien vos las enseñó" (*Epic Ballads*, p. 136, vv. 27–28). The Leonese versions of *Conde Vélez* have now been published in RGL, nos. 33.1–4 (where information concerning the collaborative collectors is specified). The Zamoran text (*a*) was collected by Diego Catalán and Alvaro Galmés. We wish to express our gratitude to Diego Catalán and to Ana Valenciano and Flor Salazar for their generosity in making these (and so many other unedited texts) available to us. For more data, see the Appendix.

It is impossible to divine exactly what this MS version represents. Most of its readings are so close to those of the *Silva* that it would seem there must be some direct relation between these two early texts. The MS's several obvious agreements with later tradition may possibly mark it as a conflation of a version identical to the printed one with some other form (or forms) current in the 16th-century oral tradition. It is, however, unlikely, if not impossible, that the writer of the MS consulted the *Silva* version itself as the basis for his conflation. From a paleographic perspective, the MS would seem to have been written considerably before the middle of the 16th century. The hand clearly belongs to the early 1500s, as becomes apparent from a comparison with contemporary dated documents (e.g., Arribas Arranz, no. 111 [1516]; Millares Carlo, no. CVII [1519]). It would serve no purpose to hypothesize about the exact relationship of these two early versions. But what is abundantly clear from this case, as from so many others, is that the printed canon is woefully incomplete and stands only in an indirect relationship to genetically related forms current in the modern *Romancero*. Even so, the modern traditions, particularly that of Morocco, have remained strikingly close to the brief, truncated 16th-century fragment, as can be seen in the following comparison. (The base text for the early tradition is the *Silva*; variants from the Bibl. Nac. MS are in parentheses; the numeration of the verses follows the *Silva*.)

1   Alabose el conde velez   en las cortes de Leon (se alabó)
     Alavóse el conde Belo,   en sus cortes s'alavó: (*E*)
     Alabóse el conde Veles,   en las cortes se alabó: (*M*)
     Alabóse conde Félix,   alabóse el gran traidor: (*L-Z*)

2   que no ay dueña (dama) ni donzella   que le negas(s)e su amor
     Que no hay ni mosa ni cazada   que s'encubra del amor;   (*E*)
     Que no hay dama ni donzeya   que reñegue el nuevo amor,   (*M*)
     Que no hay dama ni doncella   que a él le niegue el amor.   (*L-Z*)

3   sino fuera el de la infanta   que no se le (lo) demando
     aunque fuera la más honesta,   venser la vensía yo.   (*E*)
     si non fuera la infanta,   qu'él no se lo demandó,   (*M*)

4   que si se le (lo) demandara   no le dixera de no
     que si se lo demandara,   no le dijera que (de) no.   (*M*)

5   Mucho peso a los hidalgos (galanes)   quantos en la corte son

         Mucho pezó a los galanes,   cuantos en la corte son.   *(M)*

6   mucho mas peso a don Bueso   que adamaua nueuo amor

         Más y más lo sintió don Güezo,   que adoraba nuevo amor: *(M)*

         Oído le había Carlos   y muy mal le pareció: *(L)*

7   Una amiga tengo el conde   de quinze años que mas non

         Una niña tengo, Veles,   de quinse años, más no,   *(M)*

         Esposita tengo en Francia,   de quince años, que más non,   *(L-Z)*

8   que si (tu) me la engañasses(-ares)   sacas(s)esme el coraçon

         Si tú venses a la infanta,   siete sivdades te do;   *(E)*

         que si tú me la vensieras,   me sacas el corasón;   *(M)*

         que si tú me la engañases,   me sacas el corazón;   *(L-Z)*

9   y si no me la engaña(s)es   quedarias(-ases) por traydor

         y si no la venserías,   te quitaba el corasón.   *(E)*

         y si no me la vensieras,   te lo sacaría yo.   *(M)*

         y si no me la engañases,   te lo tengo sacar yo.   *(L-Z)*

10   todos fian a don bueso   y al conde ninguno non

         (Todos fian a don Bueso   quantos en la corte son)

         (y el traydor del conde Velez   no hallava fiador)

         Todos fían a don Güezo   y al traidor de Veles, no,   *(M)*

11   sino fuera vn infante   (ques) hijo de vn gran (padre) traydor

         si no fuera un renegado,   malo y de mala traisión: *(M)*

12   este (ese) fio al conde velez   en dos quentos que mas no.

         Yo fiaré al conde Veles;   yo seré el fiador.   *(M)*

The Eastern and Moroccan modalities of *Conde Vélez* embody two quite different narratives: In the East, Vélez obtains false signs or tokens of the princess' apparent infidelity (description of the palace, birth mark, ring) and triumphantly returns to court, only to be found out, through the princess' artful intervention, and pay with his life for his arrogant pretensions. In Morocco, on the other hand, Vélez undertakes a series of ostentatious displays, aimed at attracting the princess' attention and winning her love, only to be constantly scorned. When he finally does bring her to her window, with his desperate screams, as he is being taken away to be killed, he is definitively "put down": "Bueno me pareses, Veles; / conde Albar, mucho mejor." He is then dragged away to have his heart cut out, according to his agreement with Don Güezo and as a lesson to all arrogant and boastful gallants.

In its central motif, the chastity wager (AT 882), *La jactancia del conde Vélez* recalls—distantly at least—a series of ballad narratives that were once current in other branches of the Pan-European tradition—Scottish, German, Danish, Greek: In the Scottish *Twa Knights* (Child 268), the wager is about a married woman's chastity: The husband agrees to go to sea for six months, while a squire, his sworn brother, offers the lady "a coffer o gude red goud" if she will sleep with him. When she refuses, he takes counsel with his foster mother, who then persuades the lady to send away all her servants and obtains the keys to her castle, giving them to the squire. He opens the thirty-three locks and, waking the lady, informs her that: "I hae it fully in my power / to come to bed to thee." The wife escapes by means of a substitute bedfellow: Her niece, Lady Maisry, sleeps with the squire, gets the "gude red gowd . . . / and likeways white money," and finally marries him, despite his having taken her ring and cut off her ring-finger as "love-tokens."[56]

In *Redesdale and Wise William* (Child 246; Bronson, IV, no. 256), the beginning is much like *La jactancia:* Everyone is boasting and Redesdale arrogantly claims: "There is not a lady fair, / In bower wherever she be, / But I could aye her favour win / Wi ae blink o my ee" (246A.3). William wagers the chastity of his sister, offering Redesdale his "head against your land." Redesdale throws William into a "prison strang" and rides off to seduce the girl, who, however, had been forewarned in a "braid letter" sent by William. She rejects a series of offers from Redesdale, who then sets fire to her house and rides away, lamenting that the girl and her ladies will be unable to escape. But they do and Redesdale forfeits his land, admitting: "If there is a gude woman in the world, / your one sister is she" (246A.28).

The German *Wette* is like *The Twa Knights:* Künig Ecksteyn and Wolff Reyn wager first their horses and then their own heads over whether Reyn can sleep with Ecksteyn's wife. Reyn tells the wife that her husband has been found sleeping with someone else's wife and has been killed and that she should

---

56. Coffin (no. 268) lists two Anglo-American songs that may be distantly related to *The Twa Knights* (or at least cover thematically similar material) and include the chastity wager motif. For the substitute bedfellow, see n. 59.

therefore become his lover. She escapes, as in *The Twa Knights*, by substituting the beautiful servant girl, Adelheit, from whom Reyn takes two locks of hair as a token. The queen demonstrates her own innocence, by showing that her hair has not been cut. Wolff Reyn begs for his life, but: "Sein Haupt verlor er zů der selbigen stund."[57]

The Danish *Vaeddemaalet* (DgF 224; TSB D145) relates to *Redesdale and Wise William* more closely than to the other analogues we have seen, in that there are a series of offers, which are rejected, but no substitute bedfellow, no tokens, etc. Here, "Peder boasts of his power to seduce any girl he wants, but Lave says he knows one woman Peder could never get. Peder bets his estate and his life on it and rides to Ingerlill. He asks for her hand. She reminds him of all the women he has already deserted and rejects his offer of gifts. Finally he must ride off, having lost his bet." Mockery and rage await him at the king's court: He has lost house, lands, and life.[58]

In the Greek ballad, *Toũ Maurianoũ kaì tẽs aderfẽs toũ* (*Of Mavrianós and his Sister*), the king wagers his kingdom that he can sleep with Mavrianós' sister, while Mavrianós wagers his own life that he will fail. The king, in some variants, imprisons Mavrianós (as in *Redesdale*), sends rich gifts of gold and ducats to the girl, and asks for a meeting with her, but she sends in her stead a servant girl disguised in her clothes. As in *The Twa Knights*, the king cuts off the girl's ring-finger (or takes her ring) and, as in *Die Wette*, also takes a lock of hair, as proof that he has slept with Mavrianós' sister. As Mavrianós is being led to the gallows, his sister appears to prove that her hair and her hands are still intact. The king must forsake his kingdom and become the girl's slave (or

---

57. For texts, see DVM, II, no. 38; Meier, *Balladen*, II, no. 49. Note, also, Engle's useful analysis: *A Preliminary Catalogue*, II, 714–715 (no. V72). See the detailed studies in Schewe, pp. 176–186, and DVM, II, no. 38; also Taylor, "English and German Balladry," p. 28.

58. TSB D145; for Danish texts: DgF, IV, no. 224; note also Prior, III, 28–33. There is apparently no close relationship between Lave and Ingelille: She is neither his wife nor his beloved and is merely identified as "her Torloffs datter" (DgF 224*C*.4; or other similar names). In *Ridderens runeslag* (or *Her Oluf og hans forguldte Ljud*), Oluf wagers his grey charger with Her Peder that he can seduce proud Mettelil (or little Kiersten) with the help of the magical sound of his gilded horn. He succeeds, but, when the girl returns home, she stabs herself to death. Peder then sets his own sword against a stone and runs himself through. See DgF 73; TSB A10; Olrik, II, no. 9; Smith-Dampier, pp. 268–271; Dal, no. 4; Prior, III, 34–38. Note the motif: D1355.1.3. *Magic love-producing horn*; for more balladic references: *Yoná*, p. 363, n. 18.

swineherd). Sometimes the woman involved is Mavrianós' wife rather than his sister (as, for example, in Dawkins, no. 8).[59]

The Continental ballads we have just seen all embody, of course, the essential motif of the chastity wager. They attest, too, to various crucial and widely shared motifs, some of which are also present in *La jactancia del conde Vélez:* The protagonists wager their lives (or one of their lives) against or together with property (*Redesdale; Wette; Vaeddemaalet; Mavrianós; Vélez*); offers of inducements to the girl (*Knights; Redesdale; Vaeddemaalet; Mavrianós;* parallel, perhaps, to the ostentatious displays in the Moroccan *Vélez* and the golden cord in the Leonese-Zamoran texts); the old woman helper (*Knights;* corresponding to the treacherous servants in the Eastern *Vélez*); the substitute bedfellow (*Knights; Wette; Mavrianós*); false tokens (*Knights; Wette; Mavrianós;* Eastern *Vélez*). It is clear, all the same, that *Vélez* and its continental counterparts are only very distantly and indirectly related.

A study of *El conde Vélez* and its Continental ballad congeners would be incomplete if we neglected to look at medieval narratives and modern folktales embodying the motif of the chastity wager. An exploration of these analogues will be essential to clarifying the relationship of the two quite different modalities adopted by *La jactancia del conde Vélez:* The Eastern form, with its false tokens, and the Moroccan and Leonese-Zamoran types, with their ostentatious displays. The chastity wager narrative has been circulating in the European tradition at least since the high Middle Ages. The story is known in a great number of medieval and Renaissance forms, as well as in folktales current in modern tradition. We will limit our analysis of early narratives to some of the Old French renditions, to Medieval Latin and Middle English versions, and to the famous *Decameron* story (Day II:9), which together offer sufficient evidence of

---

59. The ballad is widely known in Greece, as well as in Cyprus and in the Greek-speaking community of Corsica. See Baud-Bovy, *Textes*, pp. 245–247, 303; also Dawkins, "Dōdekanēsōn," pp. 42–45 (nos. 7–8); Jeannaraki, no. 294; Kind, *Anthologie*, pp. 56–61; Legrand, *Recueil*, pp. 302–305 (= Pellegrini); Liebrecht, *Zur Volkskunde*, pp. 218–219 (concerning Jeannaraki); Lüdeke, *Griechische Volksdichtung*, pp. 217, 252; Id., *Im Paradies*, pp. 80–81; Lüdeke-Megas, nos. 36–38 (36 = Jeannaraki); Pachtikos, nos. 23–24; Pappadopoulos, p. 417*b*; Passow, no. 474; Pellegrini, *Cargese*, pp. 19–20; Pernot, *Anthologie*, pp. 87–90; Politis, *Eklogaì*, no. 81; Spyridakis, no. 60 (= Theros); Theros, I, no. 340 (= Passow). Note the study by Brewster and Tarsouli, pp. 42–44. Numerous additional versions are cited in Baud-Bovy, *Textes*, p. 245; DVM, II, 45–46. As is noted in DVM, Politis' version is a "Mischtext ohne volkskundlichen Wert" (II, 46). For more on the chastity wager motif in other European ballad traditions, see the Appendix.

the narrative's ultimately genetic relationship to *La jactancia del conde Vélez* and, at the same time, attest to the modern folktales' multi-secular traditional character.

In Old French, the narratives closest to that of *El conde Vélez* are *Le Comte de Poitiers* (late 12th to early 13th cent.), *Guillaume de Dole* (circa 1212–1213), *Roman de la Violette* (circa 1227–1229), *Le roi Flore et la belle Jehanne* (mid-13th cent.?), and the *Miracle de Oton* (circa 1380). In *Le Comte de Poitiers*, Gerart, count of Poitiers, praises the beauty and fidelity of his wife. The Duke of Normandy wagers his lands against those of Gerart that he can seduce her within a month. The Countess rejects his advances. With the help of the Countess' aged nurse, Alotru, the Duke of Normandy obtains her wedding ring, ten golden hairs from her comb, and a piece of her skirt. The Duke returns to Paris and shows these tokens of the Countess' supposed infidelity to King Pépin. Gerart sends for the Countess. The King decides she is guilty and Gerart loses his lands. He abandons the Countess in a forest. She is rescued by Harpin, the Count's nephew, who forces her to accompany him to his town. Disguised as a pilgrim, Gerart goes to Poitiers to kill the man who has dishonored him. He hears Alotru and the Duke discussing their treacherous deception and the Countess' innocence. Gerart goes directly to the town where Harpin is about to marry the Countess. Once reunited, Gerart and his wife go to Paris, where, in the King's presence, he denounces the Duke. After Gerart defeats the Duke in a judicial combat, the traitor is tied to a horse, dragged, and hanged. Alotru's nose and ears are cut off and she is confined to a convent. Gerart and his wife return to Poitiers.[60]

Guillaume de Dole or *Le Roman de la Rose* (by Jean Renart; circa 1212–1213) tells a related story, but the crucial chastity wager and other essential features are lacking: A treacherous seneschal defames Guillaume's beautiful sister, Liénor, by revealing that she has, on her thigh, a birthmark in the shape of a rose—information obtained from her unsuspecting mother. He claims that he has been Liénor's lover. Liénor appears at court and tricks the seneschal into accepting as gifts various objects, which she then accuses him of having stolen. The seneschal, claiming that he has never seen her before (*se onques més la vi!* [v. 4793]), vehemently denies her accusations. When the objects are found on his person, Liénor is vindicated and can marry the Emperor Conrad of Germany. The

---

60. We follow the detailed analyses in V.-F. Koenig's (pp. iii–v) and B. Malmberg's (pp. 9–12) eds. and in Buffum's ed. of *Le Roman de la Violette* (pp. xl–xliii) and Koenig's and Malmberg's texts. For additional data on *Le Comte de Poitiers*, see the Appendix.

evil seneschal is exiled and goes to the Holy Land to serve in the Order of the Temple.[61]

In the *Roman de la Violette* or *Gerart de Nevers* (by Gerbert de Montreuil; circa 1227–1229), Gerart de Nevers sings a song about the beauty and fidelity of his *amie*, Euriant, after which Lisiart, the treacherous Count of Forois, boasts that, if he is given eight days, he will be able to seduce her (vv. 254–267). He and Gerart wager their lands. Euriant rejects his advances. With the help of Gondrée, a false servant woman, Lisiart manages to see the beauteous, fifteen-year-old Euriant in her bath, noting that she has a purple birthmark (*violette*) under her right breast. Lisiart returns to the court at Melun, boasting of his success. Gerart sends for Euriant and, when she arrives, Lisiart reveals his knowledge of the birthmark. Gerart gives up his lands to Lisiart and abandons Euriant in a forest. She is rescued by the Duke of Metz, who falls in love with her. Gerart, disguised as a *jongleur*, visits Lisiart and hears him and Gondrée recalling their treacherous deception and speaking of Euriant's innocence. After numerous adventures, unrelated to the chastity wager narrative, Gerart manages to arrive at Metz in time to save Euriant (falsely accused of murdering the Duke's sister) from being burned at the stake, by defeating her accuser (Meliatir) in single combat. Gerart then accuses Lisiart of treason and defeats him too in another judicial duel. Lisiart is tied to a horse's tail, dragged, and hanged. Gondrée is boiled to death in a cauldron. Gerart and Euriant are married and return to Nevers.[62]

In *Le roi Flore et la belle Jehanne* (mid-13th cent.?), Messire Robiert has vowed to make a pilgrimage to the tomb of St. James immediately after marrying his young wife, Jehanne. Messire Raoul boasts: "Je vous ferai cous [= cocu] avant ke vous revigniés" and promises to provide "ensengnes ke j'arai eu part de li; si y meterai ma tière contre la vostre" (p. 98). Having agreed to the wager, Robiert departs for St. James. Raoul bribes a false old governess, *Dame* Hiersent, who sends all other servants out of the house and, while *Dame* Jehanne

---

61. See the detailed analyses in the eds. of Servois (pp. ix-xii) and Lejeune (pp. ix-xii), and in Jean Frappier, *Les romans courtois*, pp. 81–91. Note also Lacy, "'Amer par oïr dire'" and DeLooze, "The Gender of Fiction." For some medieval analogues of *Guillaume de Dole*, see the Appendix.

62. See Buffum's ed. and detailed analysis, pp. xxxvi-xliii. As Buffum shows: "Le R[oman] de la V[iolette] est dérivé directement du C[omte] de P[oitiers] avec additions et substitutions de motifs empruntés à la Rose [i.e. *Guillaume de Dole*]" (p. xl). For more data on Jean Renart (author of *Le Roman de la Rose* or *Guillaume de Dole*) and Gerbert de Montreuil (author of *Le Roman de la Violette* or *Gerart de Nevers*), see the Appendix.

is in her bath, Raoul enters and attempts to carry her to her bed. She strikes him
in the face with a stick, making a deep wound, and he leaves, but not before
noting that she has a black mole on her right thigh. When Raoul tells Robiert
about the mole, he is convinced that Jehanne has betrayed him and allows that
Raoul has won the wager. Deprived of his lands, Robiert departs. Jehanne also
leaves the castle, disguised as a man, to search for her husband, whom she finds
and, unrecognized, becomes his squire. They work as innkeepers in Marseille
(Jehanne still remaining unrecognized by her husband!). Meanwhile, the traitor
Raoul becomes ill and confesses his deception to a chaplain, who orders him to
go on a pilgrimage to the Holy Land and to confess his sin to anyone who may
ask him. He stops at the inn in Marseille, is recognized by Jehanne, and
confesses what he has done, but she says nothing, and allows him to continue
on his pilgrimage. After seven years, Robiert and his wife (still in disguise!)
return to their native land. Jehanne now reveals that Raoul has obtained
Robiert's lands by trickery. The matter is decided by a judicial combat, in which
Robiert is victorious, and Jehanne finally reveals her identity.[63]

The *Miracle de Oton, roy d'Espagne* (circa 1380) embodies the following
narrative: Oton (Ostes), nephew of the Emperor Lotaire [of Rome?], marries
Denise, daughter of King Alfons of Spain, who cedes his kingdom to the young
couple. Oton must return to Rome and leaves, with Denise, a bone from his toe
as a love token (!!!). At Rome, Berengier, who is also in love with Denise,
wagers his lands against Oton's kingdom that he can seduce her. Denise rejects
his advances. Berengier bribes her maid, *Damoiselle* Esglantine, who serves
Denise wine and, when she has fallen asleep, takes the bone to Berengier and
describes to him a mark (*saing*) on Denise's body. Oton accepts that he has lost
the wager and returns to Spain to kill his wife, but she flees, disguised as a man,
and, unrecognized, enters the service of her father, King Alfons. On learning
what has happened, Alfons declares war on Lotaire. Meanwhile, Oton has gone
to Outremer, to live as a Sarracen. Denise, in disguise, is sent to Rome as a
messenger and, along the way, meets Oton. She accuses Berengier, with whom
Oton fights a judicial duel. Defeated, Berengier confesses his crime. Denise

---

63. We follow the ed. of Moland and d'Hericault, pp. 83–157, and the analysis of
G. Paris, "Le cycle de la gageure," pp. 532–534. As Paris observes, this little prose
romance "comprend deux histoires qui n'ont aucun rapport l'une avec l'autre"—one
concerning King Flore and the other the chastity wager narrative, the latter being
"pleine de gaucheries, de contradictions et d'inutilités ... Ce récit est tout à fait
invraisemblable" (pp. 532–533).

reveals her identity and pardons her husband. Berengier and Esglantine are to be executed.[64]

In an untitled Medieval Latin *exemplum* (second half of the 13th century; Tours MS 468), a virtuous wife is mentioned in conversation among knights (*milites*). One of them states: "Ego pono terram meam quod infra quindenam faciam de ea quicquid voluero et per bona indicia hoc probabo." The husband wagers his lands to the contrary. The potential seducer attempts in vain to enter the wife's castle, but "per fraudem domicellam domine seduxit." This servant girl "ei anulum quem maritus ei dederat furata tradidit et signum vnum quod habebat in coxa reuelauit." The would-be seducer then informs the husband, who takes his wife to a country residence and throws her into the sea (eam ad quoddam manenum ducens in aquam proiecit). She escapes and, dressed in men's clothing and with the help of monks, becomes highly successful as the king's almoner (pro elemosinario). In the course of her duties, she discovers and is reconciled with her husband, who had fled [to a foreign land]. She returns home and accuses the false knight "quod eam violenter oppressit." He, however, "iurauit et negauit se unquam illam vidisse," thus vindicating the wife. She then demands justice of the king. The evil knight is hanged, the husband's land is returned to him, and he is reunited with his wife.[65]

In the mid-15th-century Middle English *Two Merchants in Rome*, one of the merchants has as his wife "a chast and a faire womman," but the other mistrusts all women. "Thei put in plegge al their possessioun: this that he shuld corrupt hir within XV daies." The would-be seducer is unsuccessful, but "hir footemayde or seruaunt with yiftes corrupt she was disceived." He gains possession of a highly prized ring and knowledge of a birthmark and, when the husband is informed, he leaves his "possessioun" and goes into exile. The wife is "outcast as advowteres" ('adulteress'). She disguises herself as a man and flees to Alexandria, where she wins great favor as an officer of the king: "The kynges Rentis wern infinytily multiplied bi his providence." When the emperor of

---

64. See the ed. by G. Paris and U. Robert, pp. 315–388, and the analysis in G. Paris, "Le cycle de la gageure," pp. 530–531. As Paris argues, Denise, disguised as a man, must originally have fought against Berengier, but to accomodate the narrative as a Marian miracle, the Virgin appears, to reproach Oton for having converted to Islam (je sers et croy Mohammet [v. 1509]); he then repents and claims his right to fight against Berengier. Denise's disguise has thus become pointless: "Tout le rôle de la femme devient inutile" (p. 531, n. 4).

65. Hilka, "Neue Beiträge," pp. 16–17 (no. XIII); Hulme, "A Middle English Addition," p. 221*a*.

Rome dies, his son calls the successful officer to Rome. "Bi hap and fortune," the disguised wife finds her husband among the poorest of the poor and they are reconciled. The treacherous merchant is "deemed into deth of his own confession." Husband and wife are reunited.[66]

Boccaccio's interpretation of the chastity wager story (*Decameron* II:9; circa 1348–1352) is well known: Bernabò da Genoa boasts of his wife's fidelity. Ambruogiuolo da Piacenza states that any woman can be seduced and undertakes to prove it by going to Genoa and "infra tre mesi dal dì che io mi partirò di qui avere della tua donna fatta mia volontà." Bernabò wagers his own head, against a thousand gold florins, on his wife's chastity, but Ambruogiuolo prefers five thousand of Bernabò's florins against his own one thousand. They sign an agreement. Ambruogiuolo goes to Genoa, bribes a poor woman who often visits *Madonna* Zinevra, to conceal him in a specially made chest which is then taken to the lady's home and left, for safekeeping, in her bedroom. When *Madonna* Zinevra falls asleep, Ambruogiuolo emerges, takes note of all the details of the room and the fact that the lady has a mole, "dintorno al quale erano alquanti peluzzi biondi come oro" (p. 209). He then takes a purse, a cloak, some belts and rings, and, after spending three days in the chest, departs, when the poor woman (la buona femina) comes to reclaim her property. On returning to Paris, Ambruogiuolo tells Bernabò that he has won the bet: he displays the objects he has taken and describes the room. When Bernabò objects that servants could have given him the belongings and provided a description of the room, Ambruogiuolo describes the mole. Bernabò is convinced of his wife's guilt and arranges to have his servant kill her, but the servant spares her life; abandoned in the wilderness, she is helped by an old woman and, disguised as a man, undergoes various adventures: She serves as a sailor on a ship that takes her to Alexandria, where she enters the service of the Sultan and becomes an important official; she meets Ambruogiuolo while on a trip to Acre; he is offering her purse and belt for sale; he tells her how he acquired them; she orders Ambruogiuolo to return with her to Alexandria; she also arranges to bring the impoverished Bernabò to Egypt; she orders Ambruogiuolo, under threat of torture, to tell his story to the Sultan, in Bernabò's presence; Bernabò reveals that he ordered his wife to be killed; she reveals her true identity; he begs her to pardon him; Bernabò and Zinevra depart for Italy; the Sultan orders Ambruogiuolo tied to a stake and smeared with honey, to be devoured by flies and wasps.[67]

---

66. Hulme, "A Middle English Addition," pp. 219–221.

67. See Branca's notes on the story's origins and analogs: pp. 1123–1124, n. 2, 1132, n. 11; Landau, pp. 135–145, 148; A.C. Lee, pp. 42–57. On Ambruogiuolo's

The Medieval French, Latin, and Middle English narratives and Boccaccio's story embody the following common stages. The numeration reflects our subsequent analysis of the modern Hispanic folktale:

1. Boast of wife's fidelity (*Poitiers; Violette; exemplum; Merchants; Decameron*).

2. Envious false friend (rival) claims all women can be seduced (*Merchants; Decameron*).

3. Wager on wife's fidelity: lands (*Poitiers; Violette; Jehanne; Oton; exemplum; Merchants*); money (husband initially offers his own head) (*Decameron*).

4. Written agreement (*Decameron*).

5. Wife rejects would-be seducer (*Poitiers; Violette; Jehanne; Oton; exemplum; Merchants*); she strikes him with a stick and injures him (*Jehanne*).

6. Old woman (nurse: *Poitiers*; false servant woman: *Violette; Oton; exemplum; Merchants;* governess: *Jehanne*; poor woman: *Decameron*) bribed and gains entry; allows would-be seducer to enter (*Jehanne*); wagerer hidden in chest (*Decameron*).

7. False tokens: wedding ring, golden hairs, piece of skirt (*Poitiers*); birthmark (*Guillaume; Violette*); mole (*Jehanne*); bone and birthmark (*Oton*); ring and birthmark (*exemplum; Merchants*); wagerer notes details of room, mole, takes purse, cloak, belts, rings (*Decameron*).

8. Husband loses wager (all, except *Guillaume*, where there is no wager).

9. Wife abandoned (*Poitiers; Violette*); leaves castle (*Jehanne*) or flees (*Oton*); thrown into sea (*exemplum*); outcast as adulteress (*Merchants*); husband orders servant to kill wife (*Decameron*).

---

punishment, see the motif: Q464. *Covering with honey and exposing to flies*; FLSJ, III, 260, n. 28. For more data, see the Appendix.

10.   Wife rescued or escapes (*Poitiers; Violette; exemplum; Merchants*);
        servant spares wife (*Decameron*).

11.   Disguised as man (*Jehanne; Oton; exemplum; Merchants; Decameron*).

12.   Becomes powerful in foreign land (*exemplum; Merchants; Decameron*).

13.   Passes test aimed at proving she is not man (*Decameron?*).

15.   Husband brings about wife's vindication (*Poitiers; Violette*); or girl or
        wife tricks would-be seducer into revealing deception by claiming he has
        stolen various objects (*Guillaume*); or by accusing him of raping her
        (*exemplum*); wife takes initiative in search for truth (*Jehanne; Oton;
        exemplum; Merchants; Decameron*).

16.   Treacherous wagerer and old woman punished: wagerer dragged and
        hanged; old woman mutilated (*Poitiers*) or boiled alive (*Violette*);
        treacherous seneschal exiled (*Guillaume*); wagerer and servant woman
        executed (*Oton*); wagerer hanged (*exemplum*); condemned to death
        (*Merchants*); wagerer tied to stake, smeared with honey, devoured by flies
        and wasps (*Decameron*).[68]

The medieval story is still widely known, throughout the Hispanic domain
and beyond, as a modern folktale, which, in one or another of its modalities,
embodies all of the narrative's essential characteristics. Here, as an example, is a
version from the Asturian tradition:

El zapato de plata

Una vez era un comerciante que fue a una población a comprar
géneros y allí se juntó en un café con varios amigos. Y el comerciante
hizo muchos elogios de la fidelidad de su mujer. Y dijo uno de la
reunión:
—¡Qué inocente eres! Las mujeres son fáciles de vencer, y yo
apuesto a vencer la tuya antes de ocho días.

---

68. For additional data on the medieval narratives, see the Appendix.

Apostaron mucho dinero. Y el comerciante quedó en aquella población, mientras el otro fue a ver si ganaba la apuesta. Cuando llegó, se puso a rondar la casa. Y ya llevaba tres días calle arriba y calle abajo, y la mujer del comerciante no salía a la calle ni se asomaba a la ventana. Él estaba desesperado, y en esto pasó por allí una vieja y le preguntó que qué tenía, y dijo él:

—¿A usted qué le importa?

—¡Quién sabe si le podré servir a usted en algo! —dijo la vieja.

Él le contó lo que pretendía. Y la vieja fue a casa de la señora a llevarle una cesta de judías y algunas mantecas, diciendo que se las mandaban sus parientes de la aldea. Y como estaba oscureciendo, la señora le dijo a la vieja que se quedara a dormir allí.

Se quedó y entró en la habitación de la señora cuando ésta se estaba acostando, y vió que tenía en el pecho un lunar con tres cabellos que le rodeaban la cintura. Y al salir le llevó un anillo que tenía encima de la mesa.

La vieja marchó al rayar el alba y entregó el anillo al pretendiente y le dio los detalles que había visto en la habitación de la señora.

El pretendiente fue donde estaba el comerciante y le dijo:

—¿Conoces este anillo?

—Sí, es nuestro anillo de boda.

—¿Y no es cierto que tu mujer tiene en el pecho un lunar con tres cabellos que le rodean la cintura?

—¡Sí, es cierto!

—Pues gané la apuesta.

Entonces el comerciante hirió de gravedad al pretendiente de su mujer y por esta causa lo metieron preso.

Y en cuanto se enteró de esto la mujer del comerciante fue a casa de un platero y le encargó un zapato de plata. Y el día que iban a sentenciar a su marido, se presentó delante del tribunal y preguntó:

—¿Cuál es el enemigo del hombre que van a sentenciar aquí?

Y le dijeron:

—Es aquél.

La mujer le dió con el zapato de plata en la cara y le dijo:

—¡Ladrón de mi cuarto! ¡Me has robado el compañero de este zapato!

Y dijo él:

—¡Señora! Eso no es verdad; ni yo estuve en el cuarto de usted, ni la he visto a usted nunca.

—¿Y jura usted delante de este tribunal que no ha estado usted jamás en mi cuarto, ni me ha visto usted nunca?

—Lo juro.

—Pues yo soy la mujer del hombre que van a sentenciar por ser usted un calumniador.

Y el pretendiente dijo al tribunal de qué medios se había valido para ganar la apuesta, y le metieron preso a él y a la vieja. Y el comerciante salió de allí cogido del brazo de su mujer.[69]

We have seen versions of this story from the following Hispanic subtraditions: Eastern Judeo-Spanish, Castilian areas of Spain, Asturias, New Mexico, Mexico, Santo Domingo, Panama, Chile, and Argentina, as well as from Portugal, Madeira, Azores, Brazil, the Cape Verde Islands, and Catalonia. The Philippine versions are clearly of Hispanic origin. Cynthia Crews' Eastern Judeo-Spanish version, from Skoplje (Macedonia), is undoubtedly patterned on a Near Eastern subtype. We have included a French Basque version (Webster) in our analysis because of its essential similarity to the Hispanic texts.[70] The following features are present in the modern Hispanic forms:

(1)   Husband boasts about wife's fidelity *bdenpxzb'i'j'n'*.
(2)   Envious false friend or rival (old man *a*) claims all women are unfaithful and easily seduced *abefginpqrswzk'l'm'*.
(3)   Wager on wife's fidelity; can involve wagerers' lives (by beheading *bcol'*; hanging *dh'm'*) *bcdob'h'l'm'*; wealth *aefipuwxd'f'k'*; property *gmnpqstxyza'b'e'i'j'k'*; property against life *kor*; *abcdefghijklmnopqrs tuvwyxz a'b'c'd'e' f g'h'i'j'k'l'm'*.
(4)   Written agreement signed *abdqrl'*.
(5)   False friend unsuccessfully attempts to speak with (seduce) wife, but she rejects him. (He does acrobatic tricks in front of house every day *f*; sets up tent, runs bulls, holds dances every evening *k*; exhibits riches during

---

69. Llano Roza de Ampudia, no. 115. The style clearly bespeaks the collector's having abbreviated and retold the story, perhaps following detailed field notes. (See our comments in the following note.) All the same, the text provides a characteristic example of many of the narrative's significant features. For more data, see the Appendix.

70. For additional data on the modern Hispanic folktale, its analogues, and the motifs it embodies, see the Appendix.

many days *b;* but wife will not look or come out *fkb';* wife rejects him, beats him on head with stick *x*) *bcdefghijklrstxyzb'c'd'e'f'h'i'j'k'n'.*

(6)   False friend (brother *v*) bribes treacherous old woman (witch *afiuvj'k'm';* wife's [husband's *z*] [old] servant woman *bpzb'd';* gypsy woman *c;* wife's former wet nurse *dowf';* go-between *m;* midwife who delivered wife as baby *x;* poor woman *a';* wife's neighbor *i';* wife's chaperone *l'*) to obtain false tokens of infidelity (old man hidden in chest left in wife's room *a;* servant woman [old witch] sees wife through keyhole *pv;* gypsy woman [old woman, witch] sleeps in wife's bedroom *ceghlmntuwc'f'm';* witch becomes mouse to enter wife's bedroom *i*) *abcdefghijklmnopqrstuvwyza' b'c'd'e'f'g'h'i'j'k'l'm'.*

(7)   Old man sees (*a*) or old woman (etc.) sees and tells false friend of mole(s) *abcdegmopquxy;* (golden) hair(s) *ghijlrf'g'i'l';* clothing *dj;* jewels *d;* birthmark(s) *nb'c'd'e'f;* writes down description of room *m';* and/or takes dress *a;* hairs *bi';* (wedding) ring *bcejkrstuwye'g'h'i'j';* wedding gown *f;* nightgown *ju;* sheet with wife's initials *j;* (golden; red) band (inscribed with wife's name) *qu;* handkerchief with husband's name *ty;* golden scissors *v;* wedding presents given to wife by husband *z;* garter *a';* pistol *d';* piece of dress *g';* golden chain inscribed with wife's name *k';* rival steals wife's underskirt *n';* *abcdefghijklmnopqrstuvwyza'b'c'd'e'f'g'h'i'j' k'l'm'n'.*

(8)   When token(s) shown, husband loses wager and property *aefgikmnopqsuve'f'i';* is condemned to death *bcdb'd'h'm'n';* *abcdefghi kmnopqsuva'b'd'e'f'h'i'j'm'n'.*

(9)   Wife is rejected and husband attempts to kill her or orders her killed by various means (she is thrown into sea [well *q;* river *we'*] in [silver *f;* glass *k*] box [coffin *q;* boat *s;* bottle *c'*] *fhiko qstvwya'c'e'g'i'j'k';* in rawhide trunk *g;* he pushes her off cliff *j;* he abandons her in the hills *l,* in wilderness *m,* on island *x,* on barren heath *z;* he takes her out of town and shoots her *n;* he orders her killed by servants, who are to cut out heart as proof, but bring deer's heart instead *p;* by shoemaker, who is to bring eyes as proof, but brings dog's eyes instead *u*); *fghijklmnopqs tuvwxyza'c'e'g'i'j'k'.*

(10) Wife manages to escape (is rescued by fishermen *fghikc';* saved by prayer to Virgin, helped by thieves and by talking bird *j;* saved by cowboys *l;* by old woman *m;* by the Virgin Mary *n;* by sailors *osi'j';* by good witch *p;* by goatherds *q;* by old man *tv;* by prince *we';* by king *y;* by pirates *a';*

by people on shore *k'*; is helped by talking goat *x*; overhears how witches have put spell on queen *z*); *fghijklmnopqrstvwxyza'c'd'e'i'j'k'*.

(11) Wife disguised as man *afghijlnoqsuvwxyza'd'e'i'j'k'l'*.

(12) Wife becomes powerful person (in foreign land) *fgijloqrwd'i'j'k'*; fights bravely in war *fgilqy*; tames horned water serpent *h*; (foreign) king (governor) sends her as king (governor) to her own country *stuy*; she cures queen of witches' spell *z*; restores sight (health *k'*) of king's daughter *a'k'*; works for king *d'*; asks king to make her judge in her own country *za'd'*; *fghijloqrstuvwyza'd'i'j'k'*.

(13) Wife passes tests aimed at proving she is not man *hijnquvwe'*.

(14) Talking water serpent (*h*) or talking bird (*j*) reveals her identity and saves her from punishment *hj*.

(15) Wife contrives to have truth revealed to/by husband (and/or to king) (She tricks old man into explaining deception *a*; accuses false friend (rival) of having stolen her [golden; silver] shoe *berb'm'*; sleeve of her dress *cdh'*; earring *j'*; he answers: "I never saw you in my life"; deception revealed *bcderb'l'* [cf. *n'*]; she speaks to [threatens *c'k'*] impoverished [deranged *c'*] husband and truth is revealed *fghijknoqtuvwya'd'e'i'k'*; talking bird reveals false friend's treachery *j*; false friend's hand squeezed in vise, he confesses *l*; good witch beats false friend till he confesses *p*; wife threatens [to shoot] false friend and he confesses *q*; false friend and old woman [former wet nurse] seized by police [soldiers] or taken before judge *xz*, confess[es] *hnsuvwxzk'*; false friend confesses *a'*; false friend and old woman [neighbor woman] forced to confess *e'i'*; wife tricks false friend into confessing *g'*); *abcdefghijklnopqrstuvwxyza'b'c'd'e'g'h'i'j'k'l'm'n'*.

(16) False friend and/or old woman punished (husband [wife *vi'*] pardons false friend *bvi'*; false friend exiled *bz*; decapitated *cm'*; hanged *dfb'h'j'l'*; imprisoned *esa'*; stabbed to death by old woman *m*; burned to death *hpyd'*; placed in boiling water *t*; torn apart by ponies *x*; shot *e'*; rival deported for ten years to lonely island *n'*; gypsy woman decapitated *c*; old woman imprisoned *efszl'*; dragged to death by horse[s] *gqt*; burned to death *hijlvyd'k'm'*; taken into custody *m*; killed *n*; "put into a cask of oil" *o*; killed by mule *r*; torn apart by [wild] ponies *uwx*; neighbor woman pardoned *i'*; old woman [witch] hanged *j'*); *bcdefghijklmnopqrstu vwxyza'b'd'e'h'i'j'k'l'm'n'*.

Sources

Eastern J.-Sp.:	*a*	=	Crews, pp. 168–177
Castilian:	*b*	=	Cortés y Vázquez, *Cuentos*, I, no. 80
	c	=	Curiel Merchán, pp. 220–222
Asturian:	*d*	=	Llano Roza de Ampudia, no. 114
	e	=	Llano Roza de Ampudia, no. 115
New Mexico:	*f*	=	J. M. Espinosa, *New Mexico*, no. 70
Colorado:	*g*	=	Parsons, *Taos*, no. 78
	h	=	Parsons, *Taos*, pp. 144–147
	i	=	Rael, no. 130
	j	=	Rael, no. 131
	k	=	Rael, no. 132
	l	=	Zunzer, no. 4
Mexico:	*m*	=	Aiken, pp. 8–12
	n	=	Foster, no. 41
	o	=	Parsons, "Mitla," no. 13
	p	=	Wheeler, no. 71
	q	=	Wheeler, no. 72
Santo Domingo:	*r*	=	Andrade, no. 268
Panama:	*s*	=	Riera Pinilla, no. 54
Chile:	*t*	=	Pino Saavedra, *Cuentos*, no. 127
	u	=	Pino Saavedra, *Cuentos*, no. 128
	v	=	Pino Saavedra, *Cuentos*, no. 129
	w	=	Pino Saavedra, *Cuentos*, no. 130
	x	=	Pino Saavedra, *Cuentos*, no. 270
Argentina:	*y*	=	Chertudi, no. 61
Portugal:	*z*	=	Castro Osório, II, 235–252
	a'	=	Leite de Vasconcellos, *Contos*, II, no. 347
Madeira:	*b'*	=	Costa Fontes, *Folktales*, no. 30 (pp. 255–264)
Azores:	*c'*	=	Braga, *Contos*, no. 76
	d'	=	Costa Fontes, uned. (Godinho)
	e'	=	Costa Fontes, uned. (Silveira)
Brazil:	*f'*	=	Romero, *Contos*, no. 13 (pp. 105–106)
Cape Verde:	*g'*	=	Parsons, *Cape Verde*, no. 57 (pp. 177–178)
Catalonia:	*h'*	=	Amades, *Rondallística*, no. 391
Mallorca:	*i'*	=	Alcover, X, 86–113
	j'	=	Alcover, XI, 96–104

Basque:	k'	=	Webster, pp. 132–136
Philippines:	l'	=	Fansler, pp. 248–251
	m'	=	Fansler, pp. 252–253
	n'	=	Fansler, p. 253

In his crucially important comparative study of folktales in a world-wide perspective, Stith Thompson gives our story short shrift, stressing its literary origins and doubting its essential traditionality:

> A favorite theme in the romantic literature of the Middle Ages was that of the wife who, in spite of misunderstandings and often of hardship and abuse, seeks her husband and at last finds him after many adventures. The tales vary only in the nature of the undeserved sufferings of the wife and of the circumstances under which the husband is recovered. They appear not only in medieval literature, but in that of the Renaissance as well; not only in the romances, but in the novelle and later in the drama. Eventually these literary tales were adapted to the purposes of the oral story-teller, though they have never become popular and cannot in any sense be thought of as a product of folklore.[71]

Here, however, Stith Thompson is wrong. It is true that the *Decameron* embodies more narrative stages in common with the modern Hispanic tale than do any of the other medieval accounts, but, at the same time, the modern story's various conformations attest to far ranging popularity and to numerous features which clearly go back to variants similar or identical to those reflected in the Old French, Latin, and Middle English texts, features which, at the same time, are

---

71. *The Folktale*, p. 109; cf. also p. 203 and n. 24. The story's history is, of course, neither totally literary nor totally oral. Liungman argues that, in the Swedish repertoire at least, the story does not really belong to oral tradition ("Dies ist ein Märchen, das eigentlich der mündlichen Überlieferung nicht angehört" [p. 231]) and he cites the influence of a 17th-century printed *Volksbuch*; but he also concedes the story's oral character in other traditions (including those of Spain and Portugal). Undoubtedly, here, as in innumerable other cases, the oral and written traditions have frequently interacted. As Farinelli has observed with regard to another Boccaccio story (Ghismonda; IV:1): "Ben può supporsi che la tradizione orale venisse, di tempo in tempo, in soccorso di quella scritta, e contribuisse alla maggiore celebrità e diffusione della novella" (*Italia e Spagna*, I, 362).

lacking in the *Decameron:* Thus many of the story's variants go into considerable detail concerning the wife's rejecting her would-be seducer (stage 5); one Chilean variant even has her strike him on the head with a stick, just as in *La belle Jehanne*. In Boccaccio's story, on the other hand, Ambruogiuolo does not even see the lady at this stage, but goes directly to the "poor woman" and offers her a bribe to help him gain access to the lady's house. Again, under stage 6, the female accomplice's identity in the modern stories is often closer to the Old French sources (servant, nurse, governess) than to the *Decameron* (merely a poor woman). Only the Judeo-Spanish text, doubtless following some Near Eastern model, attests to the wagerer's gaining entry inside a box, while other variants document details scattered through the diverse medieval French narratives: The servant woman sees the wife taking a bath (*Violette;* cf. *Jehanne*), just as, in several of the modern stories, she spies upon the wife or steals her ring while she is in her bath (stages 6–7). Among the false tokens (stage 7), there are also variants, such as golden hairs and a piece of a dress, which are already mentioned in the Old French versions, but are lacking in the *Decameron*. Under stage 15, the wife's tricking the wagerer in the modern story by accusing him of stealing her golden shoe (or a sleeve of her dress) recalls the similar accusation in *Guillaume de Dole*. The wagerer's denial is identical: "se onque més la vi!" (¡Si yo nunca he vihto a uhté hahta ahora, ni la he vihto nunca! [Cortés y Vázquez, *Cuentos*, I, no. 80]). Compare also the Latin *exemplum:* "iurauit et negauit se unquam illam vidisse." Boccaccio's story ends with Ambruogiuolo tied to a stake to be devoured by wasps and flies, but many of the modern stories atest to equally authentic medieval punishments, some of which have parallels in the narrative's Old French congeners (dragging at a horse's tail; burning at the stake; boiling alive), while others, such as tearing apart by wild horses, would also seem to go back to medieval origins. [72] Again, the treacherous wagerer is sometimes exiled, just as in *Guillaume de Dole*. In sum: To derive all these stories from written *novelle* of the Renaissance is a simplistic solution. It would be futile, too, to attempt to find each of these variants somewhere among the story's late Italian modalities, for all such a procedure would show is that the Italian stories had, in diverse ways, also drawn upon earlier oral narratives. Indeed, Boccaccio's story itself is not "literary," but is undoubtedly modeled on previous oral tradition.[73] Even though our modern Hispanic folktale may, on occasion, very well have been influenced by written

---

72. Concerning the punishments of being torn apart by horses and being boiled alive, see the Appendix.

73. For some literary treatments of the chastity wager story, see the Appendix.

sources, there is simply no way that its complex diversity of variations can be envisioned by means of a conventional stemma or reduced to any fixed "text" or unique written prototype. Just as in the case of its balladic congener, *La jactancia del conde Vélez*, the story and its traditional life resist simplification and are as characteristically protean as any other creation of the oral tradition.

We have undertaken a lengthy deviation from our study of *La jactancia del conde Vélez*, but as we shall presently see, our analysis of the medieval and modern modalities of the chastity wager story will serve to clarify the ballad's diverse conformations in the Eastern Sephardic tradition, on one hand, and in Morocco and León-Zamora, on the other. The Eastern Judeo-Spanish form of *Conde Vélez* is obviously very closely related to the Pan-Hispanic folktale. It embodies the following stages: (2) All women can be seduced; (3) wager: first proposal: seven cities against Vélez's heart; final agreement: heart for heart; (4) written agreement; (6) three consecutive slave girls are bribed; (7) they provide a description of the princess' halls, tell of a mole under her left breast, and give Vélez the princess' ring; (8) Vélez reveals information at court; (11) princess disguised as man; (14) talking parrot, first refuses to speak, but then offers advice; (15) princess accuses Vélez of having stolen golden slipper; he answers: "Me mate el Dio del sielo, / si en tu corte entré yo"; (16) Vélez's heart is to be cut out. In contrast to the folktale, where it is always a married woman's fidelity that is in question, here—and also in the other forms of *Vélez*—the object of the wager is the chastity of the unmarried *infanta*, as in *Guillaume de Dole* and *Violette* and also in various Continental ballads: *Redesdale*, *Vaeddemaalet*, *Mavrianós*. But, in general, after stage 6, the Eastern *Conde Vélez* will follow the folktale very closely, while the Moroccan and Peninsular forms, as we shall see, will opt for a quite different, but still related narrative. The motif of the talking bird is problematic. It is found in only one text of the folktale, from Colorado (Rael, I, no. 131 [= text *j*]), and, given the frequent intervention of talking birds and particularly parrots in folk-narrative, its presence in *Vélez* and in the folktale may well be polygenetic.[74] All the same, there are striking agreements: In both accounts, at first, the bird refuses to speak—on two previous occasions in the Colorado tale—but the wife/princess urges it to speak and it finally does, advising the strategem of the golden slipper in the ballad and

---

74. In the folktale's Brazilian form (Romero, *Contos*, no. 13), the entire story is one of several narrated by a parrot just as in the Persian and Indian story collections: *Tutinameh* and *Çukasaptati* (Fansler, pp. 254–255; Landau, *Die Quellen*, pp. 89–90). For more on talking parrots, see the Appendix.

revealing the wife's identity and the wagerer's treachery in the folktale. Here is the pertinent passage in the Colorado story:

> Alcario [= Alcarita] pegó con su varita donde el pájaro saltó y le dijo:
> —Alcatraz, ¿me hablarás?
> Y Alcario se retiró otro poco y dió otro salto el pájaro y repitió Alcario las mismas palabras y la tercera vez el pájaro le dijo:
> —Sí te hablaré.
> Y la reina se quiso morir del susto. Le dijo Alcario:
> —Y ¿qué dirás?
> —Te diré que tú estás engañando al pueblo y al rey que tú eres hombre, y eres mujer.
> La reina la pasó en desmayos y el rey no le importó de la reina y se enamoró de una vez de Alcario. Entonces le contó el pájaro de la traición de Federico y le dijo que Eduardo estaba en la prisión.[75]

The Eastern and North African forms of *Conde Vélez* are in essential agreement in their initial stages: (2) All women can be seduced; (3) wager: heart for heart; (4) written contract. After this point, the Moroccan form takes a very different direction. From here on, the action will center around an amplification of the folktale's stage 5: the wagerer's unsuccessful attempt to attract the wife's /princess' attention and her repeated rejection of his suit: "A todo esto, el conde Veles, / la niña no se asomó." When all his efforts fail, we then pass directly to the dénouement (stage 16) and the boastful count's punishment: "Ya yevan al conde Veles / a sacarle el corasón." All the same, the Moroccan ballad's change in orientation does not imply that it is less related to the folktale tradition than is its Eastern congener. Count Vélez's displays and spectacles aimed at attracting the *infanta* have close counterparts in certain variants of the folktale. So, in one New Mexican variant, the wagerer does acrobatic tricks in front of the wife's house, while, in another—even closer to the Moroccan ballad—he sets up a tent, runs bulls, and organizes a dance. The dance is repeated the following night, but again to no avail. Here, the first two items obviously correspond to the ballad's readings: "Otro día en la mañana, / Veles sus tiendas armó. . . . // Otro día en la mañana, / a los sien toros soltó" (vv. 17, 32). Here are the Colorado and New Mexican texts:

---

75. Rael, I, 290. Alcario is the pseudonym taken by the wife, Alcarita, while she is disguised as a man.

[El envidioso] fue y todos los días hacía maromas. Y ella no salía nunca a ver las maromas porque se entretenía con un pájaro que hablaba. (Espinosa).

El día que don Luis se jue, aquí junto al palacio de don Luis vino aquél y puso una carpa y trujo unos toros y hizo bailes a ver si iba la mujer. La mujer de don Luis no salía pa ninguna parte. Ella no conocía gente, ni quería conocer. Otro día en la nochi, volvió a hacer sus bailes y todo pa que juera ella, pero ella no jue (Rael).[76]

The Leonese-Zamoran texts of *Conde Vélez* are, in the final analysis, analogous to the Moroccan ballad: In both geographic subtypes, the narrative concentrates on the treacherous wagerer's attempt to attract the girl's attention. After initial stages similar to the ballad's other modalities (2. boast; 3. wager: heart for heart), Don Félix sets up a tent before the girl's door and hangs up a strand of golden cord (cordón de oro) which he offers "for sale," in exchange for "un beso de su cara / y un ramito de su amor." Here, in contrast to the Moroccan texts and their folktale parallels, the lady does not remain secluded in her house, but puts in an appearance, dressed in finery, with the sole purpose of rejecting Félix's offer: "Tengo yo un novio en Mombuey; / me lo ha de comprar mejor" (Ribadelago, Zamora). Just as in the differing treatments of the Eastern and Moroccan traditions, the Peninsular form, in which the wagerer offers valuable objects for sale in an attempt to attract the lady's attention, is also paralleled in the folktale narrative. Compare the following Madeiran text (from Paúl do Mar, collected in California), in which riches are offered to tempt the girl, though she chooses not to appear:

E esse gajo p'a convencer a rapariga foi. Pôs muitas, muitos lugares de ouro, muitas coisas p'a ver s'a rapariga vinha comprar. Muitas coisas que valiam uns dias a fazer aquelas grandezas todas, mas a rapariga nunca saía.[77]

---

76. The first text is from J. M. Espinosa, *New Mexico*, no. 70; the second, from Rael, I, no. 132. Note also the vestigial survival of the talking bird motif in Espinosa's text: "porque se entretenía con un pájaro que hablaba."

77. Costa Fontes, *Folktales*, no. 30, p. 259.

As we have just seen, the three different modalities of *Conde Vélez*—Eastern, Moroccan, and Peninsular—each embody a different interpretation of how the chastity wager story is to be developed and each of these diverse interpretations can also be found somewhere in the narrative's folktale versions. The Eastern ballad (with its bribed servants, false tokens, disguise in men's clothing, talking bird, and stolen slipper) is obviously closest to the folktale, while the Moroccan and Peninsular forms both choose to develop—each also following a different modality of the folktale—the scene of the wagerer's unsuccessful attempts to attract the princess. The ballad of *Conde Vélez* points up, of course, the permeability of seemingly neat and well defined generic categories in oral literature. Proverbs become songs and songs, proverbs; tales embody riddles and riddles generate tales; and ballads and tales sometimes share the same story.[78]

Though our exploration of the various forms of *Conde Vélez* has revealed much concerning the ballad's multi-secular traditional life, in elucidating its complex relationship to the folktale narrative on the same subject, it is difficult, if not impossible to establish any system of priorities as to when the ballad's multiple interactions with the folktale took place. The truncated Golden Age versions of the ballad include only two of the folktale's early stages (2. All women can be seduced; 3. wager: lover's heart against would-be seducer's condemnation as traitor) and there is no way of knowing how the song may have continued. It is tempting to theorize that the Eastern ballad, with its multiple folktale correspondences, may embody an "original" form of *Vélez*, while the Moroccan and Peninsular texts might reflect a later "deviation." But the very fact that the Moroccan and Leonese-Zamoran forms—current in widely separated areas—are in essential agreement points to the considerable antiquity of the narrative pattern they embody. It is perfectly possible, then, to envision a *Conde Vélez* first conceived as a balladic treatment of the wagerer's attempts at seduction, as in Morocco and León-Zamora, which, in the Eastern tradition, could then—at any subsequent moment or moments in the ballad's traditional life—have been (gradually?) reassimilated to the song's folktale congener. There is, as of now, no way of specifying the ballad's origins and, with no additional textual evidence at hand, it serves no purpose to engage in theorizing. What is quite apparent, however, is that the Moroccan tradition—in comparison to the Peninsular texts—has undertaken a very substantial and poetically effective elaboration of Count Vélez's ostentatious stratagems. The Leonese-Zamoran

---

78. For some examples of cross-generic contacts in folk literature, see the Appendix.

versions mention only Félix's tent and the golden cord (while its Madeiran tale analogue speaks vaguely of golden objects and "grandezas"). In the Colorado and New Mexican stories, there are acrobatic tricks or a tent, bull fights, and dances, all of which leave the virtuous wife unmoved. In contrast to such relatively simple displays, if we take into account all known Moroccan readings, we find Vélez decorating the streets with silk and brocade, setting up luxurious tents, deploying musicians, paving the streets with jewels, fighting with Moors, jousting with two hundred opponents, running bulls, and parading his brilliantly dressed Black servants—and all to no avail. At this point in the narrative, some Moroccan singer developed a poetically effective strategy for ending the narrative. In the East and in León-Zamora, Bélo/Félix, without more ado, will be taken away to have his heart cut out. But the Moroccan texts attest to his being given one last chance: His screams, as he is being dragged away (vv. 37, 40), finally attract the aloof princess' attention. Full of renewed hope, Vélez asks—breathlessly:

—¿Qué tal vos paresco, niña?   ¿Qué tal vos paresco yo?

But the virtuous and resolute *infanta* then calmly answers:

—Bueno me pareses, Veles;   conde Albar mucho mejor.

Count Vélez's defeat and punishment are thus very effectively highlighted by suggesting the possibility of a last-minute reprieve, which is then definitively snatched away from him and, in a verse identical to the earlier v. 37, he is dragged away to face his terrible, but, as the ballad implies (and in one case redundantly specifies [v. 44]), richly deserved fate:

Ya yevan al conde Veles   a sacarle el corasón.

It is this ending that has been adapted to serve as a dénouement for the Moroccan versions of *Conde Claros y el emperador* + *Conde Claros insomne*. The contamination was obviously suggested by various similarities between the *Claros insomne* and *Vélez* narratives. In both ballads, there is a gallant (or womanizing) protagonist, who rides by a lady's door to put on a display of "conspicuous consumption": Claros, in his rich attire and with bells on his horse's harness, and Vélez, in the variegated displays we have just enumerated. There is, however, a basic difference between the two narratives. In *Conde Vélez*, the story clearly favors the authentically enamored Don Bueso and the incorruptible *infanta*, while Vélez is seen as a cynical scoundrel, who ultimately receives his just punishment. But Count Claros is seen quite differently: Outrageous as his ostentatious attire may seem to some modern readers, one senses a generally favorable attitude towards him, as a paragon of gallantry, the quintessential enamored hero. A number of Moroccan versions of *Claros insomne* conserve some echo of the original unfavorable ending taken from *Vélez:* Claraniña prefers Alvar and marries him; Claros rides off or drops dead from sorrow; Claraniña jumps from the window. Yet, in others (CMP B9.15, 17; Larrea 30–31; our 10*B*), the tradition's basically favorable attitude toward the hero prevails and leads to a felicitous reelaboration: Drawing perhaps upon *El conde Sol*, Claros is made to swoon on hearing that Claraniña prefers Alvar, after which she offers assurances that she really does prefer Claros and all ends happily, as in so many other ballads in the Moroccan tradition.[79] The Moroccan ballad of *Conde Claros y el emperador* + *Conde Claros insomne* + *La jactancia del conde Vélez* offers a paradigmatic example of the complexities inherent in oral literature, as well as of the positive functions of contamination as an essential component in the dynamic creativity of ballad poetry.[80] *La jactancia del conde Vélez*, in particular, points also to the even greater complexities of multiple cross-generic contacts between narratives in verse and in prose in the oral tradition.

Musicological Commentary

For early evidence of the music of *Conde Claros insomne*, see the musical commentary to Chapter 11.

Five tunes for *La jactancia de conde Vélez* were collected in Morocco during the second decade of the 20th century. One was notated by Antonio Bustelo and the other four by Manuel Manrique de Lara. These transcriptions represent three

---

79. Compare also Zaida's initial rejection of Zaide, in Moroccan modalities of Lope's *Mira Zaide que te aviso*, followed immediately by a reconciliation and a happy ending: "Serró la dama el balcón / y al Sidi dejó en la caye. // Ya yoraba el moro Saidi, / que se quería matare. / —No yores tú, el moro Saidi, / ni te querías matare. // Tuya soy, tuya seré, / tuya soy, mi vida, Saidi" (*Epic Ballads*, p. 164, no. 4*B*). For a detailed study, see FLSJ, VIII, Chap. 32.

80. See Silverman, "La contaminación como arte"; also my "Reconstruction."

types or tune families, the first of which, comprising three melodies, can be seen in Example 1:

Example 1: Alignment of variant tunes comprising Type I

    a) Manrique de Lara B22.16*a* (from Alcazarquivir)
    b) Manrique de Lara B22.16*b* (from Alcazarquivir)[81]
    c) Bustelo (from Tetuán)[82]

---

81. The notation was published in RoH, I, p. 399.

82. This tune appeared in Manuel Ortega, *Los hebreos en Marruecos*, 1st ed. (Madrid: Editorial Hispano Africano, 1919), p. 239; 3rd ed. (Madrid: Compañía Ibero-Americana, 1929), p. 213. See also Israel J. Katz, "The Enigma of the Antonio Bustelo Judeo-Spanish Ballad Tunes in Manuel L. Ortega's *Los hebreos en Marruecos* (1919)," *Musica Judaica*, 4 (1981–1982), 32–67: p. 42.

que nohay da- ma____ ni__ don - ce -
lla___

que nohay da - ma____ ni don - ce - lla___

que nohay da - ma ni don - ce - lla

que le nie-gue____ nue-voa- mo - re___.

que le nie-gue____ nue-voa - mo re___.

que re- ñe - gue el nue - vo a - mor.

At first glance, judging from their contours, ambitus, and initial and final tones, one might conclude that all three tunes are in the same mode. Yet, upon closer scrutiny, it is clear that Examples 1*a* and *b* are in the Phrygian mode, while 1*c* is in the plagal Minor (*finalis* a). Moreover, their concurrence in the third and final melody phrases should not be surprising, since the plagal Minor tetrachord (a-g-f-e) is Phrygian. In both phrases, the cadence is preceded by (g-sharp) (the raised 3rd [Major] in the Phrygian mode; and raised 7th in the Minor).

Bustelo's example (1*c*), however, hints at a *hidjaz* cadence in the final phrase, which is somewhat rare among the Moroccan Sephardic tunes. I have discussed elsewhere the reliability and skeletal nature of Bustelo's notations, yet, if we considera the second halves of the tunes, there can be no question as to their close relationship.[83] Bustelo's notation clearly indicates the Minor mode. All three tunes adhere to the designated quatrain strophe: $ABC^{x+y}C^{x'+z}$.

The second and third types are each represented by a single tune. The second type (Ex. 2), from Tangier, is in the plagal Minor mode (*finalis* a) and bears a quatrain structure, ABCD. Notice the *overt* and *clos* cadential relationship between melody phrases B and B'.

Example 2: Manrique de Lara B22.8 (from Tangier)

The third type, from Tetuán (Ex. 3), is distinctly different from Bustelo's tune. It is in the plagal Major mode (*finalis* g) and, while its latter three phrases begin with the same three melodic progressions (d-d-b), its formal structure may be depicted as ABCC'. Like the Bustelo tune, it too displays triadic characteristics, particularly in its initial and second melody phrases.

---

83. Katz, "The Enigma," pp. 33–67.

Example 3: Manrique de Lara B22.13 (from Tetuán)

To sum up: The ballad tunes from Alcazarquivir (Exs. 1*a* and 1*b*) were also known in Tetuán (Ex. 1*c*); however, in the case of Example 1*c*, Bustelo did not perceive its rendering in compound duple meter as did Manrique in the other examples (tunes 1*a* and 1*b*). A second melody from Tetuán (Ex. 3) is profusely ornamented, which contrasts markedly with the entirely syllabic Tangier rendition (Ex. 2). Closely related to the plagal Minor of the Tetuán (1*c*) and Tangier examples is the Phrygian modality of the Alcazarquivir tunes (1*a* and 1*b*). Only the example from Tangier exceeds an octave (spanning a Major 9th). In our examples, only two quatrain structures can be distinguished: ABCC' (Exs. 1*a*–*c* and 3) and ABB'C (Ex. 2).

BIBLIOGRAPHY

Conde Claros y el emperador + *Conde Claros insomne*

EASTERN JUDEO-SPANISH

Sofía: CMP B9.1.
Salonika: Attias 31; CMP B9.2–9, 23; Crews 12.15–19; Hemsi, "Evocation," p. 1057*a* (= *Yoná*: BRI); LSO, p. 77, vv. 13–21; Mano, p. 18 (= *Yoná*: GRI); Onís B9*a*; PTJ 22 (= Attias); UR 2 (pp. 365–366; = CBU, pp. 331–332; = *Yoná*: GRI); *Yoná* 4*A*–4*B*.
Larissa: CMP B9.10.
Jerusalem: CMP B9.11.

MOROCCAN JUDEO-SPANISH

Tangier: CMP B9.12–16; Gil 31 (= MP); MP 23 (= CMP B9.12); Nahón 5; Pulido, p. 54 (= MP).
Tangier-Tetuán: Librowicz (2) (= Librowicz, *RH:Fronteras*, pp. 94–95; Katz, "Survey," pp. 453–454).
Tetuán: CMP B9.17–21; Larrea 27–31; Librowicz (2) B9.
Tetuán-Xauen: Castro MS, fols. 19, 126.
Larache-Tetuán: Amsélem MS, B9.
Alcazarquivir: MRuiz 35; PTJ 22*a* (= MRuiz).
Morocco (unlocated): CMP B9.22.

PENINSULAR TEXTS

Conde Claros y el emperador

Aragon: CGR, I*A*, 44; see above at n. 19.

Conde Claros insomne

Castilian areas: Aliste, p. 63; Catarella, *Gitano-andaluz*, no. 11.1–8; CGR, I*A*, 45–46; Díaz-Delfín-Díaz Viana, *Catálogo* (1978), I, 166; Díaz-Díaz Viana,

Castilla y León (1982), no. 17.1–7 (= *Catálogo*); Díaz Viana, "Evolución," p. 65; *Revista de Folklore*, 1:2 ([1980]), 28; Kundert, pp. 87–88 (G4, vv. 7–8); RGL 19.1–2, 4, 6–8, 16–18, 23; RPC, p. 12; RPM 58; *Voces nuevas*, I, nos. 48.6, 7, 10; our text *C*.

Asturias: Busto Cortina, nos. 36.6–8 (= Cano); Cano, nos. I*A*.1–3, I*B*.1–2, I*C*.1–2; NCR 13.1–2; 14.9.

Galician: CARG 17*a*.1–2; CPG, III, no. 44*c*.1–2.

SPANISH AMERICAN

Argentina: Moya, II, 23 (vv. 1–8).

PORTUGUESE

Portugal: Alves, p. 566; Braga, I, 306–307, 324, 325, 330; Costa Fontes, *Trás-os-Montes*, no. 43; Garrett, II, 225–226; Martins, II, p. 10 (no. 11.1–3); Pinto-Correia, pp. 176–177 (= VRP 50–51); Purcell, *Ilhas*, nos. 7.1.1–10, 7.4.1–12; Purcell, *Açores*, I, no. 7, vv. 1–12; VRP 50–51.

Azores: Cortes-Rodrigues, no. 1 (= Braga); Braga, I, 405.

Madeira: Braga, I, 334 (= Rodrigues de Azevedo, p. 94); Rodrigues de Azevedo, pp. 81–82, 89, 94.

For extensive additional Portuguese bibliography, see Pinto-Correia, *Carolíngios*, II, 137–233, BRP, nos. 402–598; RPI, no. B3.

CATALAN

Ibiza: AFC 2973 (= Aguiló); Aguiló, pp. 307–308; Macabich, pp. 13–14, 21 (pp. 13–14 = Aguiló). See Massot i Muntaner, "Aportació," p. 83.

For extensive references to all branches of the modern tradition, see RPI B3.

ARCHAIC TEXTS

Conde Claros y el emperador + *Conde Claros insomne*

— "A Missa va el emperador / a san juan dela montiña (= *Primav.* 192). Three *pliegos sueltos* are known:

a.   *Pliegos BL*, III, 977–982 (no. 54*a*); DPS 704.
b.   *Pliegos BN*, II, 293–297; DPS 729; Moll, "Tres Volúmenes," p. 301 (no. 13).
c.   *Pliegos de Praga*, I, 41–45; DPS 730.

Conde Claros y el emperador

—   "A caça va el emperador / a sant Iuan de Montiña" (= *Primav.* 191); C1550, pp. 319–321. For later printings, see MCR, II, 289*a*.

Conde Claros insomne

—   "Media noche era por filo / los gallos querian (quieren) cantar" (= *Primav.* 190). There are two *pliegos sueltos* and numerous *cancionero* printings:

a.   *Pliegos de Praga*, I, 33–39; DPS 1017.
b.   *Pliegos BN*, II, 144–151; DPS 1018.
c.   CSA, fols. 83 ro.–90 ro.
d.   C1550, pp. 168–173.
e.   *Silva* (1550), pp. 390–396.
f.   *Silva* (1561), fols. 80 vo.–87 vo.
g.   Tortajada (1652), pp. 198–209.

For additional printings, see MCR, II, 584*a*; IV, 166*b*. A text included in the *Libro en el qual se contienen cincuenta romances* doubtless represented *Media noche*: "Otro del conde Claros. Otros tanbien de amores" (*Pliegos de Morbecq*, p. 166; DPS 936). For numerous citations in *ensaladas* and musical treatments, see n. 18 above.
—   "Conde Claros con amores / non podiera reposare": Parody of *Medianoche* in Luis Vélez de Guevara, *Los hijos de la Barbuda* (1608–1609), ed. Profeti, pp. 106–107 (vv. 396–415). See n. 17 above.
—   "media noche era por filo / los gallos quieren (querian) cantar": in Agustín Moreto, *Baile de Conde Claros* (circa 1650–1660?), ed. Balbín Lucas, p. 97 (on the basis of two MS with minor variants).
—   "Dormiendo esta el conde claros / la siesta por descansar" (ASW, p. 73): *Pliegos BN*, III, 277–280; DPS, no. 423; Norton, *Descriptive Catalogue*, no. 854; Gallardo, *Ensayo*, III, no. 3338. For an *ensalada* citation, see n. 18 above.
—   "A[l] rededor del collado": Judeo-Spanish tune marker recorded in *piyûtîm* collections dating from 1584 and 1587: Avenary, "Cantos españoles," no. 21; Armistead and Silverman, "El antiguo romancero," no. 6. The relationship is possible, but rather dubious. The *incipit* could perhaps correspond to: "con trezientas piedras preciosas / al derredor del collar" or "con trezientos cascaueles / alrededor del petral" (*Media noche era por filo*: CSA = *Primav.* 190) and in some Moroccan readings: "con doscientos cascabeles / alrededor del collar" (Larrea 30; our synthetic text, v. 56). See also the Appendix, Chap. 10, n. 18.

¿Por qué no cantáis fortuna?

MOROCCAN JUDEO-SPANISH

Tangier: CMP B9.13; Nahón 5.
Tetuán: CMP B9.18, 20–21; Larrea 30; Librowicz (II) B9.
Alcazarquivir: CMP K11.1; MRuiz 35.3–4.

ARCHAIC TEXTS

— "maldita seas, ventura, / que ansi me hazes andar": *Cancionero del British Museum*, ed. Rennert, p. 34*a*, nos. 60–61.
— "Maldita seas vētura / q̄ assi me hazes andar":

    a.   *Cancionero general* (1511), ed. Rodríguez-Moñino, fol. cxxxiij vo.*a*.
    b.   *Pliegos de Praga*, I, 54*b*; DPS 654.
    c.   CSA, fol. 248 vo.
    d.   C1550, p. 298.
    e.   *Silva* (1550), p. 229.

For other printings, see MCR, I, 578.

La jactancia del conde Vélez

EASTERN JUDEO-SPANISH

Salonika: Attias 34; CMP B22.1–3; Coello 10; Crews 33; Gil 33 (= Coello); Hemsi II 7.
Larissa: CMP B22.4.
Jerusalem: CMP B22.5.

MOROCCAN JUDEO-SPANISH

Tangier: CMP B22.6–8.
Tetuán: AJE, II, no. 21*b* (= Alvar, *Textos*); Alvar, *Textos*, II, 760 (vv. 1–23) (= traditionalized rendition of Ortega); CMP B22.9–13; Boaknín MS, pp. 5–7; Idelsohn, *Gesänge der Marokkanischen Juden*, V, 16 (= Ortega); Ortega, p. 213; PTJ 120*a* (= Ortega).
Ceuta: Hassán B22*A–C*.
Larache-Tetuán: Amsélem MS B22 (= Ortega).
Larache: AJE, II, no. 21*b*; CMP B22.14–15.

Alcazarquivir: CMP B22.16–17; Martínez Torner, *Temas*, p. 54 (= CMP B22.16).
Morocco (unlocated): CMP B22.18.

PENINSULAR

León: RGL 33.1–4.
Zamora: One unedited version at the Menéndez Pidal Archive. See the synthetic text representing these two regional traditions included in the present chapter.

ARCHAIC TEXTS

— "Alabose el conde Velez / en las cortes se alabo": Bibl. Nac. (Madrid) MS 1317 (olim F-18), fol. 454*a* (16th cent.). See *Inventario*, IV, p. 168. Bonilla y San Martín (*ALE*, p. 29), who edits the MS (p. 32), dates it from the middle of the 16th century ("a mediados de dicho siglo"), but to judge by a comparison with dated contemporary documents (Arribas Arranz, no. 111 [1516]; Millares Carlo, no. CVII [1519]), the hand would seem to belong to the early 1500s.
— "Alabose el conde velez / en las cortes de Leon": *Silva* (1550), p. 443.

EUROPEAN ANALOGUES

For Scottish, German, Scandinavian, Greek, and Slavic ballad congeners, as well as medieval narratives and modern folktales embodying the same motif, see the body of the present chapter.

El nacimiento de Bernardo del Carpio (á-a) +
Conde Claros y la infanta (á) + Conde Claros fraile (á)
(The Birth of Bernardo del Carpio +
Count Claros and the Princess + Count Claros
Disguised as a Friar)
(1/A1 + 24/B10 + B12)

11A

Version from Tetuán (Morocco), sung by Luna Farache, 78 years, collected by S. G. A. and I. J. K., in Tetuán, August 13, 1962.

Ya se sa - le la prin - se - sa de sus pa - la - θios re - al_____.

¡Oy, más___ re - [e] - al!

Po-ren-cuen-tro se___ la pu - [u]-ẓo y al con-de de___ Mon-teal-bá_____.

¡Oy, mâ___ A - [a]l - bá!

¡Qué bo - ni - to va - iđ, el co - [o]n-de, pa - ra con mó - ro i - brar___!

¡Oy, má ___ lu - [u] - char!

Ya se sale la prinsesa   de sus palaθios real.
      ¡Oy, más real!

2   Por encuentro se la puẓo   y al conde de Montealbá.
      ¡Oy, mạ Albá!

    —¡Qué bonito vaiđ, el conde,   para con morọ librar!
      ¡Oy, mạ luchar!

4   —¡Más bonita sos, prinseẓa,   para conmigo folgar!
      ¡Oy, más folgar!

    —¡Qué chiquito soiđ, el conde,   para'se ofisio tomar!
      ¡Oy, más tomar!

6   —Si chiquito soy de cuerpo,   máđ y mạ lo soy de edad.
      ¡Lo soy de edad!

    La guerra de los sien moros   yo la supí aguerrear
      ¡Oy, guerrear!

8   y a los sincuenta matara   y sincuenta heridọ están.—
      ¡Oy, heridọ están!

    Tocóse mano con mano,   subióle a su rosal;
      ¡Y a su roẓal!

10   hísole cama de rosa,   cabesera de aẓahar;
      ¡Oy, aẓahar!

    cobertón con que se atapan   de hojas de un limonar.
      ¡Oy, de un limonar!

12   Hasia'yá la media noche,   prinseẓa los gritos da:
      ¡Los gritos da!

    —¡Sortéisme la mano, el conde,   que me vais a reventar!
      ¡A reventar!

14   —¡Que revientes, que te quedes   a mí poco se me da!
      ¡Oy, se me da!

Juramento tengo hecho   y en mi librito anisar:
  ¡Oy, anisar!
16 Mujer que a mi mano cae,   no la dejo arrevolar.
  ¡Oy, revolar!
Bien sabrás tú, la prinseᶎa,   que soy caᶎador legal.
  ¡Que sa legal!
18 Tú serás mi cosinera;   tú me pastorearáᶑ el ganado.—
  ¡Oy, mą́ ganá!
Como's'oyó la prinsesa,   muerta cayó en un desmayo.
20 —No desmayes tú, prinseᶎa,   ni te quieraᶑ haᶎer mal.
  ¡Oy, mą́ del mal!
Mañana por la mañana,   yo te pideré al rey, tu padre.

---

17   *refrain*: sa (*sic*).

11*B*

Version from Tetuán (Morocco), sung and recited by Luna Farache, 79 years, collected by S. G. A., in Tetuán, May 31, 1963.

[Ya se sa - le la] prin - se - ᶎa   de sus pa- la- θios le - al_____.

¡Yoy, mą́ ____ le- [e] - al!

♩ = ca. 160

v. 2: Po - ren - cuen - tro se le pu - zo y al con - de de Mon- teal- bar:

-- ¡Qué bo - ni - to vas, el con - de, pa - ra con mo - ros li - brar!

-- ¡Qué bo - ni - ta vas, prin- ce - za, pa - ra con - mi - go fol - gar!

-- ¡Qué chi - qui - to soḏ, el con - de, pa - rae - seo - fi - sio - to - mar!

-- Si chi - qui - to soy de cuer - po, más y má lo soy dee - dad.

La gue-rra de los cien mo - ros yo la pu - día gue -rre - ar; *etc.*

Ya se sale la prinseʓa   de sus palaθios leal.
    ¡Y oy má̧ leal!

2   Por encuentro se le puʓo   y al conde de Montealbar:
    —¡Qué bonito vas, el conde,   para con moros librar!

4   —¡Qué bonita vas, prinseʓa,   para conmigo folgar!
    —¡Qué chiquito sođ, el conde,   para ese ofisio tomar!

6   —Si chiquito soy de cuerpo,   más y má̧ lo soy de edad.
    La guerra de los sien moros   yo la pudía guerrear;

8   a los sincuenta matara   y sincuenta heridǫ'stán.—
    Tocóse mano con mano   y le subiera a su roʓal;

10   hí́ʓole cama de roʓa   y cabesera de aʓahar;
    cobertón con que se atapa,   con hojas d'un limonar.

12   Hasia'yá la media noche,   prinseʓa los gritos da:
    —¡Soltéisme la mano, el conde,   que me vaiđ a reventar!

14   —¡Que revientes, que te quedę,   a mí poco se me da!
    Juramento tengo hecho   y en mi librito anisar:

16   Coʓa qu'a mi mano cuae,   no la dejo revolar.
    Bien sabes tú, la prinseʓa,   que soy caʓado legal.—

18   Ya yoraba la prinseʓa,   que se quiere arreventar.
    —No yores tú, la prinseʓa,   ni quierą que te hagas mal.

20   Mañana por la mañana,   yo a tu padre te demandaré.—
    Y otro día en la mañana,   las ricas bodas se armaron.

V. 1 and its refrain were sung; the rest was recited. Vv. 2–3*a* and 4–6 were recited twice. Variants from the second recitation:

2*a*   se la puʓo.
3*a*   vađ.
4*a*   Más bonita sois, prinseʓa.
5*a*   eres.

11C

Version from Tetuán (Morocco), recited by Luna Farache, 78 years, collected by S. G. A. and I. J. K., in Tetuán, August 13, 1962.

♩ = 160

v. 2: Po - ren - cuen-tro se la pu - zo al con - de de Mon - tal - bar.

-- ¡Qué bo - ni - to vad̄, el con-de pa-ra con mo-ros gue - rre - ar!

-- ¡Más bo - ni - ta sos, prin - se - za, pa - ra con-mi - go fol - gar!

-- ¡Qué chi - qui -to sos, el con - de, pa-rae- seo - fi - sio to - mar!

-- Si chi - qui - to soy de cuer-po, má- d̄y má - d̄e soy dee - dad.

La gue - rra de los sien mo-ros yo la pu - día gue - rre - ar;

a los sin-cuen - ta ma - ta-ra;a los sin - cuen-tahe - ri - does - tá.--

[Ya se sale la prinsesa   de sus baños de bañar.]
2   Por encuentro se la puzo   al conde de Montalbar.
    —¡Qué bonito vađ, el conde,   para con moros guerrear!
4   —¡Más bonita sos, prinseza,   para conmigo folgar!
    —¡Qué chiquito sos, el conde,   para ese ofisio tomar!
6   —Si chiquito soy de cuerpo,   mád y máđe soy de edad.
    La guerra de los sien moros   yo la pudía guerrear;
8   a los sincuenta matara;   a los sincuenta heridǫ están.—
    Tocósen mano con mano   y le subiera a su vergel.
10 Hízole cama de rosa,   cabesera de azahar;
    cobertón con que se atapa,   de hojạ de un limonar.

––––––––––

1   *not picked up on recording; supplied by S. G. A.*

11D

Version from Tetuán (Morocco), recited by Luna Farache, 78 years, collected by S. G. A. and I. J. K., in Tetuán, August 7, 1962.

    Hermana tiene el buen reye   que Šimena se yamaba:
2   Un día vio a Rondales,   cabalgado'n su cabayo;
    la siya yeva dorada   y el cabayo yeva blanco.
4   —De tuđ amores, el Sidi,   estoy prendida.—
    Tocóse mano con mano,   subiera a su vergel.
6   Hízole cama de seda,   cabesera de azahar;
    cobertón con que se atapa,   de hojas de un limonar.
8   Hasia de medianoche,   hojas de un limonar.
    Por ahí pasara un pajesito,   qu'al rey se lo fue a contar.
10 —Si supierađ, pajesito,   [así Dios te guarde del mal]:
    Darte he yo sien marcos d'oro;   Jimena, los siento y más;
12 que no le digađ a mi padre   d'eso qu'has visto pasar.—
    El pajesito desfortunado   al buen rey fue a contar:
14 —Si supieras, mi señor rey,   en qué río estáđ a nadar:
    Imá Šimena, tu hija,   durmiendo con el Sidi 'stá.—
16 Ayá la mandan serrada   a unas carséles d'honda y d'escuredad;
    el agua a las rodiyạ,   que dišera la verdad.

18 Dentro de quinƶe días,   [ya la sacan a quemar].
    Pasara un pajeϴito,   que por ahí le vino a pasar.
20 —Pajeϴito, pajeϴito,   ¿qué alvisias me traerás?
    —El alvisia que te traigo,   [que te haré llorar]:
22 Que de hoy en quinƶe días,   ya te sacan a quemar.—
    Šimena, como tal oyera,   se sentara a yorar:
24 —Si encontrara yo un paje,   que s'adueliera de mi mal.
    Le yevarán estas cartas   y al conde de Montalbán:
26 Que de hoy en quinƶe días,   ya me sacan a quemar.
    No se me da por mi muerte,   ni por mi puerpo real;
28 se me da por la criatura,   que es de sangre real.—
    Ahi s'alḥadró un pajeϴito,   que a su meƶa comió pan:
30 —Yo te la yevaré, Šimena,   yo te la tengo que yevar.—
    Camino de quinƶe díá   en ocho le ha d'andar;
32 el día por los šarales   y la noche con el lunar.
    Fuese a los palasios,   donde el conde Niño está:
34 —Tome estas cartas,   [que la prinsesa vos da].—
    Conforme'l conde Niño la carta,   se puƶo al yorar.
36 Vistiérase de fraile;   a las cársel' fuera la a buscar:
    —Júrame tú, la Šimena,   y en este librito anisar,
38 que cara d'hombre no has visto;   sólo la del Montealbán.
    —Te juro a Dios del sielo   y a este librito anisal,
40 que cara d'hombre no ha visto;   sólo la del conde Albar.—
    Saliérase'l conde Albar   y fuera a los palasios de rey su padre real.
42 Pidiérase la mano.   . . . .
    Otro día en la mañana,   con Clarañina se casó.

4*b*   estoy pres . . . prendida.
8*b*   *sic.*
10*a*   Pajesit . . . el rey . . . si supieraď, el buen reye . . . no . . . Si supieraď, pajesito, que al rey se lo fuera a contar.
10*b*   *supplied from Larrea 33.38.*
18*b*   *See vv. 22b, 26b.*
20*b*   dime ¿qué alvisias me traerás?
21*b*   *supplied from Larrea 33.62.*
22*b*   *repeated.*
23*a*   Eya, la infanta, como . . . Šimena, como tal oyera.

25*b*   *repeated*: al monde de Contalbán (!).

26*a*   Que no se me da . . . Que de hoy en quinze días.

34*b*   *See our synthetic text, v. 52b.*

38*b*+   Yo te juro, mi señor padre.

43*b*+   Se casó con eya.

11E

Version from Tetuán (Morocco), recited by Luna Farache, 78 years, collected by S. G. A., J. H. S., and I. J. K., in Tetuán, August 21, 1962.

Hermana tiene el buen Sidi, que Šimena se yama:
2 'Namoróse del conde Niño, ese conde de Sandalia.
Van día y vienen días, Šimena quedó preñada;
4 preñada quedó d'un niño como la leche y la grana.
A él le mandó en prisiones y a eya la mandó enserrada;
6 el agua hasta las rodiyas, para que diga la verdad.
Van díađ y vienen días, el rey la mandó a prender.
8 Por ahí pasara un pajesito, qu'a su mesa comió pan.
—Pajesito, pajesito, ¿qué novedad me das?
10 —La novedad que te traigo, que no te la puedo dar;
que de hoy en quinze días, ya te sacan a quemar.—
12 Como es'oyó Šimena, se sentara a yorar:
—No se me da por mi muerte, ni por la mi muerte se me da;
14 se me da por la criatura, qu'era de sangre real.
Si se alḥadra aquí alguno, que se aduela de mi mal;
16 que me yeven estas cartas al conde de Montealbán.—
Y áhi se alḥadró'n pajesito, que a su mesa comió pan:
18 —Yo se la yevaré, señora; yo te la he de yevar.—
Camino de ocho díađ, en cuatro le ha de andar;
20 camino de cuatro díađ, en dọ le ha de andar;
el día con los šarales; la noche con el lunar.
22 No son dos horas pasadas, la carta en mano del conde Niño va
                   [parar.
Conde Niño la tomara; se sentara a yorar.
24 Quitárase ropa de conde; de fraile se le fuera a poner.
Fuérase para las carsélas, donde Šimena está:
26 —Si me juras tú, Šimena, en este libro anisar,
que cara d'hombre no has visto, sólo la del conde Albar.
28 —Yo le juro Dios del sielo y en este libro anisar,
que cara de hombre no he visto, sólo la de conde Albar.—
30 Ya se iba el conde Albar al palasio de su padre:
Demandando iba a Šimena, para caẓarse con eya.
32 Otro día en la mañana, las ricas bodas se armaran.

———————

2*a*+ . . . del conde Niño, me parese. . . .
21*b* *repeated.*
23*b*+ Fuérase pa sus palasios. . . .

11F

Version from Larache (Morocco), sung by Mesodi Castiel Oziel, 68 years, collected by S. G. A., J. H. S., and I. J. K., in Larache, August 25, 1962.

v. 3: Ya - hí se la pre - zen - ta - ra___

ye - [e]l mo - so del Mos-tral - var.

-- ¡Qué bo - ni - to vais___, el___ con - de___,

pa - ra's - teo - fi - sio___ to - mar!

-- ¡Qué bo - ni - to vais, el___ con - de___,

pa - [a] - ra's - teo - fi - sioa - to - mar!

-- Si soy bo - ni - to___ de___ ca - ra;

más bo - ni - to soy___ d'e - dad.

Ya se sale la prinseza   de sus baños de bañar
2   y el lustre de la su cuara,   como roza en el rozal.
Y ahí se la prezentara   y el moso del Mostralvar.
4   —¡Qué bonito vais, el conde,   para'ste ofisio a tomar!
—Si soy bonito de cara;   más bonito soy d'edad.
6   La guerra de los sien moros   ya toda soy de ganar
y a sincuenta yo matara   y a sincuenta heridos van.—
8   Tomóla'l rey de la su mano;   yevóla y a su rozal.
Hízola cama de roza;   cabesera de azahar;
10 cubierto con que se tape,   con hojuas de un limonar.
Ansina la media noche,   prinseza de gritos da:
12 —¡Sortísme la mano, 'l conde,   que me vais a arreventar!
—¡T'arrevientes, que te quedes,   y a mí poco se me da!
14 Palomo en mi mano cae,   de mi mano no's d'escapar.—
Ya se ponía la niña   de sus ojos a yorar.
16 Por ahí pas'un pajezito,   qu'a su cuaza iba a almorzar.
—Pajezito, mi buen paje,   ¿qué notisias me trairás?
18 Le dirás al rey mi padre,   que sola'stó'n este rozal.—
Ya se iba'l pajezito;   con repuesta vien' y va.
20 Camino de ocho días,   hízole de cuatro días.
Ya se iba el pajezito;   con recuesta vien' y va:
22 —Ya se lo dijí, prinseza,   ya se lo dizía yo:
Si fue coza la que volviera   y al fuego ech'a quemar.—
24 Ya se ponía la niña   de sus ojos a yorar.

Vv. 4–8, 11–17, 19–21 were repeated in singing.

Variants:

5a   Mi *instead of* Si *in the first rendition of the verse*; Si *in the repetition.*
7b   y a *omitted in repetition.*
8a   de su mano *in repetition.*
19b+   la hija del rey.

11G

Version from Larache (Morocco), sung by Sultana viuda de José Melul, 55 years (±), collected by S. G. A., J. H. S., and I. J. K., in Larache, September 1, 1962.

Ya____ se sa - le la prin- se - sa____

de_____ su____ ba - ño de ba - ñar;

co - lo - res____ de la____ su ca - ra,

co - mo_____ ro - saen el____ ro - sal.

A - hí____ se la pre - sen - ta - ra

el con - de de Mon - tal - bán:

--¡Que bo - ni - ta va - [a]is, la ni - ña,

pa - ra____ con- mi - go a fol - gar!

>   Ya se sale la prinsesa   de su baño de bañar;
> 2   colores de la su cara,   como rosa en el rosal.
>   Ahí se la presentara   el conde de Montalbán:
> 4   —¡Qué bonita vais, la niña,   para conmigo a folgar!
>   —Si bonita sois de cara,   más y máis lo soiš'n edad.
> 6   —La guerra de los sien moros   yo la solía guerrar:
>   A los sien ha muerto ya;   los cuarenta heridos están.—
> 8   Cogióla de mano'n mano;   yevóla a su roẓal.
>   La hiso la cama de pluma,   cabesera de un limonar;
> 10 cubierto con que la cubre,   con hojas d'un toronjil.
>   A eso de la media noche,   prinsesa de gritos da.
> 12 —Te revientes o te quedes,   a mí poco se me da.
>   Paloma qu'en mi mano cae,   de mi mano no se va.

11*H*

Version from Larache (Morocco), collected by Samuel Fereres, before August 25, 1962, when a copy of the collection was acquired by S. G. A., J. H. S., and I. J. K.

>   Ya se sale la princesa   de sus baños de bañar;
> 2   colores de su cara,   como rosas del rosal.
>   Allí se la presentara   el conde de Montalbán:
> 4   —¡Qué bonita vais, la niña,   para conmigo folgar!
>   La guerra de los cien moros   yo la solía guerrar;
> 6   a los cincuenta heridos;   y los treinta han muerto ya.—
>   La hizo la cama de plumo,   cabecera de un limonar
> 8   y cubierto con que se tapa   de hojas de un toronjil.
>   A eso de la medianoche,   princesa de gritos da.
> 10 —Te revientes o te quedes,   a mí poco se me da.
>   Paloma que en mi mano cae,   ya nunca más saldrá.

We conserve the original normative spelling.

5a   *original*: Las guerra.

5a, 6a–b *numerals used in original.*

7a   plumo (*sic*).

Summaries

El nacimiento de Bernardo del Carpio

M: The king's (or the Cid's) sister, Jimena, falls in love with Count Saldaña (Sandalia, Sandalla, Sandaya, Sandaria, Asaldaña(s), Asaldania, Asandalia, Andalla). They meet; she becomes pregnant. The king finds out and orders her and the count punished; he is imprisoned and Jimena is locked in a room, in a high, well guarded castle of glass (or on three hills); she gives birth to a beautiful child. Jimena laments her imprisonment and that of the count. The queen overhears her and asks what is wrong and if she is in need of money, clothing, or gifts (food, cities). She answers that she needs none of these things, but that her son is asking for his father. The queen swears that she will not eat on a tablecloth (or sit at a table) or sleep on a pillow until she has obtained freedom for the count. She goes to the king and urges him to free the count and marry him to Jimena. The king orders his knights to bring the count from prison, to the sound of musical instruments and showing him great honor. The wedding is celebrated next morning.

Conde Claros y la infanta

E: [The count addresses Blancaniña], praising her charms. He takes her to a rose arbor; the falling leaves serve as their bed; the [count] throws down his cape and Blancaniña her gown. A young page passes by; Blancaniña begs him not to reveal to her father, the king, that he has seen them there. The page refuses and goes to the king, who asks for a report concerning his vineyards. The page answers: "There were seven whores and your daughter was the greatest of all." The king orders her killed.

Conde Claros y la infanta + Conde Claros fraile

M: The princess, beautiful as a rose, is leaving the baths (or her palace). She meets Count Montalvar (Montalbán, Montealvar, etc.) and tells him that he has a fine figure for fighting against Moors. He answers that she is even better suited for making love; to which she answers that he is too young to undertake such an endeavor. He then replies that, though he may be young, he has already fought a battle against a hundred Moors, has killed fifty of them and has wounded the rest. He takes her by the hand and they go to a rose arbor; rose petals serve as their bed, orange blossoms as their pillow, and lemon leaves as their blanket. At midnight, the princess cries out: "Let me go! You are killing me!" The count answers: "It makes no difference to me! You know only too well that I am an excellent hunter and I never let my prey (or any dove that I catch) fly away." A young page happens to pass by; The princess (or the count?) begs him to keep their secret and offers him a hundred marks of gold, promising that Count Alvar (or the princess) will give him another hundred and more. The wretched page goes to the king and tells him he has seen the princess with Count Montalvar. The king orders the page killed. *Conde Claros fraile*: Women visit the princess and confirm the truth. The king orders both the lovers punished: The count manages to escape and the princess is imprisoned in a deep, dark dungeon, in water up to her knees, so she will confess (or up to her waist, so her flesh will rot). Dukes and jailers visit her, expressing their sorrow: Fifteen days from now she is to be burned at the stake. (She weeps.) At midnight, the princess cries out: "Would that someone would appear to take pity on me and carry these letters to Count Montalvar, telling him to come immediately: Fifteen days from now I am to be burned. I don't care about my own death, even though I am young, or about my abandonment; I care about my child, who is of royal blood." A young page, who ate bread at her table, appears: "I will carry the letters for you. I will make a journey of fifteen days in eight; of eight days in four; of four days in two; traveling by day through thickets and at night by moonlight, until I come to the castle of Count Montalvar." The page takes the letter, rides off to Count Alvar's castle, and gives him the letter: "Take this letter from the princess: Fifteen days from now she is to be burned." The count reads the letter and weeps (or says he doesn't care whether she is burned or not). He puts on friar's garb and goes to the princess' prison: "Swear on this prayer book (missal) that you have seen no man's face but that of Count Alvar." She answers: "I swear to God in heaven and on this prayer book (missal) that I have seen no man's face but that of Count Alvar." He takes her out of prison and carries her off to his city. The wedding is celebrated the next morning.

Motifs

Nacimiento de Bernardo del Carpio:

Cf. T31.1. *Lover's meeting: hero in service of lady's father.*
T400. *Illicit sexual relations.*
Q243. *Incontinence punished.*
Q254. *Girl punished for becoming pregnant.*
Q433. *Punishment: imprisonment.*
R41. *Captivity in tower (castle, prison).*

R41.1. *Captivity in castle.*
F771.1. *Castle of unusual material.*
F771.1.6. *Crystal castle.*
F771.1.6.1. *Castle with glass wall.*
L111.5. *Bastard hero.*
Z235. *Hero born out of wedlock.*
M151.5. *Vow not to eat or sleep until certain event is brought to pass.*

Conde Claros y la infanta:

T31.1. *Lovers' meeting: hero in service of lady's father.*
T400. *Illicit sexual relations.*
K1271. *Amorous intrigue observed and exposed.*
K2250.1. *Treacherous servant.*
P365. *Faithless servant.*
Q261. *Treachery punished.*
Q411. *Death as punishment.*

Conde Claros fraile:

T400. *Illicit sexual relations.*
Q243. *Incontinence punished.*
Q254. *Girl punished for becoming pregnant.*
Q433. *Punishment: imprisonment.*
R41.3. *Captivity in dungeon.*
Cf. R41.3.2. *Prison with stream of water in it.*
Q414. *Punishment: burning alive.*
D2122. *Journey with magic speed.*
K1826. *Disguise as churchman (cleric).*
K1826.1.1. *Lover disguised as monk or friar meets sweetheart.*
R161. *Lover rescues his lady.*
R175. *Rescue at stake.*

Textual Commentary

The use of verses from *El nacimiento de Bernardo del Carpio* as a prologue to *Conde Claros y la infanta* + *Conde Claros fraile* (our 11D.1–4) and to *Conde Claros fraile* alone (our 11E.1–5) must count as an idiosyncratic innovation in

Luna Farache's personal repertoire. We will study the *Bernardo del Carpio*
ballad at the end of the present chapter.

As with other Conde Claros ballads, the traditional life of *Conde Claros y la
infanta* and *Conde Claros fraile* is enormously variegated and complex.[1]
Sometimes in association and sometimes not, both ballads have combined with
an astounding variety of narrative themes in the various Hispanic subtraditions.
The two Sephardic branches themselves attest to considerable diversity: *Conde
Claros y la infanta* is known in very different forms both in the East and in
North Africa, while *Conde Claros fraile* is limited to the latter tradition, usually
in association with *Infanta*, but, counter to the typical close agreement between
Moroccan versions, *Fraile* occurs, in the various Moroccan communities, in
three significantly divergent avatars.

In the East, *Conde Claros y la infanta* is extremely rare, if not now, in all
probability, extinct. In our own field work, we have never collected it. Aside
from several brief contaminations, only two relatively extensive texts are
known: Attias 30, the most satisfactory, and a truncated version printed in Yacob
Yoná's *Pizmônîm de bĕrîth mîlāh* (Salonika, 1895–1896). We reproduce both
texts below (using simplified transcription systems and modifying the
punctuation). To the right of pertinent verses, corresponding verse numbers in
the 16th-century form of *Infanta* (= *Primav.* 190) and in our Moroccan synthetic
text (*M*) are listed in parentheses:

	Dulce érais, la mi siñora,	y a tan dulce en el hablar,	
2	con dulzor de vuestra boca,	a la gente hacéis pecar.	(22)
	Dos besicos has pedrido,	cuatro vos entiendo dar,	
4	que los dos eran d'amores,	los otros dos d'amistad.	
	Besóla y abrazóla,	consigo se la llevará.	
6	¿Ande ḥue sus aposamiento?;	debajo d'un bel rosal;	(47; *M*10)
	De las hojicas que cayen,	una cama ordenará.	(*M*11)
8	Por ahí pasó un pajico,	cual hubiera de pasar:	(51; *M*18)
	—¡Estéis en bonhora, Blancaniña!	—Pajico, en buen vengáis.	
10	Así biva el pajico,	así buena ventura tengáis,	(55; *M*19)
	que le digáis la mintira	y que le enieguéis la verdad.	(56; *M*20)
12	—En mi tefter no'stá escrito,	ni en el mi libro estudiar.	
	¡Estéis en bonhora, Blancaniña!	—Pajico, en buen vayáis.	
14	Yo arogaré por tus días,	que buenos caminos tengáis.	

---

1. See Chap. 10 supra.

—¡Estéis en bonhora, el buen reyes!   —Pajico, en bien vengáis.   (63)
16 ¿En qué ían las mis viñas?   Las mis viñas ¿en qué van?
—Siete putas había, siete;   vuestra hija es la caporal.—
18 Esto que oyó el buen reyes,   presto la mandó a matar.   (71; *M*26)

(Attias 30)

¡Yelikos, yelilos!
—Dulses sox, la mi senyyora,   i a tan dulse en el avlar.
2   I a los savyyos metéx boka   i a los mudos azéx avlar.—   (22)
I yyorava la Blankaninyya   i lágrimas de veluntad.
4   —¿De ké yyoráx, Blankaninyya?   I mi alma, ¿de ké yyoráx?
—Lyyoro por vos, kavayero,   ke vos vax i me dexáx.
6   Me dexáx ninyya i muchacha   i chika de la poka edad.—
Esto sintyyó el kavayero,   dexó todo i tornó atrás.
8   Se tomaron mano kon mano   i ǧuntos van un barabar.
¿I ánde era sus paseos?;   i de debaxo de un bel rozal.   (47; *M*10)
10 Las ojikas ke kaían   i por kama se echará.
El vyejo echó su kapa;   Blankaninyya su ben biá.
12 I por aí pasó un pajeziko,   el kual non era de pasar.   (51; *M*18)
—I yya si biva el pajeziko,   así me tenga buen mazal.   (55; *M*19)
14 Si vas por ande el rey mi padre   i ke le digas la verdad: (56; *M*20)
I si buxkáx a Blankaninyya,   lyya se buxkó su buen mazal.

(*Pizmônîm*, no. 4)[2]

In Yoná's *Pizmônîm* text, *Conde Claros y la infanta* is associated with *La partida del esposo* (vv. 3–7) and this juxtaposition is reflected in several other Eastern versions of the latter ballad. A rendition by the great Larissa singer, Vida de Albilansí, begins and ends with verses from *Conde Claros y la infanta* (vv. 1–4*a*, 20–21, 23):

—Dulce sox, la mi señora,   atan dulce en el hablar.
2   Tres besicos vos hay dado,   cuatro yo vos quiero dar;
los dos eran de amores,   los otros dos de amistad.—
4   Besóla y abrazóla,   sola la dexa y se vá;
la dexa niña y muchacha,   chiquita de poca edad;
6   le dexa hijos chiquitos,   lloran y demandan pan.

---

2. *Seis romancerillos*, no. PB4, p. 21. Concerning Moisés Abravanel's transcription of the *Pizmônîm* text, see the Appendix.

      Lloraba la blanca niña,   lágrimas de veluntad.
8   Por en medio del camino,   haberchís que ya le van:
      —La niña está llorando   lágrimas de veluntad.—
10   Eso que oyó el caballero,   dexó todo y tornó atrás:
      —¿Qué llorabax, blanca niña?   Mi alma, ¿por qué lloráx?
12   —Lloro por vos, caballero,   que vos vax y me dexáx;
      me dexáx niña y muchacha,   chiquita de poca edad;
14   me dexáx hijos chiquitos,   lloran y demandan pan;
      me demandaban al padre,   no sé qué respuesta les dar.
16   —Digáxme, la blanca niña,   cuálos vos hiẕieron mal;
      si vos hiẕieron mal los vuestros,   yo los vo a castigar;
18   si vos hiẕieron mal los míos,   yo los mandaré a matar.
      —Ni los vuestros, ni los míos,   ningunos no me hiẕieron mal.—
20   Ya la toma por la mano,   ya se van a pasear.
      ¿Dónde fueran sus paseos?   Debaxo de un bel roṣal.
22   Allí metieron la meṣa,   se asentaron a almorzar;
      allí hiẕieron la cama,   se echarían a folgar.

                            (RT, III, no. III.3, p. 99)[3]

The contamination explains the idiosyncratic initial verses (1–3) of another version of *La partida* printed in Yoná's *Güerta de romansas antiguas de pasatyempo* ([Salonika?], before 1908?):

      Dulse érax, la mi madre,   i atan dulse en el avlar.
2   Dos bezikos ax pedrido   i tres i kuatro entyendo a dar.
      Los dos eran de amores   i los dos de veluntad.
4   Yyorava la Blankaninyya   lágrimas de veluntad.. . .[4]

---

3. The text was collected by M. Manrique de Lara, in Jerusalem, in 1911. See CMP 16.20. Vv. 4*b*–15 pertain to *La partida del esposo*; vv. 16–19 are a migratory formulaic complex, to our knowledge otherwise unattested in the Eastern tradition, but well documented in various Moroccan ballads: *Moriana y Galván, Buena hija, Culebro raptor* (*En torno*, p. 144 and n. 31). The verses correspond to *Primavera* 121.14–17, 20–22. Since Vida de Albilansí's repertoire also included a vestige of *Moriana y Galván* (as a contamination in a version of *Galiana*: CMP, III, 9, no. 3*b*.12–14), it is quite possible that these verses may also represent another and otherwise undocumented Eastern survival of *Moriana*. See CMP B1, B21.1; III, 8, 12 (nos. 3*A* and 6).

4. *Yoná*, pp. 304, 306, n. 1; RT, III, no. III.4 (p. 100). We have simplified the transcription. For a description of the booklet: *Yoná*, pp. 24–26.

The characteristic rose arbor verses from *Conde Claros y la infanta* likewise serve to close several Moroccan versions of *La partida* from Tetuán and Tangier:

> . . . Tocóse mano con mano,   subiéralo al buen rosal.
> 20 Hízole cama de rosa,   cabecera de azahar;
> cobertor con que se tapa   de hojas de un limonar.[5]

In North Africa, *Conde Claros y la infanta* is typically associated with *Conde Claros fraile*: After their amorous repartee, the lovers repair to the rose arbor, where they are discovered by the treacherous page, who betrays them to the king. The Moroccan narrative then continues with *Fraile*: The princess, imprisoned and to be burned at the stake, sends a faithful page to summon Claros, who appears, disguised as a friar and unrecognized, to test her fidelity and then rescue and marry the girl. This combined narrative is found in a majority of Tangier and Tetuán versions collected early in this century, as well as in Larrea's no. 33, copied from a MS presumably dating from the same period (texts *abcdijklmnp* below), and also in our 11*DE* (and vestigially in 11*F*). On the other hand, *Conde Claros y la infanta* is also sung alone (our 11*ABCGH*) and there is no way of knowing whether these uncontaminated texts may have broken away from *Fraile* or, on the other hand, perhaps derive from an originally autonomous form. Such "independent" variants have been recorded in Tangier, Tetuán, and Larache (*eghoqrswa'b'*). Text *e* (= CMP B10.5) was collected by Manrique de Lara, in Tangier, in 1915, but all other such versions are of relatively late provenience, suggesting, perhaps, a recent truncation, rather than the survival of an early autonomous form. Below, we offer a synoptic version of *Conde Claros y la infanta* (vv. 1–26) + *Conde Claros fraile* (vv. 27–62). Our text strives to include every verse present in the tradition (even if

---

5. RT, nos. III.62; essentially identical verses in nos. 63, 69. Since the Moroccan texts of *La partida del esposo* are of Eastern origin (*En torno*, p. 167), the use of the rose arbor verses in this particular context probably also originated in the East (as in Vida de Albilansí's version: RT, no. III.13). Note also the presence of similar, but probably unrelated, final verses in certain other Eastern texts of *La partida:* "Ya se besan, ya se abrazan, / ya se van a caminar, // debaxo de un rosal vedre, / solombra de toronyal" (RT, nos. III.39, 41). Note the same formulaic cluster in a wedding song collected by Alberto Hemsi: "Se toman mano con mano, / ya se van a pasear, / debaxo de un rosal vedre, / solombra de toronjal" (Hemsi, no. 30; Hemsi-II, no. 112). For more on the rose arbor motif, see the Appendix.

attested in only one version) which may be considered an "authentic" part of the combined ballads' Moroccan modality. Sporadic contaminations and other irreconcilable verses are listed together with the variants. Numbers of corresponding verses in *Media noche era por filo* (for vv. 1–26), *A caza va el emperador* (for vv. 27–62), and the Eastern texts of *Conde Claros y la infanta* (preceded by *E*) are listed in the right-hand margin:[6]

	Ya se sale la princesa de los sus baños bañar:	
2	El rostro sacó hermoso como rosa en el rosal.	
	Por encuentro se lo puso al conde de Montalvar:	(27)
4	—¡Qué bonito vais, el conde, para con moros lidiar!	(28)
	—¡Más bonita sois, princesa, para contigo folgar!	(30)
6	—¡Qué chiquito sois, el conde, para ese oficio tomar!	
	—Si chiquito soy de cuerpo, más y más lo soy de edad.	
8	La guerra de los cien moros yo la supe guerrear;	(32)
	a los cincuenta matara y cincuenta heridos van.—	
10	Tocósen mano con mano; subióle a su rosal;	(47; *E*6)
	púsole cama de rosa, cabecera de azahar;	(*E*7)
12	cobertor con que se tapan, de hojas de un limonar.	
	Hacia'llá a la medianoche, princesa los gritos da:	
14	—¡Soltéisme la mano, el conde, que me vais arreventar!	
	—¡Que arrevientes, que te quedes, a mí poco se me da!	
16	Bien lo sabes tú, princesa, que soy cazador real;	(44)
	caza que en mi mano cae no la dejo arrevolar.—	(45)
18	Por áhi pasó un pajecito, por ahí vino a pasar.	(51; *E*8)
	—Por tu vida, el pajecito, así Dios te guarde de mal:	(55; *E*10)
20	En casa del rey mi padre, no descubras poridad.	(56; *E*11)

---

6. We have profited from consulting the preliminary draft of a synthetic text prepared by Diego Catalán, which, with characteristic generosity, he placed at our disposal. After v. 7, MRuiz 36 (= *d'*) cannot be reconciled with the rest of the narrative and variants are not recorded, except in the case of vv. 32–33 which supply otherwise undocumented material. The entire text of *d'* is reproduced further on in the present chapter. After v. 53, text *a* (= CMP B10.1), copied by José Benoliel, continues with non–traditional material which has not been reproduced here. On Benoliel's unfortunate tendency to "improve" his texts, see CMP, I, 51. Variants corresponding to *Conde Claros fraile* in texts *vxyzc'* are not recorded here (for reasons that are explained below), but are reproduced separately. A substantial version of *Conde Claros y la infanta*, collected by Manuel Alvar in Larache (AJE, II, no. 17; = PTJ 23, with minor variants) reached us only in 2004, after the present text was already in final form.

Darte he cien marcos de oro;   conde Alvar los ciento y más.—   (57–60)
22 Pajecito sin fortuna   al rey se lo fue a contar: (61–62)
—Si supieras tú, el buen rey,   lo que por ti hoy fu'a pasar:
24 Umá princesa, tu hija,   en gran río quiere entrar;
yo la he visto en sus palacios   con conde de Montalvar.—   (68)
26 El pajecito desfortunado   el rey lo mandó matar.   (71; *E*18)
Dueñas entran, dueñas salen: Todas dicen qu'es verdad.   (21)
28 Como es'oyó el buen rey,   los mandara castigar.
El conde s'echar'a escape;   princesa encerrada está.
30 Mandóla a carcéles hondas,   hondas y d'escuridad;   (24)
el agua hasta las rodillas,   porque diga la verdad.   (25)
32 Ya la vesitan los duques,   los duques y los alcaides: (27)
—Nos mancillamos de ti, Alda,   de tu cara y de tus males;   (28)
34 que de hoy en quince días,   ya te sacan a quemar.—   (29)
A eso de la medianoche,   princesa los gritos da:
36 —¡Si s'alḥadr'aquí alguno   que se aduela de mi mal!   (32)
Que me leven estas cartas   al conde de Montalvar.   (33)
38 Que venga pronto y aína,   de prisa y sin más tardar:
Que de hoy en quince días,   ya me sacan a quemar.
40 No se me da por mi muerte,   ni por la mi soledad;   (30)
sino por la criatura,   qu'era de sangre real.—   (31)
42 Ahi se alḥadró un pajecito,   que a su mesa comió pan: (34)
—Yo's la levaré, señora,   yo's la tengo de llevar.—   (35)
44 Camino de quince días,   en ocho lo haré andar;   (37)
camino de ocho días,   en cuatro lo haré andar;
46 camino de cuatro días,   en dos lo haré andar;
el día por los xarales,   la noche por el lunar;
48 hasta que llegue, al castillo   del conde de Montalvar.—
El paje tomó la carta;   cabalgó y s'echar'andar.   (36)
50 Fuese a los palacios   donde el conde [Alvar] está.   (38)
A mano del conde Alvar,   se la fuera a entregar:
52 —Toméis, conde, esta carta,   que princesa vos da;   (41)
que de hoy en quince días,   ya la sacan a quemar.—
54 El conde leyó la carta;   asentárase a llorar.   (42)
Quitóse ropa de conde;   de fraile la fu'a tomar;   (47)
56 fuese para las carcéles,   donde la princesa está:
—Júrame tú, la princesa,   en este libro misal,
58 que cara de hombre no viste,   sólo la del conde Alvar.

—Yo te juro a Dios del cielo,   en este libro misal,
60 que cara de hombre no vide,   sólo la del conde Alvar.—   (55)
Sacóla de las prisiones   y llevóla a su civdad.   (67?)
62 Otro día de mañana,   ricas bodas van a armar.

Sources

Tangier:						
	a	= CMP B10.1.		*q*	= our 11*A*.
	b	= CMP B10.2.		*r*	= our 11*B*.
	c	= CMP B10.3.		*s*	= our 11*C*.
	d	= CMP B10.4.		*t*	= our 11*D*.
	e	= CMP B10.5.		*u*	= our 11*E*.
	f	= CMP B10.5 (music).		*v*	= CMP B10.11.
	g	= Guzofsky B10*A*.	Larache:	*w*	= García Figueras,
	h	= Guzofsky B10*B*.			p. 106.
Tetuán:	*i*	= Bennaim MS 100.		*x*	= García Figueras,
	j	= CMP B10.6 (= Silvela			p. 107.
		MS).		*y*	= PTJ 23.
	k	= CMP B10.7.		*z*	= our 11*F*.
	l	= CMP B10.8.		*a'*	= our 11*G*.
	m	= CMP B10.9.		*b'*	= our 11*H* (=
	n	= CMP B10.10.			Fereres MS).
	o	= Larrea 32.	Alcázar:	*c'*	= CMP B10.12.
	p	= Larrea 33.		*d'*	= MRuiz 36.

Variants

1   *abcdefijklmnopqrsvwxyza'b'c'd'*
1*b*   de en los sus baños bañar *a*; de su palacio real *deo*; de sus baños de
bañar *gsvwxyzb'*; de sus palacios leal *ik*; de sus palacios real (leal) *jn*;
de los sus baños bañar *l*; de su palacio leal *p*; de sus palaθios real *qr*;
de su baño de bañar *a'*; de palazios de Almuidare *d'*.
1+   Hoy más leal (a*nd after each subsequent verse*) *o*; *note other refrains*
qr.
2   *acfgijklnpvxza'b'*
2*a*   De rostro salió hermoṣa *cf*; El brillo de su cara *g*; Su rostro *n*; colores
de la su cara *va'*; el lustre de la su cara *x*; y el lustre de la su cuara *z*;
colores de su cara *b'*.

2*b*   más que rosa en el rosal *acfkl*; como el sol y la luna *g*; como rosas del rosal *b'*.

3   *abcdegijklmnopqrsvwxyza'd'*

3*a*   Por encuentro se encontrara *a*; Por encuentro se la pusso *bdkn*; Por encuentro se la pone *cij*; Por ahí pasó el conde *g*; Por encuentro se le puso *lmord'*; Por encuentro se la pone *p*; Por encuentro se la puẓo *qr(var.)s*; Allí se le presentaba *v*; Por encontrar encontrare *w*; Allí se le presentara *x*; y ahí se la presentaba *y*; Y ahí se la preẓentara *z*; Ahí se la presentara *a'*; Allí se la presentara *b'*; En encuentro se la pusu *c'*.

3*b*   al conde de Montalbán *ap*; el conde de Montealbar *bcdlm*; que fue a las guerras a guerrear *g*; al conde de Monte Albar *ij*; el conde de Montalvá *k*; al (*or* el) conde de Montealvar *n*; el conde de Montalbán *owzb'*; (y) al conde de Montealbá(r) *qrs*; el conde de Montalvar *v*; con el conde de Montalbán *w*; y al conde de Montalbán *y*; y el moso del Mostralvar *z*; el conde de Montealvar *c'*; el conde de Montalbare *d'*.

3+   Si quierís, la niña, / venir a mandare *d'*.

4   *abcegijklmnpqrszc'*

4*a*   Qué chiquito sois *b*; Ay, qué lindo vais *g*; Qué bonito vas *mrs*; Qué bonito vais (*altered to* sois) *n*; Qué bonito vais *z*; Qué bonito sois *c'*.

4*b*   a ese oficio tomar *g*; para'ste ofisio a tomar *z*; lidar *a*; guerrear *ijps*; liviar *n*; librar *qr*; luchar *q* (*refrain*).

5   *abcijklmopqrsuva'b'c'*

5   Más bonita sois, princesa, / para conmigo folgar *almc'*; Más chiquita sois, princesa, / para conmigo folgar *b*; Más bonita vais, princesa, / para conmigo folgar *cd*; Más chiquita sois, princesa, / para contigo folgar *e*; Más bonito soy, princesa, / para contigo jugar *j*; Más bonito soy, princesa, / para contigo folgar *kmp*; Qué bonita vas, princeza, / para conmigo folgar *or*; Más bonita sos, prinseẓa, / para conmigo folgar *qs*; Qué bonita vais, la niña, / para conmigo folgar *va'b'*; Qué bonita vais, princesa, / para conmigo folgar *w*; Qué bonita sois, la niña, / para conmigo folgar *y*; Qué bonita vais, princesa, / para contigo folgar *z*.

6   *acdeijklmnopqrsvwxyc'd'*

6*a*   Aún chiquito *a*; Qué [chiquito] vais *c*; Qué chiquito vais *dk*; Muy chiquito sois *l*; Qué chiquito vas *m*; Qué chiquito sos *ors*; Qué chiquito eres *r(var.)*; Qué chequito sois *v*; Aún es chiquito el conde *d'*.

6*b*   para con damas estare *d'*; este *vyc'*.

7   *abcdegijkmnopqrsvwxza'b'c'd'*

7*a*   Si soy bonito de cara *gz*; Si bonito soy de cuerpo *k*; Si bonita sois de cara *a ′*; Si soy chiquito de cuerpo *d ′*.

7*b*   más chiquito soy de edad *bv*; más grande lo soy de edad *d*; más bonito soy de edad *gz*; más y más lo soy (estoy) de edad *n*; más lo soy de edad *p*; máď y máďe soy de edad *s*; más y más tengo de edad *vx*; más y máis lo soiš'n edad *a ′*; doble lo soy de edad *c ′*; grande de mocedade *d ′*.

8   *abcdeijklmnopqrsvwxza′b′c′*

8*b*   yo me atrevo a guerrear *m*; yo te la supe guerrear *p*; yo (*deleted*) la pude yo de ganar *v*; a todos pude ganar *x*; ya toda soy de ganar *z*; pude *acdw*; supi *i*; pudi *n*; pud *o*; supía *q*; pudía *rs*; solía *a′b′*; aguerrear *bcdkn*; pelear *w*; guerrar *b′*.

9   *abcdeijklmnopqrsvwxza′b′*

9   a los sien ha muerto ya; / los cuarenta heridos están *a′*; a los cincuenta heridos / y los treinta han muerto ya *b′*.

9*a*   cincuenta dejara muertos *a*; cincuenta tengo matados *x*; y a sincuenta yo matara *z*; cincuenta quedaron muertos *c′*; mataba *k*; he matado *mv*; mató *w*.

9*b*   *y lacking abcdemn*; cincuenta feridos van *a*; los cincuenta *delm*; y los cincuenta herido están *o*; y sincuenta heriḍ están *qr*; a los sincuenta heridos está *s*; los otros heridos van *w*; y a sincuenta heridos van *z*; cincuenta heridos están *c′*.

10   *abcdegijklmnpqrstvwxyza′c′*

10*a*   Tocóse *bcdeikmnpqrtvc′*; La cogió el conde la mano *g*; Tocara *j*; Tocósen *sw*; Cogiéronse *x*; Tomóse *y*; Tomóla'l rey de la mano *z*; Cogióla de mano'n mano *a′*.

10*b*   subiéronse al buen rosal *ad*; se subiera *b*; subiérase *cijmnp*; subióse *e*; la metió en su rosal *g*; subiéranse al buen roṣal *k*; subiéranse(?) a su roṣal *l*; subióle *q*; y le subiera *rs*; subiera *t*; llevóla y a su rosal *v*; y metióla en su hogar *w*; y la llevó *x*; yevóla y a su rosal *yz*; yevóla *a′*; subiéronse *c′*; vergel *st*.

10+   La metió de huerta en huerta, / de rosal en rosal *g*.

11   *abcdeghijklmnpqrstvwxyza′b′c′*

11*a*   Cama hicieron de rosas *a*; Hízole *bnv*; Le hizo *d*; Echóle cama de seda *e*; La hizo *gha′b′*; Pusóle corchón *i*; Púsole colchón *p*; Hísole *qrs*; Hízola *tz*; púsola *x*; le puso cama sedosa *y*; Hizo la cama *c′*; seda *t*; pluma *a′*; plumo *b′*.

11*b* y cabecera *dxb'*; (y) cabacero *gh*; (y) cabasera *rs*; cabeceron (?) *v*; azahar *bck*; aẓahar *m*; asahar *n*; aẓahar *qrstz*; un limonar *a'b'*.

12 *abcegijklmnpqrstvwxyza'b'c'*

  12 Por camas pusieron / hojitas de un limonar *w*; cubierto con que la cubre, / con hojas d'un toronjil *a'*; y cubierto con que se tapa / de hojas de un toronjil *b'*; cobertor con que se tapa / de hojas de un toronjil *c'*.

  12*a* cobertor con que s'atapa *e*; cubierto *ghy*; cobertón *qrsty*; tapa *bmnvc'*; atapan *cq*; tapen *ij*; atapa *lrst*; tape *x*; atape *y*.

  12*b* de *omitted ghx*; con *rz*; debajo de un limonar *y*; hoja *abn*; hojitas *x*; hojuas *z*.

  12+ Agarróla de la mano, / no la quería soltar *kl*; y por almohada pusieron / hojitas de azahar *w*.

13 *bcdehijklmnpqrtvwxyza'b'c'*

  13*a* A eso de la medianoche *bklnvwxa'b'*; Y a la medianoche *e*; Y a eso de la medianoche *hy*; Así a la medianoche *ij*; Haca allá, a la medianoche *m*; Hacia la medianoche *pc'*; Hasia de medianoche *t*; Ansina la medianoche *z*.

  13*b* princesa de gritos da *hvyza'b'*; hojas de un limonar *t*; la princesa gritos da *wx*.

14 *bcdehijklmpqrvwxyzc'*

  14*a* Súeltame *b*; Soltáime *dwx*; Soltísme, conde, la mano *h*; Soltenme *j*; Solteme *m*; Soltáme *p*; Sortéisme *q*; Asidme *v*; Me asís de la mano *y*; Sortísme *z*; Soltísme *a'*.

  14*b* que me voy a reventar *beij*; que me voy a arreventar *cpc'*; que me vais a reventar *hqrvwxy*; que ya me va a reventar *k*; que me quiero arreventar *lmn*.

15 *bcdhijklmnpqrvwxyza'b'c'*

  15*a* Que revientes *bqrc'*; Te revientes o te quedes *hxa'b'*; Que revientes que te pudes *k*; Que arrevientes o te quedes *v*; Que te reviente o te quedes *w*; T'arrevientes u te quedes *y*; T'arrevientes, que te quedes *z*.

  15*b* poquito se me da *h*; que a mí *y*; y a mí *z*.

  15+ Juramento tengoy hecho / en mi librito lisal *k*; Juramento tengo hecho / en mi librito missal *l*; Juramento tengo hecho / y en mi librito anisar *qr*; Juramento tengo hecho / en mi librito resal *v*; Juramento tengo hecho / en mi librito de rezar *x*; Juramento tengo y hecho / y en mi librito rezar *y*.

16 *bcdeijklmnpqc'*

16*a*   Ya sabías tú, princesa *ij*; Bien ya sabes tú, princesa *k(rep.)n*; Ya lo
       sabes tú, princesa *lm*; Ya sabrás tú, la princesa *p*; Bien sabrás tú, la
       prinseza *q*; Bien sabes tú, la prinseza *r*; Bien sabes tú, princesa *c´*.

16*b*   que casadito y leal *c´*; cazado *r*; leal *bcdijk(rep.)lmnp*; legal *qr*.

16+   Juramento tengo hecho / en mi librito resal *c´*.

17   *bcijklmnpqvwxyza´b´c´*

17   Paloma que mi mano cace / de mi mano ha de volar *v*; Paloma que
       tengo en mano / de no dejarla volar *x*; Paloma que de mi mano pase, /
       de mi mano a de volar *y*; Palomo en mano cae, / de mi mano no's
       d'escapar *z*; Paloma qu'en mi mano cae, / de mi mano no se va a´;
       Paloma que en mi mano cae, / ya nunca más saldrá *b´*.

17*a*   casa *n*; mujer *qw*; coẓa *r*; la niña *a´*; a mi mano *ijk(rep.)pq*; viene
       (*emended cae*) *j*; cuae *r*; caiga *c´*.

17*b*   deẋo *m*; revolar *bcqr*; devolar *c(var.)i*; adeudar *p*; resollar *w*.

17+   *extraneous verses qr*.

18   *abcdijklmptc´*

18   Ellos en estas palabras, / un paje que fue a pasar *a*; Un paje
       desfortunado / por ahí le vino a pasar *m*.

18*a*   Por allí *j*; pasara *t*.

18*b*   que a su meṣa comió pan *b*; por ahí le vino a passar *dp*; por allí le bino
       a pasar *i*; por allí vino a pasar *j*; que en casa del rey está *kl*; que al rey
       se lo fue a contar *t*; que no había de passar *c´*.

19   *a(a)b(a)c(a)dijk(a)l(a)m(a)pt(a)c´*

19*a*   Pajecito, pajecito *bijmp*; Si supieraḍ, pajesito *t*.

19*b*   que a mi mesa comió pan *c´*; del *ijp*.

20   *a(b)b(b)c(b)dijk(b)l(b)m(b)ptc´*

20   No deis notisia a mi padre / de esto que hoy a pasado *ij*; No deis
       noticias a mi padre / de esto que hoy ha pasado *p*; que no le digaḍ a mi
       padre / d'eso qu'has visto pasar *t*; y a las tierras de mi padre / no lo
       vayas a contar *c´*.

20*b*   no descubras puridad *a*; tú mos cubrades leal *b*; guárdame la libertad
       c; no descubras polidad (poridad) *d*; tapéisme mi mocedad *kl*; tú me
       guardas polidad *m*.

21   *abcdijklmptc´*

21   doscientos te da mi novio, / doscientos princesa da *c´*.

21*a*   Daréte cien *a*; Te daré yo cien *b*; Te daré cien *c*; Darte 100 *i*; Darte
       cien *j*; Darte he yo cien *klt*.

21*b*   la princesa ciento y más *ac*; princesa doscientos más *b*; Conde Albar
los ciento y más *d*; princesa lo(s) siento y más *ijklmp*; Jimena, los
siento y más *t*.

22   *abcdijklmnptc´*
22   Por ahí pasó un pagecito, / que al rey se lo fue a contar *n*; El pajesito
desafortunado / al buen rey fue a contar *t*.
22*a*   El page desfortunado *bd*; Sin fortuna el pajecito *c´*.

23   *abcdijklmnpt*
23*a*   Si supieras, mi señor rey *at*; Si supieres, el buen rey *b*; Si supieras tú,
el rey *ij*; Si vieras, mi señor reye *k*; Si supieras, el buen reye *p*.
23*b*   lo que por ti va a passar *b*; lo que por ti hoy ha passar *ckm*; lo que por
ti fue a passar *d*; lo que por ti hoy a pasado *ijp;* lo que por ti ha de
passar *l*; lo que por ti hoy a pasar *n*; en qué río está de nadar *t*.

24   *abcdijklmnt*
24   Tu hija la princesa / con el conde de Montalbán *a*; Lo que es princesa
tu hija / en amores quiere entrar *b*; Umá tu hija princesa / con conde
de Monte Albar *cm*; Umá princesa, tu hija, / gran traición la vide
armar *d*; Umá princesa, tu hija, / con conde de Montalvá *k*; Umás
princesa, tu hija, / con conde de Montealvar *l*; Uma princesa, tu hija, /
con conde de Montealvar *n*; DonŠimena, tu hija, / durmiendo con el
Sidi 'stá *t*.
24*a*   Una princesa *j´*.
24+   Los dados tiene en la mano, / al suelo los arronjá *k*; Dados de oro
tiene en mano, / al suelo los fue a arroĵar; // fuese para los palacios /
ande la princesa está *l*.

25   *bdijp*
25*a*   Yo la he visto en el palacio *b*.
25*b*   con el conde de Montalbán *p*; Montealbar *dij*.

26   *b*
27   *ijklmnp*
Dueños entran, dueños salen: / Todos dicen que es verdad *ij*.

28   *n*
29   *bdmnu*
29   Mandaron prender al conde / y a la princesa encerrar *d*; A él le mandó
a prisiones / y a ella mandó encerrar *m*; A él le metió en prisión / y a
ella la mandó encerrar *n*; A él le mandó en prisiones / y a ella la
mandó enserrada *u*.

30   *acdijklmnpt*

30*a*   Metióla en unas carceles *c*; La metían en carcel hondas *d*; La mandó a unas carceles *i*; La manda a unas cárceles *jp*; Metióla en carceles hondas *klmn*; Ayá la mandan serrada *t*.

30*b*   a unas carséles d'honda y d'escuredad *t*; honda *p*; oscuridad *ij*; obscuridad *p*.

30+   Los grillos en las sus manos, / porque diga la verdad; // la agua hasta las rodillas, / porque diga bien notá *d*.

31 *ijptu*

     31   la awua yegó a la sinta / porque la pudrán (*sic*) su carne *d'*.

     31*a*   La agua *ip*; el agua a las rodiya *t*.

     31*b*   que dijera la verdad *t*; para que *u*.

     31+   Por allí pasó un pajesito, / que a su mesa comi pan: // —Pajesito, pajesito, / ¿qué novedad me das? // Las novedad (*sic*) (novedades *p*) que te (*omitted p*) traigo / que te haré llorar *ijp*; Van díad y vienen días, / el rey la mandó a prender. // Por ahí pasara un pajesito, / qu'a su mesa comió pan. // —Pajesito, pajesito, / ¿qué novedad me das? // —La novedad que te traigo, / que no te la puedo dar: // Que de hoy en quinẓe días, / ya te sacan a quemar *u*.

32 *d'*

33 *c'd'*

     33   Me alegro de ver tu cara, / me atristo de ver tu mal *c'*.

34 *abcdijmnpt(a)*

     34*a*   que de allí *a*; y dentro de *b*; El otro día a la mañana *d*; Dentro de *t*.

     34*b*   sentenciada está a quemar *am*; que la saquen *b*; para sacarla *d*; ya te sacan *ip*; que te sacan *j*.

     34+   Pasara un pajeθito, / que por ahí le vino a pasar. // —Pajeθito, pajeθito, / ¿qué alvisias me traerás? // —El alvisia que te traigo, / [. . .]: // Que de hoy en quinẓe días, / ya te sacan a quemar *t*.

35 *bcdijklmnptu*

     35   Como eso oyó la princesa, / (a)sentárase a llorar *dimp*; Como eso oyó la princesa, / sentaríase a llorar *j*; Šimena, como tal oyera, / se sentara a yorar *t*; Como es'oyó Šimena, / se sentara a yorar *u*.

     35*a*   Hacia ya la media noche *kl*; Así a la media nocha *n*.

36 *abcdijklmnptu*

     36*a*   Si estuviera aquí alguno *ab*; Si se aḥadró aquí alguno *cm*; Si se alḥadra aquí alguno *du*; Si se presenta aquí alguno *ijnp*; Si estuviese aquí alguno *kl*; Si encontrara yo un paje *t*.

36*b* que de mi tenga piedad *a*; que se aduela de su mal *j*; que aduela de mi mal *p*; que s'adueliera de mi mal *t*.

37 *abcdijklmnptu*

37*a* Le yevaran estas cartas *t*; lleve *a*; lleven *bdijklmnpu*; estas cartas *aijklnpu*; esta carta *cdm*.

37*b* y al conde *t*; Montalbán *apt*; Montealbar *cdijm*; Montalbá *k*; Montealvar *ln*; Montealbán *u*.

38 *b*

39 *abijmt*

39*a* Que de aquí a quince días *a*; Que dentro de quince días *b*.

39*b* soy sentenciada a quemar *a*; me sacarán a quemar *b*; que *deleted and* ya *written above the line j*; sentenciada estó en quemar *m*.

40 *bcijmnptu*

40*a* Yo no siento por mi cuerpo *b*; No se me da por mi cuerpo *c*.

40*b* aunque soy chica y sin edad *b*; en que voy para quemar *c*; aunque soy de poca edad *mn*; ni por mi puerpo real *t*; ni por la mi muerte se me da *u*.

41 *bcijmnpt*

41*a* yo siento a la criatura *b*; se me da por la criatura *ctu*; me importa la criatura *n*.

41*b* porque es *b*; que es *cint*.

41+ Ellos en estas palabras, / conde Albar ha de llegar *c*; Acabara de decirlo, / Montesino llegará *n*.

42 *abcdklmtu*

42*a* Allí *a*; Y áhi *u*.

42*b* que en *b*.

43 *abcdijklmtu*

43*a* Yo las llevaré *al*; Yo la llevaré *bd*; Yo las levaré *ck*; Yo os la llevaré *ijp*; Yo os las llevaré *m*; Yo te la yevaré, Simena *t*; Yo se la yevaré, señora *u*.

43*b* yo la tengo que llevar *ac*; a mí me toca llevar *b*; yo la tengo que llevar *d*; yo os la tengoy que llevar *i*; yo os la tengo de (*deleted*) que (*above line*) llevar *j*; yo os las tengo que llevar *km*; yo las tengo de llevar *l*; yo te la tengo que yevar *t*; yo se la he de yevar *u*.

44 *acdijklmpt*

44*a* Camino de quince en ocho *p*; siete *c*.

44*b* en cinco le haré yo andar *a*; en tres yo le haré andar *c*; yo le haré andar *p*; le haré *ijk*; los haré *l*; le ha d'andar *t*.

45 *bdjkmu*
    45   *written in by hand on the typewritten copy j.*
    45*b*   en ocho (*sic*) *d*; le haré *jk*; le ha de *u*.
    45+   Ellos en estas palabras, / Montesino allegará *m*.

46 *bcu*
    46*a* tres *c*.
    46*b* en uno *c*; haría *b*; le haré *c*; le ha de *u*.

47 *adijklptu*
    47   la noche con el xaral / y el día por el lunar *d*.
    47*a* el día por el charcal *k*; el día por el charcale *l*; el día con los šarales *u*.
    47*b* y la noche con el lunar *tu*.

48 *a*
    48*b* Montalbán *a*.

49 *bdijkp*
    49*a* Llevara el paje la carta *b*; Alzó las cartas el paje *k*.
    49*b* en seguida se dio a andar *ip*; en seguida se dio adar (*sic*) *j*; y empezara a caminar *k*.
    49+   Libro de oro en la su mano, / que por él tiene que jurar *b*; El día por el charcale, / la noche por el lunar *k*.

50 *t*
    50*b* donde el conde Niño está *t*.

51 *ijpu*
    51   No son dos horas pasadas, / la carta en mano del conde Niño va parar *u*.

52 *adkt(a)*
    52*a* Toméis, el conde, estas cartas *kl*; Tome estas cartas *t*; aquestas cartas *a*.
    52   que la princesa os las da *a*; que la princesa vos la da *d*; que la princesa vos da *kl*.

53 *a*
    53*a* que de allí a *a*.
    53*b* sentenciada está a quemar *a*.
    53+   Que la quemen, que la dejen, / a mí poco se me da *a*.

54 *dijklptu*
    54   Conforme'l conde Niño la carta, / se puẓo al yorar *t*.
    54*a* El conde tomó la carta *l*; Conde Niño la tomara *u*; las cartas *ijk*.

54*b*   adueliéndose de su mal *i*; doliééndose (*emended in handwriting to*
        adueliéndose) de su mal *j*; demandó de cabalgar *k*; no hacía más que
        llorar *l*; aduelándose de su mal *p*; él sentara a yorar *u*.

54+   Fuérase pa sus palasios *u*.

55   *dijlpu*

55*a*   Quitóse paños de siempre *ijp*; Quitóse paños de conde *l*; Quitárase *u*.

55*b*   de fraile la hizo estar *d*; de fraile los fue a tomar *ijp*; de fraile los fue a
        buscar *l*; de fraile se le fuera a poner *u*.

56   *bdijkptu*

56   Vistióse todo de fraile / y en la cárcel fuera a entrar *b*; Vistiérase de
        fraile; / a las cársel' fuera la a buscar *t*.

56*a*   Se llega para la cárcel *d*; Se fuera para la carcel *k*; Fuérase para las
        carsélas *u*; los carseles *i*; las cárceles *jp*.

56*b*   ande *k*; donde Šimena está *u*.

57   *bcdijklmptu*

57*a*   Juráisme vos, la princesa *d*; Júrame tú, princesa *k*; Juréisme aquí,
        la princesa *l*; Yo te juro a Dios, princesa *m*; Júrame tu, la Šimena *t*;
        Si me juras tú, Šimena *u*.

57*b*   en mi librito missal *m*; en tu libro de rezar *n*; en este libro de Nisar *p*;
        y en este librito anisar *t*; missal *bcl*; a rezar *d*; de misa *ij*; lisal *k*; lissal
        l (*variant*); anisar *u*.

58   *dijklmnptu*

58*a*   no has visto *ijkntu*; no vites *lm*; *no he visto p*.

58*b*   sólo que de conde Alvar *di*; sólo que de Monte Albar *j*; sólo que de
        Montalvá *k*; más que la de Montealvar *mn*; sólo que de Montalbán *p*;
        sólo la del Montealbán *t*; sólo la del conde Albar *u*.

59   *cdijklmnptu*

59*a*   Yo te juro a ti, el conde *c*; Yo te juro a ti, el fraile *l*; Yo te juro a Dios,
        el conde *m*; Yo te juro Dios del cielo *p*; Te juro a Dios del sielo *t*; Yo
        le juro Dios del sielo *u*; Dio *n*.

59*b*   y a este librito de nisar (*altered in handwriting to* misar) *j*; y a la mi
        sangre real *k*; y a este libro lissal *l*; en tu librito missal *m*; y en mi libro
        de rezar *n*; en este librito Nisar *p*; y a este librito anisal *t*; y en este
        libro anisar *u*; missal *c*; a rezar *d*; de misa *i*.

60   *bcdijklmnptu*

60*a*   no he visto *bcjnpu*; no ha visto *ikt*.

60*b*   sólo que el conde Montalbar *b*; más que al conde de Monte Albar *c*;
        sólo que de conde Alvar *d*; sólo que de Monte Abar *i*; sólo que de

Monte Albar *j*; sólo que de Montalvá *k*; más que la de Montealvar *mn*; sólo que de Montalbán *p*; sólo la del conde Albar *t*; sólo la de conde Albar *u*.

61 *bcijl*

61   Le sale de las carseles, / para en ca de rey se fuera *i*; Se sale de las cárceles, / para en cade (de *deleted*) del (d *supplied in handwriting*) rey se va *j*; La sacara de la cárcel / y con ella se va a casar *b*; Echóla en sus ricos brazos; / con ella se hubo de casar *n*; Se sale de las cárceles / por el conde, el rey se va *p*.

61*a*   Sacóla de las carceles *c*.

61*b*   y *lacking c*; ciudad *l*.

61+   —Buenos días, señor rey. / —Conde en ella vengadeis. // —Umá prinsesa, tu hija, / yo soy el que l'ay de llevar *i*; A una princesa, tu hija, / por mujer la he de llevar *j*; —Buenos días, señor rey. / —Conde, en ellos vengáis. // —Una princesa, tu hija, / la he de llevar *p*; Saliérase'l conde Albar / y fuera a los palasios del rey su padre real. // Pidiérase la mano. / [. . .] *t*; Ya se iba el conde Albar / al palasio de su padre: // Demandando iba a Šimena, / para caẓarse con eya *u*.

62 *cdijklptu*

62*a*   El otro día a la mañana *dk*; Otro día en la mañana *ijptu*; Otro día a la mañana *l*.

62*b*   las ricas bodas se armar *dk*; las ricas bodas se harán *i*; sus ricas bodas se arman *j*; las ricas bodas se arman *p*; con Claraniña se casó *t*; las ricas bodas se armarán *u*.

As opposed to Tangier and Tetuán, the Larache tradition of *Conde Claros y la infanta + Conde Claros fraile* reflects a distinctive and quite inept treatment of the *Fraile* story. In several Larache versions (*vxyz*), the narrative is "telescoped" and the treacherous page of *Infanta* becomes identified with the faithful, helpful page of *Fraile*, thus resulting in a totally incoherent story: Claros (= Conde Niño) departs, the *infanta* remains alone in her *rosal*, the (treacherous) page appears; the rose arbor scene is then immediately followed by the (faithful) page's rapid journey (camino de ocho días, etc.) and then, abruptly and inexplicably, by the news that the princess has been condemned to be burned at the stake. We reproduce the pertinent verses (correlated, where possible, with the verse numbers of our synthetic text [= *M*]):

14 —Que arrevientes o te quedes,   a mí poco se me da.   (*M*15)
    Juramento tengo hecho   en mi librito resal: (*M*15+)
16 Paloma que mi mano cace,   de mi mano ha de volar.—   (*M*17)
    Ya se sale el conde Niño;   sola queda en el rosal.
18 Vio venir un pajecito,   que a su casa fue a almorzar: (*M*18)
    —Pajecito, pajecito, si vais por casualidad,   (*M19*)
20 le diréis al rey mi padre,   sola quedé en el rosal.
    —Camino de ocho días,   en tres le haré andar;   (*M*45)
22 que dentro de quince días,   el rey te manda quemar.   (*M*53?)
                    (Larache: *v* = CMP B10.11)

14 —Te revientes o te quedes,   a mí poco se me da;   (*M*15)
    juramento tengo hecho   en mi libro de rezar,   (*M*15+)
16 paloma que tengo en mano   de no dejarla volar.—   (*M*17)
    Ya se sale el conde Niño;   sola quedó en el rosal.
18 Vio pasar un pajecito,   que a su casa va a almorzar: (*M*18)
    —Pajecito, pajecito, si yantáis por un casual (*sic*),   (*M19*)
20 le diréis al rey mi padre,   sola quedé en el rosal.
    —Camino de doce días,   en tres lo tengo de andar;   (*M*45?)
22 y dentro de quince días,   el rey te manda quemar.   (*M*53?)
    —Que me queme, que me deje,   a mí poco se me da.   (*M*40?)
                    ([Larache]: *x* = García Figueras, p. 107)

10 —T'arrevientes u te quedes,   que a mí poco se me da: (*M*15)
    Juramento tengo y hecho   y en mi librito rezar: (*M*15+)
12 Paloma que de mi mano pase,   de mi mano ha de volar.—   (*M*17)
    Ya se iba conde Niño;   sola queda en el rosal.
14 Se asomó por la ventana,   vido avinar un paje: (*M*18)
    —Pajecito, pajecito,   [. . . . .]   (*M19*)
16 le dirás al re mi padre,   que sola quedé en el rosal.—
    Ya s'ha ido el pajecito,   [. . . . .]   (*M*49?)
18 y le dijo que su hija   está sola en el rosal.
    —Ve y dila que, dentro un día,   ya la mandaré quemar.   (*M*34?)
                    (Larache: *y* = PTJ 23)

    —T'arrevientes, que te quedes,   y a mí poco se me da: (*M*15)
14 Palomo en mi mano cae,   de mi mano no's d'escapar.—   (*M*17)
    Ya se ponía la niña   de sus ojos a yorar.   (*M*35 *var.*)

16 Por ahí pas'un pajeźito,   qu'a su cuaźa iba a almorźar.   (M18)
    —Pajeźito, mi buen paje,   ¿qué notisias me trairás?
18 Le dirás al rey mi padre,   que sola 'stó'n este roźal.—
    Ya se iba'l pajeźito;   con repuesta vien'y va.   (M49?)
20 Camino de ocho días,   hízole de cuatro días.   (M45)
    Ya se iba el pajeźito;   con recuesta vien'y va: (M49?)
22 —Ya se lo dijí, prinseźa,   ya se lo dizía yo:
    Si fue coźa la que volviera   y al fuego echá a quemar.—   (M53?)
24 Ya se ponía la niña   de sus ojos a yorar.   (M35 var.)
                              (Larache: z = our text 11F)

The Alcazarquivir tradition documents yet another modality of *Conde Claros fraile*. Following a short, but generally undifferentiated rendition of *Conde Claros y la infanta* (up to a point corresponding to v. 21 of our synthetic text), the version collected by M. Manrique de Lara, in Alcazarquivir, probably in 1916, continues with these verses:

22 . . . Sin fortuna el pajecito   al rey se lo fue a contar.   (M22)
    De aquí a unos quince días,   ya le sacan a quemar.   (M53?)
24 Dueñas entran, dueñas salen,   todas dicen que es verdad.   (M27)
    —Me alegro de ver tu cara;   me atristo de ver tu mal.   (M33)
26 —Ni se me da por mi muerte,   ni menos por mi quemar;   (M40)
    se me da por el condesito,   que es de sangre real.—   (M41)
28 Y otro día en la mañana,   princesa en la calle está.
                              (Alcazarquivir: c' = CMP B10.12)

Here vv. 23–28 belong to *Conde Claros fraile*, but v. 25, which would seem to correspond, remotely, to v. 28 of the 16th-century version: "pesa nos de vos señora / quanto nos puede pesar" (C1550, p. 320a), is unknown to forms of the ballad from other Moroccan localities. The text collected by José Martínez Ruiz (no. 36; PTJ 23a) combines a highly aberrant and poorly remembered form of *Conde Claros y la infanta* (vv. 1–7) with a text of *Fraile* which confirms the authenticity of v. 25 of Manrique's version and supplies an additional unique verse (v. 10) also present in C1550. (Where pertinent, verse numbers from the C1550 text are cited in parentheses at the right.)

    Ya se sale la prinseźa   de palazios de Almuidare.

2   Por encuentro se le puzó   el conde de Montalbare:
    —Si quierís, la niña,   venir a mandare.
4   —Aún es chiquito el conde,   para con damas estare.
    —Si soy chiquito de cuerpo,   grande de mosedade.—
6   Qui[n]se días con quinse noches,   la dama con el conde estare
    y eso de los siete meses,   la dama en sintas estare.
8   Mandalá en carseles hondas,   carseles de escuredades;   (24)
    la awua yegó a la sinta,   porque la pudran su carne.   (25)
10   Ya la vesitan los duques,   los duques y los alcaides: (27)
    —Nos mansiyamos de ti, Alda,   de tu cara y de tus males.   (28)
12   —No vos mansiyéis de mí,   ni de mí, ni de mis males,   (30?)
    mansíyavos d'esta criatura,   qu'era de sangre reale.   (31)
14   Si aquí se alḥadra alguno,   que de mi meza comió pane,   (32)
    que leve esta cartita   al Conde de Montalbare.—   (33)
16   Conde Albare que venía: [. . . . .]
    —¿Qué tienes y tú, mi alma?   ¿Qué tienes y tú, mi vida?
18   Yo te escaparé, mi vida,   del rey, tu padre.—
    Tres días no habían pasado,   las ricas bodas se armaron.
20   Ya le puzieran al niño   en manos del re su padre.
    —Y ¿qué nombre l'echarían?   El nombre del rey su padre.

$$(d' = \text{MRuiz } 36)^7$$

Here vv. 10–11 clearly represent vv. 27–28 of C1550:

    los caualleros de su casa   se la yuan a mirar
    pesa nos de vos señora   quanto nos puede pesar.

At the same time, Martínez Ruiz's text also preserves (in v. 9) the *infanta*'s punishment in its pristine brutality (el agua hasta la cinta / porque pudriesse la carne [C1550, v. 25]), while, in other Moroccan subtraditions, the corresponding reading has been softened: "El agua hasta las rodillas, / porque diga la verdad" (synthetic v. 31).[8] The Alcazarquivir texts would, then, seem to reflect, in these

---

7. We have modified punctuation and capitalization. Except for v. 19, the dénouement of Martínez Ruiz's text (vv. 16–21) is an inept and essentially non-traditional pastiche.

8. Concerning such punishments, see FLSJ, III, 258–260, n. 28; NSR, pp. 64–65 and n. 18. A verse similar to that known in Alcazarquivir also survives, as we shall see, in certain Peninsular forms of *Fraile*, as well as in the Moroccan *Cautiverio de Guarinos*

details at least, a very different modality of *Conde Claros fraile* than has survived elsewhere in Morocco.

We have already noted the complex interrelationship of Eastern versions of *Conde Claros y la infanta* and *La partida del esposo*. The Moroccan forms of *Infanta + Fraile* have experienced numerous minor and sporadic contaminations: In regard to the Count's taking Claraniña's hand (v. 10), *Juan Lorenzo* has occasionally imposed its readings: "Tomóla'l rey de la su mano; / yevóla y a su rozal" (*z* = our 11*F*.8), as also in text *g* (= Guzofsky B10*A*), which interpolates: "La metió de huerta en huerta, / de rosal en rosal."[9] Compare *Juan Lorenzo*:

> La tomó el rey de la mano   y la llevó a pase[ar].
> La llevó de huerta en huerta   y de rosal en rosal.
> (Nahón 30.14–15)

The princess' midnight cries, which replace her excuse about bathing in the 16th-century text (. . . dexame ir a los baños . . .), were undoubtedly borrowed from *Disfrazado de mujer* (polyassonant) and at an early stage in the ballad's development, since, because of the Moroccan form's distinctive beginning (Ya se sale la princesa / de los sus baños bañar), the original bath motif became redundant and could no longer be used.[10] Compare *Disfrazado de mujer*: "Hasia allá a la media noche, / la infanta los gritos daba" (Larrea 172.45–46; 173.43–44). The interpolation following vv. 15 and 16 concerning an oath on a prayer book (*libro missal, lisal, de rezar, anisar*, etc.) could well have been suggested by identical verses used later on in *Fraile* (vv. 57, 59), but it is formulaic and could also have been borrowed from some other ballad: *Robo de Elena, Gerineldo, Gritando va el caballero*.[11] At v. 22, the *á-o* assonant verse in Larrea 33.45–46 (as well as in the Bennaim and Silvela MSS—all clearly dependent on a common source), "Si supieras, el buen reye, / lo que por ti hoy ha pasado," has

---

and *Cautiverio del príncipe Francisco* (MP 52; FLSJ, III, 76–77, and n. 15; 91–92, and n. 28; 250–255, n. 15; 258–260, n. 28).

9. Verse references concerning these minor contaminations are to our synthetic text, unless otherwise specified.

10. For this excuse in other Sephardic ballads (*Silvana*; *El pretendiente burlado*), see Yoná, p. 270, n. 8; CMP T5. Compare the Thompson motif: K1227.1. *Lover put off till girl bathes and dresses.*

11. See Nahón, p. 67, nn. 7–8; Larrea 218–219. Concerning the formulaic oath taken on a prayer book, see the Appendix.

doubtless been affected by *El sacrificio de Isaac*: "Si supieras, tú, Sarah, / lo que por ti hoy ha pasado" (Larrea 42.42–43; also our 11D.14–15). *Búcar sobre Valencia* has influenced two versions at a point following v. 24:

—Si supieras tú, el buen rey,   lo que por ti ha de passar:
24   Umá princesa, tu hija,   con conde de Montealvar.—
Dados de oro tiene en mano,   al suelo los fue a arronĵar;
26   fuese para los palacios   ande la princesa está.
(Tetuán: *l* = CMP B10.8)

Text *k* (= CMP B10.7), also from Tetuán, includes only the verse about the dice: "Los dados tiene en la mano, / al suelo los arronjá." This verse and vv. 25–26 of text *l* doubtless had their immediate origin in *Búcar*:

Oído lo había el buen Cidi,   dende su sala ande estaba;
dados de oro tiene en mano   y al suelo los arronjara;
fuese para los palacios   ande la Urraca estaba.
(*Epic Ballads*, p. 243, vv. 9–11)[12]

The possibility of an interview between father and daughter presumably might have led to a further contamination with *La infanta parida* (*í–a, á–a*), as seems to have happened in some Peninsular texts of *Conde Claros y la infanta*, but in Morocco such a contamination did not take place, perhaps because, in the Moroccan *Infanta parida*, the pregnant princess is not visited by her father, but by the queen (as in *Primav.* 159), whereas a similar scene, in Castilian (*á* assonance) and Portuguese (*á* + *á–a*) forms of *Conde Claros y la infanta*, involves the king's interviewing all his daughters.[13]

---

12. The *dados* verse also occurs in *La buena hija* (Larrea 180) and *El hijo vengador* (Larrea 182). Concerning the verse's origin in *Asentado está Gaiferos* (*Primav.* 173), see *Yoná*, p. 90, n. 1, and FLSJ, V, Chap. 12.

13. See *Voces nuevas*, 48.6.22–26, 48.12.11–16; Braga, I, 365–366, vv. 20–25; VRP 54, 59, 69. Autonomous Castilian and Canarian versions of *La infanta parida* (*á-a*) also involve a confrontation between the king and his daughter (e.g. RPM 32–33; FM 81–82). The relationship between the father-daughters scene (*á* assonance) in *Conde Claros y la infanta*, the *í-a* verses from *La infanta parida* in some Castilian versions of *Conde Claros fraile* (e.g. CPE, I, 32–33, vv. 8–9), and autonomous Castilian forms of *La infanta parida* (*á-a*) needs to be investigated, but, for now, must remain enigmatic, since we lack a detailed study of the latter ballad's complex traditional life.

At v. 30, one Tangier version (*d* = CMP B10.4) augments the severity of the *infanta*'s punishment by drawing upon *El cautiverio de Guarinos*:

> La metían en carcel hondas,   hondas y de escuridad.
> Los grillos en las sus manos,   porque diga la verdad;
> la agua hasta las rodillas,   porque diga bien notá;
> el otro día a la mañana,   para sacarla a quemar.

Compare *Guarinos* :

> El agua hasta la cinta,   porque le pudra la carne;
> desposicas en sus manos,   porque pierda el bien notare.
>   (FLSJ, III, 79, vv. 11–12)

El sueño de doña Alda may have intruded upon *Conde Claros fraile* (at vv. 31 and 34), in that, in the Bennaim, Silvela, and Larrea MSS (*ijp*), as well as in our 11*D-E*, the princess asks the page for news and he warns her that it is bad:

> . . . la agua hasta las rodillas,   porque diga la verdad.
> Por ahí pasó un pajecito,   que a su mesa comió pan.
> —Pajecito, pajecito,   ¿qué novedad me das?
> —Las novedades que traigo,   que te haré llorar;
> que de hoy en quince días,   ya te sacan a quemar.
>   (Larrea 33.55–64)

Compare *Doña Alda* :

> —¿Qué novedad me traes, paje,   de mi esposo don [Rondale]?
> —La novedad que os traigo,   que da ganas de yorare:
> Por aquel xarav d'arriba,   ayí mataron a Rondale.
>   (FLSJ, III, no. 9C.33–35)[14]

At v. 31, *Virgilios*, another story of secret amours followed by rigorous imprisonment, has affected our text 11*E*.6–8:

---

14. Note, however, that this reading is limited to a single version. The majority of texts read: ". . . no te las quizera dare . . ." (FLSJ, III, 128: synthetic text, v. 27). In v. 35, *xarav* 'hill' is from Cl. Ar. *šaraf*.

el agua hasta las rodiyas,   para que diga la verdad.
Van díađ y vienen días,   el rey la mandó a prender.
Por ahí pasara un pajesito,   qu'a su mesa comió pan.

The extraneous material (v. 7) added to 11*E* is of great interest and fully vindicates the study of even the smallest and seemingly most insignificant contaminations as a potentially important source of documentation. The second hemistich of v. 7 obviously corresponds to the usual v. 1*b* of *Virgilios*: "Preso llevan a Vergico, / el rey le mandó prender" (Bénichou, p. 99). Verse 7*a* is, of course, formulaic:

Van días y vienen días,   la carne se iba dañando.
(Guardadora de un muerto: MP 110)

Pasó tiempo y vino tiempo,   su cariño la fue a dar.
(Vuelta del hijo maldecido: RT, III, no. III.69)

But in the context of a contamination from *Virgilios*, v. 7*a* cannot be viewed as a mere formulaic filler. There is no such hemistich in any of the Moroccan texts of *Virgilios*—edited or unedited—that we have seen, including Luna Farache's own version. However, various Eastern texts confirm the authenticity of v. 7*a* as a part of *Virgilios*:

Passó tiempo y vino tiempo,   ninguno se acodran dél.
("Oriente" = Sarajevo: Pulido, Españoles, p. 296)

Pasa tyenpo i vyene tyenpo   i ninguno se akodra dél.
(Bosnia: *Bosnia* A1.6)

Pasan días, vienen días,   minguno demanda por él.
(Sarajevo: *Bosnia* B1.9)

Tiempos van y tiempos vienen,   dinguno s'acodra dél.
(Salonika: Attias 7.17–18)

Pasa tyempo y viene tyempo,   dinguno s'acodra de él.
(Bucharest: Milwitzky MSS, no. 36)

Días van y días vienen   y el rey no se acodra de él.
(Salonika: LSO, p. 73)

Such Eastern verses point to the presence, in the Moroccan tradition of *Virgilios* (as attested only in our text 11 *E*, v. 7*a*), of a distinctive Judeo-Spanish variant reading, as opposed to that of both 16th-century texts:

> siete años lo tuuo preso   sin que se acordasse del
> (CSA, fol. 189 vo.)

> siete años le tuuo preso   sin nunca se acordar del
> (*pliego suelto*: Duque de T'Serclaes)[15]

At vv. 41 and 45, two Tetuán versions call, quite inappropriately, upon *Rosaflorida y Montesinos*: "Acabara de decirlo, / Montesino llegará" (*n* = CMP B10.10); "Ellos en estas palabras, / Montesino allegará" (*m* = CMP B10.9). Compare *Rosaflorida*: "Eyos en estas palabras, / Montezino yegaría" (Benardete 5.17; Larrea 36, 38; Nahón 6.18); "Y al fin de estas palabras, / Montesino allegaría" (Gallent 4.21); "Eyos en estas palabras, / Montesinos que venía" (MRuiz 38.22). The golden book mentioned following v. 49: "Libro de oro en la su mano, / que por él tiene que jurar" (*b* = CMP B10.2) recalls *Las hermanas reina y cautiva*: "libro de oro en la su mano, / las oraciones leían" (Benardete 19.6; Larrea 54–56) or an identical verse in *La buena hija* (Bénichou, p. 180; Larrea 179–181). The references to "Conde Niño" at synthetic vv. 50, 51, 54 (in our texts 11*D–E*) are non-specific, but ultimately depend on the eponymous ballad. Repeated mentions of "doña Ximena" in the same texts reflect, of course, the initial contaminations with *El nacimiento de Bernardo del Carpio* (RT, I, 177–183). The allusion to everyday clothing in the Bennaim, Silvela, and Larrea MSS (*ijp*): "Quitóse paños de siempre, / de fraile los fue a tomar" (Larrea 33.89–90) could echo either *Sancho y Urraca*: "Quitóse paños de siempre, / los de la pascua vistió" or *Búcar sobre Valencia*: "Quitóse paños de siempre, / púsose los de la pascua."[16]

---

15. We cite our transcription of a handwritten copy (at the Archivo Menéndez Pidal) of the *pliego suelto* (whereabouts now unknown), that in 1916 belonged to the library of the Duque de T'Serclaes de Tilly, in Madrid: *Romance nueuamente trobado del infante Turian . . . Com (sic) el romance de Uergilius por gentil estilo* (Barcelona, c. 1525): "Mandã tomar a Uirgili*us* / 7 a buẽ recaudo poner" (= DPS 1045). Concerning other texts of *Virgilios* and their readings, see the Appendix.

16. *Epic Ballads*, pp. 135 (v. 10), 147–148, 243–244 (vv. 13, 24); Catalán, *Siete siglos*, p. 175 (v. 37).

Our 11*A* includes an aberrant dénouement (vv. 18–21) composed of an amalgamation of diverse elements: Verse 18, "Tú serás mi cosinera; / tú me pastorearád el ganado" is sometimes connected with *El robo de Elena* and probably depends originally on the rare *Gentil porquera* (Nahón, p. 66 at v. 4), but the *cocinera* reference seems to recall *Búcar sobre Valencia*: "Su mujer, Ximena Gómes, / será la mi cozinada" (*Epic Ballads*, p. 243, v. 5). There are many fainting fits in the Moroccan *romancero* (CMP, III, 307), often followed by consolatory verses. Verse 19, "Como's'oyó la prinsesa, / muerta cayó en un desmayo," with its *á-o* assonance, may perhaps best be attributed to *El sacrificio de Isaac*, a ballad which, as we have seen, has also influenced another stage of our *Conde Claros* poem (at synthetic vv. 23–24): "Como eso oyó Sara, / muerta quedó en [un] desmayo" (Benardete 11.21; MRuiz 42*A–B*). Verse 21, "Mañana por la mañana, / yo te pideré al rey, tu padre," comes from *Melisenda insomne*: "Mañana por la mañana, / te demandaré a tu padre" (Larrea 39, 41). Both 11*D*.41–42 and 11*E*.30–31 embody an idiosyncratic elaboration which cannot be related to any other specific ballad ending.

Before going further afield to compare *Conde Claros y la infanta* with its early and modern congeners, let us look briefly at how the combined narrative, *Infanta + Fraile*, emerges in the Moroccan tradition as a poetic structure. Clearly the intervention of the two pages—one hostile and treacherous, the other friendly and helpful—are parallel and are crucial to the story's development.[17] It is possible, tentatively at least, to envision our synthetic text in terms of a characteristically balladic ring composition:

A: Prologue: Princess leaves baths (1–2)
B: Dialogue: flirtation (3–9)
C: Lovers' encounter (10–17)
D: Page to King (18–22)
E: Revelation–reaction: imprisonment (23–31)
E′: Revelation–reaction: message to Count (32–41)
D′: Page to Count (42–54)
C′: Lovers' encounter (55–56)
B′: Dialogue: confession (57–60)
A′: Epilogue: Princess leaves prison (61–62)

---

17. David Buchan notes how, in the English and Scottish ballad of *Lady Maisry*, similarly—but coincidentally—the evil kitchy-boy, who reveals Maisry's pregnancy to her hostile brother, is balanced by the helpful foot-page who takes her message to the English lord (*The Ballad and the Folk*, p. 113).

Let us now look at the 16th-century and modern Hispanic analogues of *Conde Claros y la infanta* from the perspective of their relationship to the Sephardic tradition. *Conde Claros y la infanta* has a single known 16th-century congener, printed in two *pliegos sueltos*, in the *Cancionero sin año* (our base text: *C*), and in various other later *cancioneros*. The text begins with verses reflecting *Conde Claros insomne* (vv. 1–20), continues with *Conde Claros y la infanta* (vv. 21–75), and closes with *Conde Claros preso* (vv. 76 ff.). In our Chap. 10, we have edited and studied the segment relating to *Conde Claros insomne*, which we reproduce here (but without recording variants), in order to present *Conde Claros y la infanta* in context. Here then is the CSA version (text *C*), followed by variants from six other early sources:[18]

	Media noche era por filo	los gallos querian cantar
2	conde claros con amores	no podia reposar
	dando muy grandes sospiros	que el amor le hazia dar
4	por amor de clara niña	no le dexa sossegar
	quando vino la mañana	que queria alborear
6	salto diera dela cama	que parece vn gauilan
	bozes da por el palacio	y empeçara de llamar
8	leuanta mi camarero	dame vestir y calçar
	presto estaua el camarero	para auer selo de dar
10	dierale calças de grana	borzeguis de cordouan
	dieranle jubon de seda	aforrado en zarzahan
12	dierale vn manto rico	que no se puede apreciar
	trezientas piedras preciosas	al derredor del collar
14	traele vn rico cauallo	quen la corte no ay su par
	que la silla con el freno	bien valia vna ciudad
16	con trezientos cascaueles	alrededor del petral
	los ciento eran de oro	7 los ciento de metal
18	7 los ciento son de plata	por los sones concordar
	7 vase para el palacio	para el palacio real
20	ala infanta clara niña	alli la fuera hallar

---

18. All these early texts obviously represent the same variant of *Conde Claros y la infanta*. The *pliegos sueltos* (= *AB*) reflect a slightly different subgroup (over against CSA [= *C*]). *Silva* (1550) (= *E*)—and secondarily also *Silva* (1561) (= *F*)—seems to have conflated CSA or C1550 with one of the *pliegos*. Tortajada (= *G*) is clearly based on a *pliego* (*A* or *B*), with occasional, superficial reworking and with characteristically inept euphemisms in vv. 48–49 and 70.

trezientas damas con ella   que la van acompañar
22 tan linda va clara niña   que a todos haze penar   (*E* 2)
conde claros qu[e] la vido   luego va descaualgar
24 las rodillas por el suelo   le començo de hablar
mantenga dios a tu alteza   conde Claros bien vengays
26 las palabras que prosigue   eran para enamorar
conde claros conde claros   el señor de montaluan   (*M*3)
28 como aueys hermoso cuerpo   para con moros lidiar   (*M*4)
respondiera el conde claros   tal respuesta le fue a dar
30 mi cuerpo tengo señora   para con damas holgar   (*M*5)
si yos tuuiesse esta noche   señora a mi mandar
32 otra dia enla mañana   con cient moros pelear   (*M*8)
si a todos no los venciesse   que me mandasse matar
34 calledes conde calledes   7 no os querays alabar
el que quiere seruir damas   assilo suele hablar
36 y al entrar enlas batallas   bien se saben escusar
si no lo creeys señora   por las obras se vera
38 siete años son passados   que os empece de amar
que de noche yo no duermo   ni de dia puedo holgar
40 siempre os preciastes conde   delas damas os burlar
mas dexame yr alos baños   alos baños a bañar
42 quando yo sea bañada   estoy a vuestro mandar
respondierale el buen conde   tal respuesta le fue a dar
44 bien sabedes vos señora   que soy caçador real   (*M*16)
caça que tengo enla mano   nunca la puedo dexar   (*M*17)
46 tomara la por la mano   para vn vergel se van
ala sombra de vn acipres   debaxo de vn rosal   (*E*6; *M*10)
48 dela cintura arriba   tan dulces besos se dan
dela cintura abaxo   como hombre y muger se han
50 mas la fortuna ques aduersa   que a plazeres o a pesar
por ay passo vn caçador   que no deuia de passar   (*E*8; *M*18)
52 de tras de vna podenca   que rauia deuia matar
vido estar al conde Claros   con la infanta abel holgar
54 el conde quando le vido   empeçole de llamar
ven aca tu el caçador   assi dios te guarde de mal   (*E*10; *M*19)
56 de todo lo que has visto   tu nos tengas poridad   (*E*11; *M*20)
darte yo mil marcos de oro   7 si mas quisieres mas   (*M*21a)
58 casarte con vna donzella   quera mi prima carnal

darte he en arras y en dote   la villa de montaluan
60   de otra parte del infanta   mucho mas te puedo dar   (*M*21*b*)
el caçador sin ventura   no les quiso escuchar   (*M*22)
62   va se para los palacios   a do el buen rey esta
mantenga te dios el rey   y a tu corona real   (*E*15)
64   vna nueua yo te trayo   dolorosa y de pesar
que nos cumple traer corona   ni en cauallo caualgar
66   la corona de la cabeça   bien la podeys vos quitar
si tal desonrra como esta   la ouiesseys de comportar
68   que hallado la infanta   con claros de montaluan   (*M*25)
besando la y abraçando   en vuestro huerto real
70   dela cintura abaxo   como hombre 7 muger se han
el rey con muy grande enojo   al caçador mando matar   (*E*18; *M*26)
72   porque auia sido osado   de tales nueuas lleuar
mando llamar sus alguaziles   a priessa no de vagar
74   mando armar quinientos hõbres   que le ayan de acompañar
para que prendan al conde   y le ayan de tomar . . .

Sources (Base text: *C*):

A   =   *Pliegos de Praga*, I, 33–39.
B   =   *Pliegos BN*, II, 144–151.
C   =   CSA, fols. 83 ro.–90 ro.
D   =   C1550, pp. 168–173.
E   =   *Silva* (1550), pp. 390–396.
F   =   *Silva* (1561), fols. 80 vo.–87 vo.
G   =   Tortajada (1652), pp. 198–209.

Variants:

23*a*   qua *C;* que *ABDEFG.*
23*b*   luego va a descaualgar *A*; luego fue a descaualgar *G*.
24*a*   las rodillas per (*sic*) el suelo *F*.
24*b*   la comiença de hablar *G*.
26*b*   . . . para enamorar *B* (*physical lacuna*).
30*a*   mejor le tengo señora *A*; mejor lo tengo señora *BG*.
31*a*   si yo os tuuiesse esta noche *AB*; si y'os tuviesse esta noch (*sic*) *D*; si yo
os tuuiesse señora *G*.

31*b*   esta noche a mi mandar *G*.

32*a*   y otro dia de mañana *G*.

32*b*   cien *ABG*.

33*b*   me mandassedes matar *A*; que me mandasses matar *B*; mandassedesme matar *G*.

34*a*   calleys conde calleys conde *AB*.

35*a*   los que quieren seruir damas *AB*; que el que quiere seruir damas *G*.

35*b*   assi lo suelen hablar *AB*.

36*a*   y al entrar en las batalla (*sic*) *F*.

36*b*   bien se suelen escusar *G*.

38*b*   que os comencè de amar *G*.

40*a*   siempre tuuistes el conde *AB*; Siempre lo tuuiste Conde *G*.

41*a*   mas dexad me yr el conde *ABG*.

42*b*   estare a vuestro mandar *BF*.

43*a*   alli respondiera el conde *AB*; respondiera luego el Conde *G*.

44*a*   bien sabeys vos mi señora *ABG*.

45*a*   caça que tenga en la mano *B*; caça que viene a mis manos *G*.

46*a*   tomara le por la mano *F*; Y tomòla por la mano *G*.

46*b*   y para vn vergel se van *A*.

47*a*   ala sombra de vn cipres *ABEF*; a la sombra de vn limon *G*.

47*b*   debaxo de vn verde rosal *G*.

48*a*   con grande contentamiento *G*.

48*b*   muy dulces besos se dan *G*.

49*a*   con el amor que se tienen *G*.

49*b*   que era cosa de admirar *G*.

50*a*   mas fortuna q̃ es aduersa *AG*; mas fortuna que es aduerso *B*; mas la fortuna aduersa *EF*.

50*b*   que a plazeres da pesar *ABEFG*.

51*a*   por ay passa vn caçador *B*; alli passò en (*sic*) caçador *G*.

51*b*   que no deuia de pasar *D*; que no deuiera pasar *ABEF*; que no deuia passar *G*.

52*a*   en busca de vna podenca *EF*; En busca va de vn açor *G*.

52*b*   que rauia deuiera matar *AB*.

53*b*   con la infanta al bel folgar *BF*; con la infanta al bel holgar *E*; con la Infanta a mas holgar *G*.

54*a*   el conde quando lo vido *ABG*.

54*b*   començòle de hablar *G*.

55*b*   si Dios te guarde de mal *BFG*.

56*b*   puridad *G*.

57*a*   darte he yo mil marcos d' oro *A*; darte he mil marcos de oro *BG*.

58*a*   casarte he con vna donzella *AB*; casarte he con vna dama *G*.

58*b*   que era *ABG*.

59*a*   Darte he en arras, y dote *G*.

60*a*   de otra parte la infanta *ABEFG*.

60*b*   mucho mas te puede dar *ABEFG*.

61*a*   el caçador sui (*sic*) ventura *B*.

61*b*   no los quiso escuchar *BG*.

62*b*   a donde el buen rey esta *ABFG*.

64*a*   traygo *ABF*; traigo *G*.

65*a*   q̃ no te c͠uple traer corona *A*; no te cumple traer corona *B*; Que no os
         cumple traer corona *G*.

65*b*   ni en cauallo passear *G*.

66*a*   corona dela cabeça *a*; la corona de la cabeca (*sic*) *B*.

66*b*   bien te la puedes quitar *AB*; bien os la podeis quitar *G*.

67*a*   si tal de honra (*sic*) como elta (*sic*) *B*.

67*b*   la huuiesses de comportar *AB*; la aueis de comportar *G*.

68*a*   que he hallado ala infanta *ABG*.

68*b*   hay (?; *damaged type*) Claros de Montaluan *A*.

69*a*   besandola y abraçando la *AB*; abraçandola, y besando *G*.

70*a*   de lo qual dolor no tuue *G*.

70*b*   y no quisiera ver tal *G*.

71*a*   el rey con grande enojo *AB*; el rey con el grande enojo *F*; El Rey con el
         gran enojo *G*.

71*b*   mandò al caçador matar *G*.

72*b*   de tales nueuas le dar *EF*.

73*a*   mando llamar alguaziles *AB*; Manda llamar Alguaciles *G*.

73*b*   a priessa y no de vagar *ABEFG*.

74*a*   mandar armar trecientos hombres *G*.

74*b*   para los acompañar *AB*; que los hayan de acompañar *EF*.

75*b*   ò le ayan de matar *G*.

In terms of direct evidence, we know nothing about the early traditional life of *Conde Claros y la infanta*. Given the enormous popularity of *Conde Claros insomne* (*Media noche era por filo*)—which serves to introduce our only known early text of *Infanta*—as well as of its continuation, *Conde Claros preso* (or, at least, of its fragmentary derivatives, *Pésame de vos, el conde* and *Más envidia he de vos, conde*), *Conde Claros y la infanta* must also have been a very well known ballad. But we do not even know how the early form began or how it ended, since our only known text is preceded by *Insomne* and is followed by *Preso*. To our knowledge, there are no early *ensalada* or other literary citations, though further documentary explorations may, of course, bring some to light.

We will now compare the Judeo-Spanish forms of *Conde Claros y la infanta* with their early relative. Though radically abbreviated, the Eastern texts embody important features which are unknown to the Moroccan tradition. Their initial praise of Blancaniña would seem to reflect an elaboration of the 16th-century verse, "tan linda va clara niña / que a todos haze penar" (v. 22), which has, to our knowledge, survived nowhere else in the modern tradition. The corresponding Sephardic verse is given a somewhat moralistic tone: "Del dulzor de vuestra boca, / a la gente hacéis pecar" (Attias 30.2). The Eastern tradition also preserves the treacherous page's (or hunter's) greeting to the king, which is not present in any recognizable form in the Moroccan versions (at synthetic v. 23):

> mantenga te dios el rey   y a tu corona real
> (CSA, fol. 85 ro., v. 63)

> —¡Estéis en bonhora, el buen reyes!   —Pajico, en bien vengáis.
> (Attias 30)

In the *Pizmônîm* text, the seemingly strange v. 11: "El viejo echó la kapa; / Blankaniña su ben biá" (*read* buen brial) is likewise absent from the Moroccan versions and will, as we shall see, be important in relating the Sephardic ballad to other modern traditional forms. The Eastern and Moroccan modalities share a verse specifying that the rose arbor serves as a bed for the lovers:

> De las hojicas que cayen,   una cama ordenará.
> (Attias 30.7)

> Las ojikas ke kaían   i por kama se echara.
> (*Pizmônîm*, v. 10)

> Púsole cama de rosa,   cabecera de azahar.
> (Morocco, v. 11)

The verse, attested in two such widely separated and otherwise quite different traditions, suggests that here, quite possibly an early—16th- or even 15th-century—variant reading has been preserved. The king's question about his vineyards and the page's brutally direct answer: "Siete putas había . . ." etc. are unique to the Eastern tradition, though these seven girls may somehow echo the king's seven daughters, who, in modern Castilian versions, are called together at this point to be interrogated about their chastity (for example, *Voces nuevas*, no. 48.6.23–24). In Attias' v. 18, the death sentence of the hunter has been reinterpreted to apply to the princess: "presto la mandó a matar," over against "al caçador mando matar" (*Media noche*, v. 71). Again, that the informer should be a page in both Sephardic traditions, rather than a hunter, is, as we shall see, also significant for the ballad's early history. Needless to say, the final verse of the *Pizmônîm* version, "I si buxkáx a Blankaninyya, / lyya se buxkó su buen mazal," reflects an arbitrary and cloyingly optimistic alteration.

The North African *Conde Claros y la infanta* differs at almost every stage from its early analogue, while conserving, with much greater fidelity than the Eastern tradition, most of the narrative's crucial features. As we have seen, nothing is known about our *romance*'s beginning in its early form or forms. The Moroccan texts either begin insipidly, as do various other ballads, with the princess' leaving her royal palace,[19] or by envisioning her emerging, resplendently beautiful, from the baths, paralleling, in this latter case, the courtly *Guiomar*, as well as *Melisenda sale de los baños*:

> Ya se sale guiomar   delos baños de bañar
> colorada como rosa   su rostro como cristal. . . .
> (*Pliegos de Praga*, I, 209)

> Ya se sale Melisendra   de los baños de bañar. . . .
> (*Pliegos de Praga*, I, 7a)[20]

---

19. "Ya se sale la princesa, / de sus palacios reales" (*Quejas de Jimena:* Nahón 1A); "Ya se sale el conde Niño, / de sus palacios reales" (*Conde Antores:* Nahón 22); "Ya se salió el buen reye, / de su palacio real" (*Conde Claros y el emperador:* Larrea 27). Actually, all these incipits may depend on *Conde Claros y la infanta*. Note that, in Larrea 27, the following verse is: "Por encuentro se le puso / y el conde de Montealbar." On similar ballad introductions, see *Epic Ballads*, p. 94, n. 18.

20. Compare also, of course, the elaborate description in Thomas Coenen's early Dutch translation (Scholem, p. 401) and in the modern Eastern versions of *Melisenda sale de los baños* (Attias 13–13a). See FLSJ, V, Chap. 14. On the agreement with *Guiomar*,

The early text's elaborate presentation of Claraniña, with three hundred ladies in attendance, the sufferings caused by her beauty, and Claros kneeling in homage before her, are lacking here, as we go directly to the amorous exchange between the two protagonists.[21] In the early text, Count Claros speaks first, humbly greeting Claraniña, who then pointedly observes: ". . . como aueys hermoso el cuerpo . . ." (v. 28). In Morocco, the princess is first to speak, confronting the count with her provocative initial commentary.[22] The scene deviates, in a characteristically traditional style, from the lengthy and somewhat complex conversation of the early text (vv. 23–45), to develop a brisk and suggestive repartee: "¡Qué bonito vais! . . . ¡Más bonita sois! . . . ¡Qué chiquito sois! . . . La guerra de los cien moros," etc. (vv. 4–9). Gone from the Moroccan tradition are Claraniña's objection that the bold words of amorous gallants are usually followed by pretexts (bien se saben excusar), the count's seven years of amorous suffering, and Claraniña's excuse that she must go to the baths (vv. 34–42). The elimination (or absence) of this latter motif has had important effects on the narrative, as we shall see. The count's boast about fighting Moors is quite different in the Moroccan versions. In the old text, it is pure hypothesis: "Si a todos no los venciesse / que me mandasse[s] matar" (v. 33), while, in Morocco, the feat has already been accomplished: "a los cincuenta matara / y cincuenta

---

note MRuiz, p. 127. Concerning medieval attitudes toward public bathhouses, see the Appendix.

21. A retinue of numerous ladies, in other Sephardic ballads, represents a widely used topos, as in *Sancho y Urraca; Búcar sobre Valencia* (*Epic Ballads*, pp. 135, v. 12; 244, v. 27); *Robo de Elena* (Nahón 12AB); *Expulsión de los judíos de Portugal; Preferida del rey* (*Tres calas* C5.10, A11.8). Additional examples could doubtless easily be found. In the Arthurian romance, *Jaufre*, Brunisen, on the advice of her seneschal, goes out to meet the protagonist, accompanied by one hundred maidens: "E menas de puicellas cent / De tals c'a vos fassan honor" (Lavaud and Nelli, I, 408, vv. 7100–7101). As Fernando Gómez Redondo observes: "El séquito de que se rodea un noble o una dama es el que determina la importancia social y el valor de su figura" (*Jaufre*, p. 218, n. 378; also p. 129, n. 210: with reference to the *romance* of *El sueño de doña Alda*: "Trescientas damas con ella . . ."). We may recall the immense followings who attend upon Charlemagne and King Marsile in the *Chanson de Roland*: "De dulce France i ad quinze milliers" (v. 109); "Envirun lui plus de vint milie humes" (ed. Whitehead, v. 13).

22. In many texts, it is the count who confronts the princess: "Por encuentro se la pone (puzo) / el conde de Montealbar" (variants to v. 3), but such a formulation is at odds with the fact that Claraniña is the first to speak: "¡Qué bonito vais, el conde!" (v. 4). The *infanta*'s admiring exclamation about the Count recalls a similar verse from *La guarda cuidadosa*: "¡Qué buen cuerpo tienes, Cidi, / merecéis tener amiga!" (Catalán, *Por campos*, p. 232; MP 128; *Epic Ballads*, p. 248, n. 30).

heridos van" (v. 9). In the Judeo-Spanish texts, deeds seem to speak louder than words: Claraniña is immediately convinced and they repair forthwith to the rose arbor. In the early version, Claraniña's pretext about bathing is countered by Claros' boast that he is a "good huntsman" (v. 44), but the Sephardic poem is radically different: Claraniña's objections, reformulated in terms of *Disfrazado de mujer*, and Claros' hunting metaphor have been shifted to a later stage in the narrative (vv. 13–17) and we pass directly to the rose arbor.[23] Here, the early *vergel, aciprés, rosal* and the scene's specifically erotic description (vv. 46–49) are sensitively—and effectively—replaced by evoking a bed consisting of natural components that imparts exactly the same message, but in less graphic terms: "cama de rosa, . . . cabecera de azahar, . . . cobertor de hojas de un limonar" (vv. 10–12). That such a reading is no late development, but must go back to an early variant of *Conde Claros y la infanta*, is confirmed by the similar bed of leaves evoked in the Eastern tradition: "De las hojicas que cayen, / una cama ordenará" (Attias 30.7); "Las ojikas ke kaían / i por cama se echará" (*Pizmônîm*, v. 10).

In the early version, the informer is a huntsman, who intrudes upon the love scene by following his wandering hound (de tras de vna podenca / que rauia deuia matar).[24] In Morocco, as in the East, the culprit is a page (*pajico*; *pajecito*), whose identity evokes the ballad's courtly ambience.[25] Like the detail of the bed of leaves, this page again points to the Sephardic ballad's derivation

---

23. On the influence of *Disfrazado de mujer*, see the text at n. 10 supra. On the hunt of love motif, see *Yoná*, pp. 249–250; *En torno*, pp. 204–205; *Epic Ballads*, pp. 79, n. 4; 97–98, n. 25; 176, n. 11; 182, n. 34. Note again Marcelle Thiébaux's important monograph. Note also how the count's boast about fighting a hundred Moors and Claraniña's reproach about vainglorious warriors knowing how to avoid battle have both survived in modern Asturian and Ibizan versions of *Infanta* (NCR 13A.24–25; Aguiló, pp. 308–311; Macabich, pp. 21–23).

24. Ultimately, this adapts the motifs: N774.2. *Adventures from seeking (lost) domestic animal*; N774. *Adventures from pursuing enchanted animal (hind, boar, bird)*; N773. *Adventures from following animal to cave (lower world)*; N771. *King (prince) lost on hunt has adventures*. Note that Damián López de Tortajada (p. 200), for whatever reason, replaces the hound with a goshawk (*açor*)—even though birds of prey are not normally given to hydrophobia(!)—thus suggesting the initial episode of *La Celestina* and its analogues (*Yoná*, pp. 119, n. 2, 245–251, nn. 5–7, 625).

25. In early documentation, *paje* often had menial connotations, referring to "viles personnes, comme à garçons de pie" (L. Spitzer, *ZRPh*, 42 [1922], 340–342; apud DCECH, s.v.), but in the modern oral tradition, the word is an archaism, sometimes misunderstood and transformed, and, where it still survives, there can be little doubt concerning its courtly, chivalric implications. See FLSJ, III, Chap. 9, n. 52.

from an early variant form and such a conclusion will be confirmed by Peninsular evidence. In the *pliego suelto* and *cancionero* text, it is Count Claros who offers rewards to the hunter for his silence (tu nos tengas poridad [v. 56]). The Moroccan readings of vv. 20–21 are in conflict: The allusion to "el rey mi padre" (in v. 20) indisputably identifies Claraniña as the speaker, but then, in v. 21, as she offers the page 100 marks, she promises that "la princesa" will give "ciento y más"(!). Only the isolated reading of text *d*, from Tangier, makes sense of such confusion: "Darte he cien marcos de oro, / conde Albar los ciento y más" (CMP B10.4), pointing, possibly here too, to an early variant in which it was the princess, not Count Claros, who made the offers. Such is also the case in the Eastern versions and, as a minority reading, in Brazil: "E também o Conde Elado / alguma coisa ha de dar" (Santos Neves, "Presença," p. 51). The identity of the speakers would, of course, easily be interchangeable in this context, but the princess' identical role in texts from such widely separated areas (East; Morocco; Brazil) suggests, at very least, the possibility that this may be an authentic early reading (like the bed of leaves and the page). The offers themselves are less elaborated in Morocco (100 marks and more), in contrast to the variegated inducements of the early version (1000 marks; marriage to the count's cousin; the town of Montalbán), which, as we shall see, have been better preserved in other modern traditions (Argentina, Portugal, Madeira, Brazil, Ibiza). The page's revelations in the Moroccan texts are also less elaborate than those of the early version, making use of an interesting metaphor: "Umá princesa, tu hija, / en gran río quiere entrar" (synthetic v. 24) or "Si supieras, mi señor rey, / en qué río estád de nadar" (our 11D.14). The one Eastern text to preserve this segment is, by contrast, brutally direct: "Siete putas había, siete; / vuestra hija es la caporal" (Attias 30.17). Drawing on previously specified details of the love scene (vv. 48–49, 70), the hunter, in the early text, belabors his point and thus helps seal his own doom by stressing the king's dishonor (vv. 64–70). A single Moroccan version, from Tangier, attests to the crucial v. 26: "El pajecito desfortunado / el rey lo mandó matar" (*b* = CMP B10.2). The verse is also in Attias' Salonikan text, though reinterpreted, as we have seen, to apply to Blancaniña: "Esto que oyó el buen reyes, / presto la mandó a matar" (no. 30.18). Needless to say, the early version's tiresome and redundant explanation (porque auia sido osado / de tales nueuas lleuar), the last verse which we can assign with any certainty to *Conde Claros y la infanta*, has been felicitously eliminated in all branches of the modern tradition.

In most other modern Hispanic subtraditions—just as in Morocco and the Eastern communities—*Conde Claros y la infanta* can be characterized as a notably rare ballad, which has in general only survived in combination with a variety of other narratives—all concerned, in one way or another, with the dangers attendant upon a love affair between a nobleman and a princess. Such is the case in the center of the Peninsula (Castilian-speaking areas); in Argentina; in Portugal, the Azores, and Madeira; and in Ibiza. Only in Brazil, where *Conde Claros y la infanta* is widely known and consistently occurs either alone (Silva Lima, *Folclore*, nos. 8.3, 5, 7; "Achegas" [1979], pp. 59–63) or in combination with *Conde Claros preso*, does *Infanta* achieve wide popularity in the modern tradition and a certain stability in its relation to other narratives. In rare and scattered cases—Argentina, Asturias, some Portuguese versions, Azores, Madeira, Ibiza—the tradition attests to the correlation *Insomne + Infanta + Preso*, just as in the early *pliego* and *cancionero* version, but more typical of the modern tradition is a bewildering, constantly varying and shifting alignment of *Infanta* with *Conde Claros fraile*, *Aliarda y el alabancioso*, *La infanta parida (á, á-a)*, and *La canción del huérfano*. The following list outlines our ballad's typically protean relationships. Versions from Brazil, where, as we have seen, *Infanta* is consistently found either alone or followed by *Preso*, are not listed here, but can be found in the bibliography at the end of the chapter:

Castilian Areas:

Aliste, pp. 63–64 (no. 1.13–54): *Insomne + Infanta + Fraile.*
Catarella, *Gitano-andaluz*, no. 11: *Insomne + Infanta.*
Díaz-Delfín-Díaz Viana, *Catálogo* (1978), I, 166 (vv. 9–20): *Insomne + Infanta + Fraile.*
Díaz Viana, *Rev. de Folklore*, I:2 ([1980?]), 27–29 (vv. 9–10): *Insomne + Infanta + Parida (á) + Fraile.*
Fonteboa, *Bierzo*, no. 3: *Infanta + Parida (á) + Fraile.*
Gomarín, *Cántabro*, p. 43: *Infanta + Alabanza + Fraile.*
Kundert, pp. 87–88 (G4.17–38): *Insomne + Infanta + Fraile.*
Manzano, *Leonés*, no. 740: *Infanta + Parida (á) + Fraile.*
Manzano, *Leonés*, no. 921: *Infanta + Parida (á) + Fraile.*
RGL 19.1: *Insomne + Infanta + Parida (á) + Fraile.*
RGL 19.2: *Insomne + Infanta + Parida (á) + Fraile.*
RGL 19.3: *Infanta + Fraile.*
RGL 19.4: *Insomne + Infanta + Fraile.*
RGL 19.5: *Infanta + Alabanza + Parida (á) + Fraile.*
RGL 19.6: *Insomne + Infanta + Alabanza + Fraile.*

RGL 19.8: *Insomne + Infanta + Parida (á) + Fraile.*
RGL 19.9: *Infanta + Parida (á) + Fraile.*
RGL 19.15: [. . .] *Infanta + Fraile.*
RGL 19.16: *Insomne + Infanta + Fraile.*
RGL 19.17: *Insomne + Infanta + Parida (á-(e)) + Fraile.*
RGL 19.18: *Insomne + Infanta + Parida (á) + Fraile.*
RGL 19.23: *Insomne + Infanta + Alabanza + Parida (á).*
RPC, p. 12 (vv. 7–8): *Insomne + Infanta + Fraile.*
RPM 58.3–16: *Insomne + Infanta + Fraile.*
Suárez, *Dos siglos*, p. 103: [. . .] *Infanta* [. . .].
Voces nuevas 48.5.1–12: *Infanta + Parida (á) + Fraile.*
Voces nuevas 48.6.5–21: *Insomne + Infanta + Alabanza + Infanta + Parida (á) +*
    Fraile.
Voces nuevas 48.7.6–22: *Insomne + Infanta + Alabanza + Infanta + Parida (á) +*
    Fraile.
Voces nuevas 48.10.3–12: *Insomne + Infanta + Fraile.*
Voces nuevas 48.12.1–2: *Infanta + Alabanza + Parida (á) + Fraile.*
Voces nuevas 48.16.1–7: *Infanta + Parida (á) + Fraile.*
Our text *C*: *Insomne + Infanta + Alabanza + Parida (á) + Fraile.*

Argentina:

Moya, II, 23–24 (vv. 9–23): *Insomne + Infanta + Preso.*

Asturias:

NCR 13*A*: *Insomne + Infanta + Preso.*
NCR 13*B*: *Insomne + Infanta + Alabanza + Fraile.*

Galicia:

CARG 17*a*: *Insomne + Infanta + Fraile.*
CPG, III, 44*c*: *Insomne + Infanta + Fraile.*

Portugal:

Athaide Oliveira, pp. 70–71 (vv. 1–3, 14–16): *Infanta + Alabanza + Infanta +*
    Fraile.
Athaide Oliveira, pp. 327–328 (vv. 1–3, 13–14): *Infanta + Alabanza + Infanta +*
    Fraile.

Braga, I, 309–310 (vv. 1–17): *Infanta + Fraile*.
Braga, I, 325–326 (vv. 15–44): *Insomne + Infanta + Preso*.
Braga, I, 330–331 (vv. 9–34): *Insomne + Infanta + Preso*.
Braga, I, 338–339 (vv. 1–21): *Infanta + Preso*.
Braga, I, 364–365 (vv. 1–19): *Infanta + Parida (á, á-a) + Fraile*.
Coelho, "Rom. Pop.," pp. 64–65 (vv. 1–42): *Infanta + Fraile*.
Coelho, "Rom. Pop.," p. 66 (vv. 1–33): *Infanta + Fraile*.
Costa Fontes, *Trás-os-Montes*, no. 42.1–5: *Infanta + Fraile*.
Costa Fontes, *Trás-os-Montes*, no. 43.2–3: *Insomne + Infanta* [...].
Galhoz, no. 12.1–10: *Infanta + Fraile*.
Galhoz, no. 14.17–23: *Fraile + Infanta + Parida (á) + Fraile*.
Garrett, II, 226–227 (vv. 9–27): *Infanta + Preso*.
Leite de V., "D. Carlos," pp. 189–190 (vv. 1–26): *Infanta + Preso + Huérfano + Preso*.
Lima Carneiro, "Monte Córdova," p. 57 (vv. 1–2, 5–6): *Infanta + Parida (á) + Infanta + Parida (á + á-a) + Fraile + Caballero burlado + Don Bueso*.
Martins, II, 10–11 (vv. 8–18): *Insomne + Infanta*.
Nunes, "Subsídios," pp. 161–162 (vv. 1–6, 24–27): *Infanta + Alabanza + Infanta + Fraile*.
Nunes, "Subsídios," p. 164 (vv. 1–7, 25–28): *Infanta + Alabanza + Parida (á) + Infanta + Fraile*.
Reis Dâmaso, *Encycl. Rep.*, pp. 203–204 (vv. 1–3, 9–11): *Infanta + Alabanza + Infanta + Fraile*.
VRP 50.12–13: *Insomne + Infanta*.
VRP 51.8–9: *Insomne + Infanta*.
VRP 52.1–13: *Infanta + Fraile*.
VRP 54.1–13: *Infanta + Parida (á-a) + Fraile*.
VRP 55.1–18: *Infanta + Fraile + ?*
VRP 59.1–4: *Infanta + Alabanza + Parida (á-a) + Fraile*.
VRP 69.1–2: *Infanta + Parida (á-a) + Fraile*.

Azores:

Braga, I, 405–406 (vv. 1–21): *Insomne + Infanta + Preso + Huérfano*.
Purcell, *Açores*, I, no. 7A: *Insomne + Infanta + Preso*.

Madeira:

Braga, I, 334–336 (vv. 12–31): *Insomne + Infanta + Preso*.

Rodrigues de Azevedo, p. 75 (vv. 42–43): *Bodas de sangre + Infanta + Preso* (totally reworked).

Rodrigues de Azevedo, pp. 78–80: *Infanta + Huerfano + Prisionero + Conde Niño* (totally reworked).

Rodrigues de Azevedo, pp. 81–84: *Insomne + Infanta + Preso*.

Rodrigues de Azevedo, pp. 89–91: *Insomne + Infanta + Preso*.

Rodrigues de Azevedo, pp. 94–96: *Insomne + Infanta + Preso*.

Rodrigues de Azevedo, pp. 99–100: *Infanta + Preso*.

Ibiza:

Aguiló, pp. 308–311 (vv. 30–99): *Insomne + Infanta + Preso*.

Macabich, pp. 21–23 (vv. 8–30): *Insomne + Infanta + Preso*.

The scattered instances of *Insomne + Infanta + Preso* replicate the alignments of the early text, but there are also numerous instances of *Insomne + Infanta + Fraile*—over against the latter's only known early context *Conde Claros y el emperador + Fraile*—and, just as in Morocco, of *Infanta + Fraile*, perhaps not without significance, usually from the archaic region of Trás-os-Montes (Costa Fontes; VRP 52, 55). From a thematic standpoint, the intrusion of other themes can easily be explained: In *Aliarda y el alabancioso* (abbrev.: *Alabanza*), there is an amorous dialogue similar to that of *Infanta*; in *La infanta parida*, as a consequence of her love affair, the princess is in danger of being burned at the stake (as in *Fraile*); while in *La canción del huérfano* and *Las bodas de sangre* (in Madeira), the protagonists are condemned to death for having slept with a princess (as in *Conde Claros preso*).[26] Attention to the transformations and consistencies of *Conde Claros y la infanta* in the other Hispanic subtraditions yields important evidence which helps to elucidate the ballad's characteristics in the Sephardic tradition. On the following pages, we offer representative texts from Castilian areas, Argentina, Galicia, Portugal, Madeira, Brazil, and Ibiza. The Castilian, Portuguese, and Brazilian texts are synthetic and have been drawn up on the basis of the published versions available to us. Here we have avoided a number of developments typical of these subtraditions and have stressed, rather, the survival of archaic features shared with the Sephardic text-types and with the *pliego-cancionero* version. In the case of Argentina and Madeira, only one text is known to us, and for Galicia and Ibiza we reproduce two mutually

---

26. Concerning these narratives, see CMP R1, R3, H25.

complementary versions—the only ones available. In each case, texts are correlated to corresponding verses in *Media noche*:

Castilian Areas:

	—¡Qué buen cuerpo tienes, Carlos,	para con moros pelear!	(28)
2	—Mejor lo tengo, señora,	para con damas holgar.—	(30)
	Con estas palabras y otras,	se arrimaron a un rosal;	(47)
4	don Carlos tendió la capa,	la niña el sobrial;	
	la dice unas palabras,	que eran para enamorar;	(26)
6	que siete años lleva, siete,	que no la deja de amar.	(38)
	[Por áhi pasó] un escudero,	[que] no debía pasar.	(51)
8	—Por Dios te pido, el escudero,	por Dios y por la verdad,	(55)
	de todo lo que hayas visto,	nada lleves que contar;	(56)
10	te daré mil doblas de oro,	que en la faldriquera están;	(57)
	la niñita, por su parte,	te dará otro tanto y más.—	(60)
12	El pícaro del escudero	a nadie quiso escuchar;	(61)
	a la puerta de los reyes,	allí se fue a pasear:	(62)
14	—Nuevas [te] traigo, mi rey,	nuevas de gran pesar;	(64)
	no te puedes llamar rey,	ni rey te puedes llamar;	(66?)
16	que tu hija, Claralinda,	con Montalvares está;	(68)
	hacían cosas allí	que son dignas de contar.—	(70?)
18	—Si me lo dices callando,	bien te lo [había de] paga[r];	
	pero me lo has dicho a voces;	te voy a mandar quemar. . . .	(71)

(Synthetic text)[27]

Argentina:

	A las once de la noche,	empezó el gallo a cantar;
2	se levantó el conde Claro	sobre su cama a pensar.
	Le pidió a su camarero	de vestir y de calzar.
4	Le sacó un rico vestido,	que no lo había en la ciudad
	y su caballo rosillo,	que tenía de su montar.
6	Dijeron los que lo vieron,	sin faltar a la verdad,
	en la cincha y en el freno,	equivale a una ciudad.
8	Saca su bestia y ensilla	y se va al palacio real,

27. For the sources of this synthetic Castilian text, see the Appendix.

porque sabía que la reina   se está por ir a bañar;
10 doscientas damas con ella(s),   que la van acompañar.   (21)
Tan poco que caminó,   con la reina se encontró.
12 Clavó la rodilla en tierra   y así la empezó hablar: (24)
—Diez años ha que padezco,   en este palacio real,   (38)
14 por ver si mi vida puede   de tu hermosura gozar.—
Iba pasando un cazador,   que nunca solía pasar.   (51)
16 Le hace señas con la mano   y así lo empezó a llamar: (54)
—Te voy a dar en oro y plata   y la ciudad de Montalván;   (55a; 59b)
18 una prima hermana tengo,   con ella te has de casar;   (58)
las riquezas que ella tiene   mi lengua no puede hablar.—
20 Los engaña el cazador;   se va al palacio real: (62)
—Buen día tengas,   mi Sara Real Majestad.   (63)
22 Aquí nuevas más amargas   nadie te ha de contar: (64)
La reina, yendo a los baños,   con el conde fué a encontrar. . . .
(Moya, II, 23–24)[28]

Asturias:

16 . . . Iba a ver a Claraniña,   de paseo la fue hallar,   (20)
doscientas damas con ella   para verla de acompañar.   (21)
18 —Conde Claros, Conde Claros,   el señor de Montalbán,   (27)
que lindo cuerpo tenéis   pa con moros pelear.   (28)
20 —Mejor lo tengo, señora,   para con damas holgar.   (30)
Si usté estuviera esta noche   a mi gusto y mi mandar,   (31)
22 mañana por la mañana   con cien moros pelear,   (32)
si no los venciese a todos   que me mandasen matar.   (33)
24 —Calla, conde, calla, conde,   no te sepas alabar,   (34)
cuando vas a las batallas   bien te sabes excusar.   (36)
26 Si me esperas, buen conde,   de los ríos al bañar,   (41)
cuando venga   estaré a vuestro mandar.—   (42)
28 Se agarraron del brazo   y para el jardín se van   (40)
y con gran contentamiento   grandes abrazos se dan.
30 Por allí pasó un cazador   que no debía pasar,   (51)
y el conde así que lo vio   enseguida le fue hablar: (54)

---

28. The text was collected in a Catamarca village called La Albigasta (p. 19).
Typically, Moya gives no further information. For more data, see the Appendix.

32	—Dios te guarde, cazador, y Dios te libre de mal,	(55)
	todo esto que tú has visto te pagaré por callar;	(56)
34	te daré mil marcos de oro, y si quisieras más, más;	(57)
	te casarás con una moza que es prima mía carnal.	(58)
36	y de dote os daré la villa de Montalbán.—	(59)
	El cazador enojóse y no lo quiso escuchar,	(61)
38	y se fue para palacio, para palacio real,	(62)
	a llevar la nueva al rey, nueva de tanto pesar;	(64)
40	tan afortunado fue que de paseo lo fue hallar.	
	—No mereces traer corona, ni caballos pasear,	(65)
42	pues deshonra más grande no se puede ejecutar:	(67)
	he visto yo la infantina con el conde Montalbán,	(68)
44	en el huerto se abrazaban, en tu jardín real.—	(69)
	El rey que esto oyó al cazador mandó matar,	(71)
46	tan sólo por ser osado de aquellas nuevas llevar . . .	(72)

(NCR, no. 13*A*)

Galicia:

	A la medianoche y guila, los gallos quieren cantar,	
2	Carlos, el amor que tiene, no lo puede sosegar.	
	Salen niñas y doncellas, aos balcones mirar,	
4	salió la hija del rey, hija de su majestad:	
	—¡Qué cuerpo llevas, don Carlos, para con el moro pelear!	(28)
6	—También lo llevo, señora, para con usted hablar.—	(30)
	El ya tira de capote, la niña con su sayal.	
8	Estando en estas razones, un hombre vieron pasar.	(51)
	—Por Dios le pido, buen hombre, por Dios y su caridad,	(55?)
10	que cosa que de mí viera al rey no se la ha de contar.	(56)
	—Tengo juramento hecho a la Virgen del Pilar,	
12	que cosa que de ti viera al rey se la he de contar.—	
	—Nuevas le traigo, buen rey, nuevas de su queridá,	(64)
14	que su hija la Lanzuca con Carlos la vi quedar.	(68)
	—Prender(os) a este hombre, prender, ya que no cuenta verdad.	(71?)

16 —Si no me lo cree, buen rey,   a los nueve meses lo verá.—. . .

(CARG, no. 17a)²⁹

Galicia:

Oit'a noite a media noite,   antes do galo cantar,
2 don Carlos anda d'amores,   no lo puede arremediar,
en sendo la Nerluquiña,   que lo va apaciguar.
4 Carlos va por el camino,   Nerluca por arenal
y Carlos tiende la capa,   Nerluca el verde brial.
6 Llega por allí un hombre;   no debía de llegar.   (51)
—Por Dios le pido, buen hombre,   por Dios le voy suplicar: (55)
8 Cosa que esta noche vea,   al rey no la ha de contar.   (56)
—Tengo un juramiento hecho,   a la Virgen del Pilar:
10 Cosa que esta noche vea,   al rey no se la calar.   (64)
Carta le traigo, buen rey,   cartas de grande pesar.
12 —¿Qué cartas te serán estas,   que a mí me dían pesar?
O me queiman el castillo,   o me roban la ciudá.
14 —Ni le queiman el castillo,   ni le roban la ciudá.
Que su hija Neluquiña   encinta está. . . .

(CPG, III, 44c)

Portugal:

Andando Claralinda   no jardim a passear,
2 por ali passou dom Carlos,   dom Carlos de Montalvar.
—Oh, que lindo corpo de homem,   p'ra co'os Mouros batalhar!   (28)
4 —Melhor o tem a menina,   p'ra comigo brincar!   (30)
Deixe-me, ó senhor dom Carlos,   que me quero ir lavar: (41)
6 Naquele tanque de água,   me quero desenganar.   (42?)

---

29. The text is from Goia (ay. Quiroga, p.j. Monforte de Lemos, Lugo), informant: Elisa Macía, 69 years, collected on July 16, 1982, by Beatriz Mariscal, Blanca Urgell, Ana Vian, Koldo Viguri, and Teresa Yagüe, during the Instituto Menéndez Pidal's "Encuesta Norte '82." We gratefully acknowledge the kind help of Ana Valenciano, who made this text available in advance of its publication in *Os romances tradicionais de Galicia* (= CARG). Note the euphemism: *hablar* (v. 6*b*); compare *Las quejas de Jimena* (*Epic Ballads*, p. 79, v. 8*b*).

    —Eu não a deixo, menina,   eu não a hei-de deixar:
8   Pomba que eu te tenho na mão,   não a deito a avoar.—   (45)
    Passou um pagem de el-rei,   nunca houvera de passar.   (51)
10 Disse dom Carlos ao pagem,   muito bem posto a espreitar: (54)
    —Viste o que has visto agora,   a el-rei não vas contar.   (56)
12 Dar-te-ei prata e ouro,   canto te possas gastar;   (57)
    dar-te-ei as minhas terras,   as terras de Montalvar;   (59)
14 dar-te-ei minha sobrinha,   braço de sangue real;   (58)
    e da parte da senhora,   o que ella te quizer dar.—   (60)
16 Pagem, como ignorante,   a el-rei o foi contar: (61)
    —Deus vos salve, senhor rei,   e a vossa corôa real!   (63)
18 Vossa corôa não vale nada,   nem vosso septro real.   (65)
    Aqui venho, ó seôr rei,   tristes novas lhe quero dar: (64)
20 Eu bem vi Claralinda   com dom Carlos a brincar,   (68)
    debaixo duma roseira,   debaixo dum bom rosal;   (47)
22 de bejinhos e abraços,   sem se poder apartar;   (69)
    como marido e mulher,   cada cual a redobrar.   (70)
24 —Se m'o disseras oculto,   tença te havia de dar;   (71)
    mas em prúvico lo dizes,   logo te mando matar. ...
                              (Synthetic text)[30]

Madeira:

12 —Mal empregado corpinho,   pera com mouros brigar!   (28)
    —Melhor lo tenho, senhora,   pera comvosco brincar.—   (30)
14 E foram p'r'o rosal verde,   ambos á sombra folgar.   (47)
    N'isto vem um caçador,   que não houvera passar.   (51)
16 —Escuta-me, caçador,   se me quizeres escutar: (55)
    Lo que viste aqui agora   a el-rei não vás contar;   (56)
18 prata e oiro te darei,   quanto possas carregar;   (57)
    e derei minha sobrinha,   pera comtigo casar;   (58)
20 e tambem, em dote della,   las terras de Montalvar;   (59)
    essas terras são tamanhas,   que da serra dão na mar.
22 —Não quero vossa riqueza,   nem sobrinha p'ra casar,
    nem essas tamanhas terras,   Condado de Montalvar;
24 lo que vos ouvi e vi   a el-rei lo vou contar.

---

30. For the sources of our synthetic Portuguese text, see the Appendix.

—Deus vos salve, rei senhor,   n'esse throno de reinar.   (63)

26 Aqui vos dou umas novas,   que não las quizera dar: (64)

La infanta mail lo conde   ambos los vi a brincar,   (68)

28 á sombra do rosal verde,   como não deviam estar.

—Se com verdade e secreto,   lo vieras delatar,

30 santa palavra de rei,   que tença te houvera dar;

mas prúvico lo disseste;   vaes por isso a enforcar. . . .   (71)

(Braga, I, 334–335)[31]

Brazil:

—Linda cara tem o conde,   para comigo brincar.   (28)

2 —Mais linda tendes, senhora,   para comigo casar.   (30)

Estava dona Claralinda   com dom Carlos a brincar,

4 debaixo de um arvoredo,   num fermoso roseiral.   (47)

Foi passando um caçador,   que não devia passar.   (51)

6 [Dom Carlos] pede logo   que a el-rei não vá contar: (54?)

—Vinde cá, meu caçador,   meu caçadorinho real,   (55)

8 cala a boca, mexeriqueiro,   ao rei meu não vai contar.   (56)

[Darei-te] ouro e prata,   quanto possas carregar;   (57)

10 darei-te terras de França,   para ires governar;   (59)

darei-te minha sobrinha,   para contigo casar.   (58)

12 [. . . E também o Conde Elado   alguma coisa ha de dar . . .]   (60)

—Tudo isso que eu vi   ao meu rei eu vou contar.

14 Deus vos salve, senhor rei,   e vossa corôa real!   (63)

Novas vos trago, senhor,   novas eu vos quero dar: (64)

16 Que eu vi dona Claralinda   com dom Carlos de Montealvar;   (68)

aos abraços e beijinhos,   sem se poderem apartar;   (69)

18 da cintura para cima,   eu vi eles se abraçar;   (48)

da cintura para baixo,   eu vi eles a brincar.   (49; 70)

20 —Se me contasses oculto,   muito devias ganhar;

como me contas em público,   eu te mando a enforcar. . . .   (71)

(Synthetic text)[32]

---

31. Rodrigues de Azevedo's text (*Canción del huérfano* + *Infanta* + *Conde Claros preso*) embodies only a two-verse echo of *Infanta*; the horribly mutilated protagonist of *Las bodas de sangre* informs his mother: "um treidor mexeriqueiro / que foi de mim delatar, / por me ver mail la infanta / no laranjal a brincar" (p. 75).

32. For the sources of our synthetic Brazilian text, see the Appendix.

Ibiza:

16 L'ha trobada que baxava per anar a passejar,
  gonella de seda verda y 'ls tapinets platetjats . . . [. . .]
18 —A burlarvos de les dames, jau teniu acostumat.   (40)
  —Avesat estich, senyora, amb els moros pelear; (28*b*)
20 per tenirvos tota sola una estona al meu manar, (31)
  pelearia ab cent moros y 'ls havia de matar. (32–33)
22 —Si axò es veritat, lo comte, men aniré a pendre un bany, (41)
  y com surta de banyarme, estaré a vostron manar. (42)
24 —Ja sabeu vos, Claranina, que som caçador reyal; (44)
  caça qu' está a punt de pendre no la deix escapolar. (45)
26 L'agafa per la má blanca y no lay vol amollar. (46)
  Comte Claros y l' infanta se 'n van a l' orta reyal,
28 debaix d' una llimonera, al mitg d' un tarongerar; (47)
  l'un hi va estendre la capa, l' altra hi estengué 'l brial . . .
30 Un caçador en mal'hora, en mal'hora va passar. (51)
  —Caçador, bon caçador, axí Deu te guart de mal (55)
32 y te dó mellor ventura de la que vas a cercar;
  de lo que ara 'ls teus uys veuen, a ningú n' has de parlar. (56?)
34 Vaig a donarte cent dobles, que dins la percinta guart; (57)
  te donaré per esposa a ma germana carnal; (58)
36 que te durá per adot la vila de Montalvá, (59)
  y l' infanta de part seua molt mes te podrá donar.— (60)
38 Lo caçador sens ventura res d' axò volgué escoltar, (61)
  perque diu qu' estes noticies a 'n el rey deuen anar:
40 —Me 'n vaig a dirho a 'n el rey, qu' ell molt mes me donará.—
  Ja se 'n va a cal senyor rey, d' arrambada ley comptá. (62)
42 —Bon dia tenga 'l bon rey, que Deu lo vulga guardar. (63)
  Esta corona que porta ja se la pot arrancar, (66)
44 que no li cal dur corona, ni 'ls esperons d' or calçar, (65)
  ni conversar amb la Reyna, si axò volgués comportar. (67*b*)
46 Allá té la seua infanta, a l' orta de sa reyal,
  debaix d' una llimonera, al mitg del tarongerar,
48 folgant amb el comte Claros, que burlant se d' ella está.— (68)
  Unes noves tan pesades a 'n els Reys no 's poden dar . . .
50 —Vaja el caçadó a la forca, vuy mateix l' han de penjar. . . . (71)

       (Aguiló, pp. 308–311)

Ibiza:

8 [. . . . .]   Dret a la horta reial,
    varen trobar Claranyina,   que es deixava de regar.
10 —Déu me la guard, Claranyina.   —*Dios* mo' n'ha de guardar.   (25)
    —Si pogués estar, senyora,   una *nochu* en son manar,   (31)
12 l'endemà m'atreviria   amb cent moros peleiar.   (32)
    —Això teniu, lo bon condi,   que us sabeu ben alabar,   (34)
14 i en ser prop de les batalles,   no'n sabeu ben apartar. [. . .]   (36)
    El senyor estengué la capa,   la princesa son brial.
16 I va passar un caçador,   que no deuria passar.   (51)
    —Caçador, bon caçador,   Déu te do bona ventura;   (55)
18 de lo que has vist i sentit   no en digues cosa ninguna;   (56)
    jo et daré cent *marcus* d'or,   que ara te'ls puc entregar,   (57)
20 i et casaré amb una dama   que és *mi hermana* carnal.—   (58)
    Es caçador sens ventura   res d'això volgué escoltar,   (61)
22 sinó que se'n va a cal rei   i en presència li contà: (62?)
    —Bon dia tenga, el bon rei   i la corona reial;   (63)
24 no li val portar corona,   ni espasa d'or manejar,   (65)
    ni anar per les *ventanes*   i amb les dames passejar;
26 que yo he vist la seua fiia,   dret a la horta reial,
    i hi he vist el condi Flori,   que se n'estava burlant.—   (68?)
28 El rei que va sentir això,   de raons se'n va picar,
    perquè unes noves d'aqueixes   no es van an el rei donar.
30 —Anau-me a dur es caçador,   perquè l'hi de fer penjar. . . .   (71)
                  (Macabich, pp. 21–23)

The Castilian evidence for *Infanta* is often vestigial (Díaz Viana; RPC; *Voces nuevas* 12, 16), but where relatively extensive texts have survived, they follow the order of the early version with notable fidelity and without significant elaborations (Díaz-Delfín; Kundert; RPM 58; *Voces nuevas*, nos. 48.5–7, 10). The only variation in order is the unique reading of RPM 58 (here vv. 5–6), in which the wooing of Claralinda takes place after the lovers are in the rose arbor, by shifting two verses of the early text to a later stage in the narrative: Clearly vv. 5–6 echo *Media noche*, v. 26, originally referring to Claraniña: "las palabras que prosigue / eran para enamorar" and Claros' amorous avowal: "siete años son passados / que os empecé de amar" (v. 38). The only significant amplification is a passage, not cited here, in which the informer and the princess return to the palace at the same time, the girl taking a short cut, which allows her to arrive first: "El pastor fue por la sierra, / la niña por el arenal; // cuando llegó el pastorcito, / la niña en casa está" (*Voces nuevas*, nos. 48.7, 5, 6; Kundert). Thus, when the informer announces: "la su hija, Galanzuca, / con don Carlos la vi estar," the king can truthfully answer: "Mientes, mientes, pastorcito, / que mi hija en casa está" (*Voces nuevas*, no. 48.6). But the shepherd then replies: "Quédese con Dios, buen rey, / más tarde me lo dirá" (48.7). Interestingly enough, the RPM text begins, like a few of the Moroccan ones, with the princess leaving her palace, rather than the baths: "Vio salir a Claralinda / de su palacio real; // era hermosa como el oro / por su vestir y calzar" (no. 58). The amorous dialogue, as in Morocco, has been felicitously reduced to its essentials, though the verses about Claros' youth and his battle with the hundred Moors are not in evidence. In Kundert's version, the romantic *rosal* has been replaced by a pedestrian *arenal* and, in several Leonese texts (*Voces*), the talebearer, rather than an archaic *escudero*—sometimes transformed into a popular-etymological *escuchero* (Díaz-Delfín)—is, as we have seen, a shepherd. But behind this shepherd there may lurk a medieval page (*pajecito*), as is, perhaps, suggested by the still feudalistic verse: "Ya los viera un pastorcito, / de los que comen su pan" (*Voces*, no. 48.5).[33]

Notable is our v. 4 concerning *capa* and *brial*, which we have already seen in the Salonikan version from Yoná's *Pizmônîm* chapbook and about which we will have more to say later on. In the Castilian texts, just as in the early version, it is Claros, not the princess, who attempts to bribe the informer. The last two verses of our synthetic text, in which the treacherous squire's potential secrecy is contrasted with his actual publication of the scandal is, as we shall see, an important feature of the ballad's development in both the Spanish and the Portuguese oral traditions.

It is difficult to know quite what to make of the lone Argentinian version published by Moya. It conserves the same sequence (*Insomne* + *Infanta* + *Preso*) as the early *Media noche* and is so radically different from anything else in the modern oral tradition, that, at first reading, one is tempted to attribute it to an independent traditionalization of some *pliego* or *cancionero*, exported, as so

---

33. The verse may, however, simply have been transferred from *Conde Claros fraile*, where, in this same text, a faithful page will bear Claralinda's message to Claros: "¡No viniera un pajecillo, / de los que comen mi pan!" The characterization of the informer as a hunter (as in *Media noche*) has survived in the modern tradition of Castilian areas. Note the following verses cited in CGR: "Pasó por allí un cazador, / que no había de pasare, // en busca una perra blanca / que de rabia la matare" (IA, 76).

many were, to the New World—with Carolingian themes enjoying particular
favor: Note, for example, the "25 Romanceros de romances franceses y no
castellanos," specified in a 1583 book order from Lima.[34] There are striking
verbal agreements between the lone Argentinian text and its early congener—
and in verses that are preserved nowhere else in modern tradition:

10	doscientas damas con ella(s),		21	trezientas damas con ella
	que la va a acompañar.			que la van acompañar
12	Clavó la rodilla en tierra		24	las rodillas por el suelo
	y así empezó hablar.			le començo de hablar
16	Le hace señas con la mano		54	el conde quando le vido
	y así lo empezó a llamar.			empeçole de llamar
	(Moya)			(CSA)

But here, incongruously, Claros is enamored of the queen, not the princess.
As in the *pliego-cancionero* text, a hunter discovers the lovers, but he only sees
them in conversation. Such details could, of course, easily have developed in the
course of oral transmission, but can the same be said for the notable feature of
the queen's going to the baths at the beginning of the text (porque sabía que la
reina / se está por ir a bañar), which seemingly cannot but recall the initial verse
of the Moroccan texts? After Claros is imprisoned, the king's daughter expresses
her wish to marry him and begs for his life, to which the king accedes. The death
of the treacherous hunter is alluded to in prose at the end of the narrative: "Y así
los casó el rey, / y lo agarró el cazador / y le cortó la cabeza, / pa que no vaya a
contar / lo que tan a la vista está." It is difficult to reach a satisfactory conclusion
concerning this poem. We can only surmise that this highly idiosyncratic version
may ultimately derive from print, but had long circulated in oral tradition and
may perhaps have taken over the motif of the initial baths from some oral
variant.

The notable text, probably of Leonese origin, collected by Jesús Suárez, in
Asturias, in 1991, follows the early printings so consistently and, in many cases,
with such close verbal agreement, that we are, I believe, faced with a relatively
late traditionalization of some printed source. In any event, it is interesting to
review what has been omitted from this text, as part of what I would see as an
incipient process of traditionalization: Omitted verses (numbered according to

---

34. See E. Romero, *Perú*, pp. 32–33; RoH, II, 231–232; Leonard, *Books of the Brave*,
p. 209, 224; Id., *Libros del Conquistador*, pp. 178, 189, 286 (no. 177), 291 (no. 16).

our ed. of CSA, fols. 83 ro.–90 ro.) include vv. 23–26, involving Claros' greeting to Claraniña and the unnecessary explanation of the following dialogue as erotic in character; 29, introducing Claros' answer; 37–40, concerning Claros' seven years of amorous suffering and Claraniña's response that he is a deceiver of women; 43–45: Claros' answer, involving the hunting metaphor, otherwise so well known in the tradition; 47–50, concerning the well known amorous *rosal* and the couple's lovemaking; 52–53, the hunter's searching for his hound and the unnecessary specification that he sees the lovers; 60, which explains that the princess will offer an even larger bribe; 63, the hunter's widely known greeting to the king; 66, which, in part, duplicates 65; and 70, which, like 48–49, may have been prudishly expurgated. Much of this material is either explanatory, introductory, or marginal and most of it is not essential to developing the ballad's action. At the same time, we are surprised at the absence of the hunting metaphor, the rose arbor, and the hunter's greeting to the king, all so widely known in the tradition. These other omissions reinforce our perception that this modern Leonese-Asturian text is a traditionalization of an early printing. We may also note that no new materials have been added and that the numerical sequence of CSA's verses is invariably preserved. A comparison of vv. 1–15 with the early version of *Conde Claros insomne* (*Media noche era por filo*) confirms such a perception. The reading *goryerán* (v. 8*b*) agrees with Tortajada's *gorguerán*. See our edition in Chapter 10.

The first Galician version we have chosen to reproduce (CARG, no. 17*a*) is essentially Castilian in its language. It begins with verses from *Conde Claros insomne* (1–4). Here the amorous repartee is preserved. It is initiated by the *infanta*, but, in this case euphemistically subverted by Don Carlos: ". . . para con usted hablar" (v. 6*b*). Here, as also in CPG, we have the important *capa-brial* verse and, again, the informer is described as a nondescript *hombre*. The oath made before the *Virgen del Pilar* is seemingly typical of the Galician tradition and may well be connected to *Gerineldo*. In CARG, material pertaining to *Conde Claros y la infanta* ends with a unique reading, in which the treacherous talebearer insolently contradicts the king: "Si no me lo cree, buen rey, / a los nueves meses lo verá." Our other Galician text, published in CPG, is defective and idiosyncratic, but nonetheless important. It also begins with three verses from *Conde Claros insomne*, continues by representing all the preliminaries of Claros' and the princess' amorous encounter in a single verse (v. 4) usually applied in Castilian versions to the informer and the princess. Then comes the important *capa/brial* verse, as also in Salonika and the Castilian tradition. Again, the informer is identified only as a nondescript *hombre*. His formulistic swearing to tell the king is, to our knowledge, unique in this context (v. 9), as are the letters (vv. 11–12) which are supposed to inform the king of Neluquiña's dishonor. The informer's oath and vv. 13–14 suggest borrowings from *Gerineldo*: "U me duermen con la infanta / u me roban el castillo."[35]

In the Portuguese versions, Claros meets the princess as she is strolling in her garden. Just as in the Moroccan and Castilian forms (as well as in Madeira and Brazil), the amorous dialogue is direct and to the point: "Oh, que lindo corpo de homem . . ." (v. 3). Going to the baths as an evasion survives as in the early text, together with Claros' hunting metaphor. The rose arbor has here been transferred to the talebearer's speech to the king. Just as in the Sephardic versions, it is a page that passes by (rather than a hunter, squire, etc.), but here, as almost everywhere else in the modern tradition (in agreement with the early version), it is Claros (not the princess, as in Morocco, the East, and in some Brazilian texts), who speaks to the discoverer of their secret amours. Claros' offers are well preserved vis-à-vis the early text, as is also the case in the Brazilian versions. A curious development in some Portuguese texts is an attempt to justify the page's rejection of all offers and his stubborn insistence on informing the king: The page too had wanted to sleep with Claralinda (Só queria Claralinda / três noites ao meu mandar [VRP 52, 55]). As in the Eastern Sephardic tradition, the Portuguese texts (like other modern forms, with the exception of Morocco) clearly preserve the page's (hunter's etc.) initial greeting to the king: "Deus vos salve . . ." (v. 17). As also in the Castilian, Madeiran, and Brazilian forms, the Portuguese variants develop the contrast between *oculto* and *prúvico* in the king's response to the informer's scandalous revelation, with their public nature providing an agreeable justification for his summary execution.

The lone Madeiran version is notable, principally, in agreeing with *Media noche* in that, as also in Brazil, the talebearer is a hunter—a reading we have not seen so far in any continental Portuguese text nor in the only Azorian version available to us (Braga, I, 405–406, from São Miguel). In Madeira, as in Brazil, the rose arbor retains it original position in the narrative. Other elements (direct amorous dialogue; Claros makes the offers; greeting to the king; *oculto/prúvico*) agree with the Portuguese variants.

---

35. RT, VI, I.66.9 (p. 102); also I.68.18 (p. 103). These are, however, Leonese, not Galician texts; the Galician versions in RT, VI, do not have the verse (pp. 98–101). On the other hand, the versions edited in CPG, III, nos. 42.I*b*–42.II*j* (2) (pp. 219–228), prove that the verse is a commonplace in the Galician tradition. For the oath in Galician texts of *Gerineldo*, see nos. 42.I*ac(1)g*; 42.II*ab(bis)d*, etc. Concerning both details, see Menéndez Pidal et al., *Cómo vive un romance*, pp. 19, 27–28, 152–156, 215.

These same characteristics appear also in Brazil: direct dialogue, rose arbor preserved; hunter; Claros' offers; greeting to king; *oculto/público*. The reading: "E tambem o Conde Elado / alguma coisa ha de dar" (Santos Neves, p. 51) documents a variant in which it is the princess, rather than Claros, who makes the offers, just as in the Sephardic forms, both Eastern and North African. Notable in the Brazilian texts is the retention of *Media noche*'s graphic description (vv. 48–49) of the love scene: "da cintura para cima . . ." (vv. 18–19).

More than any other branch of the modern tradition, the two Ibizan texts agree with *Media noche* in a number of details: Claros' and Claraniña's initial greeting (mantenga dios a tu alteza . . . [*Media noche*, v. 25] / Déu me la guard, Claranyina . . . [Macabich, v. 10]); Claros' boast about fighting with "cien moros" (*Media noche*, vv. 31–33; Aguiló, vv. 20–21; Macabich, vv. 11–12); Claraniña's reproach about brave words over against excuses in the face of battle (*Media noche*, vv. 35–36; Aguiló, v. 18; Macabich, vv. 13–14); the identity of the informer as a hunter; the detailed imprecations against the king: he should not wear a crown, golden spurs, etc. (*Media noche*, vv. 65–66; Aguiló, vv. 43–45; Macabich, vv. 24–25).[36] But in no sense can these Ibizan texts be considered simply as modern derivatives of the 16th-century printed text. At exactly the same juncture in the narrative as in the Eastern Sephardic, Castilian, and Galician forms, both Ibizan texts include the same verse about the Count spreading his cape and the princess her gown (Aguiló, v. 29; Macabich, v. 15), but, on the other hand, just as in Morocco, it is a lemon tree (*llimonera*) that shades the lovers (Aguiló, v. 28), while, in agreement with Portuguese tradition, Claros meets the princess as she is strolling in her garden (Aguiló, v. 16, Macabich, vv. 8–9). In sum: It is impossible to reconcile such diverse geographical correspondences with any simplistic derivation based on written sources.

Let us summarize, now, how the various other branches of the modern tradition help to elucidate the prehistory of our ballad's Judeo-Spanish forms. Just as in Morocco, several other modern subtraditions have reduced *Media noche*'s amorous dialogue (vv. 28, 30) to its basic essentials:

---

36. Such privations reflect a formulaic complex also present in *Las quejas de Jimena*. See *Yoná*, pp. 95–96, nn. 13–14; Nahón, pp. 31–32, nn. 6–7; *Epic Ballads*, pp. 84–85, n. 10, 93, n. 16. For more on such privations, either self-imposed as an oath or as part of a punishment (exile, etc.), see Gómez Redondo's useful notes in *Jaufré*, pp. 25, 68, n. 73, 86, n. 117, 107, n. 157, 122–123, n. 194, 126 et alibi.

—¡Qué bonito vais, el conde,   para con moros lidiar!
—¡Más bonita sois, princesa,   para contigo folgar!
                                    (Morocco, vv. 4–5)

—¡Qué buen cuerpo tienes, Carlos,   para con moros pelear!
—Mejor lo tengo, señora,   para con damas holgar.
                                    (Castilian, vv. 1–2)

—¡Qué cuerpo llevas, don Carlos,   para con el moro pelear!
—También lo llevo, señora,   para con usted hablar.
                                    (Galicia: CARG, vv. 5–6)

—Oh, que lindo corpo de homem,   p'ra co'os Mouros batalhar!
—Melhor o tem a menina,   p'ra comigo brincar!
                                    (Portugal, vv. 3–4)

—Mal empregado corpinho,   pera com mouros brigar!
—Melhor lo tenho, senhora,   pera comvosco brincar.
                                    (Madeira, vv. 12–13)

—Linda cara tem o conde,   para comigo brincar.
—Mais linda tendes, senhora,   para comigo casar.
                                    (Brazil, vv. 1–2)

Here, perhaps, all the subtraditions could have acted, in parallel fashion, each to reduce independently the old ballad's somewhat ponderous courtly dialogue to the verbal economy so essential to oral traditional style. Yet the close agreement between such widely separated geographic modalities seems too exact to admit of such a possibility. More convincing is the option that the dialogue may already have existed in its present succinct form in some of our ballad's earlier and otherwise undocumented avatars.

Shifting the motif of the bath to the beginning of the narrative could have taken place independently in Morocco (vv. 1–2) and in Argentina (v. 9), but it would seem difficult to attribute to independent development the presence, at exactly the same juncture in the narrative, of the *capa/brial* verse, in three widely separated geographic subtraditions (Salonika, León–Trás-os-Montes–Galicia, Ibiza):

El vyejo echó su kapa;   Blankaninyya su ben biá.
                              (Salonika: *Pizmônîm*, v. 11)

don Carlos tendió la capa,   la niña tendió el verdal.
                              (León: *Voces*, 48.5–6*)*

don Carlos tiende la capa,   la niña se tiende allá.
                              (León: *Voces,* 48.10)

Don Carlos tendió el capote,   la Galanzuca el sobriale.
                              (Tr.-os-Montes: Kundert G4, p. 87)

y Carlos tiende la capa,   Nerluca el verde brial.
                              (Galicia: CPG, III, 44*c*)

y ya tira de capote,   la niña con su sayal.
                              (Galicia: CARG 17*a*)

l'un hi va estendre la capa,   l'altra hi estengué'l brial.
                              (Ibiza: Aguiló, v. 29)

El senyor estengué la capa,   la princesa son brial.
                              (Ibiza: Macabich, v. 15)[37]

Granted the verse is formulaic,[38] but it also embodies an archaic lexical item that would seem to have become meaningless to many singers and usually survives only in a variety of deformed, fossilized forms: *biá, verdal, sobriale*, or, in *Conde Sol, brillar*.[39]

Obviously this is some article of clothing (*sobretodo* > *sobriale* = *el su brial*), but it is hard to see how such a relatively difficult, obscure verse could take on a

---

37. A Leonese version from Trascastro (ay. Peranzanes, p.j. Ponferrada) published in *Voces nuevas* offers further documentation of the verse as part of the princess' confession in *Conde Claros fraile*: "Yo no he tenido que ver con nadie, / na más con don Carlos de Montealvar; // dos fueron a mi querer / y otra fue a mi pesar, // una fue en su capa, / dos en mi verde brial" (48.13.32–34).

38. For details, see the Appendix.

39. Concerning the survival of the medieval *brial* in traditional *romances*, see the Appendix and more data in FLSJ, V, Chap. 12.

vibrant traditional life and migrate independently to five different modern subtraditions of the same ballad. A more viable explanation would place it in some early—and never printed—variant of *Media noche,* from which the modern Eastern Sephardic, Castilian, and Leonese–Trás-os-Montes–Galician ballads derive. Such a conclusion is confirmed by the variegated identity of the informer in the different branches of the modern tradition. As we have seen, *Media noche*'s hunter (*cazador*) is present in many of the subtraditions: Castile, Argentina, Madeira, Brazil, Ibiza. Some Castilian texts, however, prefer to see the informer as a squire (*escudero* [RPM 58]) and at least one clearly reflects the word's semantic impoverishment by elaborating a popular-etymological deformation: "el escuchero parlero" (Díaz-Delfín-Díaz Viana, *Catálogo* [1978], I, 166). Like the Moroccan and Eastern Sephardic versions' *paje, pajecito/pajico, pajezico,* some Portuguese texts attest to a *pagem, pajico,* or *paigezinho* and the *pastor* or *pastorcito,* who figures in some Castilian versions, may also disguise a page.[40] We can, of course, already document the huntsman's 16th-century origins in *Media noche,* but both squires and pages reflect medieval realities that are not likely to have been independently evoked at modern stages of the various geographic subtraditions.[41] Here too, as in the case of the *capa/brial* verse, the readings *escudero* and *paje,* together with *cazador,* would seem to reflect modern survivals of variant readings which already existed at an early stage in our ballad's traditional life. Once again, then, in the case of *Conde Claros y la infanta,* it is impossible to reduce the ballad's development over the centuries to the simplified scheme of a conventional stemma. The Moroccan versions of *Conde Claros fraile* and the ballad's other manifestations in the modern tradition are genetically related to the 16th-century text, *A caza va el emperador,* which embodies *Conde Claros y el emperador* (vv. 1–20) + *Conde Claros fraile* (vv. 21–68) (= *Primav.* 191). This poem was first published in the *Cancionero de romances* (1550) and was reprinted in various later collections (MCR, II, 289*a*). Here is the text according to C1550. Verse correspondences with our Moroccan synthetic text (M) and with Martínez Ruiz's distinctive Alcazarquivir variant (A) are listed in parentheses on the right. In the interest of

---

40. Concerning the words *escudero* and *paje* (or *pagem*), see the Appendix.

41. As Menéndez Pidal has shown, the figure of the *escudero* already represented an archaism in the early 1500s and, in the printed ballad repertoire of the 16th century, was systematically replaced by *caballero* ("Suerte de un arcaísmo léxico," pp. 201–202). Needless to say, given the singular importance of hunting in medieval life, especially in an aristocratizing context, the hunter too is to be considered a characteristically medieval figure.

presenting the 16th-century *Conde Claros fraile* in its original context, we
reproduce here the first 20 verses (representing *Conde Claros y el emperador*),
which have already been studied in Chap. 10:

	A caça va el emperador	a sant Iuan de Montiña	
2	con el yua el conde Claros	por le tener compañia	
	contando le yua contando	el gran menester que tenia	
4	no me lo digays el conde	hasta despues a la venida	
	mis armas tengo empeñadas	por mil marcos de oro y mas	
6	otros tantos deuo en Francia	sobre mi buena verdad	
	llamen me mi camarero	de mi camara real	
8	dad mil marcos de oro al conde	para sus armas quitar	
	dad mil marcos de oro al conde	para mantener verdad	
10	dalde otros tantos al conde	para vestir y calçar	
	dalde otros tantos al conde	para las tablas jugar	
12	dalde otros tantos al conde	para torneos armar	
	dalde otros tantos al conde	para con damas folgar.	
14	Muchas mercedes señor	por esto y por mucho mas	
	a la infanta Clara niña	vos por muger me la dad:	
16	Tarde acordastes el conde	que mandada la tengo ya	
	vos me la dareys señor	acabo que no querays	
18	porque preñada la tengo	de los seys meses o mas.	
	El emperador que esto oyera	tomo dello gran pesar	
20	buelue riendas al cauallo	y torno se a la ciudad	
	mando llamar las parteras	para la infanta mirar	(*M*27)
22	alli hablo la partera	bien vereys lo que dira	
	preñada esta la infanta	de los seys meses o mas	
24	mando la prender su padre	y meter en escuridad	(*M*30)
	el agua hasta la cinta,	porque pudriesse la carne	(*M*31; A9)
26	y perezca la criatura	que no viua de tal padre	
	los caualleros de su casa	se la yuan a mirar	(*M*32; A10)
28	pesa nos de vos señora	quanto nos puede pesar	(*M*33; A11)
	que de oy en quinze dias	el emperador os manda quemar	(*M*34)
30	no me pesa de mi muerte	porque es cosa natural	(*M*40)
	pesa me de la criatura	porque es hijo de buen padre	(*M*41)
32	mas si ay aqui alguno	que aya comido mi pan	(*M*36)
	que me lleuasse vna carta	a don Claros de Montaluan	(*M*37)
34	Alli hablo vn page suyo	tal respuesta le fue a dar	(*M*42)

	escriuilda vos señora	que yo se la yre a lleuar	(*M*43)
36	ya las cartas son escritas	el page las va a lleuar	(*M*49)
	jornada de quinze dias	en ocho la fuera a andar	(*M*44)
38	llegado auia a los palacios	adonde el buen conde esta	(*M*50)
	bien bengays el pagezico	de Francia la natural	
40	que nueuas me traeys	de la infanta como esta?	
	Leed las cartas señor	que en ellas os lo dira	(*M*52)
42	desque la vuo leydo	tal respuesta le fue a dar	(*M*54)
	vno me da que la quemen	vno me da que la maten	(*M*53+)
44	ya se partia el conde	ya se parte ya se va	
	jornada de quinze dias	en ocho la fuera a andar	
46	fuera se a vn monesterio	donde los frayles estan	
	quito se paños de seda	vistio habitos de frayle	(*M*55)
48	fuera se a los palacios	de Carlos el imperante	
	mercedes señor mercedes	querays me las otorgar	
50	que a mi señora la infanta	vos me la dexays confessar	
	ya lo lleuauan al frayle	a la infanta confessar	
52	en lugar de confessarla	de amores le fue a hablar	
	tate tate dixo frayle	que a mi no llegaras	
54	que nunca llego a mi hombre	que fuesse biuo en carne	
	sino solo aquel don Claros	don Claros de Montaluan	(*M*60)
56	que por mis grandes pecados	por el me quieren quemar	
	no doy nada por mi muerte	pues que es cosa natural	
58	mas pesa me de la criatura	porque es hijo de buen padre	
	yase yua el confessor	al emperador hablar,	
60	Mercedes señor mercedes	querays me las otorgar	
	que a mi señora la infanta	sin ningun pecado esta.	
62	Ay hablo el cauallero	que con ella queria casar	
	mentides frayle mentides	que no dezis la verdad	
64	desafian se los dos	al campo van a lidiar	
	al apretar de las cinchas	conociolo el imperante	
66	dixo que el frayle es don Claros	don Claros de Montaluan	
	mato el frayle al cauallero	la infanta librado ha	(*M*61?)
68	en ancas de su cauallo	consigo la fue a lleuar.	

(C1550, pp. 319–321)

Unlike the other Conde Claros ballads in the Sephardic repertoire—
Emperador, Insomne, Infanta—which, in other branches of the *Romancero*, are

usually little known rarities surviving often in fragmentary form and in remote outposts and archaic peripheral areas, *Conde Claros fraile* enjoys a vigorous traditional life in many Hispanic subtraditions. As well as in Morocco, the ballad has continued to be popular in Castilian-speaking regions throughout the Peninsula, in Asturias, in Galicia and Portugal, in the Atlantic islands (Canaries, Azores, Madeira), in Brazil, and in Catalonia. This is, then, a relatively common *romance*, of which a vast number of variant texts have been collected in many different areas. Our Pan-Hispanic survey of *Fraile* does not pretend, in any sense, to be exhaustive. At the Menéndez Pidal Archive alone, there are, without doubt, several hundred unedited texts from various different regions and it is also quite possible that we have passed over a number of versions recently published in little known sources. All the same we are confident that this survey of well over 300 variant texts is sufficient to provide a representative sample of the tradition. In the following chart, we list the published texts of *Conde Claros fraile* we have been able to consult and we identify the various contaminations present in each version:[42]

Castilian areas:

Aliste, pp. 63–66: *Insomne + Infanta + Fraile.*

Alvar, *Romancero viejo*, no. 175a: *Alabanza + Parida (í-a) + Fraile.*

---

42. In addition to the abbreviated designations of Count Claros ballads, we use the following short titles (identified here by the corresponding text-type numbers in CMP): *Alabanza = Aliarda y el alabancioso* (R1); *Apuesta = Apuesta ganada* (T1); *Fuente = Fuente fecundante* (R4–R5); *Parida = Infanta parida* (R3). Sporadic contaminations from other ballads, listed with full titles in the chart, can all also be identified by means of CMP: *Adúltera (ó)* (= *Blancaniña*) (M1); *Flérida* (S2); *Mala hierba* (R6); *Mala suegra* (L4); *Muerte de don Beltrán* (B4); *Silvana* (P1); *Delgadina* (P2). As an indication of the generally coherent—and creative—character of ballad contaminations, it is interesting to note that almost all of these narrative types pertain either to the Seduction of Women (R) or to related sexual themes: the Adulteress (M), Incest (P), Various Amorous Adventures (S). *La apuesta ganada* (T1), hardly known in Sephardic tradition, and *El caballero burlado* (T6) are listed under Tricks and Deceptions (T), but they too could just as well have been classified under R. Only in unique or at least very rare contaminations, such as the Carolingian *Muerte de don Beltrán* (B4) and *Venganza de Montesinos* (B19), *El conde Sol* (I7; I. The Husband's Return), and *La mala suegra* (L4; L. The Unfortunate Wife) do the narrative associations seem not to respond to the thematic logic of the "super-narrative" which multiples singers in the various oral traditions are here seeking to elaborate and recreate. On contamination as a creative process, see Silverman, "La contaminación como arte," and my "Contamination and Reconstruction."

ART, p. 221: *Fraile.*

Atero, *Cádiz*, no. 1: *Alabanza + Parida (í-a) + Fraile.*

Atero, *Cádiz*, no. 2: *Alabanza + Parida (í-a) + Fraile.*

Atero, *Cádiz*, no. 3: *Alabanza + Parida (í-a) + Fraile.*

Calvo, *Segovia*, no. 5.1: *Alabanza . . . + Fraile. . . .*

Calvo, *Segovia*, no. 5.2: *Alabanza + Parida (í-a) + Fraile.*

Casado, no. 2.1-8: *Alabanza + Parida (í-a) + Fraile.*

Casado, no. 3.1: *Fraile* + copla infantil.

Cid, "Garganta la Olla," no. 5: *Alabanza + Parida (í-a) + Fraile.*

CPE, I, 32–33: *Alabanza + Parida (í-a) + Fraile.*

CPE, II, 17–18: *Alabanza + Parida (í-a) + Fraile.*

Díaz-Delfín-Díaz Viana, *Catálogo* (1978), I, 166: *Insomne + Parida (í-a) + Parida (á) + Fraile.*

Díaz Viana, *Rev. de Folklore*, I:2 [1981], 27–29: *Insomne + Parida (í-a) + Parida (á) + Fraile.*

Feito, pp. 124–128: *Alabanza + Parida (á) + Fraile.*

Ferrer-Sanjuán, p. 167: *Alabanza + Parida (á) + Fraile.*

Flores, *Jerte*, pp. 80–81: *Alabanza + Parida (í-a) + Fraile.*

Flores, *Jerte*, pp. 81–83: *Alabanza + Parida (í-a) + Fraile.*

Fonteboa, *Bierzo*, no. 3: *Infanta + Parida (á) + Fraile.*

Fraile Gil, *Madrid*, pp. 46–47: *Alabanza + Parida (í-a) + Fraile.*

Fraile Gil, *Madrid*, pp. 48–49: *Alabanza + Parida (í-a) + Fraile.*

Fraile Gil, *Madrid*, p. 49: *Alabanza [. . .] [+ Parida (í-a) + Fraile?].*

Galindo Ocaña, "Andalucía," pp. 543–544: *Alabanza + Parida (í-a) + Fraile.*

García Matos-Crivillé, *Cáceres*, no. 13: *Alabanza + Parida (í-a) + Fraile.*

García Matos-Crivillé, *Cáceres*, no. 13B: *Alabanza + Parida (í-a) + Fraile.*

García Redondo, *Arroyano*, pp. 51–52: *Alabanza + Parida (í-a) + Fraile.*

Gil, *Rioja*, no. 41: *Fuente fecundante +Parida (í-a) + Fraile.*

Gomarín, *Cántabro*, pp. 43–46: *Infanta + Alabanza + Fraile.*

Gutiérrez Macías, pp. 344–345: *Alabanza + Parida (í-a) + Fraile.*

Iglesias Giraud, *Rebollar*, pp. 83–84: *Alabanza + Fraile.*

Kundert, pp. 87–88 (G4): *Insomne + Infanta + Parida (á) + Fraile.*

Ledesma, pp. 181-182: *Alabanza + Parida (í-a) + Fraile.*

Manzano, *Leonés*, no. 738: [. . .] *Alabanza [. . .] + Fraile.*

Manzano, *Leonés*, no. 739: [. . .] *Parida (á-a) + Fraile.*

Manzano, *Leonés*, no. 740: *Infanta + Parida (á) + Fraile.*

Manzano, *Leonés*, no. 920: *Alabanza + Parida (á) + Fraile.*

Manzano, *Leonés*, no. 921: *Infanta + Parida (á) + Fraile.*

Marazuela, *Segoviano*, pp. 332–333: *Alabanza + Parida (í-a) + Fraile.*

Martínez Ruiz, "Güéjar," pp. 362–363: *Alabanza + Parida (í-a) + Fraile.*

Mendoza Díaz-Maroto, no. 38.2: *Alabanza + Parida (í-a) + Fraile.*

Mendoza Díaz-Maroto, no. 38.5: *Alabanza + Fraile.*

Pérez de Castro, p. 478: *Alabanza + Fraile.*

RGL 19.1: *Insomne + Infanta + Parida (á) + Fraile.*

RGL 19.2: *Insomne + Infanta + Parida (á) + Fraile.*

RGL 19.3: *Infanta + Fraile.*

RGL 19.4: *Insomne + Infanta + Fraile.*

RGL 19.5: *Infanta + Alabanza + Parida (á) + Fraile.*

RGL 19.6: *Insomne + Infanta + Alabanza + Fraile.*

RGL 19.7: *Insomne + Alabanza + Parida (á) + Fraile.*

RGL 19.8: *Insomne + Infanta + Parida (á) + Fraile.*

RGL 19.9: *Infanta + Parida (á) + Fraile.*

RGL 19.10: *Alabanza + Parida (á) + Fraile.*

RGL 19.11: *Delgadina + Parida (á-a) + Fraile.*

RGL 19.12: *Alabanza + Parida (í-a) + Fraile.*

RGL 19.13: *Alabanza + Fraile.*

RGL 19.14: *Insomne + Alabanza + Parida (á) + Fraile.*

RGL 19.15: [. . .] *Infanta + Fraile* [. . .].

RGL 19.16: *Insomne + Infanta + Fraile.*

RGL 19.17: *Insomne + Infanta + Parida (á-(e)) + Fraile.*

RGL 19.18: *Insomne + Infanta + Parida (á) + Fraile.*

RGL 19.19: *Alabanza + Parida (í-a) + Fraile.*

RGL 19.20: *Delgadina + Parida (á) + Fraile.*

RGL 19.21: *Parida (á-a + á) + Fraile.*

RGL 19.22: *Adúltera (ó) + Parida (á) + Fraile.*

RGL 19.24: *Parida (á) + Fraile.*

RGL 19.25: *Alabanza + Parida (á) + Fraile.*

RGL 19.26: *Alabanza + Parida (á) + Fraile + Conde Sol + Fraile.*

RGL 19.27: *Alabanza + Parida (á) + Fraile.*

RGL 19.28: *Alabanza + Fraile.*

RGL 19.29: *Alabanza + Fraile.*

RGL 19.30: *Alabanza + Fraile.*

RPC, pp. 9–10: *Conde Sol + Fraile.*

RPC, pp. 10–11: *Fraile.*

RPC, p. 12: *Insomne + Infanta + Fraile.*

RPE, pp. 9–10: *Alabanza + Fraile.*

RPM 58: *Insomne + Infanta + Fraile.*
RPM 59: *Fraile.*
RPM 60: *Fraile.*
RTCN 30: *Alabanza + Fraile.*
RTR 4: [. . .] *Fraile* [. . .].
Schindler (music), nos. 54 and 232: *Alabanza* [. . .] (incipit) (= *Lizarda*).
Seeger, *Count Claros*, pp. 260–261: *Alabanza + Fraile.*
Voces nuevas 48.1: *Fraile.*
Voces nuevas 48.2: [. . .] *Fraile.*
Voces nuevas 48.3: *Alabanza + Parida (á) + Fraile.*
Voces nuevas 48.4: *Alabanza + Parida (á) + Fraile.*
Voces nuevas 48.5: *Infanta + Parida (á) + Fraile.*
Voces nuevas 48.6: *Insomne + Infanta + Alabanza + Infanta + Parida (á) +*
  Fraile.
Voces nuevas 48.7: *Insomne + Infanta + Parida (á) + Alabanza + Parida (á) +*
  Fraile.
Voces nuevas 48.8: *Alabanza + Parida (á) + Fraile.*
Voces nuevas 48.9: *Alabanza + Parida (á) + Fraile.*
Voces nuevas 48.10: *Insomne + Infanta + Parida (á) + Fraile.*
Voces nuevas 48.11: *Alabanza + Fraile.*
Voces nuevas 48.12: *Infanta + Alabanza + Parida (á) + Fraile.*
Voces nuevas 48.13: *Alabanza + Parida (á) + Fraile.*
Voces nuevas 48.14: *Alabanza + Parida (á) + Fraile.*
Voces nuevas 48.15: *Alabanza + Parida (á) + Fraile.*
Voces nuevas 48.16: *Infanta + Parida (á) + Fraile.*
Voces nuevas 48.17: *Mala suegra + Fraile.*
our text *C*: *Insomne + Infanta + Alabanza + Parida (á) + Fraile.*
our text *D*: *Alabanza + Parida (í-a + á) + Fraile.*
our text *E*: *Alabanza + Parida (í-a) + Fraile.*
our text *F*: *Alabanza + Parida (í-a) + Fraile.*

Asturias:
Cano, no. 1*A*: *Insomne + Alabanza + Parida (á) + Fraile.*
Cano, no. 1*B*: *Insomne + Parida (á) + Fraile.*
Cano, no. 1*C*: *Insomne + Parida (á) + Fraile.*
Cid, "Asturias," no. 8: *Alabanza + Fraile.*
CVR 6: *Alabanza + Parida (á) + Fraile.*
CVR 7: *Alabanza + Parida (á) + Fraile.*
Feito, pp. 124–128: *Alabanza + Parida (á) + Fraile.*

García López, "Degollada," pp. 13–15: *Alabanza + Parida (á) + Fraile.*
Munthe 2: *Alabanza + Parida (í-a) + Fraile.*
NCR 13.2: *Insomne + Infanta + Alabanza + Fraile.*
NCR 14.1–8: *Alabanza + Fraile.*
NCR 14.9: *Insomne + Alabanza + Fraile.*
NCR 14.10–26: *Alabanza + Fraile.*
NCR 14.27: *Fraile.*
NCR 14.28–31: *Alabanza + Fraile.*
Pérez de Castro, p. 478: *Alabanza + Fraile.*
Ruiz Granda, pp. 754–755: *Alabanza + Parida (á-a) + Fraile.*

Canary Islands:
FM 5–9: *Fraile.*
FM 78–80: *Fraile.*
FM 234–237: *Fraile.*
FM 257: *Silvana + Fraile.*
RCan 17: *Fraile* [. . .].
Trapero-Siemens, *Gran Canaria*, I, no. 13: *Fraile.*
Trapero-Siemens, *Gran Canaria*, II, no. 10.1: *Fraile.*
Trapero-Siemens, *Gran Canaria*, II, no. 10.2: *Fraile.*

Galicia:
CARG 17a: *Insomne + Infanta + Fraile.*
CARG 18a: *Mala hierba + Parida (á-a) + Fraile.*
CARG 18b: *Alabanza + Parida (á + á-e) + Fraile.*
CARG 18c: *Alabanza + Parida (á-e) + Fraile.*
CARG 18d: *Alabanza + Parida (á) + Fraile + Cab. burlado.*
CARG 15bis: *Mala hierba (á-a) + Parida (á-a) + Fraile + Venganza de Montesinos.*
CPG, III, 44a: *Alabanza + Fraile.*
CPG, III, 44b: *Alabanza + Parida (á) + Fraile.*
CPG, III, 44c: *Insomne + Infanta + Fraile.*

Portugal:
Anastácio, *Faro*, no. 1: *Apuesta + Alabanza + Fraile.*
Anastácio, *Faro*, no. 2: *Apuesta + Alabanza + Fraile.*
Anastácio, *Faro*, no. 3: *Apuesta + Alabanza + Fraile.*
Athaide Oliveira, pp. 70–73: *Infanta + Alabanza + Infanta + Fraile.*
Athaide Oliveira, pp. 74–76: *Apuesta + Alabanza + Fraile.*
Athaide Oliveira, pp. 327–330: *Infanta + Alabanza + Infanta + Fraile.*

Athaide Oliveira, pp. 330–331: *Infanta + Alabanza + Infanta + Fraile.*

Braga, I, 309–313: *Infanta + Fraile.*

Braga, I, 364–368: *Infanta + Parida (á, á-a) + Fraile + Insomne + Fraile.*

Braga, I, 368–371: *Adúltera (ó) + Alabanza + Fraile.*

Braga, I, 371-373: *Alabanza + Fraile.*

Braga, I, 376–378: *Adúltera (ó) + Alabanza + Fraile + Flérida.*

Braga, I, 382–384: *Fuente (á-a) + Parida (á-a) + Fraile.*

Braga, I, 397–399: *Parida (á-a) + Fraile.*

Buescu, 1st ed., p. 219: *Mala hierba (á-a) + Parida (á-a) + Fraile.*

Buescu, 1st ed., pp. 227–228: *Apuesta + Parida (á-a) + Fraile.*

Coelho, "Rom. Pop.," pp. 64–66: *Infanta + Fraile.*

Coelho, "Rom. Pop.," pp. 66–67: *Infanta + Fraile.*

Consiglieri Pedroso, pp. 460–462: *Apuesta + Parida (á-a) + Fraile.*

Costa Fontes, *Trás-os-Montes*, no. 42: *Infanta + Fraile.*

Costa Fontes, *Trás-os-Montes*, no. 44: *Fraile.*

Costa Fontes, *Trás-os-Montes*, no. 710: *Alabanza + Fraile.*

Costa Fontes, *Trás-os-Montes*, no. 712: *Alabanza + Fraile.*

Costa Fontes, *Trás-os-Montes*, no. 714: *Alabanza + Fraile.*

Costa Fontes, *Trás-os-Montes*, no. 715: *Adúltera (ó)+ Alabanza + Fraile.*

Costa Fontes, *Trás-os-Montes*, no. 773: *Apuesta + Fraile.*

Costa Fontes, *Trás-os-Montes*, no. 775: *Apuesta + Alabanza + Fraile.*

Costa Fontes, *Trás-os-Montes*, no. 776: *Apuesta + Parida (á-a) + Fraile.*

Cova da Beira 12.1: *Apuesta + Parida* (polyas.) *+ Fraile.*

Cova da Beira 12.2: *Apuesta + Parida* (polyas.) *+ Fraile + Parida (á-a) + Fraile.*

Cova da Beira 12.3: *Apuesta + Parida* (polyas.) *+ Fraile.*

Cova da Beira 12.4: *Apuesta + Parida* (polyas.) *+ Fraile.*

Cova da Beira 12.5: *Apuesta +* [. . .] *Parida (á + á-a)* [. . .] *+ Fraile.*

Cova da Beira 12.6: *Apuesta + Parida (á-a + í-a) + Fraile.*

Cova da Beira 12.7: *Apuesta +* [. . .] *Parida* (polyas.) [. . .] *+ Fraile.*

Cova da Beira 12.8: *Alabanza + Fraile.*

Cova da Beira 12.9: *Apuesta + Parida (í-a + á-a) + Fraile.*

Cova da Beira 12.10: *Apuesta + Alabanza + Parida (á)* [. . .] *+ Fraile.*

CTT 10*g*: . . . *Fraile.* . . .

Custódio-Galhoz, no. 1: *Alabanza + Parida (á) + Fraile.*

Delgado, *Subsídio*, 2d ed., II, 160–161: *Adúltera (ó) + Alabanza + Fraile.*

Dias, "Ourique," pp. 46–48: *Apuesta + Alabanza + Fraile.*

Dias Costa, *Murteira*, p. 318: *Apuesta + Alabanza + Fraile.*

Dias Marques, "Loures," no. 4: *Apuesta + Fraile.*

Fs. Thomas, *Velhas Canções*, pp. 29–30: *Fuente (á-a) + Parida (á-a)* + Fraile.

Fs. Thomas, *Velhas Canções*, pp. 36–39: *Apuesta + Alabanza + Fraile.*

Ferré, *Castelo Branco*, no. 4: *Apuesta + Alabanza + Fraile.*

Ferré, *Castelo Branco*, no. 5: *Mala hierba (á-a) + Parida (á-a) + Fraile.*

Ferré, *Castelo Branco*, no. 6: *Apuesta + Fraile + Flérida.*

Ferré, *Guarda*, no. 1: *Apuesta + Alabanza + Fraile.*

Ferré, *Guarda*, no. 2: *Apuesta + Parida (á-a) + Fraile.*

Galhoz 12: *Infanta + Fraile.*

Galhoz 13: *Fraile.*

Galhoz 14: *Fraile + Infanta + Parida (á-a) + Fraile.*

Galhoz 16: *Alabanza + Fraile.*

Galhoz 17: *Alabanza + Fraile.*

Galhoz 19: *Fraile.*

Galhoz 22: *Apuesta + Alabanza + Fraile.*

Galhoz 23: *Apuesta + Parida (á + á-e) + Fraile.*

Galhoz 24: *Apuesta + Alabanza + Fraile.*

Galhoz 25: *Apuesta + Alabanza + Fraile.*

Galhoz 26: *Apuesta + Alabanza + Fraile.*

Galhoz 27: *Mala hierba (á-a) + Parida (á-a) + Fraile.*

Galhoz 28: *Apuesta + Parida (á-a) + Fraile.*

Galhoz 29: *Alabanza + Fraile.*

Galhoz 30: *Apuesta + Alabanza + Fraile.*

Garrett, II, 203–213: *Apuesta + Parida (á) + Fraile.*

Giacometti-Lopes-Graça, no. 123: *Apuesta + Alabanza + Fraile.*

Gomes Pereira, "Novo Supl.," pp. 100–101: *Apuesta + Parida (á) + Fraile.*

Kundert, pp. 86–87 (H3): *Fraile.*

Lima Carneiro, "Monte Córdova," pp. 54–57: *Parida (á-a) + Alabanza + Parida (á + á-a) + Fraile.*

Lima Carneiro, "Monte Córdova," pp. 57–60: *Infanta + Parida (á-a) + Infanta + Parida (á + á-a) + Fraile + Cab. burlado + Don Bueso.*

Lopes Dias, *Beira*, VII, 49–52: *Mala hierba (á-a) + Parida (á-a) + Fraile.*

Ludovice, pp. 147–150: *Apuesta + Parida (á) + Fraile.*

Martins, I, 193–196: *Alabanza + Fraile.*

Martins, II, 34–35: [. . .] *Fraile* [. . .].

Martins, II, 40–41: [. . .] *Fraile* [. . .].

Martins-Ferré, nos. 1–8: *Alabanza + Fraile.*

Martins-Ferré, no. 1: *Alabanza + Fraile.*

Martins-Ferré, no. 2: *Alabanza + Fraile.*

Martins-Ferré, no. 3: *Alabanza + Fraile.*

Martins-Ferré, no. 4: *Alabanza + Fraile.*

Martins-Ferré, no. 5: *Alabanza + Fraile.*

Martins-Ferré, no. 6: *Alabanza + Fraile.*

Martins-Ferré, no. 7: *Alabanza + Fraile.*

Martins-Ferré, no. 8: *Alabanza + Fraile.*

Nunes, "Subsídios," no. 4: *Infanta + Alabanza + Infanta + Fraile.*

Nunes, "Subsídios," no. 5: *Infanta + Alabanza + Parida (á) + Fraile.*

Pinto-Correia, no. 44: *Apuesta + Parida (á, á-a) + Fraile.*

Pires de Lima, *Minhoto*, pp. 87–88: *Parida (á-a) + Fraile.*

Pires da Cruz, *Beira*, no. 147: *Alabanza + Fraile.*

Pires da Cruz, *Beira*, no. 149: *Parida (á-a) + Fraile.*

Pires da Cruz, *Beira*, no. 152: *Apuesta + Alabanza + Fraile.*

Pires da Cruz, *Beira*, no. 153: *Apuesta . . . + Fraile.*

Pires da Cruz, *Beira*, no. 154: *Apuesta + Parida (á-e) + Fraile.*

Pires da Cruz, *Beira*, no. 155: *Apuesta + Parida (á-e) + Fraile.*

Pires da Cruz, *Beira*, no. 157: *Apuesta + Alabanza + Fraile.*

Pires da Cruz, *Beira*, no. 158: *Apuesta + Alabanza + Fraile.*

Reis Dámaso, *Encycl. Rep.*, pp. 203–204: *Infanta + Alabanza + Infanta + Fraile.*

Reis Dámaso, *Encycl. Rep.*, pp. 215–216: *Alabanza + Fraile.*

Tavares, *Illustração*, III, 76: *Alabanza + Fraile.*

Tavares, "Romanceiro," no. 45: *Alabanza + Fraile.*

Tavares, "Romanceiro," no. 60: *Fraile.*

Thomaz Pires, "Lendas," *Tradição*, 3:2, pp. 42–43: *Apuesta + Parida (í-a, á-a) + Fraile + Flérida.*

Thomaz Pires, "Lendas," *Tradição*, 3:2, pp. 43–44: *Alabanza + Fraile.*

Thomaz Pires, "Lendas," *Tradição*, 4:2, p. 176: *Alabanza + Fraile.*

Thomaz Pires, *Lendas*, pp. 187–189: *Alabanza + Fraile.*

Vale Judeu, II, no. 1: *Parida (á-a + á) + Fraile.*

VRP 52: *Infanta + Fraile.*

VRP 53: *Parida (á-a) + Fraile.*

VRP 54: *Infanta + Parida (á-a) + Fraile.*

VRP 55: *Infanta + Fraile + ?.*

VRP 56: *Alabanza + Fraile.*

VRP 57: *Alabanza + Fraile.*

VRP 58: *Alabanza + Fraile.*

VRP 59: *Infanta + Alabanza + Parida (á-a) + Fraile.*

VRP 60: *Alabanza + Fraile.*

VRP 61: *Alabanza + Parida (á) + Fraile.*

VRP 62: *Fraile.*

VRP 63: *Alabanza + Fraile.*

VRP 64: *Alabanza + Fraile.*

VRP 65: *Fraile.*

VRP 66: *Fraile.*

VRP 67: *Fraile.*

VRP 68: *Alabanza + Fraile.*

VRP 69: *Infanta + Parida (á-a) + Fraile.*

VRP 70: *Alabanza + Fraile.*

VRP 71: *Adúltera (ó) + Alabanza + Fraile* [. . .].

VRP 72: *Alabanza + Fraile.*

VRP 73: *Fraile.*

VRP 74: *Alabanza + Fraile* [. . .].

VRP 75: *Apuesta + Alabanza + Fraile.*

VRP 76: *Apuesta + Alabanza + Fraile.*

VRP 77: *Apuesta + Alabanza + Fraile.*

VRP 78: *Apuesta + Alabanza + Fraile.*

VRP 79: *Apuesta + Alabanza + Fraile.*

VRP 80: *Apuesta + Parida (á-a ?) + Fraile + Don Bueso.*

VRP 81: *Apuesta + Parida (á-a) + Fraile.*

VRP 82: *Alabanza + Apuesta + Alabanza + Fraile.*

VRP 83: *Apuesta + Alabanza + Fraile.*

VRP 84: *Apuesta + Alabanza + Fraile.*

VRP 85: *Apuesta + Alabanza + Fraile.*

VRP 86: *Apuesta + Alabanza + Parida (á-a) + Fraile.*

VRP 87: *Apuesta + Alabanza + Fraile.*

VRP 88: *Apuesta + Alabanza + Fraile.*

VRP 89: *Apuesta + Alabanza + Fraile.*

VRP 90: *Apuesta + Fraile.*

VRP 91: *Apuesta + Fraile.*

VRP 283: *Mala hierba (á-a) + Parida (á-a) + Fraile.*

VRP 987: *Apuesta + Parida (á-a) + Fraile.*

Azores:

Braga, *Cantos*, pp. 243–246: *Parida (á-a) + Fraile.*

Braga, *Cantos*, pp. 246–249: *Fraile.*

Cortes-Rodrigues, pp. 226–228 (no. 4): *Parida (á-a) + Fraile + Don Beltrán.*

Costa Fontes, *Califórnia*, no. 1: *Adúltera (ó) + Alabanza + Fraile.*

Costa Fontes, *S. Jorge*, no. 3: *Parida (á) + Fraile.*

Costa Fontes, *S. Jorge*, no. 4: *Parida (á) + Fraile.*

Costa Fontes, *S. Jorge*, no. 5: *Parida (á-a) [. . .] + [. . .] Fraile [. . .].*

Galhoz, no. 34: *Apuesta + Alabanza + Fraile.*

Lemos de Mendonça, pp. 194–196: *Parida (á-a) + Fraile + Don Beltrán.*

Purcell, *Açores*, I, no. 8A: *Apuesta + Alabanza + Fraile.*

Purcell, *Açores*, I, no. 8B: *Apuesta + Alabanza + Fraile.*

Purcell, *Açores*, I, no. 8C: *Parida (é-a, á-a)+ Fraile.*

Purcell, *Ilhas*, no. 8.7: *Apuesta + Adúltera (ó) + Alabanza + Fraile.*

Purcell, *Ilhas*, no. 8.8: *Parida (á-a) + Fraile.*

Purcell, *Ilhas*, no. 8.10: *Parida (á-a) + Fraile.*

Purcell, *Ilhas*, no. 8.11: *[. . .] Fraile [. . .].*

Purcell, *Ilhas*, no. 8.12: *Fraile [. . .].*

Purcell, *Ilhas*, no. 8.13: *Alabanza + Fraile.*

Purcell, *Ilhas*, no. 8.14: *Parida (á-a) + [. . .] Fraile.*

Purcell, *Ilhas*, no. 8.15: *Alabanza + Fraile.*

Purcell, *Ilhas*, no. 8.16: *[. . .] Fraile [. . .].*

Purcell, *Ilhas*, no. 8.17: *Parida (á-a) + Fraile.*

Madeira:

Ferré 40: *Alabanza + Parida (á) + Fraile.*

Ferré 41: *Alabanza + Parida (á) + Fraile.*

Ferré 42: *Alabanza + Parida (á) + Fraile.*

Ferré 43: *Alabanza + Parida (í-a, á) + Fraile.*

Ferré 44: *[. . .] Fraile.*

Ferré 45: *Alabanza + Parida (á) + Fraile.*

Ferré 46: *Alabanza + Parida (á) + Fraile.*

Ferré 47: *Alabanza + Parida (á) + Fraile.*

Ferré 48: *[. . .] Fraile.*

Ferré 49: *Alabanza + Parida (á) + Fraile.*

Ferré 50: *Alabanza + Parida (á) + ?(á-a, í-a) + Fraile.*

Ferré 51: *Alabanza + Parida (á) + Fraile.*

Ferré 52: *Alabanza + Parida (í-a) + [. . .] Fraile.*

Ferré 53: *Alabanza + Parida (á) + [. . .] Fraile.*

Ferré 54: *Apuesta + Alabanza + Fraile.*

Ferré 304: *Parida (á-a) + [. . .] Fraile [. . .].*

Ferré, *Vértice*, no. 2: *Alabanza + Parida (á) + Fraile.*

Galhoz, no. 31: *Apuesta + Parida (á) + Fraile.*

Galhoz, no. 32: *Parida (á-a) + Fraile.*

Purcell, *Ilhas*, no. 8.1: *Alabanza + Parida (á) + Fraile.*

Purcell, *Ilhas*, no. 8.2: *Alabanza + Parida (á) + Fraile.*

Purcell, *Ilhas*, no. 8.3: *Alabanza + Parida (á) + Fraile.*

Purcell, *Ilhas*, no. 8.4: *Alabanza + Parida (á) + Fraile.*

Purcell, *Ilhas*, no. 8.5: *Apuesta + Alabanza + Fraile.*

Purcell, *Ilhas*, no. 8.6: *Apuesta + Alabanza(?) + Parida (á-a) + Fraile.*

Rodrigues de Azevedo, pp. 156–158: *Parida (á-a) + Fraile.*

Xarabanda, nos. 1–2: *Alabanza + Parida (á) + Fraile.*

Brazil:

Bahia 1.5.1: (unrelated prose narrative) + *Parida (á-a) + Fraile.*

Bahia 1.5.3: *Parida (á-a) + Fraile.*

Bahia 1.5.7: *Parida (á-a) + Fraile.*

Bahia 1.5.9: *Parida (á-a) + Fraile.*

Bahia 1.5.10: *Parida (á-a) + Fraile.*

Bahia 1.5.11: *Parida (á-a) + Fraile.*

Calasans B. da Silva, pp. 132–133: *Parida (á-a) + Fraile.*

Calasans B. da Silva, pp. 133–134: *Parida (á-a) + Fraile.*

Galvão, pp. 41–43: *Parida (á-a) + Fraile.*

Gurgel, pp. 44–45: *Parida (á-a) + Fraile.*

Lopes, *Presença*, pp. 148–150: *Apuesta + [?](polyas.) + Parida (á-a) + Fraile.*

Lopes, *Presença*, pp. 152–154: *Parida (á-a) + Fraile.*

Lopes, *Presença*, pp. 155–156: *[?](prose) + Parida (á-a) + Fraile.*

Lopes, *Presença*, pp. 158–159: *Parida (á-a) + Fraile.*

Lopes, *Presença*, pp. 160–162: *Parida (á-a) + Fraile + Infanta.*

Lopes, *Presença*, pp. 162–163: *Parida (á-a) + [. . .] Fraile.*

Magalhães, *Poesia*, pp. 62–63: *[. . .] [Parida (á-a)?] [. . .] + Fraile [. . .].*

Pereira da Costa, pp. 316–319: *Parida (á-a) + Fraile.*

Romero, *Cantos*, pp. 98–99: *Parida (á-a) + Fraile.*

Seeger, *Study*, pp. 289–290: *Parida (á-a) + Fraile.*

Seeger, *Study*, p. 292: *Parida (á-a) + Fraile.*

Silva Lima, "Achegas" (1991), pp. 129–130: *Parida (á-a) + Fraile.*

Silva Lima, *Folclore*, no. 9.1: *Parida (á-a) + Fraile.*

Silva Lima, *Folclore*, no. 9.2: *Parida (á-a) + Fraile.*

Silva Lima, *Folclore*, no. 9.3: *Parida (á-a) + Fraile.*

Silva Lima, *Folclore*, no. 9.4: *Parida (á-a) + Fraile.*

Silva Lima, *Folclore*, no. 9.5: *Parida (á-a)* + *Fraile.*
Silva Lima, *Folclore*, no. 9.6: *Parida (á-a)* + *Fraile.*
Silva Lima, *Folclore*, no. 9.7: *Parida (á-a)* + *Fraile.*
Silva Lima, *Folclore*, no. 9.8: *Parida (á-a)* + *Fraile.*
Silva Lima, *Folclore*, no. 9.9: *Parida (á-a)* + *Fraile.*
Silva Lima, *Folclore*, no. 9.10: *Parida (á-a)* + [. . .] *Fraile.*
Silva Lima, *Folclore*, no. 9.11: [?](prose) + *Parida (á-a)* + *Fraile.*
Silva Lima, *Folclore*, no. 9.12: *Parida (á-a)* + *Fraile.*
Silva Lima, *Folclore*, no. 9.13: *Parida (á-a)* + *Fraile.*
Vilela, no. 2.1: *Parida (á-a)* + *Fraile.*
Vilela, no. 2.2: *Parida (á-a)* + *Fraile.*
Vilela, no. 2.3: *Parida (á-a)* + *Fraile.*
Vilela, no. 2.4: *Parida (á-a)* + *Fraile.*

Catalonia:
AFC 3263: *Parida (á-a)* + *Fraile.*
Aguiló, pp. 315–328: *Fuente (á-a)* + *Parida (á-a)* + *Fraile.*
Briz, IV, 43–44: *Parida (á-a)* + *Fraile.*
Briz, IV, 44–45: [. . .] *Fraile* [. . .].
Ginard Bauçà, IV, 418–419: *Parida (í-a, á-a)* + [. . .] *Fraile.*
Milá 258: *Parida (á-a)* + *Fraile* + *Delgadina* + *Fraile.*
Milá 258*B*: *Parida (á-a)* + *Fraile.*
Milá 258*C*: *Parida (á-a)* + *Fraile.*
Milá 258*D*: *Parida (á-a)* + *Fraile.*
Milá 258*E*: *Parida (á-a)* + *Fraile.*
Milá 258*F*: *Parida (á-a)* + *Fraile.*
Milá 258*G*: *Parida (á-a)* + *Fraile.*
Milá 258*H*: [. . .] *Fraile* [. . .].
Milá 258*K*: [. . .] *Fraile* [. . .].
Milá 258*L*: *Fuente (á-a)* + *Parida (á-a)* + *Fraile.*
Milá 258*M*: [. . .] *Fraile* [. . .].

Valencia:
Rico Beltrán, no. 10: *Alabanza* + *Parida (í-a)* + *Fraile.*

In Castilian areas, though there are numerous other combinations, *Conde Claros fraile* is known in three major forms: (1) a relatively rare autonomous variant, especially characteristic of the Cantabrian coast, in which the ballad is not joined to any other narrative (ART, p. 221; RPC, pp. 10–11; RPM 59–60;

Voces 48.1; compare the Canarian tradition); (2) a type in which *Insomne* is followed by *Infanta* and then by *Fraile* (as in RPM 58; RGL 19.4; our text *C* below), also of northern and northwestern distribution; and (3), *Lisarda*, a vulgate form, by far the most common modality: *Alabanza* + *Parida* (*í-a*) + *Fraile* (our texts *DEF* below), a form which is now known all over the center of the Peninsula (note RGL 19.12, 19), but which, one might hazard a guess, on the analogy of *Gerineldo* and *Conde Sol* (Menéndez Pidal, *Cómo vive*, pp. 275–276), may perhaps have originated in some southern tradition and later have invaded the north.

Only a much more detailed study than we can undertake here—from a primarily Judeo-Spanish perspective—will perhaps offer a solution to this and other pertinent problems. In contrast to most Peninsular Castilian areas, the Canarian tradition is characterized by a monolithic uniformity, as far as contaminations are concerned: *Fraile* occurs alone as an independent narrative in all texts we have seen (except FM 257, which, exceptionally, has *Silvana* as a prologue). In Galicia, our ballad occurs in two basic modalities: either *Alabanza* + *Parida* (*á* + *á-a*) + *Fraile*, as also in some Portuguese texts, or, as in northwestern Castilian-speaking areas, *Insomne* + *Infanta* + *Fraile*. There are also sporadic contaminations from other text-types: *Mala hierba, Caballero burlado* + *Don Bueso*.

Continental Portugal and the Azores offer an enormously complex picture in regard to *Fraile*'s multiple associations with other ballad narratives. A variety of different patterns, best perceived through direct consultaion of our chart, are in evidence. The islands of Madeira, on the other hand, have generally opted to associate *Alabanza* + *Parida* (*á-a*) + *Fraile*, as in Galicia, together with rare instances of *Parida* (*á-a*) + *Fraile* and the occasional use of *La apuesta ganada* as a prologue. In contrast to Portugal and the Azores, Brazil, like the Canaries and Madeira, has decisively chosen a single modality: *Parida* (*á-a*) + *Fraile*. Strangely enough, this same association also predominates at an opposite extreme of our ballad's geographic range, in the distinctive and strikingly archaic Catalan versions, where *Fraile* is also preceded by *Parida* (*á-a*), with occasional instances of *La fuente fecundante* (*á-a*) serving as a prologue to these two associated narratives.

An exhaustive study of *Conde Claros fraile*, in all its many conformations, would necessitate an extensive book-length monograph. Here, basically, the major problem at hand is to see how the other geographic traditions may help to elucidate our Moroccan Sephardic texts in relation to *Fraile*'s 16th-century congener. Before approaching such an undertaking it may be useful to offer here some examples of the various forms in which *Conde Claros fraile* has survived in modern Castilian-speaking areas: (*A*) *Fraile* as an autonomous ballad; (*B*) *Insomne* + *Infanta* + *Fraile*; (*C*) *Insomne* + *Infanta* + *Alabanza* + *Parida* (*á*) + *Fraile*; and the vastly distributed *Lisarda*, the vulgate form, (*DEF*) *Alabanza* + *Parida* (*í-a* + (*á*)) + *Fraile*. Text *A* is taken from N. Alonso Cortes' collection (ART, p. 221); text *B* is from Cossío and Maza Solano (RPM 58); texts *C*, *D*, *E*, and *F* have, until now, remained unedited. Text *A*, as we have said, represents *Fraile* alone; in text *B*, vv. 1–2 are from *Insomne*; 3–16, from *Infanta*; and 17–47 represent *Fraile*; in text *C*, vv. 1–2 are *Insomne*; 3–5*a* are *Infanta*; 5*b*-11 are *Alabanza*; 12–18 are *Parida* (*á*); and 19–47 are *Fraile*; in *D*, vv. 1–6 are *Alabanza*; 7–13 are *Parida* (*í-a* + *á*); and 14–44 are *Fraile*; in *E*, vv. 1–6 represent *Alabanza*; 7–9 are *Parida* (*í-a*); 10–45 are *Fraile*; in *F*, vv. 1–7 belong to *Alabanza*; 8–9 are *Parida* (*í-a*); 10–32 are *Fraile*. Each text is correlated to corresponding verses in the 16th-century version of *Fraile* (*A caza va el emperador*):

A:

	Tres hijas tenía el rey	y todas tres son igual;	
2	todas visten de un vestido,	todas calzan de un calzar,	
	todas van a coger flores	la mañana de San Juan;	
4	se dicen unas a otras:	—La infanta encinta está ya.	
	¡Ay, infantita, infantita,	cómo te van a quemar!	
6	—Que me quemen, que me dejen,	a mí lo mismo me da:	(30)
	Lo siento por lo del cuerpo,	que lo es de sangre real.	(31)
8	¡Quién tuviera un pajecito,	pajecito a mi mandar,	(32)
	para escribir una carta	a don Pedro Montalván!	(33)
10	—Escriba, señora, escriba;	el pajecito aquí está.—	(35)
	Siete vueltas dio al castillo,	con don Pedro vino a dar.	
12	—Noticias traigo, don Pedro,	noticias le vengo a dar,	
	que la infanta doña Clara	hoy la sacan a quemar.	
14	—Si me lo dices de broma,	vámonos a merendar,	
	y si lo dices de veras,	vámonos a caminar.—	
16	—Lea, señor, esta carta	y en ella se lo dirán.—	(41)
	La madre, que ha oído esto,	le ha empezado a gritar:	
18	—Hijo, si al[g]o ties con ella,	a ver si la puedes salvar.—	
	Se ha vestido de fraile	y un caballo fue a montar.	(47)
20	Cuando ha llegado a la villa,	la sacaban a quemar.	
	—Deténganse, cortesanos,	deténgase la hermandad:	

22 Si esa alma no se confiesa,   esa alma se perderá.—
    La arrimó al confesonario,   la ha empezado a confesar,
24 y en medio la confesión,   un beso la quiere dar.   (52)
    —Poco a poco, fraile mío,   poco a poco y no besar.—   (53)
26 La ha cogido por los brazos   y a caballo la fue a montar: (68)
    —Case el rey las otras hijas,   que ésta bien casada está.
28 Tenga por yerno querido   a don Pedro Montalván.
    Las hogueras tenéis hechas,   los perros podéis quemar,
30 y si no quemáis los perros,   a las viejas del lugar.
                                   (Luena, Santander)[43]

B:

    Son las doce de la noche,   los gallos quieren cantar,
2   don Carlos se muere de amores,   que ni puede sosegar.
    Vio salir a Claralinda   de su palacio real;
4   era hermosa como el oro,   por su vestir y calzar.
    Don Carlos, que así la ha visto,   la llevó para el rosal,
6   y la dice una palabras   que eran para enamorar;
    que siete años lleva, siete,   que no la deja de amar.
8   Un pícaro de escudero   por allí pasó a mirar.
    —Por Dios te pido, escudero,   nada de esto tú has de hablar;
10 de lo que aquí hubieres visto,   nada lleves que contar;
    te daré mil doblas de oro,   que en la faldriquera están;
12 la niñita, por su parte,   te dará otro tanto y más.—
    El pícaro de escudero   a nadie quiso escuchar;
14 a la puerta de los reyes,   allá se fue a pasear:
    —No te puedes llamar rey,   ni rey te puedes llamar,
16 que tu hija Claralinda   con Montalvares está.—
    Entran damas, salen damas,   dicen que preñada está.   (23)
18 —Quién tuviera un pajecito,   que haya comido mi pan,   (32)
    que le llevara esta carta   a mi primo Montalván.—   (33)
20 Esto ha oído un pajecito,   que allí cerquita lo está: (34)
    —Escriba, señora, escriba,   que yo se la iré a mandar.—   (35)
22 Por donde le ve la gente,   poquito a poquito va;
    por donde no le ve nadie,   corre como un gavilán.
24 A las puerta[s] de los reyes,   allí se fué a pasear:

43. ART, p. 221. The text is from Luena (p.j. Villacarriedo, Santander).

    —No te puedes llamar rey,   ni rey te puedes llamar,
26 que a tu prima Claralinda   hoy la sacan a quemar.—
    —Si eso es cierto, pajecito,   sube, sube a merendar. [. . .]
28 Malhaya por la doncella,   doncella poco leal,
    que mete el pie en el lodo   y no le sabe sacar.—
30 Fuérase para un convento,   que allí cerquita lo está;   (46)
    dejó la ropa de rey,   la de fraile fue a tomar.   (47)
32 Por muy pronto que ha llegado,   ya la sacan a quemar.
    —Paso a paso, la justicia,   paso a paso, la hermandad,
34 que niña de quince años   no puede ir sin confesar.
    —Ya lo he confesado, padre,   ya lo he confesado, ya.
36 —Si ha confesado la niña,   se querrá reconciliar.—
    La ha agarrado de la mano,   la llevó para el altar:
38 —Confiesa tú aquí, hija mía,   confiesa tú aquí verdad.
    —Ya lo he confesado, padre,   por el paso que he de dar,
40 que sólo he estado una hora   con mi primo Montalván.—   (55)
    Eso que oyó el fraile,   de amores la quiso hablar;   (52)
42 ella con su blanca mano,   un bofetón le fue a dar:
    —No me toque ningún hombre,   ninguno me ha de tocar;
44 donde Carlos puso su honra   nadie tenga más que hablar.—
    La ha agarrado de la mano,   pa el caballo la llevar: (68)
46 —Los perros de la ribera   pueden sacar a quemar;
    el rey que case las otras,   que ésta bien casada va.

                          (Cañeda, Santander)[44]

C:

    [. . .] Don Carlos por amores   no podía sosegar. [. . .]
2 Apareja el caballo   y empieza a caminar. [. . .]
    —Buen cuerpo tienes, don Carlos,   para con moros pelear.

---

44. RPM 58; collected in Cañeda (ay. Enmedio, p.j. Reinosa, Santander). Worthy of note is the expression "a la puerta de los reyes" (vv. 14*a*, 24*a*), which, in O. Sp. and, independently, in Eastern Judeo-Spanish, could mean 'at the king's court', on the model of Ar. *bāb al-malik* (or T. *babı âli*, i.e. the Sublime Porte). It seems unlikely, but not impossible, that, in this ballad from Santander, any vestige of the O.Sp. semantic calque has survived. Note also text *C*, v. 34. See my article with James T. Monroe (*Sef*, 58 [1998]). For the expression used in v. 29, compare the *Corbacho*: "O quiçá . . . me sacara tantos pollos e pollas con que pudiera tanto multiplicar, que fuera causa de me sacar el pie del lodo" (ed. González Muela, p. 124 [2d part., Chap. I; ed. Gerli, p. 149]); more examples: Fernández Gómez, *Vocabulario de Cervantes*, p. 796*b*.

4 —Oh, mejor tú, Galanzuca,   para con [vosté gozar].
  —Eres, el conde, muy nuevo;   luego te habías de alabar.
6 —Mal fuegos quemen mis carnes,   cochillos d'un mal cortar,
  si con damas que yo duermo   las habían d'envergonzar.—
8 Desotro día de mañana,   don Carlos a los juegos va:
  —He dormido esta noche con una chica   que en el mundo no la hay tal.
10 Los ojos de la su cara   parecen el fino cristal;
  los dientes de la su boca   parecen la menuda sal.
12 —O es mi hija Galanzuca,   o en el mundo no hay verdad.—
  Fuérase el rey para casa,   sus hijas mandó a llamar:
14 —¿Cuál de vosotras, mis hijas,   cuál es la que encinta está?—
  Miran unas para otras,   todas dicen que no están,
16 si no fue la Galanzuca,   que se soltara a llorar.
  —Altos, altos, mis criados,   de los que suelgo llamar.
18 Veis a apañar la leña;   mañana se va quemar.
  —¡Quién tuviera un pajarcillo,   de los que suelgo mandar!   (32)
20 Para escribir una carta   a Carlos de Montalbar.   (33)
  Tú, si lo hallas en misa,   por Dios, déjalo acabar.
22 Tú, si lo hallas en el baile,   no lo dejes más bailar.
  Tú, si lo hallas en el juego,   no lo dejes más jugar.—
24 Cuando el pajarcillo llega,   don Carlos de misa sal.
  —Nuevas te traigo, don Carlos,   nuevas de muy gran pesar:
26 Qu'a tu esposa Galanzuca   ya la iban a quemar.
  —Se la queman, que la quemen,   que la dejen de quemar.   (43)
28 Mujeres hay por el mundo,   para mí no han de faltar.—
  Oyéralo la su madre,   d'altas salas donde está:
30 —Oh, malhaya tales hijos   que tales respuestas dan.
  —Usted, como madre mía,   un consejo m'has de dar.
32 —Sí te lo doy, mi hijo,   si tú te lo quieres tomar:
  Quítate el vesti'de conde;   póntelo de capillán.
34 A las puertas,   puertas de no sé qué [. . .].—
  Cuando don Carlos llegaba,   ya la sacan a catar.
36 —Altos, altos, los señores,   justicias d'este lugar,
  que la niña es muy nueva   y va muy mal sin confesar.
38 —Confesada vai, señor,   pero va sin comulgar.
  —Un pecado qu'ella tiene,   a mí me l'ha de confesar.—
40 La cogiera de la mano,   la llevó pa'l pie del altar:
  —¿Has dormido con alguno,   de mentira o de verdad?

42 —Ni he dormido con ninguno,   de mentira o de verdad,   (54)
si no una noche u dos   con Carlos de Montealbar.—   (55)
44 La montara en el caballo,   encomienza a caminar: (68)
—Si quieren venir a la boda,   yo ya los vengo a brindar.
46 Siete vacas tengo muertas,   otras tantas por matar.
Hasta el rabo mi caballo   vengan todos a besar.
                (Rábano de Sanabria, Zamora)[45]

D:

Se paseaba Lisarda   por los altos corredores,
2 con un vestido de seda,   que le arrastra los galones.
Pasó por allí un señor;   l'ha pretendido en amores.
4 —No, señor, que soy mu chica;   no señor, que soy muy joven.—
Al otro día siguiente,   por la corte se decía:
6 —He dormido con una dama,   la flor de la maravilla.—
Su padre que lo escuchaba: —¿Si será mi Lisardilla?
8 Y si acaso no lo fuese,   será la reina en Castilla.
Y si acaso lo fuese,   al punto la quemaría.
10 Ven acá, mis tres hijitas,   que vos quiero preguntar:
¿Quién ha dormido esta noche   con el conde Montealvar?—
12 La una lo trasmiraba;   ninguna decía nada
y la pobre de Lisarda   al punto s'echó a llorar.
14 El castigo que le dio,   no se lo dé Dios a nadie:
Fue meterla en un pozo,   para que pudran sus carnes.   (25)
16 Todos los días iba a verla   primos y tíos carnales.   (27)
Su hermano, qu'iba en el medio,   que Rondales se llamaba:
18 —Hermano, si eres mi hermano,   sácame d'este albedrío.
—Mañana te sacará,   al pueblo más inmediato;
20 al pueblo más inmediato,   te quiere padre quemar.—   (29)
—Si me queman, que me abrasen,   a mí no me importa nada.   (30)
22 Lo que importa es lo que tengo,   que es de mi sangre leal.   (31)
Si bajara un pajarito,   d'éso que pic64 el pan,   (32)
24 yo mandaría una carta   al conde de Montealvar.—   (33)
Ha bajado un pajarito,   d'éso que pican el pan: (34)
26 —Traiga, señora, la carta;   yo se la ir'a llevar.   (35)

45. Version from Rábano de Sanabria (ay. San Justo, p.j. Puebla de Sanabria, Zamora), recited by Sofía Anta, 67 years, collected by S. G. A., July 19, 1980. For more data, see the Appendix.

—Si lo coges merendando,   no lo dejes merendar.
28 Si lo coges paseando,   no lo dejes pasear.
    Y si lo coges dormiendo,   no lo dejes sosegar.
30 —¿Qué me traes, pajarito?   —La carta se lo dirá: (40*a*/41*b*)
    Que la pobre de Lisarda   mañana la quemarán.
32 —Si la queman, que la abrasen,   a mí lo mismo me da.   (43)
    Lo que importa es lo que tiene,   qu'es de mi sangre leal.—
34 H'aparejado el caballo   lo de atrás para'lante.
    Se vistió de padre cura   y l'ha salido a buscar.   (47)
36 Al llegar a la ciudá,   ya la sacan a quemar.
    —Se detenga la justicia   y también la autoridad.
38 Que Lisarda es muy joven   y la quiero confesar.—
    L'ha montado en el caballo;   l'ha'mpezado a preguntar:
40 —Dime, niña, tus pecados,   que los quiero saber ya.
    —El primer amor que tuve   fue el conde de Montealbá.   (55)
42 La gente cuenta muy bueno;   conmigo lo hizo muy mal.
    —Poco mal lo habrá hecho,   cuando en brazo de él está.
44 Y al pueblo más inmediato   nos irémos a casá.
            (Casillas de Coria, Cáceres)[46]

E:

    Se paseaba Criselda   por sus altos corredores,
2 con sus vestidos de seda,   que le tapa sus tacones.
    El conde de Montealvar   l'ha requerido de amores.
4 —No conde, que soy muy niña   y lo dirás en la corte.—
    Al otro día de mañana,   en la corte se decía:
6 —Yo dormí con una dama,   la flor de la maravilla.—
    El padre, que la escuchaba: —¿Si será mi Criseldilla?
8 Y si acaso no lo fuera,   sería la reina en Castilla.
    Y si acaso ella lo fuera,   al punto la quemaría.
10 El castigo que le diera,   no se lo dé Dios a nadie.
    Es arrojarla'n un pozo,   que se le pudran sus carnes.   (25)
12 Al otro día de mañana,   pasan tres primos carnales.   (27)
    El del medio era su hermano,   que le llaman Rondanes:
14 —Cállate, lengua infernal,   lengua de malas bondades.
    Que mañana es otro día   y ya saldrán a quemarte.   (29)

---

46. Version from Casillas de Coria (p.j. Coria, Cáceres), sung by María Gómez, 28 years, collected by S. G. A., in Madrid, June 25, 1972.

16	—Si me queman, que me quemen; a mí tanto se me da.	(30)
	Lo que siento es lo que siento; es la mi sangre real.	(31)
18	Si tuviera un pajarito, d'esos que comen el pan,	(32)
	yo le mandaría una carta al conde de Montealvar.	(33)
20	Y ha mirado para el cielo; ha visto un ángel bajar.	(34)
	—Dame la carta, Criselda, que yo se la iré a llevar.	(35)
22	—Si lo coges paseando, no lo dejes pasear.	
	Y si lo coges cenando, no le dejes y'acabar.—	
24	Cuando llegó el pajarito, en gran función están.	
	—¿Cuál de acustos señores es conde de Montealvar?	
26	—¿Qué me quieres, pajarito, que me vienes a buscar?	(40)
	—Yo, conde, no quiero nada; mi carta se lo dirá.	(41)
28	Que a la señora Criselda ya la sacan a quemar.	
	—Si la queman, que la quemen; a mí tanto se me da.	(43)
30	Lo que siento es la mi sangre, que se va por bautizar.—	
	Ha'parejado el caballo, lo de alante par'atrás.	
32	Y ha cogido los manteos; vestido de cura va.	(47)
	Y a la entrada de aquel pueblo, ya la sacan a quemar.	
34	Mandó detener la gente, la vara de la humildad.	
	—Esa niña es muy bonita y se querrá confesar.	
36	Si me la dieran sus padres, yo la supiera estimar.	
	—Cójala usted, padre cura, que en brazos de usted está.—	
38	L'ha montado en el caballo; le ha empezado a preguntar:	
	—Dime tus pecados, niña; no te quieras condeñar.	
40	—Yo se lo diré a usted, padre; empiéceme a preguntar.	
	El primer amor que tuve fue el conde de Montealvar.	(55)
42	Dicen qu'es gran caballero; conmigo lo ha hecho muy mal.	
	—No lo habrá hecho tan mal, niña, cuando en brazos de él vas.	
44	En el pueblo más cercano, nos iremos a casar.—	
	Y aquí se ha'cabado el corro de Criselda y Montealvar.	
	(Arroyo de la Luz, Cáceres)[47]	

F:

Lizarda se paseaba,   por sus lindos corredores,
2   con sus trajes de diario,   que l'arrastran lq galones
Por allí viene don Luce,   reduciéndote d'amores:

---

47. Version from Arroyo de la Luz (p.j. Cáceres, Cáceres), sung by Domitila Parra Molano, 40 years (±), collected by S. G. A., June 22, 1963.

4 —¡Quién te pillara, Izarda,   entre las dię a las doce!
   —Tú píllame cuando quieras,   que no s'enter'en las cortes.—
6 Y al otro día siguiente,   las cortes ya lo sabían,
   qu'el Niño de Montalbán,   con una niña dormía.
8 Y el pá que: —Si eso fuese mentira,   raina del mundo l'haría,
   y si eso fuese verdá,   de su sangre bebería.—
10 Y el padre l'ha'cha'o'n castigo,   qu'eso no la hace naiden,
   de meterla en un pozo,   que se le pudran sų carnes.   (24–25)
12 Dǫ hermanas, que tenía,   sų ojǫ eran dǫ mares.
   Todǫ lǫ días bajaban   a los pozǫ a rezalde: (26)
14 —Lizarda tiene la culpa   de que padre encomodarte.
   Mañana te sacarán   a lǫ campǫ a quemarte.   (29)
16 —Si vinera un pajarito,   mandado por Dios yamá,   (32)
   y le yevaría'sta carta   y al conde de Montalbán.—   (33)
18 Ya lo se presenta el pajarito,   mandado por Dios yamá.   (34)
   —Anda y yévale'sta carta   y al conde de Montalbán.
20 Si lo pillas de paseo,   tú hará por esperar,
   y si lo pillą comiendo,   de seguida se la dan.
22 —Y una carta de Lisarda,   que la sacan a quemá.
   —Si la quemen, que la quemen,   a mí nada me se dan.   (43)
24 Lo que siento qu'ę mi sangre,   dentro de su cuerpo van.—
   Y al otro día siguiente,   ya la sacan a quemá.
26 Y él s'ha vestido d'obispo,   lą cortę arriba van: (47)
   —Se detenga la justicia   y toda la artoridá:
28 Que Isarda ę muy niña   y yo la quiero confesá:
   ¿Cuántǫ besos tú l'has dado   y a los chicos de tu edad?
30 —Yo besǫ ná mą́ qu'a uno   y al conde de Montarbán.   (55)
   —Se detenga la justicia   y toda la artoridá:
32 Y anda y dile a su padre,   que Isarda ę mía ya.

                              (Zagra, Granada)[48]

As in the study of any aspect of the *Romancero*, it is necessary to take into
account all branches of the tradition, as exemplified in a substantial number—if

---

48. Version from Zagra (p.j. Loja, Granada), sung by Carmen Cervera, 78 years,
collected by S. G. A. and José Manuel Pedrosa, in Madrid (Vallecas), December 9, 1992.
Variants and observations: v. 5*b*+ Lą cortę eran de su padre; 8*a* Y el pá que: 'y el padre
[dice] que'; 13*a* bajaban *pronounced* majaman; 14*b* *sic*; 15*a* sacarán *pronounced* pacarán;
21*b*, 23*b*, 24*b*, 26*b* dan, van = *idiosyncratic nasalization*; 30*b*+ Y era él; 32*b*+ Ya'stá.

not, ideally, in fact, impossibly, an exhaustive corpus—of texts.[49] As we shall now see, in the case of *Conde Claros fraile*, the other subtraditions are indispensable in clarifying the relationship of the Moroccan versions to their 16th-century congener. Prefixed by a twenty-verse text of *Conde Claros y el emperador* (*A caza va el emperador*), the only early form of *Fraile* that has been preserved, gives us no idea of what the ballad's initial verses may have been when (and if) it was sung as an autonomous narrative in the early tradition. A minority of the Moroccan texts—seven in all—attest to the following line, as the first verse pertaining to *Fraile* in the combined ballad, *Infanta + Fraile*: "Dueñas entran, dueñas salen: / Todas dicen qu'es verdad" (synthetic v. 27). The autonomous Canarian versions, as well as one of the Cossío-Maza Cantabrian texts, prefixed by *Insomne + Infanta* (RPM 58 = text *B* above), show us beyond doubt that this rare Moroccan verse does indeed represent an authentic incipit of *Conde Claros fraile* and that, given the wide geographic separation of the various testimonies, such a beginning must be of very considerable antiquity:

> ¡Qué malita está Sidrana,   de un mal que le suele dar!
> Entran dueñas, salen dueñas,   que la van a visitar,
> y entre tantas le murmuran: —La infanta ocupada está.
>
> (FM 6.1-3)

> Entran damas, salen damas,   que la van a visitar,
> y entre las damas murmuran: —¡Princesa ocupada está!
>
> (FM 9.1-2)

> Entran dueñas, salen dueñas,   y la van a visitar;
> entran las dueñas, mormuran: —La Ausente ocupada está.
>
> (FM 236.1-2)

> . . . Entran damas, salen damas,   dicen que preñada está.
>
> (RPM 58.17)[50]

---

49. On the dangers of reaching general conclusions based on a limited corpus, see the Appendix.

50. For other Canarian texts, see also FM 78–80 and 237. FM 234 and 235 conflate the *dueñas'* visit with the later visit of "caualleros de su casa" (*A caza*, v. 27; Moroccan synth. v. 32: "Ya la vesitan los duques, / los duques y los alcaides"). Autonomous Castilian versions have a rather different beginning, reminiscent of *El sueño de doña Alda*: "Las hijas del rey Chiquito / todas andan a un igual, // todas visten un vestir, / todas calzan un calzar, // todas dicen a una voz: / La infanta preñada está" (RPM 59.1–3). See

In the early text and in the Castilian and Canarian versions, the truth about the *infanta*'s affair with Claros is revealed in very direct terms ("preñada está la infanta / de los seis meses o más" [*A caza*, v. 23]), while in the Moroccan tradition, the princess' condition is understood only implicitly: ". . . todas dicen qu'es verdad," thus exemplifying, perhaps, the Sephardic tendency to attenuate certain sexual references.[51] In the Moroccan ballad, possibly under the influence of some memory of *Conde Claros preso*, a minority of versions (four in all) have both the count and the princess imprisoned, or, as in the lone verse we have chosen for our synthetic text, in the interest of coherence, the count escapes and only the princess is jailed (v. 29). There is, of course, no such imprisonment in *A caza* and, to our knowledge, except in Morocco, the detail occurs nowhere else in the modern tradition—if we discount a probably coincidental threat against Dom Carlos in one of the Brazilian versions (Lopes, *Presença*, pp. 160–161). The *infanta*'s imprisonment in most Moroccan texts, though bad enough, has been attenuated vis-à-vis the early version: "el agua hasta las rodillas, / porque diga la verdad" (synth. v. 31). Only Martínez Ruiz's Alcazarquivir text echoes *A caza*'s cruel reading: "la awua yegó a la sinta / porque la pudran su carne" (MRuiz 36.9), while the dreadful following verse about the child's death in *A caza* (v. 26) has been universally shunned. In the Moroccan tradition, such an omission may indeed reflect the well known Sephardic trend toward attenuating cruelties,[52] but the brutal verse has, in fact, survived nowhere in the modern tradition, at least in the texts we have seen. The original reading of *A caza*'s v. 25 has, on the other hand, been preserved in various Peninsular versions, particularly in Extremadura, Andalucía, and Catalonia:

> Que la metan en un pozo   y se la pudran sus carnes.
> (Cid, "Garganta," no. 5)

> La ha metidito en un pozo,   pa que ce pudran zuh cahneh.
> (Alvar, *R. viejo*, no. 175a)

> Fa agafar la seva filla   i a la presó l'ha posada,
> amb aigua fins a mig cos   por mes aviat matar-la.
> (AFC 3263)

---

also RPC, pp. 10–11, and ART, p. 221 (= text *A* above). On *Doña Alda*, see FLSJ, III, Chap. 9.

51. See *Tres calas*, p. 108, n. 42, and the references provided there.

52. See *Tres calas*, p. 124, n. 15; 134, n. 26.

—Tancaula als sols de la torre,   de les torres la mes alta;
aygua fins a la cintura,   perque's pudresca dins l'aygua . . .
De la cintura en amunt,   de ferros l'han carregada;
de la cintura en avall,   la cubrexen d'aygua clara.

(Aguiló, p. 320)[53]

Again, *A caza*'s vv. 27–28 are present in the Moroccan tradition only in Alcazarquivir: "Ya la vesitan los duques, / los duques y los alcaides: // —Nos mansiyamos de ti, Alda, / de tu cara y de tus males" (MRuiz 36.10–11; = synth. vv. 32–33). The survival of these verses exemplifies, once again, the importance of the Alcazarquivir texts as representatives of an at least partially autonomous subtradition vis-à-vis those of other Moroccan communities. Verses concerning this same visit are present in Asturian, Castilian, Canarian, Azorian, and Catalan texts, although the identity of the visitors tends to vary between the original *caballeros* in Asturias and Catalonia and diverse relatives in the other traditions:

Fueron tres primos a verla,   todos tres primos carnales.
(Cid, "Garganta," no. 5)

Lo supo un primito hermano,   que la vino a visitar.
(FM 235)

Caballeros de su casa   la diban a visitar.
(CVR 7)

Todos os primos e primas   lá a foram visitar.
(Braga, *Cantos*, p. 244)

Molts nobles la van a veure,   molts nobles i moltes damas.
(AFC 3263)

Cavallers la'n van a veure,   cavallers y nobles dames.
(Aguiló, p. 320)[54]

---

53. See also Avenç, III, 35; Milá 258, 258*BEH*, and our texts *D* and *E* above. For more on such punishments in ballads, epics, and other traditional narratives, see FLSJ, III, 76–77, n. 15; 250–255, n. 15 (*Guarinos*); also the Appendix.

54. For additional readings, see the Appendix.

To judge by the presence of *caballeros*, not only in *A caza* (v. 27), but in such lateral areas as Asturias, Catalonia, and Alcazarquivir (*duques*), the relatives as visitors would seem, perhaps, to be a secondary development.

The additional expressions of regret, as in *A caza* ("pesa nos de vos señora / quanto nos puede pesar" [v. 28]) and in the Alcazarquivir variant, survive only exceptionally. In most cases, the visitors either say nothing or immediately announce that the princess is to be burned. We know of only two instances, from the Canaries and the Azores, in which, as in Morocco, the regrets have survived. In the Canarian version, the text has been confused and the verse in question has been assigned to the *infanta*:

> Un primito hermano,   que la viene a visitar:
> —Mucho pésame, mal primo,   y mucho me ha de pesar.
> —De eso no se le dé, prima,   bien sé que le ha de pagar.
> (FM 237)

> Seu tio a veiu vêr,   seu primo a visitar:
> —Muito me pésa, prima,   muito me pésa o seu mal.
> (Braga, *Cantos*, p. 246)

Our Moroccan v. 35 (A eso de la medianoche, / princesa los gritos da) is a filler, borrowed originally from *Disfrazada de mujer* ([polyas.]: CMP T1), but here probably transferred from *Conde Claros y la infanta*, where a similar contaminated verse has already been used (synth. v. 13). An alternative possibility is the Moroccan verse: "Como eso oyó la princesa / asentárase a llorar" (synth. v. 35, vars.). Neither verse has any counterpart in *A caza*. Most non-Sephardic forms either go on to have the princess express her courageous sentiments of not caring about her own death, but only about her unborn child (= *A caza*, vv. 30–31) or she immediately wishes for a messenger to communicate with Claros (*A caza*, vv. 32–33). In the Moroccan tradition, the various components of the *infanta*'s speech have been rearranged: Vv. 36–41 correspond to *A caza*'s vv. 32–33 (about the messenger) and 30–31 ("no me pesa," etc.), while Moroccan v. 38 is an innovative elaboration and v. 39 a repetition of v. 34:

> 38   Que venga pronto y aína,   de prisa y sin más tardar:
> 39   Que de hoy en quince días,   ya me sacan a quemar.

Most subtraditions have had trouble with the archaic and courtly figure of the page, though, just as in Morocco (v. 42), the original reading has survived in many different regions, notably in lateral areas (La Montaña, Tenerife, Asturias, Galicia, the Beiras, Madeira, Catalonia):

Ahi se alḥadró un pajecito,   que a su mesa comió pan . . .
                                    (Morocco, v. 42)

—Escriba, señora, escriba;   el pajecito aquí está . . .
                                    (ART, p. 221)

—Llámame aquel pajecillo,   que a mi mesa come pan . . .
                                    (FM 5, 234)

Allí hablara un pajecico;   tal respuesta la fue a dar . . .
                                    (CVR 7)

Por allí viene un paje,   que de Carlos comía el pan . . .
                                    (CPG, III, no. 44*b*)

—Ai, quem me dera un pagico,   que me fôra bem mandado . . .
                                    (Braga, I, 366)

—Haverá por'hi um pagem,   o qual queira do meu pão . . .?
                                    (Braga, I, 369)

—Quem me dera um paigete,   um paigete com vagar . . .
                                    (VRP 69)

—Nã havera por aí um pagem,   que meu pão queira ganhar…?—
Apareceu um pagenzito,   que o recado ia levar . . .
                                    (Purcell, *Ilhas* [Madeira], no. 8.6)

Mentre está dient axò,   un petit vaylet entrava;
vol esser patge del Rey   y fa tot lo que li manan . . .
                                    (Aguiló, p. 321)

—Qui trovés un pagecito, que la mar anés volando . . .
(Milá 258*D*)[55]

More frequent, however, is the archaizing page's popular-etymological transformation into a bird—helped no doubt by the traditional topos of the bird messenger: *pajarito* (CPE, I, 32; Milá 258); *passarico* (Costa Fontes, *Trás-os-Montes*, no. 42); *passarinho* (VRP 55; Vilela 2.4); *pasarito* (Milá 258*B*).[56] Such forms will in their turn generate other readings, such as *paloma* (FM 80); *pombinho* (Braga, *Cantos*, p. 247); *ocellet* (AFC 3263). Another frequent alternative is a thaumaturgical angel: "No bahara un anhelito / de ezoh que zuelen bahá . . ." (Alvar 175*a*); "Um anjo do ceu falou: / —Escreve, que a vou levar . . ." (Athaide Olivera, pp. 71, 75); "Deceu um anjinho do céu, / um anjinho muito leal" (Silva Lima 9.9); "Devalla un ángel del cielo, / con la corona y la palma" (Milá 258*E*).[57] Sometimes, as a derivative of the relatives who visit the princess, it is a cousin or a brother who takes the message[58] or, again, the page is simply modernized to a servant or even servants (*criado(s)*; *creado*).[59] The weakening of the page reading has further led to a variety of additional alternatives, particularly in the Portuguese and Brazilian traditions: *portador* (Braga, I, 311; Purcell, *Ilhas*, no. 8.10); *mensageiro* (Silva Lima 9.6); *peixe*(!) (Galhoz 23); *menino* (Braga, I, 385; Galhoz 26; Reis Dámaso, p. 215; VRP 88; Lopes, p. 153); *velhinha* (Galhoz 31; Ferré 41, 43, 46, 47, 49–51; Purcell, *Ilhas*,

---

55. For other instances of the page, see, among many other examples, RGL 19.1, 8, 16; RPC, pp. 9, 11; RPM 58; *Voces nuevas* 48.5; CARG 18*b* (*paxín*); Braga, I, 366, 369 (*pagico*); Consiglieri Pedroso, p. 461 (*pagemzito*); VRP 52 (*pagem*). Compare also the analogous role of the "little foot-page" in Scottish *Lady Maisry* (Child 65).

56. On the bird messenger, see FLSJ, III, 272–273, n. 52. For more data, see the Appendix.

57. Other instances of the angel (among many that could be cited): Braga, I, 391; Reis Dámaso, p. 204; Thomaz Pires, pp. 43, 188; VRP 52, 90, 91; Braga, *Cantos*, p. 246; Pereira da Costa, p. 317. In another Brazilian text, there is no specific mention of the angel, but the offer to take the message is expressed by "uma voz / lá debaixo de um altar" (Silva Lima, no. 9.8).

58. For example, *primo*: FM 78, 79, 235–237; Trapero, no. 13; Costa Fontes, *Trás-os-Montes*, nos. 44, 712; Galhoz 16–17 etc.; Martins, I, 194–195; VRP 65; Braga, *Cantos*, p. 244; *irmão*: Costa Fontes, *Trás-os-Montes*, nos. 710, 714, 715, 773, 775, 776; Ferré, *Guarda*, no. 1; Kundert H3; Tavares, no. 45; VRP 60, 72; Purcell, *Ilhas*, nos. 8.13, 15.

59. For examples of the servant, see FM 7; Athaide Oliveira, p. 75; Braga, I, 376, 383; Galhoz 29 (*criados*), 30; Lopes, p. 159; Romero, p. 98; Silva Lima, no. 9.1. In Asturias, the messenger sometimes is a shepherd (*pastorcillo*: NCR 14.23–24).

nos. 8.1-3); *rapazinho* (but later *pagem*) (Lopes, p. 153); *negro* (Silva Lima 9.13); *moleque* (Lopes, p. 161); *cachorro* (Lopes, p. 157); *demônio* (Seeger, p. 289); *correu* (Milá 258C); *passatjant* (Avenç, III, 36).[60] What seems certain is that the page, attested in *A caza* (v. 34) and in modern archaic survivals, is the only reading we can, at this point, confidently attribute to the ballad's early form, while the bird (etc.) is certainly a late development, at least in the Hispanic tradition.

The page's answer to the *infanta*'s plea has been expanded in the Moroccan tradition, with what is third person narrative in *A caza* (v. 37: "jornada de quinze dias . . ."), becoming part of the page's offer and generating two additional verses (vv. 45–46: "camino de ocho . . ., camino de cuatro . . .," etc.). The text is then further amplified with the ancient formula: "el día por los xarales, / la noche por el lunar" (v. 47). Most of the other subtraditions have tended to conserve the miraculously rapid journey at this point and, just as in Morocco, the motif, rather than being in narration, often forms part of the page's offer: "Siete leguas de camino / en un'hora los (*sic*) he de andar" (FM 5, 6); "Fosse viagem de dias, / eu á noit' hei de voltar" (Rodrigues de Azevedo, p. 157); "Viagem de quinze dias / vos farei em um jantar" (Pereira da Costa, p. 318). Only one Castilian text we have seen, like some of the Moroccan versions (v. 47), reinforces the journey's urgency with the formulaic verse about traveling roads by night and hiding in the forest by day, followed in this case by two other well known formulaic verses:

> —Escribe la carta, prima,   que yo se la iré a llevar,
> de noche por los caminos,   de día por el jaral.—
> Cuando no le veía gente,   corre como un gavilán
> y cuando gente le veía,   poco a poquito se va.[61]

---

60. In regard to the *velhinha*, note the Thompson motif: N825.3. *Old woman helper.* The role of this old woman as messenger was possibly suggested by the presence of the hero's mother as confidante in many of the ballad's Portuguese versions. For data on the Brazilian readings *cachorro* and *demônio*, see the Appendix.

61. RPM 60. The *gavilán* verses are also in CVR 7, following "jornada de quinze días," etc., and alone in RPM 58 (= our text *B* above), RPC, p. 11. In Marazuela, *Segoviano*, p. 332, and *Voces nuevas*, no. 48.11, the same formulaic verses apply to the count's journey (see below). Concerning these verses, see Yoná, pp. 84–85. For similar verses in *Conde Claros insomne*, see CGR, IA, 45–46. For more on marvelously rapid journeys, magic circumambulation, and traveling by night and hiding by day, see the Appendix.

Many modern non-Sephardic versions are amplified at this point by a series of alternatives—usually three—addressed by the *infanta* to her messenger, as in our texts *C, D, E* and *F* above, or in the following Portuguese verses:

> Se o achares deitado,   deixa-o bem levantar;
> se o achares jantando,   deixa-o bem acabar;
> se o achares passeando,   vae-lh'a logo entregar.
>
>   (Braga, I, 376)

There is no trace of such verses either in *A caza* or in the Moroccan tradition, but their very wide diffusion—in Castilian, Galician, continental and insular Portuguese, and Brazilian texts—suggests the possibility of their relative antiquity.[62]

In *A caza*, Claros greets the page, asking him what news he brings concerning the princess: "bien vengays el pagezico / de Francia la natural // que nueuas me traeys / de la infanta como esta?" (vv. 39–40). In most Peninsular texts, as in Morocco (synth. v. 52), it is the messenger who greets the count, but in some Canarian versions, whether by direct survival or coincidental development, it is Claros who first offers the greeting:

> —Tú que vienes de palacio,   ¿Oh, qué nuevas me trairás?
>
> —¿Qué nuevas traes, pastorcito,   qué nuevas vienes a trair?
>
> —Usted que viene a palacio,   ¿qué nuevas me trae acá?
>
>   (FM 236, 237, 257)

A single Moroccan version of *Conde Claros fraile* (CMP B10.1, collected—or assembled?—by José Benoliel, in Tangier, 1904–1906) attests to the uncaring response by Claros to the page's news that the princess is to be burned: "Que la quemen, que la maten, / a mí poco se me da" (variants to synth. text, v. 53+).

---

62. For other examples, see Alvar, *Rom. viejo*, no. 175*a*; Cid, "Garganta," no. 5; CPG, III, nos. 44*ac*; Braga, I, 366, 369, 372, 391; Costa Fontes, *Trás-os-Montes*, nos. 44, 47, 715; Costa Fontes, *Califórnia*, no. 1; Galhoz 24; Purcell, *Ilhas*, nos. 8.1, 5–7, 13; Pereira da Costa, p. 318; Seeger, p. 290; Silva Lima, no. 9.8, 11, among many other instances. As we shall see, a similar detail will appear in *Fraile*'s Hungarian congener, *The Dishonored Maiden*.

This callous answer, which is impossible to reconcile with the count's heartfelt reaction in most of the Moroccan texts ("El conde leyó la carta; / asentárase a llorar" [synth. v. 54]) is, of course, already present in *A caza*: "vno me da que la quemen / vno me da que la maten" (v. 43). Such a heartless attitude clashes, too, with the hero's furious efforts (a fifteen-day journey in eight) to come to his beloved's aid. But despite a certain lack of logic, the verse, like various other elements in the ballad, effectively contributes to the story's narrative tension.[63] The venerable, if illogical, reading, which is still widely distributed in the modern tradition, may originally have been attributed to Claros on the model of the princess' earlier, selfless renunciation: "no me pesa de mi muerte . . ." (v. 30), with one expression of not caring having suggested the other, but with diametrically opposite implications. The relationship and interchangeability of the two passages clearly emerge in the following Extremeño text:

> —Si me queman, que me abrasen,   que a mí lo mismo me da,
> lo que siento es lo del vientre,   que se va sin bautizar—. . .
> —Coja la carta, buen conde,   cójala su Magestad,
> que a Risaldilla esta tarde   la han tratado de quemar.
> —Si la queman que la abrasen,   que a mí lo mismo me da,
> lo que siento es lo del vientre,   que es de mi sangre real.
> (Cid, "Garganta," no. 5)[64]

Such discordant expressions of the count's insouciance occur in many areas (Castile, Canaries, Asturias, Galicia, Portugal, Azores, Madeira) and are, indeed, sometimes arrogantly elaborated and reinforced:

> Tanto me da que la queme,   ni la deje de quemar;
> que mujeres en el mundo,   para mí no han de faltar.

---

63. Other such elements which draw out the story and delay the rescue are—as we have just seen—the various alternatives expressed by the princess ("si lo coges merendando," etc. [text *E* above]); the page's formulaic—and magical—circumambulation (text *A* above, v. 11); Claros' doubts about the truth of the page's report ("Si lo dijeras de burla," etc. [CVR 7]); Claros' consultation with his mother (*Voces*, 48.17; CPG, III, no. 44c; many Portuguese versions); the encounter and dialogue with the *justicia* (texts *ABCE* above).

64. Note also Claros' earlier reaction in the Moroccan texts of *Infanta*: "—¡Que arrevientes, que te quedes, / a mí poco se me da! // Bien lo sabes tú, princesa, / que soy cazador real . . ." (synth. vv. 15–16).

> Si non lo tienen de guapas,   lo tendrán de habilidad.
>
> (CVR 6)[65]

In Catalonia, there is a somewhat different, though ultimately analogous development: The hero claims he can't be bothered and, besides, he must take care of his sick mother, but, as soon as the messenger (a bird in this case) leaves, he has his horse saddled and rushes off:

> L'ocellet ja se n'hi va   i la carta li ensenyava.
> —Digues a la Rosa Vera   que tinc la mare molt mala.
> Digues a la Rosa Vera   que no puc pas destorbar-me.—
> Així que l'ocell és fora,   mana que li ensillin l'haca,
> no pas la que va corrent,   sinó aquella que volava.
>
> (AFC 3263)[66]

The widely diffused insistence on Claros' not caring about the *infanta*'s fate clashes with another reading, which, except for Galicia, can be found in every one of the modern subtraditions and sometimes, indeed, in versions which include his initial insouciance: On hearing the news of her impending execution, the count immediately bursts into tears:

> El conde leyó la carta;   asentárase a llorar.
>
> (Morocco, v. 54)

> Más pronto cogió la carta,   más pronto se echó a llorar.
>
> (FM 257; 5)

> Al momento que la [carta] abrió,   ya encomenzó a llorar.
>
> (Munthe, no. 2)

> Saltou a ler a carta,   seus olhinhos a chorar.
>
> (VRP 80; 69, 91, 987)

---

65. In CVR 6, the text is confused and these verses would seem to be attributed to the princess(!). See, however, our text *C* above or VRP 283. For additional data, see the Appendix.

66. See, for example, also Aguiló, p. 322; Avenç, III, 36; Briz, IV, 43; Milá 258, 258*CF*.

Começou a ler a carta,   começara a chorar.
                          (Cortes-Rodrigues, *Açoriano*, p. 227)

Mas começou a ler a carta,   começou a soluçar.
                              (Ferré, *Madeira*, no. 50)

D. Carlos pegou na carta,   pegou a ler e a chorar.
                             (Lopes, p. 153)

Al descloent de la carta,   llàgrimes de sanc llançava.
                             (Avenç, III, 36)[67]

In one of the Portuguese versions, Claros' lamentations are especially developed:

—Se mo dizes a brincar,   eu vou-te dar de jantar;
se mo dizes deveras,   eu viro-me já a chorar.—
Mandou tirar o jantar,   para fingir que comia,
mas as lágrimas eram tantas   que pela mesa corriam.
Mandou fechar o seu quarto,   para fingir que dormia,
mas os soluços eram tantos,   que até palácio tremia.
                              (VRP 69)

Granted, the hero's weeping is, of course, the most logical reaction to the news of his beloved's impending death and there is nothing particularly unusual about such a detail. All the same, the readings are consistently similar throughout the modern tradition and, though the motif of weeping is absent from the 16th-century version, there would seem to be a strong possibility that it may already have been present earlier on in the ballad's traditional life.

Before starting his journey, Claros consults with his mother in many modern subtraditions and it is she who suggests that he disguise himself as a friar.[68]

---

67. For additional Portuguese, Brazilian and Catalan readings and the motif of weeping tears of blood and the Devil's sleeplessness, see the Appendix.

68. For a few examples (among many others), see ART, p. 221 (= text A above); Kundert G4; CPG, III, no. 44c; Costa Fontes, *Tr.-os-Montes*, no. 42; Martins, II, 40; Tavares, no. 45; VRP 57, 60, 76, 77, 79, 82, 283; Braga, *Cantos*, pp. 245, 247; Purcell, *Ilhas*, nos. 8.12, 13, 15.

There is no trace of the mother's intervention, either in *A caza* or in the Moroccan tradition. The mother as confidante, usually of her daughter, is, of course, a fundamentally important motif in balladry and in the early lyric, but here the mother, who advises her son concerning a disguise aimed—with whatever ultimate purpose—at uniting or reuniting him with his beloved, is probably borrowed from *La apuesta ganada*—so frequently associated with *Conde Claros fraile* —where the mother advises her son to disguise himself as a girl (*tecedeira*, etc.).[69]

In *A caza*, the count's journey is described merely by repeating the formulary verse about making a fifteen-day trip in eight (v. 45), already attributed in identical form to the page (v. 37). The Moroccan tradition, having elaborated upon the page's ride (vv. 44–48), then says nothing at all about how Claros arrives at the princess' prison (vv. 55–56). Other branches of the tradition have not only maintained the early reading, but have in various ways also worked creatively with this stage of the narrative. The marvelously rapid journey is present in Leonese, Asturian, Portuguese, Azorian, Madeiran, and Catalan texts:

Jornada de quince leguas,   en hora y media he de andar.
                    (*Voces nuevas*, no. 48.5)

Jornada de cuatro días,   en uno la fuera andar.
                    (CVR 6)

Jornada de quince días,   en ocho la fuera andar.
                    (CVR 7)

Jornada de outo dias,   esta noite se hade andar.
                    (Braga, I, 370, 377, 383)

Viage de quinze dias,   toda a noite vou andar.
                    (Costa Fontes, *Califórnia*, no. 1)

---

69. For bibliography, see CMP T1 (= *Disfrazado de mujer* [polyas.]) and, above, our chart of *Fraile*'s contaminations. See also now CSQ, I, no. 47. On the motif of disguise in balladry, see *Yoná*, p. 279, n. 6; Thompson motif: K1310. *Seduction by disguise . . .* (and other motifs listed in *Yoná*, loc. cit.). Seeger identifies a vestige of the *Tecedeira* (*Apuesta ganada*) in one of the Brazilian versions (*Count Claros*, section 5.5.1).

| Viagem de quinze dias, | em três se havia de dar. |
| | (Ferré 49; 47) |

| Alli ahunt hi ha deu horas, | ell ab cuatre las passava. |
| | (Milá 258*B*)[70] |

The rapidity or simply the dramatic quality of the count's journey has been enhanced by a variety of other means. Some Castilian and Galician versions embody formulaic verses we have already seen applied to the page's ride:

Por onde no le ve gente,	corre como un gavilán;
por onde le ve la gente,	bien a poco a poco va.
	(RPC, p. 11)

| Por donde no le ve nadie, | parece el viento volar. |
| | (RPM 60) |

Cuando iba por los altos,	parecía un águila real;
cuando iba por los bajos,	parecía un alcotán.
	(Marazuela, p. 332)

Iba por los campos arriba,	corre más que un gavilán;
por los otros de abajo,	más que polvos de alquitrán.
	(*Voces*, no. 48.11)

Por aquella cuesta arriba,	parece que cientos van;
por aquella cuesta [abajo],	más correr que no andar.
	(CPG, III, no. 44*c*)[71]

---

70. For other Leonese readings: *Voces nuevas*, nos. 48.4, 6, etc.; for Portugal: Athaide Oliveira, pp. 72, 76, 329, 333; Costa Fontes, *Tr.-os-Montes*, no. 44; Delgado, *Subsídio*, II, 161; Tavares, no. 60; Thomaz Pires, *Lendas*, pp. 44, 188; for Madeira and the Azores: Purcell, *Ilhas*, nos. 8.1, 8.13.

71. No. 44*c* reads "arriba" in the second verse, but note no. 44*b*: "por aquellas veigas abajo . . ."; also Ledesma, p. 182; *Yoná*, pp. 84–85, nn. 9–10. The hawk's speed recalls French epic antecedents: "Ist de la presse, / fuiant come falcon" (*Chanson d'Aspremont*, ed. Brandin, v. 8763). For *alcotán*, see Corriente, *Arabismos*, p. 143.

In the Canarian tradition, Claros' journey will be so rapid that, like Conde Arnaldos' miraculous song or the supposedly leprous *infanta* in the *Caballero burlado*, it will produce magical results:

> La tierra que yo pisare   no volverá a dar más pan;
> los niños tiernos de cuna   de pesar se morirán.
>
> (FM 5, 234)[72]

Certain Portuguese versions borrow a verse from *Gaiferos y Melisenda* (or from *La esposa de don García*) to stress the trip's urgency by focusing on Claros' attention to the horse's equipment:

> Chamara pelo criado,   aquele mais liberal:
> —Aparelha-me o cavalo,   depressa, não devagar;
> aperta-lhe bem a cilha,   alarga-lhe o peitoral.
> Jornadinha de três dias,   em três horas se há-de andar!
>
> (VRP 63)[73]

Some Asturian and Leonese texts allude to Claros' speaking to his horse to encourage it and sometimes, indeed, the horse answers, offering its own instructions concerning sustenance:

> —Come, el mi caballo, come,   que hoy [te] tengo 'reventar;
> jornada de quince leguas,   en hora y media has de andar.
> —Si me dieras sopa en vino,   como me la sueles dar,
> jornada de quince leguas,   en hora y media he de andar.
>
> (*Voces nuevas*, no. 48.5)

> —¡Ay mi caballito rojo!   hoy tienes que caminar,
> siete leguas en hora y media   lo menos tienes que andar;
> la cebada de tres días   hoy te la tengo de dar;
> cuatro firraduras nuebas   hoy las tienes de gastar.
>
> (Munthe 3)

---

72. Concerning these motifs, see the Appendix.

73. See also Braga, I, 312; Martins, I, 195; VRP 66, 73. For more on these verses, see the Appendix.

—Caballo, caballo mío,	Dios te libre de mal,
cuatro ferraduras nuevas	hoy las has d'espedazar.
La cebada de ocho días	te la he de dar a cenar.
Ocho ferraduras nuevas	hoy las has d'espedazar

(Pérez de Castro, p. 478)[74]

The allusion to changing the horse's shoes to stronger material is regularly developed in the Galician-Portuguese traditions (Galicia, Portugal, Azores, Madeira):

—Quítale las herraduras de oro	y ponlas de pedernal.

(CPG, III, no. 44*c*)

Ala, ala, meus creados,	cavallos ide ferrar,
com ferraduras de bronze,	que não se hajam de gastar.

(Braga, I, 370)

Alto moços, meus criados,	meu burro o mandai ferrar,
com ferradura de bronze,	que é para mai não gastar.

(Purcell, *Ilhas* [Madeira], no. 8.2)[75]

The allusion to shoeing has led, in some rare Galician and Portuguese versions, but particularly in Castilian texts from Extremadura and Segovia, to the not altogether logical introduction of another motif: putting the horse's shoes on backward to disguise one's tracks:

Mandó herrar el caballo,	lo de alante para atrás.

(Cid, "Garganta," no. 5)

---

74. See also *Voces*, nos. 48.4, 6, 7. Compare also, for example, Braga's Portuguese and Purcell's Azorian texts (Braga, I, 312; *Ilhas*, no. 8.15, vv. 34–35), where the count likewise addresses his horse. Concerning such verses in various other ballads, see *Yoná*, pp. 182–183; for talking horses, pp. 181–182 and nn. 10–11; *Epic Ballads*, p. 263, n. 59.

75. For more Portuguese instances, see, for example: Athaide Oliveira, pp. 71, 76, 333; Braga, I, 312, 373, 377, 392; Delgado, II, 160; Pinto-Correia, no. 44; Reis Dâmaso, pp. 204, 216; VRP 52, 53, 55, 69, 987, etc.; for more Madeiran examples: Purcell, *Ilhas*, nos. 8.5–6; Ferré 49, 51; for an Azorian instance: Purcell 8.7. Note how, in *El prior de San Juan*, the protagonist promises to shoe his horse with gold: "de tres me has escapado / con esta quatro seran // y si desta me escapas / de oro te hare herrar" (*Silva* [1550], p. 333, vv. 49–52). See also D. Catalán's ed., *Siete siglos*, pp. 19–20. For horses shod with silver and gold, see Child, V, 483*b*; Wimberly, p. 454*b*.

Aparejó su caballo;   lo de alante puso atrás.

(CPE, I, 33)

Com ferradurinha de ouro,   ás avessas hão de andar.

(Braga, I, 312)

Ferradinhos às avessas;   ninguem nos há-de apanhar.

(VRP 86)

Ferraduras às avessas,   que não nos possam pilhar.

(VRP 86 var.)[76]

But Claros departs from his own home, whence he can hardly expect that anyone would wish to follow him in hostile pursuit, so why should he need to disguise his tracks?

Claros' disguise as a priest is an essentially universal feature of the narrative,[77] but, in *A caza*, the count puts on friar's garb after his rapid ride (vv. 46–47), whereas, in the modern tradition, the usual (and more logical) sequence is for him to take the disguise first.[78]

After reaching his destination, the disguised count immediately goes to see "Carlos el imperante" and asks to be allowed to take the *infanta*'s confession (*A caza*, vv. 48–50). There is no trace in Morocco of this seemingly unnecessary visit to Charlemagne, but some few Peninsular texts do seem to preserve it:

—Buenos días, el buen rey,   y su corona rial:
Me han dicho que tié usté una hija,   que usté la quiere quemar.
Si no se ha confesado,   déjela usté confesar.

(RPC, p. 10)[79]

---

76. Other instances: CPE, II, 17–18; García Matos-Crivillé, nos. 13–13*a*; Gutiérrez Macías, p. 345*a*; Marazuela, *Segoviano*, p. 332; and our texts *E* and *F* edited above. Between the hemistichs cited, CPE adds the informant's observation: "Para no ser conocido" (I, 33). For other instances of reversing horseshoes, see the Appendix.

77. For the various designations used, see the Appendix.

78. For data concerning this detail, see the Appendix.

79. See also the Catalan versions: AFC 3263; Aguiló, p. 325; Avenç, III, 36; Briz, IV, 44; Milá 258, 258*BCJ*.

In *A caza*, there is no confession: "en lugar de confessarla / de amores le fue a hablar" (v. 52). In rejecting the "friar's" advances, the truth emerges about the girl's affair with "don Claros de Montaluan" (vv. 53–56). Most branches of the modern tradition include both the confession and, supported by the motif of the lecherous priest, the friar's attempt to kiss and/or embrace the princess.[80] The amorous advances and the crucial confession—the whole point of the story—are, of course, also lacking in the Moroccan ballad. Here the text has probably been subjected to a process of de-Christianization and the confession has been replaced by an oath on a prayer book (synthetic vv. 57–59).[81]

One cannot but wonder if the oath's euphemistic phraseology may perhaps reflect centuries of residence in an Islamic environment, where, except for family members, women were prohibited from seeing or being seen by men: "que cara de hombre no vide, / sólo la del conde Alvar" (synth. v. 60). In the Moroccan tradition, in compactly traditional style, Claros then frees the princess without further ado, takes her to his *sivdad*, and, with the universal happy ending formula, marries her the next day.[82]

Following the princess' revelation of her affair with Claros (vv. 54–55), *A caza* attests to a series of unique developments. In vv. 56–58, the girl essentially repeats vv. 29–31, about being burned at the stake within fifteen days and not caring for her own death, but only for that of her child. Then, instead of having Claros immediately ride off with the *infanta*, *A caza* continues with several tedious, and doubtless non-traditional, elaborations: Claros again speaks with Charlemagne, defending the princess' innocence (vv. 59–61); a knight, who also

---

80. See, for example, texts *A B* above. The amorous advances are lacking in the Canarian texts we have seen, but are abundantly attested in the other regional forms: Castile, Galicia, Portugal, Azores, Madeira, Brazil, Catalonia. On the motif of the lecherous priest, see Armistead, "Neo-Individualism and the *Romancero*," pp. 179–181; CMP, III, 319; and now Alonso Montero, "O cura," and Felgueiras, "Clérigos e Monges." Note also the allusions in the 16th-century *Coplas de las comadres* (*Pliegos BN*, III, 246*a*, 251*b*); multiple instances in Frenk, *Corpus*, nos. 1833–1864 and 1198*C* (Solo, solo, / ¿cómo lo haré yo todo?). See also n. 138 below.

81. Concerning de-Christianization of Judeo-Spanish ballads, see the Appendix.

82. On formulaic happy endings, see *Epic Ballads*, pp. 96, n. 21; 145–146, n. 28. The use of *sivdad* for 'home, homeland' in Moroccan ballads would seem to respond to the particular conditions of Jewish settlement in scattered urban communities. The resolution of Moroccan ballad narratives often includes the protagonist's return to his or her *sivdad*: "Arçó velas el navío / y volviéronse a su cibdad" (*Conde Arnaldos*: Bénichou, p. 207; CMP H15); "Caen remos y alzan velas, / se van para su ciudad" (*Princesa rescatada*: CMP H14, X24); "Muerta la dejó el morito / y fue para su ciudade" (*Moro cautivo*: CMP H7).

loves the girl, accuses the "friar" of lying (vv. 62–63); they challenge one another to battle (v. 64); the emperor recognizes Claros by the way he tightens his horse's saddle straps (vv. 65–66); the "friar" then kills the knight and frees the princess (v. 67); after which—finally—the lovers ride off together (v. 68). None of this can be documented anywhere in the later tradition, but, while the ballad's Moroccan modality is notably succinct in bringing the action to a close (Sacóla de las prisiones / y llevóla a su civdad [v. 61]), other subtraditions have elaborated the final stages of the narrative in a great variety of ways. The rescue is often tantalizingly delayed by Claros' encounter and dialogue with the *justicia* (*hermandad*, etc.) and his command that they should halt, as the princess is being taken to the stake: "Se detenga la justicia / y también la autoridad. . . ."[83] Once the count and the princess do ride off, the modern tradition has delighted in creating a plethora of spirited *despedidas*.[84]

Many versions throughout the tradition, like those of Morocco, end by evoking a wedding, though the specific wording constantly varies from text to text. The formulaic Moroccan ending would seem to be exclusive to that tradition. Here are some characteristic non-Sephardic conclusions that stress the wedding:

> Allá alante hay una ermita,   nos tenemos que casar;
> las fiestas y los torneos   ocho días durarán.
>
> (Cid, "Garganta," no. 5)

> Más alante hay una ermita;   noh tenemoh que casar,
> pa cortar la lengua al mundo   y a tuh padreh consolar.
>
> (CPE, I, 33)

> —Tan mal, niña, no lo ha hecho,   cuando en manoh d'él ehtá(s).
> En el pueblo máh cercano   nos iremos a casá(r).
>
> (CPE, II, 18)

---

83. Text *E* above; also *ABCDF*. For further examples of the order to stop and the conversation with the authorities, see the Appendix, where the princess' punishment is also discussed.

84. On the variability of ballad endings, see, for example, Bénichou, *Creación*, pp. 98–117 (*Príncipe don Juan*), 150–158 (*Búcar sobre Valencia*), 175–184 (*Cautivo del renegado*); Catalán, *Siete siglos*, pp. 204–206 (*Búcar*); Nahón, pp. 66–68 (*Robo de Elena*); *Tres calas*, pp. 33–34 (*Forzador*); *Epic Ballads*, pp. 271–273 (*Búcar*).

El rey casará a sus hijas, que ésta casadita está.
Como mujer y marido, para el palacio se van.
(RPC, pp. 10, 11)

—Me ha dado un anillo de oro, conmigo le voy llevar.
—Buenos días, Galancina, que tú mía serás ya.
(RGL 19.29)

—Padres que queman las hijas, que os dotes le quieren dar;
se quieren vir al casamento, mañana se vai casar.
Siete vacas ya están muertas y otras tantas p'a matar.
(Costa Fontes, *Tr.-os-Montes*, no. 42)

L'agafa per la mà blanca, la se'n va dur a l'altar:
Vénguen rectors i vicaris; amb ella me vui casar.
(Ginart Bauçà, p. 419)[85]

Azorian, Madeiran, and Brazilian texts frequently do not allude directly to the wedding, but prefer, in one form or another, language in which it is implied as a certainty:

Toda a filha desgraçada comigo queira embarcar;
vista-se e ande comigo, qu'eu vou para Gibaltar.
(Costa Fontes, *S. Jorge*, no. 3)

—Confesse, menina, confesse, saiba bem se confessar,
ca princesa Galaducha, pa palácio vai morar!
(Galhoz, no. 31)

Voltai, justiça do conde, minha justiça é real,
que no reino de D. Carlos D. Branca vai reinar.
(Lopes, p. 154)

—Me acompanhe, me acompanhe, quem quiser me acompanhar,
que o palácio de D. Carlos Dona Branca vai gozar.
(Vilela 2.2)[86]

---

85. See also, for example, our texts *D* and *E*; Kundert G4; VRP 68.

86. See also Braga, *Cantos*, p. 246; Lemos de Mendonça, p. 196; Ferré 40; Lopes, pp. 159, 163; Pereira da Costa, p. 319; Silva Lima 9.2, 7, 8; Vilela 2.4.

Some Portuguese conclusions embody a tentative approval of Claros' carrying off the princess, on condition of their marriage:

> —Se a levas p'ra mulher,   Deus te a deixe gozar;
> se a levas p'ra criada,   deixa-nos antes queimar.
>
> > (Ferré, *Guarda*, no. 1)

> —Se a levas para mulher,   Deus ta deixe gozar;
> se a levas para madama,   Deus ta confunda no fundo do mar.
>
> > (Galhoz 22)

> —Se a levas por amiga,   deixa que a vamos queimar;
> se a levas por esposa,   Deus te a deixe lograr.
> Amanhã são minhas bodas,   eu vos irei a chamar.
>
> > (VRP 68)[87]

In the Castilian-Leonese-Asturian tradition—and also in some Galician and Portuguese texts—an essentially identical pattern of alternate possibilities embodies the offer of a dowry, which, in turn, is firmly rejected:

> —Si la llevas por amiga,   más le valiera quemar;
> si la llevas por esposa,   vuélvela, que la he de dotar.
> —Padres que queman sus hijas,   ¡buen dote les quieren dar!
>
> > (*Voces* 48.6)

> —¡Válgale el diablo a usté ya'l dote   y lo que usted le pueda dar,
> que pa una hija que tenía   la trataba de quemar!
>
> > (NCR 14.23)

> —Se la llevas por amiga,   un rayo la va a matar;
> se la llevas por esposa,   joyas le vuelvo a buscar.
> —Padres que queiman sus hijas,   ¡qué joyas les pueden dar! . . .
> El galopín que te lleva   joyas terá que te dar.

---

87. Compare also VRP 62, 283, and a Leonese text: "¡Padre que quema a sus hijas, / qué dote les ha de dar! // Todos dicen a una voz: «Dios te la deje gozar»" (RGL 19.11). On the alternatives *por mujer o por amiga* in many ballads (*Caballero burlado, Infantina,* and others), see Devoto, "Un ejemplo de la labor tradicional," p. 389 and n. 7.

Del domingo en ocho días,   la boda volver llamar.
                              (CPG, III, 44*c*)

—Se a levais ben levada,   vem cá que t'a hei dotar;
se a levaes mal levada,   Deus não t'a deixe gozar!
—Oh! Paes que queimaes as filhas,   bom dote lhe quereis dar!
                              (Tavares, no. 45)[88]

In many texts, the *despedida* focuses on alternate uses of the bonfire: It should be used to burn dogs, old women, a cat; to roast a turkey or a sheep; to destroy the rejected dowry; or to burn one of the *justicias* or the father himself:

Las hogueras que tenéis hechas,   los perros podéis quemar
y si no quemáis los perros,   a las viejas del lugar.
                              (ART, p. 221)

—Quédese con Dios, el rey   y la su corona real,
que en esa hoguera que han hecho   un gato pueden asar;
case el rey las otras hijas,   que ésta bien casada va;
cáselas ambas con duques,   que ésta con un duque va.
                              (RPM 60)

—Quédense con Dios, señores,   justicia de este lugar.
Esa hoguera que ahí tienen,   echen un pavo a asar;
y si no, queméis uno de ellos,   que a mí lo mismo me da,
que la niña Galanzuca   no ha nacido pa quemar,
que ha nacido pa ser esposa   de Carlos de Montealvar . . .
                              (*Voces* 48.11)

Esa lumbre que ustés tienen   echen un carnero a asar,
no quemar a Galanzuca   y ésa no vale ya.
                              (RGL 19.25)

—¿Te la llevas por esposa?,   la ropa has de ir buscar;
¿te la llevas por amiga?,   de ella veas mal gozar.
—Querían quemar la niña,   ¡las ropas pueden quemar!

---

88. For similar readings, see Feito; Munthe; RGL 19.4, 5, 6, 13, 16, 17, 18, 19, 21; Ruiz Granda; *Voces nuevas*, 48.7, 8, etc.

Para la tierra que va,   ropa no la faltará.
(*Voces* 48.12)

—Ni la llevo por esposa   y no quiero su dotal,
que padres que quemáis las hijas,   ¿qué dotes les vais a dar?
Arrójenlo a la candela,   a usted y a su dotal . . .
(*Voces* 48.4)

Esa lumbre que ahí tienen   echen canes a quemar
y si no, échense ustedes,   que a mí lo mismo me da . . .
(*Voces* 48.7)

A la hoguera que han hecho   metan ustedes un can,
si no uno de vosotros,   que a mí ¿qué cuidao me da?
(NCR 14.26)

—Pois essa lenha que está cortada   a tê pai ha-de abrasar
e o palácio de tê pai   a gente o há-de usar . . .
(Galhoz 34)

El abraçou a Dona Branca: —Dom Carlos sou eu mesmo.
A caleira que o rei fez   vai servir pra ele mesmo.—
O rei subiu no palácio,   o pescoço foi quebrar.
E Dona Branca se casou   com Dom Carlos de Montevar.
(Silva Lima 9.9)[89]

Azorian and Madeiran versions prosaically suggest more practical and less aggressive solutions:

—Esta lenha que aqui está   na boda eu vou-a gastar
e os palácios de teu pai   para nós ambos gozar.
(Purcell, *Ilhas*, no. 8.7)

—Voltem, voltem para trás,   para tras devem voltar.
Levem a lenh'à sê pai   para cozer o jantar.
(Ferré 50)

---

89. For additional variants of this dénouement, see the Appendix.

Some Asturian versions focus on the wealth and well-being the girl will enjoy in her new home, as Carlos de Montealbar triumphantly announces:

```
56   ¡Maldito sea su dote,      su dote y el su dotal,
     que para una hija tienía   ya se la quiere quemar!
58   Nu le hace falta su dote,   ni tampoco su dotal,
     que tengo yo más balcones,   qui ella pueda paseyar,
60   que tengo yo más vestidos,   qui ella pueda gastar,
     que tengo yo más dinero,   qui ella pueda comprar.
                              (NCR 14.24; 14.25, 27, 30)
```

Very frequent and in several subtraditions (Canaries, Galicia, Portugal, Azores, Madeira, Catalonia) are variations on the idea: "Just try to catch me!"

```
—¡El que es guapo que se atreva   a venírmela a quitar!—
La corte le contesta:   —¡Dios se la deje gozar!
                              (FM 6)
```

```
. . .si la llevo por fantasía   soy hombre de la llevar.
Si son hombres y capaces,   venganlam' eiquí quitar.
                              (CPG, III, 44a)
```

```
Dize agora á tua tia   que te venha cá fechar!
Dize agora a teu pae   que te venha queimar!
Com a ponta da espada   o havemos de matar!
                              (Tavares, Ill. Trasm., III, 76)
```

```
—Que vingui ton pare el rei,   que vingui ara a buscar-te;
la foguera que ha fet fer,   prou tindrá ara d'apagar-la.
                              (AFC 3263)[90]
```

In several texts, the departure is marked by relatively mild insults:

90. Other readings: FM 5, 78, 79, 234, 235, 237; Trapero 13; Athaide, pp. 73, 330; Braga, I, 368; Pinto 44; VRP 52, 76, 78, et alibi; Purcell, *Ilhas*, 8.6; Ferré 54; Avenç, III, 37. In Braga, I, 399, and Rodrigues de Azevedo, p. 158, the girl tells the *justicia* to wait for her or to come get her.

—Mira, cómo va la puta,   la puta con su galán.
—Deja la puta que vaya,   que con su marido va.
—Si con su marido va,   que aguarde por el dotal.
—Padres que quemáis las hijas,   ¿qué dotes les queréis dar? . . .
                                        (RGL 19.25)

—¡Yo me cargo hasta en el dote   que usted la pueda mandar,
cuando una hija que tienen   la trataban de quemar!
                                        (NCR 14.16)

—¡Vaya al carajo su dote   y todo cuanto ustede va dar,
si una hija que tiene   usted la iba a quemar!
                                        (NCR 14.18)

—Adiós, suegros míos   y alcaldes deste lugar.
Qu'inda son ustés más tontos   que la niña pa quemar . . .
                                        (CPG, III, 44*b*)

—Quedaivos con Dios, cornudos,   cornudos de este lugar.
O pai que queima as fillas,   mal lle pode dar el dotal.
                                        (CARG 18*a*; 18*bc*)

Diz ao ladrão do teu tio   que te venha aqui trazer;
diz ao ladrão do teu pai   que te venha aqui queimar . . .
                                        (VRP 987)

More outrageous are the following readings, limited, to our knowledge, to
only two texts, one from Sanabria and the other, unidentified as to origin, but
probably from neighboring Trás-os-Montes:

—Si quieren venir a la boda,   yo ya los vengo a brindar.
Siete vacas tengo muertas,   otras tantas por matar.
Hasta el rabo de mi caballo   vengan todos a besar.
                                        (our text *C*)

Deus os guarde, meus senhores,   Deus os queira guardar,
que essa mulher que aí levam,   ela vai por confessar.
Subam-na ao meu cavalo,   que eu a quero confessar . . .

Levantem no rabo ao cavalo,   no cu o queiram beijar.
     E fugiu com ela.

(VRP 73)[91]

Up to now, we have seen a variety of different endings which have achieved a certain currency in tradition, but *Conde Claros fraile* also attests, in its *dénouements*, to various poetic experiments, which have little or no traditional diffusion and, to our knowledge, are limited to one or, at most, a handful of versions. Most are insipid and obviously deserve their lack of success, while others, such as the heroic escape (CVR 7) or the girl's taking leave of the church bells of her village (VRP 987), are poetically effective. The following examples are self-explanatory:

Tomóla el conde en sus brazos,   tercióla en el su ruán.
Siete guardias dejó muertos   por las puertas al pasar;
y en aquellos campos verdes   ¡quién los vía galopar!

(CVR 7)

Ya la pone en el caballo,   la llevó a Montealbar.
Le echan perros, le echan galgos,   no le pudón alcanzar.

(RGL 19.30)

—Appareça já um Padre,   que nos venha já casar.
Mande o recado a seu Pae,   que nos venha visitar.

(Thomaz Pires, *Lendas*, p. 189)

—Venha cá, minha menina,   comigo a hê-de levar.
Ao palácio da rainha,   lá iremos descansar.
—Meu irmãozinho mais novo   comigo hê-de levar.
Foi o que me livrou à morte,   senão eu ia a queimar!

(VRP 70)

—Cala-te aí, ó Alvaninha,   todo isso me há-des dar.
O teu irmão mais novo   para casa o vamos levar.
O teu irmão mais velho   amanhã vai-se queimar.

(Galhoz, no. 25)

---

91. Needless to say, the crucial verses here can be related to a variety of ritualized insults, punishments, and tricks current in popular tradition: for details, see the Appendix.

—Os sinos da minha aldeia   bem nos sinto tocar!
—Sentes, sentes, minha menina,   para lá não hás-de voltar.

(VRP 987)

Passára por uma rua,   a mãe á janella estava:
—Deos te guie, cavalleiro,   Deos te queira guiar;
que livraste Claralinda   d'ella não ir a queimar.

(Braga, *Cantos*, p. 249)

Ide-me pôr esta menina   no meu palácio a morar,
qu'eu é que fui o traidor,   agora lhe quero pagar.

(Purcell, *Ilhas*, no. 8.8)

—Cala a boca, minha Branca,   que eu não vim de confessar.
Eu vim de livrar do fogo   que já vinha de queimar.

(Campos Tourinho, p. 133)[92]

A limited number of versions attest to quite extensive sequels, in which the
action, so definitively concluded with the lovers' joyous escape, is nonetheless
drawn out with additional, tedious developments. Though there is no direct
relationship, such continuations cannot but recall the redundant final verses of
the 16th-century *A caza* (vv. 59–67). In several modern Leonese texts, there is a
continuation, in which, after seven years, a child appears at the grandfather's
door to reproach him for the attempted burning and to reject his offers of gifts:

58   . . . Por la puerta del rey   la espada iban a jugar.
       —¿De quién será ese niño   que tan bien la espada sabe jugar?
60   —Yo soy su nieto, mi abuelo,   que usted quería quemar.
       —Si eres mi nieto,   muchas cosas te voy dar.
62   —Yo no le quiero 'e sus cosas,   mi padre tiene que dar.
       ¡Padres que queman una hija,   no tendrán mucho que dar!

(RGL 19.2)

48   Pasaron siete años   y un niño por allí fue a pasear.
       —Dime, niño, dime, niño,   dime de quién serás.

---

92. For the intolerably redundant endings ("I'm paying my debt"; "I came to save
you") of *Ilhas*, no. 8.8, and Campos Tourinho, compare, respectively, *Ilhas*, no. 8.4, and
VRP 68; Delgado, II, 161.

50   —Soy su nieto, mi abuelo,   el que usted quería quemar.
     —Si eres mi nieto, pasa,   que te daré de almorzar.
52   —Déme su caballo, mi abuelo,   que yo se lo [s]abré montar.
     —Pasa, pasa, mi nieto,   que todo te he de dar.
54   —Déme su espada, mi abuelo,   que yo se la sabré manejar.
     —Pasa, pasa, mi nieto,   que yo todo te he de dar.
56   —Nada le quiero, mi abuelo,   [. . . . .]
     que todo eso mi padre   también me lo puede dar.

                                        (RGL 19.9)[93]

In an alternate sequel, also Leonese, Galanzuca herself appears at her parents'
door after seven years, bringing twins (*niños* or *niñas*). The parents (either father
or mother) want to take one of them, but the girl refuses, reproaching them for
having wanted to burn her:

     —Padres que quemáis las hijas,   ¿qué dote les queréis dar?—
     Siete años tardó Galanzuca   de volver a ca su padre;
     de los siete pa los ocho,   Galanzuca vuelve allá,
     con dos niñas por la mano,   parecían un cristal.
     Su padre, desque las vio,   se las quería quitar.
     —No me las quitará, padre,   no me las quitará tal,
     que la madre de estas niñas   la quería usté quemar.

                                        (*Voces* 48.11)[94]

We may contrast such rejections with a unique Leonese version, where the
girl, as she rides away, pardons her mother:

     —¡Válgame Dios de los cielos   y la Virgen del Pilar,
     que aquí la perdono yo   por la leche que me diera,
     también por los nueve meses   que en el vientre me trajera!

                                        (RGL 19.20)

---

93. RGL 19.1 also embodies a vestige of this conclusion.

94. The same ending appears in RGL 19.22, 24, 27; *Voces nuevas*, 48.2, 3. Similar
elaborate sequels also figure in *Fraile*'s German congener, *Der König von Mailand* (as
we will see below).

The Catalan tradition also attests to a prosaic sequel which insists upon the obvious:

Alante, alante, muger,   que ya 'ribem a Granada.
Alli serás ben servida   de mon pare y de ma mare.
Quant a Granada va sé,   d'un hijo s'es deslliurada.
Envian a dir al Rey   si vol[ía] sé compare.
                                           (Milá 258*c*)

Al arribar al castell,   Dona Iselda deslliurava;
n'ha parit un bell infant,   un infant com una plata.
Envian a dir al Rey   si volia esser compare.
Quan el Rey ho ha sabut,   ab gran festa ho celebrava.
                                           (Aguiló, p. 328)

In several geographic areas (León, Algarve, Madeira), the tradition has experimented with the ballad's conclusion by adding verses which differ in assonance from the rest of the poem:

Esa lumbre que ahí tienen   echen canes a quemar
y si no, échense ustedes,   que a mí lo mismo me da.
No la llevo por amiga,   ni la llevo por querida,
que la llevo por esposa,   mientras que en el mundo viva.
                                           (*Voces* 48.7)

—Tenho feito juramento,   protesto de não faltar,
d'onde o conde pós a boca   de mais nenhum me tocar.
—Este sou, minha menina,   este sou, meu coração,
que te venho aqui buscar   por mulher, que amiga não.
                                           (Nunes, no. 5)

—Não permita Deus do Céu   nem à Sua Pretindade,
aonde Conde pôs sus lábios   já cá nã põe nenhum frade.
—Esta menina é minha   que m'a deram em sentência;

foi arrematada em Roma na mesa da consciência.

(Ferré 44)[95]

We see yet another, and more interesting, indication of poetic creativity in several minor contaminations which contribute to the variability of the ballad's dénouement. One Zamoran version draws upon the well known *Conde Sol*:

Queden con Dios, los señores, casadas y por casar,
yo me voy con mi esposita, que la he venido a buscar,
que los amores primeros son muy malos de olvidar. . . .

(*Voces* 48.17)

Compare:

Quédese con Dios, la novia, con Dios se puede quedar,
que los amores primeros son muy malos de olvidar. . . .

(*Conde Sol*)[96]

In two Portuguese texts—one from Castelo Branco, the other from Elvas—the girl's departure seems to have evoked that of another departing princess in the ballad of *Flérida*. The contamination is limited to a single verse (v. 49 in both cases), though in Thomaz Pires it may also be echoed in the waiting boat:

  Montou-a no seu cavalo, começou de caminhar.
48 —Diga agora ao seu pai, que a venha aqui buscar.
  —Adeus, casa do meu pai, adeus, tanque da água fria,
50 já não torno a ouvir cantar rouxinol ao meio-dia.

(Ferré, *Castelo Branco*, no. 6)

---

95. These concluding verses in *é-a* are popular in Madeira: Ferré 43, 47–51; Purcell, *Ilhas*, no. 8.2, 3. Some versions prefix them with others in *á-o*: Ferré 46; Purcell, *Ilhas*, no. 8.1. The verses cited here from *Voces* (48.7) may have been influenced by *El caballero burlado* or *La infantina*.

96. We cite the synthetic version of *Conde Sol* representing northern Zamora, León, and Santander (RT, IV, 16, vv. 39–40). Concerning these verses, which also occur in traditional texts of *Conde Dirlos* (i.e. *Conde Antores*), see Menéndez Pidal et al., *Cómo vive un romance*, pp. 66, 240, 242; for examples: RT, III, 164–167, 170 etc.; Armistead, "Una encuesta," p. 78. For more data, see the Appendix.

```
       Diz ao barbaro de teu pae      que te venha aqui buscar;
48     com este punhal de prata       o hei de assassinar!
       —Adeus casa de meu pae,        onde o gallo canta ao meio dia.
50     —Venha-se embora, menina,      não fale com phantasia,
       que eu tenho um navio no mar,       [. . . . . . . . . .]
52     Onde canta o rouxinol,    quer de noite, quer de dia.
                              (Thomaz Pires, *Lendas*, p. 45)
```

Compare the following verses from *Flérida*:

```
       Adeus, cravos, adeus, rosas,      adeus, tanque d'água fria;
       adeus, jardim de flores,     ond'eu passava o meu dia;
       adeus, casa de meus pais,    e o espelho donde m'eu via.
                        (Costa Fontes, *Trás-os-Montes*, no. 113)[97]
```

A lone Portuguese version from Mondim da Beira equates the couple's arrival on horseback with the conclusion of the octosyllabic *Don Bueso y su hermana*:

```
       Pegou nela e aventou      com ela para palácio.
       A mãe:
       —Se vens para minha filha,      anda cá para meu braços;
       se vens para minha nora,     entra cá para esse palácio.
                                            (VRP 80)
```

Compare these verses from *Don Bueso*:

```
       Se tu trouxesses espôsa,      entravas por êsse palácio;
       se trazes hermana tua,    deita-m'aqui nos meus braços.
                                     (Martins, I, 208)[98]
```

---

97. The reference to "tanques d'água fria" is relatively rare (also Costa Fontes, *Tr.-os-Montes*, no. 720; VRP 278, 280). More frequent are fountains: "Adeus, casa de meu pai, / adeus, fontes de agua fria" (VRP 277; *Tr.-os-Montes*, nos. 719, 721-725; also Costa Fontes' extensive bibliography: II, 1350). We cannot attribute any specific source to the singing nightingale. On the motif, see Chap. 10, n. 52 above.

98. Typically, these verses, belonging to *Don Bueso,* may also conclude versions of *El caballero burlado*: VRP 203, 207, 210, 218, 219.

In many subtraditions, *El caballero burlado* is associated with verses from
Don Bueso y su hermana.[99] Some Galician versions of *Conde Claros fraile*
would seem to have combined verses from both *romances* (below, vv. 60–62
and 55–57, respectively) to create distinctive conclusions. The silent seven-
league ride could be from *El caballero burlado*, while the girl's weeping
(sighing or laughing) leads to the protagonists' mutual recognition in *Don
Bueso*. The two versions of *Conde Claros fraile* explain the weeping differently.
In CARG 18*b*, she is uncertain about the future; in 18*d*, the motif is related to
her rejection of the supposed prelate's amorous pretensions. Whether the
contaminated elements in *Conde Claros fraile* originated in some combined
version of *El caballero burlado* + *Don Bueso* or from independent forms of both
romances remains open to question. We can only note here that the three ballads
embody various common elements which undoubtedly motivated their
association: In all three, the young man carries the girl away on his horse; in
Fraile and in *Bueso* the girl either recognized Claros or the protagonists
recognize each other; in *El caballero burlado* and in *Fraile*, the girl rejects his
amorous advances; her crying (sighing, laughing), which calls for an explanation
in *Bueso*, recalls her laughing, which calls for an explanation in *El caballero
burlado*. The concluding verses of CARG 18*b* (vv. 65–67) attest to yet another
otherwise undocumented experiment:

	Padres que criai-las fillas,	¿que dotes lles podeis dar?—
60	E anduveron sete leguas	sin malhaya fala dar,
	al cabo de sete leguas	se soltara a llorar.
62	—¿Por qué lloras, Analuca,	por qué dejas de llorar?
	—Porque non sei pra onde von,	nin pra onde eu irein parar.
64	—Lévate don Carlos, nena,	don Carlos de Montealvar,
	ben ves aqueles balcois,	donde t'has apasear,
66	onde ves aqueles perros,	pronto lle[s] has dar pan,
	onde ves aqueles criados,	pronto lles has mandar.

(CARG 18*b*)

48	—Quédense con Dios, señores,	alcaldes de este lugar,
	que esta nena es muy mía,	con ela me vou casar.—
50	Bien lo vira ir su padre	de altos palacios que está.
	—Da la vuelta, caballero,	que te la quiero dotar.

---

99. See Nahón, p. 164, n. 8.

52   —No quiero que usted la dote   ni que le haga otro mal,
     para mí y para ella   haciendas no han de faltar,
54   ni tampoco llaves de oro,   las que pueda manejar.—
     Anduviera siete leguas   sin con ella palabra hablar;
56   desde las siete a las ocho,   la niña empieza a llorar.
     —¿Por qué lloras, Julianita,   o por qué es tanto llorar?
58   —Más quixera ser queimada   en un fuego de alquitrán,
     que no verme en estos montes   en brazos de un cardenal.
60   —No llores, no, Julianita,   que ya no es tiempo de llorar,
     que el que te lleva en sus brazos   es Carlos de Montealvar.

                                        (CARG 18*d*)

Corresponding verses in *El caballero burlado* and *Don Bueso* read:

Han andado siete leguas,   palabra no se decían,
mas al cabo de las ocho,   de amores la requería.

                    (*Caballero*: Ledesma, no. 10)

Anduvieron siete leguas,   sin hablar y sin dar risa;
de las siete pa las ocho,   ya la niña se sonría.
—¿De qué se ríe, la blanca?   ¿De qué se ríe, la niña?
Ríome, el caballero,   de toda su cortesía.

                    (*Caballero*: Poncet, p. 131, n. 5)

Al llegar a aquellos montes,   la mora llora y suspira.
—¿Por qué lloras, mora bella,   por qué lloras, mora linda?
—Lloro porque en otros tiempos   mi padre aquí me traía,
con mi hermano el Aguileño   y toda su compañía.

                    (*Bueso*: CARG, I, no. 78*b*)[100]

------

100. Compare also *Voces nuevas*, no. 40.16. The silent ride is, however, exceptional in Western versions of *El caballero burlado*. We have not seen it in Galicia (CARG 23–24), nor in Leonese versions (RGL 23.1, 24.1-8). *Voces nuevas*, no. 46.2, from Zamora, also lacks this motif. Ledesma's and Poncet's texts, which we have cited, are from Salamanca and Zamora, respectively. It is also possible that in *Fraile* the silent ride may have been taken from some version of *Don Bueso*, since it can also occur in that *romance* (RPM 196, 200). On the motif of the silent ride, see Devoto, "Entre las siete y las ocho," pp. 67–71.

In the Azores, *Conde Claros fraile* can conclude incongruously with verses (vv. 35–36) borrowed from *La muerte de don Beltrán*:

    —Toda a filha da Fortuna   que se queira imbarcar
34   viste-se e ande comigo,   qu'ê vou p'a Gibaltar.—
     Por milaigre de Jesus,   o cavalinho falara:
36   —Aperta-me bem a sela   e tãobém o peitoral;
     ê quero ver si a venço   a fora do arraial.
38   —Sinhor pai, sinhóra mãe,   a mão vos quero beijar.
     —Ficai-vos imbora, sogro,   sogro, qu'ela já cá vai.
                         (Lemos de Mendonça, p. 196)[101]

Compare vv. 24 and 38 of Silveira's *Don Beltrán* from the Island of Flores ("Materiais," p. 477):

    Cavalo, que estava morto,   sangrando no arenal,
34   por graça do Espir'to Santo,   logo se pôs a falar:
     —As culpas que me botais,   vos não deveis me as botar!
36   Que as vezes que retirava,   tantas me fez el' tornar;
     outras tantas deu d'esporas,   sempre a querer guerrear!
38   Seis vezes me aperta a silha,   me alargando o peitoral:
     À sete me fui em terra,   d'ua lançada mortal![102]

Three Portuguese texts end with a famous verse ultimately derived, perhaps, from *Belerma y Durandarte*: "que ojos que nos vieron yr / nunca nos veran en francia" (CSA, fol. 255 vo.; *Primav.* 181, v. 18):

    Montara-a no seu cavalo   de ligeiro caminhar.
     Olhos que a vêdes ir   não na vêdes cá voltar.
                         (Martins, II, 41)

---

101. Côrtes-Rodrigues' text (pp. 227–228) is essentially identical.

102. On the verses in question, see FLSJ, III, 273–274, n. 54. The verse about tightening the saddle (or girth) and loosening the breast-strap has become a migratory formula. Ultimately it probably comes from *Gaiferos y Melisenda* (*Primav.* 173, vv. 191, 195). Concerning these verses, as well as the motif of talking horses, see *Yoná*, pp. 179–182; also *Epic Ballads*, p. 263, n. 59.

Pegara-lhe pela mão,   pousara-a no cavalgar.
Olhos que a viram ir   não na viram cá voltar!
                                      (Tavares, no. 60)

Diga ao pai desta senhora   que a venham aqui buscar;
eu, com este meu alfange,   aqui o hei-de passar.
As terras que a vêem ir   não ha hão-de ver voltar.
                                      (VRP 91)

The verse is migratory and is also known from other ballads and songs in the modern tradition. In the Golden Age, it became proverbial and was repeatedly used in *comedias*. Gonzalo Correas cites: "Oxos ke le vieron ir, no le verán más en Franzia; oxos ke le vieron ir, no le verán más venir."[103] In Portuguese tradition, the formula occurs also in *Gaiferos y Melisenda* and *La esposa de don García*, and in an identical context: the rescue of the protagonist's beloved:

Espôsa da minha vida,   inda te vim resgatar.
Olhos que a vêdes ir   não na vêdes cá voltar.
                                      (*Gaiferos*: Martins, I, 193)

Pegara-lhe pela mão,   pusera-a no cavalgar:
—Olha que a vêdes ir,   não na vereis cá voltar!
                                      (*Gaiferos*: Tavares, no. 9)

Acudi-lhe à Milondinha,   que se vai para além do mar.
Olhos que a vedes ir,   não na vereis cá tornar.
                                      (*Don García*: VRP 625)

In sum: In their complex variability, our ballad's many different endings—a number of which are, in varying degrees, poetically effective—offer a splendid testimony to the incessant, dynamic creativity of the oral tradition.

---

103. *Vocabulario de refranes*, ed. Combet, p. 171*b*; cf. ed. Mir, pp. 371–372. Concerning the diffusion of this formula, which also occurs in Ibizan and Eastern Sephardic versions of *Celinos y la adúltera*, see Catalán, *El Poema de Alfonso XI*, pp. 94–96; *Yoná*, pp. 238–239, n. 30; *Tres calas*, pp. 74–75, n. 79.

Before continuing to other matters, a word should be said about the onomastics of *Conde Claros fraile* . The name of the female protagonist varies greatly. Many of these names seem to have been arbitrarily assigned: the widely known *Galanzuca* (and variants)[104] and the vulgate *Lizarda* type.[105] Others clearly respond to associations with other ballads, some of which on occasion have contaminated the narrative of *Conde Claros fraile* , while others are merely narrative types well known in the various traditional repertoires: *Ausênsia* comes from *La mala hierba*, which serves as a prologue to this particular version,[106] while *Moriana* clearly reflects the influence of a preceding *Apuesta ganada*.[107] *Doña Arbola* and *Narbola* (RPC, p. 10; *Voces nuevas* 48.17) echo *La mala suegra*; *Delgadina* (NCR 14.26–27; RGL 19.10), her eponymous ballad; a Canarian *Sidrana* (FM 6) obviously responds to *Silvana;* *Blancaflor* (RGL 18, 21) could reflect *Blancaflor y Filomena* or possibly *Las hermanas reina y cautiva* or, again, some folktale; and a Catalan *Adriana* (Briz, IV, 43–44) doubtless recalls the protagonist of another amorous intrigue: *La calumnia de la reina*.[108] *Griselda* or *Criselda*, in some Extremeño and Andalusian vulgate versions, would seem to respond—not very appropriately—to the widely known tale of *Griselda*, the abused and ever patient wife.[109] Other names, such as *Elena* (RGL 19.5), *Albaninha* (Galhoz 17, 22, 25; VRP 63–64 etc.), *Aninha(s)* (C. Fontes, *S. Jorge*, nos. 3–4), the Brazilian *Dona Branca* (Vilela 2.1–3 etc.) or the Canarian and Catalan *Isabel* (FM 7; Aguiló, p. 328), can only be described as characteristically balladic names, which could have originated in a variety of sources. Some few names, no doubt arbitrarily assigned, have epic origins, but can, in no sense, have anything to do with the ballad's genesis: We have already

104. See, for example, CVR 6; Kundert G4; *Voces nuevas* 48.5, 6, 8, etc.; CARG 17; Athaide, pp. 70, 328, 330; Galhoz 31; Ferré 40, etc.; Purcell, *Ilhas*, 8.1–4.

105. Alvar; CPE, I, 32–33; CPE, II, 17–18; Ledesma, p. 181; Marazuela; RPE, p. 9; our texts *D* and *F*; Braga, I, 368, 371; Costa Fontes, *Tr.-os-Montes*, 715, etc.

106. Ferré, *Cast. Branco*, no. 5. Compare *Ausenda* in Braga, I, 392–393 (= *Mala hierba + Parida* [á-a]).

107. Ferré, *Cast. Branco*, no. 4; also Consiglieri Pedroso, p. 461; Dias Costa, *Murteira*, p. 318; Galhoz 26, 28, 30, 34; Giacometti 123; Thomaz Pires, p. 43; VRP 76, 81, 86, 88, 89, 91, 987.

108. See our study in Nahón 29 and its bibliography.

109. See García Matos 13, 13*A*; our text *E*; Martínez Ruiz, p. 362 (*Griseritas*). Pertinent scholarship on the story is vast: Thompson H461. *Test of wife's patience: Griselda*; Aarne-Thompson 887. *Griselda*; Boccaccio, *Decameron*, X:10 (ed. Branca, pp. 1553–1554); Lee, *Sources*, pp. 348–356; Consoli, F79, F108; Chaucer's *Clerk's Tale* (R. P. Miller, pp. 136–152; L. K. Morris, pp. 468–469; Bryan and Dempster, pp. 80–81, 288–331).

seen *Rondale(s)* (and its variants) applied to the brother; in Morocco, by contamination with *Bernardo del Carpio*, the princess sometimes becomes *Simena* (synthetic vv. 56b, 57a, 61+) or *Alda* (v. 33) because of her sad fate (*Sueño de doña Alda*; *Muerte ocultada*). Claros himself can be *Oliveros el del Mar* (RPC, p. 9) or *Carlos Magnos* (VRP 75), the latter surely echoing, as Leite de Vasconcellos notes, the famous *librito de cordel* (VRP, I, 85, n. 1). The princess' city can be *Sansueña* (*Voces nuevas* 48.13), which ultimately responds to the pagan stronghold in the *Chanson des Saisnes* and survives in certain ballad contexts even down to the present.[110] But despite such variegated onomastics, *Conde Claros fraile* has maintained the protagonists' original names in a number of subtraditions. This is, however, not the case in Morocco, where the early *Claraniña* has become an anonymous *princesa* and *Claros* is known simply as *el conde de Mont(e)alvar*, *Montalbán* or *Conde Alvar*,[111] but *Claraniña* has survived in the Castilian tradition in its original form or as *Clara(y)linda*[112] and in Portugal, the Azores, and Madeira as *Claralinda*.[113] *Claros* has universally changed into *Carlos* (*Carles* in Catalonia), but *Montalbán*, though it has suffered many bizarre transformations, can also be found in its original form in widely separated areas (Castile, Extremadura, León, Canaries, Portugal).[114]

Unlike the other Conde Claros ballads, *Conde Claros fraile* attests to striking parallelisms with several extra-Hispanic ballads. Worthy of detailed comparison

---

110. For example: *Gaiferos y Melisenda* (*Voces* 11.1) and *Conde Niño* (Andalusian Gypsy, uned.: *Sagüeña*); *Asentado está Gaiferos* (*Primav.* 173.109 etc.) and *De Mérida sale el palmero*: "a la infanta de Sansueña / me fueron a presentar" (*Primav.* 195.39); the famous scene in *Don Quijote* (II:XXVI; ed. Rodríguez Marín, VI, 160, 165; ed. Murillo, II, 240, n. 4; ed. Lathrop, pp. 598–599). On the name's Hispanic development, see Menéndez Pidal, *Los godos*, pp. 203–206; my article (with Luis Suárez Avila) "Un nuevo fragmento del romance de *Calaínos*."

111. See synthetic vv. 3b, 24, 25, 37b, 58b, 60b; in some texts he becomes *Conde Niño* (v. 50b) or *Montesino* (41+, 45+), by means of obvious contaminations. Note how *Conde Claros y el emperador* + *Conde Claros insomne* maintains the names better: *Claraniña* (synth. vv. 24, 25, 27, 30b, 30+, 33, 60; our text 10B) and, very rarely, even *Claro(s)* (synth. v. 31).

112. See Díaz, *Catálogo*, I, 166; RPM 58; *Voces* 48.1; RGL 19.8.

113. See Braga, I, 313; Costa Fontes, *Tr.-os-Montes*, no. 42; Coelho, pp. 64, 66; Galhoz 12–13; VRP 52; also VRP 55 (*Dona Linda*); Braga, *Cantos*, pp. 244, 246; Purcell, *Ilhas*, nos. 8.12 (Azores) and 8.6 (Madeira).

114. ART, p. 221; Cid, "Garganta"; RGL 19.11; FM 7; in Portugal, *Montalvão*: Braga, I, 369, 383; Fernandes Thomas, p. 30; Ferré, *Cast. Branco*, no. 5; Galhoz 24; Thomaz Pires, p. 43; VRP 61, 71, 88.

are the Scottish and Anglo-American *Lady Maisry*, the German *König von Mailand*, and the Hungarian *Dishonored Maiden*.[115]

The Scottish texts of *Lady Maisry* embody the following story: Lady Maisry rejects the suit of all the lords in the north country; she tells them she has given her love to an English lord. Her father's kitchy-boy—"an ill death may he dee"—overhears her and tells Maisry's brother that she goes with bairn (or sister, brother, mother, father accuse Maisry of being a whore; her brother notes that her clothes no longer fit). The brother (or father) requires her to renounce her English lord, but she refuses; the brother orders servants "to pu the thistle and thorn" for the fire; her father offers her the choice of marrying an auld man or burning (or the family, father and brother, set about preparations for burning her, without attempting any arrangement). Maisry, warned of her approaching fate (by her old nurse, bower-woman), calls for a boy to carry word to England; a devoted young messenger takes her errand; he swims rivers, runs over the dry land (or the green grass), and, on arrival, leaps over the English lord's wall. He brings tokens from Maisry (right-hand glove, penknife, gold ring). The English lord asks if his biggins ('buildings') are broken, his towers won, or his lady lighter ('delivered'), and is told that his lady is to be burned that very day. Horses are instantly saddled: a black, a brown, are foundered, a milk-white [a dapple-gray]—"fair fall the mare that foaled that foal!"—holds out (or fifteen stout steeds are burst), yet the little foot-page runs aye before, crying: "Mend your pace an you may!" Maisry, in the flames, hears her lover's horse or horn, or hears his bridle ring: "Beet on, my brother dear (or mother), I value you not one straw! Mend up the fire, brother; I see him coming that will soon mend it up to thee" (or: she blesses her lover with her dying words). She cries out, when her lover appears, that, if her hands had been free, she would have cast out his young son. He leaps into the fire for a last kiss; her body falls apart. He threatens awful retaliation: He will burn (or hang) father and brother and burn mother and sister; many a wife will be widowed and many a babe left fatherless; He will burn the town. Vengeance glutted, he will throw himself into the flames (or: will take the pilgrim's cloak and staff; or he goes mad and runs over the fields). The foot-page shall be heir of his land (or: he will remember the bonny boy that ran the errand).[116]

---

115. Leader (pp. 195–197) sees the German *Ritter und Magd* (Erk-Böhme, no. 110; DVM 55) as an additional analogue, but the similarities, in my view, are coincidental. Compare Vargyas' remarks (*Hungarian Ballads*, p. 171).

116. I adapt and expand Child's summary (II, 112–113; compare Davis, *Traditional Ballads of Virginia*, p. 180), taking into account all of Child's texts (65A–*I*).

In more recent English versions (Bronson, II, nos. 65.4–11), there is no burning at the stake. The lady is merely ill, fears she will die before her lover can come to her, and sends her little foot-boy (page boy; nephew) to fetch him; both lover and lady die; the rose and sweet-briar grow from their graves and twine in a true lover's knot.

The ballad is very rare in America. The general lines of the story have survived: A girl is with child and her parents are planning to burn her at the stake. She sends her oldest brother's son to tell her lover what has happened and to get him to attend the burial. The boy goes and informs the lover, who hurries to the girl's house, blowing his bugle. The girl, hearing, is tied to the stake unafraid. The hero rushes up just in time to tear her dying form from the flames and kiss her. He then wills his land to the oldest brother's son. The same story can be told in abbreviated form and has added a cliché ending so that the man is late and can only stop the funeral, kiss the corpse, and die himself.[117]

To our knowledge, there are only three variants—widely separated in time and space—of the German ballad, *Der König von Mailand*. John Meier summarizes the ballad's situation: "Here is an example of the tenacious life of songs and their peculiar destinies! At the beginning of the 19th century [1804–1808], our ballad was transcribed in Gütenback in the Black Forest of Baden and Herr von Wessenberg transmitted it to the publishers of the *Wunderhorn*; in the middle of the same century [1836], it was found in the Canton of Zürich. In neither case, was the melody transcribed. In recent years [1928], it has been taken down at various places in the Volga Republic, together with its tune, though indeed here too it is only known to elderly people and is about to disappear."[118] In the following abstract, we combine features of the ballad's three different modalities: A lord has seven sons, but only one daughter; he organizes a great banquet and invites many guests; among them is the King (Lord) of Mailand [= Milan] (a prince). The lord's beautiful, golden-haired daughter, Anneli, with eyes bright as stars and rose-red cheeks, serves the wine. (The King of Mailand stays three days at the lord's house and meets the girl in a

---

117. I adapt the summary in Coffin and Renwick (no. 65); I have also read Bronson, II, nos. 65.12–13 (= Sharp and Karpeles); Davis, *Traditional Ballads*, nos. 16A-B; Scarborough, *Song Catcher*, pp. 137–139; Sharp and Karpeles, *English Folksongs*, nos. 17A-B. For additional data, see the Appendix.

118. Meier, *Balladen*, I, 209. For Volga Germans, who settled in Russia in the late 18th century, their dialect (Bavarian) and ballad tradition, see Schirmunski, "Wolga-Kolonien," pp. 160–161. For the ballad's three forms, see DVM, III:2, 227–228 (no. 67); also Holzapfel's type-index (DVM, X, 206, no. H10).

garden; weeping, she complains bitterly about her father's strict, ill-tempered character.) There is a nocturnal rendezvous; at his departure, the King of Mailand promises to return in forty weeks (i.e. at the time of her delivery). The girl tells her brother that she is pregnant; she wishes, in vain, that the King of Mailand were there; with the help of her brother and three maidservants, she gives birth to a son. The servant women praise the child's beauty, saying that he looks like the King of Mailand; Anneli's mother, listening through the wall, overhears them; she goes to the father and slanders the child as a monstrous offspring of the Devil. (The father hears the child crying and discovers everything.) Enraged, the father calls all the neighbors together and asks their help in constructing the gallows; he tells the daughter: "You deserve death" (or: The mother orders that the daughter should die on the gallows on Friday; or by the executioner's sword in three days' time); the child is to be drowned (in the deep sea). (Anneli turns pale as snow and faints.) The brother, who has been listening through the wall, weeps and quickly goes to his sister to inform her of the death sentence; she writes (lacking ink, she cuts her finger and uses the blood) an urgent letter to the King of Mailand; the brother himself offers to take the message (or: a rapid messenger, carrying the letter, reaches the Lord of Mailand only by the second evening; the messenger meets the king at a half-way point along the road.) (Servants tell the brother that the King of Mailand is not at home, but he persists and is able to deliver the letter.) When the king reads the letter, his eyes fill with tears (he becomes pale; he is filled with anguish); he immediately orders the servants to saddle his best horse (or saddles it himself) and rushes to help his beloved. Meanwhile, early on Friday (after three days), the girl (carrying the little child in her arms) is taken to the place of execution; the child is to be drowned. She asks the hangman to wait, because she hears (sees) a rider rapidly approaching (along the road) and is still hoping that the child's father will appear. (As she ascends each step of the gallows ladder, she asks mother, father, sister, brother, and everyone present at least to take pity on the little child, but she encounters instead the mother's mercilessly repeated death verdict.) (As she reaches the last step), the King of Mailand arrives just in time: "What are you doing with my wife and child?" He is amazed at the strange custom of wishing to hang a woman. He wraps the child in a beautiful kerchief, strikes down the fiendish mother with his sword, but spares the only moderately guilty father out of respect for his nobility (or: he consigns the mother to the Devil, but the father to Heaven; he wishes his brother-in-law perpetual good luck; and wishes everyone else well). With Anneli and the child, he rides home for the wedding. (After half a year has gone by, the King of Mailand organizes a banquet; he would like to invite Anneli's father, to show his conciliatory intentions; she is alarmed and wishes to avoid the invitation; he sets her mind at rest: Even if the father is angry, the greatest anger subsides, just as a bird's flight always leads back to earth; or: After ten years, the father appears as a beggar at Anneli's house; the King of Mailand wants to pour hot water on him, but Anneli objects: She has forgiven him and cannot turn him away or take any vengeance against him; begging forgiveness, he dies in her arms.)[119]

The Dishonored Maiden (or *The Disgraced Girl* = *Szégyenbe esett lány*) is massively documented in the Hungarian tradition.[120] In the following summary, I have selected those readings which agree most closely with one or another of the Hispanic subtraditions: "A king had twelve daughters; / the thirteenth was Dora Landorvári"; her suspicious mother asks the daughter to explain why her skirt has become shorter in the front, longer at the back, why her slender waist has grown stout. At first the girl prevaricates: The tailor did not cut the skirt well; the dressmaker did not sew it well; she has drunk cold water (river water; the Danube's water). After the mother repeats the question (three times), she confesses that she is pregnant: She met her lover "in the little flower garden, under the apple tree; I prepared a green bed for small Nicholas King; I fell in love." The mother orders the girl to be put in (the bottom of the dark, deepest) prison or has her taken straight to the place of execution: She summons constables (or her maids, servants, headsmen, hangmen, soldiers) to take her daughter away; "On the thirteenth day I myself will go to witness her death; on the thirteenth day, may she be beheaded" (or: she is to be put into hard irons for fifteen days); the mother has her daughter taken to the beheading-bridge ('scaffold'); or "from the condemned cell, to the gallows-tree"; "headsmen, take my daughter, cut off her head." Her mother (father, brother, sister) goes to the

---

119. I have translated and amplified the summary in DVM 67 (Vol. III:2, 227) and have also taken into account texts 67.1, 2, and 3, as well as the summaries in Engle, no. V115 (pp. 937–938); Künzig and Werner, no. 17; Leader, pp. 194–195 (based on Schirmunski); Schirmunski, "Wolga-Kolonien," pp. 163–164. Text 67.1 can also be read in Von Arnim's and Brentano's *Des Knaben Wunderhorn*, pp. 497–500, and in Erk and Böhme, I, no. 97; texts 67.1 and 3 are in Meier, *Balladen*, nos. 29A-B; 67.3 is in Schirmunski, Künzig and Werner, and Engle. Künzig and Werner list another Volga-German version (in a recording they published) which we have not seen (pp. 87, 275). For the relationship of *Der König von Mailand* to *The Maid Freed from the Gallows*, see the Appendix.

120. Leader lists "twenty-seven versions and some sixteen fragments" (p. 183); in *Researches*, Vargyas could cite 137 variants (p. 105); in *Hungarian Ballads* (p. 168), he lists a total of 299.

prison; a dialogue follows; the mother interprets the girl's symbolic dream about her impending death. From the prison (or before being taken to the place of execution; or before being imprisoned), the girl writes a message to her lover. She entreats a bird (in most cases a swallow) to take it to him, also giving instructions on how the letter should be delivered: The girl says she has no pen, no ink, and no messenger; the brother answers: let her fingertips be her pen, her heavy tears her ink, the swallow her messenger; she has no ink, and no pen: let her red blood be her ink, let her tiny white nails be her pen, her fine tears her ink; she prays to God that he may send one of his angels to her in the shape of a little bird, so that she may send her letter by it; she sends the letter by "a bird"; she ponders whether to send it with a raven, a magpie, a swallow, a crow, or a stork (or: she sends it by her coachman). If the bird arrives at noon, it should place the letter on the plate of her lover; if in the evening, it should place it on his pillow; in the morning, on his bedstead; at noon, on his plate, in the evening, on his table; if at lunch, on his table; at dinner, on his plate; if he is eating, on his plate; if he is drinking, in his glass; if he is walking, on his right shoulder, etc. Having received the message from his beloved, the young man orders his coachman to harness his (swiftest) horse(s) (with golden bridle and silver halter), and set off at once, anxious to arrive before it is too late (or he rides alone to his beloved). Two horses die by the time they arrive. He goes straight to his sweetheart's house and, after greeting the mother, demands to see her daughter. Now it is the mother's turn to palter with the truth (her daughter is picking flowers in the garden, at the neighbors', in church, etc.); ultimately, however, on the urging of the young man, who could not find his beloved at any of these places, the mother has to confess the truth: She had just sent her daughter to the place of execution. The young man goes to the place of execution, arriving just as she has been killed; he takes his knife and kills himself next to his beloved: "Bury my body together with hers in the same grave, let my blood and her blood run together in one stream"; "Have me buried in the front [part] of the church, have Barbara Angoli buried in the middle part of the church, have our little child buried [in front of] the altar." (In one version, he kills the mother.) "One of them was buried in front of the small altar, the other was buried in front of the big altar." "Two sprigs of rosemary (or a beautiful walnut tree) sprang from the grave of one of them, two pairs of turtle-doves hatched out on the grave of the other." Rosemary stems grow from both graves and lean toward each other. The mother goes to the grave and tears a branch from the rosemary; a drop of blood flows from it. "A little white pigeon was hatched on one [of the graves], a little white cock was hatched on the man's grave." The pigeon (or turtle-dove) coos and the cock crows, uttering curses against the girl's mother and father.[121]

As is so often the case with oral literature, a comparison of the diverse Pan-Hispanic modalities of *Conde Claros fraile* with their Scottish (English and Anglo-American), German, and Hungarian analogues suggests many more problems than it solves. Let us look briefly at some of the points of agreement between these four ballad traditions. One of the most curious aspects of the supposed parallelisms between *Conde Claros fraile* and its various extra-Hispanic congeners relates to a series of motifs present in unrelated ballads, which, as contaminations, function as prologues to the *Conde Claros fraile* narrative. Thus, in *Conde Claros y la infanta*, as prologue to *Conde Claros fraile*, as well as in the German and Hungarian songs, the lovers meet in a garden:

Tocósen mano con mano;   subióle a su rosal;
púsole cama de rosa,   cabecera de azahar;
cobertor con que se tapan,   de hojas de un limonar.
                    (Morocco: synth. vv. 10-12)

Goht mit dem [Heer] Anneli wol ine-n-und us,
Goht mit ihm im Garten uf und ab,
Si breched bim Moschi Röseli ab.
                    (Zürich: DVM, III, no. 2.6–7)

I fell in love with John Ármádi
In the little flower garden
Under the apple-tree.
                    (Leader, p. 185: texts *UV*)

I prepared a green bed

---

121. The present synopsis is based on Leader's detailed summary (pp. 184–192). I have also read and taken into account Aigner's (pp. 215–218) and Vargyas' translations (pp. 148–161, nos. 10.29–33). Though I do not agree with many points, particularly in regard to the ballads' international relationships, Leader's and Vargyas' detailed analyses are excellent and indispensable: *Hungarian Classical Ballads*, pp. 192–223; *Researches*, pp. 105–110; *Hungarian Ballads*, pp. 161–175. I feel we must be much more cautious in attempting to establish exact dates and direct relationships between the various traditions. For additional observations, see the Appendix.

For small Nicholas King;
I fell in love.
      (Leader, p. 185: texts *KQ*)[122]

Again, in *Conde Claros y la infanta* and in *Lady Maisry*, the lovers are betrayed by a social inferior (page or kitchy-boy):

Pajecito sin fortuna   al rey se lo fue a contar: . . .
—Umá princesa, tu hija,   en gran río quiere entrar;
yo la he visto en sus palacios   con conde de Montalvar.
      (Morocco: synth. vv. 22, 24–25)

Her father's kitchy-boy heard that,
An ill death may he dee!
An he is on to her brother,
as fast as gang coud he. . . .

'Your father and your mother is well,
But an your brothers three;
Your sister Lady Maisry's well,
So big wi bairn gangs she.'
      (Child 65A.6, 8)

Conde Claros fraile is introduced in Leonese, Galician, Portuguese, Madeiran, Brazilian, and Catalan texts with verses taken from *La infanta parida* (*á-a*). Here, as in the Scottish and Hungarian ballads, we find the motif of the ill-fitting clothes, and just as in the Hispanic texts, a tailor is blamed in the Hungarian song:

—Casilda, hija mía,   la basquiña se levanta.
El sastre que la cortó   ni otra corte ni otra haga.
Las tijeras se le troncen   y el dedal también le caiga.
      (RGL 19.11)

—O que é isso, D. Aurelia,   que me pareces pejada?

---

122. By pure coincidence, in Marazuela's version of *Alabanza* + *Parida* (*á-a*) + *Fraile*, the lover is also called "Don Nicolás" (*Segoviano*, p. 332).

—Nada disso é, meu pai, é da saia arregaçada.
—Venham já três alfaiates, dos melhores que ha em Braga.—
Três alfaiates chegáram; logo a saia foi virada.
—Esta saia está perfeita; não tem erro, não tem nada;
é a menina que a veste, que parece estar pejada.
(Fernandes Thomas, Velhas, p. 29)

'What's come o a' your green claithing,
Was ance for you too side?
And what's become o your lang stays,
Was ance for you too wide?'

'O he that made my claithing short,
I hope he'll make them side;
And he that made my stays narrow,
I hope he'll make them wide.'
(Child 65H)

Ilonka Londonvári,
What is the reason
That your green silken skirt
Is getting long at the back?

The tailor did not cut it properly,
The seamstress did not sew it properly,
May the Lord punish her,
She has spoiled it very much.
(Vargyas, Hungarian, no. 30)[123]

In many traditions (Azores, Madeira, Brazil, Catalonia), in verses pertaining to *La infanta parida* (á-a) and doubtless ultimately echoing *La fuente fecundante*, the girl offers the excuse that she is ill from drinking (cold) water. The same excuse is found in the Hungarian *Dishonored Maiden*:

—Que tens, ó filha Izétima, que 'tás tão decorada?

---

123. Scots *side* 'wide, long' (Warrack, s.v.); for the motif of ill-fitted clothing, see the Appendix.

—Foi um copo d'água fria,   qu'eu bebi de madrugada?
    (Purcell, *Ilhas*, no. 8.14)

—O que tendes, D. Angélica,   qu'andas tão desmaiada?
—Senhor pai, e d'água fria,   qu'ê bebo de madrugada.
    (Ferré, *R. trad.*, no. 304)

—O que é que tem Dona Branca,   de cor estais demudada?
—Foi água fria, rei me(u) pai,   que tomei de madrugada.
    (Vilela, no. 2.1)

—Qué teniu, la meva filla,   no teniu colors en cara?
—He begut en una font,   que tota m'ha reinflada.
    (AFC 3263)

—Mother, mother, mother,   Kate Vándorvári,
I have drunk river-water,   that has made me fatter.
    (Leader, text *A*, v. 8)[124]

In other variants of the Hungarian ballad, the girl is said to have drunk "cold water" or "the Danube's water" (Leader, p. 185).

Let us now look at a series of agreements between *Conde Claros fraile* itself—rather than its contaminations—and its Scottish, German, and Hungarian analogues. Some Castilian variants of *Fraile* agree with one version of *Der König von Mailand* and several of *The Dishonored Maiden* in beginning with a typical ballad incipit: "A king had X number of daughters (sons) . . .":

Tres hijas tenía el rey   y todas tres son igual;
todas visten de un vestido,   todas calzan de un calzar. . . .
    (Santander: ART, p. 221)

Weiss mir e Herr, hätt siebe Süh
Und nu-n-e einzig Töchterli. . . .
    (Schwarzwald: DVM 67.1)

---

124. For the motif of drinking cold water and the idea of conception from eating, drinking, or other supernatural causes, see the Appendix.

A king had twelve daughters,
The thirteenth was Dora Landorvári. . . .
                    (Leader, p. 184, text *N*)[125]

In isolated Portuguese texts, an aunt warns the girl of her impending punishment and a servant woman does the same in at least one Catalan version. Such figures can, perhaps, be seen as corresponding to Maisry's old nurse or bower-woman:

Uma tia que ela tinha   logo a foi avisar:
—Confessa-te, Crandolina,   que tu vais hoje a queimar. . . .
                                        (VRP 61)

So uma tia que tinha,   essa tia bem leal:
—Triste de ti, Mariana,   triste de ti, desgraçada;
hoje t'acarretam lenha,   amanhã já és queimada. . . .
                                        (VRP 88)

Hi va aná una criada   del palacio de su madre: . . .
Las noticias qu'ara corren,   que vosté ha de sé cremada. . . .
                                        (Milá, no. 258)

Then in it came an old woman,
The lady's nurse was she,
And ere she could get out a word,
The tear blinded her ee. . . .
                    (Child 65*B*.9)

Soon after spoke her bower-woman,
And sorely did she cry:
'Oh woe is me, my lady fair,
That ever I saw this day!

For your father's to the fire, Janet,
Your brother's to the whin,

---

125. For the topic ballad incipit, "A king had X number of daughters (or sons)," see the Appendix.

Even to kindle a bold bonefire,
To burn your body in.'
(Child 65C.3–4)[126]

The brother's violent hostility in the Scottish ballad can be compared to a similar attitude in Leonese and Extremeño versions of *Conde Claros fraile*:

Y un hermano que tenía,   que le llamaban Maldades:
—Asómate en hora mala,   cara de quitar pesares,
para mañana a las nueve,   vendremos a quemarte.
(RGL 19.19)

El del medio era su hermano,   que le llaman Rondanes:
—Callate, lengua infernal,   lengua de malas bondades,
que mañana es otro día   y ya saldrán a quemarte.
(Arroyo de la Luz: our text *E*)

When her brother got word of this,
Then fiercely looked he:
'Betide me life, betide me death,
At Maisry's bower I'se be. . . .

I'se cause a man put up the fire,
Anither ca in the stake,
And on the head o yon high hill
I'll burn you for his sake.'
(Child 65H.3, 14)[127]

---

126. The friendly aunt appears also in one of the Leonese texts (RGL 19.11). In Child 65C, *whin* means 'furze' (to be gathered for fuel; Vol. V, 392a; Warrack, s.v.). In both ballads, the aunt/nurse/ bower-woman represents the type of the *Old woman helper* (Thompson N825.3).

127. Compare also RGL 19.12; García Matos-Crivillé, no. 13B; and García Redondo, pp. 51-52 (the last two also from Arroyo de la Luz). The brother or brothers are also hostile, in various ways, in other areas: for example, Ledesma, pp. 181-182; FM 78; VRP 56, 85, etc. Note also Child 65ABCG (though all family members are consistently hostile in the Scottish texts).

The hostility of the mother, so pronounced in the German and Hungarian ballads, is also present in some Hispanic texts, but here her hostility, as in the Scottish song (Child 65*B*.5), is not stressed as being greater than that of other family members:

> Luego saltara su madre,   mala lengua y mal hablar:
> —Apañai leña, mis criados,   que la vamos a quemar.
> (RGL 19.2)

> La madre, cuanto lo supo,   pronto la mandó amarrar.
> (FM 7)

> A mãe, assim que o soube,   logo a mandou fechar.
> (Braga, I, 369)

By contrast, the mother in the German and Hungarian ballads is by far the most hateful and is singled out for retribution at the end of the narrative (DVM 67.1.55; Leader, pp. 191-192).

In various Catalan versions, the father is represented as hidden in a room or behind a door, as he surreptitiously listens to the revelation of his daughter's condition:

> El seu pare s'ho escoltava   amagat dintre una cambra.
> (AFC 3263)

> El senyor rey, sospitós,   a la porta ho escoltava.
> (Aguiló, p. 319)

> El rey, como es picarón,   se lo estava escuchando.
> (Milá 258*D*)

The situation recalls the hateful mother's listening behind a wall in the German ballad (Schwarzwald version):

> Die Mutter an de Wände
> Erloset de Reden en Ende.
> (DVM 67.1.17)[128]

---

128. Note that, in the German text, the very same verse is applied to the friendly brother who overhears the father's plans to have the girl hanged: "Der Brude[r] an de Wände / Erloset de Reden en Ende" (DVM 67.1.25).

In Asturian, Leonese, Galician and Portuguese texts, the father orders his servants to gather wood for the bonfire. In *Lady Maisry*, the brother does the same and, in *Der König von Mailand*, the father similarly asks his neighbors' help in building the gallows:

> Siete criados tenía,   leña les mandó apañar,
> para quemar Galanzuca,   hija del rey tan galán.
> (CVR 6)

> Su padre, desque lo supo,   triminara de a queimar
> y ha llamado cuatro mozos   para la leña cortar.
> (CARG 18*d*)

> —Altos, altos, meus criados,   que estão ao meu mandar!
> Vão roçar mato   p'ra D. Mariana queimar.
> (VRP 90)

> 'O whare is a' my merry young men,
> Whom I gi meat and fee,
> To pu the thistle and the thorn,
> To burn this wile whore wi?'
> (Child 65A.17)

> 'Nachbure, liebi Nachbure mi,
> Müend mir e Galge mure,
> Dra mue mi Tochter verfuhle.
> Ich will sie lasse hänke. . . .'
> (DVM 67.1.23–24)[129]

In many Hispanic texts (Castilian, Leonese, Asturian, Galician, Catalan), the girl writes the message to her lover in blood (or blood mixed with ink, milk, tears). The German and Hungarian messages are likewise written in blood:

---

129. For more Hispanic allusions to gathering the wood, see Kundert G4; *Voces nuevas* 48.4–11, 16; Athaide Oliveira, pp. 75, 328; Costa Fontes, *Tr.-os-Montes*, no. 42; Consiglieri Pedroso, "Poesias," p. 461. Compare also Child 65*H*.15. Scots *wile* can mean 'wild' or, as is probably the case here, 'vile' (Warrack, s.v.).

Una la escribió con tinta   y otra con sangre leal
y otra la escribió con leche,   porque viera su pesar.

(RPM 59)

Escribió una con sangre   y otra con tinta moral
y otra con lágrimas tiernas   que de sus ojos le sal.

(NCR 14.14.14–15)

La escribiera con su sangre,   para mayor pena dar.

(RGL 19.27)

Ab sanch de les sues venes,   ella n'escriu una carta.

(Aguiló, p. 321)

Das Anneli uf mit frischem Mueth,
Es haut sih in Finger und schrybt mit Bluet.

(Zürich: DVM 67.2.24)

Sie schnitt sich in' Finger 'nein, ob's weh auch tut,
Und schrieb mit ihrem eignen Blut.

(Wolga-Kolonien: DVM 67.3.10)

I have neither ink / nor pen to write with.
You will have for ink / your red blood. . . .

(Vargyas, *Hungarian*, p. 163)[130]

The bird (*pajarito*) that, through popular etymology, presumably replaces an earlier page (*paje, pajecito*), occurs in several branches of the modern tradition (Castilian, Galician, Portuguese, Brazilian, Catalan), but, except in Castilian-speaking areas, it is not a particularly strong reading and, as we have seen, it still alternates in most of these traditions with the medieval page. Yet the bird messenger is solidly established as a majority reading in the Hungarian ballad:

Si tuviera un pajarito,   d'esos que comen el pan,
yo le mandaría una carta   al conde de Montealvar.

(Arroyo de la Luz: our text *E*)

---

130. For letters written in blood, see the Appendix.

¡Quién me diera un pajarito,   que algún día le di pan! . . .
Me ha de llevar esta carta   a Carlos de Montealbar.
(CARG 17a)

Quem me dera un passarico,   destes que sabem bolar,
para escrever uma carta   a D. Carlos de Montealbare!
(Fontes, Tr.-os-Montes, no. 42.9–10)

Quem me dera um portador,   para esta carta ir levar. . . .
Ali chegou um passarinho,   con vontade de falar.
(Vilela 2.4)

Ocellet, bon ocellet,   si volguéssiu ajudar-me?
Si em portessis paper i ploma   i em volguessis dur una carta?
(AFC 3263)

Si trovas un pajarito,   qu'anés corriendo y volando,
enviaría una carta   al caballero D. Carlos.
(Milá 258.32–33)

Swallow, my little swallow, / take my letter,
Take my letter / to young Miklós Király!
(Vargyas, Hungarian, p. 151)[131]

Many modern Hispanic versions (Castilian, Portuguese, Azores, Madeira, Brazil), as we have already seen, embody what would seem to be an innovative amplification, in which the girl offers detailed instructions to the messenger, depending on what Claros happens to be doing when he arrives. There are strikingly similar verses in the Hungarian ballad:

Tú, si lo hallas en misa,   por Dios, déjalo acabar.
Tú, si lo hallas en el baile,   no lo dejes más bailar.
Tú, si lo hallas en el juego,   no lo dejes más jugar.
(Rábano de Sanabria: our text C)

Si le coges paseando,   no le dejes pasear.
Si le coges merendando,   no le dejes merendar.
(Cid, "Garganta," no. 5.22–23)

---

131. Concerning the page/bird reading, see the Appendix.

If you find him at lunch, / you will place this on the table.
If you find him at supper, / you will place this by his plate.
(Vargyas, *Hungarian*, p. 151)

If you meet him at lunch, / put it on his table.
If you meet him asleep, / put it on his pillow.
(Vargyas, *Hungarian*, p. 154)[132]

In a few versions from Castilian-speaking areas, Claros' frantic ride to rescue his beloved causes a series of horses to die of exhaustion. The same motif occurs in the Scottish and Hungarian ballads:

Siete caballos tenía,   todos siete mandó ensillar.
Todos siete reventaron,   a no ser el caballo del mar.
(RGL 19.13)

Ocho caballos tenía,   ocho mandó aparejar
y los siete reventaron,   antes del puerto llegar.
(RGL 19.28)

He left the black into the slap,
The brown into the brae,
But fair fa that bonny apple-gray
That carried this gay lord away!
(Child 65*E*.14)

It's first he burst the bonny black,
An syne the bonny brown,
But the dapple-gray rade still away,
Till he cam to the town.
(Child 65*F*.17)

Drive, coachman, drive! / the faster you drive
The surer you will get my coach / and the six black horses.

---

132. For some other Hispanic texts that include such alternatives, see n. 62 above. For other Hungarian readings (at breakfast, drinking, walking), see Vargyas, *Hungarian*, pp. 156, 160; Leader, pp. 182, 187–188.

By the time they got there, / two of the horses had died.

(Vargyas, *Hungarian*, p. 164)[133]

The parallels we have pointed out between *Conde Claros fraile*—or, in the first four instances, its contaminations with *Conde Claros y la infanta* and *La infanta parida* (á-a)—and the European ballads to which *Fraile* seems to be genetically related can be summarized in the following chart: (Tenuous agreements are placed in parentheses.)

	Fraile (or contam.)	*Maisry*	*Mailand*	*Maiden*
1. Lovers meet in garden	X		X	X
2. Betrayed by social inferior	X	X		
3. Ill-fitting clothes	X	X		X
4. She drank cold water	X			X
5. King has X daughters	X	(X)	X	X
6. Helpful aunt/servant	X	X		
7. Brother's hostility	(X)	X		
8. Mother's hostility	(X)	(X)	X	X
9. Father/mother listens	X		X	
10. Servants gather wood/ neighbors build gallows	X	X	X	
11. Writes letter in blood	X		X	X
12. Bird messenger	X			X
13. Alternative instructions	X			X
14. Horses burst	X	X		X

On one hand, there can, I believe, be no doubt about the ultimate genetic relationship between the four ballads. All, in essence, tell an identical story: A girl, imprisoned for sexual misconduct, is to be burned at the stake; a faithful messenger summons her lover, who travels at utmost speed, either to free his beloved (*Fraile, Mailand*) or to witness her death (*Maisry, Maiden*).[134] Yet what are we to make of the agreements we have previously singled out? Earlier

---

133. Scots *slap* 'a narrow pass between two hills'; *syne* (= *since*) 'then, afterward; thereupon' (Warrack, s.vv.); for horses dying of exhaustion, see the Appendix.

134. John Meier, by contrast, argues for the independence of *Der König von Mailand*: "Unsere Ballade hat aber ihre Kernmotive selbständig gestaltet" (DVM, III, 231).

scholarship has taken the first four parallels to be "authentic" components of *Fraile*, but this is not the case. All are contaminations from two other ballads (*Conde Claros y la infanta* and *La infanta parida*) and they can be shown to occur also in autonomous forms of the ballads in question. Genetically they cannot be considered as part of *Fraile*. And what about the other agreements? Though some are known to several different subtraditions, in a number of cases they are minority readings limited to relatively few and scattered versions (e.g. 5–9, 11, 14), though stages 10 (servants gathering wood), 11 (letters in blood), and 13 (alternative instructions) are indeed somewhat more widely distributed. As to the bird messenger (12), there is good reason to believe that it is a late development and that the page (*paje*)—who survives alongside the bird (*pajarito*) in almost all the subtraditions—continues to reflect the earlier reading. Taken together with the generally sparse distribution of most of these motifs, the absence of every one of them from the 16th-century form of *Conde Claros fraile* (*A caza va el emperador*), would, in this case, seem to be significant. We are obliged to ask which of these motifs are coincidental, polygenetic agreements and which are genetic features that go back to some common ancestor of all four ballads. A definitive answer must await further study. Surely a good number of these parallels could have been polygenetically suggested and independently generated by the exigencies of the traditional narrative itself.[135] This seems to have been the case with *Fraile*'s four initial motifs (1–4) borrowed from *Conde Claros y la infanta* and *La infanta parida*. They are indeed an authentic part of the variable super-narrative which oral tradition has gradually constructed out of *Fraile* plus its diverse ancillary contaminations and they certainly embody striking agreements with one or another of the European ballads, but they simply cannot go back to any imaginable common prototype. Given France's central role as an innovative purveyor of ballad narratives to culturally more conservative lateral areas of Western Europe, Lajos Vargyas' hypothesis of a common French ancestor for *Fraile*, *Maisry*, *Mailand*, and *Maiden* is very possibly correct, but I cannot believe that their relationship can be as precisely explained as he supposes.[136] Clearly these four ballads are somehow genetically

---

135. Note how the recent English versions of *Lady Maisry* (Bronson, II, nos. 65.4–11) and the Hungarian *Dishonored Maiden* (Leader, pp. 191–192) have independently acquired the commonplace of the twining plants. For more data, see the Appendix.

136. "With the French ballad as intermediary everything can be neatly explained" (*Researches*, p. 110; compare *Hungarian*, p. 173). In my view, few, if any, problems pertaining to oral literature can ever be "neatly explained." In no sense, however, do I

related, but the exact nature of that relationship cannot—perhaps ever—be worked out in terms of a specific, conventional stemma. There are too many gaps in our knowledge and too many variables in the enormous complexities of oral-traditional transmission and recreation.[137] What is clear, for now, is that sometime in the late Middle Ages a Spanish balladeer, very possibly following a now-lost French prototype, adapted the story of the condemned girl who is rescued by her lover and, with genial creativity, joined it to another ballad narrative: that of the lover as confessor.[138] The result was the ballad of *Count Claros in Friar's Garb*, which, through the centuries, has continued to attract ballad singers over the length and breadth of the Hispanic world.

A unique, idiosyncratic feature of our star informant Luna Farache's ballad repertoire provides the opportunity to include, in the present chapter, *El nacimiento de Bernardo del Carpio*, an epic ballad which is otherwise unrepresented in our collection. In Luna's texts 11*D*.1-3 and 11*E*.1-5, she uses a few verses of the *Bernardo* ballad as a prologue to *Conde Claros y la infanta* + *Conde Claros fraile*. Though I have not seen such an association elsewhere in the tradition, the three ballads' obvious thematic affinities clearly justify their juxtaposition: All three concern the discovery of clandestine amours between a knight and a princess, followed by imprisonment and, in *Fraile* and *Bernardo*, by a happy ending with the long-suffering protagonists' marriage.

In addition to its Moroccan texts, *El nacimiento de Bernardo* is known in three early versions, all of which are fragmentary. An eight-verse text was printed in the *Cancionero de 1550* (and its later editions). Another fragment of six verses forms part of a secret dispatch, written in cipher and full of interpolated verses—"para burlarse de los que interceptaban las cartas en Francia"—sent to Felipe II, on May 26, 1562, by the Spanish ambassador in Paris, Tomás Perrenot de Chantonnay. A third fragment, cited in Luis Vélez de Guevara's *El conde don Pero Vélez* (vv. 2287, 2294, 2299–2308) can be very

---

wish to demean the magnificent scholarly achievement embodied in both of Vargyas' enormously useful books.

137. Even when we actually possess numerous modern French derivatives of a Hispanic ballad's putative ancestor text—as is the case with *Roi Renaud* vis-à-vis *La Muerte ocultada*—the exact relationship of the two ballads often remains unknowable in many of its details. For more data, see the Appendix.

138. For *L'amante confessore* (or *Finto frate*), see Nigra 97; Bronzini, II, 139–170 et alibi (with extensive additional bibliography and previously unedited texts). I have also seen Balladoro, no. 231; Borgatti, pp. 7–9; Ferraro-Monferrini, pp. 98–99; Ive, pp. 322–323; Marcoaldi, pp. 158–159; Pergoli, p. 43; Pitrè, II, 85–86; Radole, *Seconda raccolta*, nos. 67*ABC*; Vettori, no. 224 (and pp. 354–355). For analogous ballads, see n. 80 above.

precisely dated in 1615: the *estreno* took place on *la Noche de San Juan* (June 24, 1615). Verse numbers (in parentheses) to the right of Chantonnay's and Vélez's texts remit to C1550.

En los reynos de Leon   el casto Alfonso reynaua
·2   hermosa hermana tenia   doña Ximena se llama
       enamorarase de ella   esse conde de Saldaña
4   mas no biuia engañado,   porque la infanta lo amaua
       muchas vezes fueron juntos   que nadie lo sospechaua
6   de las vezes que se vieron   la infanta quedo preñada
       la infanta pario a Bernaldo   y luego monja se entraua.
8   Mando el rey prender al conde   y ponerle muy gran guarda.
                                                        (C1550)

En el reyno de Leon   quando el casto rey Alfonso reynava,   (1)
2   hermossa hermana tenía,   doma Ximena se llama   (2)
       y enamoróse della   el buen conde de Saldama.   (3)
4   Andando en estos amores   la ynfanta quedó prenada   (6)
       y parió a un cavallero   que Vernaldo del Carpio se llamava, (7)
6   Y era muy gentil honbre   y de los buenos de Espana.
                                                  (Chantonnay)[139]

En Castilla y en León   el casto Alfonso reinaba.   (1) 2287–8
2   Hermosa hermana tenía,   doña Jimena se llama.   (2) 2289–90
       Hase enamorado de ella   ese conde de Saldaña,   (3) 2291–2
4   el más galán caballero   que ciñó en Castilla espada.   2293–4

---

139. For the C1550 text, I follow Rodríguez-Moñino's ed. (p. 205; = RT, I, no. 1*a*, p. 176). For subsequent reprintings, see MCR, II, 482*a*. For Chantonnay, I take into account RT, I, no. 1*b*, p. 176, but follow Catalán's reading text (giving preference, however, to certain aberrant readings present in the decipherment: *Saldama, prenada, Espana*) (see Catalán, *Cancionero en cifra*, no. 5). My thanks go to Diego Catalán for placing at our disposal a preliminary print-out of his edition and study of this crucially important collection of late 16th-century traditional poetry. For a photograph of the cypher dispatch, see RT, I, 270–271 (last plate). Concerning the document, see Gómez del Campillo, *BRAH*, 129 (1951), 306, and Catalán's forthcoming study. For Vélez de Guevara's fragment, only five hemistichs of which are traditional (vv. 2287–2294, 2299, 2302, numbered here as vv. 1, 2, 3, 5*a*, 6*b*), the other components having largely been invented. Compare Thomas E. Case's study: "Esta segunda parte del romance . . . parece ser innovación de Vélez" (p. 31).

No estaba engañado el conde,   porque si amaba a la Infanta,   (4a) 2290–2300
6 con amorosos estremos   ella mucho más le amaba.   (4b) 2301–2
  Los pensamientos se dicen   por los ojos con las almas,   2303–4
8 llegando a la posesión   de las dichosas esperanzas.   2305–6
  A pesar de mil envidias,   los hurtos de amor gozaban.   2307–8

(Vélez de Guevara)

Obviously, none of these texts in very satisfactory. Though Chantonnay's verses do not supplement the *Cancionero* fragment—his v. 6 looks as if it were a vacuous filler—they clearly do not represent an identical version. In the urgency of the moment, to find verses to confuse possible decipherers, it seems obvious that Chantonnay would not have had reference to a written text, but would merely have set down from memory whatever verses happened to come to mind.[140] But Chantonnay's seemingly invented v. 6: "Y era muy gentil honbre / y de los buenos de Espana" distantly corresponds to Vélez de Guevara's vv. 2293–2294: "el más galán caballero / que ciñó en Castilla espada" (numbered here as v. 4) and would consequently seem to be authentic.

All three texts, then, must independently reflect the 16th-century oral tradition, but not much can be done with the minimal differences between C1550, Chantonnay, and Vélez. In two cases, however, the *Cancionero* (agreeing here with Vélez) has readings which look more like the modern Moroccan tradition than do those of the Spanish ambassador. Thus, while C1550 and Vélez have "es(s)e conde de Saldaña" (3b; Morocco: "ese conde de Saldaña"), Chantonnay reads: "el buen conde de Saldama" (3b) and, against C1550's "de las vezes que se vieron" (6a; Madrid: "De las veces que salieron juntos" [infra]; Morocco: "Un día se vieron juntos"), Chantonnay has "Andando en estos amores" (4a). Many Moroccan versions have "namorado se había" (compare Vélez's "Hase enamorado" [v. 3a]), instead of C1550's "enamorarase" (3a), but a good number have "namoróse" or "se enamoró," like Chantonnay's

---

140. The same is certainly the case with pen-trials. A person wishing to test a pen is not going to look for a written text to copy, but, on the spur of the moment, will call up from memory whatever happens to suggest itself. Concerning pen-trials and their potential importance, see my paper, "¿Existió un romancero de tradición oral entre los moriscos?," pp. 224–227. The example adduced (condeclarosconamo . . .) represents "Media noche era por filo." For other, recently discovered pen-trials of significance for the study of early Hispanic poetry, see Conde López, "Otro testimonio," and M.C. García, "Romances, villancicos y refranes." For pen-trials as some of the earliest documentation of Scandinavian ballads, see Dal, *Danish Ballads*, pp. 243–244, 289–290.

"enamoróse," but such variants seem essentially insignificant. The two other early texts differ radically in regard to C1550's v. 7 (Chantonnay, v. 5), where Bernardo's name has disappeared from the modern versions. Suffice to say that, in their differences vis-à-vis C1550, Chantonnay's and Vélez's texts also embody traditional readings. We cannot, then, reduce any of this to a simplified stemma. Ximena's reclusion in a nunnery (C1550, v. 7*b*)—to become a de-Christianized imprisonment in the Moroccan tradition—ultimately recalls the ballad's chronistic antecedents: "Desy tomo a su hermana donna Ximena et metiola en orden" (PCG).[141]

In the modern *Romancero*, *El nacimiento de Bernardo* has survived only among the Spanish Jews of Morocco and in a lone version recently collected in the Province of Madrid. On October 22, 1982, Julio Camarena, Paloma Esteban, and Antonio Lorenzo Vélez collected the following *romance* from a 90-year-old shepherd woman, Juana Bordó Jiménez, in Montejo de la Sierra (p.j. Torrelaguna). Two years later, José Manuel Fraile Gil again collected this same text, on May 15, 1985, and from the same informant, who, this time, was helped in the recitation by Liboria González García, 86 years. Both women were born in Montejo de la Sierra. (Corresponding verse numbers in C1550 and in the synthetic Moroccan version [*Mo*] are listed to the right of vv. 2–7.)

	En el reino de Aragón,	el casto Alfonso reinaba.	(1)
2	Tenía una hermosa hermana,	doña Jimena se llama.	(2/*Mo*6)
	Y se ha enamorado de ella	don Rodrigo de Vivarra.	(3/*Mo*7)
4	De las veces que salieron juntos,	la infanta encinta quedara.	(5–6/*Mo*8)
	De ella nació un infantito,	como la nácar y el agua.	(7*a*/*Mo*12)
6	Le puso el nombre de Juan,	al que Juan Prin le llamaban.	(7*b*)
	A ella la llevó a un convento;	a él en un castillo encerrara.	(8/*Mo*10)
8	Al cabo de los veinte años,	cuando Juan Prin se enterara,	
	se presentó a su tío	y de este manera le hablara:	
10	—¡Si no me entregas mis padres,	te formaré una batalla!—	

---

141. Heinermann, *Unterschungen*, pp. 4–5 (= PCG, Chap. 617, p. 351*a*.9–10). Concerning *Con cartas y mensajeros* (*Primav.* 13–13*a*), see the Appendix. Lucas de Tuy and Rodrigo Ximénez de Rada also record this detail: "& sororem suam in ordine monastico trusit" (Lucas *apud* Heinermann; "y a su hermana ençerro en orden de monja" [ed. Puyol, p. 286.21–22]); "Sororem autem Semenam religioni in monasterio mancipavit" (Rodrigo X. de Rada, *De Rebus Hispania*, ed. Cabanes Pecourt, Chap. IX, p. 82*b*). The Moroccan imprisonment would therefore seem to be yet another example of de-Christianization.

Fue por su madre al convento   y a su casa la llevara;
12 fue por su padre al castillo   y de esta manera le hablara:
—Cuando entré en este castillo,   apenas tenía barba
14 y ahora, por un pecado,   la veo crecida y blanca.
—Padre, no se apure usté,   que yo le llevaré a su casa,
16 donde vivirás tranquilo   y tendrás una vida santa.[142]

This *Madrileña* version, with astounding anachronism, replaces Bernardo del Carpio with the 19th-century general and master politician, Juan Prim y Prats (1814–1870), thus making him an offspring of the Cid Campeador, "don Rodrigo de Vivarra," who, thanks to the presence of "doña Jimena" in our *romance*, will replace the Count of Saldaña as father of the hero. As Diego Catalán points out, v. 5, "De ella nació un infantito, / como la nácar y el agua," is supported by the Moroccan reading, "parida estaba de un niño, / como la leche y la grana" (v. 12), as evidence of the traditional development of this erudite, chronistic ballad (*Cancionero en cifra*). Like C1550, Chantonnay, and Vélez de Guevara, the modern Madrid version fails to clarify the ballad's early dénouement, which, in this case, is borrowed in part (vv. 13–14) from another early *romance artificioso* about Bernardo del Carpio, *Bañando están las prisiones*:

Quando entre en este castillo   apenas entre con barbas
y agora por mis pecados   la veo crecida y blanca.[143]

In Morocco, *El nacimiento de Bernardo* is not a common ballad. Except for the exiguous verses embedded in Luna Farache's *Conde Claros* texts, we were never able to record it. At the beginning of the century, Benoliel and especially

---

142. I cite the text edited by Fraile Gil, in his *Romancero tradicional de la Provincia de Madrid*, p. 39. Here I make some minor changes on punctuation and prefer the "neutral" spelling *Prin* (instead of *Prim*), suggested by Catalán in *Cancionero en cifra* (no. 5). Concerning Fraile Gil's text, see also his "Crónica de una recolección," pp. 545–546. For the initial recording by Camarena, Esteban, and Vélez, see A. Lorenzo Vélez, "Una nueva aparición."

143. *Pliegos Milán*, I, 203; RT, I, 244–245 (no. 20*a*). For the same ballad's fragmentary survival in the Gypsy tradition, see Catarella, *El romancero gitano-andaluz*, pp. 20–21, 55, and Luis Suárez Avila's monographic articles, "Bernardo del Carpio," pp. 235–237 et alibi, and *Dos siglos*, p. 98. Concerning the Gypsy tradition, see also my review of Catarella's *Romancero gitano-andaluz*, *HR*, 64 (1996), 97–99.

Manrique de Lara collected fine versions. Bénichou's and Larrea's text 1 are from oral tradition, while Larrea 1*b* is from a manuscript copy. Oro A. Librowicz's 25-verse unedited text, sung by a relatively young informant, would seem to be a splendid exception.

As Menéndez Pidal has pointed out, the ballad, in Morocco, has turned into something quite different from its 16th-century antecedents and has lost contact with the traditional narrative from which it derives. It can tell us nothing about the ballad's unknown ending in its earlier forms. In elaborating its innovative dénouements, the modern song has broken altogether with the epic tradition.[144] Menéndez Pidal's brief appreciation should be quoted at this point:

> El romance tradicional marroquí se fija especialmente en el dolor de la madre, ideando un desenlace enteramente extraño a la leyenda de Bernardo: la reina, conmovida al escuchar el llanto de su cuñada, va a pedir gracia al rey para el conde prisionero. El romance, con la adición del llanto de Ximena y la intercesión de la reina, pierde su contacto con el conjunto de la leyenda, pero gana en interés novelesco y en lirismo (RT, I, 184).

Rather than record all variants, as we have done in the case of ballads represented by many unedited texts, I reproduce below (and supplement at vv. 3+ and 10+) the most complete version (no. 1*c*) edited by Menéndez Pidal (RT, II, 177–178), correlating each verse with all known variant texts. All these readings, except those of Librowicz's still unedited version (*o*) are readily available in RT, pp. 178–183, and here in the brief fragments absorbed by our texts 11*D* and *E*. Corresponding verse numbers in C1550 and in the Madrid version (*Ma*) are listed to the right of vv. 6–12. In listing sources, we follow the order of the texts in RT (nos. 1*c*-1*n*):

	Mañanita era, mañana,	al tiempo que alboreaba,
2	gran fiestas hacen los moros	por la bella de Granada.
	Arrevuelven sus caballos,	jugando iban a la danza:
3+	[aquél del caballo blanco,	el de la silla dorada . . .];
4	aquél que amigas tenía,	allí se le señalaban;

---

144. This is not to say that this ballad's origin was ever directly connected with an epic source. Its origin is undoubtedly chronistic. Compare Heinermann, *Unterschungen*, p. 3 (= PCG, Chap. 617, p. 350). Concerning *Con cartas y mensajeros* (*Primav.* 13–13*a*), see the Appendix.

aquél que no las tenía, procuraba de ganarlas.

6 Hermana tiene el buen reye, que Ximena se llamaba;   (2/*Ma*2)

namorado se había della ese conde de Saldaña.   (3/*Ma*3)

8 Un día se vieron juntos, Ximena quedó preñada.   (5–6/*Ma*4)

El buen rey, como lo supo, un mal castigo fue a darla:

10 A él lo metió en prisiones y a ella encerró en una sala,   (8*a*/*Ma*7)

10+ [en un castillo de vidro, buen castillo y buena guardia.]   (8*b*)

Van días y vienen días, Ximena parida estaba;

12 parida estaba de un niño, como la leche y la grana.   (7/*Ma*5)

Un día empañando al niño, su madre bien le miraba:

14 —¡En qué hora nacistes, hijo, de madre tan desdichada!—

Con lágrimas de sus ojos, la cara del niño lava:

16 —Tu padre estaba en prisiones y tu madre aquí encerrada.—

Oyido lo había la reina, dende su sala ande estaba:

18 —¿Qué tienes y tú, Ximena, Ximena la mi cuñada?

Si te hace falta dinero, te daré yo oro y plata;

20 si te faltaran vestidos, te daré yo seda y grana;

si te faltaran regalos, muchos en mi mesa estaban.

22 —No me faltaba dinero, eso es lo que me sobraba;

ni me faltaban vestidos, muchos tengo yo en mi arca;

24 ni me hacen falta juguetes, muchos en la plaza estaban.

El mayor de mis cuidados, éste que ahora te contara:

26 El hijo ya tengo grande, por su padre me demanda.

—Yo te juro a ti, Ximena, y a Dios que me puso el alma,

28 ni comer pan a manterles, ni arrimarme a la almohada,

hasta que saque a ese conde de las prisiones de Italia.—

30 Fuese para los palacios, adonde el rey gobernaba.

El buen rey, como la vido, en sus ojos cayó en gracia.

32 —Buenos días, mi señor rey. —Buenos los tengas, mi amada.—

Tomó el verdugo en su mano y le pidió una demanda:

34 —¿Cuál es la tuya, la reina, y cuál es la tu demanda?

—Que me saques a ese conde de las prisiones de Italia

36 y le cases con Ximena, Ximena la mi cuñada.

—Aína, mis caballeros, armad pronto una guiñarda,

38 de toques y de torneos, músicas muy aparadas,

y me traigáis a ese conde,   en palmas muy estimadas.—
40   Otro día a la mañana,   las ricas bodas se arman.[145]

Sources

Base text: Tetuán: *c* = RT 1*c* (= CMP A1.6)

Tangier: *d*	= RT 1*d* (= CMP A1.1)		Larache: *k*	= RT 1*k* (= CMP A1.8)
e	= RT 1*e* (= CMP A1.2)		Tetuán: *l*	= RT 1*l* (= Larrea 1)
f	= RT 1*f* (= CMP A1.3)		*m*	= RT 1*m* (= Larrea 1*b*)
Tetuán: *g*	= RT 1*g* (= CMP A1.5)		Buenos Aires: *n*	= RT 1*n* (= Bénichou, pp. 29 + 40)
h	= RT 1*h* (= CMP A1.4)		Tetuán: *o*	= Librowicz (II) A1
i	= RT 1*i* (= CMP A1.7)		*p*	= our 11*D*.1–3
Alcázar: *j*	= RT 1*j* (= CMP A1.9)		*q*	= our 11*E*.1–5

Variants

1 *defghijlmno*	12 *defghijklmnoq*
2 *defghijklmno*	13 *deghijlmno*
3 *dehijk*	14 *defghijlmno*
3+ *ejkp*	15 *fhlm*
4 *deghilmno*	16–20 *defghijlmno*
5 *deghimno*	21 *defghijmo*
6 *defghijklmnopq*	22 *defghijlmo*
7 *deghijklmnoq*	23 *defghijlmno*
8 *defghijklmnoq*	24 *defghijmo*
9 *deghil(a)mn*	25 *c* only
10 *defghilmnq*	26 *dghij*
10+ *ilno*	27 *defghimno*
11 *defghijklmno*	28 *deghino(a)*

---

145. The text contains several difficult lexical items. What is the meaning of *verdugo* (v. 33*b*)? None of its academic exceptions would seem to fit this particular context. Again: What is a *guiñarda* (v. 37; *guillarda* in the variant ending, p. 178, v. 34)? Obviously it is a spectacle, a display, an *alarde* of some sort, but what is the word's origin? Neither DCECH (s.vv. *guillarse* and *guiñar*) nor DECLlC (s.v. *guinyar*) provides any leads. Concerning *torneos* (v. 38), which occurs also in *El sueño de doña Alda*, see FLSJ, III, 136, n. 12.

29 *defghino(a)*   40 *efghjlmno*
30–39 *c* only

A number of contaminations, which attest to our ballad's complex interaction with other *romances*, should be discussed first of all. Except for our fragments 11D and E, all texts of *El nacimiento de Bernardo* begin with a five- or six-verse prologue, which we have called *La sanjuanada*. These are migratory verses, which, over the centuries, have been attached to various different traditional narratives. We have already studied these verses and their variant readings in detail elsewhere (*En torno*, pp. 13–22). Here I will merely identify the verses' various traditional forms and the contexts in which they can be documented. In the 16th century, *La sanjuanada* was associated with two *romances*: the frontier ballad of *La pérdida de Antequera* and, in essentially identical form, the artistic Morisco ballad of *Jarifa y Abindarráez*. The verses attached to *La pérdida de Antequera* read as follows in a *glosa* included in the *Cancionero de Juan Fernández de Ixar*:

   La mañana de San Juan   al punto que alboreaua
2   gran fiesta hazen los moros   por la bega de Granada
   revolbiendo sus caballos,   y jugando de las lanças
4   ricos pendones en ellas   labrados por sus amadas
   ricas aljubas bestidas   de sedas y finas granas
6   ricos albornozes puestos   texidos de oro y plata
   el moro que amores tiene   señales d'ellos mostraua
8   mas quien amores no abia   alli no escaramuçaba. . . .[146]

The verses attached to *Jarifa y Abindarráez* read as follows:

---

146. *Disparates donde ay puestas muchas damas y señoras de Aragón* (Vi con muy brauo denuedo / aquella reyna Marfissa), *Cancionero de Ixar*, ed. Azáceta, II, 785–786. Azáceta provisionally specifies "el comienzo del último cuarto [del siglo XVI] . . . como tope máximo" as a possible chronology for this late section of the MS (I, xx–xxi). For variants in other early texts, see *En torno*, pp. 16–17, n. 6. The *Sanjuanada* verses may, in their turn, be genetically related to the thematically identical Mozarabic *kharja*, "¡Albo día este día, / día de al^cAnṣara ḥaqqā!," as we have pointed out in *En torno*, pp. 13–22. López Estrada's detailed study of *La sanjuanada* is crucial (*La conquista de Antequera*, pp. 21–39).

LA mañana de sant Juã al tiempo q̃ alboreaua
2 hazen gran fiesta los moros por la vega de Granada
 reboluiendo sus cauallos jugando van de las lanças
4 ricos pendones en ellas labrados por sus amadas
 ricas aljubas vestidas de seda y oro labradas
6 el moro que amores tiene alli bien se señalaua
 y el que amores no tenia alli no escaramuçaua. . . .[147]

The differences between the various early texts are quite minor. Note, however, that the ballad's Moroccan form prefers the reading "al tiempo que alboreaba" (v. 1*b*), which figures in the *Silva* (1550) and Diego Pisador, attached to *La pérdida de Antequera*, and in the Cracow *pliego* and the *Silva recopilada*, attached to *Jarifa y Abindarráez*.[148]

In the modern Peninsular tradition, one or two initial verses of *La sanjuanada* serve to introduce *El martirio de Santa Catalina*, in Castile and Catalonia, and *La fuente consagrada* (*La Virgen* [or *Jesucristo*] *y la hija del rey*), in Castile, Asturias, Galicia, and Trás-os-Montes:

La mañana de S. Juan, al punto que alboreaba,
hacen gran función los moros en la ciudad de Granada. . . .
           (*Santa Catalina*)

Manhanas de S. João, pela manhã de alvorada,

---

147. *Pliegos de Cracovia*, II, 97. For minor variants from two other early sources, see *En torno*, pp. 17–18 and n. 7. Ginés Pérez de Hita's text, in the *Guerras civiles de Granada* (1595), can be consulted in Bryant's ed. (pp. 80–81). Paula Blanchard-Demouge's earlier ed. (1913–1915) has now again become available in a photographic ed., with extensive preliminary studies by Pedro Correa and Joaquín Gil Sanjuán (1998–1999). On the wide diffusion of the migratory prologue and its early analogues and congeners, see *En torno*, pp. 16–18. Note also the following allusion in Francisco López de Úbeda's *La pícara Justina*: "Acuérdome que hice azofar a una mujer porque me dijo que madrugase la mañana de San Juan al punto que alboreaba, y que cual fuese la primera cosa que viese, tal sería mi novio" (ed. Bruno M. Damiani, p. 424).

148. See Bénichou's study, pp. 40–41. Note that the "al punto" reading also occurs in other printings of the verses prefixed to both *romances*: *En torno*, pp. 16–19, as well as in the Castilian version of *Santa Catalina*. For the *Silva recopilada*, see MCR, I, 411–489; II, 551.

Jesus Cristo se passeia   à roda da fonte clara . . .
                              (*Fuente consagrada*)[149]

Needless to say, the use of these verses as a prologue to the *Bernardo*
narrative in the Moroccan tradition invests the ballad with a new and distinctive
aura of Morisco exoticism and gallantry which further separates it from its
original epic context. *El nacimiento de Bernardo* thus participates in what we
might call a pervasive "Morisquization" of the repertoire of Moroccan epic
ballads. We have already noted a similar process in *Las almenas de Toro, El
destierro de Cid*, and *Búcar sobre Valencia*.[150] Such a trend is much more than
merely a capricious, though ultimately logical, tendency to associate what were
once high medieval heroic narratives with the final events of the Reconquest.
Here our modern Moroccan ballads continue to participate in a tendency which
was already present in much earlier stages of the epic: As the *Frontera* gradually
moved toward the south, the old narratives were in constant need of keeping
pace with contemporary events. This same pressure leads to the consecutive
relocation of the *Infantes de Lara* story ever southward until it ends up on the
outskirts of Córdoba or, again, the shifting of Don Beltrán's Carolingian
Roncesvalles to the "campos de Alventosa" in the Province of Jaén.[151]
   Text RT 1*e*, which lifts vv. 3 and 3+, with the gallant jousting and the white
horse, from their original *Sanjuanada* context and relocates them between vv. 7
and 8, stresses even more the innovative Morisco ambience of the *Bernardo*
ballad's Moroccan form. With the addition of v. 9, text 1*e* specifies what is
elsewhere only implied: Ximena falls in love with Count Saldaña because of his
knightly attributes and valiant horsemanship:

6   Namorado se había de ella   ese conde de Asaldania.   (7)
    Al revolver sus caballos,   jugando iban a la lanza,   (3)
8   ése del caballo blanco,   el de la barba dorada,   (3+)
    todas enamoran de él;   Ximena es a una banda.

---

149. The texts cited are from ART, p. 116, and Costa Fontes, *Trás-os-Montes*, no.
894. We cite various other versions in *En torno*, p. 19. Costa Fontes edits many more
Trás-os-Montes texts (nos. 895–918) and provides an extensive bibliography from
various traditions (II, 1351: *A Fonte Clara*). See now RPI U29 (*Santa Catarina*) and U41
(*Fonte Clara*).
   150. On the evocation of a Morisco ambience in traditional *romances* of epic origin,
see the Appendix.
   151. Concerning the historical actualization of epic narratives, see the Appendix.

10 Un día se vieron juntos,   Ximena encinta quedara.   (8)[152]

Looking now at some minor associations or contaminations present in
Moroccan texts of *El nacimiento de Bernardo*: Verse 12, though it fulfills the
same function as v. 7 of the C1550 text, recalls, undoubtedly, two verses from
La infanta parida (*í-a, á-a*): "Entre almenas y almenas, / a un niño parido había;
/ envolvióio en seda y grana / y asomóse a una ventana . . ." (Larrea 160.53–56).
But the same allusion to *seda y grana* also occurs in *El infante parricida* (or
Hijo vengador):

> Van días y vienen días,   la reina parió un infante;
> envolvióle en seda y grana   y a la leona le mandó echare.
>
> > (Bénichou, p. 200)

An association with these verses leads, in text 1*k*, to a unique contamination
which replaces the *Bernardo* ballad's dénouement with partially re-rhymed
verses taken from *El infante parricida*:

>   Van días y vienen días,   Ximena parida estaba;   (11)
> 8   parida estaba de un hijo,   como la leche y la grana.   (12)
>   Vistióle en grana y en seda   y a la leona se le daba;
> 10 la leona, como discreta,   conoció sangre reala;
>   quitó leche de su hijo   y al infante se lo dara.
> 12 Van días y vienen días,   l'infante y un barragane.
>   Alzó armas y caballos   y a su padre fue a matare.
> 14 Cuando a su padre mataba,   se fue a la reina su madre:
>   —No me mates tú, mi hijo,   no me mates barragane.
> 16 Te daré medio reinado   y la corona de tu padre.[153]

---

152. Text 1*e* (= RT, I, 178–179; CMP A1.2). The count's "gilded" beard may reflect
an Arab custom of decoratively staining the beard with henna (but, in available sources,
the purpose is usually to disguise the effects of age). See Armistead and Monroe, "A New
Version of *La morica de Antequera*," p. 238, n. 11. For more on the uses of henna, see
Yoná, pp. 344–345, n. 1.

153. Concerning this ballad, see Bénichou, pp. 200–201, and Catalán, "Análisis
semiótico," pp. 244–247. For published versions, see CMP G2; Nahón 15. Verse 12*b*:
"l'infante y un barragane" is obviously defective.

Verse 17, "Oyido lo había la reina, / dende su sala ande estaba," echoes any number of ballads in which someone overhears the protagonist:

Oído lo había el buen reye,   desde su alto altare. . . .
                                  (*Buena hija*: Bénichou, p. 180)

Oído lo había el buen Cidi,   dende su sala ande estaba. . . .
                                  (*Búcar*: *Epic Ballads*, p. 243)

Oyido le había el buen rey,   desde su sala reale. . . .
                                  (*Guarinos*: FLSJ, III, 79, v. 17)

Oído lo había el buen reye,   desde su rico altar. . . .
                                  (*Lavandera*: Ortega, p. 229)

Verse 25, which is unique to our base text (1c), represents a contamination from *La buena hija*. The association is probably triggered by the allusion in v. 26 to the son's having grown:

El mayor de mis cuidados,   éste que ahora te contara:
El hijo ya tengo grande,   por su padre me demanda.
                              (*Bernardo* 1c, vv. 25–26)

Compare *La buena hija*:

El mayor de mis cuidados,   hija, que te veo y grande. . . .
                              (Larrea 179.24–25)[154]

The queen's vow in vv. 27–28, attested to in many versions, suggests some recollection of *Las quejas de Jimena*. Here are some of the variant readings present in our *Bernardo* ballad:

Yo te juro a ti, Ximena,   y a Dios que me puso el alma,
ni comer pan a manteles,   ni arrimarme a la almohada. . . .
                              (1ch)

---

154. Similar readings in Alvar, *Textos*, II, 766; Arce, no. 4; Bénichou, p. 180 ("pesares" for "cuidados"); Larrea 180–181. See also CMP X2.

Por Dios te juro, Ximena,   Ximena, la mi cuñada,
que ni pan coma en manteles,   ni ponga mi cabeza en almohada. ...

(1d)

ni coma pan en manteles,   ni me arrime a la almohada. ...

(1e)

ni comer pan a manteles,   ni con el rey duerma en cama. ...

(1gi)

no comer pan a manteles,   ni acostarme en la mi cama. ...

(1n)

que no me siente a la mesa,   hasta no estés casada. ...

(1o)

Corresponding readings in *Las quejas de Jimena* are:

ni comer pan a manteles,   ni con la reina folgare. ...
ni arrimarse a la estormía,   ni en caballo acabalgarse. ...
ni arrimarse a la almoada,   ni con la reina folgare. ...[155]

Let us now briefly look at certain differences between our base text (1*c*) and the other Moroccan versions of *El nacimiento de Bernardo*: In regard to the order of vv. 13–16, text *c* is certainly defective: Verse 15 is out of place. Texts *hlm* attest to the proper order:

Un día empañando al niño,	su madre bien le miraba;	(13)
de lágrimas de sus ojos,	la cara ya al niño lava:	(15)
—¿Para qué nacistes, hijo,	a madre tan desdichada?	(14)
Tu padre estaba en prisiones	y tu madre aquí encerrada.[156]	(16)

---

155. The readings are from *Epic Ballads*, p. 87 (synthetic text, v. 12); CMP A9.9 (= *Epic Ballads*, p. 89, variants to v. 11); and CSQ, no. 17, v. 31. The form *estormía* corresponds to Moroc. Ar *ṣṭormiya* 'throw pillow; round cushion' (*Epic Ballads*, p. 93, n. 16).

156. Compare also texts *degijmo*, which have vv. 13, 14, 16, and *f*, which lacks v. 13, but follows the order 15, 14, 16.

In vv. 19–24, Ximena's possible needs and their order, as specified by the queen, vary from text to text. To those present in text *c* (*dinero, vestidos, regalos/juguetes*), other versions add *comidas* (*degimo*).[157]

Only text *f* adds to *dinero* and *vestidos* an offer and subsequent rejection of cities:

15   si necesitas ciodades,   te daré Francia y Granada. . . .

18   ni necesito ciudades,   mía es Francia y Granada. . . .

These verses are almost certainly a borrowing from *Sancho y Urraca*, a ballad which, as we shall see, has in other ways, undoubtedly had a significant impact on *El nacimiento de Bernardo*:

    —¿Si quieres Fransia o Granada   o Toledo o Aragón?

    —No quiero siudá ninguna,   todas a mi mandar son.

                     (*Epic Ballads*, no. 3B.14–15)[158]

In v. 26, the various Moroccan versions embody two quite different perspectives. Some suggest the epic motif of the father quest:

El hijo ya tengo grande,	por su padre me demanda.	(*c*)
El niño ya tengo grande,	por su padre preguntaba.	(*d*)
Me falta el padre del niño,	que su hijo le demanda.[159]	(*j*)

Texts *f* and *l* also focus on the child and the father's absence by repeating earlier verses:

. . . ni necesito ciudades,	mía es Francia y Granada.	
Aquí me ha nacido un niño,	como la leche y la grana.	(12)

---

157. Concerning the formulaic pattern of a series of questions followed by negative answers, see the Appendix.

158. For other readings, see vv. 20–23 of the synthetic text and its variants (*Epic Ballads*, pp. 136 and 139–140).

159. See also texts *hi* and the variant ending of *c* (v. 33); *g* has a similar verse (but with a nonsensical repetition of *padre*); a variant reading of *d* has: "me falta el padre del niño / que su hijo le demanda" (v. 25).

Su padre está en las prisiones	y yo estoy aquí encerrada.	(16)

(1f)

... ni me faltaba dinero,	¡cuántos en mis cofres estaban!	(23)
Que aquí me ha nacido un niño,	como la leche y la grana.	(12)
Su padre está en las prisiones,	su madre aquí está encerrada.	(16)

(1l)

Other versions, by contrast, stress the importance of freeing Ximena's lover:

Lo que quiero es a ese conde,	ese conde de Asaldañas.	(*e*)
Lo que quiero es ese conde,	ese conde de Sandalia.	(*m*)
Lo que quiero es a ese conde,	a ese conde de Sandaria.	(*n*)

Oro A. Librowicz's unedited text has the same perspective, but expresses it in a verse borrowed from *Sancho y Urraca*, pointing once again to that song's impact on our *Bernardo* ballad:

Lo que quiero es a ese conde,	lo saquéis de la prisione.	(*o*)

Compare *Sancho y Urraca*:

Lo que quiero es a mi hermano,	que saquís de prizión.

(Epic Ballads, no. 3A.20)[160]

Ultimately, the child's *demanda* concerning his father recalls the epic tradition reflected in the *Estoria de España*, though, in the chronicle text, the hero's "quest" for his father is handled very differently.[161] The emphasis on freeing the count, on the other hand, agrees with important narrative innovations characteristic of the ballad's experimental dénouements.

---

160. For other readings, see *Epic Ballads*, pp. 136 and 140 (v. 24).

161. See Heinermann, *Unterschungen*, pp. 11, 20, 24. On the hero's search for his father, see *Bosnia*, pp. 90–91 (nos. A5, B13, C19: *En busca del padre*), and CMP G4. David Bynum's "Themes of the Young Hero" is crucial. Note also my "Gaiferos' Game." See Thompson: H1385.7. *Quest for lost father*. On heroes of illegitimate birth in the Spanish (and Pan-European) epic, see my article, "Dos tradiciones épicas," and now my *Tradición épica*, pp. 17–30 and 139–151.

Perhaps the most striking feature of our *Bernardo* ballad in the Sephardic tradition is the diversity of its endings.[162] While most complete versions end with the typical deus-ex-machina wedding verse: "Otro día a la mañana, / las ricas bodas se arman,"[163] their perspectives on how such an outcome is achieved vary considerably. Several texts stop short of an elaborate ending. Texts *degino* end with the queen's promise to Ximena; *j* ends with the verse about the child asking for its father (v. 26); in *lm*, the queen simply assures Ximena that she will marry the count.

Text *h* and the variant ending of *c*, on one hand, and *f*, on the other, take the narrative further. In *c* (variant) and *h*, following the queen's promise to Ximena, the king appears and asks the queen what is wrong:

26	—Yo te juro a ti, Ximena,	Ximena la mi cuñada,	(27)
	ni comer pan a manteles,	ni arrimarme a la almohada,	(28)
28	hasta que saque a ese conde,	a ese conde de Sandalia.—	(29)
	Ellos en estas palabras,	el buen rey por allí entrara:	
30	—¿Qué tienes y tú, mi reina?	Dime lo que te pasaba.	
	—Con Ximena mi cuñada,	[. . . . .]	
32	que el niño ya tiene grande,	por su padre le demanda.—	
	Otro día en la manaña,	las ricas bodas se arman.	(40)

(1*h*)

30	Ellos en estas palabras,	el buen rey por allí entrara:
	—¿Qué tienes y tú, mi reina,	que te veo asofocada?
32	—Las prisiones de Ximena	las veo muy alteradas,
	que el niño ya tiene grande	y por su padre demanda.
34	—Aína, mis caballeros,	armad pronto una guillarda;
	id, traedme a ese conde,	a ese conde de Saldaña.
36	Agústate tú, mi reina,	ya se aceptó tu demanda.—
	Otro día en la mañana,	ricas bodas se arman.

(1*c*: variant)

---

162. For other examples, among many, of creative experimentation in ballad endings, note *El cautivo del renegado* (Bénichou, *Creación,* pp. 182–184); *El forzador* (*Tres calas,* pp. 33–34); *Robo de Elena* (Nahón, pp. 66–68); *Sancho y Urraca* (*Epic Ballads,* pp. 142–146); and, in a Pan-Hispanic perspective, *Búcar sobre Valencia* (*Epic Ballads,* pp. 270–273). For more on ballad endings, see *Epic Ballads,* p. 142, n. 21.

163. Texts *d* and *i* are exceptions. Concerning this "happy ending" formula, see *Epic Ballads,* pp. 96, n. 21; 145, n. 28.

In *f,* where we have already noted the influence of *Sancho y Urraca* (in vv. 15 and 18), the queen takes matters into her own hands, goes to the prison herself, and frees the count:

	Oídolo había la infante, desde su sala ande estaba:	(17)
12	—¿Qué tienes y tú, Ximena, Ximena la mi cuñada?	(18)
	Si necesitas dinero, yo te daré oro y plata;	(19)
14	si necesitas vestidos, yo te daré seda y grana;	(20)
	si necesitas ciodades, te daré Francia y Granada.	
16	—No necesito dinero, que yo tengo oro y plata,	(22)
	ni necesito vestidos, muchos tengo yo en mi arca,	(23)
18	ni necesito ciudades, mía es Francia y Granada.	
	Aquí me ha nacido un niño como la leche y la grana.	(12)
20	Su padre está en las prisiones y yo estoy aquí encerrada.	(16)
	—No se te importe, Ximena, Ximena la mi cuñada,	
22	yo [le] sacaré de prisiones y pronto serás casada.—	
	Otro día a la mañana, en las prisiones entrara.	
24	Lo agarrara de la mano y a su casa le llevara.	
	Mañana por la mañana, Ximena ya está casada.[164]	(40)

Such a development brings us to the elaborate and unique dénouement of text *c* (vv. 30–39). Preciada Israel's alternative ending, in which, as also in text *h,* the king first asks the queen what is wrong, suggests that the lengthy *desenlace* of text *c* may well be a personal creation of the singer. Yet its traditional underpinnings are also very strong. We have already seen how, in a number of cases, *El nacimiento de Bernardo* has been influenced by or shares formulaic verses with) a number of other ballads: *Buena hija* (Oído lo había el buen rey . . .; El mayor de mis cuidados . . .); *Búcar sobre Valencia* (Oído lo había el buen

---

164. Note how, in CMP A5.2 (version *b* of *Sancho y Urraca*), like version *f* of *Bernardo,* also sung by Hanna Bennaim of Tangier, Doña Alba (= Doña Urraca) goes to the prison and personally frees her brother. See *Epic Ballads,* pp. 143–144. For the formulaic verse so frequent in Morocco, in which the *infanta,* in her *sala,* overhears what is being said, compare the following line in an Asturian version of *Conde Claros fraile*: "bien la oyera un primo suyo / de altas murallas del mar" (NCR 14.25.17). The formula about abundant clothing saved up in chests (v. 17), also occurs in Moroccan versions of *La expulsión de los judíos de Portugal*: "no por mengua de ajuar, / que en mi arca está cumplido" (MP 13); "nin por mengua de ažuares, / en su arca los tenía" (Armistead and Silverman, "Un aspecto desatendido").

Cid . . .); *Lavandera* (Oído lo había el buen reye . . .); and, very especially, *Las quejas de Jimena* (ni comer pan a manteles . . .) and *Sancho y Urraca* (¿Si quieres Francia o Granada . . .?; Lo que quiero es a mi hermano . . .; en las prisiones entrara . . .). We might now ask what all of these ballads have in common. Obviously, all concern strong, even daring women, whose character gains them recognition by powerful figures of authority, in many cases despite initially very disadvantageous circumstances. In stressing the queen's assertiveness, text *c* is paralleled by Hanna Bennaim's text *f* and, in a broader perspective, it undoubtedly is modeled on the figure of the strong, brave woman of Biblical tradition (*'ešeth ḥayil*), as exemplified by Doña Alba in *Sancho y Urraca,* by the homonymous Ximena in *Las quejas de Jimena,* and, less directly, on the other narratives I have mentioned.[165] In *Sancho y Urraca* and in *Las quejas,* we find a similar array of identical motifs: Here too the brave woman defiantly appears at the king's court, greets the king, and voices her demand: freedom for her brother (or marriage to her father's killer). In Preciada Israel's distinctive ending to *El nacimiento de Bernardo,* the immediate model is undoubtedly *Sancho y Urraca,* but, in the queen's vow to Ximena (v. 28), the influence of *Las quejas* had already been brought to bear upon the *Bernardo* ballad by other singers (texts *deghino*). In this remarkable ending, we can, then, observe, at first hand and in process, the poetic creativity of an individual traditional singer. Here indeed we can perceive a single link in the traditional chain of transmission. We are witness to a single stage in the intricate workings of what Menéndez Pidal so rightly characterized as *el autor-legión.*[166]

Musicological commentary

In the present chapter we have discussed textual problems involving two *Conde Claros* narratives that survived among the Sephardim: *Conde Claros y la infanta* and *Conde Claros fraile,* but in our musical commentary we will, for comparative purposes, bring together all early musical documents for various *Conde Claros* ballads. We therefore also discuss here the tunes for *Conde*

---

165. Concerning the type of the strong woman (*'ešeth ḥayil*) in the Moroccan tradition, see, for now, *Epic Ballads,* p. 153 and n. 56. Rosalía Guzofsky explores the topic in detail in her *Mujeres heroicas.* For more on this crucial theme, see our study of *Melisenda insomne* (FLSJ, V, Chap. 13).

166. See, for example, RoH, I, 49–50, 233–234, 258–259. In his pathfinding book, *Creación poética,* Paul Bénichou has refined this crucially important concept and, at the same time, has provided a host of eloquent additional examples.

Claros preso (not represented in the Judeo-Spanish tradition) and *Conde Claros insomne*, whose textual tradition was already discussed in Chapter 10. While none of the tunes associated with these *romances* can be traced to earlier Iberian sources, it is noteworthy that we possess two distinct musical examples from well-known early Castilian sources that also relate to *Conde Claros*. The first is the *tiple* from the four-part setting by Juan del Encina (1468–1521): "Pésame de vos, el conde," for solo voice and instruments, which can be found in the *Cancionero musical de Palacio*.[167] The setting, closely resembling the style of the Italian *frottola*, possibly dates from the last decade of the 15th century.[168] Encina's text, which deals with the narrative of *Conde Claros preso*, constitutes the segment's earliest printed source.[169]

The second example is nothing more than a trichordal melodic distich (AA′) which appeared in Francisco de Salinas' treatise *De Musica libri septem* (Salamanca, 1577),[170] in association with the verse "Conde Claros con amores /

---

167. Madrid, Biblioteca del Palacio Real, II/1335; *olim* 2-I-5, fols. 77vo.–78 (= Barbieri, *Cancionero musical*, no. 329; Anglés, *La música en la corte*, I, no. 131). For the text, see *Cancionero musical de Palacio*, ed. Romeu Figueras, II, no. 131.

168. Most probably after 1496, the year Encina's *Cancionero* was printed in Salamanca and in which this and several other of his poems from the *Cancionero musical de Palacio* were not included.

169. Isabel Pope ("Notas," p. 397) remarked that the episode "era tan conocido en círculos aristocráticos en los primeros años del reinado de los Reyes Católicos, que el poeta Francisco de León lo glosó en su romance «La desastrada cayda» [y que] en 1495 lo cantaban las damas de la corte, como se sabe por el «Juego trobado que hizo a la reyna doña Isabel» el poeta Pinar." She added that "es muy posible que a esta misma canción de Encina se refiera Pinar en su «Juego trobado»." The "Juego trobado" to which Pope referred was actually the "Juego de Naipes trovado" (versified playing cards) by Jerónimo de Pinar, who Ramón Menéndez Pidal believed "debió jugarse hacia mayo o junio de 1495, residiendo los reyes en Madrid. Cada naipe lleva una décima dedicada ora a la Reina Católica, ora al Príncipe. . ., ora a las infantas. . ., y a todas las damas; cada naipe atribuye a cada persona ciertos emblemas y una canción. Varios de los naipes señalan como canción un romance, alguno trovadoresco, «un romance entristecido que es el de la Reina Dido», y hasta cinco romances viejos, todos de final trunco . . . [uno de que] manda cantar el tan glosado y tan asonado fragmento del Conde Claros: *Pésame de vos, el conde*" (RoH, II, 46–47).

170. Book VI, Chapter 14, p. 342 (= Kastner, *Francisco Salinas De Musica*, p. 342; for a Castilian translation, see Fernández de la Cuesta, *Francisco Salinas*, p. 597). The treatise's original title was *Francisci Sa / linae Bvrgensis / Abbatis Sancti Pancratii / de Rocca Scalegna in regno Neapolitano, & in Academia Salmanticensi / Musicæ Professoris, de Musica libri Septem, in quibus eius doctrinæ / veritas tam quæ ad Harmoniam, quàm quæ ad Rhythmum / pertinet, iuxta sensus ac rationis iudicium osten / ditur, & demonstratur* (Salmanticæ: Excudebat Mathias Gastius, M.D.LXXVII). Book

no podía reposar." Of importance here is that in the narrative of *Conde Claros y el emperador*, the Sephardim usually interpolated verses from yet another *romance*, *Conde Claros insomne*, to which Salinas' example belongs. Moreover, the same melodic distich, in a slightly different or abbreviated form, was previously utilized by several Spanish *vihuelistas* as a tenor or *cantus firmus* for their instrumental variations, known as *diferencias*.[171] Thus, prior to its inclusion by Salinas, it had already achieved revered status among the traditional melodies that were immortalized by 16th-century Spanish composers in their collective contribution to the nascent variation form.[172]

Commenting on Encina's example, Francisco Asenjo Barbieri *(Cancionero musical*, p. 166) prudently pointed out that "sería por demás prolijo y enojoso apuntar aquí todas las ediciones, variantes, aumentos y glosas que se hicieron de este popularísimo romance. . . ," adding that a similar task was undertaken by Agustín Durán in his *Romancero general* (1849-1851). Barbieri then indicated that Encina's text "es de fecha anterior á los impresos antiguamente, y por lo tanto, es de presumir que sea el más fiel traslado de la tradición oral."

A comparison of Encina's text—a fragment of *Conde Claros preso*—with its contemporary counterpart in Hernando del Castillo's *Cancionero general*

VI, Chapter XIIII, deals with meters built on poetic feet consisting of six rhythmic units or beats, primarily of the *molossus* (*moloso* = ♩♩♩) and the *antispastus* (*antispasto* = ♪♩♩♪) types. Salinas' magnificent treatise, considered the basis of modern Spanish musicology, was conceived in two parts: harmony (Books I–IV) and rhythm (Books V –VII). In Book I, which actually deals with mathematics, he treated music as one of its branches.

In the catalog, *Biblioteca Ibérica*, published by the Leipzig firm Karl W. Hiersemann (ca. 1910, p. 215), mention is made of a second edition published in 1592, which resembled the first, except for "nuevas portadas y hojas finales . . . [que] contiene . . . el principio de algunos romances y cantares antiguos." However, thanks to the clarification (in a personal communication) by my learned colleague, Jaime Moll, we learn that: "Sólo hay una edición de Salinas. Lo anunciado por Hiersemann es una emisión de la primera y única edición. Se encuentra en varias bibliotecas, entre ellas la Biblioteca Nacional. Quedaban ejemplares de la edición, que compraría el librero Claudio Curlet, el cual hizo cortar la portada y la última hoja, pegando nuevas hojas, con su nombre y el del impresor que las imprimió, con la fecha de 1592."

171. Concerning the *diferencia* both as a musical practice and form, as well as the *diferencias* based on the *Conde Claros* tune, see John Ward (*Vihuela de mano*, pp. 197– 200 and 202–204, respectively) and Cecilio de Roda's earlier comments ("La música profana," pp. 258–264).

172. The traditional melodies included such genres as the *romance* ("La bella malmaridada"), *romanesca* ("Guárdame las vacas"), and *villancico* ("A monte sale el amor," "Si tantos halcones la garza combaten," and "Y la mi cinta dorada").

(Valencia, 1511; fol. cxxxj ro.)[173] and with the later text in Martin Nucio's *Cancionero de romances sin año* (Antwerp, ca. 1548; CSA, fols. 90vo.–91),[174] illustrates the high esteem this popular segment enjoyed up through the mid-16th century. The full text, to which this segment belongs, can be found in Nucio's *Romance del conde Claros de montaluan* (CSA, fols. 83–90vo.). Although the three texts are remarkably similar, one should take note of their differences. I follow Romeu Figuera's 1965 ed. of the *Cancionero musical de Palacio* (no. 131 = fols. 77–78ro.) for Encina's text and Rodríguez-Moñino's facsimile ed. of the *Cancionero general* (1511) for Hernando del Castillo (fol. cxxxj ro.). Castillo's variant readings vis-à-vis Encina are indicated in bold letters:[175]

Encina (ca. 1490?)	Castillo (ca. 1511)
(Jones and Lee, p. 298)	(fol. cxxxj ro.)

	Encina		Castillo
	Pésame de vos, el conde,		Pesame de vos el conde
	porque vos mandan matar,		porque **assi os quiern** [*sic*] matar
2	pues el yerro que hezistes	2	porquel yerro que hezistes
	no fue mucho de culpar,		no fue mucho de culpar
	que los yerros por amores		quelos yerros por amores
	dinos son de perdonar.		dignos son de perdonar
4	Yo rrogué por vos al rey	4	**suplique** por vos al rey
	que vos mandase soltar,		**cos mandasse delibrar**
	ma*s* el rey con gran enojo		mas el rey con gran enojo
	no me lo quiso escuchar.		no me **quisiera** escuchar
6	Dixome que no rrogase,		
	que no se puede escusar;		
	la senteçia es ya dada,	6	**quela** sentencia **era** dada

173. Madrid, Biblioteca Nacional, 7-36333 (= A. Rodríguez-Moñino, *Cancionero general*, Madrid, 1958).

174. Madrid, Biblioteca Nacional, R-12985 (= CSA). Menéndez Pidal suggested that CSA was published between 1545 and 1550, the latter year being that of Nucio's second edition. Nucio entitled this poem *Otro romance del conde claros*.

175. Encina's text comprises thirty-six octosyllabic hemistichs, whose pairs, rhyming in assonance, number eighteen verses. Together with Castillo's and Nucio's texts (each containing thirteen verses), all three are actually condensed versions of the latter part of Nucio's full text, the 206-verse *Romance del conde Claros de Montaluan* (CSA, fols. 83–90vo.) (= *Conde Claros insomne* + *C. Claros y la infanta* + *C. Claros preso*; = *Primav.* 190), where "Pésame de vos, el conde" commences at v. 118. Text and music of Encina's version are conveniently available in Jones and Lee, *Poesía lírica*, pp. 297–298.

no se puede rrevocar,
8 que dormistes con la infanta
que avíades de guardar.
El cadahalso está hecho
donde os an de degollar.
10 Más os valiera, sobrino,
de las damas no curar,
que quien más las damas sirve,
tal merçed deve esperar,
12 que de muerto o perdido
ninguno puede escapar.

—Tales palabras, mi tío,
no las puedo soportar.
14 Más quiero morir por ellas
que bevir sin las mirar.
Quien a mi bien me quisiere
me cure de llorar,
16 no muero por traidor
nin por los dados jugar:
muero yo por mi señora,
que no me puede penar,
18 pues el yerro que yo fize,
no fue mucho de culpar.

no se **podia reuocar**
pues dormistes con la infante
auiendola de guardar

8 mas os valiera sobrino
delas damas no curar
que quien mas **haze por ellas**
tal **espera dalcançar**
10 que de **muerte** o **de** perdido
ninguno puede escapar
que firmeza de mugeres
no puede mucho durar
12 **que** tales palabras tio
no las puedo **comportar**
quiero mas morir por ellas
que beuir sin las mirar.

Martín Nucio (CSA, fols. 90vo.–91ro.), for his part, seems to be copying directly from Hernando del Castillo, but with several mostly minor changes and emendations (1*b*, 2*a*, 4*b*, 7*b*, 9*b*, 10*a*) and the unfortunate repetition of *morir* (in v. 13*b*): 1*b* quieren; 2*a* porque el; 4*b* que os; 7*b* con la infanta; 9*b* de alcançar; 10*a* muerto; 13*b* que morir.

As can be seen from Encina's extensive variant (Jones and Lee, pp. 297–298), he was familiar with the narrative, which, during his generation, appears to have enjoyed the status of a full-fledged ballad. The late Royston Oscar Jones, a Welsh scholar and noted specialist on the poetic works of Encina, alluded to the text's traditionality: "aunque los textos poéticos del CMP (= *Cancionero musical de Palacio*) son anónimos, cuando la música es de Encina nos parece justificado atribuirle también la poesía (con la excepción del romance «Pésame de vos, el conde»'" (Jones and Lee, *Poesía lírica*, p. 51). Yet, since Barbieri believed that Encina took his text directly from oral tradition, he was not entirely convinced about the traditionality of the tune, stating that it was "exclusivamente suya [Encina's], y no . . . la vulgar del romance del Conde Claros, que sonaba en boca del pueblo, cuya *melodía sencilla* [my italics] sirvió durante casi todo el siglo XVI de tema para que sobre ella se hicieran muchísimas *diferencias* o variaciones" (Barbieri, p. 167), about which we shall say more later.[176]

Encina's musical setting has been transcribed in modern notation by Barbieri (*Cancionero musical*, no. 329), Higinio Anglés (*La música en la corte*, no. 131), John M. Ward (*Vihuela de mano*, ex. 17), Carolyn R. Lee (Jones and Lee, *Poesía lírica*, pp. 297–298), and Jack Sage ("Early Spanish Ballad Music,"p. 210).[177] Sage, with minor modifications, modeled his transcription on Anglés'. Although each of the transcribers selected different temporal values (Anglés by half, Lee by a quarter, and Ward by an eighth of Barbieri's transcription), the differences among them are minimal. Here are their respective transcriptions of the *tiple* (*superius*) voice (Ex. 1). I have transposed Barbieri's soprano clef to the treble. Notice that Anglés employed broken bar lines and that Ward ignored barring. The ligatures from the original source have been indicated either with slurs or brackets. Both Anglés and Ward suggested the antepenultimate tone g be changed to g-sharp in the initial melody phrase, and the flattened second occurrence of b, in the third.

---

176. Neither was Pope convinced: she referred to it as "música sabia, obra de un artista muy versado en el arte contrapuntístico de la época . . . [y] la pieza, con su melodía bien desarrollada, es análoga a muchas otras del mismo *Cancionero*, compuestas para cantar romances en el estilo de la música cortesana ("Notas," p. 397).

177. Vicente T. Mendoza (*El romance español*, p. 237), offered a piano reduction of Barbieri's transcription, wherein he halved the note values and aligned the musical phrases of each verse. Anglés' edition of the *Cancionero musical de Palacio* is more readily accessible for study and performance. Moreover, the reprinting of the Barbieri edition, in 1987, by the Centro Cultural de la Generación del 27, Diputación Provincial de Málaga, has also helped to keep the *Cancionero* in the public domain.

Example 1: The *tiple* of "Pésame de vos, el Conde"

a
pues el ye - rro que he - - - - cis - tes
b
pues el ye - rro que___ vos he - sis - tes
c
vos
d
vos zis -
e
vos zis -
a
no fué mu - cho______ de cul - par___.
b
c
d
fue
e
fue

We concur with Anglés' transcription (Ex. 2),[178] which we shall treat here apart from its four-part setting. True to the traditional quatrain form (ABCD), Encina's *tiple*, discounting Angles's suggested alterations for harmonic reasons, is entirely Dorian in character. Nonetheless, Anglés' suggested b-flat, in melody phrase C, lends prominence to its alteration as the pivotal tone of transition between the Dorian and natural Minor mode. Given that each transcriber agreed that g-sharp should precede the cadential tone in melody phrase B, one might question why Barbieri and Lee ignored its possible earlier occurrence in the cadential portion of the initial phrase.

Example 2: Encina's tune for "Pésame de vos, el conde"

Returning to Barbieri's negative opinion concerning the traditionality of Encina's tune, we find that it was based solely on the distinction between the melody that was exclusively Encina's (without offering further clarification) and Salinas' notated distich (the *melodía sencilla*), to which the people sang or recited the ballad and on which the *vihuelistas* created their variations. Perhaps here we can offer two explanations concerning Barbieri's view: The first entails its comparison with another Encina tune, also a quatrain strophe (ABCD), which

---

178. Jack Sage's transcription of the *superius* voice ("Early Spanish Ballad Music," p. 210) also agrees with that of Anglés.

may serve as a clue for Barbieri's skepticism.[179] We refer here to the *tiple* of Encina's four-part setting, "¡Triste España sin ventura!" (Ex. 3), lamenting the death of Prince Juan, the only son of King Ferdinand and Queen Isabella (in Salamanca on October 4, 1497).[180]

Again, excluding the harmonic alterations suggested by Anglés, this rather doleful tune, based upon a hexachordal configuration (d-e-f/ f-sharp-g-a-b-flat that concludes on *finalis* g), bears some resemblance to "Pésame de vos, el conde."[181] This can be observed particularly in the latter portions of phrases A and C, as well as the tones preceding and including the ligated melodic arc in phrase D. More than coincidental, this suggests the possibility that certain melodic norms may have, in fact, served Encina as compositional devices for generating some of his melodies. Could this have been what Barbieri possibly had in mind?

---

179. In S. Griswold Morley's view ("Are the Spanish *Romances* Written in Quatrains?," p. 73), "all the *romances* in Barbieri['s edition] are set to three or four part airs. . . . Now, [I have been told by unnamed] competent persons that in Latin countries the presence of more than one part in a song is practically sure evidence of learned influence, popular melodies being always conceived for one voice only in southern Europe. If this be true, what stronger inference can one draw from the *Cancionero musical* than the very natural one, that Encina and his school amused themselves setting *romances* to their formal type of music, just as they made a pastime of composing poems based on the general type of the *romances viejos*, but more formal in structure?. . . In other words [he protested] that we know nothing whatever of the music to which the people sang the *romances* in the sixteenth century, unless indeed there exists some proof vastly different from that contained in the *Cancionero musical*. . . . [Yet, he added that] it may be also that Encina or others used popular melodies as a basis for some of their compositions. This remains to be proved."

180. Jones and Lee (*Poesía lírica*, pp. 212-213, 292). Barbieri's erroneous statement (*Cancionero musical*, p. 162) that the text was inspired by the death of Queen Isabella, on November 26, 1504, has, unfortunately, been repeated by other scholars. Only the first quatrain strophe was included in the *Cancionero musical*, fol. 50vo.). The entire text, published by Jones and Lee, follows a *pliego suelto* in the library of the Hispanic Society of America (= DPS 180).

181. One may wish to compare Anglés' transcription with those made by Barbieri (*Cancionero musical*, no. 317) and Lee (*Poesía lírica*, p. 292).

Example 3: Encina's tune for "¡Triste España sin ventura!" (Anglés, *La música en la corte,* no. 83)

Our second explanation coincides in substance, but not in detail, with Jack Sage's view that "Encina's version of «Conde Claros» ... is perfectly in keeping with ballad tunes [actually thirty-three in number] ... in the *Cancionero musical de palacio* and other collections up to the beginning of the 16th century" ("Early Spanish Ballad Music," p. 200).[182] Questioning whether the *Cancionero musical's* settings comprised "wholly original compositions" or "arrangements of given melodies drawn from popular tradition" (p. 196), Sage's intuitive response, based on the material he studied, "strongly ... [suggests] we have further evidence that [their composers] used pre-existing, popular melodies rather than creating popular-type or new melodies." But, here we must part paths, when Sage assumes (p. 200) that the "melodía sencilla" may have derived from the same melodic source as the initial phrase in Encina's *tiple*. We should note, however, that Sage did not base his assumption upon Salinas' example, but

---

182. Although forty-four ballads are listed in the *Cancionero musical's* index, there are actually only thirty-three. For the revised listing, see I. J. Katz ("Romancero," p. 362), where an additional non-ballad text (no. 126) was mistakenly included.

rather on the *melodía* (p. 211), as it appeared in the first of Alonso Mudarra's *diferencias* on "Conde Claros":[183]

Thus, while Sage argues for the traditionality of Encina's tune, in no way does its initial phrase, which hovers predominantly on the fifth degree (a), resemble that of Mudarra, nor any of its other instances in the *vihuela* manuals.[184]

Whether Encina's tune (Ex. 4*a*) entered the realm of oral tradition, or was itself a product thereof, is highly speculative. Yet, interestingly, Marius Schneider ("¿Existen elementos . . .?," no. 7*b*) discovered what he believed to be a possible tune analogue associated with a Galician rendition of a widely known and relatively modern Spanish ballad, *El vendedor de nabos* (CMP X31; III, 56, no. 50), whose initial text reads "Mi abuelo tenía un huerto" (Ex. 4*b*).[185] Concerning this nexus, Sage remarked that: ". . . it is one of the closest parallels between [the] ancient and modern [tradition] that [he had] met; yet apart from its vague melodic shape, in every other respect—metre, rhythm, key, mood—it constitutes a virtually different song" (p. 202). The resemblance, however, is startling, in spite of an apparent modal discrepancy. Salinas' tune is a mixture of pure Dorian and Minor modes (phrase C), whereas the Galician tune is in the natural Minor mode. Notice also the closely matched cadential portions of their first, third, and final melody phrases.

---

183. *Tres libros de música* (Seville, 1546), Book I, fol. 15vo.

184. Pope ("Notas," p. 397) had already dismissed such a relationship, particularly with regard to Salinas' "melodía." Even Ward (*Vihuela de mano*, p. 175), who had earlier suggested a "recitation formula" for the same melody phrase, took care not to link it with Salinas' "melodía," although he mentioned that its initial phrase "contains the ingredients of the recitation formula."

185. Schneider collected the ballad during a field trip to Galicia that was sponsored by the Instituto Español de Musicología. His original transcription and extended text can be found in the Instituto's *Materials inéditas*, no. 234. The text underlay for Ex. 4*b*, however, was adapted from Ana Valenciano, *Os Romances Tradicionais de Galicia*, no. 98.

Example 4: Comparison between *a*) Encina's tune and *b*) Schneider's Galician ballad

[Mi a - bue -lo   te - ní - aun huer- to   (mi a -)
to - do sem-bra - do___ de___ na - - bos
en la   co-se - cha___ de___ e - - llos
to - do se le vuel - van na - bos___.]

* * *

Isabel Pope, in her much-cited article, "Notas sobre la melodía del *Conde Claros*," was the first to attempt a serious study of Salinas' melodic distich. Beginning with the statement: "conocemos la melodía con que cantaba el antiguo romance del Conde Claros gracias al tratado de teoría musical de Francisco Salinas, publicado en 1577" (p. 395), she then proceeds to interpret Salinas' notation, as well as his comment regarding the tune. She also includes a discussion of the tune's earlier utilization as a "tenor," or theme, on which the Spanish *vihuelistas* (Luys de Narváez, Alonso Mudarra, Enríquez de Valderrábano, and Diego Pisador; plus an anonymous composer in the treatise by Luis Venegas de Henestrosa) composed *diferencias*.[186]

Also preceding Salinas' treatise, by some two decades, was the famous *Declaración de instrumentos musicales* (Osuna, 1555), by the Franciscan friar, theorist, and composer, Juan Bermudo (ca. 1510–after 1560). In Book I, he made a curious allusion to the *melodía*: "Pues no sé, si es más sabio, el que pretende contentar oydos, o por mejor dezir orejas de pueblo: al qual contentan con el canto de Conde Claros, tañido en guitarra, aunque sea destempla."[187]

The "melodía," to which Pope alludes, figures among the most interesting examples in Salinas' treatise, where it was cited primarily as a Spanish tune (*cantus apud Hispanos*)[188] accommodating the Latin verse *Virtus est fortitudo*

---

186. Listed according to the chronological order of the *vihuela* manuals, in which their respective *diferencias* appeared: *Los seys libros del Delphin de música de cifras para tañer vihuela* (Valladolid, 1538), *Tres libros del Delphin de música de cifras para tañer vihuela* (Seville, 1546), *Libro de música de vihuela, intitulado Silva de Sirenas* (Valladolid, 1547), *Libro de música de vihuela* (Salamanca, 1552), and *Libro de cifra nueva para tecla, harpa y vihuela* [Alcalá de Henares, 1557).

187. Bermudo, *Declaración,* Book I, Chap 3, fol. 3vo. The statement, taken within the context that preceded it, implies that, if one is not a true musician, one should not attempt to entertain the common public by singing "Conde Claros," even with the accompaniment of a guitar that is out of tune. This little-known citation confirms the wide popularity of our ballad. I am most grateful to my colleague Genoveva Gálvez for bringing it to my attention, in a letter dated July 10, 2000. The town of Osuna, whose university was founded in 1548, is located approximately 75 km. east of Seville. Of the aforementioned *vihuelistas*, Mudarra's manual, although published earlier in Seville (in 1546), was also printed by Juan de León, before he became "impresor de libros de la insigne Universidad [de Osuna]." Mudarra's performance skills were highly praised by Bermudo.

188. Felipe Pedrell (*Cancionero musical,* I, 69) referred to the tune as a *tonada vulgar,* while J. B. Trend (*Music of Spanish,* p. 104 and "Folk Music," p. 370) and Miguel Querol (*La música en . . . Cervantes,* p. 52) called it a *tonada.* Jack Sage's description, "melodic snippet" ("Early Spanish Ballad Music," p. 220) and Thomas Binkley's "a short sing-song phrase" (*Spanish Ballads,* p. 10) are certainly appropriate, although Binkley also mentioned "formula." He also felt that certain ballad melodies,

virtus est fortitu (*De Musica*, Book VI, Chapter 14, p. 341).[189] Salinas explained that "Ad quem cantum Hispani plurimos ex his, quos Romāces, vocant, enuntiare solent . . . (to this tune the Spaniards are accustomed to enunciate innumerable songs, which they call *Romances* . . .)," and he presented, as an example, the verse "Conde Claros con amores / no podía reposar" (see Ex. 5) after suggesting "a division of its third *semibreve* (*longa*)" to correspond with the stress patterns of each hemistich (see Ex. 6g):[190]

Example 5: Salinas (*De Musica*, VI, 342)

Conde Claros con amores no podía reposar.

Salinas' observation should not be taken lightly, for it furnishes us with an essential clue regarding an earlier practice that continued in his day. The verb *enuntiare*, which appears only once again in Chapter 1 (p. 375, line 17 up) of Book VII as a passive verb (*ita enuntietur*) in a nonmusical context, is somewhat

---

including that of *Conde Claros*, were "nothing more than template models in which infinite variation might have been employed . . . " (p. 8). However, Milá y Fontanals observed: "La palabra *melodía*, que a algunos parezca tal vez un tanto ambiciosa, es en el fondo exacta y la única que puede ahora emplearse para designar los motivos musicales que acompañan la letra de las canciones, como quiera que las de *tono* o *son* serían actualmente amfibológicas, la de *aire* es galiciana y la de *tonada* que se usa en Cataluña y en Andalucía no es admitida en esta acepción por el *Diccionario de la Academia*" (*Romancerillo catalán*, p. 431). Here, for whatever reason, our esteemed *maestro*, Milá y Fontanals, though worthy of the greatest respect, has nodded. The term *tonada* is already in the *Autoridades* (1726–1739) and it also figures in the one-volume *Academia* dictionaries, starting with the [1st ed.], 1780, the 2d, 1783, and the 3rd, 1791, up to the more recent editions: 13th, 1899; 17th, 1947, 21st ed., 1992 and the definition has remained essentially invariable: "Composición métrica, a propósito para cantarse" (*Autoridades*; 1780); "Composición métrica para cantarse" (1899; 1947; 1992). Captain John Stevens' *Dictionary* (1706) already documents: *tonada* 'tune' (s.v.).

189. The verse was given as an example of *tetrametrum catalecticum* (*tetrá-metro cataléctico*), which combines after the first *molossico rhythmo* (*moloso* rhythm = ♩♩♩) a *dipodia trochaica* (*dipodia trocaico* = ♩♩♩) and after the second, a *mínimo metro trochaico* (*metro trocaico más pequeño* = ♩♩).

190. ". . . solent secunda longa aut tertiare solutis . . ." (p. 342); "resuelta la segunda o la tercera larga . . ." (trans. Fernández de la Cuesta, p. 597).

confusing, for it appears to imply that, to the melody in question, the Spaniards suited innumerable ballad texts as a recitation formula.[191]

From a broader perspective, it should be noted that the musical examples in Books VI and VII of Salinas' treatise are, for the most part, fragmentary, and with good reason. As it was his purpose in the second part of his treatise, to which these books belong, to discuss everything a musician must know about rhythm,[192] Salinas included, among his examples, melodic snippets taken from the then traditional and popular songs and ditties, various national genres, dance tunes, and even hawkers' street cries, all of which served to illustrate the varied rhythms, meters, and metrical combinations under discussion.[193] From a

---

191. Ward (*Vihuela de mano*, p. 174) retained *enuntiare* in his translation: "to this song [*cantus*] the Spaniards are accustomed to *enunciate* [italics mine] very many of those things that they call *Romances*," while Daniels (*De Musica*, pp. 459–460) remarked that "Salinas cited the tune, to which 'the Spaniards are accustomed to *set* [italics mine] a great many of their so-called «Romances».....'" Fernández de la Cuesta posited, "con esta música *cantan* [italics mine] los españoles sus romances ... " (p. 597). While this translation appears to be the most commonly held, Ward may reflect more closely what Salinas intended. Furthermore, Ward refers to the *cantus* as one of the "short recitation-formulas" (p. 177) quoted in Salinas' treatise.

192. "Todo lo que el músico debe saber acerca del ritmo" (trans. Fernández de la Cuesta, *Francisco Salinas*, p. 30), from the sentence "Tres autem posteriores partis quoque posterioris, quæ ad rhythmum attinet, omnia, quæ necessario musicum scire visa sunt, habere deprehendantur" (Salinas, *De Música: Præfatio*, p. [xiii.]).

193. In Salinas' words (*De Música*, at the end of his prologue [p. xiv], lines 10–18; translated by Fernández de la Cuesta, p. 32):

> Subiunximus etiam metr[a] vulgaria Hispanica, Gallica, & Itala Græcis ac Latinis, vt ostenderemus versus ac metra ad omnes pertinere linguas, vel potius nullius idiomatis esse propria, quandoquidem in modulationibus absque verbis inueniuntur: & modos quibus vulgò canuntur, apposuimus, notis & figuris à practicis recentioribus inuentis delineatos, cùm vt ab omnibus in arte canendi vel mediocriter exercitatis intelligi possemus; tùm vt vulgarium linguarum syllabæ, in quibus quantitatem fixam non habent, sed omnes communes sunt, ex ipso cantu longæ ne an breues essent, dignoscerentur. Quod in Græcis ac Latinis fieri necesse non fuisset, nisi propter eos, qui cum canere sciant, syllabarum tamen quantitatem ignorant.

> [Castilian translation: A los versos latinos y griegos hemos añadido versos en lengua vulgar, española, francesa e italiana, para demostrar que los versos y el metro pertenecen a todas las lenguas, o más bien que no es exclusivo de ningún idioma en particular, siendo así que incluso se encuentra en las modulaciones sin palabras. En cuanto a los cantos y tonadas en lengua vulgar,

structural standpoint they comprise quatrain strophes, distichs, and both full and incomplete musical phrases. Several examples include either initial or latter halves of quatrain strophes. On reflecting upon the immense tonal memory of this astute blind musician whose world was dominated by sound, we should, nonetheless, be grateful that his examples were chosen from a wide variety of current and traditional tunes to which he was exposed. Yet, whatever value judgment one might care to venture regarding his selection, it is indeed unfortunate that they were not all notated in their entirety, nor with time signatures to confirm their proper metrical renderings.[194]

Books VI and VII contain 463 musical examples (370 and 93, respectively), whose scalar configurations range from reiterated unison tones through those encompassing an octave.[195]

Among the seventy tunes associated with Spanish texts,[196] only three in Book VI, can be identified as full-fledged quatrains.[197] Of the remaining sixty-seven

---

los hemos transcrito a notas y figuras modernas, tanto para poderlas cantar todos nosotros que estamos acostumbrados a ellas, cuanto para que se puedan distinguir las sílabas largas de las breves, en las lenguas vulgares que no tienen una cantidad fija, dentro del canto. Esto ni en latín ni en griego sería necesario, pero lo hacemos en gracia de aquellos que, aun sabiendo cantar, desconocen la cantidad específica de cada sílaba.]

In his dissertation, Daniels, while agreeing that "Salinas' primary purpose in these last three books [was] to present a systematic treatment of all other varieties of classical poetical feet, rhythms, meters, and verses," concluded that "the folk tunes [were] included merely to illustrate these poetical patterns [and, while many of them are fragments], no attempt [was] made to analyze them or to classify them; and there is nothing whatsoever in the entire volume to suggest that Salinas had any air of nationalistic fervor about him" (*De Musica,* p. 450).

194. Salinas employed only two note values throughout Books VI and VII, the *semibreve* (o) and *minima* (♩), which he referred to as *longa* and *breve*. In modern transcriptions they correspond either to the half- and quarter-, or to the quarter- and eighth-note, respectively. In the two instances where *minimas* are found with serif-like cross beams on their stems (Salinas, pp. 299 and 399), it appears that the stems are to be disregarded.

195. Concerning the scalar configurations of Salinas' transcriptions, see the Appendix.

196. For Pedrell's modern notations of Salinas' transcriptions, see the Appendix.

197. The three texts in question are "Penso el mal villano" and "Yo me yua mi madre" (Salinas, p. 306), both of which are *romancillos* dealing with the respective themes *La mujer engañada* and *Serranilla de la Zarzuela*, and the *cantilena* (lyrical tune) associated with "Mi grave pena crece de congoxa" (p. 362). In the latter example, the final phrase appears to be truncated. In Pedrell's transcription (*Cancionero musical,* I,

examples, consisting of two or more melody phrases, forty-one appear to be distichs, or simply the initial halves of a quatrain strophe,[198] including the long-versed *coplas*, "Caminad, señora" (p. 308), "No me digays madre" (p. 309), the derisive ditty, "Ea judios a enfardelar" (p. 312),[199] and the song referred to as "Las quexas," bearing the text: "¿A quién contaré yo mis quexas mi lindo amor / A quién contaré yo mis quexas si a vos no?" (p. 326). These four examples could, arguably, also be construed as quatrains. There is even a quintrain strophe (AABCD) for the text, "Casóme mi padre / con vn caballero. / Cada hora me llama / hija de vn pechero. / Y yo no lo soy" (p. 338; notated in quintuple meter, its last phrase appears to be a refrain).

As to the number of Spanish tunes, Pedrell cited forty-nine (see Appendix, section A), which he retranscribed into modern notation ("Folk-lore musical castillan," pp. 384–400). In the Castilian version, one will find minute rhythmic alterations for several of his earlier transcriptions (Pedrell, "Estudio sobre ...

---

76), he altered the cadential tones of the second melody phrase, as well as its concluding phrase, to match the length of the others. "Yo me yua a mi madre" has long been considered to be related melodically to "Polorum regina," a pilgrim's dance song from the 14th-century *Llibre Vermell* (Anglés, "El *Llibre Vermell*," ex. 7). See Menéndez Pidal, "Serranilla de la Zarzuela," which includes Manuel Manrique de Lara's transcription of Salinas' notation.

198. Salinas' distichs include "Milagro no hazeys, / Dama si me prendeys" (p. 298), "Milagro bien sería, / Si vos señora mia" (p. 299), "Conuiene mal dormir por bien velar" (the initial hemistich of a melodic distich; p. 300), "Mongica en religion me quiero entrar, / por no mal maridar" (p. 300); "Si le mato madre a Iuan, / Si le mato matar me han" (p. 306); "Canta tu Christiana Musa" (the initial hemistich of a melodic distich; p. 307); "Tu la tienes Pedro, / Iuro a tal no tengo" (p. 317); "Mal aya quien a vos caso, / La de Pedro borreguero" (p. 321); "Ante me beseys que me destoqueys, / Que me toco mi tía" (p. 321); "Aquel traydor ∪ / Aquel engañador" (p. 330 not repeated); "Conde Claros con amores no podia reposar" (p. 342); "Solíades venir amor, / Mas agora non venides non" (p. 344); "Oydme vn poco señora / Lo que yo quiero dezir" (p. 354); "Perricos de mi señora, / No me mordades agora" (p. 356); "Fe me condena, / amor me maltrata" (p. 362); "Las mañanas de Abril / dulces eran de dormir" (pp. 363; 398); "Rosa fresca con amores / Rosa fresca con amor" (p. 411), and "Que hare adonde yre. / Que mal vezino es el amor amargo" (p. [435]; misnumbered 437).

199. The song was, of course, most popular during the period of the expulsion of the Jews from Spain (1492). According to Salinas (p. 312), the famed Basque composer, Juan de Anchieta (1462–1523), wrote a *cantus firmus* Mass based on its tune, whose ms. still has not been recovered. Interestingly, Gil García mentioned that "Gonzalo Castrillo [Hernández, the noted Palencian choirmaster] [la] oyó tocar en la dulzaina en Medina del Campo y Villalpando en el típico baile de rueda" ("Panorama de la canción burgalesa," p. 91). See also Preciado's remarks ("Canto tradicional," p. 177).

folklore musical castellano," pp. 231–262). Among Daniels' sixty-eight transcriptions are fifty-one Spanish examples (*De Musica*, pp. 465–474), forty-five of which concur with Pedrell's; Daniels added six additional examples (see Appendix, section B). Both Pedrell and Daniels appear to have overlooked fourteen additional Spanish examples provided by Salinas (see Appendix, section C). Thus, we can account for a total of sixty-nine examples bearing Spanish texts. For more information on their formal structures and modal and scalar configurations, see the Appendix, sections D and E.

Interestingly, Salinas' notated *Conde Claros* distich contains thirteen notes (see Ex. 5), whereas its accompanying textual hemistichs consist of eight and seven syllables, respectively. To resolve this tune-text discrepancy, one would have to make the aforementioned adjustments suggested by Salinas. Still, among the twelve interpretive attempts at transcribing this unique example (see Ex. 6), several appear to have ignored Salinas' suggestion, yet, surprisingly, all are at variance with one another. Each, however, merits special attention. While their differences are noteworthy, it should be mentioned that their respective transcribers have dealt, to a greater or lesser extent, with the music of Salinas' epoch. Having aligned their transcriptions in chronological order, we shall comment on them in the ensuing discussion. Example 6 shows a chronological alignment of the interpretive transcriptions of Salinas' notation. An asterisk (*) indicates the rhythmic adjustments that were made to accomodate the text. The exponential letters 'u' through 'z' designate the variant melody phrases.

Collectively the twelve transcriptions raise several questions: 1) How did each transcriber arrive at his or her interpretation? 2) Does Salinas' notation actually represent a "melodía," as Pope suggested, or was Salinas simply registering an earlier practice, which involved reciting or singing ballads to a fixed melodic formula? 3) From what source, if any, did Salinas obtain his notated examples? And, 4) why did he ignore our ballad's initial verse, "Media noche era por filo / los gallos querían cantar," for its text underlay?

Example 6*a–l*:

1. How did each transcriber arrive at his or her interpretation?

Our initial question might best be pursued by examining how Isabel Pope arrived at her transcription (Ex. 6g) ("Notas," p. 396). Her choice of triple meter and textual underlay resulted from Salinas' comments, as well as from her metrical analysis of two other notations taken from Chapter 15 (p. 346), which related to the same ballad.[200] The first notation (Ex. 7), displaying *catalecticum* meter, embodies Salinas' suggested accommodation of the latter hemistich, "no podía reposar" (i.e., its *agudo* verse), to melody phrase A'.[201] In the second case (Ex. 8), Salinas presented the same melody phrase, slightly altered to fit the *acatalécticum* meter, giving as its text underlay the initial verse of another ballad, "Retrayda está la infanta / bien así como solía" (*Conde Alarcos*), to demonstrate its strict accomodation to the *Conde Claros* "melodía." Further on, we shall return to *Conde Alarcos*.[202]

Example 7: Salinas (*De Musica*, p. 346)

No podia reposar.

A'

no po- di - a   re- po- sar

---

200. In this chapter, Salinas discussed meters derived from the *iónico a maiori* (*jónico a mayor*) and its modalities. The *mayor* character of both notated examples differs from the *menor*, in that it begins with two *longas*, while the latter begins with two *breves*. Yet, both were derived from the *moloso*. This is how Pedrell defined *jónico* in his *Diccionario técnico*, p. 241.

201. It appears that Daniel Devoto misread the same example ("Humanisme, musicologie," p. 186). Having failed to realize that the notation, above which the text "Conde Claros, no podia reposar" was placed, referred only to the latter phrase, Devoto, nonetheless, described it as a "fragment incomplet."

202. Concerning *El conde Alarcos*, Pope remarked that "tenemos noticias aún más antiguas, pues en 1445 un poeta de la corte de Alfonso V de Aragón—Carvajal—lo imitó en [the incipit of] su romance «Retraída estaba la reina, / la muy casta doña María»" ("Notas," p. 397), which has nothing to do with Conde Alarcos, except that its initial hemistich is formulaic. According to Menéndez Pidal (RoH, II, pp. 19–20), the name of the poet in the court of Alfonso V el Magnánimo (1416-1458) was Carvajales, whose ballad entitled "Romance por la señora Reina de Aragón" was written in 1454 (perhaps inadvertently miscopied by Pope). Pedrell (*Cancionero musical*, I, p. 69) surmised that Salinas might have been unaware of Caravajales' ballad, which refers to the twenty-two-year absence of María's husband, Alfonso V.

Example 8: Salinas (*De Musica*, p. 346)

Retrayda esta la Infanta, Bien asi como solia.

Re-tra - y da es - tá la In-fan-ta,
bien a - sí co - mo so - lí - a.

Thus, it was not by chance that Pope made two rhythmic adjustments (located beneath the asterisks in Ex. 6*g*), which also apply to several other transcriptions. She mentioned Felipe Pedrell's earlier notation (Ex. 6*a*, from "Folk-lore musical castillan," p. 392), criticizing its rigid duple meter, together with its lack of coordination with the rhythmic accentuation of the verse.[203] And, although she included Anglés' transcription of *Conde Alarcos* (Ex. 10*d*), she was unaware of Cecilio de Roda's transcription (Ex. 6*b*, from *La música profana [I]*, facing p. 38).[204]

Although Juan B. Elústiza (Ex. 6*c*, from *Estudios musicales*, p. 68), J. B. Trend (Ex. 6*d*, from *The Music*, p. 225), Gonzalo Menéndez Pidal (Ex. 6*f*, from "Ilustraciones musicales," p. 387), and Thomas Binkley (Ex. 6*l*, from *Spanish Romances*, no. 23) adhered to the original sequence of pitches, they appear to have been less concerned with the tune's text underlay.[205] Both Elústiza and

---

203. Pedrell's transcription reappeared in the Castilian version ("Estudio sobre ... folklore musical castellano," p. 248) of his earlier study ("Folk-lore musical castillan") and later in both his *Cancionero musical* (I, no. 24) and "Folk-lore musical hispano" (p. 41), where he added a simple chordal accompaniment. Among the nine Salinas examples taken from Pedrell's "Folk-lore musical castillan", Abraham Idelsohn (*Gesänge*, p. 23) included "Conde Claros," but miscopied the third textual syllable as 'lla.' In his comments, Idelsohn erroneously cited Salinas' birth year as 1514 [*sic:* 1513], the publication date of his treatise as 1575 [*sic:* 1577], and its place of publication as Casablanca [*sic:* Salamanca], adding that its melodies stemmed from the 13th and 14th centuries. Calling attention to the strong Arabic character of all nine notations, Idelsohn identified the "Conde Claros" example as belonging to the *Siga maqam* (p. 21). Vicente T. Mendoza (*El romance español*, p. 235) also cited Pedrell's transcription, renotating it in 14th-century minimas and semiminimas.

204. It should be mentioned that Roda transposed his notation a whole step lower, to correspond with his transcription of Narváez's *diferencias* that followed his article.

205. Trend ("Folk Music, p. 370) presented the same rhythmic configuration. Here, however, he added, in the uppermost stave, the tune of the "melodía" and its text underlay to the accompaniment of the tenth and eleventh *diferencias* of Mudarra. Earlier (in *Music*,

Trend remained noncommittal with regard to meter. Elústiza's confused attempt resulted in an incomplete underlay for the second hemistich, but Trend, who placed the words "Claros" and "día" under their respective notes, simply implied the necessary adjustments. Menéndez Pidal, who concurred with Pedrell's duple meter, cited only the text of the initial hemistich, without providing its alignment.[206]

John M. Ward's adjustments (Ex. 6*e*, from *Vihuela de mano*, ex. 16)[207] agree with Pope's, but, like Trend, he avoided bar lines. Perhaps because the notations of Ward, Menéndez Pidal, and Pope were published during the same year, each appears to have been unaware of the others' transcriptions. Furthermore, Ward, who cited Pedrell in his bibliography, chose to ignore his metric solution.

It is strange that Miguel Querol, who mentioned Pope's article, transcribed only the first melody phrase, whose *moloso* meter he totally disregarded, thereby concluding his notated phrase on a quarter rather than an eighth note (Ex. 6*h*, "Importance historique," p. 322). Less than a decade later, Arthur M. Daniels (Ex. 6*i*, *De Musica*, p. 471) offered a solution similar to Pedrell's, but with an articulation governed by 3/2 and 3/4 metric designations. Jack Sage (Ex. 6*j*, "Early Spanish Ballad," p. 200) appears also to have based his transcriptions on Pedrell's, whose note values he doubled.[208] Moreover, for the purpose of comparing it to the *tonada* (i.e., the so-called *Conde Claros* "melodía"), upon which Alonso de Mudarra conceived his set of *diferencias*, Sage, like Roda, transposed the notation a whole step lower.[209] Finally, Thomas Binkley (Ex. 6*l*,

---

p. 226) Trend presented the ballad's initial verse followed by its ninety-first and ninety-second hemistichs (following Nucio's text, CSA?) above Mudarra's first, second, tenth, and eleventh *diferencías*.

206. Possibly as a rationale for his transcription, Gonzalo Menéndez Pidal remarked that: "Desgraciadamente, Salinas, al consignar sus ejemplos, lo hacía exclusivamente, y sólo a título de sugerencia, ya que daba por sobradamente conocido de sus lectores el villancico o romance que citaba; por eso transcribe en su libro sólo cabezas de tema y nosotros debemos completar su ulterior desarrollo" (RoH, II, 387).

207. Ward introduced his transcription with the unaltered version of *Conde Claros* bearing the Latin verse, "Virtus est fortitudo virtus est fortitu." He also acknowledged (p. 174) Curt Sachs' suggestion with regard to Salinas' phrase, *secunda longa aut tertiare solutis* (*De Musica*, p. 342), which involved *fractio modi*, meaning that "the second of the third *longa* is decomposed into *breves*." See also n. 105, in the Appendix.

208. Sage's notation was duplicated in an article by Susana Friedmann ("Tradición y cambio en el romance," p. 95).

209. See also n. 200 above. Roda explained that "para hacer una traducción verdaderamente musical, he tenido que reducir los valores . . . a la mitad y encerrar cada tres compases en uno, única manera de que pudiera resaltar la sucesión de acentos

Spanish Ballads, no. 23), who, like Elústiza, Trend and Ward, ignored bar lines, not only chose intermediary note values, but totally ignored the syllabification of "media" and "gallos" in the first verse, and "conde" and "dia" in the second. Surprisingly, Binkley was the only transcriber to provide the ballad's initial verse, which is lacking in Salinas.

Dionisio Preciado's transcription (Ex. 6*l*, from "Veteranía de algunos ritmos," p. 215), cited as an example of "aksak" rhythm, brings into focus yet another dimension concerning traditional Spanish tunes.[210] His purpose was to show that asymmetric combinations of binary + ternary rhythms, reflected in such meters as 5/8 [2+3 or 3+2], 7/8 [2+2+3, 3+2+2, or 3+2+3], etc., can be found in Andalusian, Castilian, Catalonian, Extremaduran, and Galician folk music, and that the first occurrences of 5/8 in Spanish music date from Salinas' *De Musica* and the *Cancionero musical de Palacio*. It was Constantin Brailoiu, the renowned Romanian ethnomusicologist, who coined the Turkish term "aksak" to avoid its association with any national culture wherein such asymmetric rhythms existed.[211] Brailoiu had already discovered its use among numerous Asian, North African, and European cultures, including the Basque, but did not register its existence anywhere else on the Iberian Peninsula.

---

métricos de los compases de tres por cuatro y seis por ocho. Aun así, por no reducir los valores a su cuarta parte, resultan empleados los compases de tres por dos y seis por cuatro, como amplificación de los de tres por cuatro y seis por ocho [que es un] ritmo . . . tan común en las canciones populares de nuestra patria, que puede seguirse sin dificultad desde el siglo XVI hasta hoy; las zarabandas del XVII, los zarandillos del XVIII, las guajiras del XIX, son buena prueba de ello" ("La música profana," p. 260). Even more revealing were his thoughts concerning the singing of the *Conde Claros* ballad to the accompaniment of *diferencias*: "A mi juicio cada diferencia debe ser ejecutada dos veces, como acompañamiento de los dos pies de cada verso del romance" (p. 261).

210. Together with *Conde Claros*, Preciado (pp. 213–215) included six additional tunes from Salinas' treatise, five of which bore the "aksak" rhythm 5/8: a textless tune (Salinas, p. 272), "De rosas y flores" (p. 337), "Dexadlos, mi madre" (p. 338; also transcribed in 5/8 by Torner in "Góngora y el folklore," p. 79), "Casóme mi padre . . . " (p. 338), and "Rey don Alonso . . ." (p. 339); also 3/4 + 6/8: "Retrayda está la Infanta" (p. 346).

211. Preciado mentions such Spanish musicologists and folklorists as Resurrección María Azkue, Venancio Blanco, Dámaso Ledesma, Federico Olmeda, Felipe Pedrell, Casto Sampedro, José Antonio de San Sebastián (Padre Donostia), and Eduardo M. Torner, who were acquainted with this metric phenomenon, but were not aware of Brailoiu's term; and he mentions that Manuel García Matos may have been the first to introduce the term in Spanish folkloristic literature ("Veteranía de algunos ritmos," p. 193). In Turkish, *aksak* means 'a rhythmic patttern of nine beats with a signature of 9/8', but also 'a rhythmic patttern of ten beats with a signature of 10/8' (*New Redhouse*, s.v.).

With respect to Salinas' *Conde Claros* example, Preciado linked its meter to the *petenera*, a Gypsified (*aflamencada*) dance that entered the flamenco repertoire.[212] *Peteneras* may be expressed by the metric designation 12/8 (3+3+2+2+2) or as an amalgam of the meters 6/8 + 3/4 (or 3/8 + 3/8 + 3/4), corresponding to what the ancient musical theorists called hemiola (♩.+♩. = ♩+♩+♩). Preciado points out that, in Salinas' example, "la sección binaria de corcheas precede a la ternaria, como ocurre a veces en el cancionero popular español" (p. 207). He, nonetheless, lays claim to his transcription (Ex. 6*k*) as related to the *petenera*. On the following page he states: "Los musicólogos que han escrito sobre esta melodía del *Conde Claros* no lo han presentado en ritmo de *petenera*. Tampoco nuestros viejos vihuelistas la utilizaron con el ritmo que trae Salinas" (Preciado, p. 208).

While the differences among the varied transcriptions can be seen in their note values, metric divisions, and text underlays, the most questionable transcriptions are those of Pedrell and Sage, who, unlike Daniels, failed to explain the derivation of the tone b̲ (transposed a step lower to a̲ by Sage), on which they concluded each of their melody phrases, and on which Elústiza terminated the initial phrase. Oddly enough, only Daniels—with whom I had the opportunity of discussing his transcription—appears to have heeded an additional melodic fragment (Ex. 9), provided by Salinas (*De Musica*, p. 342), which exhibited both a melodic alteration (to c̲′ in the latter note of the *moloso*) and a metric change (to *dipodia iámbica* [*dipodio iámbico*] = ♪♩♪♩, following the *moloso*), and which counts among the dozen or so Spanish examples in Salinas' Books VI and VII that display bar lines. Salinas cited it as the discant of a *gallarda*, a courtly dance (*danza*), which the Italians imported from Spain, pointing out that the cadential tones in each of its two measures were accented:[213]

---

212. According to Preciado (pp. 206–207), García Matos found an abundance of *peteneras*, as well as the *paño moruno* and *guajira*, in popular Spanish *cancioneros*, which bore the "aksak" rhythm. Yet, even though García Matos mentioned in his article ("El folklore en la Suite Española," p. 83) that the meter was already known in the 16th century in one of Salinas' examples; without naming it, we must credit its identification to Preciado. Fifty-one years earlier, Torner pointed out that its rhythm was analogous to that of the *siguiriya* ("Ritmos," p. 139).

213. Eng. *galliard/gaillard*; Fr. *gaillarde*; It. *gagliarda*. The dance, according to Curt Sachs, "appeared at the end of the 15th century in Lombardy" (*World History*, p. 358). Performed in simple triple meter, sometimes notated in 6/8, it normally followed the slow and stately pavane in duple meter. This combination may have given rise to the dance suite. In addition, each piece also served as a strictly instrumental composition. A

Example 9: Salinas (*De Musica*, VI, p. 342)

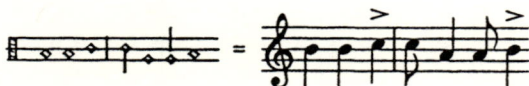

Taking into account its accentuation, together with its melodic and metric alterations, it is not entirely clear whether Salinas was referring to the *gallarda* or to the original "melodía" (Ex. 5) as the tenor, upon which ("super quem tenorem") the famous Italian composer and lutenist, Francesco Canova da Milano (1497–1543) created a series of improvisations during a performance before Pope Paul III (1468–1549), at which Salinas was present.[214] Nonetheless, Daniels, who agreed with Pedrell's melodic adjustment and textual underlay in melody phrase A, surmised that the melodic sequence of the *gallarda* fragment, which concluded on b, would best serve as the cadential phrase (B). In the process, Daniels misconstrued the fifth note a as c'.[215] Pedrell's rationale was undoubtedly different. Yet, lacking an explanation for his adjustments, we can only guess that he had in mind a kind of tonal axis, upon which each of the phrases would begin and end.

---

historical sketch of the galliard can be found in E. Markowska, "Forma galiardy." See also B. Delli, *Pavane und Galliarde.*

214. Although several of the transcribers chose to ignore this fact, Trend (*The Music*, p. 105) surmised that the fragment was a modification of the original, and that it "was the same as that of the Galliard," upon which Milano extemporized variations. Juan José Rey, an authority on Spanish medieval and Renaissance music, also agreed that "sobre la conocida melodía del Conde Claros apunta Salinas que se empleaba . . . para discantar sobre ella como tema de Gallarda" (*Danzas cantadas*, p. 33, n.15). In Rome, Salinas met and befriended Milano, sixteen years his senior, whom he considered "the prince among lutenists." The date of the performance at the Pontifical Chapel of Pope Paul III, to which Salinas alluded, has not been firmly established; however, it must have occurred sometime between Salinas' arrival in early October of 1538 and the following year when Milano retired from his papal employment in Rome. Milano died in Milan on April 15, 1543. Some interesting details concerning Milano's service to the pope can be found in Léon Dorez, "Francesco da Milano" ; see also H. Colin Slim, "Francesco da Milano," and A. J. Ness, "Francesco Canova da Milano."

215. It is unfortunate that Daniels overlooked Pope's article.

In conjunction with the aforementioned notation (Ex. 8) bearing the opening distich of *Conde Alarcos* (Ex. 10),[216] Salinas remarked that, since the latter verse was well suited to the tune of *Conde Claros* (undoubtedly referring to its initial melody phrase), upon which aged Spaniards sang *romances* recounting legends and history, its tune would also suit the text of *Conde Alarcos* (*De Musica*, p. 346).[217] This process of accommodating other ballad texts to a particular melodic formula or popular tune, sharing the same metric features, was indeed widespread, and Salinas' is but one of countless early examples of this practice.

Judging from the syllable-tone relationship, Salinas' notation (Ex. 8) does not warrant any adjustments. However, the problem of internal stress patterns must be addressed. For this purpose, a perusal of the following modern transcriptions of Salinas' notation should prove instructive (see Ex. 10).

The melody phrases accompanying each hemistich are identical, so the text's accentuation is quite clear. The accents fall on '-tá' and '-fan' in the first hemistich, and in the second, on '-mo' and '-rí', which are the fifth and seventh syllables, respectively. Yet what distinguishes this pattern from the *Conde Claros* "melodía," is that here we have a clear-cut example of a melodic stich (A), or unistrophe, whose textual hemistichs were intended to be sung or intoned *ad infinitum* throughout the entire rendition.[218] In his initial duple-metered

---

216. See Nucio (CSA, fols. 107vo.-115vo.), where the ballad is entitled *Romance del conde Alarcos y de la infanta Solisa*. Its initial distich, "Retrayda está la Infanta / bien así como solía," and the Latin verse, "Nemo volet impudico Servire diu tyranno," which Salinas placed before it, were given as examples of *dimetro acataléctico*, whose meter was based on the *jónico a mayor*. See nn. 201–202 above. Here the notation reflects the division of the last note of the *moloso* (♩♩♪♪), i.e., the *jónico a mayor* modality, to which was added a *dipodio trocaico* (♩♪♩♪), repeated twice.

217. ". . . ad quos omnes compositiones Hispanæ, quibus historiæ seu fabulæ narrantur, ab antiquis nostris canebantur" (". . . que es tambíen la [música] que sirve para los poemas que cantaban nuestros mayores contando leyendas e historias") (Fernández de la Cuesta, *Franciso Salinas*, p. 606).

218. Walter Wiora (*European Folk Song*, no. 19*b*) acknowledged this fact when he included Anglés' transcription among his examples exhibiting stichic tunes. Devoto was also convinced that the ballads in Salinas were based on phrases accompanying octosyllabic hemistichs, not on the epic verse bearing a sixteen-syllable line as Ramón Menéndez Pidal and Isabel Pope had surmised. Devoto insisted that the melody for *Conde Alarcos* should be notated as a stich [see Ex. 8], i.e., as "une seule phrase mélodique de 8 notes écrites deux foix"; however, instead of providing the text of the second hemistich, Devoto repeated that of the first ("Humanisme, musicologie," p. 186).

Example 10: A chronological alignment of interpretive transcriptions of Salinas' notation (see Ex. 8)

transcription (10*a*),[219] Pedrell ignored the accents, but years later, in another transcription (10*b*), he not only realized those on '-stá' and '-mo', but also added a simple harmonization. This was also the solution proposed by Anglés (10*d*) and Devoto (10*i*), albeit with more defined metric schemes.[220] Perhaps, to avoid the matter of internal stresses, or simply satisfied that the tone-syllable concurrence was met, Elústiza (10*c*), Ward (10*e*), and Pope (10*f*) refrained from offering a metric solution.[221] Still, one wonders why Pope did not resort to her earlier transcription (6*g*), which would have required the addition of only one note, dropping the dot from the dotted-quarter note preceding it. Only Daniels (10*g*), García Matos (10*h*), and Preciado (10*k*) emphasized the correct accentuation of each hemistich, as witnessed in their refined barring. Finally, Binkley (10*j*), uncertain about the division of syllables in the first hemistich of each of his two notated verses, awkwardly suggested "Re-tra-y-d<u>ae</u>s-tá" for the first five tones of the former, and "bivi-en-do" for the first three of the latter.

2. Does Salinas' notation actually represent a "melodía," as Pope suggested, or was Salinas simply registering an earlier practice which involved the recitation or singing of ballads to a fixed melodic formula?

Apart from the examples we have just looked at, associated with the "melodía" (Ex. 11*a* = Ex. 5) and its stichic variant (Ex. 11*b* = Ex. 8), to which the initial verse of *Conde Alarcos* was suited, Salinas provided forty-one additional trichordal examples, eight of which carry Spanish texts. The majority consist of single melody phrases, yet only three, like the "melodía" itself, can be

---

219. Pedrell, "Folk-lore musical castillan," p. 393; reprinted in the Castilian version ("Estudio sobre ... folk-lore musical hispano," p. 250).

220. It seems likely that Anglés was influenced by Roda's earlier notation (see Ex. 6*b*).

221. Elústiza's parenthetical note below his transcription: "el romance dice *Infanta*, pero he querido dejar la palabra *Reina* por respetar la transcripción de Salinas," suggests that he was uncertain about his recollection of Salinas' text underlay, which actually reads 'infanta.' For more on the transcriptions shown in Example 10, see: 10*a*: Pedrell, "Folk-lore musical castillan," p. 393; 10*b*: Pedrell, *Cancionero musical*, no. 25; 10*c*: Elústiza, *Estudios musicales*, p. 68; 10*d*: Anglés, "Das spanische Volkslied," p. 337; 10*e*: Ward, *Vihuela de mano*, ex. 16; 10*f*: Pope, "Notas," p. 396; 10*g*: Daniels, *De Musica*, p. 471; 10*h*: García Matos, "Pervivencia en la tradición," p. 80; 10*i*: Devoto, "Humanisme, musicologie," p. 186; 10*j*: Binkley, *Spanish romances*; and 10*k*: Preciado, "Veteranía de algunos ritmos," pp. 214–215.

characterized as distichs (see Exs. 11c-e).[222] Furthermore, the degree to which the "melodía" and its stichic variant differ can be seen in their cadential stress patterns. In the "melodía," the stress on the seventh (penultimate syllable) in the first hemistich conforms to the *llano* type, and that on the final (seventh) syllable in the second hemistich, to the *agudo*. Additional descriptive designations may include such terms as antecedent-consequent or *ouvert-clos*, which relate particularly to ballads in the distich category. The stress pattern of the octosyllabic *Conde Alarcos* variant (Ex. 11b), however, is of the *llano* type. Included here is Eduardo M. Torner's transcription of the popular *Gerineldo* (11f), which exemplifies a simple distich from the modern ballad tradition, although here with the addition of the *subsemitonium*.

Example 11:[223]

Conde Claros con amores no podía reposar.

Retrayda está la Infanta
Bien así como solía.

Si le mato madre a Iuan Si le mato matar me han

De mi alma De mi ánima

---

222. Examples 11d and 11e were not included among the seventy Spanish texts itemized (see Appendix, A–C). Example 11c, however, was included in Daniels' study (*De Musica*, p. 476).

223. Melody phrases from: 11a: *Conde Claros* (Salinas, *De Musica*, p. 342); 11b: *Conde Alarcos* (p. 346); 11c: "Si le mato madre a Juan /si le mato matar me han"(p. 306); 11d: "De mi alma / de mi anima" (p. 323); 11e: "Por amor de mi alma" (p. 324); and 11f: *Gerineldo* (Torner, "Indicaciones prácticas," p. 390).

Por amor de mi alma, Por amor de mi ánima

Ge - ri-nel-do, Ge - ri- nel-do, pa- je del rey tan-que-ri - do__.

With regard to their restricted trichordal ambitus, Examples 11*c-e* may be considered *bona fide* melodies, since each concludes on the lowest tone. The "melodía" (Ex. 11*a*) and its variant (11*b*) are somewhat more complicated in that their shared sequence of tones consist of a quasi reciting tone b̲, which, followed by both an upper and lower 2nd (c̲ and a̲, forming, respectively, a contrasting 3rd), strongly suggests a return to b̲ Melodic progressions of this type lack tonal resolution, yet, unlike Examples 11*c-e*, both would hardly qualify as melodies.[224] Instead, one should view their constant reiteration as a kind of *moto perpetuo*, involving a formulaic device as a vehicle for rendering ballad texts, especially those concerning historical and national themes. Surely, here we are dealing with an ancient practice, where tunes like those "assembled by Salinas . . . [of] restricted range and structural simplicity [belonged to a kind of] functional folk music [that dominated] much of the repertory of old European village life."[225]

---

224. Pedrell equated the *tonada* of *Conde Claros* with early, crudely rendered ballads, "que consiste, como en algunas recitaciones litúrgicas (por ejemplo el *tonus lectionis*), en una sencillísima figuración de dos or tres sonidos" ("Folklore musical hispano," pp. 40–41). Surely Manzano would have included this and possibly other examples from Salinas' *De Musica* in his discussion of melodies based on Minor trichords ("Estructuras arquetípicas," pp. 372–375), had he studied this source. Even Binkley *(Spanish Ballads,* p. 8) referred to it as "nothing more than a template model in which infinite variation might have been employed. . . . In such cases the model need not be thought of as a melody at all but rather as a boiler-plate structure for inventing melody."

225. Herzog, "Some Primitive Layers," p. 13. Trend was indeed calling attention to an earlier practice when referring to the *juglares*, whom he called "the inventors of the *Romances viejos*, . . . which are now known to have been the remains of long *chansons de geste*, . . . [whose] episodes were more easily remembered than the entire epics . . . [They]

Still, Sage believed that the "melodía" was actually the "first phrase of a four-phrase tune of the usual kind and that Salinas repeated it, underlaying the text of the second hemistich" ("Early Spanish Ballad Music," p. 200). Moreover, he found "no evidence in any of the ballads [in his survey, to suggest] . . . that they shared their tunes or that they were recited to a single musical phrase" (p. 201). Our reply, from our foregoing analysis, bears out the fact that Salinas, apart from the singular phrase treatment by the *vihuelistas*, presented it as a melodic distich, whose constituent melody phrases are not repeated in the literal sense, and from Salinas' aforementioned remark that Spaniards were accustomed to enunciate or to sing other ballads to this tune. We know that ballads did share tunes, albeit, in this case, using a melodic formula, or, for a better description, a formulaic device. Furthermore, in the modern oral tradition, we have discovered numerous tunes to which two or more different ballad texts were sung. Thus, it cannot be disproved that this was indeed also an earlier practice. If Salinas' "melodía" was, in fact, the first of a four-phrase tune, as Sage suggests, Salinas' notated distich would have comprised a protracted melody phrase combining two textual hemistichs, thus requiring a quatrain strophe consisting of four verses, or eight hemistichs. Strophes of this type are quite rare among traditional ballads.

It should also be pointed out that the "melodía," as notated, was not meant to be rendered verse after verse in so rigid a manner. Anyone familiar with the singing of ballads will readily understand that, whether sung to strophic tunes or melodic formulas, the addition or subtraction of textual syllables always necessitates rhythmic adjustments. And the possibility that one might find, in printed *cancioneros* and *romanceros*, examples of melodies and their entire texts, whose coordination can be accomplished without any adjustments whatsoever, is indeed a rare occurrence. Moreover, in those printed sources where one finds *romances eruditos*, it will be seen that, in the vast majority of cases, they have been altered to reflect a consistent syllable rendering.

Yet, what could be more instinctive than to suggest that strophes based on melodic stichs and distichs evolved from an earlier formulaic practice? Pedrell

---

were sung to tunes [that] might be described as a litany or psalmody, [being] simple melodic or rhythmic formulæ which could be repeated again and again" (*The Music*, p. 104). To suggest the extent to which this practice continued, Trend (in his Ex. 34) went so far as to superimpose the *tonada* above the chordal accompaniment of Mudarra's first, second, tenth, and eleventh *diferencias*, to which he set the texts of the initial and forty-sixth verse, taken presumably from Martín Nucio's *Romancero* (= CSA). Later, Trend superimposed Salinas' verses on Mudarra's tenth and eleventh *diferencias* ("Folk Music," p. 370).

was convinced that the stichic variant of the *Conde Claros* "melodía" did indeed accommodate other ballad texts. To provide an example, he suited to its melodic configuration the text of the *Romance de don Rodrigo de Lara*, a historical ballad dealing with vengeance for the deaths of the Infantes de Lara (see Ex. 12).[226] Evoking earlier juglaresque renditions, Pedrell added a simple *vihuela* accompaniment (not shown), explaining that "eso mismo harían [sus] colegas antiguos de tan lejana época, cada vez que entendían acompañar algún romance . . ." (*Cancionero musical*, I, 70).

Example 12: Pedrell (*Cancionero musical*, I, no. 26)

A	ca - zar	va	don Rod -	ri - go
Yaun don	Ro- dri -	go de	La - ra:	
Con la	gran sies -	ta que	ha - ce	
A - rri -	ma - do sehaá	un	ha - ya	
Mal - di -	cien-doś	Mu - da -	rri - llo.	
Hi - jo	de la	re - ne -	ga - da	
Que siá	las ma - nos	lehu -	bie- se	
Que le	sa - ca	- -	-	rí - ael al - ma...

Here, Pedrell aligned the hemistichs of the first four verses under the reiterated melodic stich, the even-numbered verses of which rhyme in assonance (*á-a*). Apart from the usual elisions, the rendition is entirely syllabic.[227] Notice

226. Pedrell (*Cancionero musical*, I, 68) must have been intrigued by this example when he surmised that "aunque Salinas no lo expresa, se deduce, desde luego, que había en su tiempo dos formas de entonar esas tonadas: recitándolas sobre el *ambitus* reducido de dos o tres notas musicales, o cantándolas teniendo en el oído la tonada inventada por uno o varios anónimos creadores, que por la costumbre de entonarlos hicieron que se adoptase tal tonada con preferencia a otras. Ya se comprende que aquella recitación vulgar ha de ser antiquísima, y tiene sus precedentes en las recitaciones litúrgicas, por el estilo de las llamadas *tonus simples ferialis* del rezo eclesiástico." Perhaps to justify his accompaniment, he added: "Y ¿quién de vosotros no ha oído recitar por las calles o en la plaza de un pueblo una de esas melopeas, que apenas son un canto melódicamente formulado, a un ciego, descendiente del antiguo juglar que, guitarrillo en mano, acompáñase produciendo tres o cuatro simples acordes rasgueados, y algún ramplón dibujo en el bordón del cascado y mugriento instrumento; quién de nosotros no se ha parado un momento para oír el romance que *dice* el despreciado descendiente de aquella prosapia, que empezaba en el trovador y acababa en el juglar?" (p. 68).

227. Danckert reproduced Pedrell's example, for which he also provided a German translation (*Das europäische Volkslied*, p. 279). Curiously enough, Danckert recounted

how Pedrell altered the rhythm of the concluding hemsitich by lengthening the
penultimate quarter note a̱ to a dotted-quarter, and the final eighth note a̱ to a
dotted half.

Another example (13), whose initial hemistichs were likewise sung to a
trichordal melodic stich, can be found in Rafael Mitjana.[228] The text of this
historical ballad pertains to Don Ramiro, the first king of Aragón (1035–1063).
Although it shows a more developed tripartite strophe, AAB^{n+n}, in which the
protracted latter melody phrase combines the third and fourth hemistichs, one
can readily surmise, from the reappearance of the first six tones in phrase B, that
it may have evolved from from an earlier *Cantar de gesta*, as Mitjana suggests.
A 16th-century artistic setting of the same text, for voice and *vihuela*, by Luys
de Narváez, displays a highly intricate quatrain strophe, bearing multiple internal
textual repetitions (*Los seys libros del Delphín*, fols. 65–65vo. [= 69–69vo.]).

Example 13: "Ya se asienta el Rey Ramiro"

---

the gist of George Ticknor's comments (from the German translation, *Geschichte der
schönen Literatur in Spanien*, Leipzig, 1852, I, 101, 105), concerning Esteban de
Nájera's preface to his *Primera parte de la Silva de varios Romances* (Zaragoza, 1550).
In that preface, Nájera mentioned that among the ballads that came to his attention, he
included some which he himself collected from informants whose recollections were
weak, resulting in incomplete and corrupt specimens. Danckert, interpreting these
comments as representative of the current state of oral tradition, referred to Pedrell's
example as: "Eine Probe der zumeist sehr einförmigen, orientalisch beinflussten [*sic*]
Rezitationsmelodik" (p. 279).

228. *Historia de la música*, p. 22. Mitjana included this ballad along with the initial
melodic strophes of two other ballads (*Conde Sol* or *La condesita* and the Catalan *Els
estudiants de Tolosa*). Although he mentioned Asturias as its provenience and believed it
to be traditional, he did not reveal its source. Eleven additional verses can be found in
Primavera, no. 99. *Ya se sienta el rey Ramiro* has not come down into the modern oral
tradition. See CGR, III, 551 *et alibi*.

3. From what source, if any, did Salinas obtain his notated example?

The exact source or sources—published or oral—from which Salinas obtained the so-called *Conde Claros* "melodía" cannot be ascertained. However, it can be stated unequivocally that the ballad enjoyed a wide and vibrant circulation throughout the Iberian Peninsula, prior to its adoption by the *vihuelistas*. Simultaneously the ballad's popularity spread to other European centers.

We do know that, in the fall of 1538, Salinas accompanied his relative, Don Pedro Gómez Sarmiento, then the Bishop of the Cathedral at Santiago de Compostela, to Italy, where, on October 18th, he attended the ceremony in Rome at which Don Pedro was elevated to Cardinal. Almost two weeks after that ceremony, on October 30th, the printer Diego Hernández de Córdoba completed, in Valladolid, Luys de Narváez's *Los seys libros del Delphín de música*, containing the first set of *diferencias* based on *Conde Claros*. It was during Salinas' extended sojourn in Italy (1538–1561, when he lived primarily in Rome except for a period in Naples [1553–1558]), that each of the succeeding *vihuela* books which bore the *Conde Claros* "melodía" were printed in Spain: Alonso Mudarra's *Tres libros de música en cifras para vihuela* (Seville, 1546), followed by Enriquez de Valderrábano's *Libro de música de vihuela, entitulado «Silva de Sirenas»* (Valladolid, 1547), Diego Pisador's *Libro de música de vihuela* (Salamanca, 1552), and Venegas de Henestrosa's *Libro de cifra nueva para tecla, harpa y vihuela* (Alcalá de Henares, 1557).[229]

---

229. From his introduction to *De Musica Libri Septem*, we learn that it was during this period that Salinas spent much time at the Biblioteca Vaticana (Rome) and the library of St. Mark's church (Venice), where treatises by the early Latin (primarily Boethius), and especially the Greek theorists (Aristides Quintilianus, Aristoxenus, Bacchius, Bryennius, Nicomachus, Plutarch, Ptolemy), were read to him and which were procured for him by Cardinals Rodolfo Pio from Carpi, the northern Italian cathedral city, and Francisco de Mendoza, who also served as Archbishop of Burgos. In Naples, Salinas served as organist and accompanist at the Palace of Don Fernando Álvarez de Toledo, the Duke of Alba, whose choir, under the direction of the composer Diego Ortiz, consisted primarily of Spaniards. During this period he suffered several calamities: not only did his protector, Cardinal Sarmiento, die on October 13, 1541, but also the aforementioned Cardinals, who were most helpful to him, died as well. Also, his three brothers were killed in the Italian Wars. Having earned the esteem of the Italians as a brilliant organist, Salinas was awarded, prior to his return to Spain, the title of Abbot of San Pancrazio, in Rocca Scalegna, in the Kingdom of Naples (mentioned on the title page of his treatise).

We mentioned earlier Salinas' recollection of having heard, in Rome, Francesco de Milano improvise upon *Conde Claros*. This confirms the fact that he was already familiar with the pristine melody several decades before he published his treatise. Yet, according to Sage, who surmised that Salinas "had on his desk some if not all the *vihuela* manuals" and that "his [notated] phrase is a composite version of theirs," this theory does not hold water ("Early Spanish Ballad Tunes," p. 200). If this were the case, why weren't any of the *vihuelistas* mentioned in Salinas' treatise?[230] And if, as Sage presumed, Salinas "was much more in touch [perhaps in Italy?] with cultured than with popular traditions," why is it, then, that a good-sized portion of his musical examples were taken from those popular traditions? Having spent his formative and adult years in a region that was rich in folk music and where the *Romancero* flourished, how could he possibly have ignored the local tradition?

For all his erudite learning, the facts indicate that, judging again from the examples in Books VI and VII, Salinas not only absorbed and retained countless traditional melodies during his life in Spain and travels in Italy, but he also regarded them highly. One only has to peruse his comments concerning many of the notated examples in Books VI and VII of his treatise to realize how very attuned he was to traditional music.[231] There is no question that Salinas obtained

---

More recent information concerning Salinas' life and works can be found in José María Álvarez Pérez ("El organista Fransisco de Salinas"), Arthur M. Daniels ("Microtonality and Mean-Tone Temperament"), Ricardo Espinosa Maeso ("El abad Francisco Salinas"), Ismael Fernández de la Cuesta ("Francisco de Salinas" and "General Introduction"), Dámaso García Fraile ("El acceso a una cátedra" and "La vida musical"), Macario S. Kastner (*Francisco Salinas De Musica*, Nachwort), Francisco José León Tello ("Contribución de Ramos de Pareja y Francisco Salinas"), Edward Lowinsky ("Gasparus Stoquerus and Francisco de Salinas"), Florencio Marcos Rodríguez (*El ingreso de Salinas*), Manuel Martínez Añibarro (*Intento de un Diccionario*, pp. 444–447), Paloma Otaola González (*El humanismo de Salinas*), Claude Palisca ("Francisco Salinas," "Francisco de Salinas et l'humanisme," and "Salinas, Francisco de"), and Robert M. Stevenson ("Salinas").

230. Mudarra (c.1510–1580), who died in Seville, was the only one who was alive after the publication of Salinas' treatise. The dates of the others were: Narváez (fl. c. 1505–1549), Pisador (c. 1509–1557), and Valderrábano (fl. mid- 16th century).

231. In both books, Salinas referred to folksongs as: *vulgaribus cantilenis, vulgares cantilenæ, vulgo cantebatur, cantilenæ vulgatissimæ, vulgares cantionibus, vulgarium cantilenarum, canticis autem vulgaribus, vulgarium cantionum, cantatur etiam vulgariter, cantio illa vulgatisima, vulgaribus canticis* (pp. 295, 298–299, 301–303, 308–309, 312–313, 315, 317, 320, 322–323, 325, 327–328, 335, 338, 416, 433); and he referred to Spanish songs as: *cantus apud Hispanos, Hispanæ copulæ, cantus*

his "melodía" from any source other than from the tradition with which he was most familiar.

4. Why did Salinas omit the initial verse of his *Conde Claros* ballad?

Ballad scholars familiar with the *Romance del Conde Claros de Montaluan* (= *Conde Claros insomne*), from Martin Nucio's edition (CSA, fols. 83–91vo.), know that it begins with the verse "Media noche era por filo / los gallos querían cantar."[232] Musicologists, on the other hand, appear to have overlooked this fact. Nonetheless, the question remains: Why did Salinas himself ignore the ballad's initial hemistichs, opting instead to cite the following verse: "Conde Claros con amores / no podía reposar"?[233] Three possibilities come to mind: The first concerns the tune-text relationship. We discussed how Salinas first introduced the "melodía" as a notated distich, accommodating the syllables (7+6) and stress patterns of the Latin verse, "Virtus est fortitudo virtus est fortitu" (*De Musica*, p. 342). By following his suggested metric adjustments, we saw how the second verse of *Conde Claros*, "Conde Claros con amores no podía reposar," comprising eight plus seven syllables, could be suited to the same "melodía." Had Salinas employed the first verse, one would have realized immediately that its second hemistich, "los gallos querían cantar," which comprises eight syllables, would have required the following additional modification:

Me - dia - no - che - ra   por   fi - lo / los   ga - llos   que- rí - an   can - tar.

Hispanicum, cantio Hispana, rusticæ cantionis Hispanæ, Hispani in canticis, Hispanæ notisimæ cantilenæ, etc. (pp. 305, 307, 333, 342, 346).

232. Particularly in Nucio's *Cancionero de romances* (CSA, fols. 83–91vo.) and in various other sources. *Conde Claros* was still extremely popular during the generation following Salinas (d. 1590), proof of which can be seen in Cervantes' opening of Part II, Chapter 9, of *Don Quijote* (Madrid, 1615), which begins with the ballad's initial hemistich.

233. Yet, according to Carolina Michaëlis de Vasconcelos, this verse was frequently utilized as the ballad's true beginning (*Romances Velhos*, p. 110). Of the various examples she cited, the first is included in the seventh strophe of the *Ensalada de Praga* (F.J. Wolf, *Über eine Sammlung*, p. 200 = Menéndez Pidal, *Pliegos de Praga*, I, 6).

If the above verse had been rendered in a simple duple meter, the following
alterations would have been necessary:

Me -dia - no- che̲e - ra por fi - lo / los ga - llos que- rí - an can - tar.

Secondly, a plausible explanation for beginning with the second verse may
have been Salinas' intention to mention the name of the famous ballad
protagonist, who was already immortalized by the *vihuelistas* in their
instrumental variations based on the same melo-rhythmic motif with which
Conde Claros was associated. Moreover, since the incipit, "Media noche era por
filo," also served as the initial hemistich of another ballad narrative (that of
Gaiferos: Primav. 174), Salinas may have chosen the second verse to avoid any
possible confusion.[234]

Finally, it is also likely—in view of the fact that Salinas chose the second
verse—that his "melodía" may have indeed comprised the third and fourth
melody phrases of a quatrain strophe, or perhaps the second phrase of a
protracted distich.[235]

* * *

234. José J. Labrador Herraiz and Ralph A. DiFranco (*Tabla*, p. 186) cite four distinct
sources for the initial hemistich, plus a variant that begins "Media cena era por filo."
Asensio (*Cancionero musical luso-español*, p. 61) cites the initial hemistich,
"Medianoche era por filo," which he found in an unedited sixteenth-century *Cancionero*.
Unfortunately Asensio's musical notations lack text underlays.

235. It was Sage who suggested earlier that Mudarra and other *vihuelistas* utilized
"only the first phrase of the ballad tune for «Conde Claros» . . . in order to show their
facility in creating instrumental variations (*diferencias*) upon a short theme" ("Early
Spanish Ballad Music," p. 200). Yet, Sage suggested (p. 201) that "the fact that . . .
[Salinas repeated] the same phrase, underlying the words of the next line of the ballad,
could be explained by the unusual but not unique repetition of phrase in ballad tradition
. . . or even by the reiteration of the same phrase in the *diferencias* in the *vihuela* books,"
which also led Sage to explain that "the phrase is only the first . . . of a four-phrase tune
of the usual kind" (p. 200).

In our search for examples from the modern oral tradition, we encountered three non-related tunes (14*a-d*), whose narrative segments also deal with *Conde Claros insomne*. While we cannot state with any certainty how long these tunes have existed in the modern tradition, nor can we pinpoint their origin, we do know that they were collected in such regions as the Balearic Islands, Castile (Valladolid), and Asturias (Zarréu/Degaña). Only the first (sung in Catalan) and third examples attest to survivals of the original incipit, "Media noche era por filo, / los gallos querían cantar." A fourth tune, the Portuguese example from the Azorean island of Flores begins like Salinas' text: "Conde Claros, por amores, / não podia repoisar." Collectively, all four tunes constitute quatrain strophes, yet their differences are quite striking. The first (Ex. 14*a*) adheres to an AA'BC structure, whose melody phrases exhibit a quasi-isorhythmic relationship. Its tune, combining mixed duple and triple meters, may be described as a Phrygian tetrachord (*finalis* e), whose reiterated *subtonium* (d) figures prominently in the last melody phrase.

Example 14*a*: M. Aguiló y Fuster (*Romancer popular*, no. 31; reprinted in J. Amades, *Folklore de Catalunya*, p. 578)[236]

236. Below his notation, Aguiló cited Briz's *Cançons de la terra* as his source. Yet, having examinined all five volumes of Briz's collection, published in Barcelona by Joan Roca y Bros et al. (1866-1877), I find that the tune does not appear. Aguiló's text (p. 305) appears to be a conflation of two or three versions from oral tradition which he collected in the Balearic islands of Ibiza and Formentera. Aguiló specifies that the text was not known on the Continent.

The Castilian tune (Ex. 16*b*), whose text is somewhat varied — mentioning "don Carlos" instead of "Conde Claros" — was rendered as a quasi triple-metered quatrain (ABCD) strophe with noticeable and and occasional duple-metered interpolations. Here we have a Phrygian pentachord (*finalis* e̲), plus *subtonium*. Most prominent are the biphrasal melo-rhythmic antecedent-consequent relationships. The last two phrases are restricted to a perfect 4th, extended by the *subtonium* d̲. Joaquín Díaz also reported a circular dance bearing the text of *Conde Claros* ("El romance en las danzas circulares," p. 10).

Example 14*b*:[237]

Ae̲- so de la me - dia no - che,   cuan - do los ga - llos can - tar,

don Car-los de mal dea - mo-res̲   no po - dí - a so - se - gar.

---

237. Collected by Joaquín Díaz, in June 1977, in the village of La Overuela (Valladolid), where his seventy-two year old informant, Amalia Gómez, was born (Joaquín Díaz, et al., *Catálogo folklórico*, II, 275); shown here in a slightly altered and transposed retranscription by I. J. Katz. According to Díaz' commentary, Amalia learned this and many other ballads from her parents and grandparents, who lived in Cigales, about thirteen kilometers north of Valladolid (*Catálogo folklórico*, I, 166-167). In comparing her rendition — comprising fifty-five and a half verses — with the version printed in Nucio's edition (CSA, fols. 83ro.–91ro.), Díaz concluded: "viene a probar que, en contra de las opiniones de algunos estudiosos, en el caso de [su] versión no se puede decir que, [quoting from Manuel Alvar, p. 112] 'de [sus] textos primitivos ... apenas queda en la tradición oral otra cosa que el relato novelesco y la rima en á.'" The ballad's text and tune were republished in *Romances tradicionales* (pp. 64–70). The original recording (K/5.65), housed at the Centro de Etnográfico "Joaquín Díaz" (Ureña [Valladolid]), is listed in Carlos A. Porro Fernández (*Fonoteca de tradición oral*, p. 32) as belonging to the narrative episode *Conde Claros fraile* rather than *Conde Claros insomne*. Upon closer scrutiny, however, the actual text consists of *C. Claros insomne* (vv. 1–7) + *C. Claros y la infanta* (8–20) + *C. Claros fraile* (21 ff.). We are most grateful to Joaquín Díaz for providing us with a copy of the entire rendition, dubbed from his original field tape. On the cassette that was issued with the publication, only vv. 3 through 14 were included. The informant repeated the latter two melody phrases of each strophe, either with or without hemistichal repetitions.

The example from Asturias (Ex. 16*c*), or more exactly, Asturias-León, conveys nothing more than a simple triple-metered quatrain strophe (ABAB′) in the Major mode (*finalis* c). What is curious is that its transcriber placed f-sharp in the key signature, which, if intended for subsequent strophes, would have presented us with a rare example in the Lydian mode.[238]

Example 14*c*: Version from Cerredo (Zarréu; *parroquia* of Santa María de Cerredo, *consejo* of Degaña) [239]

Finally, here is a duple-metered Portuguese example (14*d*), from the island of Flores in the Azores, which represents a quatrain strophe (ABCB). The tune's Major modality appears to gravitate toward the lower unstated *finalis* c.[240]

Example 14*d*: Version from Fajãzinha (*consejo* of Lajes das Flores, Azores), sung by Maria Rosa, July 23, 1969, collected by Joanne B. Purcell. Transcribed

---

238. This mode is quite prevalent in Galicia, particularly among the octosyllabic *alalás* (short melodies with refrains).

239. On August 31, 1991, Jesús Suárez López recorded the rendition from a woman named Celia (?), some 70 years of age, who was born in San Miguel de Laciana, in the province of León. See Suárez López (*Nueva colección,* no. 13.1); transcribed by Susana Asensio Llamas (music: p. 688).

240. To my knowledge this is the only Portuguese tune that has been collected for *Conde Claros insomne* (= *Conde Claros Insone*). Tune versions and variants can be found for the narratives *Conde Claros fraile* (= *Conde Claros Vestido de Frade*) and *Conde Claros y la princesa acusada* (= *Conde Claros e a Princesa Acusada*). See Costa Fontes, *O Romanceiro Português,* I, 68–72, and II, 409 (= RPI); Nascimento, "Conde Claros na tradição portuguesa"; and Seeger, *Conde Claros: Study of a Ballad Tradition.*

by I. J. Katz. See Armistead et al., *Romanceiro Tradicional das Ilhas dos Açores*, I, no. 7A (= RTIA).

None of the four tunes cited here attest to even the remotest link to Salinas' trichordal distich. Yet, curiously enough, Manuel García Matos suggested a melodic descendant (Ex. 15) for Salinas' variant of *Conde Alarcos* (see Ex. 8 *supra*), rather than the original "melodía" (Ex. 5), which he recorded sometime between the summer of 1944 and the end of autumn 1947, from the modern oral tradition, in La Hiruela, a border village in the province of Madrid.[241]

Example 15: García Matos ("Pervivencia," no. 12)

---

241. García Matos explained the ballad's function in the village, located slightly southeast of the northernmost point of the province of Madrid, where "se practica el Domingo de Ramos en solicitud de pecuniaria ayuda para sufragar los gastos de la cera que en el templo se consume en el alumbrado del *Monumento* del día de Jueves Santo, [adding that here] no es improbable que tengamos un caso de auténtica *convergencia* [con la de *Conde Alarcos*] antes que de parentesco o relación de *tema y variante-derivada*, ya que en el tan reducido ámbito de una *tercera* en que se desenvuelven hácese bien posible la incidencia en la semejanza al margen de cualquier parentesco, [he cautiously concludes that] ello, empero, sería arriesgado afirmarlo sin razón más decisiva" ("Pervivencia," p. 80). The notation for Example 15 was taken from García Matos' earlier collection (*Cancionero popular*, III, no. 668, which coordinates with text 383*b* in Vol. II, 129). An additional tune variant from Prádena del Rincón can be found in Vol. II, no. 303, coordinating with the text of no. 383. However no. 303's range comprises a Minor 4th (*finalis* a̲), plus raised *subtonium*. For additional information concerning *canciones de Cuaresma y de Semana Santa*, to which both variants belong, see Vol. I, xxi–xxiii.

* * *

Yet to be exhaustively explored is the extent to which narrative episodes of *Conde Claros* appeared in the Spanish theater of the Golden Age. Surely there were allusions to the notorious count in both dramatic and comic stage productions, yet we possess scant information about the ballad's role in such performances. We do know, of course, that traditional ballads and songs were incorporated, along with newly composed songs, in the varied genres of the Spanish court and popular theaters of the 17th and 18th centuries, which include *autos, bailes, comedias, entremeses, jácaras, loas, máscaras, mojigangas, sainetes* and *zarzuelas*.[242]

Several instances, dealing with the ballad's theatrical setting within a musical context, have been documented. Among them is the *comedia Aulegraphia* (Act III, scene 1), by the 16th-century Portuguese playwright Jorge Ferreira de Vasconcellos (c. 1515–1585), in which a page named Dinardo Pereira announces to his friend, while tuning his guitar, that he is about to sing the ballad *O rapaz do conde Daros*. Not only does he intentionally mispronounce Claros, but goes on to sing instead—to the melody of "Conde Claros"—the ballad of *La doncella guerrera*.[243]

---

242. Although the composed theatrical songs (*tonadas*)—basically strophic in form and declamatory in style—were conceived for specific works within a given genre, many of them were utilized, indiscriminately, in other works within the same genre or a different one, in which such texts were often parodied. Louise K. Stein's excellent and most recent study of music and theater in 17th-century Spain (*Songs of Mortals*) discusses the varied genres. See also Emilio Cotarelo y Mori (*Colección de entremeses, loas, bailes*). And, from María C. García de Enterría, we learn that she encountered in the *villancico* repertory, "numerosas resonancias de [romances antiguos] a los [que] alude siempre como a textos, o cantos o coplas muy añejos: Gayferos, Calaínos, el Conde Claro . . . entre [otros] personajes del romancero . . . y otras veces, se reproducen versos . . . los romances básicos—genotextos o hipotextos—sobre los que se construían nuevas composiciones, transformadas para dar una dirección nueva a la lectura y la audición. Así: *Media noche era por filo, etc. etc.*" ("Bailes, romances, villancicos," p. 183). Unfortunately, García de Enterría does not provide concrete examples.

243. It appears that this comedy premiered posthumously in Lisbon in 1619 (Ferreira de Vasconcellos, *Comedia Avlegrafia*, pp. 84–85). See Michaëlis de Vasconcelos (*Romances Velhos*, p. 146; = RVP) and Mele ("Due canti spagnuoli," p. 204, n. 1). Mele (pp. 204 and 212) found an occurrence of the same obvious mispronunciation in L. Tansillo's *Capitoli giocosi e satirici*, specifically in the *terzina* (p. 111, vv. 10–12): "Io feci come fa quel di Fragola / che suona il conde daro [*sic*] e canta l'appia / per far come

In the *Auto do Desembargador,* by António Prestes, a Portuguese author of *comédias* and *autos* who flourished during the first third of the 16th century, a *portero* reflects:

> por terceiros vem os senhores;
> também nossa casa está
> terceira; a feito vae jâ
> *Conde Claros con amores*[244]

Another citation figures in the *Bayle de la boda de Foncarral,* preceding the first act of the *comedia, De la vengança honrosa,* by the Valencian poet Gaspar de Aguilar (1561–1623), who served as secretary to the Duke of Gandía. Here a group of musicians

> pidieron al nobio todos
> que sacase a la madrina
> ques es la muger del alcayde
> harto bizarra y pulida,
> y como siempre en los viejos
> se halla la cortesia
> con el sombrero en la mano
> ansi dançando dezia,
> Conde Claros con amores
> no podia reposar . . . [245]

---

fan gli altri a la spagnuola," Obviously Tansillo was unaware of the tune. See also Michaëlis de Vasconcelos, "Miscelánea," pp. 379–381.

Ferreira de Vasconcellos worked as a clerk in the Royal Treasury and the House of India. Later he was elevated to knighthood in the Order of Christ. He was known for his play in prose, *Eufrosina* (1616), which imitated Fernando de Rojas' erotic *tragicomedia, Celestina* (1499), and for *Ulissipo,* a largely insignificant interlude, which, however, described 16th-century Portuguese customs and included a prodigious quantity of Portuguese proverbs and sayings. Cf. *Indice biográfico de España, Portugal e Iberoamérica* (2000). See also Diogo B. Machado, *Biblioteca Lusitana,* pp. 805–806.

244. António Prestes, *Primeira parte dos autos e comédias portuguesas,* p. 206; cited also in RVP, p. 110.

245. See Francisco de Ávila (*Flor de las comedias de España,* quinta parte, p. 110), and Cotarelo y Mori (*Colección de entremeses,* I, pp. 481–482). Both Castro Escudero ("Bailes y danzas," p. 27) and Ruiz Mayordomo, in her brief entry on "Conde Claros," in

Las hazañas del Cid, y su muerte, con la tomada de Valencia, attributed to Lope de Vega, was first published in 1603, in his *Seis comedias*.[246] Its second act begins with the Cid giving audience to the Moors of Valencia, during which his wife, Jimena, enters and is welcomed by a chorus of *moriscos*. The stage direction following the chorus' verses reads:

> (*Repitelo algunas veces, volviendo a su algazara, y tras esto entra el* CID *y* JIMENA *de la mano y sus hijas, cercado de los fidalgos, y delante el juglar tañendo "el Conde Claros," y sientanse todos, y dice el* CID *después de sentado cabe* JIMENA)

And, again, moments later, after the Cid requests: "Cantes, el juglar de buen romance, alguna trova nueva bien guisada, de amor un chiste, o de lidiar un lance," there follows the direction:

> (*El* JUGLAR, *tocando "el Conde Claros," dice de repente:*)

> Si estades, Cid, escuchando
> repertirvos he un cantar
> de amor que plugo trovar
> l infante don Fernando.
>   Y, por vuestra bien querencia
> oid dicir mi cantar:
> que Dios vos deje gozar
> esta ciudad de Valencia . . . [247]

---

the recently published *Diccionario de la música española e hispanoamericana* (III, 867), cite its author as "anónimo."

246. *Seis comedias de Lope de Vega Carpio*, Lisbon: Pedro Crasbeeck, 1603. For some interesting notes concerning this *comedia*, see the Real Academia Española's edition, *Obras de Lope de Vega*, Vol. XI, ix–xi.

247. Real Academia Española, *Obras de Lope de Vega*, Vol. XI, p. 27. J. Castro Escudero ("Bailes y danzas," pp. 27–28) had already pointed out that "en el parlamento y canto del juglar que sigue a la acotación citada, no se alude a esta danza ni al nombre del personaje del romance que la titulada."

Yet, in another *comedia*, *La villana de Getafe*, by Lope de Vega, "Conde Claros" is alluded to as a dance, in a dialogue involving three characters.[248] Asked by the character Inés what dance they would like to perform, the following are proposed: "*vacas*" (pertaining to the *romanesca* "Guárdame las vacas"), "*folías*," "*canario*," "*villano*," and finally "Conde Claros," to which she replies: "Puede ser / gusto a quien tuviere amores / si es verdad que con amores / no podía reposar."[249] Again, in a *baile* from *Boda de Foncarral*, a *comedia* by Gaspar de Aguilar (1561–1623), a bridegroom sings "Conde Claros con amores no podía reposar." Obviously "Conde Claros" and the aforementioned dances were indeed highly popular in court circles during the first half of the 17th century.[250]

In the *Auto de Dom André*, a clumsy peasant, dressed as a jester (*pagem de arte*), plays "Conde Claros" on a guitar.[251]

The *Bayle de Conde Claros*, written by the renowned dramatist and lyric poet Agustín Moreto y Cabaña (1618–1669), was intended as a parodied version of *Conde Claros insomne*.[252] Its cast includes several speaking roles (La infanta

---

248. Printed in the *Parte catorze de las comedias de Lope de Vega Carpio*, . . . *descrito en el Archivo Romano y Familiar del Santo Oficio de la Inquisición* (Madrid: Juan de la Cuesta; a costa de Miguel de Syles, 1620), fols. 28ro.-55ro., preceded by the *dedicatoria*, fols. 26vo.–27vo. See Cotarelo y Mori, *Colección de entremeses*, p. ccxxxix.

249. Mele ("Due canti," p. 211) and Pope ("Notas," p. 401) confirm the fact that *Conde Claros* and *Guárdame las vacas* were also known as dances in Italy.

250. S. G. Armistead cites, in the present volume, a brief parody of *Conde Claros insomne*, in Luiz Vélez de Guevara's play, *Los hijos de la Barbuda* (1608–1610).

251. The *auto* was attributed to Gil Vicente de Almeida, grandson of Gil Vicente, the founder of the Portuguese theater. It premiered in Lisbon in 1625. However, at the Biblioteca Nacional (Lisbon), the MS bears the attribution 'António Alves'. See Michaëlis de Vasconcelos (*Romances Velhos*, p. 108) and Mele ("Due canti," p. 210). It should be pointed out that Dona Carolina discovered numerous fragments of Castilian *romances* which Portuguese playwrights of the 16th and 17th centuries inserted in their theatrical works, principally in the musical *intermezzi*, either in their original tongue or in translation.

252. Felipe Pedrell defined the genre, *baile del teatro antiguo*, as an "intermedio de antiguas comedias, que venía a ser una especie de sainete o farsa, escrita en verso con recitado, canto y baile" (*Diccionario técnico*, p. 37). Two distinct copies of Moreto's *baile* are preserved in the Departamento de Manuscritos at the Biblioteca Nacional (Madrid). The first, entitled *Bayle de Conde Claros* (Ms. 14856, fols. 156–159), comprises 160 hemistichs. The second, *Bayle burlesco del Conde Claros* (Ms. 16291, fols. 96–103), consists of 172 hemistichs, of which thirty-one (itemized in Rafael de Balbín Lucas, "Tres piezas menores," p. 116) vary textually from the former copy. Although as this *baile* was also·attributed to Calderón, Balbín Lucas convincingly

Clara, el Conde Claros, el rey, una doncella, una dueña y un músico), plus a group of musicians. The initial pair of hemistichs, "Media noche era por filo / los gallos quieren cantar," sung by a musician, is followed by the third and fourth hemistichs, "conde claros con amores / no podía reposar," rendered by the entire cast. This alternation between soloist and chorus of odd- and even-numbered verses continues through the first five strophes, after which varied members are assigned specific hemistichs to sing (or recite) from the remaining text. Only in three instances (hemistichs 30–31, 46–47, and 126–127), does the entire cast again intercede as a unisonal chorus, amid the exchanges of the principal figures. Moreto transformed the ballad's traditional narrative setting, by means of his characteristically novel interpolations, replacing the tragic with a comic ending and concluding with a *seguidilla* (hemistichs 159–176).[253]

From these examples alone, one can appreciate the varied ways in which *Conde Claros* had penetrated both the Spanish and Portuguese theater of the Golden Age. Other ballads also continued to be suited to its melody and it also served as a dance. As Eugenio Mele observed: "canto, melodia e ballo era dunque el *conde Claros*" ("Due canti," p. 212). It is unfortunate, however, that the music used in such presentations was not preserved in notated form, and the instruments that were used were only mentioned in exceptional cases.[254]

Bailes (popular dances) and *danzas* (more formal or courtly dances) were considered the principal attractions of theatrical performances.[255] Yet what the

---

identifies Moreto as its author ("Tres piezas," p. 81). This work, and two other *bailes burlescos*, *Don Rodrigo de la Cava* and *Lucrecia y Tarquino*, "tienen de común el tratar bufonamente el asunto y están salpicados de versos tomados de romances muy conocidos. Al primero [*Conde Claros*] le llama el autor [Moreto] «baile burlesco», «baile entremesado» al segundo, y no lleva calificativo especial el último" (Cotarelo y Mori, *Colección de entremeses*, p. cxcii). Listings of Moreto's published and unpublished theatrical works can be found in Cayetano A. de la Barrera y Leirado (*Catálogo bibliográfico y biográfico*, pp. 275–281). *El Conde Claros* is cited twice in the righthand column (p. 276) as a *baile* (*burlesco*), the first of which indicates that it is a "manuscrito antiguo [inédito]." See also Cotarelo y Mori, "La bibliografía de Moreto," and Ciria Matilla, "Manuscritos y ediciones."

253. For a succinct analysis of this *baile*, see Balbín Lucas ("Tres piezas," pp. 85–86).

254. Bagpipes, harps, guitars, lutes, *vihuelas*, castanets, tambourines without jingling discs (*sonajas*), and single-headed frame drums (*panderos*) were highly popular instruments in the theater.

255. José Deleito y Piñuela devotes four short, yet informative, chapters to theatrical and recreational dances during the Golden Age (*También se divierte*, pp. 67–86). Distinguishing between *danzas* and *bailes* from a choreographic standpoint, Deleito states that *danzas* "son de movimientos más mesurados y graves, en donde no se usa de los

public truly enjoyed were the racy lyrics accompanying individual *bailes* and *danzas*, which included such lascivious dances as the *capona, chacona,* and *zarabanda*. Their inclusion, in fact, almost caused a complete shut-down of theatrical performances by both local government and church authorities. Attesting to the decadence of those times and pointing out that the lively dances and *seguidillas* replaced the earlier serious and restrained dances, the poet Francisco Quevedo mentioned several *danzas de cuenta,* including "Conde Claros," in his long satirical *romance,* "Lindo gusto tiene el Tiempo" (vv. 125–172), presented here with two hemistichs per line:[256]

---

brazos, sino de los pies solos, [while *bailes*] admiten gestos más libres de los brazos y de los pies juntamente." *Danzas* were further differentiated as *danzas de cuenta* ("de ceremonia y buena sociedad"), *danzas de cascabel* ("descompuestas y populares"), and as *danzas mixtas* ("que participaron del carácter de ambas") (p. 69, quoting from J. A. González de Salas, *Nueva idea de la tragedía antigua,* p. 171). In the short introduction to his contribution, "Castilla y León" (pp. 187–189), in *Tradición y danza en España* (Madrid, 1992), Joaquín Díaz treats the delicate question, "¿Baile o danza?" An ongoing and most enlightening polemic, distinguishing *danzas de cuenta* from *danzas de cascabel* in the 16th and 17th centuries, was printed intermittently in the Madrid-based periodical, *La Ilustración Española y Americana,* from August 1874 through December 1878. The polemicists, Francisco Asenjo Barbieri and Julio Monreal, a lawyer and amateur musicologist, after a lengthy dispute, appear to have confused rather than clarified the matter. For a carefully presented overview, see Carmen García Matos Alonso's "Una polémica." To obtain a sense of how *bailes* and *danzas* were integrated into the varied theatrical productions of Lope de Vega, iduring the generation preceding Moreto, see José Castro Escudero ("Bailes y danzas"). Castro also comments on their distinguishing features. References to the various courtly and popular dances, together with the genres in which they were included, can be found in Louise K. Stein (*Songs of Mortals,* p. 555 et alibi). Among the forty titles she lists under *bailes* (p. 552), the only *baile* cited is Moreto's *Baile de Lucrecia y Tarquino.* José Subirá (*Historia de la música teatral,* p. 94), itemized the eighty-four *bailes* and thirty *danzas* from Cotarelo's *Colección de entremeses* (Chap. III: Bailes, pp. clxiv–cclxxiii), in which the *canario* and *folías* were placed in both categories.

256. Mele, "Due canti," p. 211. Deleito y Piñuela informs us that "poco a poco los bailes se alejaron de las comedias para pasar a los entremeses, como su principal y creciente atractivo, acabando por formar un género cómico especial, mixto de entremés y baile, y al que se dió este último nombre, por ser su parte coreográfica la más destacada. Altos ingenios le cultivaron . . . [such as] Quevedo, con tipos de hampa y frases truhanescas de *germanía*. Pero muchas más hizo Quiñones de Benavente, rey de este género como del entremés y de todas las piezas cómicas menores. A unos llamó *bailes*, a otros, *entremeses cantados*" (*También se divierte,* p. 212).

... Las fiestas y los saraos   nos los trueca a mojigangas;
y lo que entonces fue culpa   hoy nos lo vende por gracia.
Los maestros de danzar,   con sus calzas atacadas,
yacen por esos rincones   dirigiendo telarañas.
Floretas y cabrïolas   bellacamente lo pasan
después que las castañetas   les armaron zangamangas.
Con un rabel, un barbado   como una dueña danzaba,
y, acoceando el *Canario*,   hacía hablar una sala.
Mesuradas, las doncellas   danzaron con una arpa:
que una cama de cordeles   mucho menos embaraza.
Usábanse reverencias   con una flema muy rancia
y de *gementes et flentes*   las veras de la *Pavana*.
Salía de *Pie de gibao*,   tras mucha carantamaula,
con más cuenta y más razón   que tratante de la plaza.
Luego la *Danza del peso*,   una *Alta* y otra *Baja*;
y, con resabios de entierro,   la que dicen *De la hacha*.
El conde Claros, que fue   título de las guitarras,
se quedó en las barberías,   con *Chaconas* de la gaya.
El Tiempecillo, que vio   en gran crédito las danzas,
pues viene, toma, y ¿qué hace?;   para darles una carda,
suéltales las *Seguidillas*,   y a *Ejecutor de la vara*,
y a la *Capona*, que en llaves   hecha castradores anda.
De la trena a *Escarramán*   soltó, sin llegar la Pascua;
y al *Rastro*, donde la carne   se hace, bailando, rajas.
Vanse, pues, tras los meneos,   los dos ojos de las caras,
los dineros de las bolsas,   de las vajillas la plata . . . [257]

---

257. José Manuel Blecua, ed., *Francisco de Quevedo: Obra poética*, III, no. 757, vv. 125–176, pp. 34–35; Id., *El Parnaso español*, pp. 607–609, Musa VI, Romance 82. María Teresa Cacho Palomar describes the context of Quevedo's verses ("Quevedo, los bailes y los cancioneros," pp. 275–277). Cotarelo y Mori, who also includes the same verses, sums up Quevedo's sentiments: "las *danzas* serias y graves se olvidaron desde que aparecieron los *bailes* populares, alegres y de castañeta o castañuelas, como hoy se llaman" (*Colección de entremeses*, p. clxvi). Emilio Carilla documents us of the frequent occurrence of *romances* in *El Parnaso español*: "si bien [Quevedo] rehuyó (y en eso se apartó de Lope, Góngora, y Cervantes) el culto a la moda de los romances pastoriles y moriscos, que en ese tiempo y con la ayuda de la música, gozaran de gran popularidad. Fuera de unos pocos romances amorosos, los demás tienen carácter satírico y burlesco, y entre ellos hay que colocar, con marbete aparte, las famosas jácaras. Quevedo prefirió la

and in another *romance burlesco* ("Pues ya los años caducos"), Quevedo wrote:

> Sepa que los condes Claros,
> que de amor no reposaban,
> de los amantes del uso
> se han pasado a las guitarras.[258]

Interestingly, Ramón Menéndez Pidal, while discussing *romances* bearing *estribillos*, pointed out that: "En las canciones épico-líricas francesas, el estribillo es mirado como parte indefectible de las canciones destinadas a la danza, a diferencia de las que se cantan en otras ocasiones. Pero en España no es así. El romance que sabemos sirvió aquí más para la danza, el del *Conde Claros*, no se cantaba con estribillo. . . . Sin embargo, también hay bailes en que el canto del romance es coreado" (RoH, I, 147). Speaking of dances sung to texts which lingered on in the modern tradition, Menéndez Pidal contributed the following enlightening paragraph:

> Es sabido que en algunos pueblos y en época antigua se acompañaba el baile con canto narrativo, de donde el vocablo *balada* («bailada») recibió el sentido de «poema breve que refiere una historia o leyenda», sentido que se propagó de la lengua inglesa y alemana (*ballad, ballade*) a las lenguas románicas en el siglo XIX, por influjo del romanticismo. Pero más general es usar en el baile canciones amorosas, por lo que el provenzal *balada* y el italiano *ballata* significan canción lírica de una sola estrofa o de pocas, y tan rápidamente decayó el uso de la danza con canción narrativa que hoy subsiste sólo por raro arcaísmo, citándose como caso notable el que la practiquen los aldeanos bretones o que en las islas Feroë se use el baile en corro, donde cogidos de las manos los danzadores entonan una balada heroica de Sigurd o moderna de asunto local sobre alguna desgracia de pescadores. En cambio, el baile al son de una canción lírica es usado en todas partes. En España y América los bailes con canto de una copla lírica son incontables (sevillanas, seguidillas, jota, bolero, giradilla, habanera, cielito, zamacueca . . .),

---

punzante descripción de costumbres y la burla de personajes típicos de los romances serios" ("Quevedo y el «Parnaso español»," p. 379).

258. Quevedo, *Obras completas*, ved. Blecua, III, no. 778, vv. 77–80. Quevedo, *Las tres últimas musas castellanas*, p. 65, Musa VII, Romance 5.

mientras que los bailes con canto narrativo son rarísimos. Pocos restos se conservan de la costumbre que sabemos existió en el siglo XVI (baile del *Conde Claros* y demás romances viejos) y en el XVII (baile de *Escarramán* y demás jácaras) (Menéndez Pidal, *Estudios sobre el Romancero*, pp. 437–438).

Menéndez Pidal also discussed how peasants amused themselves by singing ballads to accompany their dances. He suggests that the origin of this practice can be traced to aristocratic circles from the early 12th century, particularly in France (RoH, II, 98–101). A unique example, in a *mojiganga*, alluding to Conde Claros' reputed amorous adventures and intricately woven into a poetic dialogue embellishing the root "clar," was conceived as a vocal duet by Antonio de Zamora:[259]

Sargento:	Clara divina.
Sacristán:	Clara más que humana.
Sargento:	Clara, Clarea,
Sacristán:	Clara, Claríana
Sargento:	Clara, por cuios ojos [bellos], raros
	se muriera de amor el Conde Claros.
Sacristán:	Claríssima veldad, que se promete
	de la cuba de amor vino clarete.
Sargento:	Clara, que eres por veldad suprema
	de los huevos del sol clara sin yema.
Sacristán:	Clariquea, por quien mi pecho es Troia.
Sargento:	Clara, clarín.
Sacristán:	Y Clara, claraboia.
Sargento:	Digo, señor colegial, cesse el clareo,
	que de oír tanta clara me mareo.

---

259. Antonio de Zamora (1660/64–1728), *Moxiganga de los gigantones*, BN (Madrid), MS 14.0904, fols. 32ro.–41ro. (s. XVIII). It was written in 1711 for a "fiesta de Corpus en Madrid." Concerning the rare modern survival of traditional dances accompanied by the singing of ballads, see *El Romancero de La Gomera*, ed. Maximiano Trapero, especially the detailed studies by José Manuel Fraile Gil, Isidro Ortiz, and M. Trapero (pp. 107–146); also S. G. Armistead, pp. 391–392, nn. 23–24. The volume is accompanied by a splendid CD: "Las últimas danzas romancescas de España," with texts edited and commented by Fraile Gil and Trapero (pp. 413–421). For photographs of modern traditional dances accompanied by *romances*, see Menéndez Pidal, *Cómo vivió y cómo vive el Romancero*, pp. 44–45, 52–57; comment: pp. 76–81.

Sacristán: Usted, señor capitán, con essa cara
es quien me enfada a mí, pues se declara.

Zamora and José de Cañizares (1676–1750), both of whom were disciples of Calderón, were considered to be the most outstanding librettists of the early 18th century. In an article by P. Bolaños Donoso and M. de los Reyes Peña, we are provided with interesting details concerning the performances of Cañizares' *zarzuela, Las nuevas armas del amor* (with music by Sebastián Durón [1660–1716]), displaying a notable Italian influence, and the *Moxiganga*, on October 17, 1724.[260] Contrasting their performances, the authors wrote:

> La espectacularidad escenográfica y el sazonado componente musical de [*Las nuevas armas* . . .], que tienen el correlato literario en su tema mitológico y en su refinado lenguaje (si bien el gusto barroco por la tragicomedia lo hacen descender en ocasiones a profundas simas), contrastarían fuertemente con la carencia de escenografía—tan sólo era necesaria un arca—, la escasa intervención de la música, la banalidad del tema y la grosería del lenguaje presentes en la *Mojiganga de los gigantones*, . . . que la acompaño y éxito estaba cifrado de forma exclusiva en la profesionalidad de los actores: dominio de la palabra, de la gestualidad y del movimiento escénico.[261]

In France, it was not by chance that *Conde Claros* came to the attention of Mellin de Saint-Gelais (1491–1558) and Pernette du Guillet (ca. 1518–1545), two highly esteemed 16th-century poets.[262] Intrigued by their incorporation of

---

260. See their article, "Teatro español en Lisboa." For Cañizares' work, see BN (Madrid), MS 15.079 (43 hs. 4.º l.s. XVIII) and 17.4489. The premiere performance of this unedited work took place, as far as is presently known, at the Corral del Príncipe de Madrid, on November 25, 1711. The *zarzuela,* however, was performed earlier, in Lisbon, on Dec. 18, 1721.

261. For an informative introduction to the *mojiganga,* see Antonio Todera, "Historia y mojiganga del teatro." One should also examine the *entremés burlesco,* in which classical, medieval, Carolingian, and contemporary myths were parodied. The medieval figures included Conde Claros, Conde Alarcos, the Cid, and the myth of Rey Rodrigo y la Cava. See Javier Huerta Calvo, "De mitología burlesca."

262. Mellin, the son of Octavien de Saint-Gelais (1468-1502), was also an accomplished musician and was likewise competent in Greek and Latin. Although it has not been proven conclusively that he spent any time in Spain, his interest in Spanish literature, and most likely his first encounter with the *Romancero*, resulted from his close

the count's name in the original titles of their respective *chansons*, the eminent French scholar, Verdun L. Saulnier, devoted an article to unraveling the connection between their respective poems and the "Conde Claros" tune ("Mellin de Saint-Gelais"). For Saint-Gelais' "Laissez la verde couleur," which comprised forty strophes and which bore, in the original manuscript, the title "Lamentations de Vénus en la mort d'Adonis, pour reciter en façon de conte clare d'Espagne" (MS BN [Paris] n.a. fr. 1158, fol. 156), Saulnier suggested that it evoked "l'idée d'une musique d'accompagnement (plutôt qu'une forme particulière de déclamation)," together with which his poem was to be recited (p. 526).[263] Pernette's poem, "Amour avecques Psyches," retitled "Conde Claros de Adonis" in later editions, appears to have been written with the same tune in mind, as a sequel to Saint-Gelais' *chanson*.[264] However, both poems, which had nothing to do with *Conde Claros* nor with Spain, were inspired by the Greek myth of Venus and Adonis. The two poems were printed together in 1545, and, curiously enough, they preceded, by three years, Martin Nucio's *Cancionero de romances sin año* (CSA), which included the narrative segment *Conde Claros insomne*. Still, we may assume that Saint-Gelais had in mind the melodic

---

friendship with the renowned French Hispanist, Nicolas de Herberay des Essarts, who may have, in fact, discussed with him the ballad of *Conde Claros de Montalbán*, from among countless other ballad themes which were then circulating in the oral tradition.

263. Not an entirely curious remark, when one learns from Christine Collen-Jimack's brief entry on Saint-Gelais that he 'specialized in reading aloud or singing his own compositions" (Peter France, ed., *The New Oxford Companion*, p. 733). Moreover, Frank Dobbins' entry in S. Sadie (ed.), *The New Grove Dictionary of Music and Musicians* (London, 1980, Vol. XIV, 390–391) notes that he was an accomplished lutenist, whose playing was "compared with that of Alberto de Ripa," and that, although the musical compositions attributed to him have not survived, the music of his strophic poetry "may have been based on existing dance tunes."

264. This poem was included among the seventy-seven collected poems, which Pernette's husband had entrusted to Antoine de Moulin, after her premature death from the plague. It is probable that her husband also suggested the title for Du Moulin's edition: *Rymes de [la] gentile et vertueuse dame D. Pernette du Guillet* (Lyon: Jean de Tournes, 1545), which was reprinted the following year in Paris, and again, in Lyon, in 1552. For a modern edition, see *Les rymes de Pernette du Guillet*, edited by Victor Graham (Geneva: Droz, 1968). See also Verdun L. Saulnier, "Étude sur Pernette du Guillet et ses *Rymes*," *Bibliothèque d'Humanisme et Renaissance*, 7 (1944), 7-119. Saulnier deduced that it was a sequel, based on the same tune, from MS 1158 (Bibliothèque Nationale, Paris), claiming that Saint-Gelais' *chanson* was apparently written in the same spirit as the Castilian ballad text, which must have also indirectly influenced that of Guillet.

prototype upon which Narváez based his *diferencias*, seven years earlier, in *Los seys libros del Delphin* (Valladolid, 1538).[265]

* * *

The extent to which *Conde Claros* penetrated instrumental music throughout Western Europe is a matter that may never be fully explored. We do not possess any musical sources earlier than the 16th century that are linked to the *Conde Claros* melody.[266] Of the aforementioned *vihuelistas* who composed sets of *diferencias* based on the *melodía*, Valderrábano wrote an additional duet for *vihuelas*, based on the *melodía*, which has generally been overlooked.[267] There is also an anonymous 16th-century *vihuela* manuscript, containing three *diferencias* on *Conde Claros*, preserved at the Archivo General de Simancas.[268]

---

265. Both appeared, successively, at the beginning of Antoine du Moulin's compilation, entitled *Déploration de Vénus sur la mort du bel Adonis, avec plusieurs autres compositions nouvelles* (Lyon: Jean de Tournes, 1545). Demand for the collection was such that it occasioned numerous subsequent printings. The poems also appeared in *Le Discours du voyage de Constantinople* (Paris: L'Angelier, 1546; and 1548, in a second printing of *Le Discours*, under a new title, *Le Livre de plusieurs pièces*, printed in Lyon). Du Moulin gathered together the poems of his collection while in the service of Margaret of Angoulême (1492–1549), consort of Henry II, King of Navarre (1542-1549). Margaret, herself a poet of note, formed her own literary circle. An interesting biographical essay on du Moulin can be found in Alfred Cartier and Adolphe Chennevière, "Antoine de Moulin, valet de chambre de la Reine de Navarre."

266. Curiously, Manuel de Falla returned to the *melodía*, incorporating it as an orchestral theme in the second *cuadro* (scene) of his opera, *El Retablo de Maese Pedro* (*Master Peter's Puppet Show*), which premiered in Seville on March 23, 1923, in concert form. De Falla did not take it from the initial measures of Mudarra's *diferencia*, as Pope suggested ("Notas," p. 402), but from the first edition (1919) of Pedrell's *Cancionero musical* (I, no. 25), as García Matos pointed out, which was actually the Conde Alarcos variant, "Retraída está la infanta, / bien así como quería" (Pedrell's underlay). Pope, nonetheless, described how de Falla incorporated the *melodía* in this scene, where the puppet character Melisendra is being held captive in the Moorish king's "Torre del homenaje del Alcázar de Sansueña," adding that "la intención de Falla parece bastante clara: eligió la melodía como el medio musical perfecto para dar una vaga sensación de misterio y evocar un ambiente lejano en el tiempo y en el espacio" ("Notas," p. 402). Concerning the episode, see FLSJ, V, Chap. 12, pp. 9–64.

267. Listed as a *canción* in the fourth book (fols. 48–48vo.) of Valderrábano's *Libro de música de vihuela, intitulado Silva de Serenas* (Córdoba, 1537). Ward, who provided a succinct analysis of this piece, described it as a "three-voice fantasia with discant ostinato" (*Vihuela de mano*, p. 184).

268. The manuscript was discovered by Cristina Bordas Ibáñez and can be found under the signature *Casa y Sitios Reales, Legajo 394, folio 130*. For further details see Antonio Corona-Alcalde, "A Vihuela Manuscript," pp. 3–20.

In their treatment of "Conde Claros," according to John Ward, the *vihuelistas* began their variation sets with:

> a simple chordal setting of the theme ["melodía"], which is remarkably brief, consisting of six *compases*, or, transliterated, three 2/4 measures. Two rhythmic figures constitute the more notable features of the theme, which is actually a recitation formula: an initial two measures of ♩♩ are followed by a measure containing the syncopation, ♪♩♪, characteristic of many *romance* tunes. The syncopation is "resolved" on the first beat of the next variation; as a consequence, the *Conde Claros* sets are continuous variations consisting of 3+3+3 . . . measure variations +1 measure containing the final "resolution" of the syncopation (*Vihuela de mano*, pp. 202–203).

While Ward does not provide us with a musical illustration, his description fits the melodic transcription of the "melodía" offered by Gonzalo Menéndez Pidal (Ex. 6*f*). However, Cecilio de Roda, who transcribed the initial phrase of Narváez's *diferencia* (*La música profana*, facing p. 38; see also Ex. 6*b*), presented it in two measures, the first in 3/2 and the second in 6/4, thereby obscuring the syncopation that characterizes this and other ballad tunes. Roda's transcription of Narváez reads:

Yet, according to Ward's description, the same phrase should have been interpreted as:

Ward also referred to the repeated harmonic sequence I-IV-V of the *bergamasca*, which was commonly utilized for variations.[269] As his example, he cited but did not include the *Moresca quarta deta la Bergamasca* from Giulio Cesare Barbetta's *Intavolatura de liuto* (Venice, 1585, p. 14), pointing out that such "*ostinato* harmonies are more apparent to the ear than the discant tune, which is usually figured or merely hinted at" (*Vihuela de mano*, p. 203). The initial four phrases of Matteo Coferati's *bergamasca* melody, as printed in Fabrizio Costanzo's *Fior novello, libro primo* . . . (Bologna, 1627), illustrate the harmonic progressions in question.[270] Notice that, while each *diferencia* concludes on the dominant chord, each phrase of the *bergamasca* concludes on the tonic:

G: [I   IV   V   I   ]

Two published harmonizations of the "melodía" deserve mention here. The simpler, made by Querol (*La música en* . . . *Cervantes*, p. 53), based on the same harmonic progressions, assigned the "melodía" to the 3rd degree (e) in the Major mode (C):

Me - dia   no-chee - ra   por fi - lo

I   IV   V

---

269. The *bergamasca* is an Italian dance which originated in the northern district of Bergamo during the late 16th century. Later, in the 17th century, the term was applied to instrumental works, particularly those for the guitar. Paul Nettl ("Die Bergamasca") undertook the first serious study of its history. Judith Cohen, an Israeli musicologist, presents some interesting facts concerning its possible Jewish links ("The Bergamasca").

270. See Richard Hudson's entry on the *bergamasca* in *The New Grove Dictionary of Music and Musicians* (1980), Vol. II, 541–542.

Pedrell, on the other hand, ventured a modal rendition, whose constituent tones (d-e-f-g-sharp-(a)-b-c') evoke the Mixolydian mode. Here, however, he placed the melody on the second degree (of *finalis* a) (*Cancionero musical*, I, no. 24). Strummed on a guitar, it would likewise evoke the flavor of an indigenous Spanish setting:

In his article, Roda discussed the *diferencia* and its treatment by the *vihuelistas*, especially Narváez, who used it either as an accompaniment for *villancicos, romances,* and other melodies, or as a purely instrumental composition ("La música profana," p. 33). For the *romances* in particular, the variations were essentially harmonic, constructed upon a bass, which was repeated implicitly or explicitly throughout the entire composition. The variations were well developed, displaying a high degree of ornamentation. For the *diferencias* accompanying *romances*, which constituted brief and monotonous melodies (like *Conde Claros*), Roda ventured a hypothesis that the *vihuelistas* probably seized the opportunity to construct a series of counterpoints and variations around them. Thus, already created, the *diferencia* evolved smoothly, accompanying *villancicos* and other song genres, and thereafter solely as purely instrumental compositions.

Roda deduced three important facts concerning the *diferencias* accompanying *romances* (particularly *Conde Claros*): 1) that the repeated bass followed, almost explicitly, the harmonic progression I-IV-V, thus constituting a true *passacale*, which remained unaltered during the entire composition; 2) that the variations were constructed upon a harmonic rather than a contrapuntal bass, which is important, given the fact that the rules of harmony were not fully developed in this epoch; and 3) that the *diferencias* accompanying *romances* and other song genres constitute "una verdadera *monodia accompañada*" (a true accompanied monody) for which the Florentine Camarata was credited as creator at the end of the 16th century (Roda, p. 34).[271]

Additional instrumental works utilizing the *Conde Claros* "melodía" can be found in five settings contributed by Guillaume Morlaye (c. 1510–after 1558), a French lutenist and composer,[272] and in a *ricercare* by the aforementioned Italian lutenist, Francesco Canova da Milano.[273] English settings were included

---

271. For additional comments on the *vihuelistas* and their settings of *romances*, see Daniel Devoto, "Poésie et musique," pp. 89–96, and Judith Etzion, "The Spanish Polyphonic Ballad."

272. The first setting, entitled "Conte clare," was published in his *Le premier livre de tablature de leut, contenant plusieurs chansons, gaillardes, pavanes . . .* (Paris: Robert Granjon and Michel Fezandat, 1552; no. 22, fol. 24vo.); the second, "Conteclare," and third, "Conte clare," in his *Second livre. . .* (Paris: Michel Fezandat, 1553; nos. 29–30, fols. 29 and 29vo., respectively), and the fourth and fifth, each entitled "Contreclare," in his *Quatriesme livre . . .* (Paris: Michel Fezandat, 1552; fols. 18vo.-19ro. and 27vo. [for solo cittern], respectively). Modern transcriptions of the second and fourth settings can be found in *The Musical Quarterly*, 46:4 (1960), p. 464, and in John Ward, *Music of Elizabethan Lutes*, vol. 2, no. 43, respectively. I am most grateful to John Ward for providing me with these citations.

273. An informative article by Rodrigo de Zayas ("La musica a Napoli," pp. 93–103) provides us with an interesting excursus pertaining to this work. In 1938, his father, Marius de Zayas, purchased from the antiquarian bookseller Leo S. Olschki, of Florence, a *Canzoniere di Mateo Bezon* (Biblioteca Zayas [Seville], A.IV.8), compiled in Naples in 1599. This is one of two rare copies; the other belongs to the Fondo Chigi of the Biblioteca Vaticana. The Zayas manuscript comprises a collection of verses with alphabetical intabulations for a five-string guitar, which was popularly known as the "chitarra spagnola." Among the twenty-nine *canzoni* with guitar accompaniment included there, four are in Italian, twenty-two are in Castilian, two are intermixed with Castilian and Italian verses, and one is in Latin (a *lamentazione*). Among the twenty-one pieces for solo guitar, one *passacaglia*, three *romancesche*, three *sarabande*, one *villano*, one *sfessania napoletana*, one *sfessania spagnola*, one *pavaniglia di Spagna*, and one *gagliarda* complete the poetry section. Zayas suggests, from the manuscript he owns, that Mateo Bezon was a teacher of guitar, song, and dance and that he used his *canzoniere* for the purpose of instruction. This Zayas surmised from the inscribed name 'Anton', a student who began lessons with Bezon on September 7, 1600 (date also inscribed). Now, what Zayas appears to have uncovered is that Bezon's *passacaglia* evidently predates the first *passacaglia* that Richard Hudson ("Passacaglia," p. 268) traced to Girolamo Montesardo's *Nuova inventione d'intavolatura* (Florence, 1606). The "passos" or "ritornelli" of Bezon's *passacaglia*, comprising short imitative phrases that were repeated continuously above the harmonic formula or tenor (I-IV-V-I), are similar to the *diferencias* and other forms (disregarding technique) which were created during the first half of the 17th century upon the "tenor" of *Conde Claros*. Furthermore, we learn that Francesco Canova de Milano himself composed a *ricercare* (a continuous set of

in two manuscript collections: the James Marshall and Marie-Louise Osborn Collection, MS 13, fols. 41vo.–42vo. (dating from the 1560s) at the Beinecke Rare Book and Manuscript Library, Yale University (New Haven), and the Francis Willoughby lute book, MS Mi LM 15, fols. 38ro.–39vo. (dating from the 1570s) at Nottingham University Library. Both are titled, "Quando claro, quando claro," the former consisting of fifteen variations; the second, twenty-two.[274]

Taking into account Isabel Pope's musicological legacy, it is appropriate that we should close this section with her concluding remarks concerning the "melodía," whose validity has remained unchallenged for almost five decades:

> ... podemos decir ... que esta melodía, si no fue la original del romance del Conde Claros—aunque sea quizá tan antigua o más—, llegó a ser una especie de molde melódico y rítmico que se prestó a multitud de transformaciones a lo largo de los años, sin perder su identidad, ni en fin de cuentas, su asociación con el mismo romance ("Notas," p. 402).

---

diferencias on the same "tenor" for the *vihuela de mano*) which was included in the second book (fol. 5) of his *Intavolatura de viola o vero lauto composto per lo eccellente e Unico Musico Francesco Milanese non mai più stampata. Libro primo e libro secondo de la Fortuna* (printed by Joannis Sultzbach [Johann Schultbach], in Naples, May 25, 1536; also available from Minkoff Reprint, Geneva, 1977). Canova's *Intavolatura* was published just two years prior to both Luys de Narváez's first published set of *diferencias* and Salinas' trip to Rome.

274. The English settings are included in John Ward's *Music for Elizabethan Lutes*, Vol. II (nos. 117 and 146, respectively). In his comprehensive view of Elizabethan lute music from the second half of the 16th censtury, Ward includes a veritable storehouse of documentation with cross references to other collections bearing the same or related items. He explains the inclusion of *Conde Claros* in English manuscripts as either having been brought to England by way of France, or directly by Spanish musicians who accompanied Prince Felipe of Spain during his visit to England in the 1550s. See Ward ("Spanish Musicians," especially p. 363, n. 27).

Lisarda

Lacking tunes associated with *Conde Claros fraile* in the Moroccan
Sephardic tradition, we must turn to the ballad's persistent presence in the
modern Iberian repertoire, under such titles as *Lisarda, Elisarda, Luisarda,
Griselda*, etc. The Peninsular tunes that have been collected to date attest to the
ballad's wide circulation in Asturias, León, Castile, Extremadura, Andalucía,
Cataluña, and Valencia. Of questionable identity is a ballad tune for *Dona
Mariana*, from the province of Algarve in Portugal, whose text comprises a
succession of three distinct ballad themes, the final and substantial portion of
which does pertain to *Conde Claros fraile*. Nonetheless, from the various
published collections, including two examples from our own as yet unedited
field recordings, , we have brought together twenty-five distinct tunes to which
the ballad has been sung.

Two variant Catalan texts, from Barcelona, bearing the titles "L'infanta" and
"La infanta Rosa Vera" (Exs. 1*a* and 1*c*, respectively), share the same tune,
comprising a quatrain strophe (AABC) in the Minor mode (*finalis* d̲). Their
extended texts are contaminated with verses from *La infanta parida* (cf. CMP
R3). Of the forty-one verses in Francesc Pelay Briz's example, and fifty-three in
Joan Amades', we should point out that the sole textual concurrence between
them can be found in the verse "L'infanta n'està molt mala: / Lo segon metge
que ve," which, oddly enough, coordinates with melody phrases C and A in
Example 1*a*, and with B and C in Example 1*c*.[275] Example 1*b* represents Adolfo
Carrera's revision of Briz's notation.[276] Amades, who mentioned that he
collected the ballad from his mother (Teresa Gelatz), appears to have suited her
verses to Carrera's notation, which must have resembled her rendition. Be that
as it may, Amades' textual substitution exemplifies a manipulative form of
contrafaction. Notice that he also added a metronomical tempo designation and
that he altered the cadential tones—encircled in melody phrase B—to
accommodate the text.

---

275. Briz (*Cansons*, IV, 43, vv. 10*b*–11*a*) and Amades (AFC 3263, vv. 9*b*–10*a*). In
Briz's text (p. 43), the second hemistich also reads: "Lo segon metge que ve."

276. Briz's published notation carried the erroneous key signature of three flats (b̲, e̲,
and a̲), to which Carreras correctly added d̲-flat He also altered Briz's rhythmic values
and text underlay, whose orthography he revised to conform with current standards. He
also appended a tempo designation.

Example 1: *a*) Briz (*Cansons*, IV, p. 43); *b*) Carrera (*Cançons populars*, III, p. 34); *c*) Amades (AFC, p. 739)

Seven melodic versions of *Lisarda* (Exs. 2–8) were obtained in Castile and León (Avila, León, Madrid, Salamanca, and Segovia). From Avila (Ex. 2), we have a quatrain strophe (ABCB′) in the plagal Major mode (*finalis* g). Notice the quasi-sequential relationship between melody phrases A and B.

Example 2: Schindler (*Folk Music,* no. 54)

In the province of León, Miguel Manzano Alonso collected three distinct versions, the first from Pedregal (Ex. 3) whose rendition Manzano described as *declamado* ("declaimed"). It is in the plagal Minor mode (*finalis* g).[277] Its initial verse was not recorded. However, in this example, melody phrase A bears a recitation tone (d'), on which the first textual hemistich and the initial portion of the second were intoned.[278] This rendition closes with a descending half cadence on a. Melody phrase B comprises what appear to be three non-rigid descending sequential segments (indicated as 'x', 'y', and 'z'), the latter of which concludes, via a Phrygian cadence, on the lower fifth degree (d).

Example 3: Manzano (*Cancionero leonés*, II, no. 738)

---

277. According to Manzano (*Cancionero leonés*, II, p. 56), its mode is the the Phrygian mode (*modo de mi*). Although this may be the correct nomenclature, the matter has much to do with one's personal perception. Admittedly, Manzano's contention is worth considering, except when looking at the later Examples, 15c, containing an internal Phygian cadence, and 25, ending on a Phrygian cadence. In both, the modal inference appears to gravitate toward g.

278. For a most interesting study of traditional tunes based on melodic recitation formulas, see Manzano, "Estructuras arquetípicas."

Structurally, we have a distich (AB), whose meter is basically duple and whose protracted phrases A and B each contain two hemistichs. Its range spans a Major 9th.

The notation of this simple quatrain strophe (ABCD) from Llamazares (ay. Valdelugueros, p.j. La Vecilla) (Ex. 4), exhibits a plagal Minor mode (*finalis* g), in which d′ is only faintly heard in the first of the paired grace notes in melody phrase C. It is not clear why Manzano offered the time signature 3/4 2/4 for a tune which he clearly notated in strict triple meter. Perhaps it was intended for subsequent strophes. Notice also the quasi-sequential melodic relationship between phrases A and C.

Example 4: Manzano (*Cancionero leonés*, II, no. 739)

Manzano's third Leonese tune (Ex. 5a), from Castrocalbón (p.j. La Bañeza), exhibits several interesting features: its ambitus comprises a Major hexachord (*finalis* f); each of its textual hemistichs are repeated throughout; and the alignment of its first two melody phrases yields a two-measure isorhythmic pattern that continues through the ultimate or penultimate syllable. Note also that the initial measures of phrases A and B bear a distinct sequential relationship. From a metric standpoint, the stress pattern 2+2+3 is reflected in the measures designated under 'x' and 'y', but not 'z'.

Example 5a: Manzano (*Cancionero leonés*, II, no. 740)[279]

Interestingly, a highly popular Portuguese tune *contrafact* (Ex. 5b), whose melodic and rhythmic features are unquestionably similar, was collected on September 19, 1988, by I. J. Katz and Zília Osório de Castro, in Nozedo de Cima (c. Vinhais), in the northeastern sector of Trás-os-Montes. Its text, which represents Blancaniña (*La adúltera* [ó]), deals with the theme of adultery, one of the most unpardonable and forbidden social transgressions of traditional Iberian society. Of the various ballads dealing with this theme, here the unfortunate Claralinda has long served as a reminder of the consequences of infidelity. Whether the tune itself was of Castilian or Portuguese origin is difficult to ascertain. In this variant the ambitus is extended to a Major 7th (as seen in melody phrase B).

---

279. Another, yet untranscribed example bearing the incipit, "Se paseaba don Carlos, / don Carlos del monte Abraham," is listed in Porro Fernández's *Fonoteca* under K/90.20. Porro Fernández recorded the ballad in Abastas (p.j. Frechilla, Palencia), on August 26, 1987.

Example 5*b*: Armistead et al. (CTT, 17*f*); transcribed by I. J. Katz

José Manuel Fraile Gil's collection of traditional ballads from the province of Madrid contains two examples of *Lisarda* from the villages of Robregordo de la Sierra (Ex. 6) and Canencia de la Sierra (Ex. 7), both villages in the p.j. of Torrelaguna, that were transcribed by Eliseo Para García. Example 6 appears to comprise a succession of distichs (AB, A'B, CD, and A'B), the latter phrases of which conclude with Phrygian cadences (*finalis* b). The contrasting melody phrases C and D, which bring into play the Major 3rd (d-sharp) and ascent to the Minor seventh degree (a'), evoke a transitional nuance that is virtually Andalusian in character, with its stately reinforcement of the Phrygian mode. Another reading of the tune's formal structure suggests an alternative scheme: ABA'BCD, i.e., a tripartite strophe, wherein AB, its repetition (A'B), and CD would have more suitably, if not more convincingly, depicted the tune's constituent units. The stringent duple-triple-duple metric alignment of the text and the tune is quite rare in the Hispanic ballad tradition. To fully comprehend the formal and metric aspects of this rendition, one would have to hear the entire rendition from the actual recording.

Example 6: Fraile Gil (*Madrid*, M-52)

A
Gi - se - la se pa - se - a - ba____

B
por los al - tos co - rre - do - res

A'
con sus ves - ti - dos de___ ga - la - [a]s

B
a - rras-tran - do sus fal - do - nes

C
y_el con - de de Mon - te_Al - va - [a]r

D
la_ha pre - ten - di - do_en a - mo - res.

A'
--No se - ñor, que soy muy___ ni - ña____

B
¿qué di - rí - an en las___ Cor - tes?

Example 7: Fraile Gil (*Madrid*, M-81/82)

The notated transcription of Fraile Gil's second tune (Ex. 7), from Canencia de la Sierra, likewise exhibits a rather novel rendition:

```
A  B  A  B  C  A  B  D
a  b  c  d  eef g  g  h
```

Like the previous example, it attests to a repeated melodic distich (AB, rendered here in triple meter), which proceeds to a duple-metered extended melody phrase C that carries the text of the third verse, including its reiterated initial hemistich.

Through melody phrase C, we have, in effect, a formal structure which closely resembles the earlier Troubadour *canso*:

A   A   B

a b c d <u>e</u><u>e</u><u>f</u>

Our rendition, however, continues with yet another appearance of the initial melodic distich (AB), together with a concluding phrase (D), based on the same rhythmic pattern, and ending on the *finalis* b-flat. The isorhythmic pattern of the triple-metered phrases is strictly adhered to. Here again the metric distinctions between the opening, middle, and final phrases demand an audition of the original recording to confirm the structure of the entire rendition.

Dámaso Ledesma's notation (Ex. 8), from Villarmayor (p.j. Ledesma, Salamanca), comprises two melodic strophes, rendered as ABCC ADCC, respectively, in the plagal Minor mode (*finalis* g). Taking note of the melodic and rhythmic differences between melody phrases B and D, one wonders whether the remaining text was sung in accordance with Ledesma's bistrophic notation; nor is it clear whether the first appearance of Ledesma's notated tone <u>f</u>, in phrase D, was sung as f-sharp, as in the previous measures. However, the second repetition of <u>f</u>, in the same phrase, was correctly notated as f-natural, suiting its role in the characteristic Phrygian cadence which is the hallmark of plagal Minor modes. Here we have an additional example of a circular tune, ending on the raised seventh degree (f-sharp).

Example 8: Ledesma (*Folk-lore*, p. 190)

The following triple-metered Segovian tune (Ex. 9), which spans a Minor pentachord (d̲-e̲-f̲-g̲-a̲, actually comprises a Phrygian tetrachord (based on *finalis* e̲), preceded by the *subtonium* d̲. Its formal structure is fundamentally a protracted unistrophe (A), two of which were notated (AA'). The *subtonium*'s second appearance is followed by a leap of a perfect 4th; thereupon the melodic line hovers around g̲, before concluding on the Phrygian cadence. Each melody phrase carries a line of verse (comprising two hemistichs).

Example 9: Marazuela Albornós (*Cancionero segoviano,* no. 171)

A single example (Ex. 10) from Andalusia was recorded in Madrid, in 1992, from an informant from Zagra (p.j. Loja, Granada). Here, we have transcribed the first three melodic strophes (ABC ABC'DC' ABC), in the second of which the informant added the refrain-like phrases DC', sung at a somewhat faster tempo, which she repeated again at v. 22 for the text "Lo que siento qu'ę mi sangre, / dentro de su cuerpo va." Given the erratic appearance of melody phrases DC', the tripartite strophic division (ABC) most convincingly characterizes the tune's formal structure. However, we note that our informant adhered to two distinct performance practices, the first of which entailed an extended melody phrase A, accomodating a full verse, while phrases B and C each carried a textual hemistich. This practice was followed at vv. 1, 4, 14, 16, 20, 22, 25, and 27. In the second instance, melody phrase A accompanied the initial hemistich, whereas extended phrase B carried the second hemistich of the preceding and the first of the following verse, allowing the tune to conclude with phrase C. This latter practice was followed at vv. 6, 8, 10, 12, 18, 29, and 31. The mode is Major (*finalis* c̲), with a final cadence on e̲, and an internal cadence on d̲.

Example 10: Sung by Carmen Cervera, 78 years old. Collected by S.G.A. and
J.M. Pedrosa, in Madrid (Vallecas), on December 9, 1992; transcribed by I.J.K.

Extremadura appears to be one of the regions where our ballad theme is most
popular. Eleven examples, including variants, constitute the following regional
grouping: seven are from Cáceres (Exs. 11*b–e*, 12a, and 13*a–b*) and four are
from Badajoz (Exs. 11*a*, 12*b*, 13*c* and 14).

The examples (11*a–e*) constitute a group that shares not only the same modal
characteristics and concluding Phrygian cadence, but also, except for 11*e*, the
same phrasal cadences a, e, d, and e. Commenting on the first tune (Ex. 11*a*,
from Oliva de Mérida), Gil García described it as an "interesante ejemplo del
tono oriental menor con un rasgo modulatorio en el penúltimo período" (CPE,
II, Parte musical, 3).[280] Essentially, it is a quatrain strophe (AB^{x+y}CD^{y+z}),

---

280. According to Josep Crivillé i Bargalló, in his critical editionn of Manuel García
Matos (*Cancionero popular*, p. xxxii, n. 30), the opening two phrases would suit the
appellation "gama española."

whose second and final melody phrases conclude with Phrygian cadences. The so-called "modulatory" third phrase is, in spite of the reiterated tones a̱, a sequential repetition of the opening phrase, a 5th degree lower.

The second example (11*b*) was transcribed from a field recording of María Gómez, from Castillas de Coria (p.j. Coria), who sang twenty strophes, predominantly in the quatrain form $ABC^{x+y}D^{x+z}$. The second (at v. 3), fourth (v. 8), ninth (v. 19), thirteenth (v. 28), fourteenth (v. 32) and seventeenth strophes (v. 38) were rendered as $ABC^{x+y}D^{x+z}C^{x+y}D^{x+z}$, whose latter phrases C and D repeated the same textual hemistichs as the former.

Examples 11*c* and 11*d*, both from Arroyo de la Luz (p.j. Cáceres), are additional variants of the previous tune (11*b*). Francisca García Redondo's description of Example 11*d* as a "muy bella melodía en la gama andaluza," is somewhat unclear (*Cancionero arroyano*, p. 51). Each of the examples in this group contain the raised 3rd (g̱-sharp) and 6th (c-sharp) degrees, their predominant scalar configuration conforming to the Phrygian mode. The raised 3rd appears only in melody phrase A as its initial (Exs. 11*b–d*) and penultimate tones (Exs. 11*a–d*), whereas the raised 6th, appearing in phrase D (Exs. 11*a–d*), functions as a lower neighbor. Also note its occurrence in phrase C of Example 11*e*. If the chromatically altered raised 3rd had appeared in scalar segments similar to the so-called "oriental" or *hidjaz* tetrachord (a̱-g̱-sharp-f̱-e̱), then one surely could have described them as belonging to the "gama andaluza," an appellation which appears to have gained wide acceptance among Spanish musicologists.[281] However, the alteration noted here does not appear as a scalar progression; therefore such usage might not be suitable. Inasmuch as the melodic similarity of the initial phrases A and D (in 11*d*) is unquestionable, their metric differences are significant. In Example 11, the informant appears to have adhered predominantly to 5/8 $\frac{[3+2]}{8}$ metric unit, while in Example 11*c*, there is evidence to support an inclination toward the same meter, given the sporadic succession of mixed meters 3/8 + 2/8. Example 11*d*, however, is solely in duple meter.

Most startling is the example (11*e*) collected by Kurt Schindler in Arroyo del Puerco (= Arroyo de la Luz) (November 1932). Although it appears to be a simpler quatrain strophe (ABCD), in the Phrygian mode (*finalis* e̱), its melodic

---

281. Crivillé i Bargalló (*Cancionero arroyano*, pp. xvii–xx, xxvii–xviii, xxi–xxxii; and *El folklore musical*, pp. 311–316) discusses the alterations in the basic Greek Dorian (= medieval Phrygian), leading to the so-called Spanish and Andalusian scales. See also García Matos (*Lírica popular*, pp. 26–34), as well as J. A. Donostia's fundamental study ("El modo de *mi*").

relationship to the preceding examples can be seen in phrases CD and AB, which were rendered in a reversed manner.

Example 11: *a*) Gil García (CPE, II, p. 3, no. 6); *b*) Sung by María Gómez, 28 years old, from Castillas de Coria, collected by S.G.A. in Madrid, June 25, 1972, transcribed by I.J.K.; *c*) García Matos (*Cancionero popular*, no 23); *d*) García Redondo (*Cancionero arroyano*, p. 51); *e*) Schindler (*Folk Music*, no. 232)

Example 12 (from Herrera del Duque, p.j. Herrera del Duque, Badajoz) bears a remote resemblance to the previous grouping, particularly in the first phrase. Rendered in the plagal Minor mode (*finalis* g), it is a simple quatrain strophe (ABCD), with an ambitus of a Major 9th.

Example 12: Gil García (CPE, II, "Parte musical," pp. 2–3, no. 5)[282]

Se pa - se- a -ba Li - sar- da____ por sus al - toh *co- rre-do- re(s)___*

con un veh-ti- do de se - da_, que le ta - pa loh *ta - co- ne(s).*

The following two Extremaduran tunes (Exs. 13*a–b*) stem, unquestionably, from the same melodic mold. They are in the Minor mode (based on *finalis* e). Except for phrase B, they share respective cadential tones (e, b, and e). Peculiar to the former (13*a*) are the raised 3rd (g-sharp and 6th (c-sharp) degrees in phrase B.[283]

Example 13: *a*) Gil García (CPE, I, "Parte musical," 34, no. 77);[284] and *b*) *Idem.* (CPE, II, "Parte musical," p. 2, no. 3)

Li - sar - da se pa - se - a - ba____

por los *al* -toh co - rre - do - re____

con un ves - ti - do de se - da____

que le *ye g'a* loh ta - co - ne____

---

282. Gil García mentions that it is sung on Christmas Eve (CPE, II, pp. 2–3, no. 5).

283. Gil García (CPE, II, pp. 170–171) called attention to the altered 6th degree in the Minor mode, as well as the tune's termination on the tonic.

284. Gil García remarked that in this version, the second hemistich is always repeated (CPE, I, 32).

Allegro

b)

Li - sar-da   se   pa - se-a-ba____

por sus   al- toh   co - rre-do - re(s)____

con   za -pa -   ti - llah deHo- lan - da   y

veh - ti - doh   de   rah - tro- ne(s)__.

The last of the Extremaduran tunes is exhibited here in three variant forms. All three share a bipartite strophe (AB), the first protracted melody phrase of which carries two textual hemistichs. They also share the cadential tones d̲ and g̲. Both triple-metered Cáceres tunes (14*a–b*), from La Madroñera (p.j. Trujillo) and Calzadilla de Coria (p.j. Coria), are in the Major mode (*finalis* c̲/[c̲]). The basically duple-metered tune from Herrera del Duque (Badajoz), on the other hand, subscribes to the plagal Minor mode (*finalis* g̲).

Example 14: *a*) Gil García (CPE, I, Music, p. 13: no. 25)[285]

♩ = 176

a)

A

Lui - sar - da   se   pa - se - a - ba   por sus   *al - toh   co - rre - do - re,*

B

por   sus   *al - toh   co - rre - do- re.*

---

285. Gil García confirmed that its concluding tone (g̲) represents the 5th degree (CPE, I, 169, no. 25).

Example 14: *b*) García Matos (*Cancionero popular*, no. 14); and *c*) Gil García
(CPE, II, 2, no. 4)[286]

From Asturias, we have nine musical examples from the recently published
collection of Jesús Suárez López, whose widely ranging field work throughout
the province, from 1987 to 1994, has yielded a rich harvest of ballads, including
rarely heard ones. The following examples, 15 through 23, were transcribed by
Susana Asensio Llamas, musicologist and Director of the Museo Internacional
de la Gaita (Gijón).

---

286. This version was sung while undertaking household chores. The names *Griselda*
and *Griseldilla* (Exs. 11*c–e*, 14*b*), without any particular justification in regard to the
ballad lady's personality, undoubtedly originate in the famous "patient wife" story, so
well known from Boccaccio's *Decameron* (10:10) and Chaucer's *Clerk's Tale*. There is a
vast bibliography concerning both stories and their analogues: See Branca's ed., pp.
1553–1554, and his *Boccaccio medievale*, pp. 388–394 et alibi; Bryan and Dempster,
Sources and Analogues, pp. 288–331; Weever, *Name Dictionary*, pp. 160–161;
Cummings, *Indebtedness*, p. 176 (Chaucer's debt to Boccaccio is indirect; he followed
Petrarch, mostly through contemporary French translations). Note also the Medieval
French play (1395), *L'Estoire de Griseldis* (ed. Barbara Craig). For ample additional
bibliography, see Bliss, "The Renaissance Griselda"; also Lee, *Sources*, pp. 348–356.

The simplest tune (Ex. 15, from Bustellón, c. Tinéu) comprises a duple-metered and protracted unistrophe, based on a Major tetrachord (g-a-b-c), whose cadential tone g is preceded by the *subtonium* f. Here Asensio Llamas' notation carries a textual underlay of two verses.

Example 15: Suárez López (NCR 14.14)

Ga - lan - ci - na, Ga - lan - ci - na, hi - ja del con - de Ga - lán,
¡quién te tu - vie - ra tres no - ches a mi gus -toy mi man-dar.

Example 16 (from Rubayer, c. Ayer) comprises a quatrain strophe (AA'BB). Here we have a duple-metered Minor pentachord (*finalis* c). Notice the informant's textual distribution: the hemistichs of the initial verse are sung to the same melody phrase, while the ensuing verse, sung to an extended B phrase, is repeated. Notice the initial chromatic succession of tones.

Example 16: Suárez López (NCR 14.7)

Ga- ran - ti- na, Ga-ran - ti - na____,
hi - ja deun con-de Ga - - lán,

¡quién pu-die-raes-tar tres no - ches a tu ve - ra yo go - zar!
¡quién pu-die-raes-tar tres no - ches a tu ve - ra yo go - zár!

Two quatrain strophes, whose distinct isorhythmic melody phrases were sung as AABC (Ex. 17, from Pendones, c. Casu) and ABBA (Ex. 18, from Cangues D'Onis, c. Llabra), respectively, are based on Minor and Major hexachords (*finalis* c).

Examples 17 and 18: Suárez López (NCR 14.5 and 14.2)

What follows here is a series of simple quatrain strophes (ABCD) that are similar to isorhythms. The first two examples (19 and 20, from Zarréu, c. Degaña and Los Corros, c. Valdéz, respectively) comprise Minor pentachords (based on *finalis* a), the latter of which extends downward to the penultimate *subtonium* in the final melody phrase. They are also differentiated by their respective meters.

Examples 19 and 20: Suárez López (NCR 14.29 and 14.17)

The next two (Exs. 21 and 22, from Montoubu, c. Miranda, and Fontalba, c. Tinéu, respectively), also predominantly isorhythmic, share the same Minor mode (based on *finalis* c̲), but differ with regard to meter. Example 21 exemplifies the ancient practice of sustaining the cadential tone in each phrase.

Examples 21 and 22: Suárez López (NCR 14.9 and 14.15)

Our final triple-metered Asturian tune (Ex. 23, from Astierna, c. Ibias) bears out the same isorhythmic feature. However, its structure conforms to the quatrain strophe ABCC. It is in the plagal minor mode (*finalis* g̲).

Example 23: Suárez López (NCR 14.31)

Examples are numerous concerning ballads that, within their textual verses, either allude to specific exploits of Conde Claros or exhibit marked similarities to other traditional versions. Their accompanying tunes do not justify a historical link with any of the ballads in the Conde Claros cycle. As an example, we cite a Portuguese tune (Ex. 24) which was collected, in 1961, by Fernando Lopes-Graça in the village of Aljezur, located near the city of Faro, in the southern province of Algarve. The ballad's initial theme concerning *Apuesta ganada* (vv. 1–18), moves briefly to *Aliarda* (vv. 19–23), and settles in on *Conde Claros fraile* (vv. 24–55), whose verses 24–25 we have substituted for Lopes-Graça's original text underlay. To which of these themes, if any, the tune was originally associated, is difficult to ascertain. Nonetheless, given that the tune constitutes a distich (AB), Lopes-Graça's notation indicates that it was rendered as a tripartite strophe (ABB), in which the textual hemistichs in melody phrase B are also repeated. It is in the plagal Minor mode (*finalis* g), as well as in the Phrygian, as Lopes-Graça supposed. His informant appears to have altered the 3rd degree (*b*), in the second melody phrase, and the 7th (f-sharp), in the final phrase. The tune's conclusion on a Phrygian cadence (g, f, e-flat, d) contributes to its circularity. In his comments, Lopes-Graça pointed out that: "A informadora deste interessante romance cantavão de uma forma tanto caprichosa, variandolhe constantemente o desenho melódico (o que constitui uma das mais valiosas características dos cantares tradicionais de certo desenvolvimento transmitidos oralmente). Não sendo possivel . . . consignar todas as variantes da bela melodia, apontámos-lhe apenas algumas e, no geral, optámos por uma notação por assim dizer média."[287]

Example 24: Lopes-Graça (*A Canção Popular*, no. 31; reproduced in Giacometti and Lopes-Graça, *Cancioneiro Popular Português*, no. 123)

v. 24: Seu ir-mão, que is - to ou-viu, a seu pai ve - io lo - go con - ta - r(e):

--Man-de ma-tar__ Ma - ri - a - na, ai, que se dei - xou en - ga- na- r(e)__.

The foregoing observations can be synthesized in the following discussion. To begin with, we can only assume that each of the musical examples taken from their respective published sources represent the manner in which their initial strophes may have been sung. For a ballad theme like *Conde Claros fraile*, which was so widely diffused throughout the Peninsula, one would expect it to have been associated with a wide variety of tune versions and variants, whose distinct or shared formal structures, modal and scalar configurations, and meters, may have had some historical basis.

Formal structure: It is clear that *Conde Claros fraile,* however it may be known in the modern Peninsular tradition, prevailed as a quatrain strophe, albeit with notable exceptions. The two rare monostrophes (Exs. 9 and 15, from Castile and Asturias, respectively) are very probably of an earlier vintage. Their protracted phrases, confined to an ambitus of a perfect 5th, each carry, without a breath pause, a full textual verse. Examples 1 (from Catalonia), 6 (from Castile), and 14a–c (from Extremadura) are distinctly bipartite in structure. Melody

---

287. Lopes-Graça's comments (*A Canção Popular*, p. 133) were slightly altered in the 1981 publication, which, however, reproduces the original melody (Giacometti and Lopes-Graça, *Cancioneiro Popular Português*, no. 123).

phrases A and B of Example 6, and phrase A of Examples 14*a–e*, like those of Examples 9 and 15, are also extended. Example 6, discussed earlier, is somewhat problematic, but arguably falls in the category of distich strophes.

The tripartite examples (3 from León, 11 from Andalusia, and 24 from Portugal) represent quite unique renditions. The protracted phrases B, in the first, A in the second, and both A and B in the third example, each carry two textual hemistichs. A simple quatrain strophe (ABCD) predominates in eleven instances (Exs. 1*a–c* [Catalonia], 4 [León], 11*a–e*, 12, 13*a–b* [Extremadura], 19, 20, 21, and 22 [Asturias]). Additional, yet varied, occurrences can be found in Examples 2 (ABCB′) from Castile, 16 (AABB), 17 (AABC), and 18 (ABBC) from Asturias, and 24 (ABCC), from Portugal. In the Asturian Example 16, the protracted melody phrase B is repeated together with the text of each even-numbered verse.

Example 8 (from Castile) appears to have been rendered as combined quatrain strophes (ABCC and ADCC), whose distinction is borne out by their second melody phrases B and D, respectively. Phrase D, which concludes with a Phrygian cadence, provides a meaningful contrast to what would otherwise have been a monotonous rendering.

The notation of Example 7 (from Castile) indicates an extremely rare formal structure. Apart from the extended phrase C, which carries three hemistichs, the first two of which are repeated, the remaining phrases articulate a simple isorhythmic pattern. In essence, the tunes begin with a repeated distich (AB), continue through phrase C, return to the initial distich (AB), whose respective hemistichs are reiterated, and conclude on phrase D.

Modes and scalar configurations: Seven examples exhibit tetrachordal (9 and 15), pentachordal (16 and 18) and hexachordal (5*a*, 17 and 18) configurations. The majority were found in Asturias, but Example 9 (from Castile) comprises a Major tetrachord, plus *subtonium*, and Example 5*a* (from León), a Major hexachord. Minor and Major modes appear to be equally distributed: the Minor, in both its authentic (Exs. 1, 13*a–b*, 19, 21, and 22) and plagal (Exs. 3, 8, 12, 14*c*, and 24) forms; and the Major (Exs. 5*b*, 6, 10, and 14*a–b*) in its plagal configuration (Exs. 2, 4, 7, and 23). The examples from León (3 and 8), Castile (9), Badajoz (11*a–e*) and the Algarve region of Portugal (24), all conclude with Phrygian cadences.

Ambitus: Six examples exceed the range of an octave (6, 11*b–d*, 12, 21, and 24). Six comprise an octave (Exs. 2, 3, 7, 8, 11*e*, and 22), two a Major 7th (5*b*, and 19), and seven a Minor 7th (Exs. 4, 13*a–b*, 14*b–c*, and 23). Among the remaining examples, their ranges constitute a diminished octave (1*a–c*), a diminished 7th (11*a*), Major 6ths (5*a*, 10, 14*a*, and 18), Minor 6ths (17 and 20), and Perfect 5ths (9, 15, and 16).

Meter: According to the Synoptic Table for the tunes, it will be seen that fourteen examples were rendered in triple meter (3/4 and 3/8); six in duple (2/4); six in compound duple (6/8); and one in compound triple (9/8). The remainder comprise mixed meters. In the following synoptic table, one will notice the distribution of phrasal isorhythmic patterns based on dotted-quarter and quarter note *takts*.

Synoptic table of phrasal isorhythmic patterns:

a) based on a dotted quarter-note *takt*:

b) based on a quarter-note *takt*:

———————— • ————————

Bernardo del Carpio

Tunes for the ballad *El nacimiento de Bernado del Carpio* in the Judeo-Spanish tradition are extremely rare. Of the twelve Moroccan texts (1*c-n*) published in the first volume of Ramón Menéndez Pidal's RT (I, 177–183), two (1*l* and 1*n*) were preceded by their respective melodic notations. A third tune (1*k* = Ex. 2 below), erroneously inserted above a text collected in Larache by Manuel Manrique de Lara, in 1916, pertains to another ballad: *El hijo vengador*.[288]

Both tunes (1*l* and 1*n*), representing the tradition of Tetuán, were reprinted from the earlier publications of Larrea (M1) and Bénichou (p. 379), respectively.[289] The tune that Bénichou recorded in Buenos Aires in the early 1940s was transcribed and notated by Daniel Devoto (see Ex. 1*a*).[290] Its initial four verses, however, pertain to the ballad *De la pérdida de Antequera*. Larrea's transcription (Ex. 1*b*) should have been rendered in 6/8, i.e., without interpolating the 3/4 measures to interrupt the normal rhythmic flow, thus maintaining the hemiola effect:

————————

288. Menéndez Pidal himself admitted that "por error, . . . como si fuera la música de la versión 1*k*, una melodía cantada también por Sada Abecera, que pertenece a otro romance" (RT, I, 270).

289. First published in Bénichou, *RFH*, 6 (1944), 379, no. XXI.

290. From a personal communication from Daniel Devoto, dated July 14, 1969.

Likewise the sixth measure should have been notated as

mo - ros___ por la

or more likely as

mo - [o] - ros___ por la

The melody, spanning an octave, is in the Major mode, and comprises a quatrain structure ($A^{x+y}A^{x+y}BC$).

Judging from Devoto's transcription, Bénichou's tune appears even more erratic in its metric divisions. Ballads rendered in triple meter are known in the Moroccan tradition, but in the eastern Mediterranean tradition, this meter is quite rare. While it is also in the Major mode and slightly greater in ambitus (minor 9th), its quatrain strophe can be depicted as ABCD. A closer comparison of Bénichou's phrase B and Larrea's phrase A reveals a much closer affinity with the latter structure, thus confirming the erratic nature of the informant's rendering.

Bénichou's tune was collected less than a decade before Larrea's and it displays a greater sense for ornamented cadences, although it does not retain a steady metric flow. This was more likely the practice within the Moroccan tradition. Still, the two tunes are related melodically, particularly in their second and third phrases, as well as in the cadential portions of their initial and final phrases. For comparative purposes, here is an alignment of both tunes, whereby their similarities can be more readily observed:

Example 1: *a*) Bénichou (p. 379); *b*) Larrea (M1)

a. Her - ma - na tie - neel buen Ci - di,
b. Ma - ña - ni - tae - ra ma - ña - na,

a. que Xi - me - na se lla - ma - ba
b. al tiem - po queal - bo - re - a - ba

a. na - mo - ra - do seha - bí - a dee - lla
b. gran fie - sta ha - cen los mo - ros

a. es - te con - de de San - da - ria.
b. por la be - lla de Gra - na - da.

Example 2: Manrique de Lara (A1.8) (Larache, 1915–1916), vv. 15–16. Sung by
Sada Abecera, 74 years.

BIBLIOGRAPHY

Conde Claros y la infanta

EASTERN JUDEO-SPANISH

Salonika: Attias 30; PTJ 23*b* (= Attias); *Seis romancerillos*, no. PB4.
Larissa: RT, III, 99, no. III.3.1–3 (= CMP I6.20).

MOROCCAN JUDEO-SPANISH

Tangier: CMP B10.1–5; Guzofsky B10*A–B*; MP 24 (= CMP B10.1).
Tetuán: Bennaim MS 100; CMP B10.6–10; Larrea 32–33.
Larache: AJE, II, no. 17 (= PTJ 23, with minimal variants); CMP B10.11; Fereres MS 14 (= our 11*H*); García Figueras, fol. 205 (no. 8/106) and (no. 8/107); PTJ 23.
Alcazarquivir: CMP B10.12; MRuiz 36; PTJ 23*a* (= MRuiz).

PENINSULAR

Castilian areas: Aliste, pp. 63–64 (no. 1.13–54); Catarella, *Gitano-andaluz*, no. 11.9–33; Díaz-Delfín-Díaz Viana, *Catálogo* (1978), I, 166 (vv. 9–20); Díaz-Díaz Viana, *Rom. trad. de Castilla y León* (1982), no. 17 (pp. 64–67) (= *Catálogo*, I, 166); Díaz Viana, *El romancero oral . . . de Valladolid* (Ph.D. diss.), no. 6 (p. 207) (= *Catálogo*); Díaz Viana, "Evolución," pp. 65, 67–68 (= *Catálogo*); Díaz Viana, *Rev. de Folklore*, I:2 ([1980?]), 27–29 (vv. 9–13); Fonteboa, *Bierzo*, no. 3.1–12; Gomarín, p. 43 (vv. 1–6); Kundert, pp. 87–88 (G4.17–38); Manzano, *Leonés*, nos. 740, 921; RGL 19.1–6, 8–9, 15–18, 23; RPC, p. 12 (vv. 7–8); RPM 58.3–16; Suárez Avila, *Dos siglos*, p. 103; *Voces nuevas* 48.5.1–12, 48.6.5–21, 48.7.6–22, 48.10.3–12, 48.12.1–2, 48.16.1–7; our text *C*, vv. 1–7.
Asturias: NCR 13*A*–13*B*.

SPANISH AMERICAN

Argentina: Moya, II, 23–24 (vv. 9–23).

GALICIAN – PORTUGUESE

Galicia: CARG 17a.5–16; CPG, III, 44c.1–30.
Portugal: Athaide Oliveira, pp. 70–71 (vv. 1–3, 14–16), 327–328 (vv. 1–3, 13–14);
Braga, I, 307–308 (vv. 9–26); 309–310 (vv. 1–17); 314–315 (vv. 1–11); 325–326 (vv.
15–44); 330–331 (vv. 9–34); 338–339 (vv. 1–21); 364–365 (vv. 1–19); 390 (vv. 1–2, 10–
11); (307–308 = Garrett; 314 = Leite de Vasconcellos, "D. Carlos"; 390 = Reis Dâmaso);
Coelho, "Rom. Pop.," pp. 64–65 (vv. 1–42), 66 (vv. 1–33); Costa Fontes, *Trás-os-
Montes*, nos. 42.1–5, 43.2–3; Galhoz 12.1–10, 14.17–23; Garrett, II, 226–227 (vv. 9–27);
Hardung, I, 188–189 (= Braga, I, 364–365); Leite de Vasconcellos, "D. Carlos," pp. 189–
190 (vv. 1–26); Lima Carneiro, "Monte Córdova," p. 57; Martins, II, 10–11 (vv. 8–18);
Nunes, "Subsídios," pp. 161–162 (vv. 1–6, 24–27), 164 (vv. 1–7, 25–28); Reis Dâmaso,
Encycl. Republicana, pp. 203–204 (vv. 1–3, 9–11); VRP 50.12–13, 51.8–9, 52.1–13,
54.1–13, 55.1–18, 59.1–4, 69.1–2, 986 (986 = "D. Carlos").
Azores: Braga, I, 405–406 (vv. 1–21); Cortes-Rodrigues, pp. 217–219 (= Braga);
Purcell, *Ilhas*, no. 7.4; Purcell, *Açores*, I, no. 8C.
Madeira: Braga, I, 319 (vv. 42–43); 321–322, 334–335 (vv. 12–31), 338–339 (319 =
Rodrigues de Azevedo, p. 75; 321 = Rs. Azevedo, pp. 78–79; 334–335 = Rs. Azevedo,
pp. 94–96; 338–339 = Rs. Azevedo, pp. 99–100); Purcell, *Ilhas*, no. 7.1–3; Rodrigues de
Azevedo, pp. 75 (vv. 42–43), 78–79, 81–84, 89–91, 94–96, 99–100.
Brazil: *Bahia* 1.6.1–6; Boiteaux, *RIHGB*, pp. 20–21; 2d ed., pp. 116–117; Braga, I,
351–352 (vv. 1–23), 354–355 (vv. 1–15) (= Romero); Brandão, *Alagoas*, pp. 114–116
(vv. 1–13); Lopes, *Presença*, pp. 161–162, 239–241, 242–245; Magalhães, pp. 99–100 (=
Romero, pp. 95–97); Pereira da Costa, pp. 313–314, 319–321 (vv. 1–28) (313–314 =
Romero, pp. 95–97); Romero, *Cantos*, pp. 90–93 (vv. 1–23), 95–97 (vv. 1–15); Romero,
Estudos, pp. 79–80 (= Romero, *Cantos*, pp. 90–92); Santos Neves, "Presença," p. 51 (vv.
1–3; 1–5); Seeger, *Study*, pp. 290–291 (vv. 1–16); Silva Lima, *Folclore*, nos. 8.1–8 (8.8 =
Romero, pp. 90–94); 8.4, 8.5, 8.6, 8.6.1., 8.7, 8.8 (= Romero); Silva Lima, "Achegas"
(1979), pp. 59–63; Vilela, *Romanceiro Alagoano*, no. 7.1.1–13.

CATALAN

Ibiza: AFC 2973 (= Aguiló); Aguiló, pp. 308–311 (vv. 30–99); Macabich, pp. 13–14,
21–31 (vv. 8–30) (13–14 = Aguiló).
For extensive references to all branches of the modern tradition, see RPI B2.

ARCHAIC TEXTS

— "Media noche era por filo / los gallos querían (quieren) cantar" (= *Primav.* 190). *Conde Claros y la infanta* corresponds to vv. 21–72 (of our ed. based on the CSA version). Two *pliegos sueltos* and numerous *cancionero* printings are known:

a.	*Pliegos de Praga*, I, 33–39; DPS 1017.
b.	*Pliegos BN*, II, 144–151; DPS 1018.
c.	CSA, fols. 83 ro.–90 ro.
d.	C1550, pp. 168–173.
e.	*Silva* (1550), pp. 390–396.
f.	*Silva* (1561), fols. 80 vo.–87 vo.
g.	Tortajada (1652), pp. 198–209.

For additional printings, see MCR, II, 584*a*; IV, 166*b*. Compare the bibliographical data in Chap. 10 for *Conde Claros insomne* (which corresponds to vv. 1–20 of "Media noche era por filo").

Conde Claros vestido de fraile

MOROCCAN JUDEO-SPANISH

Tangier: CMP B10.1–5.
Tetuán: Bennaim MS 100; CMP B10.6–10; Larrea 32.
Larache: García Figueras, no. 8/107.
Alcazarquivir: MRuiz 36; PTJ 23*a* (= MRuiz).

PENINSULAR

Castilian areas: Aliste, pp. 63–65; Alvar, *Romancero viejo*, nos. 175–175*a*, 178–178*a* (175 = ART; 175*a*: uned.; 178 = ASW; 178*a* = Pérez de Castro); ART, p. 221 (reproduced above: text *A*); ASW 179–182, 377–378 (= CVR, Milá); Atero, *Cádiz*, nos. 1–3; Calvo, *Segovia*, nos. 5.1–5.2; Casado, *Extremadura*, nos. 2.1–8, 3.1; Cid, "Garganta la Olla," no. 5; CPE, I, 32–33; II, 17–18; Díaz-Delfín-Díaz Viana, *Catálogo* (1978), I, 166–167; Díaz-Díaz Viana, *Rom. trad. de Castilla y León* (1982), no. 17 (pp. 64–67) (= *Catálogo*, I, 166); Díaz Viana, *El romancero oral . . . de Valladolid* (Ph.D. diss.), no. 6 (p. 207) (= *Catálogo*); Díaz Viana, "Evolución," pp. 65, 67–68 (= *Catálogo*); Díaz Viana, *Rev. de Folklore*, I:2 ([1980?]), 27–29; Ferrer-Sanjuán, p. 167; Flores, *Jerte*, pp. 80–83; Fonteboa, *Bierzo*, no. 3; Fraile Gil, "Crónica," pp. 544–545 (= *Madrid*, pp. 48–49); Fraile Gil, *Madrid*, pp. 46–49; Galindo Ocaña, "Andalucía," pp. 543–544; García López, "Degollada," pp. 13–15; García Matos-Crivillé, *Cáceres*, nos. 13, 13*B*; García

Redondo, *Arroyano*, pp. 51–52; Gil, *Rioja*, no. 41 (p. 310); Gomarín, *Cantabria*, pp. 43–46; Gutiérrez Macías, pp. 344–345; Iglesias Giraud, *Rebollar*, pp. 83–84; Kundert, pp. 87–88 (G4); Ledesma, pp. 181–182; Manzano, *Leonés*, no. 738–740 and 920–921 (pp. 279–284); Marazuela, *Segoviano*, pp. 332–333; Marazuela, *Castilla*, pp. 336–337 (= *Segoviano*); Martínez Ruiz, "Güéjar," no. 1; Mendoza Díaz-Maroto, *Albacete*, nos. 38.2, 38.5 (cf. Id., *Introducción*, p. 398); Piñero-Atero, *Romancero andaluz*, no. 36 (= Martínez Ruiz, "Güéjar"); Piñero-Atero, *Tradición moderna*, no. 4 (= ART); RGL, nos. 19.1–30; RPC 9–10, 12; RPE, pp. 9–10; RPM 58–61 (61 = ART; 58 reproduced above = our text *B*); RTCN 30; RTO 14 (= RPM 59); RTR 4; Ruiz Granda, pp. 754–755; Salazar-Valenciano, *RH: Fronteras*, pp. 396–397 (= *Voces nuevas* 48.10); Schindler, nos. 54 and 232 (music); Seeger, *Count Claros*, pp. 260–261; *Voces nuevas* 48.1–17; our texts *C, D, E, F* (above). See also the indispensable analysis in CGR, IA, 45–51.

Asturias: Cano, nos. 1A–1C; Cid, "Asturias," no. 8; CVR 6–7; Feito, pp. 124–128; García López, "Degollada," pp. 13–15; Munthe 2; NCR 13*B* (= 13.2), 14.1–31; Pérez de Castro, "Nuevas variantes," p. 478; PNCR, pp. 215–216 (no. 2) (= Munthe). See also Busto Cortina, pp. 138–141 (nos. 36.1–10).

CANARIAN

Espinosa, *Romancero canario*, pp. 47–48 (= FM 9); FM 8 (nos. 5–9, 78–80, 234–237, 257); RCan 17; Trapero, *Romancero tradicional canario*, no. 14 (= FM 234); Trapero-Siemens, *Gran Canaria*, I, no. 13; *Gran Canaria*, II, nos. 10.1–2.

GALICIAN – PORTUGUESE

Galicia: CARG 15 *bis*, 17*a*, 18*a-d*; CPG, III, 44*a*-44*c*; Schubarth-Santamarina, *Escolma*, pp. 115–116 (no. 79) (= CPG 44*c*).

Portugal: Anastácio, *Faro*, nos. 1–3 (no. 2 = Lopes-Graça, *Canção*, 2d ed.; Lopes-Graça-Redol; various previous editions; see Anastácio, pp. 31–32); Athaide Oliveira, pp. 70–76, 327–336 (332–336 = Reis Dâmaso); Braga, I, 309–313, 356–373, 376–387, 390–392, 397–399, 417–419 (356–364 = Garrett; 378–382 = Athaide Oliveira, pp. 70–73; 384–387 = Reis Dâmaso, pp. 215–216; 390–392 = Reis Dâmaso, pp. 203–204; 417–419 = Athaide Oliveira, pp. 74–76); Buescu, 1st ed., pp. 219 (no. 9), 227–228 (no. 17); Buescu, 2d ed., pp. 167 (no. 7), 173–174 (no. 15); Coelho, "Romances Populares," pp. 64–66; Consiglieri Pedroso, "Poesias," pp. 460–462; Costa Fontes, "Novo Romanceiro," pp. 373–374 (= *Trás-os-Montes*, no. 714); Costa Fontes, *Trás-os-Montes*, nos. 42, 44, 710, 712, 714–715, 773, 775–776; *Cova da Beira*, nos. 12.1–12.10; CTT 10*g*; Custódio-Galhoz, no. 1; Delgado, *Subsídio*, II, 135–136; 2d ed., II, 160–161; Dias, "Ourique," pp. 46–48; Dias Costa, *Murteira*, p. 318; Dias Marques, "Loures," no. 4; Dias Marques and

Reis da Silva, pp. 1–2, 53–54; Fernandes Thomas, *Velhas Canções*, pp. 30–31, 36–39; Ferré, *Castelo Branco*, nos. 4–6; Ferré, *Guarda*, nos. 1–2; Galhoz 12–14, 16–17, 19, 22–30; Garrett, II, 203–213; Giacometti-Lopes-Graça, no. 123; Gomes Pereira, "Novo Suplemento," pp. 100–101; Hardung, I, 188–192, 198–204 (= Braga, I, 364–371, 382–384); Kundert, pp. 86–87 (H3); 87–88 (G4); Lima Carneiro, "Monte Córdova," pp. 54–60; Lopes Dias, *Etnografia da Beira*, VII, 49–52; Lopes-Graça, *Canção*, 2d ed. no. 31 (= Anastácio, no. 2); Lopes-Graça-Redol, pp. 470–472, no. 335 (= Anastácio, no. 2); Ludovice, pp. 147–150; Martins, I, 193–196; II, 34–35, 40–41; Martins-Ferré, *Beja*, nos. 1–8; Nunes, "Subsídios," nos. 4–5; Pinto-Correia (1984), pp. 178–187 (nos. 42 [= Garrett]; 43 [= VRP 52]; 44: uned.); Pinto-Correia (2003), pp. 215–228 (nos. 56–58 [= Pinto-Correia 1984: nos. 42–44 [= Garrett; VRP 52; Pinto-Correia, no. 44]; no. 59 [= Giacometti-Lopes-Graça, no. 123], et alibi); Pires da Cruz, *Beira Baixa*, nos. 147, 149, 152–155, 157–158; Pires de Lima, *Minhoto*, pp. 87–88; Reis Dâmaso, *Encycl. Republicana*, pp. 203–204, 215–216; Rosado, *Algarvia*, pp. 228–231; Tavares, *Ilustração Trasmontana*, 3 (1910), 76; Tavares, "Romanceiro," nos. 25, 45, 60 (no. 25 = *Ilustr. Trasmontana*); Thomaz Pires, *A Tradição*, 3:2 (March 1901), 42–43 (= *Lendas*, pp. 42–49); Thomaz Pires, *Lendas*, pp. 42–49, 187–189 (46–49 = Braga, I, 376–378); *Vale Judeu*, II, no. 1; VRP 52–91, 283, 986.

Azores: Braga, I, 399–404 (= *Cantos*, pp. 243–249); Braga, *Cantos*, pp. 243–249; Cortes-Rodrigues, pp. 220–228 (nos. 2–4; 2–3 = *Cantos*); Costa Fontes, *Califórnia*, no. 1; Costa Fontes, *S. Jorge*, nos. 3–5; Galhoz, no. 34; Hardung, I, 192–198 (= Braga, *Cantos*, pp. 243–249); Lemos de Mendonça, pp. 194–196; Purcell, *Ilhas*, nos. 8.7–8, 8.11–17; Purcell, *Açores,* I, nos. 8A–8C.

Madeira: Ferré, 40–54, 304; Ferré, *Vértice*, no. 2; Galhoz, nos. 31–32; Purcell, *Ilhas*, nos. 8.1–6; Rodrigues de Azevedo, pp. 156–158; *Xarabanda*, nos. 1–2.

Brazil: *Bahia* 1.5.1, 3, 7, 9–11; Braga, I, 407–408 (= Romero); Calasans B. da Silva (Campos Tourinho, *Recôncavo*), pp. 132–134; Galvão, pp. 41–42; Gurgel, pp. 44–45 (also p. 30); Lopes, *Presença*, pp. 147–163; Magalhães, *Poesia*, pp. 62–63 (fragments); Pereira da Costa, pp. 315–319 (315–316 = Romero, pp. 98–99); Romero, *Cantos*, pp. 98–99; Romero, *Estudos*, pp. 81–82 (= Romero, *Cantos*); Seeger, *Study*, pp. 289–290, 292; Silva Lima, *Folclore*, nos. 9.1–14 (14 = Romero, pp. 98–99); Silva Lima, "Achegas" (1991), pp. 129–130; Vilela, nos. 2.1–4.

CATALAN

Catalonia: AFC 3263; Aguiló, pp. 317–328; Avenç, III, 34–37 (= Briz, IV, 43–44); Briz, IV, 43–45; Ginart Baucà, IV, 418–419; Milá 258, 258*B–M*; Paloma, p. 181 (= Milá 258).

Valencia: Rico Beltrán, no. 10.

For extensive references to all branches of the modern tradition, see RPI B4. For the Portuguese tradition, note now also the exhaustive collective ed. brought together by Pere

Ferré in RPOM, I, nos. 119–201, and abundant references in BRP 402-598. Note also the crucial analyses of Bráulio do Nascimento, *QP*, 11–12 (1982), 139–187, and "Conde Claros Confesor."

ARCHAIC TEXTS

— "A caça va el emperador / a sant Iuan de Montiña" (= *Primav.* 191): C1550, pp. 319–321. The text of *Conde Claros vestido de fraile* corresponds to vv. 21–68. For later printings, see MCR, II, 289*a*. Compare, in Chap. 10, data for *Conde Claros y el emperador* (corresponding to "A caça va el emperador," vv. 1–20).

EUROPEAN ANALOGUES

Lady Maisry

Scottish: Child 65*A–I*.
English: Bronson, II, nos. 65.4–11.
Anglo-American: Bronson, II, nos. 65.12–13; Coffin and Renwick, no. 65; more data: nn. 116–117 above.

Der König von Mailand

German: DVM 67.1–3; more data: nn. 118–119 above.

Szégyenbe esett lány (*The Dishonored Maiden*)

Hungarian: Aigner, pp. 215–218; Leader, pp. 179–223; Vargyas, *Researches*, pp. 105–110; Id., *A magyar népballada*, II, 122–139 (no. 10); Id., *Hungarian Ballads*, II, 148–175 (no. 10); also nn. 120–121 above.

El nacimiento de Bernardo del Carpio

MOROCCAN JUDEO-SPANISH

Tangier: RT, I, nos. 1*def* (= CMP A1.1–3); MP 1 and 8 (= no. 1*d* = CMP A1).
Tetuán: RT, I, nos. 1*cghijlm* (= CMP A1.6, 5, 4, 7; *lm* = Larrea 1–1*b*); Larrea 1–1*b*; Librowicz (II) A1.
Buenos Aires (= Tetuán ?): RT, I, no. 1*n* (= Bénichou); Bénichou, pp. 29 + 40.
Larache: RT, I, no. 1*k* (= CMP A1.8).
Alcazarquivir: RT, I, no. 1*j* (= CMP A1.9).

All known Moroccan texts (except that of Librowicz) are brought together in RT, I, 176–184 (texts 1*a*–1*n*).

PENINSULAR

Castilian: Catalán, *Cancionero en cifra*, no. 5; Fraile Gil, "Crónica," pp. 545–546; Id., *Madrid*, p. 39; Lorenzo Vélez, "Una nueva aparición" (all texts from same informant and essentially identical).

ARCHAIC TEXTS

— "En los reynos de Leon / el casto Alfonso reynaua": C1550, p. 205 (= RT, I, no. 1*a*; = Durán 619; *Primav.* 8). For later reprintings, see MCR, II, 482*a*.

— "En el reyno de León, / quando el casto rey Alfonso reynaba" (text written in cipher, included in a secret dispatch sent to Felipe II, on May 26, 1562, by the Spanish ambassador in Paris, Tomás Perrenot de Chantonnay): RT, I, no. 1*b* (and pp. 270–271: last plate). See also Gómez del Campillo, "De Cifras," p. 306; and now Catalán, *Cancionero en cifra*, no. 5.

— "En Castilla y en León / el casto Alfonso reinaba": Luis Vélez de Guevara, *El conde don Pedro Vélez*, Act III, vv. 2287–2294 and 2299–2308, pp. 185–186; see also Case's study pp. 30–32; ed. Manson and Peale (2202); first performance: June 24, 1615.

La sanjuanada

MOROCCAN JUDEO-SPANISH

See the initial verses of all texts listed for *El nacimiento de Bernardo del Carpio*.

PENINSULAR

The first two verses are used as an introduction to Castilian and Catalan versions of *El martirio de Santa Catalina*. The initial verse survives prefixed to *La fuente consagrada* (= *La Virgen* [or *Jesucristo*] *y la hija del rey*: *En torno*, p. 19 and nn. 9–13; RPI U29 and U41). Similar verses also introduce modern traditional versions, from Cádiz, of the learned *morisco* ballad about Gazul: *Estando toda la corte / de Abdilí, rey de Granada* (Durán 46). See *Gazul rejonea un toro (á-a)* (CGR, II, no. 57, p. 303).

ARCHAIC TEXTS

— We have seen three *pliegos sueltos*, four *cancionero* texts, and a *vihuelista* version of *La pérdida de Antequera* (Presented here in the order in which these texts are arranged in *En torno*, pp. 16–17, n. 6):

a. "la mañana de San Juan / al punto que alboreaua": glossed in *Disparates donde ay puestas muchas damas y señoras de Aragón*: "Vi con muy brauo denuedo / aquella reina Marfissa," *Cancionero de Juan Fernández de Íxar*, ed. Azáceta, II, 785–794 (BN, Madrid, MS 2882 [olim M-275]: late segment of the MS: last quarter of the 16th century [Azáceta, I, xx–xxi]); ballad text also edited by López Estrada, *La conquista de Antequera*, pp. 21–22.

b. "La mañana de sant Juan / al punto que alboreaua": *Pliegos de Praga*, II, 218; DPS 683.

[*b'.*] "La mañana de sant Juan / al punto que alboreaua": *Pliegos de Cracovia*, II, 74; Porębowicz, p. 7 (no. 88); López Estrada, p. 26, n. 10; DPS 919 (Granada: Hugo de Mena, 1573).

c. "La mañana de sant Joã / al punto que alboreaua": *Pliegos BN*, II, 341–342; Gallardo, *Ensayo*, I, no. 1121 ("Puede que la impresión sea de Burgos, hecha a mediados del siglo XVI por Felipe de Junta"); López Estrada, p. 25, n. 10; DPS 679.

d. "La mañana de sant Juan / al tiempo que alboreaua": *Silva* (1550), pp. 319–320; López Estrada, p. 24; *Primavera* 75; MCR, II, 551.

e. "La mañana de sant Juan / al tiempo que alboreaua": Lorenzo de Sepúlveda, *Romances nuevamente sacados de historias antiguas dela Cronica de España* (Antwerp: Philippo Nucio, 1566), no. 123; transcription of the text: López Estrada, p. 23; MCR, I, 257–266; II, 551.

f. "la mañana de san Iuan / al t͂po q͂ albore[aua]": Diego Pisador, *Libro de mvsica de vihvela* (Salamanca: Diego Pisador, 1552), Libro I, fol. v vo.; Morphy, *Luthistes*, II, 178–179; López Estrada, pp. 25–26, n. 10; Querol Gavaldá, "Importance," pp. 310–311, 323; Binkley, pp. 72–74 (use with caution; see S.G.A.'s review: *Hispania*, 79 [1996], 782); The ballad music for *La mañana de Sant Juan*, attributed by Morphy (*Luthistes*, II, 112) to Alonso de Mudarra, *Tres libros de música en cifra para vihuela* (Seville: Juan de León, 1546), is in fact that of Diego Pisador. See A. Mudarra, *Tres libros*, ed. E. Pujol, p. 77 (no. 55). *En torno*, p. 16, n. 6, should be emended.

g. "La mañana de sant Joan / al punto que alboreaua": Juan Timoneda, *Rosas de romances (Valencia, 1573)*, ed. Rodríguez-Moñino and Devoto, «Rosa Española», fol. lij vo.-liij vo.

For later *cancionero* printings: MCR, II, 551; for additional MSS texts: *Tabla*, p. 168; for *a lo divino* contrafacts and later *romances* that adapt the *Sanjuanada* verse, see *En torno*, pp. 16–17, n. 6.

We have seen the following texts of *Jarifa y Abindarráez* (presented here in the order they are listed in *En torno*, pp. 17–18, n. 7):

a. "LA mañana de san Iuã / al tiempo q̃ alboreaua": *Pliegos de Cracovia*, II, 97; (Granada: Hugo de Mena, 1573); Poębowicz, pp. 8, 14–15, 34–35 (no. 91); López Estrada, pp. 33–34; DPS 1010.

b. "La mañana de Sant Iuan / al tiempo que alboreaua": *Silva recopilada* (Barcelona: Jaime Sendrat, 1582); MCR, I, 411–415 (no. 5); II, 551; transcription of the *romance*: López Estrada, p. 34 (see n. 2).

c. "La mañana de San Juan / al punto que alboreava": Ginés Pérez de Hita, *Guerras civiles de Granada: Primera Parte* (1595), ed. Blanchard-Demouge, I (1913), 79–80; ed. Blanchard-Demouge, I (1998), 79–80; ed. Bryant, pp. 80–81; López Estrada, pp. 36–37; Durán 80.

For later reworkings of *Jarifa y Abindarráez*, see *En torno*, p. 18, n. 7. *Jarifa y Abindarráez* (= *Fátima y Jarifa*) survives, separately from its *Sanjuanada* prologue, in the modern Judeo-Spanish tradition of Morocco. See CMP D4 and FLSJ, VIII, Chap. 31.

APPENDIX: SUPPLEMENTARY NOTES

10. *Conde Claros y el emperador*:

Chap. 10, n. 1: On Reinaldos' presence in the Roncesvalles epic, see FLSJ, III, Chaps. 7 and 9. For the French epic tradition of *Renaud de Montauban* (who does not die at Roncevaux, as in the Spanish *Roncesvalles* and related ballads), see Riquer, *Les chansons de geste*, pp. 251–258. *Renaud de Montauban* survived for centuries in popular tradition through the prose adaptation printed and reprinted in the vastly diffused *Bibliothèque Bleue*, as *Les quatre fils Aymon* (Mandrou, *De la culture populaire*, pp. 37, 47, 146–148, 155–156, 188, 201). In this form, *Renaud* reached America and reentered oral tradition in the memories of 19th- and early 20th-century French-speaking settlers in Missouri: "One hears often at Old Mines of several *conteurs* who used to be asked by miners working in the same field to tell the famous story of Renaud de Montauban. As this modern version of the old medieval favorite took a whole day to tell, the listeners got together and gave the story-teller a big pile of barite [the mineral produced at Old Mines] before he would begin. No longer can any one be found in Old Mines who knows the tale from beginning to end" (Carrière, *Tales*, p. 16, n. 10). Does the name *Claraniña* in our ballads somehow distantly recall Princess *Clarisse*, sister of King Yon of Bordeaux, who marries Renaud in the *chanson de geste*? That Count Claros in our *romances* is the emperor's nephew reflects the ancient uncle-nephew motif of Medieval French and Spanish epicry and, like other elements we have discussed, may well have been worked into the narrative to authenticate its Carolingian ambience. (On the topic, see n. 19 below.) For three late Carolingian *romances* about Reinaldos de Montalbán, see *Día era de Sant Jorge (Primav.* 187), *Estábase don Reinaldos* (188), and *Ya que estaba Reinaldos* (189). None entered oral tradition and, rather than following any early epic antecedents, they are based on 16th-century Italian narrative poems. See TRV (1926), II, 431–433; TRV (1944), II, 320–322; RoH, I, 264–265.

Chap. 10, n. 2: *Pésame de vos el conde* was very widely known. First printed in the *Cancionero general* of Hernando del Castillo (ed. Rodríguez-Moñino, fol. cxxxj ro.*a*, with *glosa*), it is reproduced in the *Segunda parte del Cancionero general* (Zaragoza, 1552), ed. Rodríguez-Moñino, pp. 98–103; in CSA, fols. 90 vo.–91 ro.; in C1550, p. 173; and in many other early collections. See MCR, II, 659*b*. There is a *pliego suelto* printing: *Pliegos de*

Praga, I, 48; DPS, no. 654. There are also manuscript versions: *Cancionero musical de Palacio*, ed. Romeu Figueras, Vol. 3*B*, no. 131 (with important commentary and bibliography; for the music: RoH, I, 374; Anglés [ed.], *Cancionero musical*, no. 131, p. 158); *Cancionero del Brit. Mus.*, ed. Rennert, p. 44 (no. 95); Dutton, *Católogo-Indice*, II, 22 (no. 0811; also *Tabla*, p. 227*a*). The fragment is recalled in the *Glosa peregrina*: "Que los yerros por amores / dignos son de perdonar // . . . Que la sentencia esta dada / no se puede reuocar" (*Pliegos BN*, II, 283–284; Piacentini, no. 37). The first of these verses is also present in *Media noche* (*Primav.* 190, p. 438), but the other is only distantly paralleled: "¿La sentencia que yo he dado / vos la queréis revocar?" (p. 441), while, in *Pésame de vos, el conde*, the reading is basically identical: "que la sentencia era dada / no se podia (*or* podie) reuocar" (*Cancionero general*, fol. cxxxj ro.*a*, vo.*a*). Like *Media noche era por filo*, the first hemistich became proverbial: "Pésame de vos, el konde. Kedó en rrefrán del kantar viexo" (Correas, ed. Combet, p. 466*a*; ed. Mir, p. 392*a*). *Pésame de vos* was also much cited in Portugal during the 16th century, especially the famous verse: "que los yerros por amores / dignos son de perdonar." See RVP, pp. 111–114, 190, 259, n. 2, 270, n. 4, 274. On *Pésame de vos*, see also RoH, II, 43–44, 47, 52, 84; Menéndez Pidal, *Estudios sobre el Romancero,* p. 188.

Another fragmentary treatment, *Más embidia he de vos, conde, / que manzilla ni pesar*, was likewise very popular and was printed and reprinted in association with *Pésame de vos*. See *Cancionero general*, ed. Rodríguez-Moñino, fols. cxxxj vo.*c*–cxxxij ro.*c*; CSA, fol. 91 ro.–vo.; C1550, pp. 173–174; MCR, II, 581–582; DPS, no. 654 (= *Pliegos de Praga*, I, 51); also Dutton, *Catálogo-Indice*, II, 19 (no. 0683); RoH, II, 28; for other manuscript versions: *Tabla,* p. 185*b*. Gonzalo Correas gives further evidence of this song's popularity: "Más enbidia de vos, Konde, ke manzilla ni pesar. Kedó de un kantar viexo: 'Si es ansí komo se kanta / ke dormistes kon la Infanta, / más enbidia [de vos, Konde, / ke manzilla ni pesar]'" (ed. Combet, p. 533*a*; ed. Mir, p. 294*b*; Cejador, *Verdadera poesía*, I, no. 758). For early Portuguese citations, see RVP, pp. 110–111; Michaëlis de Vasconcelos, "Neues," p. 416. Dona Carolina compares the initial verse with the proverb, *Antes envidia que manzilla*: "Das spanische Sprichwort . . . ward entweder aus der Romanze abstrahiert oder schon in der selben verwertet" (p. 416). The latter is perhaps more likely the case. Note the numerous variants listed in Martínez Kleiser: *Háganme envidia y no mancilla; Mejor es ser envidiado que amancillado;* and others (p. 239*a*:21.745–6); also O'Kane, *Refranes y frases*, p. 191*b*: *Envidia me ayáys y no piedad*; Rodríguez Marín, *Más de 21.000*, p. 34*b*: *Antes envidiado que* *compadecido*. Concerning these fragmentary texts and the ballad's "latent state," Diego Catalán's important commentary should be taken into account: *"Pésame de vos el Conde* y *Más envidia he de vos, Conde* fueron glosados, contrahechos y armonizados repetidas veces . . ., mucho antes que los impresores diesen acogida al texto completo" (*Por campos*, p. 92). See also Menéndez Pidal, "Poesía popular y Romancero," p. 258; *Estudios sobre el Romancero*, p. 188; Catalán, *¡Alça la voz, pregonero!*, pp. 166–167.

Chap. 10, n. 16: Two Arabisms require clarification: *el ayás* (v. 28*b*)— variously rendered as *la halláz, la yas, la yaz, el hallás, el hallar; el hayás*—is defined by Manrique de Lara as 'esperanza' (marginal notes to uned. texts in the Archivo Menéndez Pidal). The phrase "no te cortaré el ayás" (etc.) corresponds exactly to the Morocc. Ar. expressions: *qteᶜ l-iyas men* 'to despair of'; *ma-teqteᶜ-š l-yas* 'Don't give up hope!' (Sobelman and Harrell, pp. 50*a*, 101*a*); *qtaᶜ l-iyas* 'désespérer'; *ka i-qtaᶜ l-iyas* 'désespérant'; *qāṭaᶜ l-iyas* 'désesperé' (Mercier, pp. 86*a*, 167*b*), composed of *qteᶜ* 'cut' and *iyas* 'hope' (Sobelman and Harrell, pp. 43*a*, 101*a*). See also Lerchundi, p. 273. An earlier hypothesis proposed in Nahón (p. 245) should be abandoned. In v. 43*b*, *maromas*, despite its Hispanic appearance, reflects the meaning of Morocc. Ar. *mremma, mṛemma, mramma, meramma* 'métier à broder' (Mercier); 'loom' (Harrell); 'telar' (Lerchundi; Benéitez Cantero); also Alg. Ar. *mramma* 'métier de fabricant de soieries' (Abdelkader, p. 842). In Moroccan J.-Sp., *maroma* is also used in its Spanish sense ('rope'), as in: "Todas barcas y maromas, / al conde lo sacarían" (*Muerte del duque de Gandía*: Larrea 15.28–29); "Sogas y maromas, / para sonsacarlo" (*Bonetero de la trapería*: Nahón 65A.14). Corominas and Pascual list Vulg. Ar. *mabrūma* as the etymon for Sp. *maroma* (*DCECH*, s.v.), from the verb *barama* 'to twist, twine (a rope)' (Wehr and Cowan, s.v.). In St. Ar., *silk mabrūm* is 'wire rope, cable.' The form *desherdar* (v. 5*b*, variant: text *b* = CMP B9.13) could be taken as an authentic survival of the Portuguesisms that entered North African Judeo-Spanish during the first century of the Moroccan *gālûth*. (See n. 47 infra.) All the same, it should be remembered that José Benoliel spoke and wrote fluent Portuguese. Forms such as *teneryo* (v. 8*b*, variant in text *u* = MRuiz 35: "Mis cabayeros s'irían / por no teneryo que dar") are, in general, rare in the corpus of Moroccan *romances*, but they still abound in the unedited texts transcribed by Américo Castro, in Xauen and Tetuán (Winter-Spring, 1922–1923). In v. 52, Claros' fine jacket, of scarlet cloth (*grana*), is lined with tanned goat skin (*cordobán*), but variant readings have *gorgorán* 'tela de seda con cordoncillo' (*Dicc. Autoridades*), perhaps from English *grogram* 'a coarse fabric of silk' (*OED*) or directly from O.Fr. *grosgrain*

(DCECH, III, 197*a*; other references: Steiger, "Mozaraber," p. 683). Note that, in *Media noche era por filo* (v. 11), the Arabism *zarzahán* (CSA etc.) alternates with *gorgueran* (Tortajada); for *zarzahán*: Dozy, *Vêtements*, p. 369, n. 3; *Supplément*, I, 585*a–b*; Corriente, *Arabismos*, p. 477*b*; add to DCECH, Covarrubias: *çarçahán* 'especie de seda delgada, como tafatán y vareteada, tela morisca' (*Tesoro*, p. 396*a*).

Chap. 10, n. 18: *Media noche era por filo* enjoyed great popularity during the 16th century. The incipit is cited in the *Vida del estudiante pobre* (*Pliegos de Milán*, I, 244; Piacentini, no. 90): "media noche era por filo / los gallos querian cantar," but we cannot be certain that this pertains to *Conde Claros insomne*, since the verse "quando el Infante Gayferos / salio de cautiuidad" appears three pages further on (p. 247; cf. *Primav.* 174). The initial verse is also cited in Diego Sánchez de Badajoz's *ensalada*, "¡Padre santo, Padre santo, / señor, humíllome a ti," with the reading: "Media noche era por hilo, / los gallos quieren cantar" (ed. Weber de Kurlat, p. 547, vv. 105–106); given the great popularity of *Conde Claros insomne*, there can be little doubt concerning the verse's identity. The *Ensalada de Praga* cites the second verse: "Conde Claros con amores / no podia reposar" (*Pliegos de Praga*, I, 6; Piacentini, no. 64). Castillo Solórzano's *Fuerza de Lucrecia* includes the internal verses: "Conde Claros con amores / no podia reposar" and "Salto diera de la cama / que parece un gavilán" (*En torno*, p. 83, n. 1; Piacentini, nos. 133–134; Bernadach). A determined exploration of other *ensaladas* would doubtless uncover numerous additional references. The ballad's fame was also reinforced by the popularity of the fragments, *Pésame de vos, el conde* and *Más envidia he de vos, conde*. Note Piacentini, nos. 37 and 85. Lope de Vega cited the ballad in his *comedias* (Moore, *The 'Romancero'*, p. 156). The incipit, "Media noche era por filo," was, in fact, to become proverbial: "Para dezir que era justamente el punto de la media noche, dize el romance viejo: *Media noche era por filo, / Los gallos quieren cantar*, etc." (Covarrubias, *Tesoro*, ed. Riquer, s.v. *filo*; Triwedi, "Las citas," s.v.). When Cervantes began Chap. IX of *Don Quijote*, Part II, with the words: "Media noche era por filo, poco más o menos . . .," he was well aware that his readers (or listeners) would immediately call to mind the famous *romance* of Conde Claros (rather than that of Gaiferos [*Primav.* 174], which has an identical first verse). Clearly the initial words set the balladic tone for a chapter in which *El cautiverio de Guarinos* will later be brought into play: "Mala la hubisteis, franceses, / en esa de Roncesvalles" (ed. Murillo, pp. 99, 102). For a pen trial, "conde claros con amo . . .," discovered in the binding of a late 16th- or early 17th-century Morisco MS, see Armistead, "¿Existió un romancero . . .?," pp. 224–227. There are also various early Portuguese citations. See RVP, pp. 107–110. A Sephardic *piyûtîm* incipit, dated 1587 and 1594: "A[l] rededor del collado" may also echo *Media noche era por filo*'s reading "trescientas piedras preciosas / al derredor del collar" (*Primav.* 190.13) or the Moroccan verse: "con doscientos cascabeles / alrededor del collar" (Larrea 30.54–55). See Avenary, "Cantos," no. 21; Armistead and Silverman, "El antiguo romancero," no. 6.

The Salinas citations read: "Conde Claros con amores / no podía reposar" and "Conde Claros, No podia reposar" (ed. Kastner, pp. 342, 346; trans. Fernández de la Cuesta, pp. 597, 606; also Trend, *The Music*, p. 255; Id., "Biblioteca Medinaceli," p. 532; Querol, "Importance," pp. 312–313, 321–322; Pedrell, I, no. 24; J. M. Ward, *The 'Vihuela de mano'*, no. 16B (musical examples). Binkley's arrangement of Salinas (p. 76, no. 23) should be used with caution (see S. G. A.'s review). The tune of *Conde Claros* came to be a favorite among *vihuelistas* for the elaboration of *diferencias* ('variations'). It was adapted by Luys de Narváez, *Los seys libros del Delphin* . . . (Valladolid, 1538), ed. Pujol, no. 49 (also p. 53); by Alonso Mudarra, *Tres libros de música* . . . (Seville, 1546), ed. Pujol, no. 13 (also p. 67); Morphy, *Les luthistes*, II, 96; Trend, *The Music*, p. 226 (with text underlay supplied); by Enríquez de Valderrábano, *Silva de Sirenas* (Valladolid, 1547), ed. Pujol, no. 29 (also pp. 60–61); by Diego Pisador, *Libro de música para vihuela* (Salamanca, 1552), fols. i ro.–ii vo.; and by Luys Venegas de Henestrosa, *Libro de cifra nueva para tecla, harpa y vihuela* (Alcalá de Henares, 1557), ed. Anglés, pp. 180, 185 (no. 117). On the tune and its variations, Isabel Pope's article ("Notas sobre la melodía") is indispensable; also Trend, *The Music*, pp. 104–106, 225–226; Querol Gavaldá, *La música en las obras de Cervantes*, pp. 51–53; RoH, I, 147; II, 26–27, 87. Quevedo was well aware of the vast musical popularity of *Conde Claros insomne*: "Sepa que los condes Claros, / que de amor no reposaban, / de los amantes del uso / se han pasado a las guitarras. // . . . *El conde Claros*, que fue / título de las guitarras, // se quedó en las barberías, / con *Chaconas* de la gaya" (*Obra poética*, ed. Blecua, III, pp. 126, 34; in the *romances*: "Pues ya los años caducos, / que tejen edades largas" and "Lindo gusto tiene el Tiempo; / notable humorazo gasta" [nos. 778, 757]; in RVP, p. 108, nn. 8–9, there are slightly different readings). Luis Barahona de Soto's poem, "Cuán propio le es al quebrantado viejo," characterizes different social types and, among them, both noblemen and students are typified by their performance of Conde Claros ballads: "Al caballero, y aun al estudiante, [le es propio] / componer y tañer un Conde Claros" (Rodríguez Marín, *Estudio*, pp. 725–726). Rodrigo Caro, in his *Días geniales o lúdicros*, cites "el Conde Claros, que es tonadilla y cantar juntamente, que comienza: Conde Claros con amores / no podía reposar" (ed. Etienvre, II, 245 and n. 11). *Conde Claros*, as attested in various Golden Age *comedias*, was also a dance (Castro Escudero, pp. 27–28, no. X). Lope alludes to our *romance* in his *Noche de San Juan*: ". . . porque cuando el amor danza, / no hay Conde Claros, Inés, / que así salte de la cama" (ed. Stoll, pp. 49 [Act I, vv. 160–162] and 154, n. 18).

There was, in fact, no need to annotate the tune: Everyone knew what it was. So a *pliego* printing of *Coplas nueuamẽte hechas al caso acahescido en ytalia*: *en la batalla de pauia* ("Cessa tu furia frances / ni soberuia tan sobrada") need only state: ". . . las quales se pueden cantar al tono del Conde claros" (*Pliegos BN*, V, 251; DPS, no. 817). Such was, of course, the case with many other *romances* in a predominantly oral society such as that of the late Middle Ages and the Siglo de Oro, as is borne out by numerous Sephardic *piyûtîm* incipits, as well as by many other cases of contrafaction. See our "Antiguo romancero" and especially John Crosbie's article: "Medieval 'Contrafacta.'" As Eugenio Mele has shown, Conde Claros was also referred to in contemporary Italian poetry, as in the following verses by Luigi Tansillo (1510?–1568)—long a faithful servant of the Spanish viceregal court of Don Pedro de Toledo at Naples: "Io feci come fa quel de la Fragola, / Che suona il conde [cl]aro e canta l'appia / Per far come fan gli altri a la spagnuola" ("Due canti spagnuoli," p. 204). Mele also lists additional contemporary Spanish and Portuguese references to Conde Claros. Note too RoH, II, 52, 196, 200, 207, 211. The *Disparates de Saravia* include the citation: "Durmiendo esta el conde claros / la siesta por descansar" (Piacentini, no. 14; British Library *pliego*). Various *romances* begin *Durmiendo esta(ba)* . . ., but such an enormously popular poem as "Durmiendo estaua el cuydado / qu*e*l pesar lo adormescia" (*Cancionero general* [1511], ed. Rodríguez-Moñino, fol. cxxxiiij*a*; DPS, nos. 936, 1038–1039; MCR, II, 442*a*), despite the difference in assonance, may have suggested, at least to some contemporary reader/listeners, an "a lo amoroso" contrafact of the Conde Claros ballad. The inital verses (1–14) of *Bernaldino*, "Ya piensa don Bernaldino / su amiga visitar" (*Primav.* 149), are a transparent imitation of *Conde Claros insomne,* attesting yet again to our ballad's impressive popularity. Concerning *Bernaldino*, see Serrano Poncela, "Dos «Werther»," pp. 91–92. In *Floriseo y la reina de Bohemia*, Floriseo, like Count Claros, is restless, but in this case it is from joy: "Que con su grande alegría / no podía reposar" (Durán 287). In the same context, the *romance* will use another verse also associated with Conde Claros: the proverbial "Que los yerros por amores / dignos son de perdonar."

On the topic of starting the action of ballads at the dramatic and crucial hour of midnight (or midday), see *En torno*, p. 72, n. 21. Note also *El prior de San Juan*: "media noche era por filo, / los gallos quieren cantar, // quando entraua por Toledo, / por Toledo essa ciudad; // antes quel gallo cantasse / a Consuegra fue a llegar" (Catalán, *Siete siglos*, pp. 18 [vv. 29–31], 50; *Primav.* 69). Compare also, in the modern tradition, *El conde Sol*: "A las doce de la noche, / los gallos quieren cantar, // cuando el conde y la condesa / a misa del gallo van" (RT, IV, 121: no. V.125). Such special concerns with midnight (and midday) reflect widely held beliefs. See Gillet, "El mediodía y el demonio meridiano en España," and "Further Additions to the *Diablo meridiano*," as well as Rivers, "Cassian's *Meridianum Daemonium*." I owe the references to Rivers, "The Pastoral Paradox," p. 135, n. 5. At an opposite extreme of Europe, compare Oinas, "Russian *Poludnica* 'midday spirit,'" *Essays on Russian Folklore*, pp. 103–110. Note also the S. Thompson motifs: D791.1.8. *Disenchantment at midnight after owl hoots three times*; E587.5. *Ghosts walk at midnight*; G303.6.1.1. *Devil appears at midnight*; N555.1. *Between midnight and cockcrow best time for unearthing treasure*; but note also E587.1. *Ghosts walk at midday*. For further data on midnight and midday beliefs, see *En torno*, p. 72, n 21, and FLSJ, V.

Chap. 10, n. 19: *Conde Claros y el emperador* shares several elements in common with *Don García*: a close relationship between the protagonist and the king, who bestows gifts on the hero, including the castle of Urueña, and has given him his daughter, doña María, in marriage ("por muger y por yguale"). In addition, both ballads are in *á-(e)* assonance. Verses pertinent to the siege of Montalbán attest to close verbal similarities with *Don García*:

```
cercaron me lo los moros     la mañana de sant juane
siete años son passados      el cerco no quieren quitare . . .
en el castillo de vrueña     no ay sino solo vn pan . . .
si lo como yo mezquino       los mios se quexaran
               (Don García: CSA, fols. 251 vo.–252 ro.)
```

```
los moros melo hã cercado    la mañana de san Juan
tienen lo tambien cercado    q̃ no lo basto yo a descercar . . .
que en todos mis palacios    no entiendo aya vn pan
si yo melo como rey          los otros que comeran
               (A misa: Pliegos BL, III, 977–978)
```

A shorter version of *Don García*, recently discovered by H. G. Jones in a 15th-century Vatican MS, embodies yet another verbal parallel which may also have helped suggest the contamination: "Diéramelo por mi biene / y tomelo por mi male" (*Don García: La Corónica*, 10:1 [1981], 96). Compare "distes me lo por bien / yo tomélo por mi mal" (*A misa*, v. 6). There can be little doubt, then, that some version of *Don García de Urueña* has influenced this particular form of *Conde Claros y el emperador*, but that, at the same time, the contamination did not carry over to the modern tradition. It is worth noting that the loaf of bread is crucial to the narrative of *Don García*, while in *Conde Claros* its role is gratuitous or at least much less important. In *Don García*, the hero throws the last remaining loaf into the enemy camp, thus convincing the Moors that there are still ample supplies in the besieged castle. Concerning this and similar motifs (women who make cheeses from their own milk and throw them at the enemy; sending a calf gorged with grain to the besiegers' camp; etc.), see especially O. M. Johnston, "Sources of the Spanish Ballad on Don García"; Pitré, "Stratagemmi," as well as the notes by Zingarelli and Giannini with the same title; P. Meyer, "La légende de *Girart de Roussillon*," pp. 196–199; Id. (trans.), *Girart de Roussillon*," pp. xxxi-xxxii and nn. 1–2; M. R. Lida de Malkiel, "El romance de la misa de amor," pp. 25–26 and n. 1; Luttrell, "Girolamo Manduca . . . in Maltese Historiography," pp. 121–122. Also pertinent is the legend of Tudmīr, in which women carrying reeds are stationed on the battlements so the city will appear well defended. See Dubler, "Los defensores de Teodomiro"; R. Menéndez Pidal, *Epopeya y Romancero*, in *Reliquias*, 2d ed., pp. 21–22. Similarly, in the *Embajada a Tamorlán*, Ruy González de Clavijo tells how the Mongol leader ordered that the women among his followers "se pusiesen alfamares [= alfaremes] en las cabeças porque paresciesen omnes" to deceive his enemy Totamix, emperor of Tartalia (ed. López Estrada, p. 320). Note also Herodotus' story of Thrasybulus of Miletus and the messenger from Sardis: Grain is poured onto the street to give the impression that the Milesians have a surfeit of available food (*The Histories*, I:20, trans. Sélincourt, p. 20). See also Stith Thompson: motif K2365.1. *Enemy induced to give up siege by pretending to have plenty of food.* The authors of *Tirant lo Blanc*, always keenly sensitive to military strategies, tell of similar procedures: ". . . totes les dones e donzelles així velles com jóvens . . . per les finestres e per los terrats posen draps a l'entorn . . . e cascuna d'estes tinga una armadura de cap. E com los ambaixadors passaran, veuran l'arnès lluir, pensaran que tot és gent d'armes" (ed. Riquer, I, 137 [Chap. XIV]); ". . . de continent ordenaren que li fossen tramesos [al gran Soldà] quatre-cents pans calents així con eixiren del forn, vi e confits de mel e de sucre, tres parells de pagos, gallines e capons, mel, oli e totes les coses que havien portades" (I, 327 [Chap. CV]). In a later, American context, compare the following examples from Francisco López de Gómara's *Historia de la conquista de México* (1552): During Cortés' siege of Mexico City, one of the Spaniards addressed the Indians, telling them that "los tenían cercados y se morirían de hambre; que se diesen. Replicaron que no tenían falta de pan; pero cuando la tuviesen, comerían de los españoles y tlaxcaltecas que matasen; y arrojaron luego ciertas tortas de *centli*, diciendo: 'Comed vosotros si tenéis hambre; que nosotros ninguna, gracias a nuestros dioses . . .'" (ed. Gurria Lacroix, Chap. 126, p. 198); "Estando [Cortés] así platicando con el faraute, se puso en el baluarte un viejo anciano, y a vista de todos sacó muy de su espacio de una mochila pan y otras cosas, que comió, dando a entender que no tenían necesidad" (Chap. 141, p. 223). For Nahuatl *centli* 'cured and dried ear of corn,' see Campbell, p. 59*a*; Mex. Sp. *cenclina, centlinna* 'una planta de tierra caliente . . ., que los indios emplean como febrífugo' (Santamaría, I, 345*b*).

On the uncle/nephew relationship between the Emperor and Count Claros, see *Yoná*, pp. 91–92, n. 3; Nahón, pp. 126, n. 1; *Epic Ballads*, p. 207, n. 22. Note also A. C. Murray, *Germanic Kinship Structure*, pp. 22–26 et alibi. In regard to different early versions of the ballad of *Don García*, note the variant incipit recorded by Piacentini: "Se passea don Garcia / por vna sala adelante" ("Romances en 'ensaladas'," p. 1154, no. 102).

Chap. 10, n. 22: Such triadic patterns often respond to the necessity of detailing the activities of three persons, the characteristics or purposes of three objects, the features of three moments in time, etc. So, in *Riberas de Duero arriba*: "El uno viene de negro / y el otro viene de blanco // y el otro viene de verde, / dicen que es enamorado" (*Primav.* 42*a*). Innumerable examples could be cited from both early and modern traditional *romances*. Note the various instances in *El sueño de doña Alda* (FLSJ, III, Chap. 8) or in *La fuga del rey Marsín*: "ni me lo retraiga en villa, / ni me lo retraiga en Francia, // ni en cortes del emperador, / estando comiendo a la tabla" (ASW, p. 67; FLSJ, III, Chap. 7). For some modern instances, note: "una bes por la mañana, / otra bes ar medio día, // otra bes ayá a tarde, / cuando er sor se trasponía" (*Lucas Barroso*: QRA, no. 3, p. 13); for many others, see *El prisionero* (Attias 8.5–8, 15–18); *Difunta pleiteada* (RPM 236); *Virgen y la infanta* (RPM 364, 367–370); *Devota del rosario* (RPM 375–376); *Fe del ciego* (RPM 428); *Nacimiento de Jesús* (*í-a*) (RTR 32); *La Pasión* (*á-o*) (RTR 41); *Nau Catrineta* (VRP 601–603); *La barbera de Francia* (Milá 224.16–17); and, for additional instances, *Yoná*, pp.

123–124 and n. 5. The pattern has been perceptively studied by Mercedes Díaz Roig ("Un rasgo estilístico"). There are similar patterns in Anglo-Scottish ballads: "And first came out the thick, thick blood, / And syne came out the thin, / And syne came out the bonny heart's blood; / There was nae mair within" (*Sir Hugh*: Child 155A.8); also *Willie o Winsbury* (Child 100A.2–3; *Yoná*, p. 124, n. 5).

Chap. 10, n. 29: The name of St. John's morning (*mañana de San Juan*), so important to the action of many Hispanic ballads, takes on a variety of forms in the Eastern Sephardic tradition: *Sanjiguale, Sangǐguare, Sangǐeruán* (*Gaiferos jugador*: Attias 26.28; *Yoná* 5.12; uned., Salonika; *Falso hortelano*: Attias 10.18; *Conde ¿por qué no casaste?*: Attias 55.1). See also *Yoná*, pp. 92–94. In *Conde Claros y el emperador*, though the reference is obviously to St. John's morning, the form *Ǧenar* must derive ultimately from *Januarius*, which is, indeed, the name of at least two sainted Christian martyrs: Bishop Januarius (d. 305?) and Januarius, son of St. Felicitas (d. 110?). (The legend of St. Felicity, like that of St. Symphorosa, is a Christian adaptation of the martyrdom of Hannah, "la buena judía," and her seven sons.) See Attwater, *Dictionary*, pp. 128, 148; Voragine, *The Golden Legend*, p. 347 (July 10); *Epic Ballads*, pp. 65–67 and n. 59. The allusion to *San Juan* in Attias' version of *Conde ¿por qué no casaste?* is particularly interesting: "En el mes de Sanjiguale, / cuando las ovejas paren" (no. 55.1). The Sephardic text embodies an alternative designation for the month of June which is still current in certain areas of Portugal, Galicia, and Asturias, where *São João, San Xoan, San Xuan* indicate, *pars pro toto*, the entire month in which the saint's day occurs: "Só no mês de S. João, / que estão os trigos com rama, / se podem tomar amores, / e os craveiros com flores" (Basto, "'Sortes' Amorosas," p. 163, n. 3); "En San Xoan a sardiña molla o pan" (*BTPE*, IV [1884], 18). For more on *San Juan* 'junio,' see D. Alonso, "*Junio y Julio* en Galicia y Asturias"; L. Castañón, "Los meses en el refranero asturiano," p. 395. With regard to the Canary Islands, S. Jiménez Sánchez observes: "Las fiestas de San Juan . . . [son] de tanto sabor y arraigo en el alma del pueblo, que han servido hasta para designar y sobreentender el mes de junio" ("El mes de San Juan," p. 180). Concerning *San Juan* 'junio,' see also my article "Portuguesismos," pp. 509–510. For more on *San Juan* and *la mañana de San Juan*, see Armistead and Monroe, "*Albas, Mammas*, and Code-Switching," pp. 176–177 and 197, nn. 15–18, and FLSJ, V, Chap. 14.

Two other minor contaminations in the Eastern versions should be mentioned here: Instead of *Aligornar* (etc.), CMP B9.6 calls the count, to whom Blancaniña is betrothed, "conde Alimar." *Alimá(r)(e)* or *Alemane* (etc.) (CMP,

III, 330) occurs in various Eastern ballads: *Conde Niño* (CMP J1), *Conde Alemán y la reina* (M13), and *El chuflete* (X11). *Aligornar* ('from Livorno') is, of course, not the "original" form either. Compare the adj. *aligornés* in *Rico Franco* (Attias 9.24; *Yoná* 18.11*b*). A *misa* specifies "don Beltrán" (v. 39*b*), while, in *A caza*, the emperor simply says "mandada la tengo ya," without mentioning to whom (v. 16*b*). The Moroccan tradition has caused irreparable mischief by designating Claros' rival with the same name as the hero himself: *el conde de Montealbán* or *Mont(e)alvar* (synthetic v. 26*a*). In variants of v. 28 (in our synthetic text), the ladies in several versions call the knight "este moro franco." The reading doubtless offers an echo of Eastern versions of *Rico Franco*, where the abductor is designated as a 'European Moor' (*moro franco*), though here the meaning may perhaps be taken simply as 'foreign Moor.' See *Yoná* 18.11; *Tres calas*, A9, C7 (and p. 61).

Chap. 10, n. 31: Regarding horses decorated with bells, the *CMC* alludes to "buenos cauallos / a petrales 7 a cascaueles" (ed. Menéndez Pidal, v. 1508 [paleographic ed.]). Don Ramón provides massive medieval and Golden Age documentation for the custom (III, 561–563). See too Alberto Montaner's ed., p. 695 (Lámina III). Compare also the Provençal epic of *Rollan a Saragossa*, where the beauteous Muslim queen Braslimonda (am lo cors covinant), hearing of Roland's bravery, puts on all her finery and rides out to meet the invincible French hero: "La cella fon de vori ['ivory'] trasgitat amb arjant, / e la sotcella d'un pali affrican; / e lo peytral meravelhos e gran: / mil esquilletas hi ac d'aur ressonant, / totas corron por dos filetz d'arjant" (ed. C. Alvar, vv. 553–556). So again in the *Ronsasvals,* the breast strap of Turpin's horse is decorated with little bells: "de sonalhetas fon ornat son peytral" (ed. Roques, v. 447; note also v. 387). In *Fierabras*, there is a magical steed, which bears melodious golden bells: ".C. campanetes d'or i pendent de tous lés. / Quant le cevaus galope, ki tant est abreievés, / Li sons de campanetes est tans dous et soués, / N'i vaut [lai] ne vielle .ii. deniers monées" (ed. Kroeber and Servois, vv. 4118–4121). In the Provençal rhymed romance of *Flamenca*, bells worn by the horses (els sonals quel caval porteron) sound with varied notes (ed.-trans. Hubert and Porter, vv. 7701–7702). For various additional instances in Provençal poetry and interesting commentary, see Riquer, "La fecha del *Ronsasvals,*" pp. 226–228. Similarly, in *Tirant lo Blanc*: "Ixque ab uns paraments que lo rei de França li havia dats, tots brodats de lleons ab grossos sancerros d'or que al coll portaven . . . e los poquets fills portaven campanetes d'argent. E com lo cavall se movia era un plaent so d'oir que los sancerros feien" (ed. M. de Riquer, II, 30 [Chap. 189]). For a late 13th-century Italian testimony to "sweet-sounding brass belles . . .

attached to the breasts of . . . horses," see Goitein, *Mediterranean Society,* I, 109, 421, n. 59. In Chaucer's *Nun's Priest's Prologue,* the Host, addressing the Monk, alludes to the "clynking of youre belles / That on youre bridel hange on every syde" (ed. Fisher, vv. 2794–2795). These bells are prominently illustrated in the Ellesmere MS (Hussey, *Chaucer's World,* p. 57). See also Bowden, *Commentary,* p. 111. Note also *Willie's Lady:* "And at ilka tet of that horse's main, / There's a golden chess ['strap'] and a bell ringing" (Child 6A.15); also *Lord Thomas and Fair Annet* (73F.18; see Mead, "Colour," p. 332) and *Thomas O Yonderdale* (253.18cd). For other instances and commentary, see Wimberly, pp. 186–187. In the Old Norse *Atlakviđa,* Atli rides "a steed with a ringing mane" (i.e. hung with bells or rattles; ed. U. Dronke, I, 9 [v. 29b], 62). Such bells may indeed be supernatural (as Wimberly suggests) and have had a magic function for protection against evil spirits (*Ruodlieb,* ed. Zeydel, pp. 19–20, 108–109 [v. 122]). Note also in a poem by Ibn Gabîrôl: "tú que llevas colmadas de campanillas las orlas de tu falda / y túnicas con cascabeles de oro a modo de granadas" (*En honor de Yequtiel Aben Hasan,* trans. F. Pérez Castro, "Aproximación," p. 69) and in another by Yĕhûdāh ha-Lēvî: "Oh, after my death, let me still hear the sound of the golden bells on the hem of your skirt" (Carmi, p. 344). Such descriptions, seemingly exaggerated to modern tastes, doubtless correspond to the reality of medieval usage. So at the battle of Olmedo (1445), Don Alvaro de Luna's knights are described as follows: "E otros yban ende que llevaban çençerras de oro e de plata con gruessas cadenas a los cuellos de los caballos" (*Crónica de don Alvaro de Luna,* ed. Mata Carriazo, p. 166.9–10; other examples: Tuchman, pp. 244, 441). From the perspective of medieval delight in color, pageantry, and luxurious display, Claros' ostentatious clothing and extravagant adornments (*ropa roçegante*) seem less outrageous than they might to a modern reader. In this regard, compare the following passage (one among many that could be cited) from the *Hechos del condestable don Miguel Lucas de Iranzo*: "El señor Condestable leuaua vestido vn jubón de muy fina chapería de oro todo cubierto, de muy nueua 7 discreta manera ordenado, y sobre aquel vna ropa de estado en demasía roçagante, de vn carmesí velludo morado, forrada de muy presçiadas 7 valiosas cebellinas, en la cabeça vn capello negro de muy nueua guisa, con vn muy rico joyel en el rollo, bordado de muy ricas jemas, con vna guarniçión de oro de mucho valor en somo los onbros; muy bien calçado. En todo como graçioso y desenbuelto galán, ençima de vn hobero trotón bien fermoso, las crines del qual muy mucho erizadas, 7 bien troçada su cola, con vna guarniçión asaz rica 7 bien pareçiente, delantera 7 grupera de muy fino oro sobre vn terçiopelo negro, de nueua 7 muy discreta ynvençión; vn bastón en la mano" (ed. Mata Carriazo, pp. 41–42; also pp. 53, 60, 189–190, 192 etc.). Carmen Bernis Madrazo's *Indumentaria medieval española* offers abundant iconographic confirmation of such descriptions. On clothing and social status in the Middle Ages, note Le Goff's characteristically perceptive observations (*La civilisation*, pp. 441–442) and note also Milá y Fontanals' extensive observations (*De la poesía*, pp. 366–369; ed. Riquer and Molas, pp. 456–460).

The bells that ornament Claros' horse have come over into modern Brazilian versions of *Conde Claros y la infanta*, where the hero offers his horse to the treacherous *mexeriqueiro* in exchange for not telling the king of his tryst with Claralinda: "E o meu cavallo dou-te / selladinho como está, // com trezentos cascaveos / e arreios do peitoral, // tudo de ouro e prata / e do mais fino metal" (Pereira da Costa, p. 319; Silva Lima 8.3.11–18; Vilela, p. 67). In an unedited version of *Celinos y la adúltera*, from Castrillo de Rucios (ay. Gredilla de la Polera, Burgos), Celinos, just like Conde Claros, goes to visit the countess, riding a horse decorated with three hundred bells: ". . . de su casa en casa (d)el conde, / buenas correndidas da, // con trescientos cascabeles / alrededor del metral. // Los unos cien son de oro, / los otros cien de metal; // los otros cien son de plata / para mejor tresonar" (uned., Archivo Menéndez Pidal). The scene involving Claros' calling his servant to bring him luxurious clothing ornamented with courtly *motes* is imitated in the ballad of *Bernaldino*: "Ya piensa don Bernaldino / su amiga visitar" (*Primav.* 149). Francisco Rico has given us a definitive study of *motes* and their social and literary contexts (*Texto y contextos*, pp. 189–230).

Chap. 10, n. 32: On rue and its beneficent properties in Sephardic tradition, see *Yoná*, pp. 262–264, n. 7, 277 (v. 7). Note also HDA, VII, 542–548; Erich and Beitl, s.v. *Raute*; Hand et al., *Ohio*: "For high fever, beat up some rue and put it on a cloth, then put it in a handkerchief and bind it on the wrist" (no. 9522); also Hyatt, *Adams County*, nos. 4450, 4646. In *A misa* and *Dormiendo*, the rue adorns the servants' clothes (not Claros'). Concerning the erotic implications of women sewing or embroidering garments, see *Yoná*, p. 303, n. 14; Librowicz, p. 24; on clothing as a "love-bond" and its importance in courtship and seduction, Rogers, *The Perilous Hunt*, pp. 67–71, 87 et alibi. On the apparent incongruity of Claros' putting on sumptuous finery to court Claraniña, but then riding into battle against his rival, see the perceptive commentary in Librowicz, p. 24. A single Moroccan text from Tangier (CMP B9.16) has preserved the motif of the servants who accompany the hero, here hypertrophically transformed into "trescientos mil negritos." These black servants (instead of the twelve *mozos* of *A misa* and *Dormiendo*) may well have been suggested by those who figure in the hero's ostentatious displays in *La jactancia del conde Vélez*. In *La jactancia*, Count Vélez parades his black servants before the house of the princess, whom he is unsuccessfully attempting to seduce:

> Otro día, en la mañana,   negros y negras vistió,
> vestidos a la Turquía   y joyas de gran valor.
> A todo eso, el conde Velo,   la niña no se asomó.
>   (Ortega, p. 214)

At the same time, that the servants should be no less than three hundred thousand in number clearly echoes a Tangier version of the enigmatic ballad of *El Mostadí*:

> Cuando el Mostadí partiera   de Constantina a la mar,
> tres naciones con él trae,   que más no pudo llevar:
> árabes, rifeños, bárbaros,   no se podían contar,
> con trescientos mil negritos,   que más no pudo llevar.
>   (MP 16 = CMP C19.2)

These 300,000 Black soldiers ultimately reflect an actual circumstance of importance to Moroccan history: the formation, during the reign of Sultan Muley Ismā^{c}īl (1672–1727), of a special, permanent fighting force composed of Black slaves (^{c}abīd). These soldiers, who were the personal property of the sultan, constituted a numerous and powerful force and were distributed throughout the kingdom: "Mulay Ismaïl doubtless had towards the end of his reign from thirty to fifty thousand black soldiers who formed the main part of his army and were garrisoned in the qasbas that the sultan had built here, there and everywhere to guard the roads and on the borders of counties in active dissidence" (Terrasse, *History*, p. 135). Estimates as to the number of soldiers in Muley Ismā^{c}īl's army vary considerably. J. M. Abun-Nasr suggests 150,000 men (*A History*, p. 227). For more details, see Terrasse, *Histoire*, II, 256–257, 280–281; Laroui, *History*, pp. 272–273; FLSJ, VIII, Chap. 20, nn. 11, 15. Blacks—*gnawa*, of sub-Saharan origin, and *haratin* (*ḥraṭen*), possibly "indigenous"—have, in any event, been a part of Moroccan society for millenia (Coon, *The Living Races*, pp. 115–118; Brunot, *Au seuil*, pp. 21–23). For other instances of Blacks in the Judeo-Moroccan *Romancero*, note *Rosaflorida y Montesinos*, where Rosaflorida offers to give her beloved "los cien negritos /

vestidos a la Turquía" (Larrea 37.31–32). In *La expulsión de los judíos de Portugal*, the evil queen is punished for her persecution of the Jews by undergoing a miraculous transformation: "A la entrada de la puerta, / a una negra le paresía; // a la entrada más adentro, / a una al-ignawía" (Tetuán: uned., Guzofsky collection). As Diego Catalán has shown, the "criados negros y negras," who figure in *La prisión del duque de Bernáx*, are a distant echo of 15th-century historical fact ("Don Alvaro de Luna y su paje Moralicos," pp. 130–132; *Arte poética*, II, 216).

Chap. 10, n. 43: The expression *altas torres* occurs in numerous ballads: "Xerifá que está en altas torres, / las más altas que Turquía" (*Moro de Antequera: En torno*, p. 65); "Aí la olyyó la esfuegra, / de altas tores de ande estare" (*Mala suegra: Yoná* 14.6); "D'ahí la llamó la ama, / d'altas torres d'ahí arriba" (*Hermanas reina y cautiva*: Attias 11.49–50); "D'ahí la oyó su padre, / d'altas torres d'ahí arriba // . . . D'ahí la oyó su madre, / d'altas torres d'ahí arriba" (*Silvana*: Attias 41.7–8, 29–30); "Oyérala el hijo del rey, / altas torres donde está" (*Buena hija*: uned., Uña de Quintana, Zamora; also RTCN 25); "Asomárase el buen rey, / de altas torres donde estaba" (*Toros y cañas*: CVR, p. 201); "Ouviu-o a filha de el rei, / d'altas torres d'onde estava" (*Jesucristo y la hija del rey* [*Fuente consagrada*]: Braga, I, 69); "Subiérame a una torre, / la más alta que tenía" (*Emperatrices y reinas: Primav.* 102–102a); "Sevilla está en una torre, / la más alta de Toledo" (*Cabalgada de Peranzules: Primav.* 128); "Oído lo había una morica, / que en altas torres está" (*Media noche era por filo* [*Gaiferos*]: *Primav.* 174). That the knight should accept defeat and turn back (as in Molho's text) recalls one of various possible endings of the Eastern *Forzador*, but the agreement may well be coincidental. See *Yoná*, p. 259; *Tres calas*, pp. 33–34.

Chap. 10, n. 49: Note, for example, *La novia abandonada*: "Y la niña, que oyó esto, / y se empesó desmayar. // Y ni con vinos, ni con agro, / la niña no se aretorná, // y sino con dos palavricas, / que el cavayero le havló" (*Novia abandonada*: uned., Rhodes); "Esto que sintió el caballero, / desmayado quedaría. // Dio la niña un salto; / con su habla dulce l'aretornaría" (*Caballero burlado*: Attias 17.49–52); "El hijo del rey que la vido, / ya cayó y se desmayó. // Ni con aguas, ni con huesmos, / él no se aretornó; // sólo con tres palabricas, / qu'ella al oído le habló" (*Doncella guerrera*: Attias 40.49–54; Bénichou, p. 178); "El conde, desque lo vio, / cayó desmaya'o pa atrás; // ni con agua ni con vino, / le podían consolar, // sino con palabras dulces, / que la princesa le da" (*Conde Sol*: RT, V, 254; RPM 88–90, etc.). Note Stith Thompson: T24.2. *Swooning for love*.

Chap. 10, n. 51: The occasional use of Flores (texts *ag*) for Niño (= Claros) probably reflects the influence of *Hermanas reina y cautiva* (Larrea 54.17, 55.9, 56.9, 57.11; Bénichou, pp. 219–226); another possibility would be *Conde Sol* (Larrea 240.3, 242.3). The seven lots thrown in Nahón's Tangier version (*f*) originate in *El cautiverio de Guarinos* (FLSJ, III, Chap. 8). On the widely used formula, "La cabeza entre los hombros . . .," used in the same text, see *Epic Ballads*, p. 260 and n. 55. We know of no specific origin for the dreadful, pedestrian verse that concludes Martínez Ruiz's version: "Las sinco no habían pasado / cuando l'intierro pasó" (*u*).

The term *primo, prima* 'beloved' used in the *Conde Claros* ballad requires comment. In his ed. of Moroccan Judeo-Spanish wedding songs, Manuel Alvar calls attention to the similar usage of *hermano, hermana* in early and modern Spanish traditional lyric poetry (*Cantos de boda*, pp. 314–315). In the wedding songs, *prima* is used in the same sense as in our *romance*: "Desía el aguadero: / —Y arriba, prima, / mujer que d'eya bebe, / al año parida" (p. 289, no. 38.7–10); "Y a la media noche, / prima la yamaba: / —Más blanca sois, prima, / que la rosa fina" (p. 294, no. 40.29–32). Note also that in the songs' parallelistic rhymes, *hermana* and *prima* are synonyms (*Cantos*, pp. 86, 203, 290). It is, then, quite possible that this usage of *prima* may have Peninsular origins. All the same, we may propose an alternate possibility. Since early times, Arab tribal society has been endogamous: It was greatly preferred, for economic and "political" reasons, to keep marriageable women within the tribe. Hence, Bedouin custom holds that marriage between paternal cousins is especially honorable (Monroe, *The Art of al-Hamdhānī*), p. 32; Robertson-Smith, *Kinship*, pp. 100, 164, 192, 194). Such preferences continue even today. With regard to a modern Iraqi village, Elizabeth W. Fernea observes: "Tribesmen boasted with pride that they never let their womenfolk marry outside the kin group or the larger circle of the tribe. Among the merchants of the village the codes were less strict, but still the preferred marriage was that between first cousins on the father's side. The boy always had first claim to one of his father's brother's daughters (*bint ᶜamm*), and if for some reason the girl was to marry another relative, the boy cousin (*ibn ᶜamm*) first had to relinquish his claim" (*Guests*, pp. 155–156; also 44, 159, 296). For similar customs in Yemen and additional bibliography, see Dorsky, *Women of ᶜAmran*, pp. 104–105. Such cousin marriages are also practiced among Muslims in Morocco (Westermarck, *Ritual*, I, 164). It seems possible, then, that the distinctive use of *primo* and *prima* in the Sephardic songs may reflect an acquaintance with the Islamic custom or, if it is indeed of Peninsular origin, that at least it has been reinforced by such an acquaintance. That *primo* and *prima* may be semantic calques of Ar. *ibn ᶜamm* and *bint ᶜamm* is further suggested by the use of *tío* in a similar erotic sense in text *k* (CMP B9.20). In Arabic, *ᶜamm* 'paternal uncle' is used in poetry with exactly the same connotation. Compare the following Colloquial Arabic *kharja* in a medieval Hebrew *muwashshaḥ*: "bus bus bus bi-fammī / wa-daᶜ sawādak yā ᶜammī" (Kiss, kiss, kiss my mouth, / and put aside your melancholy, dear) (Monroe and Swiatlo, "Ninety-Three Arabic *Kharjas*," no. 35). The 14th-century *Ğayš at-Tawšiḥ* of Ibn al-Ḫatib offers another instance: A drunken youth sings: "qubbaylah fī l-ḫālī / ya ḫālī / fa-qāla fī fammī / yā ᶜammī" ("[May I give you] a kiss on the mole of your cheek, / O maternal uncle?" / He replied: "On my mouth, O paternal uncle" (Monroe, "Studies on the *Kharjas*," no. 27; in a *muwashshaḥ* by Abū Bakr Yaḥya as-Saraqusti al-Jazzār). As Monroe has pointed out, the refusal of ᶜAbla's father to allow her to marry her cousin, the hero ᶜAntar, is one of the major motivations of the *Sīrat ᶜAntar* (*The Art of al-Hamdhānī*, pp. 32–33).

Chap. 10, n. 52: In CMP B25, *Las salas de París* was tentatively classified as a separate ballad, but, as we have now reconstructed the Eastern *Jactancia*, it would seem to fulfill an essential function within that narrative. But again, who is Parizi? He plays no other part in the story and would seem, perhaps, to be an extraneous echo of *El juicio de Paris* or *El robo de Elena* (CMP F4–F5), though the halls themselves may recall a famous Carolingian incipit: "En las salas de París, / en un palacio sagrado" (*Oliveros y Montesinos*: *Primav.* 177–177*a*). Note also the Eastern *Bodas en Paris*: "Grandes bodas hay en Francia / y en las salas de París" (CMP M14.11; *Yoná* 2A-B; FLSJ, III, Chap. 7). For the nightingale that sings at the ear of a sleeping person, compare "A l'espona del llit, / hi canta una calandria // y á n-el capsal del llit, / el rossinyol hi canta" (Milá 558*B*); "Aux quatre coins du lit le rossignol y chante" (Daymard, pp. 49, 54; V. Smith, *Romania*, 2 [1873], 70). In regard to the different times of day, note: "Tres veces el confesor / lo va a ver al día: // una vez por la mañana, / otra vez al medio día, // otra vez a la noche, / mientras la gente dormía" (*Penitencia del rey Rodrigo* [RT, I, 14*bb*, etc.]); "uno reza a la mañana, / otro por el mediodía, // y otro por la media noche, / mientras la gente dormía" (*Devota del rosario* [RPM 372, 375, 378–379, 386]; also *Caballero burlado* [Cuscoy, p. 88]). For now, the identity of verses remains an enigma. Even so, we have advanced considerably beyond the analysis offered in "Sobre los romances . . . recogidos por C. M. Crews," p. 30 (no. 33). We may note, in passing, two sporadic contaminations in the Eastern *Jactancia del conde Vélez*: CMP B22.2 (= *c*) takes its first verse from *Almerique de Narbona*: "Aquel conde y aquel conde." (See FLSJ, III, Chap. 7.) In introducing "el gran Cides" (synthetic v. 4*a*), the Larissa text (CMP B22.4 = *g*) borrows from *Las almenas de Toro*: "De ahí saltó el gran Sidi: / —No hagáx mal a esta donzeya" (*Epic Ballads*, p. 168, v. 13). For the motif of cities offered as a reward (synthetic v. 7), compare *Sancho y Urraca* (*Epic Ballads*, p. 136, vv. 20–23) and for the formula: "Yo no quiero tus sivdades, / que mejor las tengo yo," compare a far-traveled parallel: "Yo no quiero ese cabayo, / que mejor lo tengo yo" (*Blancaniña*: Armistead, "Romances . . . de Luisiana," no. 3*A*.3). The black mule mentioned only in text *c* (CMP B22.2; at synthetic v. 11: "Se subiera en mula preta") is probably a contamination. Compare Salonikan versions of *La muerte del príncipe don Juan*, where the doctor also rides a black mule—here probably suggesting an ominous portent: "Subido en mula preta" (Attias 82.11). Note that, in Izmir versions of *La muerte de don Juan*, the appearance of the mule is accompanied by a prodigious journey: "Syete mulas i kavalyyos / por el kamino dexaras. // Kamino de kinze días / en syete los ayegava" (*Seis romancerillos*, p. 39). The similar description of fast riding in *La jactancia* may have suggested the contamination: ". . . que bola a la raya del sol. // Camino de quinze días, / en siete los ayegó" (synthetic vv. 11–12). For the famous motif of the sorrel horse (*caballo alazán/alazare*), see *En torno*, pp. 118–123. In regard to the pattern embodied in the verses about the nightingale (vv. 20–21), compare the three singing serpents in Venezuelan versions of *El caballero burlado*: "una canta en la mañana / y la otra canta al medio día, / la otra a las seis de la tarde, / cuando ya el sol se metía" (Almoina de Carrera, *Diez romances*, pp. 72–77: no. II). For the punishment of cutting out a person's heart, compare: "sáquente el corazón / por el siniestro costado" (*Jura de Santa Gadea: Primav.* 52.15); "ahí le maten los moros / y le saquen el corazón" (*Blancaniña*: Larrea 108.17–18). In the Old Norse *Atlakvida*, Atli's men cut out the hearts of the cowardly Hialli and of the heroic warrior Hogni; in the *Atlamál*, Hialli is saved at Hogni's behest and only the hero has his heart cut out (ed. U. Dronke, pp. 7–8 [vv. 21–25], 19, 88–89 [vv. 56–62], 99, n. 1). Note the motif: S139.6. *Murder by tearing out heart.*

When the present chapter was already in final form, I was able to consult a previously unedited version of *La jactancia del Conde Vélez* from Salonika, collected by Alberto Hemsi, in Alexandria, Egypt, in 1933 (= Hemsi-II 7). This excellent 24-verse text embodies various interesting readings: "Allí se topó Gran Cides," as in the Larissa version (CMP B22.4 = *g*), under the influence of *Las almenas de Toro*; "Malaña a tus civdades, / más munchas tenía yo!": the same formula as in *Sancho y Urraca* (*Epic Ballads*, p. 136, vv. 20–23); there is a "caballo castado, / que bola la raya del sol" (= synth. v. 10); the 15-day journey is accomplished in seven days (= synth. v. 11). Belo rides around eight cities (= magic circumambulation), before he encounters the princess' slave girl: "Rodeó siete civdades, / por ande entrar no topó. // Atornó por la de ocho, / con la esclava encontró" (compare synth. vv. 22–23). Belo takes both a golden slipper (*chapín de oro*) and a ring as tokens (= synth. vv. 28, 48). This muddles the traditional story, since the *chapín de oro* involves a strategy invented by the *infanta* and Belo has in fact never seen it, before she accuses him of stealing it. (See our summary of the Eastern versions.) Hemsi's version ends with three inmpenetrably enigmatic verses: "—¡Aparéjate, Parize; / te arranquí el tu coraçón! // que al que me habíax mandado, / que sepáx que me venció; // tres noches durmí con él; / preñada ya me dexó." None of this fits the traditional narrative: Parize would seem to have been identified as the other wagerer (= el Gran Duque, el Gran Cides, Don Bueso) and here he, not Belo, is the loser, while the *infanta* seems to be boasting of having been seduced by Belo. Compare Cynthia Crews' version (n. 53 infra). Concerning magic circumambulation (D1791. *Magic power of circumambulation*), see *En torno*, pp. 105–109; *Epic Ballads*, p. 263, n. 59; FLSJ, III, 163, n. 55. Note yet another instance in Virgil's *Eclogue* VIII: "terque haec altaria circum effigem duco" (and thrice around this altar I bear the effigy) (ed. and trans. Guy Lee, vv. 74–75). For circumambulation in Jewish tradition, note Psalms 26:6: "I wash my hands in innocence and walk around Your altar" (*Kithubim* [J.P.S.]); for circumambulation (of a sacred object) in Islamic tradition, see Buhl, "*Ṭawāf*," *EI-1*, VIII, 702*b*–703*a*.

That the wagerer in the ballad is called Count Vélez must be seen in relation to another widely known early ballad, *La prisión del conde Vélez*, which has also survived in the Moroccan Sephardic tradition and on the Island of Tenerife. Here also, Count Pero Vélez distinguishes himself in an amorous escapade and is punished for it. An early version begins: "Alterada esta castilla / por vn caso desastrado // quel conde don Pero Vélez / en palacio fue hallado // con vna prima carnal / del rey don Sancho el desseado // y el rey con el grande enojo / manda que sea degollado . . ." (*Silva* [1550], p. 453). In Timoneda (*Rosa Gentil*, fol. lii vo.), the situation is even more compromising. The ballad has been exhaustively studied by Diego Catalán (*Por campos*, pp. 167–185). Note also Luis Vélez de Guevara, *El conde don Pero Vélez*, ed. Manson, Peale, and Case, pp. 28–30, 214–215, vv. 2980–2987, 2992–2999.

Both the early versions of *La jactancia* and those of the modern tradition insist on the treacherous character of Count Vélez: "quedarias por traydor" (*Silva*

[1550], p. 443); "el traydor del conde Velez" (16th-cent. MS; also Morocco); "Alabóse conde Félix, / alabóse el gran traidor" (Zamora-León). There is probably no connection, though we cannot but think of the treacherous counts, Rodrigo and Iñigo Vela (or *Velaz, Veilaz*, in 11th-century documents), who assassinate the Castilian prince, García, during his visit to León in the *Romanz del infant García*. See Menéndez Pidal, *Historia y epopeya*, pp. 38–45, 47–48, 61, 64.

Chap. 10, n. 54: For the contaminated hemistich, in one of the Moroccan versions of *La alabanza del conde Vélez*: "Y al alzar de los manteles" (text *s* = CMP B22.17; at synthetic v. 40*a*), compare *La calumnia de la reina*: "Y al arzar de los manteles, / de las mujeres se habla" (Nahón 29.21). The hemistich: "más mi marido (siempre) es mejor" (text *m*: Hassán B22*B*; at synthetic v. 42*b*) suggests *La mujer del pastor*: "Por más que dijeran, / mi marido es mi señor" (Larrea 101.17–18; similar readings: RT, IX, 240–252). The repetition of synthetic vv. 2–3 at the end of the ballad in text *r* (= CMP B22.16) suggests a minimal form of ring composition and achieves a bitterly ironic effect. On irony in traditional poetry, see *Epic Ballads*, pp. 269–270, n. 69, and further observations in FLSJ, V, Chap. 13 (*Melisenda insomne*). In regard to Count Vélez's decorating the streets with silk and brocade, note the following passage, concerning a ceremonious welcome of royal visitors, in the 15th-century romance, *Carlos Magnes y la emperatriz Sevilla*: "E quando los de la villa sopieron que venían, encortinaron las rúas de muy ricos paños de seda & echaron juncos por las calles e saliéronlos a resçibir grandes & pequeños con muy grant fiesta" (ed. Benaim de Lasry, p. 170.8–11). Just so in the Provençal Arthurian romance, *Jaufre*, Brunisen decks out her castle with rich and luxurious fabrics to honor the protagonist's arrival: "E viratz lur apparellar / Palis et samitz et condatz / Don fo-l castelz encortinaz" (Lavaud and Nelli, I, vv. 7116–7118; Gómez Redondo, p. 219 and n. 379). The sumptuous character of Vélez's spectacular displays, implying an extreme of luxurious ostentation, closely recall the actual circumstances of 15th-century and Golden Age festivity: "Variopinta se presentaba la fisonomía de las celebraciones italianas de este período: permisividad en disfraces y máscaras, suntuosos desfiles presididos por artísticos carros alegóricos, coros que recitaban versos escandalosos, juegos de carácter guerrero en la Plaza Nuova de Roma con combates entre jinetes y desfiles de ciudadanos armados" (Campa et al., "Breve corpus," p. 91). As Campa points out, there are numerous additional examples, in Burckhardt, *Civilization*, pp. 299–317 (Part V); further instances: Oliveira Marques, *Sociedade*, pp. 202–208; *Daily Life*, pp. 262–268. The extreme stipulations of the wager in all modalities of *El conde Vélez* are quite in agreement with a good number of *chansons de geste* and other Old French narratives, where protagonists may wager their own heads, or parts of their bodies, or their lands and their wives. See Strohmeier, "Das Schachspiel," pp. 392–393.

Chap. 10, n. 55: In the Leonese-Zamoran *Conde Vélez* a valuable or priceless golden sash (*cordón de oro*)—variants: *bordón, gordón* (vv. 9–10, 13, 17; variants vv. 15, 16)—parallels the multiple attractions brought forward in our ballad's Moroccan modalities. As Alan Deyermond has insightfully shown, belts, sashes, girdles, and similar cinctures are traditional symbols for a woman's chastity. See his pathfinding articles: "*Hilado-cordón-cadena*" and "Traditional Images,", pp. 11, 16–17 and n. 8. Compare the *châtelaine's* willingly offered and crucially important gift of her girdle, "I schal gif you my girdel . . ." (v. 1829), secretly accepted by Sir Gawain (pp. 68–69)—against better judgment, we may suppose—but essential to our subsequent equivocal view of the protagonist's ambivalent knighthood (*Sir Gawain and the Green Knight*, ed. Gollancz; ed. Tolkien and Gordon). In the modern Hispanic tradition, the lecherous Fray Pedro's rope belt (*cordón*) takes on a more obvious meaning in the bawdy Argentinian and Moroccan Sephardic *romance* of *Paipero*. See my article, "Expurgation and Bowdlerization," pp. 25–28, no. 2*b*–2*c*.

Chap. 10, n. 59: Schirmunski studies Slavic (Serbocroatian, Bulgarian, Russian) ballads on the chastity wager theme: In *Die Wette des Königssohnes Marko*: "Der Nebenbuhler des Helden mit Unterstützung einer gedungenen Helferin sich in den Besitz von Beweisstücken für seine angeblichen Liebesbeziehungen zu der Frau bezw. Schwester des Helden bringt" (*Vergleichende Epenforschungen*, I, 107, no. 8; also Erich Seemann's references in Lüdeke, "Griechische Volksdichtung," p. 252). The Russian *bylina* of *Staver Godinovich* clearly belongs to the same basic type, but involves a wager on the cleverness of the hero's young wife, who, he claims, can outwit all the princes and boyars of Kiev, and even Prince Vladimir himself. Staver is thrown into prison, but manages to send a message to his wife (as in *Redesdale and Wise William*). She dresses in men's clothing and outwits Vladimir, despite a series of tests similar to those used in *La doncella guerrera* (including a visit to a steam bath), and frees Staver from prison. See Chadwick, *Russian Heroic Poetry*, pp. 124–133. The Rumanian *Iencea Sibiencea* is also a chastity wager ballad, but it is apparently not related to the songs and stories here under consideration. It involves essentially the same narrative as the Hispanic *Apuesta ganada*: Iencea, having attempted without success (or having made a wager) to seduce a certain (Turkish) girl, asks his mother for advice; he dresses as a woman; is received at the girl's house; will not sleep anywhere except in the girl's bed; at dawn he reveals the trick; and the girl concedes she has been conquered. See Amzulescu, I, no. 240; Rechnitz's detailed study, pp. 277–282, 370–376, 631–632; also Stein, p. 39. Another Rumanian ballad, *Călugăriţa înşelată* (*The Deceived Nun*), in some variants also involves a wager and a young man's disguise in woman's (or monk's) clothing. See Amzulescu, I, no. 253; Rechnitz, p. 641; Stein, pp. 39–40. The Hispanic analogue, *La apuesta ganada* (*á*) also involves a chastity wager: "Apostado tengo, madre, / con el rey de Portugal // de dormir con Marianita / antes los gallos cantar" (*Voces nuevas* 45.2). The polyassonant Moroccan *Disfrazado de mujer* is very similar, but there is no wager (CMP T1; T1.10 has been influenced by *La apuesta ganada*). The confident and deceptive girl in *El caballero burlado* sometimes wagers on her own chastity: "Aposté con mis hermanos / castillos de plata fina, // de entrar doncella en el monte / y a que doncella salía" (RGL 24.8, p. 153). Likewise the bold maiden in *The Broomfield Hill* makes a bet with her knight: "'I'll wager a wager wi you,' she said, / 'A hundred pounds and ten, / That I will gang to the Broomfield Hills, / A maiden return again'" (Child 43*C*.3). And, with the help of an "auld witch-wife," she achieves her purpose by magic means. Concerning the Hispanic *Apuesta ganada*, see Yoná, p. 279, n. 6; CMP T1; and Rechnitz's detailed comparative discussion: pp. 370–376.

The French, French Canadian, and Provençal song of *Les anneaux de Marianson* involves false tokens pointing to the wife's supposed infidelity, but there is no wager. See Arbaud, II, 82; Davenson 2; Decombe, p. 259; Doncieux, pp. 215–232; Gagnon, p. 135; Haupt, pp. 96–101; Legrand, *Romania*, 10 [1881], 376; Roy, pp. 125–127, 309; more bibliography: Vargyas, *Hungarian Ballads*, I, 218 (no. 4). The same story is reflected in the Italian ballad of *Gli anelli* (Nigra 6). For further versions and analogues, see Bronzini, I, 41; II, 236, n. 10. The motif of the substitute bed-partner in several of the European ballads (*Twa Knights, Wette, Mavrianós*) is a major feature that distinguishes them from *Conde Vélez* and from its medieval analogues and modern folktale parallels. For the motif in Pan-European balladry and other parallels, see Yoná, pp. 269–270 (à propos of *Silvana*); G. Paris, "Le cycle de la gageure," p. 48. Note also *Decameron*, III:6, 9; VII:8; VIII:4, and Branca's notes, pp. 1163, 1185, 1386, 1418; Stith Thompson motifs: K527. *Escape by substituting another person in place of the intended victim;* K1223.5. *King's daughter deceives king by substituting her maid;* K1840. *Deception by substitution;* K1843. *Wife deceives husband with substituted bedmate;* K1911. *The false bride (substitute bride);* now also extensive treatment in Doniger, *The*

Bedtrick. Note too the sanguinary detail of cutting off the ring finger in *The Twa Knights* and *Mavrianós*: K1512.1. *Cut-off finger proves wife's chastity;* K2112.1.1. *Fingers as false token of wife's unfaithfulness.* In regard to these motifs (substitute bedfellow; ring finger as token), the episode of Elphin and Rhun in *The Tale of Taliesin* (*Mabinogi*, trans. P. K. Ford, pp. 167–169) is particularly reminiscent of the ballads. *Taliesin* seems to be a late addition to the *Mabinogi* (Ford, p. 1). The substitute bedfellow is central to the legend of the birth of King Jaume I of Aragon (Delpeche, *Histoire et légende*, pp. 22–24). Another far-traveled example of the substitute bedfellow shows up in a Caucasian (Abaza) *Nart saga* (Colarusso, p. 189).

   Chap. 10, n. 60: Concerning the date of *Le Comte de Poitiers*, Koenig states: "L'oeuvre a pu être écrite vers la fin du XIIe siècle ou au commencement du XIIIe siècle. . . . La seule chose certaine, c'est que le *Comte de Poitiers* fut écrit avant 1229, *terminus ad quem* du *Roman de la Violette*" (p. xviii). Malmberg argues for a later date: "entre 1235 et 1240" (p. 101). The scene (vv. 854–1048), in which the Count interrupts Harpin's marriage to the Countess, ultimately embodies the same story as the ballads of *El conde Dirlos* and *El conde Sol.* Notice the motifs of the pilgrim disguise (here removed [v. 854], rather than put on) and the questioning of a squire (= *vaquerito*) (v. 900). This does not imply, of course, that there is any direct relationship between *Le Comte de Poitiers* and the Spanish ballads; both represent vastly diffused Pan-European types. See *Yoná*, pp. 314–318. Note *Decameron* X: 9, which ultimately embodies the same story as *Dirlos*. See Branca's ed., pp. 1541–1542; A. C. Lee, pp. 343–348; Landau, pp. 193–218. For the motif of pilgrim disguise and other disguises, see *Yoná*, p. 279, n. 6; *Decameron* III:7, 9; S. Thompson motif: K1817.2. *Disguise as palmer (pilgrim);* K2357.2. *Disguise as pilgrim to enter enemy's camp.* For the Duke's punishment, note Q416.2. *Punishment: dragging to death by a horse*; Q416.2.1. *Punishment: drawing at the tails of horses*; S117. *Death by dragging behind horse.* (See nn. 70 and 72 below.) The golden hairs from the Countess' comb may suggest her royal ancestry: H71.2. *Golden (silver) hairs as sign of royalty.* For Alotru's punishment, compare motif S172. *Mutilation: nose cut off.* . . . As also in the following summaries, here we have omitted numerous features which are not pertinent to our comparative study of the chastity wager narrative in *La jactancia del conde Vélez.*

   Chap. 10, n. 61: The 15th-century French prose narrative, which we will call *Ysmarie de Voisines*, embodies an analogous story to that of *Guillaume de Dole*, which also lacks the chastity wager: Enguerrand de Coucy, *conseiller* and *chambelan* of King Claudin, advises him to marry. Jacques de Voisines proposes his beautiful sister, Ysmarie, as a suitable match, but Enguerrand resents Jacques' intervention and bribes *demoiselle* Robine, cousin and friend of Ysmarie, to arrange for him to see the girl "toute nue." Robine hides Enguerrand in Ysmarie's closet. Having seen a birthmark on Ysmarie's leg, he then goes to the king, claiming that he has slept with her in exchange for 1,000 gold pieces and that she is not as beautiful as certain other women he knows. The king believes Enguerrand's claims and sends Jacques into exile; Jacques reproaches his sister and departs for unknown lands. Ysmarie goes to the king and demands justice of Enguerrand, who cannot prove his case. The king wishes to punish Enguerrand, but Ysmarie intervenes on his behalf. The king then marries Ysmarie and Enguerrand departs in search of Jacques, whom he finds on the Island of Rhodes. Both return to court, where Jacques is treated with great honor. See Langlois, "Notices," pp. 226–229. Malmberg designates this story as *La nouvelle de Sens* (*Le Roman du Comte de Poitiers*, p. 18, n. 4). We have not seen the Latin account (second half of the 13th century; Tours MS 468, fol. 33 vo.), which, to judge by Rita Lejeune-Dehousse's detailed analysis, also embodies a story quite similar to *Guillaume de Dole*: There is no wager; treacherous *maréchal;* nurse unwittingly reveals *signe*: "Non est in ea macula nisi in destro femore quasi quaedam rosa sed eam unquam vidit aliquis"; *maréchal* also obtains ring; denounces girl to emperor as unworthy to be his wife; girl decides on vengeance; accuses *maréchal* of having raped her; "I never saw this woman"; emperor, "admirans pulchritudinem et sapientiam puellae," decides to marry her (*L'oeuvre de Jean Renart*, pp. 54–57). R. Lejeune argues that this Latin story is an adaptation of *Guillaume de Dole*, "le décalque moralisé d'une oeuvre littéraire" (p. 54).

The "Story of the Rose" in the adventure romance of *Perceforest* involves a distantly similar narrative to that of our chastity wager text-type, but here the rose is a flower taken by the husband when he leaves on a journey, as a magical index of the wife's fidelity which will remain fresh as long as she is faithful. Note G. Paris' study of parallel narratives: "Le conte de la rose," pp. 102–116. Compare motifs: H430. *Chastity index;* H432. *Flower as chastity index;* H432.1. *Rose as chastity index;* 434.1. *Apple as chastity index: shines as long as woman is chaste.*

An English translation of *Guillaume de Dole*, with good notes and bibliography and an informed introduction, was published in 1993 (Terry and Durling).

Chap. 10, n. 62: For more data on Jean Renart (*Le Roman de la Rose* or *Guillaume de Dole*) and Gerbert de Montreuil (*Le Roman de la Violette* or *Gerart de Nevers*) and additional pertinent bibliography, see Baldwin, "The Image of the Jongleur," espec. pp. 635, n. 2, 638, n. 9, 641, n. 23, 659, 662–663 et alibi. For Gerart's disguise as a minstrel, compare the motifs: K1817.3. *Disguise as harper (minstrel)*; K1817.3.1. *Disguise as poet;* K2357.1. *Disguise as musician to enter enemy's camp*; also Baldwin, "The Image," pp. 652, 659. There is also a prose version—extant in two MSS written before 1467—of the *Roman de la Violette*, which is based on the rhymed form and follows it closely. As Lowe observes: "The only important deviations from the subject matter of the poem [are] an added episode and certain differences in the itinerary of the hero" (*Gérard de Nevers: A Study*, p. v; on the date: p. 10). In 1928, Lowe published an ed. of the prose redaction. We have not taken into account this derivative form.

Chap. 10, n. 67: Concerning the motif: Q464. *Covering with honey and exposing to flies*; note an apparently historical instance, involving the crusade adventurer, Reynald of Châtillon, Prince of Antioch, who used this punishment as a means of persuading the Patriarch, Aimery of Limoges, to help fund a pillaging expedition against Byzantine communities on Cyprus: Having been cruelly beaten on the head, [the Patriarch's] "wounds were then smeared with honey, and he was left for a whole summer day chained in blazing sunshine on the roof of the citadel to be a prey for all the insects of the neighborhood" (Runciman, II, 347). Needless to say, the Patriarch paid up. See also Maalouf, p. 156. Juan del Encina may perhaps be alluding cryptically to the same puninshment in his *Almoneda trobasda*: "un buen arnés / de Milán todo de pluma, / y de miel, con mucha espuma . . ." (Márquez Villanueva, "Los disparates," p. 377; n. 60; Encina, *Obras completas*, II, no. xxxix, p. 3). Apropos of the servant who spares Madonna Zinevra's life, note the motif: K512. *Compassionate executioner* (variants: K512.0.1–K512.4). Concerning another motif, Zinevra's "peluzzi biondi come oro" may hint at royal lineage: H71.2. *Golden (silver) hairs as sign of royalty*. See n. 60 above.

Chap. 10, n. 68: Stage 13 is barely hinted at—if at all—in the *Decameron*, when Zinevra (disguised as "Sicurano") tells Ambruogiuolo: "Tu ridi forse perché vedi me uom d'arme andar domandando di queste cose feminili" (ed. Branca, p. 214.50), as she is asking him about her belt and purse, which she has recognized among other precious objects in the possession of Venetian merchants at Acre. That the disguised girl should not be attracted by womanly objects is an important feature of the tests she undergoes in *La doncella* *guerrera* and its analogues. See *Bosnia* B14; CMP X4; motifs: H1578.1. *Test of sex of girl masking as man*; H1578.1.3. *Test of sex of girl masking as man: choosing flowers*. Note also Chevalier, "Un cuento," p. 37 at n. 18. A major difference between *Le Comte de Poitiers* and *Le Roman de la Violette* as opposed to the majority of the narratives (ballads; *Guillaume, Jehanne, Oton*; Latin *exemplum*; Middle English *Merchants*; Boccaccio; modern folktales) is the relative passivity of the female protagonist over against her vigorous and successful initiatives in most of the story's modalities. G. Paris' comparative monographic article ("Le cycle de la gageure") remains indispensable. Note also the later studies of Greenlaw, "The Vows of Baldwin"; Hilka and Söderhjelm, "Vergleichendes"; Lawrence, "The Wager in *Cymbeline*"; R. Levy, *"Le Roi Flore et la belle Jehane."* Malmberg's introductory study to his ed. of *Le Roman du Comte de Poitiers* offers a brief, but comprehensive listing of the various medieval chastity wager narratives.

The abandoned wife's sufferings in some of the medieval chastity wager narratives and in many of the modern folktales suggest the ordeals experienced by accused queens, such as Chaucer's virtuous Constance (*Man of Law's Tale*) and her numerous unjustly persecuted medieval sisters: treacherous seneschal, etc.; false accusation; adventures on the sea; rudderless boat; encounter with pirates; adventures in the East; womanly courage; eventual vindication. Margaret Schlauch's monograph is crucial, as is her chapter in Bryan and Dempster (pp. 155–206); also L. K. Morris (pp. 137–140); and, for a ballad analogue, Fowler, "An Accused Queen in *The Lass of Roch Royal* (Child 76)," and *A Literary History* (pp. 218–234). Note the S. Thompson motifs: D1523.2.7.1. *Self-guiding rudderless boat*; Q466.O.1. *Embarkation in rudderless boat as punishment.*

Chap. 10, n. 69: In the medieval narratives we have seen and in many of the modern folktales, the would-be seducer has the help of a woman with some personal connection to the chaste wife (servant, governess, etc.). The chance encounter—as in Llano Roza's text—with a crafty old bawd who solves the suitor's problem, evokes the same situation as in the famous medieval *exemplum, De canicula lacrimante*: Pedro Alfonso, *Disciplina Clericalis*, ed. González Palencia, pp. 32–34, 126–129 (no. XIII); Clemente Sánchez de Vercial, *Libro de los exenplos por A.B.C.*, ed. J. E. Keller, pp. 235–236 (no. 234); *Sendebar*, ed. Lacarra, pp. 108–111 (no. 10; substantial bibliography).

Chap. 10, n. 70: The modern folktale and its early analogues have been discussed in detail by Fansler (pp. 253–257). The following sources provide indispensable bibliographical leads pertinent to the Hispanic versions: Chertudi,

Cuentos (I), p. 176; Chevalier, *Cuentos folklóricos*, p. 100; Id., "Un cuento," pp. 33–34; Costa Fontes, *Folktales*, p. 262; Haboucha, *Judeo-Spanish Folktales*, no. 882; Pino Saavedra, *Cuentos*, II, 337; Robe, *Index of Mexican Folktales*, no. 882. The story corresponds to Aarne-Thompson 882. *The Wager on the Wife's Chastity*. Again, Gaston Paris' exhaustive comparative study of early analogues is fundamental ("Le cycle de la gageure"); also Malmberg's observations (*Le roman du Comte de Poitiers*, pp. 14–19).

Cynthia Crews' version clearly depends on an Eastern Mediterranean model. Note its various agreements with Littmann's Arabic text (*Arabische Märchen*, pp. 212–217): Whoever loses the bet must serve the other (trez mezes tyenis ke fazer hezmét a mí [Crews, p. 168]; . . . as a slave [Arabic, p. 213]); the false friend obtains entrance to the wife's bedroom by being hidden in a box or chest (a ti ti vo miter dyentro el dulap [Crews, p. 169; Arabic, p. 213]); the old woman's excuse for leaving the chest at the wife's house is that she is going on a pilgrimage (yo mi vo yir fazer izyara [Crews, p. 169; Arabic, p. 213]); her excuse for removing the chest is that she has decided not to go on the pilgrimage after all (yo n'ankalsí a luz yolǧís, kedí yo aki agora [Crews, p. 170; Arabic, p. 214]); the wife, disguised as a man, intoxicates (with *rakí* or *banj*) the "false friend" figure and then has him branded (with a mark identifying him as her slave; motif: P171. *Branding person makes him one's slave for life*), as a step toward revealing his deception and regaining her husband's lost fortune (Crews, pp. 174–175; Arabic, p. 216). Again, in one of Eberhard and Borotav's Turkish tales (no. 378), the dispossessed husband works as a water carrier (un sakaǧi de agwa [Crews, pp. 172, 174]) and the branding of the false friend is also mentioned (Danach brandmarkt sie ihn am Hintern). Note, finally, how, in the Greek ballad of *Mavrianós*, the king, who loses the wager, will also become the hero's sister's slave (motif: L410.5. *King overthrown and made servant*). There can, then, be little doubt about the Judeo-Spanish text's close affinity to the narrative's Eastern Mediterranean modalities. The motif of hiding in a chest is also present in Turkish forms of the story (Eberhard and Borotav, no. 272; cf. nos. 250, 378; Jason and Schnitzler, p. 66), though it is, of course, not exclusive to the Near Eastern traditions, as can be seen in Boccaccio's story and in the Swedish text-type (Liungman, no. 882). See now Haboucha's exhaustive analysis (no. 882). For the action of branding, which makes a person one's slave for life, note a Moroccan Djehá story, where the trickster succeeds in branding four thieves "sobre sus nalgas," leading the *qāḍi* to condemn them to work for Djehá "hasta su muerte" (García Figueras, *Cuentos de Yehá*, pp. 91–92 and 248: no. 139).

Various texts included in our analysis of the story's Hispanic sub-type require comment. Parson's three versions (*Taos*; "Mitla"), translated into English, were originally narrated in Indian languages (Taos, Zapoteca), as was Foster's text (Sierra Popoluca). Zunzer's and Aiken's Spanish texts have been translated into English. Pino Saavedra's no. 128 is translated in his *Folktales*, no. 37. Fansler's Philippine versions and Parson's Cape Verdean text (of which the Creole Portuguese original is not provided) are in English translation. Webster's text (*Basque Legends*, pp. 132–136) is from Labourd and so, strictly speaking, cannot be considered Hispanic, but we have included it in our analysis because of its essential similarity to other Hispanic versions.

The language of Llano Roza de Ampudia's versions, as we have observed, would seem to indicate that they have been retold in the collector's more literate idiom. Castro Osório's long Portuguese text is an acknowledged retelling in learned style (*Histórias Maravilhosas . . . recolhidas e contadas por . . .*). Romero's Brazilian text is incomplete and ends with the false friend's winning the wager. After the wife's abandonment at sea in a glass casket, Parson's fragmentary Cape Verdean version continues with an unrelated story. J. M. Espinosa's New Mexican text no. 67 lacks the motif of the chastity wager, although it embodies many features in common with our story: King proclaims: "el que adivinara qué tenía en el cuerpo la hija . . . se casaba con ella"; *vieja hechicera* sleeps in princess' room; sees her undress; tells *marqués* of *pelo de oro*; *marqués* reveals fact at court; marries princess; he tells her how he found out, she tells king; king orders *marqués* and *hechicera* burned to death. We have not included this story in our analysis. Amades' no. 372 pertains only to our story's later stages: Wife defamed by *una mala veïna*; husband throws wife into sea; saved by fishermen; disguised as man; works as doctor; cures king's daughter; becomes *virrei* of city where husband lives; husband confesses killing wife; reunion; "van fer penjar la mala veïna . . . i van viure per sempre més feliços." We have also omitted this text from our analysis.

The Argentine songs collected by Carrizo (*La Rioja*, II, 453–455:nos. 869, 869*a-b*) and R. Cano (*Del tiempo de Ñaupa*, pp. 249–251), which Chertudi (*Cuentos*, pp. 176–177) connects with Aarne-Thompson 882, actually pertain to an essentially different narrative type which lacks the chastity wager and other basic features. See Carrizo's analysis of a Brazilian-Portuguese version. The story's point of departure is Thompson motif H931.1. *Prince envious of hero's wife assigns hero tasks*. The happy dénouement growing out of the protagonists' proper interpretation of enigmatic verses alluding to a vineyard recalls the *Sendebar* story of *The Lion's Track*. See Epstein, *Tales of Sendebar*, pp. 98–

101; Keller, *El libro de los engaños*, pp. 12–14; Braga, *Contos*, I, no. 59; Aarne-Thompson 891*B. The King's Glove.* Note Perry's exhaustive study: "'La huella del león' in Spain."

The versions included in our abstract embody numerous stages and motifs which are of no significance to the story's relationship to its medieval congeners or to the ballad of *Conde Vélez* and we have, consequently, omitted such features from our analysis. The story often begins by narrating diverse circumstances under which husband and wife are married: Often, to escape a storm at sea, he promises to marry the poorest girl he can find. Viegas Guerreiro's text (*Contos*, no. 60) concerns only this early segment of our story and consequently it has not been taken into account in our repertory of texts.

Our story has numerous congeners in other European and Near Eastern languages and there is also scattered evidence from India and Indonesia. For an extensive listing, see Aarne-Thompson, Type 882. To these materials should be added the Cornish version listed by Baughman, *Type and Motif Index*, p. 370 (N15. *Chastity wager*); the German text in Ranke, *Folktales of Germany*, no. 38 (and notes pp. 213–214); the Moroccan Judeo-Arabic version (from Fez) in Noy, *Contes*, no. 24; the Yemenite Jewish version edited by Noy in *Jefet Schwili erzählt*, no. 80 (pp. 192–195). There are additional unedited Jewish texts in the Israel Folktale Archive. See Jason, "Types of Jewish-Oriental Oral Tales," p. 174 (nos. 882–882*C); Noy, "The First Thousand," p. 107; Schwarzbaum, *Studies*, p. 455. The version in English collected by Parsons in Trinidad (*Folklore of the Antilles*, no. 254) is strikingly close to the Hispanic narratives. Note also Arabic analogues: El-Shamy, I, 279 (N15).

The Hispanic folktale embodies the following notifs: (3) N15. *Chastity wager*; N2. *Extraordinary stakes at gambling*; (6) K2250. *Treacherous servants*; K2252. *Treacherous maid-servant*; N825.3. *Old woman helper*; D100. *Transformation: man to animal*; D117.1. *Transformation: man to mouse*; (7) K2112.1. *False tokens of woman's unfaithfulness*; H51.1. *Recognition by birthmark*; H75. *Recognition by hair*; H75.4. *Recognition by golden hair*; H80. *Recognition by tokens*; H86.2. *Articles of clothing with name embroidered on them taken as tokens*; H86.3. *Ring with names inscribed on it*; H86.4. *Handkerchief with name on it*; H93. *Identification by jewel*; H94. *Recognition by ring*; H110. *Identification by cloth or clothing*; H111. *Identification by garment*; H113. *Identification by handkerchief*; H117. *Identification by cut garment*; H125. *Identification by weapons*; (9) K2110.1. *Calumniated wife*; K2112. *Wife slandered as adulteress . . .*; S410. *Persecuted wife*; S431. *Cast-off wife exposed in boat*; S432. *Cast-off wife thrown in water*; S435. *Cast-off*

wife abandoned in pit; Q465.3. Punishment: pushing into well; Q466.0.2.
Punishment: setting adrift in boat; S331. *Exposure of child in boat (floating box)*; K512. *Compassionate executioner: A servant charged with killing hero (heroine) arranges escape of the latter*; K512.2. *Compassionate executioner: substituted heart*; K512.2.0.2. *Eyes of animal substituted as proof for eyes of children*; (10) B211.1.2. *Speaking goat*; B540. *Animal rescuer*; R131.3.1. *Shepherd . . .*; R131.3.2. *Goatherd . . .*; R131.3.3. *Cowherd . . .*; R131.4. *Fisher[man] rescues abandoned child*; (11) K1837. *Disguise of woman in man's clothes*; (12) K1837.6. *Disguise of woman as soldier*; (13) K1578. *Test of sex: to discover person masking as of other sex*; K52.4.1.1. *Girl escapes in male disguise*; (14) B211.3. *Speaking bird*; B211.6.1. *Speaking snake (serpent)*; (15) F823.1. *Golden shoes*; F823.4. *Silver shoes*; K1825.2. *Woman masks as lawyer (judge) and frees her husband*; S451. *Outcast wife at last united with husband . . .*; (16) Q413. *Punishment: hanging*; Q413.3. *Hanging as punishment for imposture*; Q414. *Punishment: burning alive*; Q414.0.6. *Burning as punishment for impostor*; Q414.1.1. *Punishment: boiling in oil (lead, tar)*; Q416. *Punishment: drawing asunder by horses*; Q416.0.1. *Quartering by horses as punishment for impostor*; Q416.2. *Punishment: dragging to death by a horse*; Q416.2.1. *Punishment: drawing at the tails of horses*; S117. *Death by dragging behind horse*; Q421. *Punishment: beheading*; Q428.3. *Drowning as punishment for adultery*; Q431. *Punishment: banishment (exile)*; Q433. *Punishment: imprisonment*; Q433.4. *Imprisonment for imposture.* For dragging as a punishment in ballads and in medieval texts, see *Tres calas*, pp. 41–42, n. 42a. For drawing asunder by horses, see nn. 60 above and 72 below.

Chap. 10, n. 72: We have only to recall the fate of Ganelon in the *Chanson de Roland* (ed. Jenkins, vv. 3963–3973 and p. 275, n., where various analogues are listed). See also Brault's ed., II, 332–333, 474, nn. 13–18. For a 14th-century miniature of the quartering of Ganelon (Bibl. Nat. fr. 2813, fol. 124), see R. S. Loomis, *A Mirror of Chaucer's World*, plate 130. For numerous additional examples, see the Thompson motif: Q416. *Punishment: drawing asunder by horses*; also Q416.0.1–3; Q469.12. This punishment (and dragging) inspired a stock phrase in Old French literature: 'I would rather be torn apart by horses than . . .': "Certes, l'an me devroit detreire / a chevax, se je vos creoie" (Chrétien de Troyes, *Le Chevalier de la Charrette*, ed. M. Roques, vv. 3454–3455); "Par cele foi que je ai Deu portee, / mieuz vodroie estre a chevaus traïnee . . ." (Bertrand de Bar-sur-Aube, *Girart de Vienne*, ed. van Emden, vv. 1417–1418). There is general agreement that Ganelon is torn to pieces by horses in the Oxford *Roland* and his fate is made even more explicit in some of the later versions: *Venice-IV* (ed. Mortier, II, 172, v. 5999), *Paris* (ed. Mortier, VI, 183, vv. 6815–17), *Cambridge* (ed. Mortier, VII, 159, vv. 5682–85). In Konrad's *Rolandslied*, however, Ganelon is clearly dragged to death rather than being immediately torn apart: "Genelunen si bunden / mit fuzen unt mit handen / wilden rossen zu den zagelen: / durh dorne unt durh hagene, / an dem buche unt an dem rucke / brachen si in zestucke" (ed. Wesle and Wapnewski, vv. 9009–9014; Kartschoke, p. 604). In the Norse *Saga af Runzivals bardaga*, Ganelon also seems to be dragged to death, "lié entre deux chevaux indomptés, qui le traînèrent en de nombreux endroits en France," though ultimately he is dismembered (Aebischer, *Rolandiana boréalia*, p. 237). The same punishment is applied to the traitor, Vellido Dolfos, in late chronistic narratives of the *Cerco de Zamora*, doubtless based on oral tradition (Vaquero, "The Tradition of the *Cantar de Sancho II*" and *Tradiciones orales*, pp. 88–93, 95, 103, n. 35; and my comments in "Chronicles and Epics," pp. 103–105, where I point out analogues in modern *romances*). Note also the same punishment in *Enrique fi de Oliva* (Menéndez Pidal, *Infantes de Lara*, p. 35, n. 1) and in the *Sentencia de Carloto* (En el nombre de Jesus / que todo el mundo ha formado) (*Primav.* 167.39–45; Larrea 216.982–995). For the punishment of being boiled alive (Q414.1.1), compare the horrendous dénouement of the Old Spanish *Sendebar* (*Libro de los engaños*): "E el Rey mandóla quemar en una caldera en seco" (ed. María Jesús Lacarra, p. 155 [Story 23] and n. 8, for diverse punishments in different redactions). But in the *1001 Nights* (trans. Payne, V, 345: N606), the treacherous stepmother is—characteristically—forgiven.

Chap. 10, n. 73: Branca (ed. *Decameron*), p. 1123, lists various early Italian treatments which we have not been able to consult. Mateo Bandello's *novella* XXI (ed. Brognoligo, I, 260–281), learned and literary in style, embodies almost none of the features that characterize the oral tale, except for the chastity wager itself (pp. 270–272). Yet Bandello has managed to combine two analogous motifs that both go back to medieval sources and both will turn up again in modern folk literature: the chastity wager and the chastity index (as in the *Perceforest* "Story of the Rose"; motif: H430. *Chastity index*; Type 888. *The Faithful Wife*). In Bandello's novella, the chastity index is a magic image, created by "un vegliardo polacco, che aveva fama d'essere grande incantatore" (p. 266). The image will change color depending on the wife's fidelity: "Se la moglie tua no ti romperá la fede maritale, vedrai sempre la imagine si bella e si colorita come io la fabricherò, . . . ma se per sorte ella pensasse sottoporre a chi si sia il corpo suo, la imagine diverrá pallida, e venendo a l'atto che facesse ad altrui di sé copia, subito essa imagine diverrá nera come spento carbone e putirá di maniera che il puzzo si farà d'ogn'intorno meravigliosamente sentire" (p. 267; H439.1. *Picture as chastity index: indicates by its color*). The same feature will show up in the folklore motif H430. *Chastity index* (and its avatars: H431– H439.2) and as part of the tale-type 888. *The Faithful Wife*: II. *The Chaste Wife. (a) [Husband] has a shirt (or handkerchief) that remains white as long as his wife at home remains true to him*. The oral and literary manifestations of the motif are discussed in admirably learned detail by Child, à propos of *The Boy and the Mantle* (no. 29; I, 257–271). There can be no question concerning the medieval origins of Bandello's story and, though it was indeed translated and adapted (Child, pp. 268–269), the motif's later manifestations depend as much, if not more, on an ongoing oral tradition, rather than on written literary antecedents. The same, clearly, is also the case with the multifarious conformations of the chastity wager narrative. I have not seen Francesco Sansovino's story in *Cento novelle scelte* (Rotunda, p. 148: N15).

There are several 16th- and 17th-century Spanish literary treatments of the chastity wager story: Lope de Rueda's *Comedia llamada Eufemia* (ed. Moreno Villa, especially pp. 46–47, 61, 68, 70, 85–86; Eufemia accuses Paulo of having stolen a jewel; he answers: "Ni la conozco ni la vi en mi vida") and Juan Timoneda's *Patrañuelo* (ed. Ruiz Morcuende or ed. Ferreres, no. 15) stay relatively close to the story's earlier sources. The *Novela del envidioso* by Cristóbal de Tamariz (ed. McGrady, pp. 93–147) eliminates the chastity wager, but preserves a series of elements based either on Boccaccio, on Timoneda, or on oral sources: The wife is disguised as a man; cures the daughter of the king of France; the husband confesses to the wife (as agent of the king). As M. Chevalier has shown ("Un cuento," p. 37), the role of the disguised wife as doctor indisputably has its origin in some form of the folktale; he cites Amades, *Rondallística*, no. 372, and Leite de Vasconcellos, *Contos*, no. 347; the same motif is also present in Castro Osório's retold version (p. 244) and in Webster's French Basque story (pp. 134–135), in which, respectively, the wife cures the queen and the king's daughter. In Rumanian-Gypsy and Turkish forms, the wife likewise achieves a position of power by curing, respectively, a blind king or a princess (Landau, *Die Quellen*, p. 140; Eberhard and Borotav, no. 272). María de Zayas y Sotomayor's *El juez de su causa* (ed. González de Amezúa, pp. 373– 400) concerns only the traditional story's later stages, in which the wife (*novia* in this case) disguises as a man, and, as *virrey*, judges the case of her imprisoned beloved. Doña María probably took into account both Timoneda's *patraña* 15 and Lope's *Fortunas de Diana* (first of the stories dedicated to Marcia Leonarda; ed. Rico, pp. 27–72). Concerning these late narratives, see

McGrady's perceptive analysis of the *Licenciado* Tamariz's *Envidioso* (ed., pp. 29–37); Senabre Sempere's article on María de Zayas' sources for *El juez*; and, especially, M. Chevalier's splendid study of all these Golden Age narratives, which conclusively demonstrates the influence of oral folktales on the Golden Age texts. As Chevalier observes: "Parece poco dudoso que cuento de tan extensa difusión en el área de lengua española y portuguesa fue en efecto cuento folklórico oral en la España del Siglo de Oro" ("Un cuento," p. 34). Concerning *El patrañuelo*, see also Chevalier, *Cuentos folklóricos*, no. 55. Lope de Vega's *Embustes de Celauro* (ed. Acad. Nueva, Vol. XII, 96–134) retains only a few elements pertaining to the traditional story; such as the *lunar* as token (pp. 114a, 132b) and the rejected wife's disguise—but as a *serrana*, not as a man (p. 125b)—but the wager itself is lacking. Note also María Rosa Lida de Malkiel's observations: *El cuento popular* (1941), p. 42; (1976), p. 45; Arróniz, *La influencia italiana*, pp. 90–94. C. B. Bourland's study ("Boccaccio and the *Decameron*," pp. 84–91) continues to be useful. J. M. Martín Morán, intrigued by uninformed innovation, undertakes a semiotic analysis and comparison of Boccaccio's and Timoneda's stories (*Ginevra y Finea*), but, to the detriment of his conclusions, ignores all previous scholarship.

    Chap. 10, n. 74: There are talking parrots in numerous different folktales: Aarne-Thompson 243. *The Parrot Pretends to be God*; 546. *The Clever Parrot*; 1352A. *Seventy Tales of a Parrot prevent Wife's Adultery*; 1422. *Parrot Unable to Tell Husband Details of Wife's Infidelity* (= motif J1154.1); also the motifs: B211.3. *Speaking bird*; B211.3.4. *Speaking parrot*; other talking birds: B211.3.1–9. Note the Spanish story *El papagayo blanco* (Hernández de Soto, "Cuentos de Extremadura," *BTPE*, 10, pp. 175–185) and the talking parrot in the *Libro de los engaños* (ed. Keller, pp. 15–16; ed. Lacarra); also Câmara Cascudo, *Contos*, pp. 224–233; Athaide Oliveira, *Contos*, I, 251–256 (no. 105); Leite de Vasconcellos, *Contos*, I, nos. 80–81; Silva Soromenho and Caratão Soromenho, *Contos*, I, nos. 48–50. Note also the voluble talking parrot in the late medieval French romance, *Le Chevalier du Papegau* (ed. Heuckenkamp; trans. Vesce). There are tell-tale or helpful talking birds in Child's *Lady Isabel and Elf-Knight* (4C.13–17; 4D.9–12), *Young Hunting* (68A.7–11), and in numerous other Anglo-Scottish ballads (Wimberly, pp. 44–45, 145). In the *1001 Nights* an informative parrot reveals the wife's infidelity in *The Merchant's Wife and the Parrot*, but is later deceived by her and pays with its life for its loquacity (trans. Payne, V, 265–266, Night 579). For talking birds and complex bird symbolism in modern Palestinian folktales, see now the perceptive commentary in Muhawi and Kanaana, *Speak, bird, speak again*, nos. 9, n. 7; 10, n. 9; 11, n. 5; 13, n. 11; et alibi.

Chap. 10, n. 78: Margit Frenk has studied the complex intertwining of proverbs and early Hispanic lyric poetry ("Refranes cantados"; *Estudios*, pp. 154–171). There is, to my knowledge, no study of riddle-stories in a Hispanic context, though plenty of primary material exists. See, for example, A. M. Espinosa, *Cuentos populares españoles*, I, nos. 16–30, 63; Amades, "Les contes-devinettes de Catalogne"; Leite de Vasconcellos, *Contos*, I, 275–307, 681–683; Silva Soromenho and Caratão Soromenho, *Contos*, I, nos. 172–212. Note the numerous instances of riddling in folktales listed in Aarne-Thompson (p. 577*b*); among the most famous: 851. *The Princess who Cannot Solve the Riddle* and 851A. *Turandot*. On some of the problems involved, see Abrahams, "A Note on Neck-Riddles," espec. pp. 85–86 and 92–93. María Rosa Lida de Malkiel briefly discusses some of the parallels—including *Conde Vélez* and *Doncella guerrera*—between ballads and folktales (*El cuento popular y otros ensayos*, pp. 44–46). For the English and Scottish ballads, see Morokoff, "Whole Tale Parallels." For multiple perspectives on genre problems, see Ben-Amos (ed.), *Folklore Genres*. For how ballads and lyric poetry coalesced during the 16th century, see Margit Frenk's pathfinding article, "Los romances-villancico." For an example of the interrelation of proverbs and folktales, note our article (with R. Haboucha), "Words Worse than Wounds," and Harriet Goldberg's perceptive analysis and extensive bibliography in "The Judeo-Spanish Proverb and its Narrative Context."

11. *Conde Claros fraile*:

Chap. 11, n. 2: Moisés Abravanel, claiming, as was his wont, that he had collected the ballad with great effort from oral tradition, actually copied it verbatim (with an occasional inaccuracy) from Yoná's chapbook and sent his copy to Menéndez Pidal around 1905. Before the discovery of *Pizmônîm*, Abravanel's copy was then edited in RT, III, no. III.5 (pp. 100–101) together with textual commentary concerning his supposed informants' understanding of the difficult v. 11*b*: ". . . disen los unos. . . ." For Menéndez Pidal's comments on Abravanel's "notables versiones"—he had no way of knowing that none of them were collected directly from oral sources—see MP, pp. 1046, 1056–1057. Concerning Abravanel's plagiaristic attraction to the printed word, see CMP, I, 47 and n. 32. In simplifying our transcription of the *Pizmônîm* text here, we render both *sin* and *shin* as *x*.

Chap. 11, n. 5: The rose arbor in Sephardic ballads inevitably suggests the *vergel de amor* familiar to medieval lyric poetry: "Dentro en el vergel / moriré, / dentro en el rrosal / matarm'an. / Yo m'iva, mi madre, las rrosas coger, / hallé mis amores / [dentro en el vergel]" (Frenk, *Corpus*, 308*B*; *Cancionero musical de Palacio*, ed. Romeu Figueras, no. 66; ed. Barbieri, no. 237); "Del rosal vengo, mi madre, / vengo del rosale. / A riberas d'aquel vado, / viera estar rosal granado. / Vengo del rosale. / . . . Viera estar rosal florido, / cogí rosas con sospiro. / Vengo del rosale." (Frenk, *Corpus*, 306; Gil Vicente, *Triunfo do Inverno*); "—Donde vindes, filha, / branca e colorida? / —De láa venho, madre, / de ribas de hum rio: / achey meus amores / en hum rosal florido" (Frenk, *Corpus*, 307; Gil Vicente, *Auto da Lusitánia*; also Cummins, *Spanish Traditional Lyric*, p. 68; with significant commentary). We must recall here too a paradigmatic Provençal *alba*: "En un vergier sotz fuella d'albespi / tenc la dompha son amic costa si, / tro la gayta crida que l'alba vi. / Oy Dieus, oy Dieus, de l'alba! Tan fost ve!" (Appel, *Provenzalische Chrestomathie*, no. 53; Hill and Bergin, I, no. 178) and the following verses by Walther von der Vogelweide: "Under der linden / an der heide, / dâ unser zweier bette was, / dâ mugt ir vinden / schône beide / gebrochen bluomen unde gras. / Vor dem walde in einem tal, / tandaradei! / schône sanc diu nahtegal" (Under the lime tree / on the meadow, / where we two had our bed, / you still can see / lovely broken flowers and grass. / On the edge of the woods, in a vale, / *tandaradei!* / sweetly sang the nightingale) Bartsch and Golther, p. 117, vv. 562–570; trans.: Goldin, no. 46. In the Judeo-Spanish tradition, the *rosal* has various different connotations: FLSJ, III, 140–141. On the motif of picking flowers (Frenk, no. 308*B*) and its implications, note the following poem: "¿Quál es la niña / que coge las flores / si no tiene amores?" (Frenk, *Corpus*, no. 11; Gil Vicente, *O Velho da Hora*; *Cancionero musical*, ed. Romeu Figueras, I, 111). For more on the topic, see FLSJ, V, Chap. 12.

Chap. 11, n. 11: The reading *anisar* (elsewhere: *nisán*, as in *Gritando va el caballero* [Larrea 218–219]) probably reflects an attempt at de-Christianization (*En torno*, p. 138). The variant *libro de rezar* (for *libro misal*) can be documented in Christian sources and so need not be a "neutralization" inspired by Judaic avoidance of a Catholic missal—though in Moroccan texts it undoubtedly is (*En torno*, pp. 137–138). But compare the Portuguese *Nau*

Catarineta: "Tenho feito juramento / no me livro de rezar" (Braga, I, 10, 15) and a Brazilian version of *Conde Claros fraile*: "Jura aqui, minha menina, / neste livro de rezar" (Vilela, no. 2.2). In Morocco, the oath on a missal also occurs as a contamination in *El robo de Elena* and in *Gerineldo (Nahón*, pp. 67–68 and nn. 7–8; Larrea 47, 49). The formula is widely used in early juglaresque ballads: *Ya se salen de Castilla* (RT, II, 100, vv. 85, 102); *Melisenda insomne* (Menéndez Pidal, *Estudios sobre el Romancero*, p. 26); *Conde Dirlos* (RT, III, 71, v. 118; 73, v. 193; 80, v. 64). For more on this, see Nahón, p. 67, n. 7; and for similar oaths in modern *romances* from other traditions, note: "Juramento tengo hecho / en el vino y en el pan" (*Infancia de Montesinos*: RPM 51); ". . . no le querrá quebrar" (RPM 52); ". . . en la punta de su puñal" (RPM 53); also *Infancia de Gaiferos* (RPM 54); "Tengo juramento jecho, / a ley de no quebrantarlo" (*Conde Grifos Lombardo*: FM 2.1); "Tengo juramento jecho, / en un libro consagrado" (*Prisión del conde Vélez*: FM 10.8).

Chap. 11, n. 15: The *pliego* texts of *Virgilios* in the Biblioteca Nacional (*Pliegos BN*, II, 89) and Prague (*Pliegos de Praga*, II, 98), described in DPS 1005–1006, agree with CSA and C1550 (p. 252) in this regard. Here the Castilian and Portuguese (Trás-os-Montes) versions seem to be following the same tradition as the *pliegos*: "Siete años ha estado allí, / nadie le vaya a ver" (RPC, p. 125; RTCN 114); "Sete anos esteve preso, / sem ninguém o ir a ver" (VRP 293). A unique, recently published Azorian version reads: "Sete anos jazeu em cárcere, / sete anos a padecer" (Silveira, "Mais alguns Romances," no. II). The relatively abundant, recently discovered Canarian versions (Trapero, *Hierro*, nos. 1–6) begin at a later point in the narrative. For another, otherwise unattested feature of the Moroccan form of *Virgilios*, documented in another contamination (in *Sancho y Urraca*), see *Epic Ballads*, pp. 148–150. Concerning *Virgilios*, see now Maximiano Trapero's indispensable monograph.

Chap. 11, n. 20: On going to the baths as an opportunity for an amorous encounter, note the medieval Provençal verse romance of *Flamenca*. Here, however, there is not simply a meeting on the way to or from the baths, but the situation is much more complex and the lover must dig a tunnel from his own apartments to the bathhouse to gain access to his lady (ed.-trans. Hubert and Porter, vv. 5812 ff.). Compare the Thompson motifs: K1344. *Tunnel entrance to guarded maiden's chamber;* K1523. *Underground passage to paramour's house.* Medieval attitudes connected baths and bathing with licentiousness and such an implication is doubtless present in the verses from *Conde Claros y la infanta*, *Guiomar*, and *Melisenda*. On the sinfulness of baths, see Oliveira Marques, *Daily Life in Portugal*, p. 139; Dillard, pp. 151–153; Otis, pp. 98–99;

Rossiaud, pp. 5–6 el alibi; FLSJ, V, Chap. 14. Note the motif: K1587. *Adulteress uses public baths as a meeting–place with her lover.* On the implications of cleanliness and disarray in balladry, see the perceptive treatment in Rogers, *The Perilous Hunt*, pp. 90–108. For further comments, see *Cancionero musical de Palacio*, ed. Romeu Figueras, I, 113.

Chap. 11, n. 27: Our synthetic Castilian text is based on the following sources (for complete references, see the bibliography at the end of this chapter): v. 1: *Voces nuevas* 48.5, 6, 7, 10, 12. •*2a*: *Voces nuevas* 48.5, 6, 7. •*2b*: RPC, p. 12; Díaz Viana; *habrare*: Kundert; *praticar*: Díaz-Delfín-Díaz Viana; *casar*: *Voces nuevas* 48.5, 7; *pasar*: *Voces nuevas* 48.10; *manejar*: *Voces nuevas* 48.12; *gozar*: *Voces nuevas* 48.10. •*3*: *Voces nuevas* 48.5, 6, 7. •*4a*: *Voces nuevas* 48.5, 6, 7. •*4b*: *Voces nuevas* 48.5, 6, 10 + Kundert: *la niña tendió el berdal*: *Voces nuevas*; *la Galanzuca el sobriale*: Kundert. •*5–6*: RPM 58. •*7*: RPM 58 + Kundert G4: *Un picaro de escudero / por allí pasó a mirar*: RPM; *Pasara por allí un hombre / no debía pasar*: Kundert; *el escuchero parlero / él escuchándolo está*: Díaz-Delfín; *Ya los viera un pastorcito / de los que comen su pan*: *Voces nuevas* 48.5. •*8*: Díaz-Delfín, p. 166; *pastor*: *Voces nuevas* 48.6, 7, 10. •*9a*: *Voces nuevas* 48.7. •*9b*: RPM 58. •*10–13*: RPM 58. •*14*: Kundert: *Nuevas le traigo, mi rey, / nuevas de muy gran pesare.* •*15–16*: RPM 58. •*17*: Kundert: *contare.* •*18a*: Díaz-Delfín, p. 166. •*18b*: Díaz-Delfín, p. 166: *bien te lo hubiera pagado.* •*19*: Díaz-Delfín, p. 166. Kundert's text (G4) was recorded in Guadramil (Bragança, Portugal), but, like many ballads sung in these border communities, this version is almost completely Castilian. Note the similar results obtained from another Guadramil informant, interviewed by S. G. A., in Rio de Onor, in July 1980 ("Una encuesta romancística," p. 72, at n. 13). The text recorded by the Instituto Menéndez Pidal team in Candín (p.j. Ponferrada, León) is in a mixture of Castilian and Galician (*Voces nuevas*, no. 48.16).

Chap. 11, n. 28: Moya's version of *Conde Claros y la infanta* continues with *Conde Claros preso.* "Sara Real Majestad" is based on "Sacra Real Magestad"; a similar deformation of the formula (*Sacarrial*) is much used in Spanish American folktales (Pino Saavedra, *Cuentos*, I, 356; Robe, *Los Altos*, p. 578). The supposed "variante criolla recogida en una estancia de nuestro país por Don Ciro Bayo," to which Moya alludes (as usual, without specifying any sort of bibliographical data, much less a page number), is no ballad variant, though it does provide interesting evidence of the persistence of Claros' name, and the memory of his amours with the princess in Argentine oral tradition. The verses read: "Don Claros con la infantita / está bailando en palacio; / él viste terno de seda, / ella falda de brocado. / A cada paso de danza, / va diciendo el conde Claros: / —A la huellita huella, / dame la mano . . ." (Bayo, *Romancerillo*, pp. 43–45). The insistent repetition of variations on this *huellita huella* replaces whatever narrative continuation may once have been associated with this "variante criolla." Bayo then goes on to cite further variations, one of which, as Margit Frenk has shown, is related to a 16th-century *villancico*. Bayo's verses read: "A la huellita huella, / ¡ay! que no puedo, / decirte con palabras / lo que te quiero" (p. 45). The early version, included in Juan Vásquez' *Villancicos i canciones* (Osuna, 1551) and numerous subsequent sources, reads: "¡Ay, que non oso / mirar ni hazer del ojo! / ¡Ay, que no puedo / deziros lo que quiero!" (Frenk, *Corpus*, no. 1656).

Chap. 11, n. 30: The following sources were used in elaborating our synthetic Portuguese text of *Conde Claros y la infanta*: •1: VRP 56. •2: Reis Dámaso, p. 203. •3a: Braga, p. 325; other readings: VRP 51–52. •3b: VRP 50; other readings: Braga, p. 325; VRP 51; Martins, p. 10. •4: VRP 50; *abraçar*: VRP 50; *brigar*: Braga, p. 330; *brincar*: Reis Dámaso, p. 203; other readings: Braga, p. 325; Martins, p. 10. •5: VRP 986; other readings: Braga, p. 330. •6–8: VRP 986. •9: Braga, I, 310; *pagico*: Braga, p. 364; *onzeneiro*: Braga, p. 330; *mexeriqueiro*: Braga, p. 325 et alibi; *paigezinho*: Martins, II, 10. •10–11: Braga, p. 310. •12: VRP 55; other readings: Braga, p. 310; VRP 52, 59; *as terras de Montalvar*: Braga, pp. 326, 338. •13a: VRP 55; Braga, p. 338; *que eu por dote vos darei*: Braga, p. 326. •13b: Braga, pp. 338, 326; *las terras*: Braga. •14: VRP 55. •15–16: Braga, p. 365. •17: Braga, p. 365; other readings: Braga, p. 326. •18: Braga, p. 310; other readings: VRP 52, 54. •19: Reis Dámaso, p. 204. •20a: VRP 54. •20b: Braga, p. 310; VRP 52. •21: VRP 54. •22: Braga, p. 310; VRP 52. •23: Braga, p. 338. •24: Braga, p. 310; VRP 52, 54; Martins, p. 11. •25a: Braga, pp. 326, 331; VRP 52, 54; Martins, p. 11. •25b: Braga, p. 310; *enforcar*: Braga, pp. 310, 331, 365; *degolar*: VRP 55; *matar*: Braga, p. 326; VRP 52, 54; Martins, p. 11.

Chap. 11, n. 32: The following sources were used in elaborating our synthetic Brazilian text of *Conde Claros y la infanta*: •1–2: Romero, p. 95. •3: Brandão, p. 114; other readings: Pereira da Costa, p. 319. •4: Pereira da Costa, p. 319; Vilela, p. 67. •5: Brandão, p. 114. •6: Pereira da Costa, p. 319: *Felizardo*. •7: Brandão, p. 114; Romero, p. 95; other readings: Santos Neves, p. 51. •8: Vilela, p. 67; other readings: Romero, p. 90; Santos Neves, p. 51; Seeger, p. 291; Silva Lima 8.1–7; Silva Lima, "Achegas," p. 60. •9: Romero, p. 90; *qu'eu te darei*: Romero, p. 90; other readings: Pereira da Costa, p. 319; Seeger, p. 291; Silva Lima 8.2, 4, 6 et alibi. •10: Brandão, p. 114; other readings:

Romero, p. 95. •11: *dareite*: Romero, p. 95; *minha sobrinha*: Romero, p. 91; Santos Neves, p. 51; other readings: Brandão, p. 114; Pereira da Costa, p. 319; Seeger, p. 291; *prima*: Silva Lima 8.7. •12: Santos Neves, p. 51. •13: Silva Lima 8.4; other readings: Brandão, p. 114; Pereira da Costa, p. 319; Silva Lima 8.2; Vilela, p. 67. •14: Pereira da Costa, p. 320; other readings: Boiteux, p. 20; Brandão, p. 114; Silva Lima 8.4, 6; Silva Lima, "Achegas," p. 61. •15: Romero, p. 91. •16*a*: Silva Lima 8.4; *Clarasmina*: Silva Lima 8.4; *Clara Aninha*: Boiteux, p. 20. •16*b*: Silva Lima 8.3; *a brincar*: Boiteux, p. 20; Brandão, p. 114; Romero, pp. 91, 95; Santos Neves, p. 51 et alibi; *a conversar*: Seeger, p. 291; *a namorar*: Silva Lima 8.1. •17: Boiteux, p. 20; other readings: Brandão, p. 114; Romero, p. 95; Santos Neves, p. 51; Silva Lima 8.6. •18–19: Silva Lima 8.3; other readings: Pereira da Costa, p. 320; Romero, pp. 91, 95; Silva Lima 8.1, 2, 4, 6; Silva Lima, "Achegas," pp. 59–60, 62. •20–21: Boiteux, p. 20; other readings: Brandão, p. 114; Pereira da Costa, p. 320; Silva Lima 8.1, 2, 6, 7; Silva Lima, "Achegas," p. 61; *degolar*: Brandão, p. 114; Pereira da Costa, p. 320; Romero, pp. 91–92, 95; Seeger, p. 291; Silva Lima 8.4; *a morte te mando dar*: Silva Lima 8.6; *a forca tu vai ganhar*: Silva Lima, "Achegas," pp. 61, 63.

Chap. 11, n. 38: The *capa/brial* verse also occurs in *Conde Sol*: "El conde tiende [tira] / a [su] capa, / la condesa su brillar" (RT, IV, nos. V.158–161, pp. 151–153), but the reading is exceptional. No. 158 is from Vegas de Matute (p.j. Segovia) and 159–161 are all from the same village in Avila: Peguerinos (p.j. Cebreros). It would be easy to consider this verse as extraneous to *Conde Sol*. What is the point of the count throwing down his cape and the countess her gown, when what will immediately follow is the revelation of his departure for at least seven years, and perhaps forever? In *Conde Claros y la infanta*, on the other hand, the verse, as prelude to a love scene, is fully functional and harmonizes with the exquisite allusion to the bed of rose petals or lemon leaves. It seems probable that, in these few *Conde Sol* versions, the verse is a borrowing from *Conde Claros y la infanta*. In *La condesa traidora*, the aged count and his countess rest from their travels "debaxo de un verde pino," where: "La condessa tendió el manto / y el buen conde su mantillo" (Bénichou, p. 145); "El conde tendió su capa, / la condesa su [mantillo]" (MP 85*bis*); "El conde tendió su manto, / la condesa su rocino"(!) (Nahón 37.6). For more on this verse and on the topic of the old man in *Yoná*'s *Pizmônîm* version of *Conde Claros y la infanta*, see *Seis romancerillos*, pp. 17–18.

Chap. 11, n. 39: The form *brial* would seem to have survived intact in the Ibizan texts because, in Catalán, the word has been retained in popular usage, whereas in Castilian it would seem to have been relegated primarily to literary texts, as an archaism: "Ben entès el mot ha acabat per designar una peça del vestit popular de la dona, sobretot en terres valencianes . . .; però això és un resultat secundari de la popularitat que conferí la moda al vestir de les grans dames dels Ss. XIV–XV" (DECLlC, II, 229*a*). Concerning the medieval *brial* and the word's origin, see *DCECH*, s.v.; Menéndez Pidal, *CMC*, II, 513–515. For the medieval *brial*, see Gómez Redondo's informative note (*Jaufre*, p. 176, n. 306). In regard to medieval Portugal, Oliveira Marques observes: "The term *brial* began to disappear around the middle of the fourteenth century and came to be used only in poetic language" (*Daily Life*, p. 77). In Carré's *Diccionario galego-castelán*, *brial* 'sayo o vestidura antigua' is designated as an archaism; see also García and González, *Dicc. da Real Ac. Galega*, s.v. The form *brial(e)*—written in local MSS as *brillal(e)*—occurs in various Moroccan Judeo-Spanish ballads. While, in some cases, the word may still denote some remnant of the original meaning, several of the following examples indicate that, in Morocco, *brial* has become a meaningless fossil: "La garsa, por guareserse, / entróse en mi briale" (alternating with *rosal(es)*) (*El sueño de doña Alda*: FLSJ, III,128, synth. v. 16); "Tocóle mano con mano, / subióle a su briale" (*Por la calle de su dama*: Larrea 21.36–37); "tiróse una sayita, / no la tapa su brillare" (*Melisenda insomne*: Larrea 40.11–12; 41.11–12); "porque, con la sangre, / no se manche el brillale" (*Mujer de Arnaldos*: Nahón 28.20); "Los ojos trae llorosos / y el brillal desarreglado" (CSQ, I, 50.4; Catalán, *Por campos*, pp. 74–76: *brial(e)*). For more on this, see FLSJ, V, Chap. 13.

Chap. 11, n. 40: Various *lectiones faciliores* which replace *escudero* or *pagem* attest to the singers' difficulties with forms that no longer reflect living realities in a 19th- or 20th-century context: "un hombre" (Kundert; CPG; CARG); "onzeneiro" (Braga, I, 330); "mexeriqueiro" (Braga, I, 325). The page could, of course, have been borrowed by *Infanta* from *Fraile* (see n. 32 supra), at least in the Moroccan tradition and in some Castilian and Portuguese versions, but, in such a case, how then would we explain the page's presence in the Eastern Sephardic texts representing a tradition where *Fraile* has never been collected? Concerning the word *paje* and its implications, see n. 25 supra and FLSJ, III, 272–273.

Chap. 11, n. 45: In regard to vv. 1–2 of the version from Rábano de Sanabria (Zamora), the informant was hesitant and indicated that there might have been more to the story than she was able to provide. She could not remember (or preferred not to remember?) the ending of v. 4*b*; it is supplied here, without any assurance that this is in fact the correct reading, from *Voces nuevas*

48.16 (from Candín, p.j. Ponferrada, León). In regard to the defective v. 34, compare text *B*: "a la puerta de los reyes, / allí se fue a pasear" (v. 14). The informant offered the words "a llamar" as an alternative to "a brindar" (v. 45*b*). In 1980, the vocabulary and certain phonological features of the original Leonese dialect were still alive, at least as a substrate to the current Castilian speech, among older residents of the Sanabrian villages. This will explain such forms as *se* 'si' (v. 27), *suelgo* (vv. 17, 19), *veis* (v. 18), *vai* (v. 38) and the archaism *desotro* (v. 8). The form *u* (v. 43) should rank as a widely distributed vulgarism (Bénichou, "Observaciones," p. 256*c*). On *se*, see Díaz Castañón, *Cabo de Peñas*, p. 245; Rodríguez-Castellano, *Aspectos del Bable Occidental*, p. 251; for *suelgo*, Maldonado de Guevara, *La Ribera*, p. 142; for the forms of *(d)ir*, Maldonado, p. 146; Zamora Vicente, *Dialectología*, p. 196. *Essotro* figures, for example, in *La Celestina* (ed. D. S. Severin, pp. 231, 271 [auctos IX and XII]); in Quevedo ("Cerrar podrá mis ojos la postrera"; ed. Crosby, no. 78); and in countless other early texts.

Chap. 11, n. 49: Concerning the danger of basing sweeping conclusions—Wm. J. Entwistle's, in this case—on a limited corpus, see Catalán and Galmés, "El tema de la boda estorbada," especially pp. 74–75, 77–78, 80, et alibi. Entwistle's work is admirable and his vast knowledge of Pan-European balladry sometimes made possible crucial discoveries (see, for example, *En torno*, pp. 50–60), but his faith in the definitive character of the printed or handwritten word—which has inspired a generation of neo-individualist scholars—can and has, in some instances, led to a distorted vision of the basic nature of both epic and ballad and their genetic relationship. For more on limited bibliographical repertoires, see Armistead, "Neo-Individualism and the *Romancero*," particularly p. 181.

Chap. 11, n. 53: The sad record of early modern and modern penology still brings us reports of punishments strikingly similar to those visited upon the *infanta* in *C. Claros fraile*, that were in effect on Norfolk Island (Australia) during the late 19th century: "There was also . . . a water pit below the ground where prisoners would be locked, alone, naked, and unable to sleep for fear of drowning, for forty-eight hours at a spell" (Hughes, *The Fatal Shore*, p. 115). For all their barbarity and seeming exaggerations, the descriptions of medieval punishments in literature may well have been closer to contemporary reality than we moderns might wish to suspect at first glance. Note also that, in the Bosnian epic of *The Captivity of Djulic' Ibrahim*, the protagonist is thrown into an icy dungeon of horrors, filled with snakes and scorpions, where "the reeds grew waist high and there was water to our knees" (SCHS, I, 92). These lines were written well before the enormities of Abu Ghraib and Guantánamo brought us new evidence of human—and, to our disgrace, specifically American—barbarism.

Chap. 11, n. 54: Alternative readings concerning the identity of the *infanta*'s visitors during her imprisonment specify: "amigas" (Díaz Viana, *Rev. de Folklore*); "muchachas de su tiempo" (Munthe 3; RGL 19.29); "amigas de su pueblo" (RGL 19.30). See also our texts *E* and *F* above, where "tres primos carnales" or "primos y tíos carnales," as well as the *infanta*'s brother, *Rondanes* or *Rondale(s)*, all visit her. Here, of course, we have *Roldán*—complete with paragogic *-e* (*Rondale* in CPE, I, 32–33; *Rondales* in Gutiérrez Macías, p. 345*a*; *Rondanes* in García Matos-Crivillé, no. 13*B*). The Carolingian reference is undoubtedly coincidental, rather than somehow reflecting a survival of the ballad's already superficial Carolingian patina in the 16th-century text. Note how Gaiferos has become *don Roldán, don Ruindá, Ruidán*, in Canarian versions of *La infancia de Gaiferos* (FM 4, 5, 74, 75, 230, 336). A distantly similar verse about noble visitors going to see a lady in distress occurs in the Catalán *Testament d'Amèlia*: "Comtes la van a veure, / comtes i noble gent" (OCPC, II, 167; AFC 2998); "Ya la van a veure, comtes, / comtes y barons y reys" (Milá 220).

Chap. 11, n. 56: Note also the bird messenger in *El prisionero*: "Mas quién ahora me diese / un pájaro hablador, // siquiera fuese calandria, / o tordico o ruiseñor: // criado fuese entre damas / y avezado a la razón, // que me lleve una embajada / a mi esposa Leonor" (*Primav*. 114*a*). Note also Melibea's song: "Papagayos, ruyseñores, / que cantáys al alborada, / llevad nueva a mis amores, / cómo espero aquí assentada" (*Celestina*, ed. Severin, p. 322, auto XIX; Frenk, *Corpus*, nos. 570–571). In Canarian and Azorian texts, *pajecito/pagem* seems to have led, not to a bird, but to a shepherd as messenger: *pastorcito* (FM 237); *pastorinho* (Purcell, *Ilhas*, no. 8.8). But note also how pages become birds in a Canarian version of *Delgadina*: "¡Ocurran, los pajarcillos, / y tránquenla en una sala!" (FM 258). For the nightingale as messenger, see now two 15th-century Catalan and French songs and also, of course, the famous later song, *Lo rossinyol* (Romeu i Figueras, *Corpus*, no. 101; Capmany, *Cançoner*, no. xxxix: Me levay un domatin / matinet denant l'alba; M'y levay par ung matin, / plus matin que ne souloye; Rossinyol, que vás á França, rossinyol, / encomanam á la mare, rossinyol).

Chap. 11, n. 60: Concerning the Brazilian readings *cachorro* and *demônio*, note Seeger's perceptive observations: "In the single text, from Maranhão, in which the messenger is a dog, he is probably the Devil himself, who, in popular speech is frequently called *O Cão* (The Dog) to avoid summoning him accidentally by mentioning his name" (*Count Claros*, p. 95). Seeger suggests that the demon may have originated in the Bahian *candomblé* tradition. That the Devil may appear when mentioned is recalled in the Spanish proverb: *En nombrando el ruín de Roma, luego asoma* (Campos-Barella, no. 2669), though today its original implications apparently have been lost. In English, the saying's meaning remains clear: *Speak of the Devil and he appears* (Flores, pp. 111). Compare Thompson: C12.5. *Devil's name used in curse. Appears*; G303.6.1.2. *Devil comes when called upon.* Note also Röhrich's comments (*Lexikon*, IV, 1066*b*). The Devil's name is taboo all over Europe, giving rise to a plethora of apotropaic circumlocutions (such as, indeed, *el ruín de Roma*): *Old Nick, the Old Gentleman, Old Scratch, Auld Clootie*, the *Auld Chield, el Patas, el Rabudo, el Quemado, el Colorado, el Mandinga, hŏstis antīquus* (> *estantigua*), etc. (Opie and Tatum, pp. 118–119; A. Jones, p. 140*a*; Erich and Beitl, p. 751; Kany, pp. 1–4). The Scots designation of the Devil as *Auld Clootie* refers to his cloven hoof: *cloot* 'a division of the hoof of cattle, sheep, pigs, etc.; the hoof, foot; *in pl.* the devil.' The Devil was very much present in everyday popular belief: *Clootie's craft* 'the devil's croft' or 'the goodman's field' was "a small portion of land set apart for the devil and left untilled" (Warrack, p. 103*b*). For a comprehensive overview and bibliography of evil spirits with anomalous feet, see Pedrosa et al., *Héroes, santos, moros y brujas*, p. 32, n. 2. One immediately calls to mind, of course, Luis Vélez de Guevara's *El Diablo Cojuelo.* Similar taboos hold for the names of certain dangerous or destructive animals: e.g., bears and wolves (HDA, I, 881–882; IX, 716–717: s.vv. *Bär, Wolf*). So, in Russian, Serbo-Croatian, and Bulgarian (dialects), the bear is *medved', mèdvjed, medved* 'the one who eats (knows about or sees) the honey' (*mëd*) (Skok, II, 398; Georgiev, III, 710), while in the northwest of the Iberian Peninsula, he is sometimes known as *García*, to avoid an unwanted appearance (as remembered from some long-ago reading I am now unable to specify). One cannot but wonder if the use of this particular name may not somehow echo a distant memory, surviving in oral tradition, of a Pre-Roman (Celtic) etymon, as in Gaulish *artos*, Middle Irish *art*, Welsh *arth* 'bear' (compare Gk. *'árktos*) (Pokorny, p. 875; Boissacq, pp. 78–79; Walde, p. 861). For more on linguistic taboos and euphemisms, see Bloomfield, pp. 155–156, 396, 400–402, 507–508; Iordan-Orr, pp. 305–306 & n. 1; Iordan-Alvar, pp. 549–550 & nn. 53–54; Jespersen, pp. 255–259; Sturtevant, pp. 124–126; Kany; E. Montero. In Spain, we are, of course, well aware of the need—still very much alive even today—of exclaiming *¡Lagarto, lagarto!*, so as to counteract the bad luck brought on by hearing, or uttering, the word *culebra*, to avoid which it is also sometimes customary to use the euphemistic expression *nombrar la bicha* (Sánchez Pérez, pp. 97–98; Costa-Roldán, pp. 65–166; especially: E. Montero, pp. 159–161). For enigmatic and richly variegated linguistic taboos surrounding the weasel (Sp. *comadreja*, Port. *doninha*), see Menéndez Pidal, *Orígenes*, 3rd ed., pp. 396–405; Kany, p. 8; E. Montero, pp. 153–162. Alfonso el Sabio was already cognizant of such a taboo. The Virgin Mary, by a great miracle (un miregre grande), saves from death his beloved pet weasel: "h̄ua bestiola . . . a que chaman donezÿa [= donezinha] os galegos" (*Cantigas*, ed. Mettmann, III, no. 354.10–12). Concerning wolves and foxes, see DCECH, IV, s.v. *raposa*, pp. 783–784; Kany, p. 8; E. Montero, pp. 150–153. Such taboos are clearly of very ancient origin. Pokorny comments on certain derivatives of I.E. *ulkuos* and *ulp-*: "Es handelt sich zweifellos um verschiedene tabuistische Umbildungen" (I, 1178–1179). One would further suspect that Latin *fūro, furonis, furonem*, cited by St. Isidore, which equates ferrets with thieves (Sp. *hurón*) may also reflect another such taboo (Blaise, 369*b*); but concerning St. Isidore's citation, see DECLIC, IV, s.vv. *fura* or *furó*, p. 234*a*, lines 17–22. The Judeo-Spanish proverb, *El lovo y la oveja, todos dos una negra conseja*, nonsensical in its present form, must mask an earlier fossilized *vulpeja* 'fox' (later replaced by *oveja*), reflecting, even in a primarily urban society, popular fear and disdain for predatory animals (Saporta, *Refranero*, pp. 180–181).

Chap. 11, n. 61: Concerning swift journeys in the *Romancero*, see RoH, I, 272; Webber, *Formulistic Diction*, pp. 208–209; *Tres calas*, p. 35, n. 33; *Epic Ballads*, pp. 50–51, n. 18. About the *camino/jaral* formula we will have more to say in our study of *Gaiferos y Melisenda* (in FLSJ, Vol. V, Chap. 12). For now, see our article, "*Gaiferos y Waltharius*: Paralelismos adicionales." Note also how, in *Thidrek's Saga*, King Thidrek, traveling secretly to Amlungland, to regain his kingdom or die, makes his way through the Luruforest: ". . . and they spent the day in the forest and traveled by night" (trans. Haymes, p. 242 [Chap. 398]). In Catalonia, the page's ride is dramatized in that the horse makes the earth shake and strikes sparks from the stones: "Venta esperons al caball, / que la terra tremolava; // can passava pels carrers, / les pedres ne foguejaven. // El camí, llarch de tres dies, / l'ha fet en una jornada" (Aguiló, pp. 321–322). For similar verses in other Catalan ballads, see *Yoná*, p. 85, n. 10. In some Castilian and Leonese versions, the page's arrival is further dramatized by means of his seven ritual circumambulations of the *palacio*, before finding Don Carlos: "Siete vueltas dio al palacio, / sin saber por donde entrar; // al cabo' las siete vueltas, / a don Carlos vio pasar" (*Voces*, 48.8, 48.4; ART, p. 221 [= text *A* above]). Concerning this formula, see, especially,

Devoto, "Entre las siete y las ocho"; *En torno*, pp. 105–109; *Epic Ballads*, p. 263, n. 59; S. Thompson: D1791. *Magic power of circumambulation.*

Chap. 11, n. 65: For Count Claros' apparent insouciance concerning the princess' impending execution, compare also the Canarian reading: "Po' esas nuevas y otras nuevas, / no dejaré de almorzar" (FM 80). The count's shrugging off the girl's execution is then sometimes followed by (or alternates with) his flippant suggestion of different possibilities (probably patterned again on the *infanta*'s instructions to the page: "If you find him sleeping . . ., if you find him eating . . .," etc.): "Si me lo dices de broma, / vámonos a merendar, // y si lo dices de veras, / vámonos a caminar" (ART, p. 221 [= text *A* above]); "Si lo dijeras de burla, / mandárate prisionar; // si lo dijeras de veras, / yo te diera de almorzar" (CVR 7). There are similar verses in Galicia (CPG, III, no. 44*a*) and in many Canarian texts.

Chap. 11, n. 67: For other Portuguese readings, see, for example, Costa Fontes, *Tr.-os-Montes*, nos. 710, 715, 773, 776; Galhoz 23, 28, 30; Martins, I, 195; Tavares, no. 60; Thomaz Pires, *Lendas*, p. 44; from the Azores: Braga, *Cantos*, p. 247; Purcell, *Ilhas*, nos. 8.8, 8.15; for Brazil: Pereira da Costa, p. 318; Romero, p. 99; Seeger, *Study*, pp. 290, 292; Silva Lima, *Folclore*, nos. 9.1, 2, 4, 9; Vilela, nos. 2.1–4; from Catalonia: Milá 258, 258*B*, 258*F*. In a Galician version, it is the page, rather than Claros, who bursts into tears (CARG 18*d*). In addition to (or instead of) weeping, Claros sometimes faints, as in Tenerife (FM 8), Trás-os-Montes (VRP 65), and Catalonia (Aguiló, p. 322; Milá 258*B*), or grows pale (Aguiló; Milá 258). In one Tenerife version, he reverently kisses the letter: "Cogió la carta y la lee, / la besó y la guardará" (FM 234). In one of Silva Lima's Brazilian versions (9.9, vv. 25–32), there is an attempt to reconcile the conflicting readings. For the motif of shedding tears of blood from extreme grief, as in the Catalan version (Avenç), compare: "Al baixant de l'escala, / de sos ulls plorava sanc" (*Guardadora de un muerto*: Catalán, *Por campos*, p. 203); "Esto oyó Blancaniña, / lágrimas de sangre ya echaría" (*Vuelta del marido* [polyassonant]: Molho, *Literatura*, p. 81); "Lágrimas de sangue vivo / andava en sempre a chorar" (*Loa* from Trás-os-Montes: Martin, I, 162); "The teares he for his master wept / were blend water and bloud" (*Old Robin of Portingale*: Child 80.8); "Pă mine m-or plînge / cu lăcrami de sînge" ('[The sheep] will weep tears of blood for me' [Fochi, *Miorița*, p. 778]). In the Serbian ballad, *Marko Kraljević Recognizes his Father's Sword*, the enraged hero sheds tears of blood (Low, p. 73, v. 127; Vuk, no. 56, p. 217). In the *Nibelungenlied*, Kriemhilde weeps tears of blood over the body of Siegfried: "diu ir vil liehten ougen / vor leide wéinéten ten bluot" (ed. Bartsch, v. 1069*d*). See also the *villancico*: "Los ojos de la niña / lloran sangre; / aora venirá / quien los acalle" (Frenk, *Corpus*, no. 437). Note also the learned song, "Lágrimas de sangre lloro / encarcelado en cadenas" (*Silva* [1550], ed. Rodríguez-Moñino, p. 407). Foreseeing the fall of Granada and the destruction of Muslim Spain, the Hispano-Arabic poet, al-Bastī (from Baza) gives voice to the intensity of his emotions: "The eyes that used to shed only tears / will soon be shedding blood" (Mustapha Kamal, "Al-Bastī, the Last Arab Poet of al-Andalus"), See S. G. Armistead, "Arabic, Hebrew, & Spanish Literature," *La Corónica*, 32:1 (Fall 2003). For further references, see the Thompson motif: F1041.21.1.1. *Tears of blood from excessive grief*. The intensity of the hero's emotions is further stressed in the Canarian tradition by adding a curious invocation and rejection of Satan (which further supposes that Claros' priestly disguise will imply a permanent avocation): "Se metió para su cuarto, / donde él solía estar, // llamando por el enemigo, / llamando por Satanás. // Satanás, como no duerme, / pronto a su llamada está. // —¡Anda allá, perro maldito, / no me vengas a tentar, // que la ropa que me pongo / no me la vuelvo a quitar!" (FM 79; 8–9, 235; Trapero, no. 13). For the Devil's sleeplessness, compare the proverbs: *El diablo no duerme*; *El diablo no duerme, pero se hace el dormido cuando le conviene*; *El diablo no duerme, y todo lo añasca*; *El diablo es el que no se cansa* (Martínez Kleiser, p. 194*b*, nos. 17.600–603); *O diabo não tem sono* (Chaves, *Rifoneiro*, p. 147, no. 497); also *Poema de Fernán González*: ". . . Non es *tal* vyda sy non pora pecados / que andan noche e día e nunca son cansados" (ed. Zamora Vicente, vv. 334*b-c*) and the sensationalistic late-16th-century ballad, *La fratricida por amor* (El cielo estaua nublado, / la luna no parecia): "mirad los enrredos que haze / satanas que no dormia // al que halla muy vicioso / presto le da çancadilla" (Sutherland, *OT*, 8:2 [1993], 317, vv. 77–80; also p. 293). Ruy González de Clavijo, witnessing the frantic, unflagging efforts of Tamerlane's architects, striving to transform the city of Samarkand, undoubtedly recalls this same belief: "E los unos a derrocar casas, e otros a llanar el suelo, e otros a fazer, fazían atan grand ruido, así de día como de noche, que parecían diablos" (ed. López Estrada, p. 306). The same concept applies to the tireless urgency with which the Mongol conqueror's indefatigable horsemen covered seemingly incredible distances: "E en verdat no es de creer sino a quien lo viese lo que estos malditos andan de día e de noche" (p. 224). Note also the Thompson motif: F564.1. *Person of diabolical origin never sleeps*.

Chap. 11, n. 72: Concerning Arnaldos' (and Niño's) magic singing, which usually produces positive results, see *Yoná*, pp. 352–365, where we also take up the motif in numerous other ballads. See also Rogers, *Perilous Hunt*, pp. 109–134, and the Thompson motif: D1275.1. *Magic music*. In Morocco, Conde Niño's song can also be adverse (mujeres que están en cinta, / de suyo habrán de abortar [Larrea 64]) and, in a still unedited version of *El Mostadí*, the song is said to produce disastrous results (CMP J1.34). In Moroccan and Portuguese forms of *El caballero burlado*, the girl, claiming to be leprous, convinces the knight that she will blight any grass she steps on. See Nahón, pp. 162–164. In the Serbian ballad, *Marko Kraljević and Djemo the Mountaineer*, the Christian lords warn Djemo not to hang Marko, lest wine or wheat no longer be brought forth (Low, p. 135, v. 100; Vuk, no. 67, p. 259). In another Serbian ballad, *Vidičudo pre neviđeno* (*Look at the Marvel Never Seen Before*), the green forest withers wherever a girl, who has attempted to seduce her traveling companion, passes by (Brkić, pp. 139–140; Gesemann, no. 150, p. 227). See also Archer Taylor's note on "Attila and Modern Riddles," concerning the proverb: *Where the Turk's (Attila's) horse has trod, grass never grows.*

Chap. 11, n. 73: For the presence, in Portuguese versions of *Gaiferos* and *Don García*, of the verse about the horse's girth and breast strap, see, for example, Braga, I, 218; VRP 625; for more on this verse and its origin, *Yoná*, pp. 179–181. In Braga, I, 313, the verse is followed by a reminiscence of *Conde Claros insomne*: "Alarga-lhe a contracilha, / estreita-lhe o atafal; // vinte e cinco campainhas / todas a um peitoral." Compare *Media noche*: "con trezientos cascaueles / alrededor del petral" (*Pliegos de Praga*, I, 33–39; or v. 16 of our ed., Chap. 10 above). While we are concerned with contaminations from *Conde Claros insomne*, note Vilela's Brazilian text of *Fraile*, where Claros rides to the rescue with "vinte e cinco cavalheiros, / para com ele viajar" (no. 2.1). Compare *A missa va el emperador*: "con doze moços despuelas / para le acompañar" (v. 78 of our ed., Chap. 10, above). Brazilian versions of *Fraile* have also been influenced by *Insomne*, in that, after receiving the letter (hardly the moment to sleep!), the protagonist: "Dava pinotes na cama / como a baleia no mar" (Lopes, p. 153; Silva Lima 9.6, 14; Vilela 2.3 and other texts). See our Moroccan synthetic text, Chap. 10, v. 33+. Concerning Port. *atafal* 'cincha', see Corriente, *Arabismos*, pp. 235–236.

Chap. 11, n. 76: The motif of reversing the horse's shoes is famous in traditional narrative: "He has shod them a' their horse, / He's shod them siccer and honestly, / And he as turned the cawkers backwards oer, / Where foremost they were wont to be" (*Archie o Cawfield*: Child 188A.9, B.7). *Cawker* is a variant of *calker*, which is the same as *calkin* 'the turned-down ends of a horse-shoe which raise the horse's heels from the ground; also a turned edge under the front of the shoe' (*OED*); *cauker* 'the hind-part of a horseshoe sharpened and turned down' (Warrack, s.v.). The same device is used in *Jock o the Side* (Child 187*B*.8) and in the Scandinavian *Frederik den anden i Ditmarsken* (TSB D436; Heggstad and Grüner Nielsen, *Utsyn*, no. 195). The motif also occurs in Slavic ballads: *Der Ehemann befreit seine entführte Frau*; *Geschwister entfliehen aus der Gefangenschaft*; *Krali Marko* (Kumer, *Tipi . . . slovenskih . . . pesmi*, nos. 221.1*A*, 224*A*). Compare also the classical legend of the infant Hermes, who stole Apollo's cattle and, "lest he should be detected by the tracks, . . . put shoes on their feet" (Apollodorus, *The Library*, III.x.2, ed. Frazer, II, 6–9). Clearly some sort of reversal of the shoes is intended (De Vries, *Heldenlied*, p. 300; Id., *Heroic Song*, p. 225), but in Hesiod's *Great Eoiae*, Hermes rather fastens "to the tail of each one brushwood to wipe out the footmarks of the cows" (ed. Evelyn-White, pp. 264–265). According to St. Isidore, lions, said to be friendly by nature(!), "when they walk about, . . . obliterate their tracks with their tails that the hunter may not find them" (*Etymologies*, Chap. II; trans. Brehaut, p. 224). In the prosified account of *Maynete* (*Enfances de Charlemagne*) absorbed by one MS in the *Primera Crónica General*, the young hero covers his tracks when escaping from Toledo by reversing the shoes of his mounts: "E entre tanto Morante . . . que ferrase las bestias aviesas, porque sy algunos fuesen en pos dellos e fallasen el rastro, que toviesen que era de torno" (Gómez Pérez, "Leyendas medievales," p. 129). For additional analogues in medieval and modern traditional narratives, see Child's characteristically learned and far ranging references (III, 476, n. [3]) and Thompson: K534.1. *Escape by reversing horse's (ox's) shoes.* For numerous additional examples of the reversed horseshoes, see also Pedrosa et al., *Héroes, santos, moros y brujas*, pp. 87–88, 154, n. 2, 162, 201.

Chap. 11, n. 77: The term *fraile* is used in Morocco and in many Castilian and Canarian versions (our texts *AB* above; FM 6, 7, 234, etc.); other readings (not an exhaustive list): *capillán* (our text *C* above); *padre cura* (text *E*); *obispo* (text *F*); *monje* (Alvar, no. 175*a*); *abad* (CVR 6); *religioso* (FM 79, 235); *cura* (FM 80); *buen religioso* (CPG, III, no. 44*a*); *cardenal* (CARG 17*a*; CPG, III, no. 44*b*); *padre* (VRP 76; Costa Fontes, *S. Jorge*, no. 3; Purcell, *Ilhas*, nos. 8.8, 15–17; Seeger, pp. 290, 292; Vilela, no. 2.1); *frade* (Braga, *Cantos*, p. 248; Cortes-Rodrigues, no. 4; Purcell, *Ilhas*, nos. 8.2, 3; R. de Azevedo, p. 157; Lopes, p. 159); *clérigo* (Braga, *Cantos*, p. 245); *sacerdote* (Purcell 8.7); *frare* (AFC 3263; Aguiló, p. 324; Ginart, IV, 418). In certain texts, the specific allusion to the priest disguise is lacking (for example, FM 5, 9, 78; CPG, III, 44*c*; Ferrer-Sanjuán, p. 167).

Chap. 11, n. 78: CVR 7, however, agrees with *A caza* in this detail and various other versions also allude to Claros' visiting a monastery along the way (*Voces*, no. 48.3; VRP 55; Milá 258; AFC 3263; Avenç, III, 36; Briz, IV, 43). On the importance of disguises in balladry, see again *Yoná*, p. 279, n. 6; CMP, III, 305–306. Add the following extra-Hispanic instances: pilgrim's disguise: *Gjord Borggreve*; *Esbern og Sidsel* (DgF 248, 250; TSB D194, D195); *Der edle Moringer* (Meier, *Balladen*, I, no. 8); monk's disguise: *Der Ehemann befreit seine entführte Frau* (Kumer, *Tipi . . . slovenskih . . . pesmi*, no. 221.2A); minstrel disguise: *Omeri der Sohn des Muji* (Lambertz, *Volksepik der Albaner*, pp. 26–27); in the Bosnia epic of *Mujo and Captain Dojčić*, Mujo disguises himself as a *guslar* (SCHS, I, 148). Multiple disguises are crucially important in Bosnian and Albanian epics. See, for example, *Bihać*, pp. 479, 686–687, 689, 692, 693, 697, 713, 742, etc.; Kolsti, pp. 280, 338.. See also Child's (V, 477*a*) and Leader's (p. 355*b*) references; S. Thompson: K1826. *Disguise as churchman (cleric)*; and innumerable other instances that could be cited. Some obvious Hispanic examples of the pilgrim disguise are *El conde Sol*, *La mujer del pastor* (RT, IX, 235, no. II.19, v. 5), and Eastern Sephardic forms of *Bernal Francés*, where the disguised husband becomes "el pelegrino" (*Bosnia* B9; CMP M9). Note also how, in the chronicle prosification of the *Poema de Fernán González*, Doña Sancha arranges to free the Count, who is imprisoned in León, by pretending to be on a pilgrimage to Santiago: ". . . et fuesse ella pora Leon con dos cavalleros et non más, et su esportiella al cuello et su bordon en la mano como romera. Et fizolo saber al rey de como yua en romeria a Sant Yague" (Menéndez Pidal, *Reliquias*, p. 155.5–6; PCG, II, 420*b*.30–34).

Chap. 11, n. 81: On de-Christianization, see *En torno*, pp. 127–148. Note that the word *misal* is also de-Christianized in many texts (*nisar, anisar, lissal, a rezar*, etc.; variants to vv. 57, 59). Though the Jewish ambiance in which the Moroccan versions developed undoubtedly played a role in replacing the confession with the *infanta*'s oath, it is worth noting that in some Portuguese and Brazilian texts—thoroughly Christian, it is to be presumed—in addition to confessing, the princess swears, in a formula essentially identical to that used in Morocco, her fidelity to Carlos de Montealbar: "Eu fiz trinta juramentos / lá nas folhas do missal, // onde Carlos poz a boca, / outro não ha de beijar" (Athaide, pp. 72–73); "Tenho feito juramento, / na folhinha do missal, // bocca que beijou o conde / frade não hade beijar" (Braga, I, 370); "Foi juramento que fiz, / aos santinhos do altar, // ond'o duque pô'los beiços, / oitre não lh'há-d'embarrar" (VRP 70). In Brazil, just as in Morocco, the "senhor padre" actually asks her to swear: "Jura aqui, minha menina, / neste libro de rezar, // se o firme amor que tu tens / só é a Carlos de Montavar" (Vilela, no. 2.2). The confession and its equivocal character—the girl does not know the identity of her confessor—can be connected to several other ballad narratives. There is the late, seemingly semi-learned *Doncella que se confiesa con su galán* (RPM 329–330; Díaz Viana-Díaz-Delfín, *Catálogo*, II, 157–158, represents a rather different, enumerative form), which has apparently achieved a certain traditionality in Castile, and, in Catalonia, *Lo confès fingit* (AFC 2956; Avenç, II, 37–40; Briz, II, 153–154; Llorens de Serra, no. 64). *Lo frare blanch y la donzella* (Bertran y Bros, pp. 179–180; Llorens de Serra, no. 22; Serra i Vilaró, p. 59) is not really the same thing: The priest simply uses the confession to attempt—unsuccessfully—to seduce the girl. In another Catalan ballad, *El frare*, the priest is successful: "Frare de Sant Francisco / del més polítics que hi ha. // Per confessar una monja, / set hores hi va estar. // Ja hi va l'abadessa, / prou confessada está. // El mal que en té la monja, / als nou mesos curará" (Amades, *Cançons populars amoroses*, pp. 76–77). The Italian *Amante confessore* (Nigra 97) can be compared to *Lo confès fingit*, in that the lover is disguised as a "padre capüssin," but here the girl is not deceived and recognizes him as her "prim amur" (more bibliography: *Yoná*, p. 83, n. 7; and here in n. 138 infra). In the English *Queen Eleanor's Confession*, the queen confesses her adultery and other sins to King Henry and to her lover, Earl Martial, both disguised as "two fryars of France" (Child 156). Child (III, 258) discusses a number of tale parallels, including Boccaccio's *Decameron* VII.5 (useful notes in Branca's ed., p. 1374, and in Lee, *Sources*, pp. 190–203). Note the Thompson motifs: J1141. *Confession obtained by a ruse*; J1545.2. *Four men's mistress: A husband disguises as a priest to hear his wife's confession*; K1528. *Wife confesses to disguised husband*. The ballad of *El fraile fingido*, in two parts, edited by Durán (nos. 1357–1358) from a late *pliego suelto* does not reflect the same motif (Aguilar Piñal, *El romancero popular del siglo XVIII*, nos. 697–699; A. Lenz, *RHi*, 40 [1917], 256–259).

Inasmuch as *Conde Claros fraile* and the above-mentioned analogues involve deception (of the beloved), they bring to mind another rather different motif: the equivocal oath. The most famous example is Yseut's deceptive oath (Béroul, *Le Roman de Tristan*, ed. Muret, vv. 4205–4209; also ed. Ewert, I, 125–126; II, 251-252), but the motif is widely distributed. See Thompson: K1513. *The wife's equivocal oath*; M105. *Equivocal oaths*. As is well known, *Lazarillo de Tormes* ends with a splendidly equivocal oath, sworn by Lázaro in regard to the (dubious) virtue of his new wife, who continues, at the same time, to be the mistress of the *Arcipreste* of San Salvador: "Que yo juraré sobre la hostia consagrada que es tan buena mujer como vive dentro de las puertas de Toledo" (Tratado VII; ed. Ricapito, pp. 203–204; see Deyermond's very apposite comments on the *Lazarillo*'s many ambiguities). Concerning de-Christianization, see now also my article, "The Memory of Tri-Religious Spain," pp. 273–279.

Chap. 11, n. 83: For more examples of the order to stop and the conversation with the authorities, see CPE, I, 33; II, 18; Gutiérrez Macías, p. 345a; Kundert G4; Ledesma, p. 182b; Munthe 3; Pérez de Castro, p. 478; *Voces* 48.1, 3–5 etc.; FM 5, 6, 9, 78, 79 etc.; CPG, III, no. 44b; VRP 52, 54–58, 60–61, 63, etc.; Costa Fontes, *Califórnia*, no. 1; Id., *S. Jorge*, no. 4; Purcell, *Ilhas*, nos. 8.7–8, 11, 13–15, 17; Ferré, *Madeira*, 40, 43, 45–47, 50–51 etc.; Lopes, *Presença*, pp. 154, 156, 159, 162; Silva Lima 9.3–4, 11-13; Vilela 2.1-4. Since, in the Catalan version, Claros speaks to the king, the order to halt the procession and the conversation with the authorities is lacking in the versions we have seen.

As a rule, the princess is to be burned at the stake, but sometimes, in the Canaries, Portugal, and Brazil, she is to be hanged (for instance, FM 5–7; Delgado, *Subsídio*, II, 161; Lopes, p. 161; Seeger, p. 292) or beheaded (Galhoz 30: *degolar*); also in FM 257, "la llevan a degollar" (v. 36). The "Law of Scotland" is, of course, a commonplace, in the sentimental novel. See Matulka, *The Novels of Juan de Flores*, pp. 55–71, 190–193, and also the useful note in *Amadís de Gaula*, ed. Cacho Blecua, I, 243, n. 31 (Chap. 1). For more on burning at the stake in ballads, see *Yoná*, pp. 207–209 and nn. 8–10; CMP, III, 320; S. Thompson: Q414.0.3. *Burning as punishment for incest (incontinence)*; Q414. *Punishment: burning alive.*

Chap. 11, n. 89: For additional instances of burning dogs, see ART, p. 221; CVR 6; Díaz et al., *Catálogo*, I, 166; Díaz Viana, *Rev. de Folklore*; Munthe 3; RGL 19.20, 24, 26; RPM 58; burning the clothes: *Voces nuevas*, 48.13, 15. One of Seegers's Brazilian texts ends like a folktale: "A fogueira estava feita para ela. O pai dela—pã—caiu dentro da fogueira, morreu queimado. E ele casou com ela; estão vivendo até hoje" (p. 290). So also in Campos Tourinho's version: "A moça subiu na carruagem do padre e foi viver mais êle. Os parentes caiu tudo dentro do fogo e morreu queimado" (Calasans et al., *Bahia-Recôncavo*, p. 133). That the evil father should break his neck on returning to his palace (as in Silva Lima 9.9) recalls—doubtless coincidentally—the similar fate of the evil queen who persecutes the Jews in *La expulsión de los judíos de Portugal*: She is transformed into a goat, falls to pieces, or drops dead as she attempts to enter the palace of the King of Castile, whom she has just married: "La bašada de la bestia, / a pedasos se cairía. // La subida de la escalera, / mala toze le daría. // Eso todo se le haze / el que mal quiere los žudiós" (Armistead and Silverman, "Un aspecto desatendido, p. 189; CMP C13). In one Portuguese version of *Conde Claros fraile*, the father is threatened with burning if he appears on Claros' land: "Se o seu pai apar'cer na terra, / eu o mandarei queimar" (VRP 80).

Chap. 11, n. 91: See, for example, Voretzsch, *Altfranzösisches Lesebuch*, p. 3 (no. 1*c*.5: 10th-cent. German-Latin gloss); Delbouille, "Problèmes d'attribution," p. 68 (*Aïol et Mirabel*, ed. Foerster, vv. 9642 ff.); Roudil, *Les Fueros d'Alcaraz et d'Alarcón*, I, 243 (nos. 82 and 286); Id., *El Fuero de Baeza*, p. 115 (no. 305); Cummins, *The Hound and the Hawk*, p. 184; Francisco López de Gómara, *Historia de las Indias*, ed. BAAEE, XXII, 220*b*.21-30; Brandes, *Metaphors*, pp. 173–174; and, of course, also Chaucer's *Miller's Tale*. This particular ending of *Conde Claros fraile* may perhaps have had its origin in a folktale. In a cumulative tale from the province of Madrid, which ends with a burro (which drinks the water, which quenched the fire, etc.), then concludes with this formula: "Alzale el rabo y bésale el culo" (Fraile Gil, *Cuentos de la tradición oral madrileña*, p. 214).

Chap. 11, n. 96: In *Conde Sol*, the *amores primeros* verse is sometimes introduced by the formula: "Siempre lo he oído decir / y ahora veo que es verdad . . ." (*Cómo vive*, p. 242), thus confirming its proverbial nature. See Catalán, *Poema de Alfonso XI*, pp. 100–101; Yoná, p. 232, nn. 9 and 10; Benardete, pp. 100–101. There are, in effect, numerous paremiological parallels. Gonzalo Correas, working in the late 1500s and early 1600s, records: *El amor primero xamás se olvida, pepita le keda por toda la vida* (ed. Combet, p. 86*a*; ed. Mir, pp. 46*a-b*). Compare also: *Amor primero, el único verdadero*; *Amor primero, nunca olvidado, pero no postrero* (Rodríguez Marín, *Los 6.666 refranes*, p. 22*b*); *Amores, los primeros los mejores* (Id., *Todavía 10.700 refranes*, p. 29*a*); *Sopa y amores, los primeros, los mejores* (Sintes, *Dicc. de aforismos*, p. 66, with various analogues in other European languages).

A further intrusion of *Conde Sol* occurs in one of the Leonese versions of *Fraile*. After the messenger travels eight leagues toward Don Carlos' *palacio*: "de las siete pa las ocho, / una torre vio asomar. // —Si aquella torre es de moros, / allí me cautivarán; // y si es de cristianos, / allí darán vino y pan.— // Siete vueltas dio al palacio, / por ver si podía entrar // . . ." (RGL 19.27). The text thus uses verses from *El conde Sol* to create suspense by delaying the action and to amplify the motif of the magical numbers seven and eight which announce a threshold of renewed activity (see Devoto's article and *En torno*, pp. 105–109). For these verses in *El conde Sol*, see Menéndez Pidal et al., *Cómo vive un romance*, p. 226 (and map no. 6); RT, IV, 54–55 (nos. V.41-42 et alibi).

Like the *amores primeros* verse that concludes *Conde Sol*, there are also plenty of spirited *desenlaces* in Anglo-Scottish ballads, as the protagonists savor their having escaped once and for all against seemingly insurmountable odds. A personal favorite is: "They sought her baith by bower and ha', / the ladye was not seen! She's o'er the border and awa / wi Jock o'Hazeldean" (*John of Hazelgreen*: Bronsonn, IV, nos. 293.13, 15, 16; *The Singing Tradition*, no. 293.16). Equally satisfying is the conclusion of one Moroccan version of *Virgilios*, from Larache, in which the long-imprisioned protagonist, certain now at last he will marry his Isabel after all, is taken before the king and served a princely banquet: "Ya yevan al Veržico / a los palasios del rey, // a comer ricas gaínas / y beber vino fransés" (Alvar, *El judeo español*, II, no. 12a; Nahón, p. 73).

Chap. 11, n. 117: Davis, *Folk-Songs*, p. 12 (no. 19), is merely a cross-reference to his *Traditional Ballads* (no. 16). Barry, Eckstorm, and Smyth record a vestigial memory, of Irish origin, from Maine. It evokes something of the singing context of ballads of earlier times and is worth quoting, not only for its own sake, but also because it stresses the fierce hostility of the brother (and perhaps other family members), so characteristic of the ballad's Scottish form: "Mrs. Fred W. Morse of Islesford could recall that when she was a young child, old Andy, the strolling singer of ballads in Ireland, used to sing a song which she had overheard by stealth through the floor or when her grandparents were nodding by the fire, about a brother who called his sister a whore. There was something in it about a mother, or father, and a brother and sister, but she could recall nothing but the one objectionable word and she never could understand why the song was barred to the children and could only be heard surreptitiously" (*British Ballads from Maine*, p. 448). Concerning *Lady Maisry*, note also Bronson, *The Singing Tradition*, pp. 171–173.

Chap. 11, n. 119: Both the girl's cry to the hangman (Nachrichter, liebe Nachrichter mi, / O wart du nu-n-e kleine Wil! [DVM 67.1.47; 67.2.34]) and her successive pleas to various family members, as she ascends each step of the gallows (67.3.16 ff.) strongly suggest some relationship to *The Maid Freed from the Gallows*: "O hangman, hold thy hand, / And hold it for a while . . ." (Bronson, II, no. 95.4; Child 95; and Eleanor Long's crucial monograph). One notes, however, that, in the German tradition of *The Maid Freed from the*

Gallows, it is not a hangman, but a boatman who threatens the girl (Erk-Böhme, I, no. 78; Long, pp. 109–111), just as in the ballad's Spanish and Italian modalities. Needless to say, incremental constructions based on the enumeration of family members (e.g., *Delgadina*) need not be genetically distinctive. For Hispanic analogues of *The Maid Freed from the Gallows*, see CMP H13 and *En torno*, p. 234, n. 34.

Chap. 11, n. 121: In many Hungarian texts, the mother interprets a symbolic, prophetic dream which presages the girl's death (Leader, p. 186). The same motif is central to the Greek ballad, *Tò 'óneiron tês kórēs* (*The Maiden's Dream*), though here the girl counters with a happy interpretation (*En torno*, pp. 157–159, apropos of the Judeo-Spanish *Sueño de la hija*). There is also a Bulgarian form (Strausz, *Bulgarische Volksdichtungen*, pp. 171–172, no. 33: *Das Mädchen träumt von zwei Tauben*), but here the prediction is exclusively favorable. One can certainly support Leader (pp. 204–206) in supposing that, in the Hungarian ballad, the dream and its interpretation represent a later accretion. Whether or not the Hungarian, Greek, and Bulgarian instances perhaps represent a Pan-Balkan ballad type deserves further study. The girl's bidding farewell to her flowers (Leader, p. 187) suggests an altogether coincidental parallel with the Portuguese and Moroccan Judeo-Spanish *Flérida*: "Adiós, mis ricos vergeles, / donde yo pasearía" (Nahón 49; CMP S2). In the Hungarian song, both the girl's and the mother's false explanations represent the evasive answers motif (as in *Blancaniña* and many other ballads). See *Yoná*, pp. 210–211, n. 11. In this case, Vargyas convincingly establishes the connection between the verse "Let my blood flow in one stream with yours . . ." (at the end of the Hungarian ballad) and Central Asiatic Turkic antecedents (*Hungarian*, II, 174–175).

Chap. 11, n. 123: For the ill-fitted clothing in contaminations from *Parida* (á-a), see, for example, CARG 18b; Braga, I, 366; Fontes, *Tr.-os-Montes*, no. 776; Ferré, *Cast. Branco*, no. 5; Galhoz 14; Lima Carneiro, "Monte Córdova," pp. 55, 58; Ludovice, p. 148; VRP 80, 81, 987; Purcell, *Ilhas*, no. 8.6 (Madeira); Silva Lima 9.6, 8, 11, 12; Vilela 2.4; AFC 3263; Avenç, III, 35; Milá 258F. For the same motif in autonomous versions of *Parida* (á-a), see Braga, I, 388–390; VRP 282. Concerning *La infanta parida*, see CMP R3. Note Vargyas' perceptive comment on the Scottish verses (*Hungarian*, p. 172). Needless to say, the motif of the ill-fitting clothes is widely known and its presence in *Ritter und Magd* (DVM, III, no. 55) and *Schwabentöchterlein* (DVM, IV, no. 73.1b, v. 11) is no reason at all to connect these ballads to the Hungarian song. Vargyas provides an extensive international list of ballads which contain the motif (*Hungarian*, p. 170). One could add the Anglo-American *Careless Love*: "Once my apron strings were long . . ., you passed my cabin with a song." For some versions and references (but without the pertinent verse), see Randolf, IV, no. 793; Ives, pp. 192–193.

Chap. 11, n. 124: For other Hispanic instances of the girl's drinking cold water in contaminations with *Conde Claros fraile*, see, for example, Braga, *Cantos*, p. 243; Lemos de Mendonça, p. 194; Purcell, *Ilhas*, 8.7, 8.10; Rodrigues de Azevedo, p. 156; C. Tourinho, pp. 132, 133; Lopes, *Presença*, pp. 149, 151, 152, 155, 158, 161; Silva Lima, nos. 9.1–9, 11, 13; Vilela 2.2–4; Aguiló, p. 317; Avenç, III, 35; Milá 258*DFG*. Vargyas, *Hungarian*, no. 10.29, translates the same version as Leader, text *A*. *La fuente fecundante* (*á-a*) is sometimes associated with *La infanta parida* (*á-a*), whether or not the latter is associated with *Conde Claros fraile* (e.g. Braga, I, 382–384, 387–390; note Costa Fontes' observation, *Tr.-os-Montes*, II, 1352). Concerning the two forms of *La fuente fecundante*, in *á-a* and *í-a*, see CMP R4–5. An allied motif is that of *La mala hierba* (*á-a*) (CMP R6). The idea of conception from eating or drinking (or by other supernatural means) is vastly diffused. In the present context, I will cite just a few references: For impregnating apples and pears, see Seemann, "Deutsch-litauische Volksliedbeziehungen," p. 199 (no. 84: *Die Brombeerbrockerin*); *Volsunga Saga*, ed. Finch, pp. 2–3 (pregnancy from eating apple); Dronke, "The Rise of the Medieval *Fabliau*," p. 281 and n. 14 (*L'enfant qui fu remis au soleil*; conception from eating snow); Chadwick and Zhirmunsky, *Oral Epics*, p. 175 (pregnancy from foam of a certain lake); *David of Sassoon*, trans. Shalian, pp. 13–14 (pregnancy from drinking from spring or lake); Reckert, *Lyra Minima*, p. 53, n. 24; *Chrysanthemums*, pp. 57–58 (impregnation by wind); two notable Hispanic examples: "pisó por su ventura / yerva fuert enconada, // quando bien se catido, / fallóse embargada" (Berceo, *Milagros*, ed. Dutton, vv. 507*c–d*; for *catido*, pret. of *catar*, see ed. Solalinde, p. 122; compare *estido* 'estuvo'); "allí nace un arboledo / que azucena se llamaba, // cualquier mujer que la come / luego se siente preñada" (*Ferido está don Tristán: Primav.* 146–146*a*). Note the peculiar variant of drinking tears in 146*a*. Devoto's learned monographic study of the Berceo instance controls a vast bibliography (pp. 11–46). For still more references, see *HDA*, II, s.v. *Empfängnis*; Briffault, *The Mothers*, III, 751 (s.v. *Conception*); Leach and Fried, *Standard Dictionary*, II, pp. 661-662 (s.v. *magical impregnation*); Fraser, *Golden Bough* (1935), XII, 315*b* (impregnating water, etc.); Thompson: T511. *Conception from eating*; T511.1. . . . *from eating fruit*; T511.1.1. . . . *from eating apple*; T512. . . . *from drinking*; T512.3. . . . *from drinking water*; T524. . . . *from wind* (also Bowra, *Heroic Poetry*, pp. 157–158). Note how the

Catalan ballad, *La madrastra*, uses the same excuse as *La infanta parida* (*á-a*): "—Qué m'en dirá el meu pare / quan tan grosseta em veurà? // —Digues que n'has begut aigua / de la font d'aquest joncar" (AFC 3329). For various Indian instances, see Beck, nos. 20 (p. 72), 21 (pp. 73–74), 23 (p. 80), 58 (p. 200). Florencia Pinar's amorous partridges reflect a Bestiary tradition which claimed that the female birds would become pregnant merely if the wind blew toward them from the males (Deyermond, "The Worm and the Partridge," p. 6 and n. 14; T. H. White, *The Book of Beasts*, p. 137; "Destas aues su nacion es cantar con alegria": Hernando del Castillo, *Cancionero general*, ed. Rodríguez-Moñino, fol. cxxv vo.–cxxvj ro.). Concerning the erotic symbolism of the wind, Alan Deyermond's incisive analysis in indispensable: "Traditional Images," pp. 14, 17–22. For an additional recently discovered Moroccan Sephardic example, its 16th-century congener, and some additional instances, see my article, "Seis cantos de boda," pp. 182 (no. 6, vv. 5–6), 187–189, and nn. 15–16.

Chap. 11, n. 125: For similar Castilian beginnings, see RPC, p. 10; RPM 59, 60; *Voces nuevas*, 48.1; and n. 50 above. In Hungarian, there are a number of analogous beginnings: "Lady Landorvári had twelve daughters, / the twelfth daughter was Dora Landorvári"; "A queen had . . ."; "A widow had . . ." (Leader, p. 184; Vargyas, *Hungarian*, p. 150). Needless to say, the incipit is formulaic. We need not go beyond a few Judeo-Spanish examples: "Tres hermanas eran ellas, / hijas del rey Dolonginos . . ." (*Expulsión de los judíos de Portugal*: CMP C13.1); "Un buen rey que tenía tres ijas, / tres ijas muy regaladas . . ." (*Delgadina*: P2.13); "Y el rey de Francia / tres hijas tenía . . ." (*El sueño de la hija*: S6.12); "Siete hijas tenía la reina, / sin dingún hijo varón . . ." (*Doncella guerrera*: Rhodes, uned.); "Aquel rey de Inglaterra / hijos no tenía, non. / Tiene siete hijas beyas / y sin dingún hijo varón . . ." (*Doncella guerrera*: Salonika, uned.). In the Scottish *Lady Maisry*, some versions specify that she is an only child: "Lady Margery was her mother's ain daughter, / And her father's only heir . . ." (Child 65*DE*).

Chap. 11, n. 130: For the motif of writing letters in blood, see also Feito, p. 125; Kundert G4; RGL 19.8, 11, 13, 22; Ruiz Granda; *Voces nuevas* 48.1, 3, 17; CARG 18*b*; Briz, IV, 44; Milá 258, 258*K*. The reading in Briz and in Milá 258*K*, in which she writes with blood from her tongue (y ab sanch de la seva llenga / ella escrivia una carta), is clearly influenced by *Blancaflor y Filomena*: "La tinta te servirá / la sangre de mi lengua" (*Voces nuevas* 34.7, 8; CMP F1); and for a Mallorcan version, compare: "Pero [= para] tinta le pondrás / de mi sangre de mis venas" (Massot, "El romancero tradicional español en Mallorca," no. 14.21; cf. *Voces nuevas* 34.2). In the Hungarian ballad, just as in some Hispanic texts, tears are sometimes used instead of blood: "Let your heavy tears / be your ink!" (Leader, pp. 181, 187; Vargyas, *Hungarian*, p. 159, vv. 12*de*). In a Leonese version of *Gaiferos y Melisenda*, she writes a letter: "La mitá escribió con tinta, / la mitad con sangre real" (RGL 17.1.45). Concerning letters written in blood, see FLSJ, III, 149, 271, n. 43 (*El sueño de doña Alda*); Thompson: M201.1. *Blood covenant: contract written (or signed) with blood* and the other pertinent motifs cross-referenced there. Add also Ibn Quzmān's *zajal* no. 112, where the poet, addressing his beloved Umm al-Ḥakam, promises to answer her letter by writing with his own blood (*bi-dammī*) and using his bones as a pen (García Gómez, *Todo ben Quzmān*, II, 578; Corriente, *Cancionero*, p. 256). In the South Slavic epic of *Osmanbeg Delibegović i Pavičević Luka,* a letter affirming the adoption of Luke as a blood brother is written in blood (SCHS, VI, xxxv). In *Zaim Ali Bey in Jail*, the imprisioned protagonist writes to his mother, in desperation, having bitten his own arm to obtain blood as a writing material (*Bihać,* p. 253, vv. 176–178).

Chap. 11, n. 131: While there are many instances of the *pajarito* (*pajarcito*, etc.) in Castilian-speaking areas (Martínez Ruiz; RGL 19.2, 3, 5, 12, 17; RPE; *Voces nuevas* 48.9, 10), the page has also vigorously survived (RGL 19.1, 8, 16; RPC, pp. 9, 11; RPM 58; *Voces nuevas* 48.5); so also in Galicia: *pagharito* (CPG 44*a*) vs. *paje* (44*b*); in Portugal: *passarinho* (VRP 52) vs. *pagem* (in the same text) or *paigete* (VRP 69); in Catalonia: *pasurito* or *gavilán*(!) (Milá 258*BL*) vs. *pagecito* (Milá 258*D*). Though the *passarinho* reading can be documented in Brazil (Vilela 2.4), the *pagem* seems to have disappeared. For other Hungarian readings, including a debate over which type of bird to send, see Vargyas, *Hungarian*, pp. 154, 156, 159–160; Leader, pp. 181, 187. Concerning the page/bird reading, see also nn. 55–56 above and FLSJ, III, 272–273, n. 52.

Chap. 11, n. 133: Díaz, *Catálogo*, I, 167 (En el medio del camino, / cuatro reventados van); Ruiz Granda; RGL 19.26, 29, 30. For other Scottish readings, see Child 65*BCD*; *B* and *C* devote three whole stanzas to the successive deaths of the horses. The word *slap* (Child 65*E*.14*a*) is 'a narrow pass between two hills' (Vol. V, 376*b*; Warrack, s.v.). In the Hungarian tradition, the motif would seem to be rare. Leader lists only one version in which "two horses die by the time they arrive" (p. 189); Vargyas does not identify the text he cites (*Hungarian*, p. 164). In Hispanic tradition, fatal exhaustion of steeds on a heroic ride doubtless embodies a migratory motif. Compare an Izmir version of *La muerte del príncipe Don Juan*: "Syete mulas i kavayyos / por el kamino dexaras. // Kamino de kinze días / en syete los ayegava. / Ala entrada dela puerta,

/ la mula ke areventava; // la mula la más ermoza, / la ke el rey enbineava" (*Seis romancerillos*, p. 39; also Galante 13; *enbineava* < T. *binmek* 'to ride').

Chap. 11, n. 135: On the motif of the twining branches, see *Yoná*, pp. 161–163, n. 9; Thompson: E631.0.1. *Twining branches grow from graves of lovers.* Note too how the motif of the girl's saying goodbye to her flowers has independently entered both the Hispanic ballad (as a contamination from *Flérida*; n. 121 above) and its Hungarian counterpart (Leader, p. 187: "she asks her mother to wait while she says goodbye to her flowers . . ."), though admittedly at two different stages in the narrative.

Chap. 11, n. 137: As Beatriz Mariscal has incisively observed: "Al examinar la tradición española en el contexto europeo, nos damos cuenta de que *La Muerte ocultada* no es una mera traducción de *Le Roi Renaud* y de que la relación entre las diferentes tradiciones es mucho más compleja que la pretendida derivación en línea recta" (RT, XII, 55). How are we to explain, for instance, the Catalan and Eastern Judeo-Spanish names *Olalbo* and *Ofico* (RT, XII, nos. 20–24), which are lacking in French sources, but which clearly relate to *Olaf, Oleff, Olof*, the protagonist of the Spanish ballad's Scandinavian analogue: *Elveskud* or *Herr Olof och älvorna* (DgF, II, no. 47; Landstad, no. 40; TSB A63; Forslin). As Beatriz Mariscal notes, the ballad's onomastics show "lo difícil que es pensar en líneas únicas de derivación cuando se estudia la poesía de transmisión oral de grandes comunidades humanas. . . . Esta coincidencia del nombre del heroe (nombre bien extraño en la onomástica peninsular) . . . es un indicio de la llegada hasta la Península Ibérica de formas antiquísimas de la balada pan-europea de las que no quedan huellas en la Europa continental" (RT, XII, 56 and n. 23). See also my review: *JAF*, 100 (1987), 231-233.

Chap. 11, n. 144: *Con cartas y mensajeros* (*Primav.* 13–13a), on the other hand, depends directly on an oral epic source (RT, I, 151–175). A reworking of the ballad lives on today in the distinctive repertoire of Andalusian Gypsies (RT, I, 160–162; Vega, *Los corridos*, p. 16). Concerning this tradition, see, now, *Epic Ballads*, pp. 78–79, n. 2, Teresa Catarella's article, "A New Branch," and now her *Romancero gitano-andaluz* (specifically pp. 20–21, 51–56). Luis Suárez Avila's intervention, as collector of texts and music from the Gypsy, has been uniquely important

Chap. 11, n. 150: Something similar also occurs in *Las almenas de Toro*, which functions as a prologue to the Zaide ballads, *Por la calle de su dama* + *Mira Zaide que te aviso* and is also contaminated by the *fronterizo* ballad of *Portocarrero. El destierro del Cid*, which shares verses with *Garcilaso de la Vega*, also *fronterizo*, participates in the same process and

Búcar sobre Valencia, prefixed by verses from *Garcilaso*, takes on a similar *fronterizo* tone. See *Epic Ballads*, pp. 178–179, 214–216, 248–249.

Chap. 11, n. 151: Concerning historical actualization of epic materials, see Menéndez Pidal, *La leyenda de los infantes de Lara*, pp. 204, 491–492, 524–525 (or *Los godos y la epopeya*, pp. 237–239); Avalle-Arce, *Temas hispánicos medievales*, pp. 124–134; also our *Epic Ballads*, p. 205, n. 16; FLSJ, III, 174, 280–281, n. 67. As part of such a process, Alfonsine historiography's persistent updating of its prosified epic narratives, to keep them in line with current developments in the oral tradition, can be seen as an integral part of the on-going creativity of medieval *juglaría*. To suppose, as does D. G. Pattison (*From Legend to Chronicle*), that Alfonso X's compilation may be based on prosified epics (how could it possibly be denied?), but that all subsequent variations must somehow be the imaginative work of monkish *refundidores* and learned historiographers, is simply untenable. (See my review article, "From Epic to Chronicle.") That Castilian historiography did indeed continue to absorb epic material right up to the end of the Middle Ages has now been conclusively demonstrated by Mercedes Vaquero ("The Tradition of the *Cantar de Sancho II*"; and her book, *Tradiciones orales en la historiografía*). See also my note, "Chronicles and Epics in the 15th Century." This is not to say that Pattison's book is not a thoroughly admirable, incalculably useful, and indispensable contribution. It most certainly is.

Chap. 11, n. 157: The series of questions followed by negative answers recalls those of the Eastern Sephardic *Esclavo que llora por su mujer*: "—¿De ké yoras, pobre esklavo? / ¿De ké yoras? ¿Ké te kexas? // ¿U no komes u no beves, / u t'asotan kuando duermes? // —Yo ya bien bevo, ya bien komo; / ni m'asotan kuando duermo. // Yoro yo por una amiga / . . ." (*En torno*, p. 160; CMP H20). Identical questions and answers figure in the Judeo-Spanish ballad's Greek ancestor text, *Ho niópantros sklábos* (*The Recently Married Galley Slave*) (*En torno*, pp. 160–161). These verses exemplify a well known formulaic pattern. Compare, for example, the following verses from *La princesa rescatada* (= CMP H14; uned., Tetuán, collected by S. G. A. and I. J. K., August 5, 1962):

—¿Qué tenid, digo, la niña,	qué querid, aunque mandáis?
¿Si queréis beber del vino	o queréis comer del pą?
¿Queréis beber agua dulse,	por no beber de la mar?
—Sastisfecha'stoy del vino,	sastisfecha estoy del pą,
sastisfecha di agua dulse;	yo no bebo de la mar.
¿Si [t]e plase, mi señor rey,	de mandarme a mi sivdá?

For other instances, compare *La infancia de Gaiferos* (FM 3, 230; RPM 54–55; RTO 12; CVR 21) and *Moriana y Galván* (*En torno*, p. 144; Nahón, no. 7; FLSJ, VII, Chap. 17). For further examples, in an international perspective, see *Yoná*, pp. 123–124 and n. 5.

Another problem is the possible connection between the Sephardic *Esclavo* song and a splendid, previously unknown *cautivo* ballad recently discovered by Maximiano Trapero in the repertoire of an aged singer on the island of Gran Canaria (Trapero, "Hunting for Rare *Romances*," pp. 533–541). That the Judeo-Spanish poem is related to the Greek ballad seems beyond dispute; whether both are also related to the Canarian song is another matter. It is worth noting that we have almost no information concerning the narrative context of the Sephardic song and we have no assurance that the person who sets the captive free is, as is the case with the Canarian song, the wife of his captor (as also in *El cautivo del renegado*); on the other hand, we cannot be certain either that, in the Sephardic song, it is the captain of a galley who sets him free, as in the Greek ballad. All the same, the radical differences between the Canarian and the Greek ballads in regard to essential features of the narrative need to be taken into account: In the Canarian text, we have a Moorish lady who is enamored of the captive and who, in defiance of her husband, sets him free and sends him back to his wife and children. In the Greek song, on the other hand, we have a galley master who takes pity on a galley slave and sends him home to his wife and children. Just as there are various features of the Greek ballad which do not come over into its Sephardic derivative (as Trapero, p. 540, has observed), there are just as many in the Canarian song which are likewise lacking in its putative Judeo-Spanish parallel. Given the almost certain direct connection between the Greek and the Sephardic ballads, I remain doubtful that the latter can be genetically related to Trapero's splendid Canarian *romance*. Essentially, we must ask whether the question "¿Qué tienes, cristiano mío . . .?" (or "¿De qué lloras, pobre esclavo . . .?"), the captive's weeping and his longing for a beautiful wife and little children, and his subsequently being set free really are sufficiently distinctive and really constitute sufficient grounds for connecting the Canarian and the Sephardic ballads. Or are these all simply "Folklore motifs which appear in an infinity of popular, universal stories, whether *romances* or not" (Trapero, p. 540)? Again, the brevity of the Judeo-Spanish versions need not indicate a long development in oral tradition, as Trapero argues (p. 539). These are all very defective texts; their brevity may simply indicate that this ballad, which since 1911-1912 has never again been collected from oral tradition, had at that moment simply reached the end of its traditional life in gravely eroded form. I continue to believe that the Judeo-Spanish song depends directly on the Greek and that its agreements, striking as they may be, with the Canarian ballad may well be coincidental. None of this detracts in the very least from the great value of Maximiano Trapero's dramatic discovery or from the splendid, insightful article in which he has developed it. For the four known texts of the Sephardic *Esclavo que llora por su mujer*, see CMP, III, 28–30 (nos. 19, 21*A*, 21*B*) and Trapero, pp. 537–538.

I note, in passing, the correlation between v. 20 of text 1*c* of our *Bernardo* ballad (ni me faltaban vestidos, / muchos tengo yo en mi arca) and a similar verse in *La expulsión de los judíos de Portugal*: "nin por mengua de azuares, / en su arca los tenía" (Armistead and Silverman, "Un aspecto desatendido," p. 188, no. 4); "no por mengua de ajuar, / que en mi arca está cumplido" (MP 13); "ni's por halta de asware, / que en mi cofre lo he tenido" (MRuiz 102). See also CMP C13; *Tres calas* C5 (pp. 128–130).

Chap. 11, n. 195: All but sixteen transcriptions are notated on three-line staves. Among them, twelve were notated on five-line and four on four-line staves. In the following itemization, one will observe that all the examples fall within the range of an octave, and that tetrachords and pentachords prevail:

unisonal	2	= .0043%	pentachordal	194	= .4190
bichordal	15	= .0323	pentachordal		
bitonic	1	= .0021	+ *subtonium*	8	= .0173
trichordal	41	= .0885	hexachordal	37	= .0799
trichordal			hexachordal		
+*subtonium*	1	= .0021	+ *subtonium*	18	= .0389
tritonic	1	= .0021	hexatonic	3	= .0064
tetrachordal	118	= .2548	heptachordal	1	= .0021
tetrachordal	1	= .0021	heptatonic		
+ *subtonium*	6	= .0130	octaval	7	= .0151
tetratonic	9	= .0194			

Each of the itemized ranges can be further subdivided according to their *finalis* or lowest notated tone:

bichordal	(b̲ = 14; f̲ = 1)
bitonic	(e̲->g = 1)
trichordal	(a̲ = 14; b̲ = 15; c̲ = 4; d̲ = 1; e̲ = 1; f̲ = 1; g = 5)

trichordal +	
subtonium	($\underline{a}$ = 2; $\underline{c}$ = 12; $\underline{d}$ = 2; $\underline{e}$ = 2)
tritonic	($\underline{c}$-$\underline{d}$-›$\underline{f}$ = 1)
tetrachordal	($\underline{a}$ = 20; $\underline{b}$ = 9; $\underline{c}$ = 36; $\underline{c}$, with Minor 3rd = 1; $\underline{d}$ = 1; $\underline{f}$ = 1; $\underline{g}$ = 50)
tetrachordal +	
subtonium	($\underline{c}$ = 5; $\underline{g}$ = 1)
tetratonic	($\underline{c}$-$\underline{d}$-$\underline{e}$-›$\underline{g}$ = 3; $\underline{c}$-›$\underline{e}$-$\underline{f}$-$\underline{g}$ = 5; $\underline{g}$-›$\underline{b}$-$\underline{c}$-$\underline{d}$ = 1)
pentachordal	($\underline{a}$ = 96; $\underline{c}$ = 89; $\underline{g}$ = 8)
pentachordal	
+ *subtonium*	($\underline{a}$ = 4; $\underline{c}$ = 4)
hexachordal	($\underline{a}$ = 16; $\underline{c}$ = 5; $\underline{d}$ = 4; $\underline{g}$ = 11; $\underline{g}$, with *finalis* on $\underline{c}$ = 1)
hexachordal	
+ *subtonium*	($\underline{c}$ = 1)
hexatonic	($\underline{a}$-›$\underline{c}$-$\underline{d}$-$\underline{e}$-$\underline{f}$-$\underline{g}$ = 2; $\underline{a}$-$\underline{b}$-$\underline{c}$-$\underline{d}$-$\underline{e}$-›$\underline{g}$ = 1)
heptachordal	($\underline{c}$ = 1)
heptatonic	($\underline{d}$-$\underline{e}$-›$\underline{g}$-$\underline{a}$-$\underline{b}$-$\underline{c}$-$\underline{d}$ = 1)
octaval	($\underline{a}$ = 1; $\underline{c}$ [plagal] = 2; $\underline{c}$ = 3; $\underline{f}$ = 1)

Chap. 11, n. 196: Pedrell cited forty-six quatrains in his essay ("Folk-lore musical castillan," pp. 372–400), in which he retranscribed Salinas' music into modern notation. Listed by their textual *incipits*, according to Pedrell's order of presentation, they include: 1) "Milagro no hazeys . . ." (Salinas, p. 298); 2) "Milagro bien sería . . ." (p. 299; *contrafact*); 3) "Conviene mal dormir por bien velar" and "Mongica en religión . . ." (p. 300; the latter is a *contrafact*); 4) "Digades la casada cuerpo garrido" (p. 301); 5) "Meteros quiero monja . . ." (p. 302); 6) "Pensó el mal villano . . ." (p. 306); 7) "Yo me yua mi madre . . ." (*ibid.*) 8) "Si le mato madre a Juan . . ." (*ibid.*); 9) "Canta tu christiana musa" and "A cauallo va Bernardo" (p. 307; both *contrafacts*); 10) "Caminad, señora, si quereys caminar . . ." (p. 308); 11) "No me digays madre mal . . ." (p. 309); 12) "Tango vos yo el mi pandero . . ." (*ibid.*); 13) "En la ciudad de Toledo . . ." (p. 309); 14) "Ea judios a enfardelar . . ." (p. 312); 15) "Tu la tienes Pedro . . ." (p. 317); 16) "Mal aya quien a vos casó . . ." (p. 321); 17) "Ante me beseys que me destoqueys . . ." (*ibid.*); 18) "Ay amor como soys puntoso . . ." (*ibid.*); 19) "Qué me queréys el cauallero . . ." (p. 325); 20) "Aunque soy morenica . . ." (*ibid.*); 21) "Que amor tengo que me servirá" (p. 326); 22) "A quien contaré yo mis quexas mi lindo amor" (*ibid.*); 23) "Aquella morica garrida . . ." (p. 327); 24) "Aquel porfiado . . ." + "Que en toda aquesta noche . . ." (p. 330); 25) "Donde son estas serranas . . ." (p. 333); 26) "Dexadlos mi madre mis ojos llorar . . ." + "Pues fueron amar" (p. 338); 27) "Casó mi pardre con un cauallero . . ." (*ibid.*); 28) "Rey don Alonso" (p. 338); 29) "Conde Claros con amores . . ." (p. 342); 30) "Cata el lobo do va . . ." (p. 343); 31) "Soliades venir amor . . ." (*ibid.*); 32) Segador tírate afuera . . ." (*ibid.*); 33) "Retrayda está la Infanta . . ." (p. 346); 34) "Guárdame las vacas . . ." (p. 348); 35) "De las honduras llamo a tí . . ." (p. 350); 36) "Oydme un poco señora" + "Lo que yo quiero decir" (p. 354); 37) "Aunque me abraso y quemo . . ." (*ibid.*); 38) "Quién te me enojó Ysabel" (p. 356); 39) "Que con lágrimas te tiene" (*ibid.*); 40) "Yo hago voto solene" (*ibid.*); 41) "Que pueden doblar por él" (*ibid.*); 42) "Mi grave pena crece de congoxa . . ." (p. 362); 43) "Fe me condena, amor me maltrata" (*ibid.*); 44) "Las mañanas de Abril . . ." (p. 363); 45) "Si mis amores no me valen . . ." (p. 386); and 46) "Si jugastes a noche amore non señora none" (p. 422).

A. Daniels (*De Musica*, p. 452), who studied the folk tunes in Books VI and VII of Salinas' treatise, criticized Pedrell for citing only the Spanish melodies in his 1900 essay, and for failing "to include the French, German, and Italian, as well as a few Spanish melodies (without texts) which Salinas mentions." Among Daniels's sixty-eight transcriptions are fifty Spanish examples, forty-seven of which concur with Pedrell's. Daniels, like Pedrell, joined three of the examples: "Aquel porfiado," "Dexadlos mi madre mis ojos llorar," and "Oydme un poco señora" (Salinas, pp. 330, 338, and 354, respectively) to their immediate successors, yet their respective transcriptions differ only from a metrical standpoint. And, while Salinas transcribed the melodies accompanying the protracted texts: "Cata el lobo do va, Juanica, cata el lobo do va," "Solíades venir de amor, Mas agora non venides non," and "Segador tírate afuera dexa entrar la espigaderuela" (Salinas, p. 344), Daniels transcribed the shorter versions: "Cata el lobo do va," "Solíades venir amor," and "Segador tírate afuera" (Salinas, p. 343), the first of which bears no melodic resemblance to Salinas' longer example. (Concerning the protracted text "Cata el lobo do va, Juanica, cato el lobo do va," see García Matos, "Pervivencia," p. 72.) Be that as it may, Pedrell also included "Canta tu christiana musa," the initial hemistich of Juan de Mena's (1411–1456) *Coplas de los siete precados mortales* (Salamanca, 1500), and "A Cauallo va Bernardo," both cited as *contrafacts*, preceding a melody whose meter accomodates Spanish *coplas* of the *arte real* [or *octavas reales*] type (Salinas, p. 307*f*: see also Pedrell, *Cancionero popular*, no. 27), while Daniels added "Afición grande me haze por ti sola padescer," "Perricos de mi señora, no me mordades agora," and a slight variant of "Las mañanas de abril dulces eran de dormir" (Salinas, pp. 355, 356, and 398, respectively), bringing the total to fifty-four. Yet both Pedrell and Daniels appear to have overlooked thirteen additional Spanish examples provided by Salinas, which bring the total to sixty-seven. These include:

1) a melody phrase for the text "Contemplando, tan callando" (p. 305) (see García Matos, "Pervivencia," p. 69). Curiously, Pedrell also included it in his *Cancionero musical* (ex. 27);

2) a melody phrase for "Dama si quereys amor, amad" (Salinas, p. 307);

3) a melodic distich for "Yo bien puedo ser casada mas de amores moriré" (p. 313) (see García Matos, p. 70). Pedrell (*Cancionero musical*, I, ex. 75) included the tune of this text, with a simple harmonic accompaniment, for which he substituted the ballad text from *El Cid en las cortes*;

4) a melodic strophe for "Mi graue pena, Cresce de congoxa. Fe me condena" (p. 316), the complete musical strophe of which appears later (p. 362). Pedrell included the latter (*Cancionero musical*, I, ex. 76) and added a harmonic accompaniment;

5) a melody phrase from a well known song, to which the verse "Que era mala la usança" was notated (p. 324);

6) the opening melody phrase for "Feriré el cabello ferirélo" (p. 324);

7) the initial melody phrase for "Una moçuela desta villa" (p. 325);

8) a melody phrase for "De rosas y flores que cría el verano" (p. 337);

9) "Llamáis me villana y yo no lo soy" (p. 338);

10) the melody phrase relating to the *Conde Claros* hemistich "No podía reposar" (p. 346);

11) a variant tune fragment for the text "Oyd me un poco señora lo que yo quiero deziros" (p. 354);

12) a melodic distich for "Yo me yua madre, a Villa reale," which was also cited as a *contrafact* to the hymn "Ave maris stella Dei mater alma" (p. 397); and

13) a distich from "Rosa fresca con amores, / Rosa fresca con amor" (p. 411).

The percentages below reflect the distribution of scalar configurations among the sixty-seven Spanish examples:

trichordal	8	= .119%	tetratonic	3	= .045
trichordal			pentachordal	21	= .313
+ *subtonium*	3	= .045	hexachordal	8	= .119
tritonic	1	= .015	hexatonic	1	= .015
tetrachordal	15	= .223	heptachordal	1	= .015

tetrachordal   octaval   5   = .075
+ *subtonium*   1   = .015

Both Higinio Anglés and José Subirá (*Catálogo musical* I, p. 171), mentioned that Jesús Bal y Gay was preparing a study concerning the ballads and popular songs in Salinas' treatise. Bal (d. March 3, 1993) was an astute scholar of 16th-century Spanish music. Lamentably, the study was not found among his unpublished manuscripts.

Musicological Commentary

Section A

Spanish texts and tunes cited by Salinas and retranscribed by Pedrell, "Folklore musical castillan," pp. 384–400. Number citations, preceded by an equal sign (=), in Sections A, B, and C, remit to Margit Frenk, *Corpus de la antigua lírica popular hispánica (Siglos XV a XVII)*, Madrid: Castalia, 1987.

    1. "Milagro no hazeys, . . ." (Salinas, *De Musica*, p. 298) = no. 336.

    2. "Milagro bien sería, . . ." (p. 299; also transcribed by García Matos, "Pervivencia," ex. 7).

    3. "Conuiene mal dormir por bien velar" and its contrafaction (p.300) = no. 2019.

    4. "Mongica en religión me quiero entrar . . ." (p. 300) = no. 215A.

    5. "Digades la casada cuerpo garrido" (p. 301) = no. 2227.

    6. "Meteros quiero monja . . ." (p. 302) = no. 211; to whose tune Pedrell (*Cancionero musical*, I, ex. 68), set the text, "No quiero ser monja . . . ," from Barbieri. ex. 398. Pedrell continued this practice with other tunes (*Cancionero musical*, I, exs. 69–72, 75); see also García Matos, "Pervivencia," ex. 10.

    7. "Pensó el mal villano . . ." (p. 306).

    8. "Yo me yua mi madre . . ." (p. 306); also transcribed by Trend, "Salinas: A Sixteenth-Century Collector," p. 20; Torner, "La canción tradicional española," p. 130, below which he presented an Asturian dance tune as an analogue; and García Matos, "Pervivencia," ex. 6.

    9. "Si le mato madre a Juan . . ." (p. 306) = no. 186.

    10. "Canta tu Christiana Musa" (p. 307).

    11. "A cauallo va Bernardo" (p. 307).

12. "Caminad señora si quereys caminar . . ." (p. 308; see also García Matos, "Pervivencia," ex. 3) = no. 1010.

13. "No me digays madre mal . . ." (p. 309) = no. 1840*B*.

14. "Tango vos yo el mi pandero . . ." (p. 309; also transcribed by García Matos, "Pervivencia," ex. 9) = no. 1474.

15. "En la ciudad de Toledo . . ." (p. 309; also transcribed by García Matos, "Pervivencia," ex. 11).

16. "Ea judíos a enfardelar . . ." (p. 312) = no. 900.

17. "Tu la tienes Pedro . . ." (p. 317) = no. 1824*ABC*.

18. "Mal aya quien a vos casó" (pp. 32--321; the first hemistich also appeared on p. 318) = no. 239*ABC*.

19. "Ante me beseys que me destoqueys . . ." (p. 321) = no. 1685.

20. "Ay amor como soys puntoso . . ." (p. 321) = no. 42.

21. "Qué me queréys el cauallero . . ." (p. 325; also transcribed by García Matos, "Pervivencia," ex. 5) = no. 697.

22. "Aunque soy morenica . . ." (p. 325; both tunes appear to be related) = no. 130; also 131, 133, 139, 140.

23. "Que amor tengo que me seruirá" (p. 326) = no. 130.

24. "A quien contaré yo . . ." (p. 326; also transcribed by Trend, "Salinas," p. 20) = no. 380.

25. "Aquella Morica garrida . . ." (p. 327) = no. 497*AB*.

26. "Aquel porfiado . . ." (p. 330).

27. "Dónde son estas serranas " (p. 333; Salinas provided two variants, one notated with breves, the other with semibreves; also transcribed by García Matos, "Pervivencia," ex. 8) = no. 1477.

28. "Dexadlos mi madre mis ojos llorar. . ." (p. 338; also transcribed by Torner, "Góngora y el folklore," p. 79, and Trend, "Salinas," p. 21) = no. 596.

29. "Casóme mi padre con vn cauallero . . ." (p. 338; Pedrell's transcription connects its text with "Cada hora me llama hija de vn pechero" and "Y yo no lo soy," and, in his *Cancionero musical,* I, ex. 89, he sets the combined texts to the tune which bears the Latin underlay, "Dignare me virgo laudare te semper"); note Cejador y Frauca, *La verdadera poesía,* I, no. 9.

30. "Rey don Alonso . . ." (p. 338; also transcribed by Trend, "Salinas," p. 22; however, Daniels' transcription in 5/4, *De Musica,* p. 470, is metrically correct; see additional variants on p. 361) = nos. 891 and 892.

31. "Conde Claros con amores . . ." (p. 342).

32. "Cata el lobo do va, Juanica . . ." (p. 344; also transcribed by García Matos, "Pervivencia," ex. 4*bis*) = no. 1136.

33. "Solíades venir amor . . ." (p. 344; also transcribed by Trend, "Salinas," p. 15) = no. 574.

34. "Segador tírate afuera . . ." (pp. 344–345; also transcribed by Trend, "Salinas," p. 15; López-Chavarri, *Música popular*, p. 49; and García Matos, "Pervivencia," ex. 4) = no. 1102.

35. "Retrayda está la Infanta . . ." (= *Conde Alarcos*) (p. 346; this is a contrafaction for "Conde Claros con amores"; also transcribed by García Matos, "Pervivencia," ex. 12).

36. "Guárdame las vacas . . ." (p. 348; also transcribed by Trend, "Salinas," p. 22) = no. 1683*A*.

37. "De las honduras llamo a ti . . ." (p. 350; given as a contrafaction for a German tune, "Aus hertzen grondt . . .").

38. "Aunque me abraso . . ." (p. 354).

39. "Oyd me vn poco señora . . ." (p. 355; for another tune version, see p. 354).

40. "Quién te me enojó Ysabel" (p. 356) = no. 449.

41. "Que con lágrimas te tiene" (p. 356).

42. "Yo hago voto solene" (p. 356).

43. "Que pueden doblar por él" (p. 356; note that Pedrell linked each phrase to form a quatrain, *Cancionero musical*, I, ex. 85; it should also be noted that Fernández de la Cuesta inadvertently exchanged the musical examples for "Que con lágrimas . . ." and "Yo hago voto . . ." in *Francisco Salinas*, p. 624; note also the similarity between the notation for "Que pueden doblar por él" and the second phrase of "Perricos de mi señora, . . ." which is no. 54) (p. 356).

44. "Mi graue penna crece de congoxa . . ." (p. 362; see the abridged version, p. 316).

45. "Fe me condena, amor me maltrata" (p. 362).

46. "Las mañanas de abril . . ." (p. 363; repeated on. p. 398; also transcribed by García Matos, "Pervivencia," ex. 8*bis*) = nos. 1268*ABC*.

47. "Si mis amores no me valen . . ." (p. 386) = no. 612.

48. "Si jugastes anoche amore . . ." (p. 422) = no. 576.

49. "Que haré adonde yré . . ." (p. 437: read 435) = no. 747*B*.

Section B

Daniels included six additional texts in his dissertation, which are the shorter variations of:

50. "Cata el lobo do va" (Salinas, p. 343) = no. 1136.

51. "Solíades venir amor" (p. 343) = no. 574.

52. "Segador tírate afuera" (p. 343) = no. 1102.

53. "Afición grande me haze . . ." (p. 355).

54. "Perricos de mi señora . . ." (p. 356) = no. 1670.

55. A melodic variant for "Las mañanas de abril . . ." (p. 398; for the earlier transcription, see no. 46), thus bringing the total to fifty-five; = no. 1268*ABC*.

It should be noted that Pedrell transcribed the melodies accompanying the full texts, "Cata el lobo do va, Juanica, / cata el lobo do va," "Solíades venir de amor, / mas agora non venides non," and "Segador tírate afuera / dexa entra la espigaderuela" (from Salinas, 344–345). The first of these was also transcribed by García Matos, "Pervivencia," p. 72. M. Querol, *La música en Cervantes*, p. 86, cited Cervantes' picaresque novelette, *Coloquio de los perros*, as the source of its text. The novelette concerns a conversation between two dogs, Cipión and Berganza, the latter of whom states: "Si los míos [pastores] cantaban, no eran canciones acordadas y bien compuestas, sino un *Cata el lobo do va, Juanita*, y otras cosas semejantes. . . ." Daniels' shorter version of "Cata el lobo do va" bears no melodic resemblance to Salinas' longer example; = nos. 1136, 574, 1102.

Section C

Pedrell and Daniels omit fourteen Spanish texts and their music cited by Salinas:

56. A melody phrase for the text, "Contemplando, tan callando" (Salinas, p. 305; see also García Matos, "Pervivencia," ex. 1). Pedrell also included it in his *Cancionero musical*, I, ex. 27.

57. "Que auedes que U mal de amores he" (p. 305; Salinas suggested that this was a contrafaction of the French song, "Diste qu'aues vous fay mal aux genoux").

58. A melody phrase for "Dama si quereys amor, amad" (Salinas, p. 307) = no. 2220.

59. "Yo bien puedo ser casada mas de amores moriré" (Salinas, p. 313; see García Matos, "Pervivencia," ex. 2). Pedrell, *Cancionero,* I, ex. 75, replaced its text with that of the ballad, *El Cid en las cortes*, also adding a simple harmonic accompaniment; = no. 219.

60. A melody phrase for the well known song, "Amigo si me bien queredes" (Salinas, p. 319) = no. 2207.

61. The initial protracted melody phrase for the popular song, "Mas me querría vn çatico de pan . . ." (Salinas, p. 320) = no. 1213.

62. A melody phrase from another well known song to which the verse "Que era mala la vsança" was underlaid (Salinas, p. 324).

63. A melody phrase for "Feriré el cabello ferirélo" (Salinas, p. 324) = no. 590.

64. A melody phrase for "Vna moçuela desta villa" (Salinas, p. 325) = no. 1719.

65. A melody phrase for "Y pues me hizieron . . ." (Salinas, p. 331).

66. A melody phrase for "Amores que quieren . . ." (Salinas, p. 331).

67. A melody phrase for "Amores me dieron . . ." (Salinas, p. 331).

68. A protracted melody phrase for "De rosas y flores que cría el verano" (Salinas, p. 337).

69. A melodic distich for "Rosa fresca con amores / rosa fresca con amor" (p. 411). The latter example, included among the five ballads alluded to in the "Juego de Naipes trovado" (see n. 169, in the text), bears the following verses: "el cantar con gran dulzor / un romance, aunque es antigo, / que por mi pasión lo digo: *Rosa fresca y con amor.*" Thus, we can account for a total of seventy-one examples bearing Spanish texts in Salinas' *De Musica Libri Septem.*

Section D

Formal structure:

Singular melody phrases comprising texts or hemistichs of 6 syllables (no. 50), 7 syllables (nos. 40, 43), 8 syllables (nos. 41–42, 51–52, 56, 62), 9 syllables (nos. 23, 64), 10 syllables (nos. 45, 63, 65), 11 syllables (nos. 60, 66), 12 syllables (nos. 38, 67), 13 syllables (no. 36), and 15 syllables (nos. 22, 32). Total: 21.

Protracted melody phrases comprising hemistichs of 9 (5+4) syllables, the fourth of which carries two tones (no. 30); 12 (6+6) syllables (nos. 17, 68); 14 (7+7) syllables (no. 2); 15 (8+7) syllables (nos. 14–15, 27, 58); 15 (9+6) syllables (nos. 20, 61); 16 (11+5) syllables (no. 48); 16 (8+8) syllables (nos. 18, 39, 53); 16 (9+7) syllables (no. 37); 17 (10+7) syllables (no. 19); 19 (9+10) syllables (no. 21); and 20 (9+11) syllables (no. 25). Total: 18.

Distichs (AA) comprising hemistichs of 8 syllables (no. 35) and 12 syllables (text given only for the initial hemistich) (no. 5). Total: 2.

Distichs (AA′) comprising hemistichs of 8 syllables (text of the initial hemistich only) (nos. 10, 11); 8+7 syllables (nos. 31, 59, 69); 13 syllables (no. 24). Total: 6.

Distichs (AB) comprising hemistichs of 5 syllables (no. 57); 6 syllables (no. 1); 6+7 syllables (nos. 26, 46, 55); 7 syllables (no. 9); 7+8 syllables (no. 33); 7+11 syllables (no. 49); 8 syllables (no. 54); 8+9 syllables (no. 34); 9+7 syllables (no. 47); 10+6 syllables (no. 4); 10 syllables (text of the initial hemistich only) (no. 3); 11+5 syllables (no. 28); 15+9 syllables (no. 6). Total: 15.

Protracted distich (AB) comprising 10 (5+5) + 11 (6+5) syllables (no. 16). Total: 1.

Protracted distichs (AA′) comprising 12 (6+6) + 11 (6+5) syllables (no. 12); 13 (7+6) + 14 (7+7) syllables (no. 13). Total: 2.

Quatrain strophes (ABCD) comprising hemistichs of 6 syllables (nos. 7 and 8). Total: 2.

Quatrain strophes ($A^{x+z}B^{y+z}CD$) comprising hemistichs of 11+11+11+5 syllables (no. 44). Total: 1.

Five-phrase strophe (AABCD) comprising hemistichs of 6 syllables (no. 29). Total: 1.

Section E

Modal and scalar configurations:

Bichordal (no. 65). Total: 1.

Trichordal (Major) (nos. 9, 42, 50). Total: 3.

Trichordal (Minor) (nos. 31, 35, 40, 67). Total: 4.

Trichordal (Major + *subsemitonium*) (nos. 30, 36). Total: 2.

Trichordal (Minor + *subtonium*) (nos. 5, 6, 63). Total: 3.

Tritonic (no. 43 c-d-›f). Total: 1.

Tetrachordal (Major) (nos. 29, 45, 48, 56, 59, 64, 69). Total: 7.

Tetrachordal (Minor) (nos. 17, 41, 49, 54, 60). Total: 5.

Tetrachordal (Major / Minor + *subsemitonium*) (no. 28 b-c-d-e/ e-flat - f, *finalis* c). Total: 1.

Tetrachordal (Minor + *subtonium*) (no. 12). Total: 1.

Tetratonic (nos. 32 a-b-c-›e, 51 g-›b-›d-›e, and 52 a-b- c-›e). Total: 3.

Pentachordal (Major) (nos. 3–4, 18–19, 37–38, 47, 58, 61–62). Total: 10.

Pentachordal (Minor) (nos. 1–2, 10–11, 13, 15–16, 20, 26–27, 39, 53, 68). Total: 13.

Hexachordal (Major) (nos. 14, 33). Total: 2.

Hexachordal (Minor) (nos. 21–22, 25, 46, 55–57, 66). Total: 2.

Hexatonic (no. 34 a̲-b̲-c̲-d̲-e̲-›g, *finalis* c̲). Total: 1.

Heptachordal (Major) (no. 23). Total: 1.

Octaval (Major) (nos. 8, 24). Total: 2.

Octaval (Major plagal) (no. 44). Total: 1.

Octaval (Minor) (no. 7, a circular tune, based on *finalis* a̲). Total: 1.

BIBLIOGRAPHY

Bibliography

A. Abbreviations of Journals, Serial Publications, and Organizations

ACCP =	*Arquivos do Centro Cultural Português*, Paris.
AFE =	*El Crotalón: Anuario de Filología Española*, Madrid.
AfM =	*Archiv für Musikforschung*, Leipzig.
AJA =	*American Jewish Archives*, Cincinnati, Ohio.
AIPhHOS =	*Annuaire de l'Institut de Philologie et d'Histoire Orientales et Slaves*, Brussels.
AlAn =	*Al-Andalus*, Madrid.
ALE =	*Anales de la Literatura Española*, Madrid.
ALM =	*Anuario de Letras*, Mexico City.
ALV =	*Archiv für Literatur und Volksdichtung*, Lahr, Baden.
AMu =	*Anuario Musical*, Barcelona.
ANF =	*Arkiv för Nordisk Filologi*, Lund.
AO =	*Archivum*, Oviedo.
ASNS =	*Archiv für das Studium der Neueren Sprachen und Literaturen*, Freiburg im Breisgau–Munich.
ASTP =	*Archivio per lo Studio delle Tradizioni Popolari*, Palermo.
BAAEE =	*Biblioteca de Autores Españoles*, Madrid.
BAAL =	*Boletín de la Academia Argentina de Letras*, Buenos Aires.
BAMS =	*Bulletin of the American Musicological Society*, New York.
Berceo =	*Berceo*, Logroño.
BHi =	*Bulletin Hispanique*, Bordeaux.
BHR =	*Bibliothèque d'Humanisme et Renaissance*, Geneva.
BHS =	*Bulletin of Hispanic Studies*, Liverpool.
BICC =	*Thesaurus: Boletín del Instituto Caro y Cuervo*, Bogotá.
BIEA =	*Boletín del Instituto de Estudios Asturianos*, Oviedo.
BIHIT =	*Boletim do Instituto Histórico da Ilha Terceira*, Angra do Heroísmo.
BRAE =	*Boletín de la Real Academia Española*, Madrid.
BRAH =	*Boletín de la Real Academia de la Historia*, Madrid.
CB =	*Cuadernos Bibliográficos*, Madrid.
CE =	*Cultura Española*, Madrid.
C.E.H. =	Centro de Estudios Históricos, Madrid.

CIF =	*Cuadernos de Investigación Filológica*, Logroño.
CN =	*Cultura Neolatina*, Modena.
Consort =	*The Consort* (Dolmetch Foundation), Haslemere, Surrey, U.K.
C.S.I.C. =	Consejo Superior de Investigaciones Científicas, Madrid.
C.S.M.P. =	Cátedra-Seminario Menéndez Pidal, Madrid.
CST =	*Concelho de Santo Tirso: Boletim Cultural*, Santo Tirso.
DL =	*Douro Litoral*, Oporto.
E.E.T.S. =	Early English Text Society, London.
ER =	*Estudis Romànics*, Barcelona.
ESef =	*Estudios Sefardíes*, Madrid.
Extremadura =	*Extremadura: Boletim de Junta de Província*, Lisbon.
FA =	*Folklore Américas*, Los Angeles, California.
Fabula =	*Fabula*, Göttingen.
FAm =	*Folklore Americano*, Lima.
FFC =	*Folklore Fellows Communications*, Helsinki.
Fil =	*Filología*, Buenos Aires.
FMLS =	*Forum for Modern Language Studies*, St. Andrews.
Folklore =	*Folklore*, London.
FrRev =	*The French Review: Journal of the American Association of Teachers of French*, Santa Barbara, California.
FSt =	*French Studies*, Oxford.
Hispania =	*Hispania*, Los Angeles, California.
HLF =	*Histoire Littéraire de la France*, Paris.
HR =	*Hispanic Review*, Philadelphia, Pennsylvania.
Ilerda =	*Ilerda*, Lérida.
I.S.H.I. =	Institute for the Study of Human Issues, Philadelphia, Pennsylvania.
ISM =	*Israel Studies in Musicology*, Jerusalem.
IT =	*Ilustração Trasmontana*, Porto.
JAF =	*Journal of American Folklore*, Washington, D.C.
JAL =	*Journal of Arabic Literature*, Leiden.
JAOS =	*Journal of the American Oriental Society*, Baltimore, Maryland.
JFR =	*Journal of Folklore Research*, Bloomington, Indiana.
JHPh =	*Journal of Hispanic Philology*, Tallahassee, Florida.
JHR =	*Journal of Hispanic Research*, London.
JIFMC =	*Journal of the International Folk Music Council*, Kingston, Ontario.
J.P.S. =	Jewish Publication Society, Philadelphia, Pennsylvania.
JS =	*Le Judaïsme Séphardi*, London.
KRQ =	*Kentucky Romance Quarterly*, Lexington, Kentucky.
La Corónica =	*La Corónica*, Winston-Salem, North Carolina.
Lletres Asturianes =	*Lletres Asturianes: Boletín Oficial de l'Academia de la Llingua Asturiana*, Oviedo.
LNL =	*Les Langues Néo-Latines*, Paris.

Laog =	*Laografía*, Athens.
LR =	*Les Lettres Romanes*, Louvain.
Lute =	*The Lute: The Journal of the Lute Society*, London.
MAe =	*Medium Aevum*, Oxford.
MAHDB =	*Memorias Arqueológico-Históricas do Distrito de Bragança*, Porto.
MDisciplina =	*Musica Disciplina*, Rome.
MedRom =	*Medioevo Romanzo*, Naples.
ML =	*Music and Letters,* London.
M.L.A. =	Modern Language Association, New York.
MLN =	*Modern Language Notes*, Baltimore, Maryland.
MLQ =	*Modern Language Quarterly*, Seattle, Washington.
MLR =	*Modern Language Review*, Coventry.
MME =	*Monumentos de la Música Española*, Barcelona.
Mosaic =	*Mosaic*, Winnipeg, Manitoba.
MPh =	*Modern Philology*, Chicago, Illinois.
MR =	*Marche Romane*, Liège.
Nassarre =	*Nassarre*, Zaragoza.
NphM =	*Neuphilologische Mitteilungen*, Helsinki.
NRFH =	*Nueva Revista de Filología Hispánica*, Mexico City.
Olifant =	*Olifant*, Austin, Texas.
OTrad =	*Oral Tradition*, Columbia, Missouri.
Parergon =	*Parergon: Bulletin of the Australian and New Zealand Association for Medieval & Renaissance Studies*, Sydney.
PCPh =	*Pacific Coast Philology*, Eugene, Oregon.
PhQ =	*Philological Quarterly*, Iowa City, Iowa.
PMLA =	*Publications of the Modern Language Association of America*, New York.
QP =	*Quaderni Portoghesi*, Pisa.
RABM =	*Revista de Archivos, Bibliotecas y Museos*, Madrid.
RBelge =	*Revue Belge de Philologie et d'Histoire*, Brussels.
RBFo =	*Revista Brasileira do Folklore*, Brasília.
RBN =	*Revista de Bibliografía Nacional*, Madrid.
RCIM =	*Revista Colombiana de Investigación Musical*, Bogotá.
RDTP =	*Revista de Dialectología y Tradiciones Populares*, Madrid.
REJ =	*Revue des Etudes Juives*, Paris.
ReM =	*Revue Musicale,* Paris.
RevMusicol =	*Revista de Musicología*, Madrid.
RF =	*Romanische Forschungen*, Cologne.
RFCSH =	*Revista da Faculdade de Ciências Sociais e Humanas*, Lisbon.
RFE =	*Revista de Filología Española*, Madrid.
RFH =	*Revista de Filología Hispánica*, Buenos Aires.
RFolk =	*Revista de Folklore*, Valladolid.
RHC =	*Revista de Historia Canaria*, La Laguna.
RHi =	*Revue Hispanique*, Paris.

RHLF =   *Revue d'Histoire Littéraire de la France*, Paris.

RIHGB =   *Revista do Instituto Histórico e Geográphico Brazileiro*, Rio de Janeiro.

RL =   *Revista Lusitana*, Lisbon.

RLC =   *Revue de Littérature Comparée*, Paris.

RLM =   *Rivista di Letterature Moderne*, Florence.

RLNS =   *Revista Lusitana* (Nova Série), Lisbon.

RLR =   *Revue des Langues Romanes*, Montpellier.

RMB =   *Revista Musical Bilbao*, Bilbao.

RN =   *Romance Notes*, Chapel Hill, North Carolina.

ROcc =   *Revista de Occidente*, Madrid.

Romania =   *Romania*, Paris.

RPh =   *Romance Philology*, Berkeley, California.

RR =   *Romanic Review*, New York.

S.A.T.F. =   Societé des Anciens Textes Français, Paris.

Sef =   *Sefarad*, Madrid.

Sefunot =   *Sefunot*, Jerusalem.

SFM =   *Studi di Filologia Moderna*, Catania.

Shevet va'Am =   *Shevet va'Am*, Jerusalem.

SIMG =   *Sammelbände der Internationalen Musik-Gesellschaft*, Leipzig.

S.M.P. =   Seminario Menéndez Pidal, Madrid.

Speculum =   *Speculum,* Cambridge, Massachusetts.

SS =   *Scandinavian Studies*, Menasha, Wisconsin.

StMed =   *Studi Medievali*, Spoleto.

StPh =   *Studies in Philology*, Chapel Hill, North Carolina.

TI =   *Tribuna Israelita*, Mexico City.

UCPMPh =   *University of California Publications in Modern Philology*, Berkeley–Los Angeles, California.

Viator =   *Viator*, Los Angeles, California.

VR =   *Vox Romanica,* Bern.

Yeda-'Am =   *Yeda-'Am*, Tel Aviv.

YIFMC =   *Yearbook of the International Folk Music Council*, Kingston, Ontario.

Yuval =   *Yuval: Studies of the Jewish Music Research Centre,* Jerusalem.

ZfM =   *Zeitschrift für Musikwissenschaft*, Leipzig.

ZFSL =   *Zeitschrift für Französische Sprache und Literatur*, Jena.

ZRPh =   *Zeitschrift für Romanische Philologie*, Halle.

B. Published Sources

Aarne, Antti, and Stith Thompson, *The Types of the Folktale: A Classification and Bibliography*, 2d revision, Helsinki: Academia Scientiarum Fennica, 1961.

Abdelkader, Noureddine, *Dictionnaire français-arabe*, 4th ed., Algiers: Jules Carbonel, 1954.

Abrahams, Roger D., "A Note on Neck-Riddles in the West Indies as They Comment on Emergent Genre Theory," *JAF*, 98 (1985), 85–94.

Abun-Nasr, Jamil M., *A History of the Maghrib*, 2d ed., Cambridge: Cambridge University Press, 1975.

ACS =   *Actas del Congreso Internacional: España en la Música de Occidente, Salamanca, 1985*, ed. Emilio Casares Rodicio, Ismael Fernández de la Cuesta, and José López-Calo, Madrid: Ministerio de Cultura, 1987.

Adams, Kenneth, "Castellano, judeoespañol y portugués: El vocabulario de Jacob Rodrigues Moreira y los sefardíes londinenses," *Sef*, 26 (1966), 221–228, 435–447; 27 (1967), 213–225.

Aebischer, Paul, *Rolandiana borealia*, Lausanne: F. Rouge, 1954.

AFC =   Joan Amades, *Folklore de Catalunya: Cançoner (Cançons-refranys-endevinalles)*, Barcelona: Selecta, 1951.

Aguilar Piñal, Francisco, *Romancero popular del siglo XVIII*, Madrid: C.S.I.C., 1972.

Aguiló i Fuster, Marian, *Romancer popular de la terra catalana: Cançons feudals cavalleresques*, Barcelona: Alvar Verdaguer, 1893.

Ahmed, Salahuddin, *A Dictionary of Muslim Names*, Washington Square: New York University Press, 1999.

Aigner, Ludwig, *Ungarische Volksdichtungen*, 2d ed., Budapest: Ludwig Aigner, [1872].

Aiken, Riley, "Fifteen Mexican Tales," *A Good Tale and a Bonnie Tune*, ed. Mody C. Boatright et al. (Dallas: Southern Methodist University Press, 1964), pp. 3–56.

Alcalá Venceslada, Antonio, *Vocabulario andaluz*, Madrid: Gredos, 1980.

Alcalá Venceslada, Antonio, *Vocabulario andaluz*, ed. Ignacio Ahumada, facsimile ed. of the 1951 imprint, Jaén: Universidad de Jaén, 1998.

Alcover, Antoni Maria, *Aplec de rondaies mallorquines*, Vols. X–XI, Palma de Mallorca: Editorial Moll, 1973–1978.

Alexander, Jeffrey, and Robert Spencer, *The Willoughby Lute Book*, Kilkenny, Ireland: Boethius Press, [1978].

Alfonso, Pedro, *Disciplina Clericalis*, ed. Angel González Palencia, Madrid: C.S.I.C., 1948.

Aliste, Paule, *Survivances de la tradition orale dans la région d'Aliste*, ed. Narciso Alba, Perpignan: Université de Perpignan, 1988.

Almoina de Carrera, Pilar, *Diez romances hispanos en la tradición oral venezolana*, Caracas: Universidad Central de Venezuela, [1975].

Alonso, Dámaso, "*Junio* y *Julio* en Galicia y Asturias," *RDTP*, 1 (1944–1945), 429–454.

Alonso Garrote, Santiago, *El dialecto vulgar leonés hablado en Maragatería y tierra de Astorga*, Astorga: P. López, 1909.

Alonso Garrote, Santiago, *El dialecto vulgar leonés hablado en Maragatería y tierra de Astorga*, 2d ed., Madrid: C.S.I.C., 1947.

Alonso, Martín, *Enciclopedia del idioma*, 3 vols., Madrid: Aguilar, 1982.

Alonso Montero, Xesús, "O cura no cancioneiro popular galego," *Homenaje al profesor Hans-Karl Schneider*, ed. José María Navarro et al. (Hamburg: Helmut Buske, 1975), pp. 333–336.

Alvar, Carlos (ed.), *Roldán en Zaragoza: Poema épico provenzal*, Zaragoza: Institución "Fernando el Católico," 1978.

Alvar, Manuel, *El dialecto aragonés*, Madrid: Gredos, 1953.

Alvar, Manuel, *Textos hispánicos dialectales: Antología histórica*, 2 vols., Madrid: C.S.I.C., 1960.

Alvar, Manuel, *Cantos de boda judeo-españoles*, Madrid: C.S.I.C., 1971.

Alvar, Manuel, *El romancero viejo y tradicional*, Mexico City: Porrúa, 1971.

Alvar, Manuel, "Una recogida de romances en Andalucía (1948–1968)," *El romancero en la tradición oral moderna*, ed. Diego Catalán et al. (Madrid: C.S.M.P., 1972), pp. 95–116.

Alvar, Manuel, *El español en el Sur de Estados Unidos: Estudios, encuestas, textos*, Alcalá de Henares: Universidad de Alcalá, 2000.

Alvar, Manuel, *El judeo español*, vol. I: *Estudios sefardíes*, vol. II: *Romancero sefardí de Marruecos*, Alcalá de Henares: Universidad de Alcalá–La Goleta, 2003.

Álvarez Pérez, José María, "El organista Francisco de Salinas: Nuevos datos a su biografía," *AMu*, 18 (1963), 21–44.

Alves, Francisco Manuel, "Cancioneiro popular bragançano," *MAHDB*, 10 (1938), 347–585.

Amades, Joan, *Cançons populars amoroses i cavalleresques*, Tárrega: F. Camps Calmet, 1935.

Amades, Joan, *Folklore de Catalunya: Rondallística*, Barcelona: Selecta, 1950.

Amades, Joan, "Les contes-devinettes de Catalogne," *Fabula*, 4 (1961), 199–223.

Amador de los Ríos, José, "Poesía popular de España: Romances tradicionales de Asturias," *Revista Ibérica*, 1 (1861), 24–51.

Amzulescu, Al. I., *Balade populare romîneşti*, 3 vols., Bucharest: Editura pentru Literatură, 1964.

Anastácio, Vanda, *Romanceiro Tradicional do Distrito de Faro*, Santiago do Cacém: Real Sociedade Arqueológica Lusitana, 1988.

Andolz, Rafael, *Diccionario aragonés*, Zaragoza: Mira, 1992.

Andrade, Manuel J., *Folk-Lore from the Dominican Republic*, New York: American Folk-Lore Society, 1930.

Andrews, J. Richard, *Introduction to Classical Nahuatl*, Austin: University of Texas Press, 1975.

Andriōtēs, Nikolaos P., *Etymologikò lexikò tēs koinēs neohellēnikēs*, Athens: Institut Français d'Athènes, 1951.

Anglés, Higinio, "Das Spanische Volkslied," *AfM*, 3 (1938), 331–362.

Anglés, Higinio (ed.), *La música en la Corte de los Reyes Católicos*, I: *Polifonía religiosa*, Barcelona: C.S.I.C., 1941; 2d ed., 1960 (= *MME* 1).

Anglés, Higinio (ed.), *La música en la Corte de Carlos V con la transcripción del "Libro de cifra nueva para teclas, harpa y vihuela" de Luys Venegas de Henestrosa (Alcalá de Henares, 1557)*, Barcelona: C.S.I.C., 1944.

Anglés, Higinio, and José Subirá, *Catálogo musical de la Biblioteca Nacional de Madrid*, 3 vols., Barcelona: C.S.I.C., 1946–1951.

Anglés, Higinio (ed.), *La música en la Corte de los Reyes Católicos: Cancionero musical de Palacio (Siglos XV–XVI)*, II: *Polifonía profana*, 2 vols., Barcelona: C.S.I.C., 1947–1951 (= *MME* 5 and 10).

Anglés, Higinio, "El «Libre Vermell» de Montserrat y los cantos y la danza sacra de los peregrinos durante el s. XIV," *AMu*, 10 (1955), 44–70.

Apollodorus, *The Library*, ed. and trans. James George Frazer, 2 vols., Cambridge, Massachusetts: Harvard University Press, 1976–1979.

Appel, Carl, *Provenzalische Chrestomathie*, Leipzig: O. R. Reisland, 1902.

Arbaud, Damase, *Chants populaires de la Provence*, 2 vols., Aix-en-Provence: A. Makaire, 1862–1864.

Arce, Agustín, "Cinco nuevos romances del Cid," *Sef*, 21 (1961), 69–75.

Archivo General de Simancas, *Casa y Sitios Reales*, Legajo 394, fol. 130.

Armistead, Samuel G., and Joseph H. Silverman, "Jud.-Sp. *alazare*: An Unnoticed Congener of Cast. *alazán*," *RPh*, 21 (1968), 510–512.

Armistead, Samuel G., and Joseph H. Silverman, "Un aspecto desatendido de la obra de Américo Castro," *Estudios sobre la obra de Américo Castro*, ed. Pedro Laín Entralgo and Andrés Amoros (Madrid: Taurus, 1971), pp. 181–190.

Armistead, Samuel G., "¿Existió un romancero de tradición oral entre los moriscos?," *Actas del Coloquio Internacional sobre Literatura Aljamiada y Morisca*, ed. Alvaro Galmés de Fuentes (Madrid: Gredos, 1978), pp. 211–236.

Armistead, Samuel G., "Romances tradicionales entre los hispano-hablantes del estado de Luisiana," *NRFH*, 27 (1978), 39–56.

Armistead, Samuel G., and Joseph H. Silverman, "Sobre los romances y canciones judeoespañoles recogidos por Cynthia M. Crews," *ESef*, 2 (1979), 21–38.

Armistead, Samuel G., "Neo-Individualism and the *Romancero*," *RPh*, 33 (1979–1980), 172–181.

Armistead, Samuel G., and Joseph H. Silverman, "El Romancero entre los sefardíes de Holanda," *Etudes de Philologie Romane et d'Histoire Littéraire offertes à Jules Horrent*, ed. Jean Marie d'Heur and Nicoletta Cherubini (Liège: Gedit, 1980), pp. 535–541.

Armistead, Samuel G., and Joseph H. Silverman, "Three Hispano-Jewish *romances* from Amsterdam," *Medieval, Renaissance and Folklore Studies in Honor of John Esten Keller*, ed. Joseph R. Jones (Newark, Delaware: Juan de la Cuesta, 1980), pp. 243–254.

Armistead, Samuel G., and Joseph H. Silverman, "El antiguo romancero sefardí: Citas de romances en himnarios hebreos (Siglos XVI–XIX)," *NRFH*, 30 (1981), 453–512.

Armistead, Samuel G., Reginetta Haboucha, and Joseph H. Silverman, "Words Worse than Wounds: A Judeo-Spanish Version of a Near Eastern Folktale," *Fabula*, 23 (1982), 95–98.

Armistead, Samuel G., and James T. Monroe, "*Albas, mammas*, and Code-Switching in the *Kharjas*: A Reply to Keith Whinnom," *La Corónica*, 11:2 (1983), 174–207.

Armistead, Samuel G., and James T. Monroe, "A New Version of *La morica de Antequera*," *La Corónica*, 12:2 (1983–1984), 228–240.

Armistead, Samuel G., and Joseph H. Silverman, "Sephardic Folkliterature and Eastern Mediterranean Oral Tradition," *Musica Judaica*, 6:1 (1983–1984), 38–54.

Armistead, Samuel G., "Una encuesta romancística: Trás-os-Montes, julio 1980," *QP*, 11–12 (1982) (=1984), 67–85.

Armistead, Samuel G., "From Epic to Chronicle: An Individualist Appraisal," *RPh*, 40 (1986–1987), 338–359.

Armistead, Samuel G., "Schoolmen or Minstrels?: Rhetorical Questions in Epic and Balladry," *La Corónica*, 16:1 (1987–1988), 43–54.

Armistead, Samuel G., Review: Beatriz Mariscal de Rhett, *La Muerte ocultada*, Madrid: S.M.P., 1984–1985, *JAF*, 100 (1987), 231–233.

Armistead, Samuel G., "The Paragogic -*d*- in Judeo-Spanish *Romances*," *Hispanic Studies in Honor of Joseph H. Silverman*, ed. Joseph V. Ricapito (Newark, Delaware: Juan de la Cuesta, 1988), pp. 57–75.

Armistead, Samuel G., and James T. Monroe, "'Mjs moros mortaricaca': Arabic Phrases in the *Poema de Alfonso XI* (Strophe 1709*b–d*)," *La Corónica*, 17:2 (1988–1989), 38–43.

Armistead, Samuel G., and Joseph H. Silverman, "*Gaiferos y Waltharius*: Paralelismos adicionales," *Homenaje al profesor Antonio Vilanova*, 2 vols., ed. Adolfo Sotelo Vázquez and Marta Cristina Carbonell (Barcelona: Universidad de Barcelona, 1989), I, 31–43.

Armistead, Samuel G., "Chronicles and Epics in the 15th Century," *La Corónica*, 18:1 (1989–1990), 103–107.

Armistead, Samuel G., "Gaiferos' Game of Chance: A Formulaic Theme in the *Romancero*," *La Corónica*, 19:2 (1990–1991), 132–144.

Armistead, Samuel G., "Romanceiro e historia: *La pérdida de don Sebastián,*" *Actas del Coloquio Romancero-Cancionero (UCLA) 1984*, ed. Enrique Rodríguez Cepeda and S. G. Armistead, 2 vols. (Madrid: José Porrúa, 1990), II, 265–292.

Armistead, Samuel G., "Judeo-Spanish Traditional Poetry in the United States," *American Jewish Archives*, 44 (1992), 357–377.

Armistead, Samuel G., "Portuguesismos en dos dialectos españoles de Luisiana," *RFE*, 72 (1992), 491–524.

Armistead, Samuel G., *The Spanish Tradition in Louisiana*, I: *Isleño Folkliterature*, Newark, Delaware: Juan de la Cuesta, 1992.

Armistead, Samuel G., "Los siglos del Romancero: Tradición y creación (Estudio preliminar)," Paloma Díaz-Mas, *Romancero* (Barcelona: Crítica, 1994), pp. ix–xxi.

Armistead, Samuel G., "Three Jewish-Spanish Joseph Narratives," *RPh*, 49 (1995–1996), 34–52.

Armistead, Samuel G., Review: Teresa Catarella, *El romancero gitano-andaluz de Juan José Niño* (Seville: Fundación Machado, 1993), *HR*, 64 (1996), 97–99.

Armistead, Samuel G., Review: Thomas Binkley and Margit Frenk, *Spanish Romances of the Sixteenth Century* (Bloomington: Indiana University Press, 1995), *Hispania* (Washington, D.C.), 79 (1996), 782.

Armistead, Samuel G., and James T. Monroe, "J.-Sp. *puertas de rey(es) 'royal courts'*," *Sef*, 58 (1998), 227–241.

Armistead, Samuel G., and Luis Suárez Avila, "Un nuevo fragmento del romance de Calaínos," *RFE*, 79 (1999), 159–170.

Armistead, Samuel G., "The Memory of Tri-Religious Spain in the Sephardic *Romancero*," *"Encuentros" & "Desencuentros": Spanish-Jewish Cultural Interaction Throughout History*, ed. Carlos Carrete Parrondo et al. (Tel Aviv: University Publishing Projects, 2000), pp. 265–286.

Armistead, Samuel G., "Seis cantos de boda judeo-españoles (MSS. de Américo Castro)," *La eterna agonía del Romancero: Homenaje a Paul Bénichou*, ed. Pedro M. Piñero Ramírez et al. (Sevilla: Fundación Machado, 2001), pp. 179–193.

Armistead, Samuel G., "Contamination and Reconstruction in the Judeo-Spanish *Romancero*," *Proceedings of the Twelfth British Conference on Judeo-Spanish Studies, 24–26 June, 2001*, ed. Hilary Pomeroy and Michael Alpert (London: Queen Mary and Westfield College, 2004), pp. 93–109.

Armistead, Samuel G., "Expurgation and Bowdlerization in Hispanic Traditional Poetry," *Wine, Women, and Song: Hebrew and Arabic Poetry in Medieval Iberia*, ed. Michelle M.

Hamilton, Sarah J. Portnoy, and David A. Wacks (Newark, Delaware: Juan de la Cuesta, 2004), pp. 15–32.

Armistead, Samuel G., *La tradición hispano-canaria en Luisiana* [2d ed.], trans. Manuel Wood Wood, ed. Maximiano Trapero, Las Palmas de Gran Canaria: Anroart, 2007.

Arnim, L. Achim von, and Clemens Brentano, *Des Knaben Wunderhorn: Alte deutsche Lieder*, Munich: Winkler, 1957 (orig. 1806–1808).

Arribas Arranz, Filemón, *Paleografía documental hispánica*, 2 vols., Valladolid: Sever-Cuesta, 1965.

Arróniz, Othón, *La influencia italiana en el nacimiento de la comedia española*, Madrid: Gredos, 1969.

ART =   Narciso Alonso Cortés, "Romances tradicionales," *RHi*, 50 (1920), 198–268.

Asensio, Eugenio, *Cancionero musical luso-español del siglo XVI antiguo e inédito*, Salamanca: Departamento de Literatura, Universidad de Salamanca, 1989.

Asín Palacios, Miguel, *Contribución a la toponimia árabe de España*, 2d ed., Madrid–Granada: C.S.I.C., 1944.

Askins, Arthur L.-F. (ed.), *Cancioneiro de Corte e de Magnates: Ms. CXIV/2–2 da Biblioteca Pública e Arquivo Distrital de Évora*, Berkeley–Los Angeles: University of California Press, 1968.

ASW =   Marcelino Menéndez Pelayo, "Apéndices y suplemento a la *Primavera y flor de romances* de Wolf y Hoffmann," *Antología de poetas líricos castellanos*, IX, "Ed. Nac.," XXV, Santander: C.S.I.C., 1945.

Atanasova, T., et al., *Bălgarsko-angliĭski rečnik*, 2 vols., Sofia: Nauka, 1990.

Atero Burgos, Virtudes, *Romancero de la Provincia de Cádiz*, Cádiz: Fundación Machado, 1996.

Athaide Oliveira, F. Xavier d', *Contos Tradicionaes do Algarve*, 2 vols., Tavira: Typographia Burocrática, 1900.

Athaide Oliveira, F. Xavier d', *Romanceiro e Cancioneiro do Algarve (Lição de Loulé)*, Oporto: Typographia Universal, 1905.

Attias =   Moshe Attias, *Romancero sefaradí: Romanzas y cantes populares en judeo-español*, 2d ed., Jerusalem: Ben-Zewi Institute, 1961.

Attwater, Donald, *The Penguin Dictionary of Saints*, Baltimore: Penguin, 1965.

Avalle-Arce, Juan Bautista, "Los romances de la muerte de don Beltrán," *Temas hispánicos medievales* (Madrid: Gredos, 1974), pp. 124–134.

Avenary, Hanoch, "Cantos españoles antiguos mencionados en la literatura hebrea," *AMu*, 25 (1971), 67–79.

Avenary, Hanoch, "Contacts between Church and Synagogue Music," *Proceedings of the World Congress on Jewish Music (Jerusalem, 1978)*, ed. Judith Cohen (Tel Aviv: Institute for the Translation of Hebrew Literature, 1982), pp. 89–107.

Avenç, II =   *Segona serie de cançons populars catalanes*, Barcelona: Biblioteca Popular de "L'Avenç," 1909.

Avenç, III =   *Tercera serie de cançons populars catalanes*, Barcelona: Biblioteca Popular de "L'Avenç," 1910.

Avila, Francisco de, *Flor de las comedias de España, de diferentes autores. . .*, Barcelona: Sebastián de Cormellas al Call, 1616.

Azáceta, José María, *Cancionero de Juan Fernández de Íxar*, 2 vols., Madrid: C.S.I.C., 1956.

Azevedo, Álvaro Rodrigues de, *Romanceiro do Arquipélago da Madeira*, Funchal: «Voz do Povo», 1880.

Bacri, Roland, *Trésors des racines pataouètes*, Paris: Belin, 1983.

Badger, George Percy, *An English-Arabic Lexicon*, Beirut: Librairie du Liban, 1980.

Bahia =   Doralice Fernandes Xavier Alcoforado and Maria del Rosário Suárez Albán, *Romanceiro Ibérico na Bahia*, Salvador–Bahia: Livraria Universitária, 1996.

Balbín Lucas, Rafael de, *Tres piezas menores de Moreto, inéditos*, Madrid, 1942.

Balbín Lucas, Rafael de, "Bayle del Conde Claros; Baile de Lucrecia y Tarquino; Entremés del Vestuario," *RBN*, 3 (1942), 80–116.

Baldwin, John W., "The Image of the Jongleur in Northern France around 1200," *Speculum*, 72 (1997), 635–663.

Balladoro, Arrigo, *Folklore veronese: Canti*, Torino, 1898 (reprint: Bologna: Forni, 1969).

Ballarín Cornel, Angel, *Vocabulario de Benasque*, Zaragoza: Instituto «Fernando el Católico», 1971.

Bandello, Matteo, *Le novelle*, ed. Gioachino Brognoligo, 5 vols., Bari: Giuseppe Laterza & Figli, 1910–1912.

Barbeau, Marius, and Edward Sapir, *Folk Songs of French Canada*, New Haven: Yale University Press, 1925.

Barbeau, Marius, *Le rossignol y chante: Répertoire de la chanson folklorique française au Canada*, Ottawa: Musée National du Canada, 1962.

Barbetta, Giulio Cesare, *Intavolatura de liuto dove si contiene padoane, arie, balletti, pass'e mezi, saltarelli, per ballar à la Italiana, & altre cosa*, Venice: A. Gardano, 1585.

Barbieri, Francisco Asenjo, *Biografías y documentos sobre música y músicos españoles,* ed. Emilio Casares Rodicio, Madrid: Fundación Banco Exterior, 1986.

Barbieri =   Francisco Asenjo Barbieri (ed.), *Cancionero musical de los siglos XV y XVI*, Madrid: Tipografía de los Huérfanos, 1890; 2d ed., Málaga: Gráficas Urania, 1987.

Barrera y Leirado, Cayetano Alberto de la, *Catálogo bibliográfico y biográfico del teatro antiguo español, desde sus orígenes hasta mediados del siglo XVIII*, Madrid: M. Rivadeneyra, 1860; facs. ed., Madrid: Gredos, 1969.

Barry, Phillips, Fannie H. Eckstorm, and Mary W. Smythe, *British Ballads from Maine*, New Haven: Yale University Press, 1929.

Bartsch, Karl, and Wolfgang Golther, *Deutsche Liederdichter des zwölften bis vierzehnten Jahrhunderts*, 4th ed., Berlin: B. Behr, 1901.

Basto, Cláudio, "'Sortes' Amorosas no 'S. João'," *RL*, 32 (1934), 161–233.

Batalha, Graciete Nogueira, *Glossário do Dialecto Macaense: Notas linguísticas, etnográficas e folklóricas,* Macao: Instituto Cultural de Macau, 1988.

Baud-Bovy, *Textes* = Samuel Baud-Bovy, *La Chanson populaire grecque du Dodécanèse, I: Les textes,* Paris: "Les Belles Lettres," 1936.

Baud-Bovy, Samuel, "La chanson cleftique," *JIFMC,* 1 (1949), 4–45.

Baud-Bovy, Samuel, "Sur la strophe de la chanson 'cleftique'," *AIPhHOS,* 10 (1950), 59–78.

Baud-Bovy, Samuel, *Etudes sur la chanson cleftique,* Athens: Institut Français d'Athènes, 1958.

Baughman, Ernest W., *Type and Motif-Index of the Folktales of England and North America,* The Hague: Mouton, 1966.

Bayo, Ciro, *Romancerillo del Plata,* Buenos Aires: Institución Cultural Española, 1943.

Beck, Brenda E. F., et al., *Folktales of India,* Chicago: University of Chicago Press, 1987.

Ben–Amos, Dan (ed.), *Folklore Genres,* Austin: University of Texas Press, 1976.

Benaim de Lasry, Anita (ed.), *"Carlos Maynes" and "La emperatrís de Roma,"* Newark, Delaware: Juan de la Cuesta, 1982.

Benardete = Samuel G. Armistead and Joseph H. Silverman, *Judeo-Spanish Ballads from New York* (collected by Mair José Benardete), Berkeley–Los Angeles–London: University of California Press, 1981.

Bendayán de Bendelac, Alegría, *Diccionario del judeoespañol de los sefardíes del norte de Marruecos,* Caracas: Centro de Estudios Sefardíes, 1995.

Bender, Harold H., *A Lithuanian Etymological Index,* Princeton: Princeton University Press, 1921.

Benéitez Cantero, Valentín, *Vocabulario español-árabe-marroquí,* 2d ed., Tetuán: Editorial Casado, 1952.

Benharroch B., Isaac, *Diccionario de haquetía,* Caracas: Asociación Israelita de Venezuela, 2004.

Bénichou, Paul, "Romances judeo-españoles de Marruecos," *RFH*, 6 (1944), 36–76, 105–138, 255–279, 313–381.

Bénichou, Paul, "Observaciones sobre el judeo-español de Marruecos," *RFH*, 7 (1945), 209–257.

Bénichou =   Paul Bénichou, *Romancero judeo-español de Marruecos*, Madrid: Castalia, 1968.

Bénichou, Paul, *Creación poética en el romancero tradicional*, Madrid: Gredos, 1968.

Bennett, Philip E., "The Storming of the Other World: The Enamoured Muslim Princess and the Evolution of the Legend of Guillaume d'Orange," *Guillaume d'Orange and the "Chanson de geste": Essays presented to Duncan McMillan . . .*, ed. Wolfgang van Emden and Philip E. Bennett (Reading, England: Société Rencesvals–British Branch, 1984), pp. 1–14.

Benoliel, José, "Dialecto judeo-hispano-marroquí o hakitía," *BRAE*, 13 (1926), 209–233, 342–363, 507–538; 14 (1927), 137–168, 196–234, 357–373, 566–580; 15 (1928), 47–61, 188–223; 32 (1952), 255–289.

Berceo, Gonzalo de, *Milagros de Nuestra Señora*, ed. Antonio G. Solalinde, 6th ed., Madrid: Espasa-Calpe, 1964.

Berceo, Gonzalo de, *Obras completas*, ed. Brian Dutton, London: Tamesis, 1967.

Bermudo, Fray Juan, *Declaración de instrumentos musicales*, Osuna: Juan de León, 1555; ed. M.S. Kastner, Kassel: Bärenreiter, 1957.

Bernadach, Moïse, "Castillo Solórzano et ses fantaisies prosodiques (À propos d'une ingénieuse utilisation des romances)," *RLR*, 80 (1973), 149–175.

Bernis Madrazo, Carmen, *Indumentaria medieval española*, Madrid: C.S.I.C., 1956.

Béroul, *Le Roman de Tristan,* ed. Ernest Muret, New York: Johnson Reprint, 1965 (orig. Paris: Firmin Didot, 1903).

Béroul, *The Romance of Tristran,* ed. A. Ewert, 2 vols.,New York: Barnes & Noble, 1971.

Bertran y Bros, Pau, *Cansons y follíes populars (inédites) recullides al peu de Montserrat*, Barcelona: A. Verdaguer, 1885.

Bertrand de Bar-sur-Aube, *Girart de Vienne*, ed. Wolfgang van Emden, Paris: A. & J. Picard, 1972 (S.A.T.F.).

Biberstein Kazimirski, Albert de, *Dictionnaire arabe-français*, 2 vols., Paris: Maisonneuve, 1860.

Biblioteca Nacional, *Inventario general de manuscritos de la Biblioteca Nacional*, Vol. IV (1101–1598), Madrid: Ministerio de Educación Nacional, 1958.

Bibliotheca Iberica et Latino-Americana: Being a choice collection of books and manuscripts, maps, and periodicals . . ., ed. Karl W. Hiersemannn, Leipzig: Privately printed, 1913.

Bierhorst, John, *A Nahuatl-English Dictionary and Concordance to the Cantares Mexicanos*, Stanford: Stanford University Press, 1985.

Bihać =   David E. Bynum, *Serbo-Croatian Heroic Poems: Epics from Bihać, Cazin, and Kulen Vakuf*, New York: Garland, 1993.

Binkley, Thomas, and Margit Frenk, *Spanish Romances of the Sixteenth Century*, Bloomington: Indiana University Press, 1995 (Publications of the Early Music Institute).

Blaise, Albert, *Dictionnaire latin-français des auteurs chrétiens*, Strasbourg: "Le Latin Chrétien," 1954.

Blake, Robert J., "Sobre las vocales *e* y *o* en la documentación leonesa del siglo XIII," *Orígenes de las lenguas romances en el reino de León: siglos IX–XII*, ed. José María Fernández Catón (León: Centro de Estudios e Investigación San Isidro, Archivo Histórico Diocesano, 2004), pp. 543–553.

Blecua, José Manuel (ed.), *Francisco de Quevedo: Obra poética*, 4 vols., Barcelona: Castalia, 1969–1981.

Bloch-von Wartburg = Oscar Bloch and Walther von Wartburg, *Dictionnaire étymologique de la langue française,* 2d ed., Paris: Presses Universitaires de France, 1950.

Bloomfield, Leonard, *Language*, New York: Henry Holt, 1933.

Bloomfield, M., "On Talking Birds in Hindu Fiction," *Festschrift Ernst Windisch zum siebzigsten Geburtstag am 4. September 1914* (Leipzig: Otto Harrassowitz, 1914), pp. 349–361.

Boccaccio, Giovanni, *Decameron (Tutte le opere di Giovanni Boccaccio*, Vol. IV), ed. Vittore Branca, Milan: Arnoldo Mondadori, 1976.

Boer, Harm den, *La literatura sefardí de Amsterdam*, Alcalá de Henares: Universidad de Alcalá, 1996.

Boerio, Giuseppe, *Dizionario del dialetto veneziano*, 2d ed., Venice: Giovanni Cecchini, 1856 (reprint: Florence: Giunti, 1993).

Boissacq, Émile, *Dictionnaire étymologique de la langue grecque*, 2d ed., Heidelberg–Paris: Carl Winter–C. Klincksieck, 1923.

Boiteux, Lucas A., "Poranduba Catarinense," *RIHGB*, 184 (1944), 1–92.

Boiteux, Lucas A., *Poranduba Catarinense*, [2d ed.], Florianópolis: Comissão Catarinense de Folklore, 1957.

Bolaños Donoso, Piedad, and Mercedes de los Reyes Peña, "Teatro español en Lisboa durante la temporada de 1724–25: La fiesta de *Las nuevas armas de amor*," *Música y literatura en la Península Ibérica: 1600–1750*, ed. M. A. Virgili Blanquet et al. (Valladolid: Andrés Martín, 1997), pp. 13–47.

Bonilla y San Martín, Adolfo, "Romances antiguos," *ALE* (1900–1904), 29–46.

Boretzky, Norbert, *Der türkische Einfluss auf das Albanische, Teil 2: Wörterbuch der albanischen Turzismen*, Wiesbaden: Otto Harrassowitz, 1976.

Borgatti, Mario, *Canti popolari emiliani raccolti a Cento*, Florence: Leo S. Olschki, 1962.

Bosnia =   Samuel G. Armistead and Joseph H. Silverman, with the collaboration of Biljana Šljivić-Šimšić, *Judeo-Spanish Ballads from Bosnia*, Philadelphia: University of Pennsylvania Press, 1971.

Bourland, Caroline B., "Boccaccio and the Decameron in Castilian and Catalan Literature," *RHi*, 12 (1905), 1–232.

Bowden, Muriel, *A Commentary on the General Prologue to the Canterbury Tales*, New York: MacMillan, 1962.

Bowra, Cecil Maurice, *Homer*, London: Gerald Duckworth, 1979.

Braga =   Theóphilo Braga, *Romanceiro Geral Portuguez*, 2d ed., 3 vols., Lisbon: Manuel Gomes–J. A. Rodrigues, 1906–1909.

Braga, Theóphilo, *Cantos Populares do Arquipélago Açoriano*, Oporto: Livraria Nacional, 1864.

Braga, Theóphilo, *Contos Tradicionaes do Povo Portuguez*, 2 vols., Oporto: Magalhães & Moniz, n.d.

Branca, Vittore, *Boccaccio medievale e nuovi studi sul Decamerone*, 5th ed. Florence: Sansoni, 1981.

Brandão, Théo, *Folclore de Alagoas*, Maceió-Alagoas: Casa Ramalho, 1949.

Brandes, Stanley, *Metaphors of Masculinity: Sex and Status in Andalusian Folklore*, Philadelphia: University of Pennsylvania Press, 1985.

Brault, Gerard J. (ed.), *The Song of Roland*, 2 vols., University Park: Pennsylvania State University Press, 1978.

Brazão Gonçalves, Eduardo, *Dicionário do Falar Algarvio*, 2d ed., Faro: Algarve em Foco, 1996.

Brehaut, Ernest, *An Encyclopedist of the Dark Ages: Isidore of Seville*, New York: Burt Franklin, 1972 (orig. 1912).

Brewster, Paul G., and Georgia Tarsouli, "Two English Ballads and their Greek Counterparts," *JAF*, 69 (1956), 41–46.

BRI =   Yacob Abraham Yoná, *Brošura de romansas 'importantes*, Salonika: published by the author, 1913.

Briffault, Robert, *The Mothers: A Study of the Origins of Sentiments and Institutions*, 3 vols., New York: MacMillan, 1927.

Briz =   Francesch Pelay Briz, *Cansons de la terra: Cants populars catalans*, 5 vols., Barcelona–Paris: E. Ferrando Roca–Alvar Verdaguer–Maisonneuve, 1866–1877.

Brkić, Jovan, *Moral Concepts in Traditional Serbian Epic Poetry*, The Hague: Mouton, 1961.

Bronson, Bertrand Harris, *The Traditional Tunes of the Child Ballads with their Text, according to the Extant Records of Great Britain and America*, 4 vols., Princeton: Princeton University Press, 1959–1972.

Bronson, Bertrand Harris, *The Singing Tradition of Child's Ballads*, Princeton: Princeton University Press, 1976.

Bronzini, Giovanni B., *La canzone epico-lirica nell'Italia centro-meridionale*, 2 vols., Rome: Angelo Signorelli, 1956–1961.

Brown, Francis, S. K. Driver, and Charles A. Briggs (ed.), *A Hebrew and English Lexicon of the Old Testament*, Oxford: Clarendon, 1962 (orig. 1907).

Brown, Howard Mayer, *Instrumental Music Printed before 1600*, Cambridge, Massachusetts: Harvard University Press, 1965.

Brown, Kenneth L., *People of Salé: Tradition and Change in a Moroccan City, 1830–1930*, Cambridge, Massachusetts: Harvard University Press, 1976.

BRP = Pere Ferré and Cristina Carinhas, *Bibliografia do Romanceiro Português da Tradição Oral Moderna (1828–1996)*, 5 vols., Lisbon: Universidade Nova de Lisboa, 1996.

Bruerton, Courtney, "Eight Plays by Vélez de Guevara," *RPh*, 6 (1952–1953), 248–253.

Brunot, Louis, *Au seuil de la vie marocaine*, Casablanca: Farairre, 1950.

Bryan, W.F., and Germaine Dempster, *Sources and Analogues of Chaucer's Canterbury Tales*, New York: Humanities Press, 1958.

BTPE = *Biblioteca de las tradiciones populares españolas*, ed. Antonio Machado y Alvarez, 11 vols., Seville–Madrid: Francisco Alvarez–Fernando Fe, 1883–1886.

Buchan, David, *The Ballad and the Folk*, London: Routledge & Kegan Paul, 1972.

Buescu, Maria Leonor Carvalhão, *Monsanto: Etnografia e Linguagem*, [1st ed.], Lisbon: Centro de Estudos Filológicos, 1961.

Buescu, Maria Leonor Carvalhão, *Monsanto: Etnografia e Linguagem*, 2d ed., Lisbon: Editorial Presença, 1984.

Bugeja, Paul, *Kif titkellem bl-Ingliż: Dizzjunarju Malti-Ingliż*, Sliem, Malta: "The Book Shop," 1956.

Burckhardt, Jacob, *The Civilization of the Renaissance in Italy*, trans. S. G. C. Middlemore, ed. Ludwig Goldschneider, New York: Modern Library, 1954.

Burney, Charles, *A General History of Music, from the Earliest Ages to the Present Period*, 4 vols., London: Printed for the author, 1776–1789; reprinted with critical and historical notes by Frank Mercer, London: G. T. Foulis, 1935; New York: Dover, 1957.

Buschmann, Sigrid, *Beiträge zum etymologischen Wörterbuch des Galizischen*, Bonn: Universität, 1965.

Busto Cortina, Juan, *Catálogo índice de romances asturianos*, [Oviedo]: Principado de Asturias, 1989.

Busuttil, E.D., *Kalepin (Damm il-kliem) Malti-Ingliż*, Valletta: Aquilina, 1949.

Bynum, David E., "Themes of the Young Hero in Serbocroatian Oral Epic Tradition," *PMLA*, 83 (1968), 1296–1303.

C1550 =   Antonio Rodríguez-Moñino (ed.), *Cancionero de romances (Anvers, 1550)*, Madrid: Castalia, 1967.

Cacho Palomar, María Teresa, "Quevedo, los bailes y los cancioneros musicales mediceos," *Música y literatura en la Península Ibérica: 1600–1750*, ed. M. A. Virgili Blanquet et al. (Valladolid: Andrés Martín, 1997), pp. 275–286.

Calasans Brandão da Silva, José, Julio Santana Braga, and Maria Antonieta Campos Tourinho, *Folclore Geo-Histórico da Bahia e seu Recôncavo*, Rio de Janeiro: Campanha de Defesa do Folclore Brasileiro, 1972.

Calvo, Raquel, with Diego Catalán, *Romancero general de Segovia: Antología [1880]–1992*, Segovia: S.M.P.–Diputación Provincial, 1994.

Câmara Cascudo, Luís da, *Contos Tradicionais do Brasil*, Rio de Janeiro: "Coleção Brasileira de Ouro," 1967.

Cambel, R. Joe, *A Morphological Dictionary of Classical Nahuatl*, Madison: H.S.M.S., 1985.

Campa, Mariano de la, Delia Gavela, and Dolores Noguera, "Breve corpus documental para el estudio de los festejos públicos y su dimensión teatral a finales del siglo XVI en Madrid," *Edad de Oro*, 16 (1997), 89–98.

Cameron, D. A., *An Arabic-English Vocabulary for the Use of English Students of Modern Egyptian Arabic,* London: Bernard Quaritch, 1892.

Campos, Juana G., and Ana Barella, *Diccionario de refranes,* Madrid: Real Academia Española, 1975.

Cano, Ana María, "Contribución al romancero asturiano," *Homenaje a Alonso Zamora Vicente,* 2 vols. (Madrid: Castalia, 1988–1989), II, 337–338.

Cano, Rafael, *Del tiempo de Ñaupa (folklore norteño),* Buenos Aires: L. J. Rosso, 1930.

Capmany, Aureli, *Cançoner popular,* 3 series, Barcelona: La Renaixensa–«L'Avenç», 1901–1913.

[Capmany, Aureli], and Carrera, Adolf, *Cançons populars catalanes,* 2d ed., 4 vols., Barcelona: Biblioteca Popular «L'Avenç», 1909–1916.

CARG =   Ana Valenciano et al., *Os romances tradicionais de Galicia: Catálogo exemplificado dos seus temas,* Madrid–Santiago de Compostela: Fundación Ramón Menéndez Pidal, 1998. (The abbreviation reflects an earlier Castilian title: *Catálogo-Antología del Romancero de Galicia.*)

Carilla, Emilio, "Quevedo y «El Parnaso Español»," *BAAL,* 65 (1948), 373–408.

Carmi, T., *The Penguin Book of Hebrew Verse,* New York: Penguin, 1981.

Carney, Elizabeth, "Fact and Fiction in *Queen Eleanor's Confession,*" *Folklore,* 95:2 (1984), 167–170.

Caro, Rodrigo, *Días geniales y lúdicros,* 2 vols., ed. Jean-Pierre Etienvre, Madrid: Espasa-Calpe, 1978.

Carré Alvarellos, Leandro, *Diccionario galego-castelán e vocabulario castelán-galego,* 3rd ed., La Coruña: Roel, 1951.

Carrera, Adolf, *Cançons populars catalanes (tercera serie),* Barcelona: Biblioteca Popular «L'Avenç», 1910.

Carreras y Candi, F., *Folklore y costumbres de España.* 3 vols., Barcelona: Alberto Martín, 1931–1934.

Carrière, Joseph Médard, *Tales from the French Folk-Lore of Missouri,* New York: AMS, 1970.

Carrizo, Juan Alfonso, *Cancionero popular de La Rioja*, 3 vols., Buenos Aires: Universidad Nacional de Tucumán, 1942.

Cartier, Alfred, and Adolphe Chennevière, "Antoine de Moulin, valet de chambre de la Reine de Navarre," *RHLF*, 2 (1895), 466–491; 3 (1896), 90–106 and 218–244.

Casado de Otaloa, Luis, with Diego Catalán, *El romancero tradicional extremeño: Las primeras colecciones (1809–1910)*, Mérida: Fundación Ramón Menéndez Pidal, 1995.

Casares Rodicio, Emilio et al. (ed.), Francisco Asenjo Barbieri, *Bibliografía y documentos sobre música y músicos españoles*, Madrid: Fundación Banco Exterior, 1986.

Castañón, Luciano, "Los meses en el refranero asturiano," *RDTP*, 18 (1962), 395–415.

Castillo, Hernando del, *Cancionero general* (Valencia, 1511), ed. Antonio Rodríguez-Moñino, Madrid: Real Academia Española, 1958.

Castro, Américo, "Romance de la mujer que fue a la guerra," *Lengua, enseñanza y literatura* (Madrid: Victoriano Suárez, 1924), pp. 259–280.

Castro Escudero, J., "Bailes y danzas en el teatro de Lope de Vega," *LNL*, 156 (1961), 52–64; 185 (1968), 25–42; 188–189 (1969), 7–32; 202 (1972), 20–33.

Castro Osório, Ana de, *Histórias Maravilhosas da Tradição Popular Portuguesa*, Lisbon: Sociedade de Expansão Cultural, [1955].

Castroviejo, José María, *Apariciones en Galicia*, Santiago de Compostela: Porto, 1955.

Catalán, Diego, *Poema de Alfonso XI: Fuentes, dialecto, estilo*, Madrid: Gredos, 1953.

Catalán, Diego, and Alvaro Galmés, "El tema de la boda estorbada: Proceso de tradicionalización de un romance juglaresco," *VR*, 13 (1953), 66–98.

Catalán, Diego, *Siete siglos de Romancero (Historia y poesía)*, Madrid: Gredos, 1969.

Catalán, Diego, *Por campos del Romancero: Estudios sobre la tradición oral moderna*, Madrid: Gredos, 1970.

Catalán, Diego, *¡Alça la voz, pregonero!: Homenaje a don Ramón Menéndez Pidal*, Madrid: C.S.M.P., 1979.

Catalán, Diego, "El romancero medieval," *El comentario de textos*, 4 (Madrid: Castalia, 1983), pp. 451–489.

Catalán, Diego, "The Artisan Poetry of the *Romancero*," *OTrad*, 2 (1987), 399–423.

Catalán, Diego, "Don Alvaro de Luna y su paje Moralicos (1453) en el romancero sefardí," *Hispanic Studies in Honor of Joseph H. Silverman*, ed. Joseph V. Ricapito (Newark, Delaware: Juan de la Cuesta, 1988), pp. 109–135.

Catalán, Diego, *Arte poética del romancero oral*, 2 vols., Madrid: Siglo XXI, 1997–1998.

Catalán, Diego, *Cancionero en cifra de Perrenot, embajador de Felipe II en Francia (1562)* (in preparation).

Catarella, Teresa, "A New Branch of the Hispanic *Romancero*," *La Corónica*, 17:1 (1988–1989), 23–31.

Catarella, Teresa, *El romancero gitano-andaluz de Juan José Niño*, Seville: Fundación Machado, 1993.

CBU =   Arcadio de Larrea Palacín, "El cancionero de Baruch Uziel," *VR*, 18 (1959), 324–365.

Cejador y Frauca, Julio, *La verdadera poesía castellana: Floresta de la antigua lírica popular*, 9 vols., Madrid: Arco, 1987.

Cepas, Juan, *Vocabulario popular malagueño*, 3rd ed., Málaga: Caja de Ahorros–C.S.I.C., 1973.

Cervantes Saavedra, Miguel de, *El ingenioso hidalgo don Quijote de la Mancha*, ed. Francisco Rodríguez Marín, 8 vols., Madrid: La Lectura, 1911–1913.

Cervantes Saavedra, Miguel de, *El ingenioso hidalgo Don Quijote de la Mancha*, ed. Luis Andrés Murillo, 3 vols., 3rd ed., Madrid: Castalia, 1984.

Cervantes Saavedra, Miguel de, *El ingenioso hidalgo don Quijote de la Mancha*, ed. Tom Lathrop, Newark, Delaware: Juan de la Cuesta, 2003.

CGR =   *Catálogo General del Romancero: El Romancero panhispánico: Catálogo general descriptivo (The Pan-Hispanic*

Ballad: General Descriptive Catalogue), ed. Diego Catalán, J. Antonio Cid, Beatriz Mariscal, Flor Salazar, Ana Valenciano, and Sandra Robertson, 4 vols., Madrid: S.M.P., 1982–1988.

Chadwick, Nora K., *Russian Heroic Poetry*, Cambridge: Cambridge University Press, 1932.

Chadwick, Nora K., and Victor Zhirmunsky, *Oral Epics of Central Asia*, Cambridge: Cambridge University Press, 1969.

Chardavoine, Jean, *Le Recueil des plus belles et excellentes chansons en forme de voix de ville*, Paris: Chez Claude Micard, 1576; Geneva: Minkoff Reprint, 1980.

Chaucer, Geoffrey, *The Poetical Works of Chaucer*, ed. F. N. Robinson, Cambridge: Riverside Press, 1933.

Chaucer, Geoffrey, *The Complete Poetry and Prose*, ed. John H. Fisher, New York: Holt, Rinehart and Winston, 1977.

Cherbonneau, A., *Dictionnaire français-arabe pour la conversation en Algérie*, Paris: Imprimerie Nationale, 1872.

Chérézli, Salomon Israel, *Nouveau petit dictionnaire judéo-espagnol-français*, 2 vols., Jerusalem: A. M. Luncz, 1898–1899.

Chertudi, Susana, *Cuentos folklóricos de la Argentina: primera serie*, Buenos Aires: Instituto Nacional de Filología y Folklore, 1960.

Chevalier, Maxime, "Un cuento, una comedia, cuatro novelas (Lope de Rueda, Juan Timoneda, Cristóbal Tamariz, Lope de Vega, María de Zayas)," *Essays on Narrative Fiction in the Iberian Peninsula in Honor of Frank Pierce*, ed. R. B. Tate ([Oxford]: Dolphin, 1982), pp. 27–38.

Chevalier, Maxime, *Cuentos folklóricos en la España del Siglo de Oro*, Barcelona: Editorial Crítica, 1983.

Child, Francis James, *The English and Scottish Popular Ballads*, 5 vols., New York: Dover, 1965.

Chouraqui, André, *Les juifs d'Afrique du Nord*, Paris: Presses Universitaires de France, 1952.

Chouraqui, André, *L'Alliance Israélite Universelle et la renaissance juive contemporaine (1860–1960)*, Paris: Presses Universitaires de France, 1965.

Chrétien de Troyes, *Le Chevalier de la Charrette*, ed. Mario Roques, Paris: Honoré Champion, 1974.

Cid, Jesús Antonio, "Romances de Garganta la Olla (Materiales y notas de excursión)," *RDTP*, 30 (1974), 467–527.

Cid, Jesús Antonio, "El romancero oral de Asturias: Materiales de Josefina Cela y E. Martínez Torner: Inventario, índices, antología," *RDTP*, 48 (1993), 175–245.

Cioranescu, Alejandro, *Diccionario etimológico rumano*, 6 fasc., Madrid–La Laguna: Gredos–Universidad de La Laguna, 1958–1961.

Ciria Matilla, María Soledad, "Manuscritos y ediciones de las obras de Agustín Moreto," *CB*, 30 (1973), 75–128.

Clarity, Beverly E., Karl Stowasser, and Ronald G. Wolf, *A Dictionary of Iraqi Arabic*, Washington, D.C.: Georgetown University Press, 2003.

CMC = Ramón Menéndez Pidal (ed.), *Cantar de Mio Cid: Texto, gramática y vocabulario*, 3 vols., Madrid: Espasa-Calpe, 1944–1946.

CMP = Samuel G. Armistead, with the collaboration of Selma Margaretten, Paloma Montero, and Ana Valenciano, and with musical transcriptions by Israel J. Katz, *El romancero judeo-español en el Archivo Menéndez Pidal (Catálogo-índice de romances y canciones)*, 3 vols., Madrid: C.S.M.P., 1977.

Coelho, F. Adolpho, "Romances Populares e Rimas Infantís Portuguezes," *ZRPh*, 3 (1879), 61–72, 193–199.

Coello = Marcelino Menéndez Pelayo, "Romances castellanos tradicionales entre los judíos de Levante," *Antología de poetas líricos castellanos*, IX, "Ed. Nac.," XXV (Santander: C.S.I.C., 1945), 387–439 (nos. 1–4, 6, 8–12, collected by Carlos Coello y Pacheco).

Coffin, Tristram P., *The British Traditional Ballad in North America*, 2d ed., Philadelphia: American Folklore Society, 1963.

Coffin, Tristram P., with Roger de V. Renwick, *The British Traditional Ballad in North America*, 3rd ed., Austin: University of Texas Press, 1977.

Cohen, Judith, "The *Bergamasca*: Some Jewish Links?," *Yuval*, 7 (2002), 397–423.

Cohen, Martin N., and Abraham J. Peck (ed.), *Sephardim in the Americas: Studies in Culture and History*, Tuscaloosa: University of Alabama Press, 1993.

Colarusso, John, et al. (ed. and trans.), *Nart Sagas from the Caucasus: Myths and Legends from the Circassians, Abazas, Abkhaz, and Ubykhs*, Princeton: Princeton University Press, 2002.

Colin =   Zakia Iraqui Sinaceur, *Le Dictionnnaire Colin d'arabe dialectal marocain*, 8 vols. Rabat: al-Manahil, Ministère des Affaires Culturelles, 1994.

Collen-Jimack, Christine, "Saint-Gelais, Mellin de," *The New Oxford Companion to Literature in French*, ed. Peter France (Oxford: Clarendon, 1995), p. 733.

Conde López, Juan Carlos, "Otro testimonio-manuscrito de un villancico tradicional," *JHR*, 1 (1992–1993), 203–206.

Consiglieri Pedroso, Z., "Contribuições para um Romanceiro e Cancioneiro Popular Português," *Romania*, 10 (1881), 100–116.

Consiglieri Pedroso, Z., "Poesias Populares Portuguesas," *RHi*, 9 (1902), 455–467.

Consoli, Joseph P., *Giovanni Boccaccio: An Annotated Bibliography*, New York: Garland, 1992.

Coon, Carleton S., with Edward E. Hunt, Jr., *The Living Races of Man*, New York: Alfred A. Knopf, 1969.

Copeland Biella, Joan, *Dictionary of Old South Arabic: Sabaean Dialect*, [Cambridge, Massachusetts]: Harvard Semitic Studies, 1982.

Corona-Alcalde, Antonio, "A *Vihuela* Manuscript in the Archivo de Simancas," *The Lute*, 26 (1986), 3–20.

Correas, Gonzalo, *Vocabulario de refranes y frases proverbiales*, [ed. Miguel Mir], Madrid: "Revista de Archivos, Bibliotecas y Museos," 1924.

Correas, Gonzalo, *Vocabulario de refranes y frases proverbiales (1627)*, ed. Louis Combet, Bordeaux: Université de Bordeaux, 1967.

Correas, Gonzalo, *Vocabulario de refranes y frases proverbiales*, prologue by Miguel Mir, ed. Víctor Infantes, Madrid: Visor, 1992.

Corriente, Federico, *Gramática, métrica y texto del cancionero hispanoárabe de Aban Quzmán*, Madrid: Instituto Hispano-Arabe de Cultura, 1980.

Corriente, Federico (trans.), Ibn Quzmān, *El cancionero hispanoárabe*, Madrid: Editora Nacional, 1984.

Corriente, Federico, *Diccionario de arabismos y voces afines en iberorromance*, Madrid: Gredos, 1999.

Cortes-Rodrigues, Armando, *Romanceiro Popular Açoriano*, ed. J. Almeida Pavão and Pere Ferré, Ponta Delgada: Instituto Cultural–Pax, 1987.

Cortés y Vázquez, Luis L., *Cuentos populares salmantinos*, 2 vols., Salamanca: Librería Cervantes, 1979.

Costa Fontes, Manuel da, *Portuguese Folktales from California*, Ph.D. dissertation, University of California, Los Angeles, 1975.

Costa Fontes, Manuel da, "A Sephardic Vestige of the Ballad *Floresvento*," *La Corónica*, 10:2 (1981–1982), 196–201.

Costa Fontes, Manuel da, *Romancero da Ilha de S. Jorge*, Coimbra: Universidade, 1983.

Costa Fontes, Manuel da, *Romancero Português dos Estados Unidos, 2: Califórnia*, Coimbra: Universidade, 1983.

Costa Fontes, Manuel da, with Maria-João Câmara Fontes, *Romanceiro da Província de Trás-os-Montes (Distrito de Bragança)*, with musical transcriptions by Israel J. Katz, 2 vols., Coimbra: Universidade, 1987–1988.

Costanzo, Fabrizio, *Fior novello: libro primo di concerti di diverse sonate, sinfonie e correnti da sonare conuna, con due, con tre, e con quattro chitarre alla spagnuola*, Bologna: Nicolò Tebaldini, 1627.

Costa-Roldán = Isabel P. Costa and Gregorio Roldán, *Enciclopedia de las supersticiones*, Barcelona: Planeta, 1997.

Cotarelo y Mori, Emilio, *Colección de entremeses, loas, bailes, jácaras y mojigangas desde fines del siglo XVI a mediados del XVII*, 2 vols., Madrid: E. Bailly-Baillière, 1911.

Cotarelo y Mori, Emilio, "La bibliografía de Moreto," *BRAE*, 14 (1927), 449–494.

Cottino-Jones, Marga, *Order from Chaos: Social and Aesthetic Harmonies in Boccaccio's "Decameron,"* Washington, D.C.: University Press of America, 1982.

Cova da Beira =   Maria da Ascensão Gonçalves Carvalho Rodrigues, *Cancionero: Cova da Beira: 2.º Volume: Romanceiro, Parte I,* Covilhã: «Jornal do Fundão», 1990.

Covarrubias, Sebastián de, *Tesoro de la lengua castellana o española según la impresión de 1611, con las adiciones de Benito Remigio Noydens publicadas en la de 1674,* ed. Martín de Riquer, Barcelona: S. A. Horta, 1943.

CPE =   Bonifacio Gil [García], *Cancionero popular de Extremadura,* 2 vols., Badajoz: Diputación Provincial, 1956–1961.

CPG =   Dorothé Schubarth and Antón Santamarina, *Cancioneiro Popular Galego, Volumen III: Romances Tradicionais,* La Coruña: Fundación «Pedro Barrié de la Maza Conde de Fenosa», 1987.

Craig, Barbara M. (ed.), *L'Estoire de Griseldis,* Lawrence: University of Kansas Press, 1954 (*Humanistic Studies,* no. 31).

Crespo Pozo, José S., *Contribución a un vocabulario castellano-gallego,* Madrid: Revista «Estudios», 1963.

Crews, Cynthia M., *Recherches sur le judéo-espagnol dans les pays balkaniques,* Paris: E. Droz, 1935.

Crews, Cynthia M., "Textos judeo-españoles de Salónica y Sarajevo con comentarios lingüísticos y glosario," ed. Iacob M. Hassán, *ESef,* 2 (1979), 91–258.

Crighton, William, *Méga hellēno-agglikón lexikón,* 2 vols., Athens: E. & A. Mandalopoulos, [c. 1960].

Crivillé i Bargalló, Josep, *El folklore musical,* Madrid: Alianza Música, 1983.

Crosbie, John, "Medieval 'Contrafacta': A Spanish Anomaly Reconsidered," *MLR,* 78 (1983), 61–67.

CSA =   *Cancionero de romances impreso en Amberes sin año,* ed. Ramón Menéndez Pidal, Madrid: C.S.I.C., 1945.

CSQ =   Oro Anahory Librowicz, *Cancionero séphardi du Québec,* I, Montreal: Cégep du Vieux Montréal, 1988.

CTT = Samuel G. Armistead, Manuel da Costa Fontes, et al., *Cancioneiro Tradicional de Trás-os-Montes*, Madison, Wisconsin: H.S.M.S., 1997.

Cummings, Hubertis M., *The Indebtedness of Chaucer's Works to the Italian Works of Boccaccio*, Cincinnati, Ohio: Collegiate Press, 1916 (*University of Cincinnati Studies*, X:2).

Cummins, John G., *El habla de Coria y sus cercanías*, London: Tamesis, 1974.

Cummins, John G., *The Spanish Traditional Lyric*, Oxford: Pergamon, 1977.

Cummins, John G., *The Hound and the Hawk: The Art of Medieval Hunting*, London: Weidenfield and Nicolson, 1988.

Curiel Merchán, Marciano, *Cuentos extremeños*, Madrid: C.S.I.C., 1944.

Cuscoy, Luis Diego, *Tradiciones populares*, II: *Folklore infantil*, La Laguna de Tenerife: Instituto de Estudios Canarios, 1943.

CVR = Juan Menéndez Pidal, *Poesía popular: Colección de los viejos romances que se cantan por los asturianos en la danza prima, esfoyazas y filandones* (Madrid: Hijos de J. A. García, 1885), ed. Jesús Antonio Cid et al., 2d ed., Madrid: S.M.P., 1986.

CVR = Juan Menéndez Pidal, *Poesía popular: Colección de los viejos romances que se cantan por los asturianos en la danza prima, esfoyazas y filandones* (Madrid: Hijos de J. A. García, 1885), 3rd ed., Jesús Antonio Cid, *El Romancero asturiano de Juan Menéndez Pidal: La colección de 1885 y su compilador,* Madrid: F.R.M.P.–S.M.P., 2003, pp. [158] ff.

DAA = Federico Corriente, *A Dictionary of Andalusi Arabic*, Leiden: Brill, 1997.

Dal = Erik Dal, *Danske viser: Gamle folkeviser, Skaemte, Efterklang*, Copenhagen: Rosenkilde and Bagger, 1962, and *Danish Ballads and Folksongs*, trans. Henry Meyer, Copenhagen–New York: Rosenkilde and Bagger, 1967.

Damiani, Bruno (ed.), *La pícara Justina*, Potomac, Maryland: Studia Humanitatis, 1982.

Danckert, Werner, *Das europäische Volkslied,* Berlin: B. Hahnefeld, 1939; 2d ed., Bonn: Bouvier, 1970.

Daniels, Arthur, *De Musica Libri Septem of Francisco Salinas*, Ph.D. dissertation, University of Southern California, 1961.

Davenson, Henri, *Le livre des chansons*, 3rd ed., Neuchâtel–Paris: La Baconnière–Seuil, 1955.

Davids, William, "Bijdrage tot de studie van het Spaansch en Portugeesch in Nederland naar aanleiding van de overblijfselen dier talen in de taal der Portugeesch Israëlieten te Amsterdam," *Handelingen van het Zesde Nederlandsche Philologencongress gehouden te Leiden op woensdag 30 en donderdag 31 maart 1910* (Leiden: A. W. Sijthoff, 1910), pp. 141–154.

Davis, Arthur K., *Traditional Ballads of Virginia*, Cambridge, Massachusetts: Harvard University Press, 1929.

Davis, Arthur K., *Folk Songs of Virginia: A descriptive Index and Classification*, Durham, North Carolina: Duke University Press, 1949.

Dawkins, Richard M., "Tragoúdia tōn Dōdekanēsōn," *Laog*, 13 (1950), 33–99.

Daymard, Joseph, *Vieux chants populaires recueillis en Quercy*, Cahors: J. Girma, 1889.

DCECH =   Joan Corominas, with José A. Pascual, *Diccionario crítico etimológico castellano e hispánico*, 6 vols., Madrid: Gredos, 1980–1991.

Deak, Etienne and Simone, *Grand Dictionnaire d'Americanismes*, 4th ed., Paris: Dauphin, 1966.

De Bussy, Roland, *Dictionnaire français-arabe et arabe-français*, Algiers: Adolphe Jourdan, 1910.

DECLlC =   Joan Corominas, *Diccionari Etimològic i Complementari de la Llengua Catalana*, with Joseph Gulsoy and Max Cahner, 10 vols., Barcelona: Curial, 1983–2001.

Decombe, Lucien, *Chansons populaires recueillies dans le département d'Ille-et-Vilaine*, Rennes: H. Cailliäre, 1884.

De Gorog, Ralph, "Una concordancia del *Poema de Fernán González*," offprint *BRAE*, 1970.

De Gorog, Ralph and Lisa S., *Concordancias del "Arcipreste de Talavera*," Madrid: Gredos, 1978.

Delbouille, Maurice, "Problèmes d'attribution et de composition: I. De la composition d'*Aiol*," *RBelge,* 11 (1932), 45–75.

Deleito y Piñuela, José, *También se divierte el pueblo: Recuerdos de hace tres siglos,* 3rd ed., Madrid: Espasa-Calpe, 1966.

Delgado, Manuel Joaquim, *Subsídio para o Cancioneiro Popular do Baixo Alentejo,* [1st ed.], 2 vols., Lisbon: Alvaro Pinto, 1955.

Delgado, Manuel Joaquim, *Subsídio para o Cancioneiro Popular do Baixo Alentejo,* 2d ed., 2 vols., Lisbon: Instituto National de Investigação Científica, 1980.

Delli, Bertrun, *Pavane und Galliard zur Geschichte der Instrumentalmusik im 16. und 17. Jahrhundert* . . . Ph.D. dissertation, Berlin Universität, 1957.

De Looze, Laurence, "The Gender of Fiction: Womanly Poetics in Jean Renart's *Guillaume de Dole,*" *FrRev,* 64 (1991), 598–606.

DELP =   José Pedro Machado, *Dicionário Etimológico da Língua Portuguesa,* 6th ed., 5 vols., Lisbon: Horizonte, 1990.

Delpech, François, *Histoire et légende: Essai sur la genèse d'un thème épique aragonaise,* Paris: Presses de la Sorbonne Nouvelle, 1993.

Dent, Anthony, *Lost Beasts of Britain,* London: Harrap, 1974.

Deshen, Shlomo, *The Mellah Society: Jewish Community Life in Sherifian Society,* Chicago: University of Chicago Press, 1989.

Devoto, Daniel, "Sobre el estudio folklórico del Romancero español: Proposiciones para un método de estudio de la transmisión tradicional," *BHi,* 57 (1955), 233–291.

Devoto, Daniel, "Poésie et musique dans l'oeuvre des vihuelistes (notes méthodologiques)," *Annales Musicologiques,* 4 (1956), 85–111.

Devoto, Daniel, "Entre las siete y las ocho," *Fil,* 5 (1959), 65–80.

Devoto, Daniel, *Textos y contextos: Estudios sobre la tradición,* Madrid: Gredos, 1974.

Devoto, Daniel, "Humanisme, musicologie et histoire littéraire: Nebrija (1492) et Salinas (1577)," *L'Humanisme dans les lettres espagnoles,* ed. Agustín Redondeo (Paris: J. Vrin, 1979), pp. 177–191.

De Vries, J., and F. de Tollenaere, with A. J. Persijn, *Etymologisch woordenboek,* Utrecht: Het Spectrum, 1997 (orig. 1958).

De Vries, Jan, *Heldenlied und Heldensage,* Bern–Munich: Franke, 1961.

De Vries, Jan, *Heroic Song and Heroic Legend,* trans. B. J. Timmer, London: Oxford University Press, 1963.

Deyermond, Alan D., *Lazarillo de Tormes: A Critical Guide,* London: Grant & Cutler–Tamesis, 1975.

Deyermond, Alan D., *Hilado-cordón-cadena:* Symbolic Equivalence in *La Celestina,*" *Celestinesca,* 1:1 (1977), 6–12.

Deyermond, Alan D., "The Worm and the Partridge: Reflections on the Poetry of Florencia Pinar," *Mester,* 7:1–2 (1978), 3–8.

Deyermond, Alan D., "Traditional Images and Motifs in the Medieval Latin Lyric," *RPh,* 43 (1989–1990), 5–28.

DgF = Sven Grundtvig, with Axel Olrik, Hakon Grüner-Nielsen, et al., *Danmarks gamle Folkeviser,* 12 vols., Copenhagen: Universitets–Jubilaeets Danske–Samfund, 1966–1976.

Dias Costa, Maria Rosa, *Murteira: Uma Povoação do Concelho de Loures: Etnografia, Linguagem, Folclore,* Lisbon: Junta Distrital de Lisboa, 1961.

Dias, Maria da Conceição, "Tradições Populares do Baixo Alentejo (Ourique)," *RL,* 14 (1911), 41–61; 20 (1917), 129–136.

Dias Marques, José Joaquim, and Maria Angélica Reis da Silva, "Para o Romanceiro Português," *RLNS,* 5 (1984–1985), 73–133; 8 (1987), 105–176.

Dias Marques, José Joaquim, "Romances Tradicionais do Concelho de Loures," *RFCSH,* 4 (1989), 79–98.

Díaz Castañón, María del Carmen, *El Bable del Cabo de Peñas,* Oviedo: Instituto de Estudios Asturianos, 1966.

Díaz, Joaquín, José Delfín Val, and Luis Díaz Viana, *Catálogo folklórico de la Provincia de Valladolid: Romances tradicionales*, 2 vols., Valladolid: Institución Cultural Simancas, 1978–1979.

Díaz, Joaquín, and Luis Díaz Viana, *Romances tradicionales de Castilla y León*, Madison, Wisconsin: H.S.M.S., 1982.

Díaz, Joaquín, "Castilla y León," *Tradición y danza en España*, ed. N. A. Albaladejo Imbernón (Madrid: Consejería de Cultura, Comunidad de Madrid, Ministerio de Cultura, 1992), pp. [185]–208.

Díaz, Joaquín, "El romance en las danzas circulares," *Bailes de ruedo, II Muestra de Música Tradicional «Joaquín Díaz»*, ed. J.. Sánchez Taberno (Valladolid: Universidad de Valladolid, 1994), pp. 15–20.

Díaz Roig, Mercedes, "Un rasgo estilístico del Romancero y de la lírica popular," *NRFH*, 21 (1972), 79–94.

Díaz Viana [= Díaz González], Luis, *El romancero oral en la Provincia de Valladolid: Recopiliación y estudios*, Ph.D. dissertation, Universidad de Valladolid, [1976?].

Díaz Viana, Luis, "Evolución tradicional de un romance carolingio: 'El conde Claros'," *CIF*, 4 (1978), 57–72.

[Díaz Viana, Luis], "Canciones y cuentos," *Revista de Folklore*, 1:2 (1981), 27–30.

Dicc. Autoridades = Real Academia Española, *Diccionario de Autoridades*, facsimile ed., 3 vols., Madrid: Gredos, 1963 (orig. 1726–1737).

Dijkhoff, Mario, *Dikshonario-Woordenboek: Papiamentu-ulandes / Ulandes-papiamentu . . .*, Amsterdam: Walburg, 1994.

Dillard, Heath, *Daughters of the Reconquest: Women in Castilian Town Society, 1100–1300*, Cambridge: Cambridge University Press, 1989.

DMEH = *Diccionario de la música española e hispanoamericana*, 10 vols., ed. Emilio Casares Rodicio et al., Madrid: Sociedad General de Autores y Editores, 1999–2002.

Dobbins, Frank, "Saint-Gelais (Sainct-Gelays), Mellin (Merlín)," NGDMM, XVI, 390–391 *(see below)*.

Doncieux, George, *Le Romancéro populaire de la France: Choix de chansons populaires françaises*, Paris: Emile Bouillon, 1904.

Doniger, Wendy, *The Bedtrick: Tales of Sex and Masquerade*, Chicago: University of Chicago Press, 2000.

Donostia, José Antonio de, "El modo de *mi* en la canción popular española (Notas breves para un estudio)," *AMu*, 1 (1946), 153–179.

Dorez, León, "Francesco da Milano et la Musique du Pape Paul III," *ReM*, 9 (193), 104–113.

Dorsky, Susan, *Women of ᶜAmran: A Middle Eastern Ethnographic Study*, Salt Lake City: University of Utah Press, 1986.

Dozy, Reinhart, *Dictionnaire détaillé des noms des vêtements chez les arabes*, Beirut: Librairie du Liban, [1969?] (orig. Amsterdam: Jean Müller, 1845).

Dozy, Reinhart, *Supplément aux dictionnaires arabes*, 2 vols., Beirut: Librairie du Liban, 1981.

DPC = Lloyd A. Kasten and John J. Nitti, *Diccionario de la prosa castellana del Rey Alfonso X*, 3 vols., New York: H.S.M.S., 2002.

DPS = Antonio Rodríguez-Moñino, *Nuevo diccionario bibliográfico de pliegos sueltos poéticos, siglo XVI*, ed. Arthur L.-F. Askins and Víctor Infantes, Madrid: Castalia, 1997.

DRAE = Real Academia Española, *Diccionario de la Lengua Castellana*, 13th ed., Madrid: Hernando, 1899.

DRAE = Real Academia Española, *Diccionario de la Lengua Española*, 2 vols., 21st ed., Madrid: Real Academia Española, 1999.

DRAE = Real Academia Española, *Diccionario de la Lengua Castellana*, 2 vols., 22d ed., Madrid: Real Academia Española, 2001.

DRH = Samuel G. Armistead and Joseph H. Silverman, *Diez romances hispánicos en un manuscrito sefardí de la Isla de Rodas*, prologue by Ramón Menéndez Pidal, Pisa: Università, 1962.

Dronke, Peter, "The Rise of the Medieval *Fabliau*: Latin and Vernacular Evidence," *RF*, 85 (1973), 275–297.

Dronke, Ursula (ed. and trans.), *The Poetic Edda: Heroic Poems*, 2 vols., Oxford: Clarendon, 1969–1999.

Dubler, C.-E., "Los defensores de Teodomiro (Leyenda mozárabe)," *Études d'orientalisme dediées à la memoire de*

Lévi-Provençal, I (Paris: Maisonneuve & Larose, 1962), 111–124.

Duggan, Joseph J., "Oral Performance, Writing, and the Textual Tradition of the Medieval Epic in the Romance Languages: The Example of the *Song of Roland*," *Parergon*, 2 (1984), 79–95.

Du Guillet, Pernette, *Rymes de gentile et vertueuse dame D. Pernette Du Guillet,* ed. A. Du Moulin, Lyon: Jean de Tournes, 1545; see the modern ed. by Victor Graham (Geneva: Droz, 1968).

Du Moulin, Antoine, *Déploration de Vénus sur la mort du bel Adonia, avec plusieurs compositions nouvelles*, Lyon: Jean de Tournes, 1545.

Durán, Agustín, *Romancero general o Colección de romances castellanos anteriores al siglo XVIII*, 2 vols., Madrid: Atlas, 1945 (*BAAEE* 10 and 16).

Durante, D., and Gf. Turato, *Vocabolario etimologico veneto-italiano,* Padua: Galiverna, 1995.

Dutton, Brian, et al., *Catálogo-Indice de la poesía cancioneril del siglo XV*, 2 vols. in 1, Madison, Wisconsin: H.S.M.S., 1982.

DVM = John Meier, Erich Seemann, Walter Wiora, H. Siuts, et al., *Deutsche Volkslieder mit ihren Melodien: Deutsche Volkslieder: Balladen*, 10 vols., Berlin–Leipzig–Freiburg im Breisgau: Walter de Gruyter–Deutsches Volkslied-archiv–Peter Lang, 1935–1996.

Eberhard, Wolfram, and Pertev Naili Boratav, *Typen Türkischer Volksmärchen*, Wiesbaden: Franz Steiner, 1953.

Ehrhart, Margaret J., *The Judgment of the Trojan Prince Paris in Medieval Literature*, Philadelphia: University of Pennsylvania Press, 1987.

El-Shamy, Hasan M., *Folk Traditions of the Arab World: A Guide to Motif Classification*, 2 vols., Bloomington: Indiana University Press, 1995.

Elústiza, Juan B., *Estudios musicales: Artículos, estudios folklóricos, trabajos de investigación histórica, críticas, ensayos, etc.*, Seville: Guía Oficial, 1917.

Encina, Juan del, *Obras completas*, 4 vols., ed. Ana M. Rambaldo, Madrid: Espasa-Calpe, 1978–1983,

Engle, David G., *A Preliminary Catalogue and Edition of German Folk Ballads*, 2 vols., Ph.D. dissertation, University of California, Los Angeles, 1985.

En torno =   Samuel G. Armistead and Joseph H. Silverman, with an ethnomusicological study by Israel J. Katz, *En torno al romancero sefardí (Hispanismo y balcanismo de la tradición judeo-española)*, Madrid: S.M.P., 1982.

Entwistle, William J., and W. A. Morison, *Russian and the Slavonic Languages*, 2d ed., London,: Faber & Faber, 1964.

Epic Ballads =   Samuel G. Armistead, Joseph H. Silverman, and Israel J. Katz, *Judeo-Spanish Ballads from Oral Tradition: I. Epic Ballads*, Berkeley–Los Angeles–London: University of California Press, 1986 (= FLSJ, II).

Epstein, Morris (ed. and trans.), *Tales of Sendebar*, Philadelphia: The Jewish Publication Society of America, 1967.

Erich, Oswald A., and Richard Beitl, *Wörterbuch der deutschen Volkskunde*, 2d ed., Stuttgart: Alfred Kröner, 1955.

Erk-Böhme =   Ludwig Erk and Franz M. Böhme, *Deutscher Liederhort*, 3 vols., Hildesheim–Wiesbaden: Georg Olms–Breitkopf & Härtel, 1963 (orig. 1893–1894).

Espinel, Vicente [Martínez], *La vida del escudero Marcos de Obregón*, Madrid: Juan de la Cuesta, 1618; facsimile ed. Barcelona: Círculo del Bibliófilo, 1979.

Espinosa, Agustín, et al., *Folklore isleño: Romancero canario (Antiguos romances tradicionales de las Islas)*, Santa Cruz de Tenerife: Librería Hespérides, [1940].

Espinosa, Aurelio M., *Cuentos populares españoles*, 3 vols., Madrid: C.S.I.C., 1946–1947.

Espinosa, José Manuel, *Spanish Folk-tales from New Mexico*, New York: American Folk-Lore Society, 1937.

Espinosa Maeso, Ricardo, "El abad Francisco Salinas, organista de la Catedral de León," *BRAE*, 13:62 (1926), 186–193.

[Etzion], Judith Z. Evans, *The Spanish Polyphonic Ballad from c. 1450–c. 1650*, Ph.D. dissertation, Columbia University, 1975.

Etzion, Judith Z., "The Spanish Polyphonic Ballad in 16th-century *Vihuela* Publications," *MDisciplina*, 35 (1981), 179–197.

Falk, H. S., and Alf Torp, *Norwegisch-dänisches etymologisches Wörterbuch*, 2 vols., Heidelberg: Carl Winter, 1910–1911.

Fansler, Dean S., "Metrical Romances in the Philippines," *JAF*, 29 (1916), 203–281.

Fansler, Dean S., *Filipino Popular Tales*, Hatboro, Pennsylvania: Folklore Associates, 1965.

Farinelli, Arturo, *Italia e Spagna*, 2 vols., Turin: Fratelli Bocca, 1929.

Feito, José María, "Romances de la tierra somedana," *BIEA*, 12 (1958), 288–304; 13 (1959), 121–132.

Felgueiras, Guilherme, "Clérigos e Monges na Literatura Popular," *RL*, 3 (1982–1983), 103–115.

Fernandes Thomas, Pedro, *Velhas Canções e Romances Populares Portuguêses*, Coimbra: França Amado, 1913.

Fernández de la Cuesta, Ismael, "General Introduction to the *De Musica Llibri Septem* of Francisco Salinas, and its First Translation," *The Consort*, no. 31 (1975), 101–108.

Fernández de la Cuesta, Ismael, *Francisco Salinas: Siete libros sobre la música (Primera versión castellana)*, Madrid: Alpuerto, 1983.

Fernández de la Cuesta, Ismael, "Francisco de Salinas en el entorno de Fray Luis de León," *San Juan de la Cruz and Fray Luis de León: A Commemorative International Symposium (1991)*, ed. Mary Malcolm Gaylord and Francisco Márquez Villanueva (Newark, Delaware: Juan de la Cuesta, 1996), pp. 55–67.

Fernández Gómez, Carlos, *Vocabulario de Cervantes*, Madrid: Real Academia Española, 1962.

Fernea, Elizabeth W., *Guests of the Sheik: An Ethnography of an Iraqi Village*, Garden City, New York: Anchor, 1969.

Ferraro, Giuseppe, *Canti popolari monferrini*, Bologna: Forni, 1967.

Ferreira de Vasconcellos, Jorge, *Comedia Avlegrafia, Agora novamente impressa à custa de Dom António de Noronha, Dirigida ao Marquez de Alemquer, Duque de Fancauilla, do Estado de sua Magestade, Visorry, & Captão General destes Reynos de Portugal*, Lisbon: Pedro Crasbeeck, 1619.

Ferré, Pere, et al., *Romanceiro Tradicional do Distrito de Castelo Branco*, Lisbon: Estar Editora, 1987.

Ferré, Pere, et al., *Romanceiro Tradicional do Distrito de Guarda*, Lisbon: Real Sociedade Arqueológica Lusitana, 1987.

Ferrer-Sanjuán, Agustín Tomás, *Romances de tradición oral: Una recogida de romances en la provincia de Albacete*, Albacete: Diputación Provincial, 1993 (= *Zahora: Revista de Tradiciones Populares*, 17 [1993]).

Finch, Ronald G. (ed. and trans.), *Volsunga Saga: The Saga of the Volsungs*, London–Edinburgh: Thomas Nelson, 1965.

Fisher, John H., *The Complete Poetry and Prose of Geoffrey Chaucer*, New York: Holt, Rinehart and Winston, 1977.

Flores de Manzano, Fernando, *Una cala en la tradición oral extremeña: Estado actual del Romancero en el Valle del Jerte*, Madrid: Asamblea de Extremadura, 1995.

Flores, Sergio Recio, *Diccionario comparado de refranes y modismos: Español-English*, Mexico City: "Libros de México," 1968.

FLSJ =　　Samuel G..Armistead, Joseph H. Silverman, and Israel J. Katz, *Folk Literature of the Sephardic Jews*, 5 vols. (ongoing), Berkeley–Los Angeles: University of California Press, 1971–1994 (Vols. I–III); Newark, Delaware: Juan de la Cuesta, 2005–2008 (Vol. IV–V); Vols. VI–IX in preparation (*Yoná* = Vol. I; *Epic Ballads* = Vol. II).

FM =　　Diego Catalán et al., *La flor de la marañuela: Romancero general de las Islas Canarias*, 2 vols., Madrid: C.S.M.P., 1969.

Fochi, Adrian, *Miorița: Tipologie, circulație, geneză, texte*, Bucharest: Editură Academiei Republicii Populare Romîne, 1964.

Foerster, Wendelin (ed.), *"Aïol et Mirabel" und "Elie de Saint Gille,"* Heilbronn: Gebr. Henninger, 1876–1882.

Foley, John Miles, *"Beowulf* and Traditional Narrative Song: The Potential and Limits of Comparison," *Old English Literature in Context: Ten Essays*, ed. John D. Niles (London and Totowa, New York: D. S. Brewer–Rowman & Littlefield, 1980), pp. 117–136, 173–178.

Fonteboa, Alicia, *Literatura de tradición oral en El Bierzo*, musical transcriptions by Miguel Manzano, Ponferrada: Peñalba, 1992.

Ford, Patrick K. (trans.), *The Mabinogi and Other Medieval Welsh Tales*, Berkeley–Los Angeles–London: University of California Press, 1977.

Forslin, Alfhild, "Balladen om riddar Olof och älvorna: En traditionsundersökning," *ARV*, 18–19 (1962–1963), 1–92.

Foster, George M., *Sierra Popoluca Folklore and Beliefs*, Berkeley–Los Angeles: University of California Press, 1945.

Fowler, David C., "An Accused Queen in *The Lass of Roch Royal* (Child 76)," *JAF*, 71 (1958), 553–563.

Fowler, David C., *A Literary History of the Popular Ballad*, Durham, North Carolina: Duke University Press, 1968.

Fraile Gil, José Manuel, *Romancero tradicional de la Provincia de Madrid*, musical transcriptions by Eliseo Parra García, Madrid: Comunidad de Madrid, 1991.

Fraile Gil, José Manuel, *Cuentos de la tradición oral madrileña*, musical transcriptions by Eliseo Parra García, Madrid: Comunidad de Madrid, 1992.

Fraile Gil, José Manuel, "Crónica de una recolección romancística en la Provincia de Madrid," *Actes del Col.loqui sobre Cançó Tradicional: Reus setembre 1990*, ed. Salvador Rebés (Barcelona: Abadia de Monserrat, 1994), pp. 535–549.

Francesco Canova da Milano, *Intavolatura de viola o verso lauto composto per lo eccelente e Vnico musico Francesco Milanese non mai più stampata, Libro primo e libro secondo de la Fortuna*, Naples: [Johannis] Sultzbach [Germani], 1536; Geneva: Minkoff Reprint, 1977.

Frappier, Jean, *Les romans courtois*, Paris: Larousse, 1943.

Frazer, James George, *The Golden Bough: A Study in Magic and Religion*, 3rd ed., 12 vols., New York: MacMillan, 1935.

Frenk, Margit, "Refranes cantados y cantares proverbializados," *NRFH*, 15 (1961), 155–168.

Frenk, Margit, *Estudios sobre lírica antigua*, Madrid: Castalia, 1978.

Frenk, Margit, "Los romances-villancico," *Homenaje a Gustav Siebenmann*, ed. José Manuel López de Abiada and Augusta López Bernasocchi (Madrid: José Esteban, 1984), pp. 141–156.

Frenk, Margit, *Corpus de la antigua lírica popular hispánica (Siglos XV a XVII)*, Madrid: Castalia, 1987; 2d ed. 1990.

Frenk, Margit, *Nuevo corpus de la antigua lírica popular hispánica (Siglos XV a XVII)*, 2 vols., Mexico City: U.N.A.M.– Colegio de México–Fondo de Cultura Económica, 2003.

Freytag, Georg W., *Lexicon Arabico-Latinum*, 4 vols., Halle: C. A. Schwetschke, 1830–1837.

Friedmann, Susana, "Tradición y cambio en el romance y algunas consideraciones sobre su proyección en América Latina," *RCIM*, 1:1 (1985), 93–107.

Gagnon, Ernest, *Chansons populaires du Canada*, 6th ed., Montreal: Beauchemin, 1925.

Galante, Abraham, "Quatorze romances judéo-espagnols," *RHi*, 10 (1903), 594–606.

Galhoz, Maria Aliete Dores, *Romanceiro Popular Português*, 2 vols., Lisbon: Instituto Nacional de Investigação Científica, 1987–1988.

Galindo Ocaña, Esperanza, Maria Carmen de la Vega de la Muela, and Karl Heisel, "Hacia una exploración sistemática del Romancero de Andalucía Occidental," *El Romancero: Tradición y pervivencia a fines del siglo XX: Actas del IV Coloquio Internacional del Romancero (Sevilla–Puerto de Santa María– Cádiz, 23–26 de junio de 1987)*, ed. Pedro M. Piñero et al. (Cádiz: Fundación Machado–Universidad de Cádiz, 1989), pp. 521–548.

Gallardo, Bartolomé José, *Ensayo de una biblioteca española de libros raros y curiosos*, 4 vols., Madrid: M. Rivadeneyra, 1863– 1889; Madrid: Gredos, 1968.

Galvão, Helio, *Romanceiro: Pesquisa e Estudo*, ed. Deífilo Gurgel, Natal: Universidade Federal do Rio Grande do Norte, 1993.

García, Constantino, Manuel González González, et al., *Diccionario da Real Academia Galega,* 2d ed., A Coruña: Real Academia Galega, 1998.

García, Constantino, *Léxico de la comarca compostelana,* Santiago de Compostela: Universidad, 1974.

García de Enterría, María Cruz, "Bailes, romances, villancicos: modos de reutilización de composiciones poético-musicales," *Música y literatura en la Península Ibérica: 1600–1750,* ed. M. A. Virgili Blanquet et al. (Valladolid: Andrés Martín, 1997), pp. 169–184.

García Figueras, Tomás, *Cuentos de Yehá,* 2d ed., Tetuán: Editora Marroquí, 1950.

García Fraile, Dámaso, "El acceso a una cátedra universitaria de música en el siglo XVI," *Miscel.lània Oriol Matorell,* ed. X. Aviñoa (Barcelona: Universitat de Barcelona, 1996), pp. 35–58.

García Fraile, Dámaso, "La vida musical en la Universidad de Salamanca durante el siglo XVI," *RevMusicol,* 33:1 (2000), 9–74.

García Gómez, Emilio, "La canción famosa Calvi vi calvi / Calvi aravi," *AlAn,* 30 (1956), 1–18.

García Gómez, Emilio, *Todo Ben Quzmān,* 3 vols., Madrid: Gredos, 1972.

García Gómez, Emilio, *Las jarchas romances de la serie árabe en su marco,* 2d ed., Barcelona: Seix Barral, 1975.

García López, María Esther, "Romances de La Degol·lada (Valdés) y Las Tabiernas (Tinéu)," *Lletres Asturianes,* 34 (1989), 7–16.

García, Mari Carmen, "Romances, villancicos y refranes en unos garabatos del siglo XV al XVI," *La Corónica,* 22:2 (1993–1994), 123–132.

García Matos Alonso, Carmen, "Una polémica en torno a las danzas de cuenta y los bailes de cascabel de los siglos XVI y XVII," *Nassarre,* 12:2 (1996), 121–134.

García Matos, Manuel, *Lírica popular de la alta Extremadura,* Madrid: Unión Musical Española, 1944.

García Matos, Manuel, *Cancionero popular de la Provincia de Madrid,* ed. Marius Schneider and José Romeu Figueras, 3 vols., Barcelona–Madrid: C.S.I.C.–Instituto Español de Música, 1951–1960.

García Matos, Manuel, "El folklore en la Suite Española de Pérez Casas," *Música: Revista Trimestral de los Conservatorios Españoles,* 14 (1956), 73–86.

García Matos, Manuel, "Pervivencia en la tradición actual de canciones populares recogidas en el siglo XVI por Salinans en su tratado *De Musica Libri Septem*," AnM, 18 (1963), 67–84.

García Matos, Manuel, *Cancionero popular de la Provincia de Cáceres (Lírica popular de la Alta Extremadura, Vol. II)*, ed. Josep Crivillé i Bargalló, Barcelona: C.S.I.C., 1982.

García Redondo, Francisca, *Cancionero arroyano*, Cáceres: Diputación Provincial, 1985.

Garrett = João Baptista deAlmeida Garrett, *Romanceiro*, 3rd ed., 3 vols., Lisbon: Empreza da História de Portugal, 1900–1901.

Gauthier-Villars, Marguerite, *Chansons populaires recueillies au Villard-de-Lans*, Paris: B. Roudanez, 1929.

GDMM = *Grove's Dictionary of Music and Musicians*, ed. Eric Blom, 5th ed., 10 vols., London–New York: Macmillan–St. Martin's Press, 1954.

Georgiev, Vladimir, et al., *Bâlgarski etymologič en rečnik*, 6 vols. (ongoing), Sofia: Bâlgarska Akademija na Naukite, 1971–2002.

Gerbert de Montreuil, *Le Roman de la violette ou de Gerart de Nevers*, ed. Douglas Labaree Buffum, Paris: Honoré Champion, 1928 (S.A.T.F., Vol. 73).

Gerbert de Montreuil, *Le Roman de la violette*, trans. Gonzague Truc, Paris: H. Piazza, 1931.

Gerhardt, Mia I., *The Art of Story-Telling: A Literary Study of the Thousand and One Nights*, Leiden: E. J. Brill, 1963.

Gerli, E. Michael, Review: Martín Morán, *Ginevra y Finea*, HR, 57 (1989), 85–86.

Gesemann, Gerhard, *Erlangenski rukopis starih srpskohrvatskih narodnih pesama*, [Belgrade]: Srpska Kraljevska Akademija, 1925.

Gesenius, Wilhelm, *Hebrew and Chaldee Lexicon to the Old Testament Scriptures*, trans. Samuel P. Tregelles, Grand Rapids, Michigan: Wm. B. Eerdmans, 1969 (orig. 1846).

Giacometti, Michel, with Fernando Lopes Graça, *Cancioneiro Popular Português*, Lisbon: Círculo de Leitores, 1981.

Giannini, G., "Stratagemmi leggendari di città assediate," *ASTP*, 22 (1903), 416–417.

Gil =   Rodolfo Gil, *Romancero judeo-español*, Madrid: Imprenta Alemana, 1911.

Gil García, Bonifacio, "Panorama de la canción burgalesa," *AnM*, 18 (1963), 85–102.

Gil García, Bonifacio, *Cancionero popular de la Rioja*, ed. José Romeu Figueras, Juan Tomás, and Josep Crivillé i Bargalló, Barcelona: C.S.I.C., 1987.

Gili Gaya, Samuel, *Tesoro lexicográfico (1492–1726)*, I: *A–E*, Madrid: C.S.I.C., 1960.

Gillet, Joseph E., "El mediodía y el demonio meridiano en España," *NRFH*, 7 (1953), 307–315.

Gillet, Joseph E., "Further Additions to the *Diablo meridiano*," *HR*, 23 (1955), 294–295.

Gil Vicente, *Farces and Festival Plays,* ed. Thomas R. Hart, Eugene: University of Oregon, 1972.

Ginard Bauçà, Rafel, *Cançoner Popular de Mallorca*, 4 vols., Mallorca: Editorial Moll, 1966–1975.

Glare, P. G. W., *Oxford Latin Dictonary*, Oxford: Clarendon, 1985.

Goitein, Shelomoh D., *A Mediterranean Society,* 6 vols., Berkeley–Los Angeles: University of California Press, 1967–1993.

Goitein, Shelomoh D., *Letters of Medieval Jewish Traders,* Princeton: Princeton University Press, 1973.

Goldberg, Harriet, "The Judeo-Spanish Proverb and its Narrative Context," *PMLA*, 108 (1993), 106–120.

Goldin, Frederick, trans., *German and Italian Lyrics of the Middle Ages*, Garden City, New York: Anchor Books, 1973.

Gollancz, Israel (ed.), *Sir Gawain and the Green Knight*, London: E.E.T.S., 1940.

Gomarín Guirado, Fernando, *Romancerillo cántabro,* introduction by Diego Catalán, Santander: Ayuntamiento de Santa María de Cayón, 1997.

Gomes Pereira, A., "Novo Suplemento às Tradições Populares e Linguagem de Vila Real," *RL,* 13 (1910), 95–109.

Gómez del Campillo, Miguel, "De Cifras," *BRAH,* 129:2 (1951), 279–308.

Gómez Pérez, José, "Leyendas medievales españolas del ciclo carolingio," *Anuario de Filología: Facultad de Humanidades y Educación* (Universidad del Zulia, Maracaibo, Venezuela), 2–3 (1963–1964), 7–136.

Gómez Redondo, Fernando (ed. and trans.), *Jaufré,* Madrid: Gredos, 1996.

González de Clavijo, Ruy, *Embajada a Tamorlán*, ed. Francisco López Estrada, Madrid: Castalia, 1999.

González de Salas, Jusepe Antonio, *Nueva idea de la tragedia antigua o ilustración última al libro singular de Poética de Aristóteles Stagerita*, Madrid: Martínez, 1633; 2d ed. Madrid: Sancha, 1778.

Graham, Victor E. (ed.), Pernette Du Guillet, *Rymes*, Geneva: Droz, 1968.

Greenlaw, Edwin A., "The Vows of Baldwin: A Study in Medieval Fiction," *PMLA*, 21 (1906), 575–636.

GRI =   Yacob A. Yoná, *Gu'erta de romansos 'inportantes,* [Salonika], 1920.

Griffini, Eugenio, *L'arabo parlato della Libia*, Milan: Ulrico Hoepli, 1913.

Griffiths, John, "Vihuela," DMEH, X, 878–883.

Gurgel, Deífilo, *Romanceiro de Alcaçus*, Natal: Universidade Federal do Rio Grande do Norte, 1994.

Gutiérrez Macías, Valeriano, "Fiestas cacereñas," *RDTP*, 16 (1960), 335–357.

Guzofsky, Rosalía, *Mujeres heroicas en el romancero judeo-español*, Ph.D. dissertation, University of Pennsylvania, Philadelphia, 1990.

Haboucha, Reginetta, *Types and Motifs of the Judeo-Spanish Folktales*, New York: Garland, 1992.

Hackett, W. Mary (ed.), *Girart de Roussillon*, 3 vols., Paris: A. & J. Picard, 1953–1955.

Hand, Wayland D., Anna Casetta, and Sondra B. Thiederman, *Popular Beliefs and Superstitions: A Compendium of American Folklore: From the Ohio Collection of Newbell Niles Puckett*, 3 vols., Boston: G. K. Hall, 1981.

Hardung, Víctor Eugénio, *Romanceiro Português*, 2 vols., Leipzig: F. A. Brockhaus, 1877.

Hassán, Iacob M., "Las *Coplas de Yosef* sefardíes y la poesía oral," *De Balada y Lírica: Actas del 3er Coloquio Internacional sobre el Romancero*, ed. Diego Catalán et al., 2 vols. (Madrid: F.R.M.P., 1994), II, 271–282.

Haupt, Moriz, *Französische Volkslieder*, Leipzig: S. Hirzel, 1877.

Hawkins, Sir John, *A General History of the Science and Practice of Music*, 5 vols., London: Printed for T. Payne, 1776; facsimile ed., with a new introduction by Charles Cudworth, 2 vols., New York: Dover, 1963.

Haymes, Edward R. (trans.), *The Saga of Thidrek of Bern*, New York: Garland, 1988.

HDA =   Eduard Hoffmann-Krayer and Hanns Bächtold-Stäubli, *Handwörterbuch des deutschen Aberglaubens*, 10 vols., 2d ed., Berlin–Leipzig: Walter de Gruyter, 1987.

Heartz, Daniel, "Parisian Music Publishing under Henri II: A propos of Four Recently Discovered Guitar Books," *MQ*, 46 (1960), 448–467.

Heger, Klaus, *Die bisher veröffentlichten Harǧas und ihre Deutungen*, Tübingen: Max Niemeyer, 1960.

Heinermann, Theodor, *Untersuchungen zur Entstehung der Sage von Bernardo del Carpio*, Halle (Saale): Max Niemeyer, 1927.

Hemsi, Alberto, *Coplas sefardíes (Chansons judéo-espagnoles) [pour chant et piano]*, 10 fascicles, Alexandria, Egypt–Aubervilliers, France: Edition Orientale de Musique–privately printed, 1932–1973.

Hemsi, Alberto, "Evocation de la France dans le folklore séphardi," *JS*, 24 (July 1962), 1055–1057, 1059; 25 (Dec. 1962), 1091–1093.

Hemsi II = Alberto Hemsi, *Cancionero sefardí*, ed. Edwin Seroussi et al., Jerusalem: Hebrew University, 1995.

Hernández de Soto, Sergio, *Cuentos populares de Extremadura*, Madrid: Fernando Fe, 1886 (= *BTPE*, X).

Herodotus, *The Histories*, trans. Aubrey de Selincourt, London–New York: Penguin, 1996.

Herzog, George, "Some Primitive Layers in European Folk Music," *BAMS*, 9–10 (1947), 11–14.

Hesiod, *The Homeric Hymns and Homerica*, ed. and trans. Hugh G. Evelyn-White, Cambridge, Massachusetts–London: Harvard University Press–William Heinemann, 1927.

Heuckenkamp, Ferdinand (ed.), *Le Chevalier du Papegau*, Halle: Max Niemeyer, 1896.

Hilka, Alfons, "Neue Beiträge zur Erzählungsliteratur des Mittelalters," *Jahres-Bericht der Schlesischen Gesellschaft für vaterländische Cultur*, 90:4 (1912), 1–24.

Hilka, Alfons, and W. Söderhjelm, "Vergleichendes zu den mittelalterlichen Frauengeschichten," *NphM*, 15 (1913), 1–22.

Hill, Raymond T., and Thomas G. Bergin, *Anthology of the Provençal Troubadours*, 2d ed., 2 vols., New Haven: Yale University Press, 1973.

Holtrop, John, *Dutch and English Dictionary*, ed. A. Stevenson, Amsterdam–Dordrecht: J. van Esveldt Holtrop, 1824.

Hony, H. C., and Fahir İz, *A Turkish-English Dictionary*, 2d ed., Oxford: Clarendon, 1957.

Horrent, Jacques, "Les noms *Rodlane* et *Bertlane* dans la *Nota Emilianense*," *MR*, "numéro spécial" (1973), 231–249.

Hubert, Merton Jerome, and Marion E. Porter (ed. and trans.), *The Romance of Flamenca*, Princeton: Princeton University Press, 1962.

Hudson, Richard, "Bergamasca," *NGDMM*, II, 541–545.

Hudson, Richard, "Passacaglia," *NGDMM*, XIV, 268.

Hudson, Richard, *The Folia, the Saraband, the Passacaglia, and the Chaconne:The Historical Evolution of Four Forms that Originated in Music for the Five-Course Spanish Guitar*, Neuhausen–Stuttgart: American Institute of Musicology, 1982.

Huerta Calvo, Javier, "De mitología burlesca, mito y entremés," *Actas de las jornadas sobre teatro popular en España*, ed. J. Álvarez Barrientos and A. Cea Gutiérrez (Madrid: C.S.I.C., 1987), pp. 289–307.

Hughes, Robert, *The Fatal Shore: The Epic of Australia's Founding*, New York: Vintage, 1988.

Hulme, W.H., "A Middle English Addition to the Wager Cycle," *MLN*, 24 (1909), 218–222.

Hussey, Maurice, *Chaucer's World: A Pictorial Companion*, Cambridge: Cambridge University Press, 1967.

Hyatt, Harry Middleton, *Folk-lore from Adams County, Illinois*, New York: Alma Egan Hyatt Foundation, 1935.

Idelsohn, Abraham Zvi, *Gesänge der orientalischen Sefardim*, Jerusalem–Berlin–Vienna: Benjamin Harz Verlag, 1923 (*Hebräisch-orientalischer Melodienschatz*, Vol. IV).

Idelsohn, Abraham Zvi, *Thesaurus of Hebrew Oriental Melodies*, 10 vols. in 4, New York: Ktav, 1973 (orig. 1914–1932).

Iglesias Giraud, Cécile, and Ángel Iglesias Ovejero, *Romances y coplas de El Rebollar*, Salamanca: Centro de Estudios Salmantinos, 1998.

Índice biográfico de España, Portugal e Iberoamérica, 3rd ed., ed. Victor Herrero Mediavilla, Munich: K. G. Saur, 2000.

Inventario = [José López de Toro], *Inventario de Manuscritos de la Biblioteca Nacional*, IV *(1101 a 1598)*, Madrid: Ministerio de Educación Nacional, 1958.

Iordan-Alvar = Iorgu Iordan, *Lingüística románica: Evolución-corrientes-métodos*, ed. Manuel Alvar, Madrid: Ediciones Alcalá, 1967.

Iordan-Orr = Iorgu Iordan, *An Introduction to Romance Linguistics: Its Schools and Scholars*, trans. and ed. by John Orr, with a supplement by Rebecca Posner, *Thirty Years on*, Berkeley–Los Angeles: University of California Press, 1970.

Irmandades da Fala, *Vocabulario castellano-gallego de las Irmandades da Fala,* La Coruña: Moret, 1933.

Ive, Antonio, *Canti popolari istriani raccolti a Rovigno,* Turin: Ermanno Loescher, 1877.

Ives, Burl, *The Burl Ives Song Book,* New York: Ballantine Books, 1953.

Jambou, Louis, "Las formas instrumentales en el siglo XVI," ACS, I, 293–307.

Jansen, G. P., *Nederlands-Papiaments Handwoordenboek,* Scherpenheuvel: St. Vincentiusgesticht, 1947.

Jason, Heda, "Types of Jewish–Oriental Oral Tales," *Fabula,* 7 (1964–1965), 115–224.

Jason, Heda, and O. Schnitzler, "The Eberhard-Boratav Index of Turkish Folk Tales in the Light of the New Revision of Aarne-Thompson's *Types of the Folktale,*" *Folklore Research Center Studies* (Jerusalem), 1 (1970), 43–71.

Jeannaraki, Anton, *Ásmata krētikà metà distichōn kaì paroimiōn: Kretas Volkslieder nebst Distichen und Sprichwörtern,* Wiesbaden: Martin Sändig, 1967.

Jenkins, T. Atkinson (ed.), *La Chanson de Roland,* Boston–New York: D.C. Heath, 1924.

Jesperson, Otto, *Growth and Structure of the English Language,* Garden City, New Jersey: Doubleday, 1956.

Jiménez Sánchez, Sebastián, "De folklore canario: El mes de San Juan y sus fiestas populares," *RDTP,* 10 (1954), 176–189.

Johnston, Oliver M., "Sources of the Spanish Ballad on Don García," *RHi,* 12 (1905), 281–298.

Jonens, R[oyston] O[scar], and Carolyn R. Lee (ed.), *Juan del Encina, Poesía lírica y cancionero musical,* Madrid: Castalia, 1975.

Jones, Alison, *Dictionary of World Folklore,* Edinburgh: Larousse, 1996.

Jones, Harold G., "The Romance 'Atal anda don García / por una sierra adelante'," *La Corónica,* 10:1 (1981), 95–98.

Kamal, Mustapha, "Al-Basṭī, the Last Arab Poet of al-Andalus," *Arabic, Hebrew, & Spanish Literature in the Iberian Peninsula:*

A Symposium in Memory of Américo Castro, organized by James T. Monroe, reported by S. G. Armistead, *La Corónica*, 32:1 (2003), 357–368.

Kantor, Sofia, "*Blanc* et *noir* dans l'épique française et espagnole: Dénotation et connotation," *StMed*, 25 (1984), 145–199.

Kany, Charles E., *American Spanish Euphemisms*, Berkeley–Los Angeles: University of California Press, 1960.

Kartschoke, Dieter (ed. and trans.), *Das Rolandslied des Pfaffen Konrad*, Stuttgart: Philipp Reclam, 2001.

Karttunen, Frances, *An Analytical Dictionary of Nahuatl*, Austin: University of Texas Press, 1983.

Kasten, Lloyd A. (ed.), *Poridat de las poridades*, Madrid: University of Wisconsin, 1957.

Kastner, Macario Santiago (ed.), *Francisco Salinas, De Musica*, Kassel–Basel: Bärenreiter, 1958.

Katz, Israel J., "A Survey of the Ballad Tunes presented during the Symposium: Transcriptions and Commentary (Including transcriptions by Christina Braidotti)," *RH: Fronteras*, pp. 451–474.

Katz, Israel J., "The Enigma of the Antonio Bustelo Judeo-Spanish Ballad Tunes in Manuel L. Ortega's *Los hebreos en Marruecos* (1919)," *Musica Judaica*, 4 (1981–1982), 33–67.

Katz, Israel J., "Romancero," DMEH, IX, 361–370.

Keller, John E. (ed.), *El libro de los engaños*, Valencia: Castalia, 1959.

Kind, Theodor, *Anthologie neugriechischer Volkslieder*, Leipzig: Veit, 1861.

Kithubim, trans. Moshe Greenberg, Jonas C. Greenfield, et al., Philadelphia: J.P.S., 1982.

Kluge, Friedrich, *Etymologisches Wörterbuch der deutschen Sprache*, 11th ed., Berlin–Leipzig: Walter de Gruyter, 1934.

Knežević, Anton, *Die Turzismen in der Sprache der Kroaten und Serben*, Meisenheim am Glan: Anton Hain, 1962.

Knuchel, Eduard Fritz, *Vogel Gryff: Die Umzüge der Klein-Basler Ehrenzeichen, ihr Ursprung und ihre Bedeutung*, Basel: A. Apel, 1944.

Koenig, V.-Frédéric (ed.), *Le Conte de Poitiers: Roman du treizième siècle*, Paris: E. Droz, 1937.

Kolsti, John, *The Bilingual Singer: A Study in Albanian and Serbo-Croatian Oral Epic Traditions*, New York: Garland, 1990.

Kontopoulos, N., *Lexikón hellēnoagglikón kai aglohellēnikón*, Smyrna: B. Tatikiános, 1869.

Kontopoulos, N., *Neón lexikón hellēnoagglikón*, 3rd ed., Athens: K. Antoniades, 1880.

Kosover, Mordecai, *Arabic Elements in Palestinian Yiddish: The Old Ashkenazic Jewish Community in Palestine: Its History and its Language*, Jerusalem: Rubin Mass, 1966.

Koukoules, Anastasia I., "*Ho Maurianós ki' ho Basigeás* (Dēmōdes krētikòn āsma)," *Laografia*, 1 (1909), 685–687.

Koulákēs, Giánnēs Sp., *To megaló etymologikó lexikó tēs koinēs neohellēnikés glōssas*, Salonika: A. Malliarēs, 1993.

Krappe, Alexander Haggerty, "Le songe de la mère de Guillaume le Conquérant," *ZFSL*, 61 (1938), 198–204.

Kroeber, Auguste, and Gustave Marie Joseph Servois (ed.), *Fierabras: Chanson de geste*, Paris: F. Vieweg, 1860.

Kumar De, Sushil, *Early History of the Vaisnava Faith and Movement in Bengal*, 2d ed., Calcutta: Firma K. L. Mukhopadhyay, 1961.

Kumer, Zmaga, *Vsebinski tipi slovenskih pripovednih pesmi / Typenindex slowenischer Erzähllieder*, Ljubljana: Slovenska Akademije Znanosti in Umetnosti, 1974.

Kundert, Hans, "Romancerillo sanabrés," *RDTP*, 18 (1962), 37–124.

Künzig, Johannes, and Waltraut Werner, *Volksballaden und Erzähllieder: Ein Repertorium unserer Tonaufnahmen*, Freiburg im Breisgau: Institut für Ostdeutsche Volkskunde, 1975.

Kynoch, Douglas, *Scottish (Doric)-English / English-Scottish (Doric) Concise Dictionary*, New York: Hippocrene, 1992.

Labrador Herraiz, Jose J., and Ralph A. DiFranco, *Tabla de los principios de la poesía española*, Cleveland, Ohio: Cleveland State University, 1993.

Labrador Herraiz, Jose J., Ralph A. DiFranco, and Antonio López Budia (ed.), *Cancionero sevillano de Lisboa: Poesías Varias de Diversos Authores em Castellano (LN F.G. Cod. 3072)*, preface by Begoña López Bueno, Seville: Universidad de Sevilla, 2003.

Lacarra, María Jesús (ed.), *Sendebar*, Madrid: Cátedra, 1989.

Lacy, Norris J., "'Amer par oïr dire': *Guillaume de Dole* and the Drama of Language," *FrRev*, 54 (1981), 779–787.

Lamano y Beneite, José de, *El dialecto vulgar salmantino*, Salamanca: El Salmantino, 1915.

Lambea, Mariano, *Incipit de poesía española musicada ca. 1465–ca. 1710*, Madrid: Sociedad Española de Musicología, 2000.

Lambertz, Maximilian, *Die Volksepik der Albaner*, Halle (Saale): Max Niemeyer, 1958.

Landau, Marcus, *Die Quellen des Dekameron*, Wiesbaden: Martin Sändig, 1971.

Landstad, Magnus B., *Norske folkeviser*, Christiania: Chr. Tönsberg, 1853.

Lane, Edward William, *An Arabic-English Lexicon*, 8 vols., Beirut: Librairie du Liban, 1980 (orig. 1863–1893).

Langlois, Ernest, "Notices des manuscrits français et provençaux de Rome antérieurs au XVIe siècle," *Notices et Extraits des Manuscrits de la Bibliothèque Nationale et autres Bibliothèques*, 33 (Paris: Imprimerie Nationale, 1889), 1–229.

Lapesa, Rafael, *De la edad media a nuestros días*, Madrid: Gredos, 1967.

Laroui, Abdallah, *The History of the Maghrib: An Interpretive Essay,* trans. Ralph Manheim, Princeton: Princeton University Press, 1977.

Larrea =   Arcadio de Larrea Palacín, *Romances de Tetuán*, 2 vols., Madrid: C.S.I.C., 1952.

Lavaud, René, and René Nelli (ed. and trans.), *Les troubadours*, 2 vols., Bruges: Desclée de Brouwer, 1960–1966.

Lawrence, William W., "The Wager in *Cymbeline*," *PMLA*, 35 (1920), 391–431.

Leach, Maria, and Jerome Fried (ed.), *Standard Dictionary of Folklore, Mythology, and Legend*, 2 vols., New York: Funk & Wagnall's, 1949–1950.

Leader, Ninon A. M., *Hungarian Classical Ballads and their Folklore*, Cambridge: Cambridge University Press, 1967.

Lecoy, Félix (ed.), Jean Renart, *Le Roman de la rose ou de Guillaume de Dole*, Paris: Honoré Champion, 1962.

Ledesma, Dámaso, *Folk-lore o Cancionero salmantino*, Madrid: Imprenta Alemana, 1907.

Lee, A. Collingwood, *The Decameron: Its Sources and Analogues*, New York: Haskell, 1972 (orig. 1909).

Le Goff, Jacques, *La Civilisation de l'Occident Médiéval*, Paris: B. Arthaud, 1964.

Le Goff, Jacques, *La Civilisation de l'Occident Médiéval*, Paris: Flammarion, 1982.

Legrand, Émile, *Recueil de chansons populaires grecques*, Paris: Maisonneuve, 1874.

Legrand, Émile, "Chansons populaires recueillies en octobre 1876 à Fontenay-le-Marmion, arrondissement de Caen (Calvados)," *Romania*, 10 (1881), 365–396.

Leite de Vasconcellos, José, "Romance Popular de D. Carlos," *RL*, 4 (1896), 189–191.

Leite de Vasconcellos, José, *Contos Populares e Lendas*, 2 vols., ed. Alda da Silva Soromenho and Paulo Caratão Soromenho, Coimbra: Universidade, 1963–1969.

Lejeune–Dehousse, Rita, *L'oeuvre de Jean Renart: Contribution à l'étude du genre romanesque au Moyen Age*, Paris: "Les Belles Lettres," 1935.

Lejeune–Dehousse, Rita (ed.), Jean Renart, *Le Roman de la rose ou de Guillaume de Dole*, Paris: E. Droz, 1937.

Lemos de Mendonça, Elsa Brunilde, "Ilha de S. Jorge: Subsídio para Estudo da Etnografia, Linguagem e Folclore Regionais," *BIHIT*, 19–20 (1961–1962), 1–347.

Leonard, Irving A., *Books of the Brave*, Cambridge, Massachusetts: Harvard University Press, 1949.

Leonard, Irving A., *Los libros del Conquistador*, Mexico City: Fondo de Cultura Económica, 1953.

León Tello, Francisco José, *Estudios de historia de la teoría musical*, Madrid: Instituto Español de Musicología–C.S.I.C., 1962.

León Tello, Francisco José, "Contribución de Ramos de Pareja y Francisco Salinas a la formación de la escala musical europea," *RevMusicol*, 5:2 (1982), 287–296.

Lerchundi, José, *Vocabulario español-arábigo del dialecto de Marruecos*, Tangier: Misión Católico-Española, 1892.

Leslau, Wolf, *Lexique Soqoṭri (Sudarabique moderne): Avec comparaisons et explications étimologiques*, Paris: C. Klincksieck, 1938.

Lévi, Albert, *Les vestiges de l'Espagnol et du Portugais chez les Israelites de Bayonne*, Bayonne: Imp. du «Courier», 1936.

Levy, Emil, *Petit dictionnaire provençal-français*, 5th ed., Heidelberg: Carl Winter, 1973.

Levy, Raphael, "Le Roi Flore et la belle Jehane," *PhQ*, 14 (1935), 253–262.

Lewis, Ivor, *Sahibs, Nabobs and Boxwallahs: A Dictionary of the Words of Anglo-India*, New Delhi: Oxford University Press, 1997.

Libiez, Albert, *Chansons populaires d l'ancien Hainaut*, 5 vols. (Vol. V, ed. Roger Pinon), Brussels: Schott, 1939–1958.

Librowicz, Oro Anahory, "Florilegio de romances sefardíes de la Diáspora: Breve panorama de una colección judeo-malagueña," *RH: Fronteras*, pp. 91–97.

Librowicz, Oro Anahory, *Florilegio de romances sefardíes de la Diáspora (Una colección judeo-malagueña)*, Madrid: C.S.M.P., 1980.

Lida [de Malkiel], María Rosa, *El cuento popular hispano-americano y la literatura*, Buenos Aires: Universidad de Buenos Aires, 1941.

Lida de Malkiel, María Rosa, "El romance de la misa de amor," *RFH*, 3 (1941), 24–42.

Lida de Malkiel, María Rosa, *El cuento popular y otros ensayos*, [ed. Yakov Malkiel], Buenos Aires: Losada, 1976.

Liddell, Henry George, and Robert Scott, *A Greek-English Lexicon*, ed. Henry Stuart Jones, Roderick McKenzie, et al. With a supplement, 1968, Oxford: Clarendon, 1976.

Liebrecht, F., *Zur Volkskunde: Alte und neue Aufsätze*, Heilbronn: Henninger, 1879.

Lima Carneiro, Alexandre, "Do Cancioneiro de Monte Córdova: Considerações sobre Música e Letra," *CST*, 6 (1958), 7–177.

Littmann, Enno, *Arabische Märchen*, Leipzig: Insel, 1957.

Liungman, Waldemar, *Die schwedischen Volksmärchen: Herkunft und Geschichte*, Berlin: Akademie–Verlag, 1961.

Llano Roza de Ampudia, Aurelio de, *Cuentos asturianos*, Madrid: C.E.H., 1925.

Llatas, Vicente, *El habla del Villar del Arzobispo y su comarca*, 2 vols., Valencia: Institución Alfonso el Magnánimo, 1959.

Llorens de Serra, Sara, *Folklore de la Maresma*, Vol. I: *El Cançoner de Pineda: 238 cançons populars amb 210 tonadas*, Barcelona: Joaquim Horta, 1931.

Llorente Maldonado de Guevara, Antonio, *Estudio sobre el habla de La Ribera (Comarca salmantina ribereña del Duero)*, Salamanca: C.S.I.C., 1947.

Lombard, Maurice, *Les textiles dans le monde musulman VIIe–XIIe siècle*, Paris–The Hague: Mouton, 1978.

Long, Eleanor, *"The Maid" and "The Hangman": Myth and Tradition in a Popular Ballad*, Berkeley–Los Angeles: University of California Press, 1971.

Loomis, Roger Sherman, *A Mirror of Chaucer's World*, Princeton: Princeton University Press, 1965.

Lopes   =   Antônio Lopes, *Presença do Romanceiro: Versões Maranhenses*, Rio de Janeiro: "Civilização Brasileira," 1967.

Lopes Dias, Jaime, *Etnografia da Beira*, Vol. VII, Lisbon: Minerva, 1948.

Lopes Graça, Fernando, *A Canção Popular Portuguesa*, 2d ed., [Lisbon]: Publicações Europa-América, 1974.

Lopes Graça, Fernando, and Alves Redol, *Romanceiro Geral do Povo Portugués*, Lisbon: Iniciativas Editoriais, 1974.

López-Chavarri, Eduardo, *Música popular española*, Barcelona: Labor, 1927.

López de Gómara, Francisco, *Hispania Victrix: Primera y segunda parte de la Historia General de las Indias*, ed. Enrique de Vedia and Guillermo Morón, *Historiadores primitivos de Indias*, 3 vols. (Madrid: Atlas, 1946–1965), I, 155–455 (= *BAAEE*, Vols. XXII, XXVI, CVII).

López de Gómara, Francisco, *Historia de la conquista de México*, ed. Jorge Gurria Lacroix, Caracas: Biblioteca Ayacucho, [1979].

López Estrada, Francisco, *La conquista de Antequera en el romancero y en la épica de los Siglos de Oro*, Seville: Real Academia Sevillana de Buenas Letras, 1956.

Lord, Albert B., "Interlocking Mythic Patterns in *Beowulf*," *Old English Literature in Context: Ten Essays*, ed. John D. Niles (London–Totowa, New York: D. S. Brewer–Rowman & Littlefield, 1980), pp.137–142.

Lorenzo Vélez, Antonio, "Una nueva aparición de un romance cíclico," *De Balada y Lírica: Actas del 3er Coloquio Internacional sobre el Romancero*, ed. Diego Catalán et al., 2 vols. (Madrid: F.R.M.P., 1994), II, 125–129.

Low, David H., *The Ballads of Marko Kraljević*, Westport, Connecticut: Greenwood, 1968.

Lowe, Lawrence F. H. (ed.), *"Gérard de Nevers": A Study of the Prose Version of the "Roman de la Violette,"* Princeton: [Princeton University], 1923; 2d ed. 1928.

LSO =   Michael Molho, *Literatura sefardita de Oriente*, Madrid–Barcelona: C.S.I.C, 1960.

Lucas, Obispo de Túy, *Crónica de España*, ed. Julio Puyol, Madrid: "Revista de Archivos, Bibliotecas y Museos," 1926.

Lüdeke, Hedwig, *Im Paradies der Volksdichtung: Erinnerungen an meine volkskundlichen Sammel- und Forschungsreisen im griechischen Sprachgebiet*, Berlin: Minerva, 1948.

Lüdeke, Hedwig, "Griechische Volksdichtung," *ALV*, 1 (1949), 196–250; supplement by Erich Seemann, pp. 251–254.

Lüdeke-Megas = Hedwig Lüdeke and Georgios A. Megas, *Neugriechische Volkslieder*, II: *Übertragungen*, Athens: Akadēmía Athēnōn, 1964.

Ludovice, Licínia de Conceição, "Subsídios para o Estudo do Cancioneiro Popular Alenquerense," *Extremadura*, 23 (1950), 89–94, 325–331; 26–28 (1951), 201–207; 41–43 (1956), 135–150.

Luria, Max A., *A Study of the Monastir Dialect of Judeo-Spanish Based on Oral Material Collected in Monastir, Yugo-Slavia*, New York: Instituto de las Españas, 1930.

Luttrell, Anthony T., "Girolamo Manduca and Gian Francesco Abela: Tradition and Invention in Maltese Historiography," *Melita Historica* (Malta), 7:2 (1977), 105–132.

Maalouf, Amin, *The Crusades through Arab Eyes*, trans. Jon Rothschild, New York: Schocken, 1984.

Macabich, Isidor, *Romancer tradicional eivissenc*, Palma de Mallorca: Editorial Moll, 1954.

Machado, Diogo Barbosa, *Bibliotheca Lusitana: Historia, Critica, e Cronologia*, Lisbon: Ignacio Rodrigues, 1747.

Macrea, Dimitrie, et al. (ed.), *Dicţionarul Limbii Romîne Moderne,* Bucarest: Academia Republicii Populare Romîne, 1958.

Magalhães, Celso de, *A Poesia Popular Brasileira*, ed. Braulio do Nascimento, Rio de Janeiro: Biblioteca Nacional, 1973.

Maigne d'Arnis, W.-H., *Lexicon Manuale ad Scriptores Mediæ et Infimæ Latinitatis*, Paris: Garnier, 1890.

Malkiel, Yakov, "Castilian *albricias* and its Ibero-Romance Congeners," *StPh*, 43 (1946), 498–521.

Malkiel, Yakov, *Three Hispanic Word Studies: Latin "macula" in Ibero-Romance; Old Portuguese "trigar"; Hispanic "lo(u)çano,"* Berkeley–Los Angeles: University of California Press, 1947.

Malkiel, Yakov, "The Fluctuating Intensity of a 'Sound Law': Some Vicissitudes of Latin ĕ and ŏ in Spanish," *RPh*, 34 (1980), 48–63.

Malmberg, Bertil (ed.), *Le Roman du Comte de Poitiers: Poème français du XIIIe siècle*, Lund–Copenhagen: C. W. K. Gleerup–Ejnar Munksgaard, 1940.

Mandrou, Robert, *De la culture populaire aux 17ᵉ et 18ᵉ siècles: La Bibliothèque bleue de Troyes*, Paris: Imago, 1985.

Mano =   Guy Levis Mano (ed. and trans.), *Romancero judéo-espagnol*, Paris: GLM, 1971.

Manzano Alonso, Miguel, "Estructuras arquetípicas de recitación en la música tradicional," *RevMusicol*, 9:2 (1986), 357–397.

Manzano, Miguel, and Angel Barja, *Cancionero leonés, volumen II, tomo I: Cantos narrativos*, León: Diputación Provincial, 1991.

Marazuela Albornós, Agapito, *Cancionero segoviano*, Segovia: Jefatura Provincial del Movimiento, 1964.

Marazuela Albornós, Agapito, *Cancionero de Castilla*, Madrid: Delegación de Cultura de la Diputación de Madrid, 1981.

Marcoaldi, Oreste, *Canti popolari inediti umbri, leguri, piceni, piemontesi, latini, raccolti e illustrati*, Genoa: Co' tipi del R. I. de' Sordo-Muti, 1855.

Marcos Rodríguez, Florencio, *El ingreso de Salinas en la Universidad de Salamanca y su órgano realejo*, Salamanca: Universidad de Salamanca, 1987.

Markowska, Elzbieta, "Forma galiardy," *Muzyka*, 16:4 (1978), 73–84.

Márquez Villanueva, Francisco, "El mundo poético de los *Disparates* de Juan del Encina," *Jewish Culture and the Hispanic World: Essays in Memory of Joseph H. Silverman*, ed. S. G. Armistead and Mishael M. Caspi (Newark, Delaware: Juan de la Cuesta, 2001), pp. 351–379.

Martínez Añibarro y Rives, Manuel, *Intento de un Diccionario Biográfico y bibliográfico de la Provincia de Burgos*, Madrid: Fundación de Manuel Tello, 1899; facsimile ed. Valladolid: Consejería de Cultura y Turismo, 1993.

Martínez de Toledo, Alfonso, *Arcipreste de Talavera o Corbacho*, ed. Joaquín González Muela, Madrid: Castalia, 1970.

Martínez de Toledo, Alfonso, *Arcipreste de Talavera o Corbacho*, ed. Michael Gerli, Madrid: Cátedra, 1979.

Martínez Kleiser, Luis, *Refranero general ideológico español*, Madrid: Real Academia Española, 1953.

Martínez Ruiz, Juan, "Romancero de Güéjar Sierra (Granada)," *RDTP*, 12 (1956), 360–386, 495–543.

M[artínez] Torner, Eduardo, "Indicaciones prácticas sobre la notación musical de los romances?," *RFE*, 10 (1923), 389–394.

M[artínez] Torner, Eduardo, "La canción tradicional española," *Folklore y costumbres de España*, ed. F. Carreras y Candi (Barcelona: Alberto Martín, 1931), II, 7–166.

M[artínez] Torner, Eduardo, "El cancionero asturiano," *Temas folklóricos* (Madrid: Faustino Fuentes, 1935), pp. 35–47.

M[artínez] Torner, Eduardo, "Góngora y el folklore," *Temas folklóricos* (Madrid: Faustino Fuentes, 1935), pp. 71–83.

M[artínez] Torner, Eduardo, "Ritmos," *Temas folklóricos* (Madrid: Faustino Fuentes, 1935), pp. 129–141.

M[artínez] Torner, Eduardo, *Temas folklóricos: Música y poesía*, Madrid: Faustino Fuentes, 1935.

M[artínez] Torner, Eduardo, "La rítmica en la música tradicional española," *Nuestra Música*, 3:9, Suplemento 3 (1948), 55–68.

Martín Morán, José Manuel, *Ginevra y Finea: Novela y cuento ("Decameron", II, 9/"Patraña XV" del "Patrañuelo")*, Pisa: Giardini, 1986.

Martins, Ana Maria, and Pere Ferré, *Romanceiro Tradicional do Distrito de Beja*, Santiago do Cacém: Real Sociedade Arqueológica Lusitana, 1988.

Martins, Firmino A., *Folklore do Concelho de Vinhais*, 2 vols., Coimbra–Lisbon: Imprensa da Universidade–Imprensa Nacional, 1928–1938.

Martorell, Joanot, and Martí Joan de Galba, *Tirant lo Blanc*, ed. Martín de Riquer, 2 vols., Barcelona: Seix Barral, 1969.

Massot i Muntaner, Josep, "Aportació a l'estudi del romancer balear," *ER*, 7 (1959–1960), 63–155.

Massot i Muntaner, Josep, "El romancero tradicional español en Mallorca," *RDTP*, 17 (1961), 157–173.

Mata Carriazo, Juan de (ed.), *Crónica de don Alvaro de Luna, condestable de Castilla, maestre de Santiago*, Madrid: Espasa-Calpe, 1940.

Mata Carriazo, Juan de, *Hechos del condestable don Miguel Lucas de Iranzo (Crónica del siglo XV)*, Madrid: Espasa-Calpe, 1940.

Mathews, Mitford M., *A Dictionary of Americanisms on Historical Principles*, Chicago: University of Chicago Press, 1951.

Matisoff, James A., *Blessings, Curses, Hopes, and Fears: Psycho-Ostensive Expressions in Yiddish*, 1st ed., Philadelphia: Institute for the Study of Human Issues, 1979; 2d ed., Stanford: Stanford University Press, 2000.

Matulka, Barbara, *The Novels of Juan de Flores and their European Diffusion: A Study in Comparative Literature*, New York: New York University, 1931.

McGregor, R. S., *The Oxford Hindi-English Dictionary*, Oxford –Delhi: Oxford University Press, 1997.

MCR =   Antonio Rodríguez-Moñino, with Arthur L.-F. Askins, *Manual bibliográfico de cancioneros y romanceros*, 4 vols., Madrid: Castalia, 1973–1978.

Mead, William E., "Colour in the English and Scottish Ballads," *An English Miscellany: Presented to Dr. Furnivall in Honour of his Seventy-Fifth Birthday* (Oxford: Clarendon, 1901), pp. 321–334.

Meier, Eugen A., *Vogel Gryff: Geschichte und Brauchtum der Drei Ehrengesellschaften Kleinbasels*, Basel: Litera, 1986.

Meier, John, *Balladen*, 2 vols., Darmstadt: Wissenschaftliche Buchgesellschaft, 1964.

Mele, Eugenio, "Due canti spagnuoli nella società ispano-napoletana del cinquecento," *RLM*, 2:3–4 (1947), 204–217.

Mena, Juan de, *Coplas de los siete pecados mortales*, Salamanca, 1500.

Mendoza Díaz-Maroto, Francisco, *Introducción al romancero oral de la Provincia de Albacete*, Albacete: Excma. Diputación, 1989.

Mendoza Díaz-Maroto, Francisco, *Antología de romances orales recogidos en la Provincia de Albacete*, Albacete: Excma. Diputación, 1990.

Mendoza, Vicente T., *El romance español y el corrido mexicano: Estudio comparativo*, Mexico City: U.N.A.M., 1939.

Menéndez Pidal, Gonzalo, "Ilustraciones musicales," RoH, I, 367–402.

Menéndez Pidal, Ramón, "Serranilla de la Zarzuela," *StMed*, 11 (1905), 263–270.

Menéndez Pidal, Ramón, "Poesía popular y romancero," *RFE*, 1 (1914), 357–377; 2 (1915), 1–20, 105–136, 329–338; 3 (1916), 233–289.

Menéndez Pidal, Ramón, *Historia y epopeya*, Madrid: C.E.H., 1934.

Menéndez Pidal, Ramón, *Cómo vivió y cómo vive el Romancero*, Valencia: López Mesquida, [1945].

Menéndez Pidal, Ramón, "Suerte de un arcaísmo léxico en la poesía tradicional," *QIA*, 8 (1948), 201–203.

Menéndez Pidal, Ramón, *Orígenes del español*, 3rd ed., Madrid: Espasa-Calpe, 1950.

Menéndez Pidal, Ramón, Diego Catalán, and Alvaro Galmés, *Cómo vive un romance: Dos ensayos sobre tradicionalidad*, Madrid: C.S.I.C., 1954.

Menéndez Pidal, Ramón, *Los godos y la epopeya española: "Chansons de geste" y baladas nórdicas*, Madrid: Espasa-Calpe, 1956.

Menéndez Pidal, Ramón, *El dialecto leonés*, ed. Carmen Bobes, Oviedo: Instituto de Estudios Asturianos, 1962.

Menéndez Pidal, Ramón, *La leyenda de los infantes de Lara*, 3rd ed., Madrid: Espasa-Calpe, 1971.

Menéndez Pidal, Ramón, "Cómo vivió y cómo vive el Romancero," *Estudios sobre el Romancero* (Madrid: Espasa-Calpe, 1973), pp. 403–445.

Menéndez Pidal, Ramón, *Estudios sobre el Romancero*, Madrid: Espasa-Calpe, 1973.

Menéndez Pidal, Ramón, *Reliquias de la poesía épica española, acompañadas de "Epopeya y Romancero, 1,"* ed. Diego Catalán, 2d ed., Madrid: Gredos, 1980.

Mercier, Henry, *Dictionnaire arabe-français*, Rabat: "Editions La Porte," 1951.

Mettmann, Walter (ed.), Afonso X, o Sábio, *Cantigas de Santa Maria*, 4 vols., Coimbra: Universidade, 1959–1972.

Meyer, Gustav, *Etymologisches Wörterbuch der albanesischen Sprache*, Strassburg: Karl J. Trübner, 1891.

Michaëlis de Vasconcelos, Carolina, "Neues zum Buche der kamonianischen Lieder und Briefe," *ZRPh*, 7 (1883), 407–453.

Michaëlis de Vasconcelos, Carolina, "Miscelanea: MA Maneira do Apiahá," *RL*, 1:4 (1887–1889), 379–381.

Migliorini, Bruno, and Aldo Duro, *Prontuario etimologico della lingua italiana*, Torino: G. B. Paravia, 1958.

Miklosich, Franz, "Die türkischen Elemente in den südost- und osteuropäischen Sprachen," *Denkschriften der Kaiserlichen Akademie der Wissenschaften: Philosophisch-Historische Classe* (Vienna), 34 (1884), 239–338; 35 (1885), 105–192; 37 (1889), 1–88; 38 (1890), 1–194.

Milá = Manuel Milá y Fontanals, *Romancerillo catalán: Canciones tradicionales*, 2d ed., Barcelona: Alvaro Verdaguer, 1882.

Milá y Fontanals, Manuel, *De la poesía heroico-popular castellana*, Barcelona: Alvaro Verdaguer, 1896.

Milá y Fontanals, Manuel, *De la poesía heroico-popular castellana*, ed. Martín de Riquer y Joaquín Molas, Barcelona: C.S.I.C., 1959.

Millán Urdiales, José, *El habla de Villacidayo (León)*, Madrid: Real Academia, 1966.

Millares Carlo, Agustín, *Tratado de paleográfica española*, 2d ed., 2 vols., Madrid: Victoriano Suárez, 1932.

Miller, Robert P., *Chaucer: Sources and Backgrounds*, New York: Oxford University Press, 1977.

Mitjana, Rafael, *Historia de la música en España*, ed. Antonio Álvarez Cañibano, Madrid: Instituto Nacional de las Artes Escénicas y la Música, Ministerio de Cultura, 1992.

Moland, L., and C. d'Héricault (ed.), *Nouvelles françoises en prose du XIIIe siècle*, Paris: P. Jannet, 1856.

Molina, Alonso de, *Vocabulario en lengua castellana y mexicana y mexicana y castellana*, ed. Miguel León-Portilla, 2d ed., Mexico City: Porrúa, 1977.

Moneva y Puyol, Juan, *Vocabulario de Aragón*, ed. José Luis Aliaga Jiménez, Zaragoza: Prensas Universitarias, 2004.

Monner Sans, Ricardo, "Refranero gatuno," *Estudios eruditos in memoriam de Adolfo Bonilla y San Martín (1875–1926)*, 2 vols. (Madrid: Viuda e Hijos de Jaime Ratés, 1927), I, 319–346.

Monroe, James T., "Hispano-Arabic Poetry during the Almoravid Period: Theory and Practice," *Viator*, 4 (1973), 65–98.

Monroe, James T., and David Swiatlo, "Ninety-three Arabic Kharjas in Hebrew Muwashshaḥs: Their Hispano-Romance Prosody and Thematic Features," *JAOS*, 97 (1977), 141–163.

Monroe, James T., "Studies on the 'Kharjas': The Arabic and the Romance 'Kharjas'," *Viator*, 8 (1977), 95–125.

Monroe, James T., *The Art of Badīᶜ az-Zamān al-Hamadhānī as Picaresque Narrative*, Beirut: American University of Beirut, 1983.

Montaner, Alberto (ed.), *Cantar de Mio Cid*, estudio preliminar de Francisco Rico, Barcelona: Crítica, 1993.

Montero, Emilio, *El eufemismo en Galicia: Su comparación con otras áreas romances*, Santiago de Compostela: Universidade, 1981 (*Verba: Anuario Galego de Filoloxia*, Anexo 17).

Montesardo, Girolamo, *Nuova inventione d'intavolatura pero sonare li balletti sopra la chitarra spagniuola senza numeri e note*, Florence: C. Marescotti, 1606.

Moore, Jerome Aaron, *The "Romancero" in the Chronicle-Legend Plays of Lope de Vega*, Philadelphia: University of Pennsylvania, 1940.

Morlaye, Guillaume, *Le Premier livre de chansons, gaillardes, pavannes, bransles, almandes, fantaisies, reduictz en tabulature de guiterne*, Paris: Robert Granjon and Michel Fezandat, 1552.

Morlaye, Guillaume, *Quatriesme livre contenant plusieurs fantasies, chansons, gaillardes, paduanes, bransles, reduictes en tabulature de guyterne*, Paris: Michel Fezandat, 1552.

Morlaye, Guillaume, *Le Second livre de chansons, gaillardes, padvanes, bransles, almandes, fantaisies, reduictz en tabulature de guiterne*, Paris: Michel Fezandat, 1553.

Morley, S. Griswold, "Are the *Romances* Written in Quatrains?," *RR*, 7 (1916), 42–82.

Morokoff, Gene E., "Whole Tale Parallels of the Child Ballads as Cited or Given by Child or in *FFC* 74," *JAF*, 64 (1951), 202–206.

Morphy y Ferriz de Guzmán, Guillermo, *Les luthistes espagnols du XVe siècle (Die spanischen Lautenmeister des 16. Jahrhunderts)*, 2 vols., Leipzig: Breitkopf & Härtel, 1902.

Morris, Lynn King, *Chaucer Source and Analogue Criticism: A Cross-Referenced Guide*, New York: Garland, 1985.

Mortier, Raoul (ed.), *Les textes de la Chanson de Roland*, 10 vols., Paris: "La geste francor," 1940–1944.

Mortillaro, Vincenzo, *Nuovo dizionario siciliano-italiano*, 2 vols., Palermo: Giornale Letterario–Oretea, 1838–1844.

Moser, Hugo, and Helmut Tervooren, *Des Minnesangs Frühling*, 37th ed., 3 vols. in 4, Stuttgart: S. Hirzel, 1981–1982.

Moya, Ismael, *Romancero: Estudios sobre materiales de la colección de folklore*, 2 vols., Buenos Aires: Universidad de Buenos Aires, 1941.

MP =   Ramón Menéndez Pidal, "Catálogo del romancero judío-español," *CE*, 4 (1906), 1045–1077; 5 (1907), 161–199.

MRuiz =   Juan Martínez Ruiz, "Poesía sefardí de carácter tradicional (Alcazarquivir)," *AO*, 13 (1963), 79–215.

Mudarra, Alonso, *Tres libros de música en cifra para vihuela (Sevilla, 1546)*, ed. Emilio Pujol, Barcelona: C.S.I.C., 1949.

Muhawi, Ibrahim, and Sharif Kanaana, *Speak, bird, speak again: Palestinian Arab Folktales*, Berkeley–Los Angeles: University of California Press, 1989.

Munthe, Åke W., "Folkpoesi från Asturien," *Språk-vetenskapliga Sällskapets i Upsala Förhandlingar (Sept. 1885-May 1888): Upsala Universitets Årsskrift: Filosofi, Språkvetenskap och Historiska Vetenskaper*, 5 (1887), 105–124.

Murray, Alexander C., *Germanic Kinship Structure*, Toronto: Pontifical Institute of Mediaeval Studies, 1983.

Nájera, Esteban de, *Prima parte de la Silva de varios romances*, Zaragoza, 1550.

Nahón =   Samuel G. Armistead and Joseph H. Silverman, with the collaboration of Oro Anahory Librowicz, *Romances judeo-españoles de Tánger (recogidos por Zarita Nahón)*, Madrid: C.S.M.P., 1977.

Narváez, Luys de, *Los seys libros del Delphin de música de cifra para tañer vihuela* (Valladolid, 1538), ed. Emilio Pujol, Barcelona: C.S.I.C., 1945; 2d ed. 1971.

Nascimento, Bráulio do, "Conde Claros na Tradição Portuguesa," *QP*, 11–12 (1982), 139–187.

Nascimento, Bráulio do, "Conde Claros Confessor," *Oral Tradition and Hispanic Literature: Essays in Honor of Samuel G. Armistead*, ed. Mishael M. Caspi (New York: Garland, 1995), pp. 549–581.

Navaza Blanco, Gonzalo, et al., *Pequeño Dicionario Xerais da Lingua*, Vigo: Xerais, 2005.

NCR =   Jesús Suárez López, *Nueva colección de romances (1987–1994)*, with Mariola Carbajal Álvarez, musical transcriptions by Susana Asensio Llamas, Oviedo–Madrid: Fundación Menéndez Pidal, 1997.

Nehama, Joseph, *Dictionnaire du judéo-espagnol*, ed. Jesús Cantera, Madrid: C.S.I.C., 1977.

Neira Martínez, Jesús, *El habla de Lena*, Oviedo: Instituto de Estudios Asturianos, 1955.

Ness, Arthur J., "Francesco Canova da Milano," *NGDMM*, XII, 771–772.

NGDMM =   *New Grove Dictionary of Music and Musicians*, ed. Stanley Sadie, 20 vols., London: Macmillan, 1980.

Nigra, Costantino, *Canti popolari del Piemonte*, Turin: Giulio Einaudi, 1957.

Noreen, Adolf, *Altisländische und altnorwegische Gramatik unter Berücksichtigung des Urnordischen*, 2d ed., Halle: Max Niemeyer, 1892.

Norton, Frederick John, *A Descriptive Catalogue of Printing in Spain and Portugal 1501–1520*, Cambridge: Cambridge University Press, 1978.

Noy, Dov, "The First Thousand Folktales in the Israel Folktale Archive," *Fabula*, 4 (1961), 99–110.

Noy, Dov (ed.), *Jefet Schwili erzählt: Hundertneun-undsechzig jeminitische Volkserzählungen aufgezeichnet in Israel 1957–1960*, Berlin: Walter de Gruyter, 1963.

Noy, Dov, *Contes populaires racontés par des juifs du Maroc*, Jerusalem: Dispersion et Unité, 1965.

NSR =   Samuel G. Armistead and Joseph H. Silverman, "A New Sephardic *Romancero* from Salonika," *RPh*, 16 (1962–1963), 59–82.

Nunes, José Joaquim, "Subsídios para o Romanceiro Português (Tradição Popular do Algarve)," *RL*, 6 (1901), 151–188.

Ocampiana =   Florián de Ocampo, *Las quatro partes enteras dela cronica de España que mando componer el Serenissimo rey don Alonso llamado el sabio*, Zamora: Augustín de Paz y Juan Picardo, 1541.

OCPC =   *Obra del cançoner popular de Catalunya: Materials*, ed. Francesc Pujol, Josep Massot i Muntaner, et al., 11 vols., Barcelona: Fundació Concepció Rabell i Cibils, vda. Romaguera–Abadia de Montserrat, 1926–2001.

OED =   *The Compact Edition of the Oxford English Dictionary*, 2 vols., Oxford: Oxford University Press, 1971.

Oinas, Felix J., *Essays on Russian Folklore and Mythology*, Columbus, Ohio: Slavica, 1985.

O'Kane, Eleanor S., *Refranes y frases proverbiales españolas de la Edad Media*, Madrid: Real Academia Española, 1959.

Oliveira Marques, António Henrique R. de, *Daily Life in Portugal in the Late Middle Ages*, trans. S. S. Wyatt, Madison: University of Wisconsin Press, 1971.

Oliveira Marques, António Henrique R. de, *A Sociedade Medieval Portuguesa: Aspectos de vida quotidiana*, 5th ed., Lisbon: Sá da Costa, 1987.

Olrik, II = Axel Olrik, *Danske folkeviser i udvalg: Anden samling*, Copenhagen–Kristiania: Gyldendalske Boghandel–Nordisk Forlag, 1909.

Onions, C. T., *The Oxford Dictionary of English Etymology*, Oxford: Clarendon, 1978.

Opie, Iona, and Moira Tatem, *A Dictionary of Superstitions*, Oxford: Oxford University Press, 1989.

Orel, Vladimir, *Albanian Etymological Dictionary*, Leiden: Brill, 1998.

Ortega, Manuel L., *Los hebreos en Marruecos*, 1st ed., Madrid: Editorial Hispano Africano, 1919; 3rd ed., Madrid: Compañía Ibero-Americana de Publicaciones, 1929.

Orwell, George, "Marrakech," *A Collection of Essays* (Garden City, New York: Doubleday, 1954), pp. 186–193.

Otaola González, Paloma, "Francisco Salinas y la teoría modal en el siglo XVI," *Nassarre*, 11:1–2 (1995), 367–385.

Otaola González, Paloma, *El humanismo musical en Francisco de Salinas,* Pamplona: Newbook Ediciones, 1997.

Otis, Leah L., *Prostitution in Medieval Society: The History of an Urban Institution in Languedoc*, Chicago: University of Chicago Press, 1987.

Öztopçu, Kurtuluş, et al., *Dictionary of the Turkic Languages*, London: Routledge, 1999.

Pachtikos, Georgios D., 260 Demódē hellēnikà 'ásmata 'apò toū stómatos toū hellēnikoū laoū, Athens: P. D. Sakellarios, 1905.

Pagis, Dan, *Hebrew Poetry of the Middle Ages and the Renaissance*, Berkeley–Los Angeles: University of California Press, 1991.

Palisca, Claude, "Francisco de Salinas (1513–90) as Humanist," *ACS*, I, 165–170.

Palisca, Claude, "Francisco de Salinas et l'humanisme italien," *Musique et humanisme à la Rennaissance* (Paris: Presses de l'Ecole Normale Superieure, 1993), pp. 37–45.

Palisca, Claude, "Salinas, Francisco de," DMEH, IX, 598–602.

Palmer, E. H., *A Concise Dictionary of the Persian Language*, 12th printing, London: Kegan Paul, 1944 (orig. 1876).

Paloma, Joan Antoni (ed.), *Romancer català: Text establert per Manuel Milà i Fontanals*, Barcelona: Edicions 62, 1980.

Papahagi, Tache, *Dicționarul dialectului aromîn general și etimologic,* Bucharest: Acadamie Republicii Populare Romîne, 1963.

Papo, Joseph M., "The Sephardim in North America in the Twentieth Century," *AJA*, 44 (1992), 267–308 (also reprinted in Cohen and Peck, *Sephardim in the Americas*).

Pappadopoulos, G. G., "'Ásmata dēmotikà tōn en Korsikē Hellēnōn," *Pandṓra* (Athens), 15:353 (1864), 413–420.

Paris, Gaston, and Ulysse Robert (ed.), *Miracles de Nostre Dame*, Paris: Firmin Didot, 1879 (S.A.T.F., Vol. 6:4).

Paris, Gaston, "Le conte de la rose dans le Roman de Perceforest," *Romania*, 23 (1894), 78–140.

Paris, Gaston, "Le cycle de la gageure," *Romania*, 32 (1903), 481–551.

Parsons, Elsie Clews, *Folk-Lore from the Cape Verde Islands*, 2 vols., Cambridge, Massachusetts–New York: American Folk-Lore Society, 1923.

Parsons, Elsie Clews, "Zapoteca and Spanish Tales of Mitla, Oaxaca," *JAF*, 45 (1932), 277–317.

Parsons, Elsie Clews, *Taos Tales,* New York: The American Folk-Lore Society, 1940.

Parsons, Elsie Clews, *Folk-Lore of the Antilles, French and English*, Part III, New York: The American Folk-Lore Society, 1943.

Pascu, Giorge, *Dictionnaire étymologique macédo-roumain*, 2 vols., Iași: Cultura Naţională, 1918–1925.

Passow, Arnold, *Tragoúdia romaïkà: Popularia carmina Graeciae recentioris*, Athens: Carl Wilberg, 1860.

Pattison, David G., *From Legend to Chronicle: The Treatment of Epic Material in Alphonsine Historiography*, Oxford: S.S.M.L.L., 1983.

Payne, John (trans.), *The Book of the Thousand Nights and One Night*, 9 vols., London: privately printed, 1884.

PCG =   *[Estoria de España]: Primera Crónica General de España*, ed. Ramón Menéndez Pidal, 2 vols, Madrid: Gredos, 1955.

Pedrell, Felipe, *Diccionario técnico de la música*, 2d ed., Barcelona: Isidro Torres Oriol [1894?]; facsimile ed., Valencia: Librerías «París-Valencia», 1992.

Pedrell, Felipe, "Folk-lore musical castillan du XVIe siècle," *SIMG*, 1 (April–June 1900), 372–400.

Pedrell, Felipe, "Estudio sobre una fuente de folk-lore musical castellano del siglo XVI," *Lírica nacionalizada: Estudios sobre el folk-lore musical* (Paris: Paul Ollendorff, 1913), pp. 211–263.

Pedrell, Felipe, "Folklore musical hispano: I. Orientaciones sobre el folklore musical: El criterio etnográfico en la clasificación," *Arxiu d'Etnografia i Folklore de Catalunya: Estudis i Materials*, no. 1 (Barcelona: Oliva de Vilanova, 1916), pp. 23–48.

Pedrell, Felipe, *Cancionero musical popular español*, [1st ed.,] 4 vols., Valls: Eduardo Castells, 1919–1922.

Pedrell, Felipe, *Cancionero musical popular español*, 3rd ed., 4 vols., Barcelona: Boileau, 1958.

Pedrosa, José Manuel, César Javier Palacios, and Elías Rubio Marcos, *Héroes, santos, moros y brujas (Leyendas épicas, históricas y mágicas de la tradición oral de Burgos): Poética, comparatismo y etnotextos*, Burgos: Tentenublo, 2001.

Pellegrini, Astorre, *Canti popolari dei greci di Cargese (Corsica)*, Bergamo: Bolis, 1871.

Penny, Ralph J., *El habla pasiega: Ensayo de dialectología montañesa*, London: Tamesis, 1970.

Pensado, José Luis (ed.), *Papeletas de un diccionario gallego, I: Texto*, Orense: Insituto de Estudios Orensanos «Padre Feijóo», 1979.

Pereira da Costa, Francisco Augusto, "Folk-lore Pernambucano," *RIHGB*, 70:2 (1907), 3–641.

Pérez Castro, Federico, "Aproximación a la poesía de Ibn Gabirol," *Hispania Judaica*, ed. Josep M. Solá-Solé et al. (Barcelona: Puvill, 1982), pp. 59–74.

Pérez de Castro, José Luis, "Nuevas variantes asturianas del Romancero hispánico," *RDTP*, 16 (1960), 477–481.

Pérez de Castro, José Luis, "Nuevas variantes asturianas del Romancero hispánico (II)," *RDTP*, 23 (1967), 315–337.

Pérez de Hita, Ginés, *Guerras civiles de Granada*, ed. Paula Blanchard-Demouge, 2 vols., Madrid: E. Bailly-Baillière, 1913–1915.

Pérez de Hita, Ginés, *Guerras civiles de Granada: Primera Parte*, ed. Shasta M. Bryant, Newark, Delaware: Juan de la Cuesta, 1982.

Pérez de Hita, Ginés, *Guerras civiles de Granada*, ed. Paula Blanchard-Demouge, 2 vols., with preliminary studies by Pedro Correa and Joaquín Gil Sanjuán, Granada: Universidad de Granada, 1998–1999.

Pergoli, Benedetto, *Saggio di canti popolari romagnoli*, Forlì: L. Bordandini, 1894.

Pernot, Hubert, *Anthologie populaire de la Grèce moderne*, 2d ed., Paris: Mercure de France, 1910.

Perry, T. Anthony, "'La huella del león' in Spain and in the Early Sindibad Tales: Structure and Meaning," *Medieval, Renaissance and Folklore Studies in Honor of John Esten Keller*, ed. Joseph R. Jones (Newark, Delaware: Juan de la Cuesta, 1980), pp. 39–52.

Piacentini, Giuliana, "Romances en *ensaladas* y géneros afines," *AFE*, 1 (1984), 1135–1173.

Pickering, David, *Dictionary of Superstitions*, London: Cassell, 1995.

Pickering, David, *Dictionary of Folklore*, London: Cassell, 1999.

Pino Saavedra, Yolando, *Cuentos folklóricos de Chile*, 3 vols., Santiago de Chile: Universidad de Chile, 1960–1963.

Pino Saavedra, Yolando, *Folktales from Chile*, Chicago: University of Chicago Press, 1967.

Pinto-Correia, João David, "Le Cycle des romances du *Conde Claros*: Proposition de systematisation," *Litterature Oral Traditionelle Populaire: Actes du Colloque: Paris, 20–22 novembre 1986*, ed. José-Augusto França (Paris: Fondation Calouste Gulbenkian, 1987), pp. 301–311.

Pinto-Correia, João David, *Os Romances Carolíngios da Tradição Portuguesa*, 2 vols., Lisbon: Instituto Nacional de Investigação Científica, 1993–1994.

Pinto-Correia, João David, *Romanceiro Oral da Tradição Portuguesa*, Lisbon: Duarte Reis, 2003.

Piñero, Pedro M., and Virtudes Atero, *Romancero andaluz de tradición oral: Folklore*, Seville: Biblioteca de la Cultura Andaluza, 1986.

Piñero, Pedro M., and Virtudes Atero, *Romancero de la tradición moderna,* Seville: Fundación Machado, 1987.

Piñero, Pedro M. (ed.), *Segunda parte del Lazarillo*, Madrid: Cátedra, 1988.

Pires da Cruz, José, *Estudos sobre o Romanceiro Tradicional Português: Tradição Oral das Beiras*, Ph.D. dissertation, University of California, Davis, 1988.

Pires da Cruz, José, *Romanceiro Tradicional da Beira Baixa*, Idanha-a-Nova: Câmara Municipal, 1997.

Pires de Lima, Joaquim Alberto, and Fernando Castro Pires de Lima, *Contribuïção para o Estudo do Romanceiro Minhoto*, Oporto: Portucalense, 1943.

Pisador, Diego, *Libro de música de vihuela* (Salamanca, 1552), Geneva: Minkoff, 1973.

Pitré, Giuseppe, "Stratagemmi leggendarii di città assediate," *ASTP*, 22 (1903), 193–211.

Pitré, Giuseppe, *Canti popolari siciliani*, 2 vols., Rome: Società Editrice del Libro Italiano, 1940–1941.

Platts, John T., *A Dictionary of Urdū, Classical Hindī, and English*, New Delhi: Munshiram Manoharlal, 1997 (orig. 1884).

Pliegos BN =   *Pliegos poéticos góticos de la Biblioteca Nacional*, 6 vols., Madrid: Joyas Bibliográficas, 1957–1961.

Pliegos de Cracovia = *Pliegos poéticos españoles de la Biblioteca Universitaria de Cracovia*, ed. María Cruz García de Enterría, 2 vols., Madrid: Joyas Bibliográficas, 1975.

Pliegos de Milán = *Pliegos poéticos españoles en la Biblioteca Ambrosiana de Milán*, ed. María Cruz García de Enterría, 2 vols., Madrid: Joyas Bibliográficas, 1973.

Pliegos de Praga = *Pliegos poéticos españoles en la Universidad de Praga*, prologue by Ramón Menéndez Pidal, 2 vols., Madrid: Joyas Bibliográficas, 1960.

PNCR = Jesús Antonio Cid, *Primeras noticias y colecciones de romances en el s. XIX*, Madrid: F.R.M.P.–Seminario Menéndez Pidal, 1999.

Pokorny, Julius, *Indogermanisches Etymologisches Wörterbuch*, 2 vols., Bern–Munich: Francke, 1959–1962.

Politis, Nikolaos G., *Eklogaì apò tà tragoúdia toū hellenikoū laoū*, 4th ed., Athens: E. G. Bagionakis & T. Gregoropoulos, 1958.

Pomeroy, Hilary S., *An Edition and Study of the Secular Ballads in the Sephardic Ballad Notebook of Halia Isaac Cohen*, Ph.D. dissertation, University of London, Queen Mary and Westfield College, 2001.

Poncet y de Cárdenas, Carolina, "Romancerillo de Entrepeñas y Villar de los Pisones," *RHi,* 57 (1923), 286–314.

Poncet y de Cárdenas, Carolina, "Romancerillo de Entrepeñas y Villar de los Pisones," *AFC,* 3 (1928), 121–154.

Poncet y de Cárdenas, Carolina, *Investigaciones y apuntes literarios*, ed. Mirta Aguirre, Havana: Letras Cubanas, 1985.

Pope, Isabel, "Notas sobre la melodía del *Conde Claros*," *NRFH*, 7 (1953), 395–402.

Porębowicz, Edward, *Zbiór nieznanych hiszpańskich ulotnych druków*, Krakow: Uniwersytet Jagiellońska, 1891.

Porro Fernández, Carlos A., *Fonoteca de tradición oral: cintas 1 a 100*, Valladolid: Castilla Ediciones, 1977.

Preciado, Dionisio, "Veteranía de algunos ritmos «aksak» en la música antigua española," *AnM*, 39–40 (1984–1985), 189–215.

Preciado, Dionisio, "Canto tradicional y polifonía en el primer Renacimiento español," ACS, I, 171–183.

Prestes, António, et al., *Primeira Parte dos Autos e Comédias Portuguesas*, Lisbon: Lysia, 1973; 1st ed. 1587.

Primav. =   Fernando J. Wolf and Conrado Hofmann, *Primavera y flor de romances*, 2d ed., Marcelino Menéndez Pelayo, *Antología de poetas líricos castellanos*, VIII, "Ed. Nac.," XXIV, Santander: C.S.I.C., 1945.

Pring, J. T., *Oxford Dictionary of Modern Greek*, Oxford: Clarendon, 1982 (orig. 1965).

Prior, R. C. Alexander, *Ancient Danish Ballads*, 3 vols., London–Edinburgh: Williams and Norgate, 1860.

PTJ =   Manuel Alvar, *Poesía tradicional de los judíos españoles*, Mexico City: Porrúa, 1966.

Pulido =   Angel Pulido Fernández, *Intereses nacionales: Españoles sin patria y la raza sefardí*, Madrid: E. Teodoro, 1905.

Purcell, Joanne B., *Novo Romanceiro Português das Ilhas Atlânticas*, ed. Isabel Rodríguez-García, with Joãn A. das Pedras Saramago, Madrid: Seminario Menéndez Pidal, 1987.

Qafisheh, Hamdi A., *A Basic Course in Gulf Arabic*, Tucson: University of Arizona Press, 1975.

QRA =   Carlos Petit Caro, *Quince romances andaluces*, Seville: Librería Hispalense, 1946.

Querol Gavaldá, Miguel, *La música en las obras de Cervantes*, Barcelona: Comitalia, 1948.

Querol Gavaldá, Miguel, "Importance historique et nationale du romance," *Colloques Internationaux du Centre National de la Recherche Scientifique: Sciences Humaines*, V: *Musique et poésie au XVIe siècle*, ed. Jean Jacquot (Paris: Centre National de la Recherche Scientifique, 1954), pp. 299–327.

Querol Gavaldá, Miguel, *Transcripción e interpretación de la polifonía española de los siglos XV y XVI*, Madrid: Comisaría de la Música, 1975.

Quevedo Villegas, Francisco de, *El parnaso español, monte en dos cumbres dividido con las nueve musas castellanas,* ed. Jusepe Antonio González, Madrid: Diego Díaz de la Carrera, 1648.

Quevedo Villegas, Francisco de, *Las tres últimas musas castellanas: Segunda cumbre del parnaso español,* Madrid: Pedro Aldrete, 1670.

Quevedo Villegas, Francisco de, *Obra poética,* ed. José Manuel Blecua, 4 vols., Madrid: Castalia, 1969–1981.

Quevedo Villegas, Francisco de, *Poesía varia,* ed. James O. Crosby, Madrid: Cátedra, 1981.

Radford, Edwin and Mona A., *Encyclopedia of Superstitions,* ed. Christina Hole, London: Hutchinson, 1980.

Radole, Giuseppe, *Canti popolari istriani: Seconda raccolta,* Florence: Leo S. Olschki, 1968.

Rael, Juan B., *Cuentos españoles de Colorado y Nuevo Méjico,* 2 vols., Stanford: Stanford University Press, [1957].

Ranke, Kurt, *Folktales of Germany,* trans. Lotte Baumann, Chicago: University of Chicago Press, 1966.

RCan =   Mercedes Morales and María Jesús López de Vergara, introd. by Diego Catalán, *Romancerillo canario: Catálogo-manual de recolección,* La Laguna: Universidad de La Laguna, 1955.

Rechnitz, Florette M., *Hispano-Romanian Ballad Relationships: A Comparative Study with an Annotated Translation of Al. I. Amzulescu's "Index of Romanian Ballads,"* 2 vols., Ph.D. dissertation, University of Pennsylvania, Philadelphia, 1978.

Reckert, Stephen, *Lyra Minima: Structure and Symbol in Iberian Traditional Verse,* Portsmouth, England: Eyre & Spottiswoode, 1970.

Reckert, Stephen, *Beyond Chrysanthemums: Perspectives on Poetry East and West,* Oxford: Clarendon, 1993.

Reckert, Stephen, *Más allá de las neblinas de noviembre,* Madrid: Gredos, 2001.

Redhouse, Sir James W., *New Redhouse Turkish-English Dictionary,* ed. U. Bahadır Alkıim, Sofi Huri, Andreas Tietze et al., Istanbul: Redhouse Press, 1968.

Reis Dámaso, António, "Tradições Populares (Collecção do Algarve," *Encyclopedia Republicana* (Lisbon: Nova Minerva, 1882), pp. 154–156, 171–173, 184; variant title: "Tradições Populares do Algarve," pp. 201–204, 215–216, 232–237.

Reliquias =   Ramón Menéndez Pidal, *Reliquias de la poesía épica española, acompañadas de "Epopeya y Romancero, 1*," ed. Diego Catalán, 2d ed., Madrid: Gredos, 1980.

Rennert, Hugo A., *Der spanische Cancionero des Brit. Mus. (MS. Add. 10431)*, Erlangen: Fr. Junge, 1895 (offprint: *RF*, 10 [1895]).

Rennert, Hugo A., *Der spanische Cancionero des Brit. Museums (Ms. add. 10431)*, *RF*, 10 (1899), 1–76.

REW =   Wilhelm Meyer-Lübke, *Romanisches Etymologisches Wörterbuch*, 5th ed., Heidelberg: Carl Winter, 1968.

Rey [Marcos], Juan José, *Danzas cantadas en el renacimiento español*, Madrid: Sociedad Española de Musicología, 1978.

RGL =   Diego Catalán, Mariano de la Campa, et al. (ed.), *Romancero general de León: Antología 1899–1989*, 2 vols., Madrid: S.M.P. and Diputación Provincial de León, 1991.

RH: Fronteras =   *El Romancero Hoy: Nuevas fronteras*, ed. Antonio Sánchez Romeralo, Diego Catalán, Samuel G. Armistead, et al., Madrid: C.S.M.P., 1979.

RH: Historia =   *El Romancero Hoy: Historia, comparatismo, bibliografía crítica*, ed. Samuel G. Armistead, Antonio Sánchez Romeralo, Diego Catalán, et al., Madrid: C.S.M.P., 1979.

RH: Poética =   *El Romancero Hoy: Poética*, ed. Diego Catalán, Samuel G. Armistead, Antonio Sánchez Romeralo, et al., Madrid: C.S.M.P., 1979.

Ricapito, Joseph V. (ed.), *Lazarillo de Tormes*, 2d ed., Madrid: Cátedra, 1976.

Rico Beltrán, Amparo, "Recopilación de romances de Alpuente (Valencia)," *Historia, reescritura y pervivencia del Romancero: Estudios en memoria de Amelia García-Valdecasas*, ed. Rafael Beltrán (Valencia: Universitat de València, 2000), pp. 229–242.

Rico, Francisco, "Del *Cantar del Cid* a la *Eneida*: Tradiciones épicas en torno al *Poema de Almería*," *BRAE*, 65 (1985), 197–211.

Rico, Francisco, *Texto y contextos: Estudios sobre la poesía española del siglo XV*, Barcelona: «Crítica», 1990.

Riera Pinilla, Mario, *Cuentos folklóricos de Panamá*, Panamá: Ministerio de Educación, 1956.

Riquer, Martín de, *Los cantares de gesta franceses (Sus problemas, su relación con España)*, Madrid: Gredos, 1952.

Riquer, Martín de, *Les chansons de gestes françaises*, 2d ed., trans. Irénée Cluzel, Paris: Nizet, 1968.

Riquer, Martín de, "La fecha del *Ronsasvals* y del *Rollan a Saragossa* según el armamento," *BRAE*, 49 (1969), 211–251.

Rivers, Elias L., "Cassian's *Meridianum Daemonium*," *HR*, 23 (1955), 292.

Rivers, Elias L., "The Pastoral Paradox of Natural Art," *MLN*, 77 (1962), 130–144.

Robertson-Smith, W., *Kinship & Marriage in Early Arabia*, London: Adam and Charles Black, 1903.

Robe, Stanley L., *The Spanish of Rural Panama: Major Dialectal Features*, Berkeley: University of California Press, 1960.

Robe, Stanley L., *Mexican Tales and Legends from Los Altos*, Berkeley–Los Angeles: University of California Press, 1970.

Robe, Stanley L., *Index of Mexican Folktales*, Berkeley–Los Angeles: University of California Press, 1973.

Robson, J., "Abū Hurayra al-Dawsī al-Yamānī," *Encyclopédie de l'Islam*: New Ed., I (Leiden: Brill, 1960), pp. 132–133.

Roda, Cecilio de, *La música profana en el reinado de Carlos I: Conferencias dadas en el Ateneo de Madrid*, Bilbao: "El Nervión," 1912.

Roda, Cecilio de, "La música profana en el reinado de Carlos I," *RMB*, 4:7 (1912), 165–170; 4:11 (1912), 258–264.

Rodrigues de Azevedo, Alvaro, *Romanceiro do Archipélago da Madeira*, Funchal: "Voz do Povo," 1880.

Rodríguez-Castellano, Lorenzo, *Aspectos del Bable Occidental*, Oviedo: Instituto de Estudios Asturianos, 1954.

Rodríguez de Montalvo, Garci, *Amadís de Gaula*, 2 vols., 2d ed., ed. Juan Manuel Cacho Blecua, Madrid: Cátedra, 1991.

Rodríguez Marín, Francisco, *Luis Barahona de Soto: Estudio biográfico, bibliográfico y crítico*, Madrid: Sucesores de Rivadeneyra, 1903.

Rodríguez Marín, Francisco, *Más de 21.000 refranes castellanos no contenidos en la copiosa colección del maestro Gonzalo Correas . . .*, Madrid: "Revista de Archivos, Bibliotecas y Museos," 1926.

Rodríguez Marín, Francisco, *Los 6.666 refranes de mi última rebusca . . .*, Madrid: C. Bermejo, 1934.

Rodríguez Marín, Francisco, *Todavía 10.700 refranes más . . .*, Madrid: «Prensa Española», 1941.

Rodríguez-Moñino, Antonio, "El Cancionero manuscrito de Pedro del Pozo (1547)," *BRAE*, 29 (1949), 453–509; 30 (1950), 123–146, 263–312.

Rodríguez-Moñino, Antonio (ed.), *Segunda parte del Cancionero general* (Zaragoza, 1552), Valencia: Castalia, 1956.

Rogers, Edith Randam, *The Perilous Hunt: Symbols in Hispanic and European Balladry*, Lexington: University Press of Kentucky, 1980.

RoH =   Ramón Menéndez Pidal, *Romancero hispánico (hispano-portugués, americano y sefardí)*, 2 vols., Madrid: Espasa-Calpe, 1953.

Rohlfs, Gerhard, *Dizionario dialettale delle tre Calabrie*, 3 vols., Halle (Saale)–Milan: Max Niemeyer–Ulrico Hoepli, 1932–1939.

Rohlfs, Gerhard, *Estudios sobre el léxico románico*, ed. Manuel Alvar, Madrid: Gredos, 1979.

Röhrich, Lutz, *Lexikon der sprichwörtlichen Redensarten*, 4 vols., Freiburg im Breisgau: Herder, 1986 (3 vols., Herder, 1992).

Rojas, Fernando de, *La Celestina*, ed. Dorothy S. Severin, 8th ed., Madrid: Cátedra, 1994.

Romero, Emilia, *El romance tradicional en el Perú*, Mexico City: El Colegio de Mexico, 1952.

Romero, Sílvio, *Contos Populares do Brasil*, 2 vols., ed. Luís da Câmara Cascudo, Rio de Janeiro: José Olympio, 1954.

Romero, Sílvio, *Estudos sobre a Poesia Popular do Brasil*, 2d ed., Petrópolis: Editora Vozes, 1977.

Romeu Figueras, José (ed.), *Cancionero musical de Palacio (Siglos XV–XVI)*, 2 vols., Barcelona: C.S.I.C., 1965 (= *MME* 14.1–2).

Romeu Figueras, José, *Corpus d'antiga poesia popular*, Barcelona: Barcino, 2000.

Roques, Mario, "Ronsasvals: Poème épique provençal," *Romania*, 58 (1932), 1–28, 161–189; 66 (1940–1941), 433–480.

Rosado, Fátima, *Tradição Oral Algarvia, 1: Poesia Recolhida na Fraguesia de Querença*, Faro: Universidade do Algarve, 1993.

Rossiaud, Jacques, *Medieval Prostitution*, trans. Lydia G. Cochrane, Oxford: Basil Blackwell, 1988.

Ross, Thomas W. (ed.), Geoffrey Chaucer, *The Miller's Tale*, Norman: University of Oklahoma Press, 1983 (*Variorum Chaucer*, Vol. II).

Rotunda, D. P., *Motif-Index of the Italian Novella in Prose*, Bloomington: Indiana University Publications, 1942.

Roudil, Jean (ed.), *El fuero de Baeza*, The Hague: G. B. van Goor Zonen, 1962.

Roudil, Jean (ed.), *Les fueros d'Alcaraz et d'Alarcón*, 2 vols., Paris: C. Klincksieck, 1968.

Roy, Claude, *Trésor de la poésie populaire française*, Paris: Seghers, 1954.

RPC =   Narciso Alonso Cortés, *Romances populares de Castilla*, Valladolid: Eduardo Sáenz, 1906.

RPE =   Bonifacio Gil [García], *Romances populares de Extremadura*, Badajoz: Diputación Provincial, 1944.

RPI =   Manuel da Costa Fontes, *O Romanceiro Português e Brasileiro: Índice Temático e Bibliográfico (Com uma bibliografia Pan-Hispânica e Resumos de Cada Romance em Inglês)*, 2 vols., musical transcription and commentary by Israel J. Katz, index of Pan-European analogues by Samuel G. Armistead, Madison, Wisconsin: H.S.M.S., 1997.

RPM =   José María de Cossío and Tomás Maza Solano, *Romancero popular de La Montaña: Colección de romances tradicionales*, 2 vols., Santander: Sociedad Menéndez y Pelayo, 1933–1934.

RPOM =   Pere Ferré, with Cristina Carinhas, Ramón dos Santos de Jesus e Eva Parrano, *Romanceiro Português da Tradição Oral Moderna: Versões Publicadas entre 1828 e 1960*, Vol. I, Lisbon: Fundação Calouste Gulbenkian, 2000.

RT =   Ramón Menéndez Pidal and María Goyri de Menéndez Pidal, *Romancero tradicional de las lenguas hispánicas (Español-portugués-catalán-sefardí)*, ed. Diego Catalán et al., 12 vols., Madrid: C.S.M.P., 1957–1985.

RTCN =   [María Goyri de Menéndez Pidal], *Romances tradicionales y canciones narrativas existentes en el folklore español (Incipit y temas)*, Barcelona: Instituto Español de Musicología, 1945.

RTIA =   Samuel G. Armistead, Cristina Carinhas, Pere Ferré, Manuel da Costa Fontes, *Romanceiro Tradicional das Ilhas dos Açores: Recolha de Joanne B. Purcell, I: Corvo e Flores*, Angra do Heroísmo-Lisboa: Governo Regional dos Açores–Universidade Nova de Lisboa, 2002.

RTO =   José María de Cossío, *Romances de tradición oral*, Buenos Aires–Mexico City: Espasa-Calpe, 1947.

RTR =   Bonifacio Gil García, "Romances tradicionales de La Rioja," offprint *Berceo* (Logroño, 1962); *Berceo,* 64 (1962), 311–326; 65 (1962), 383–398; 66 (1963), 51–68.

          Rubio, Samuel, *Desde el "ars nova" hasta 1600*, Madrid: Alianza Música, 1983.

          Rueda, Lope de, *Comedia Eufemia*, ed. Jesús Moreno Villa, Madrid: Espasa-Calpe, 1983.

          Ruiz Granda, Emilio, "Breve contribución al folklore asturiano (romances de Villayón)," *BIEA*, 128 (1988), 751–778.

          Ruiz Mayordomo, María José, "Conde Claros," DMEH, III, 867.

          Runciman, Steven, *A History of the Crusades*, 3 vols., Cambridge: Cambridge University Press, 1952–1955.

RVP =   Carolina Michaëlis de Vasconcelos, *Estudos sôbre o Romanceiro Peninsular: Romances Velhos em Portugal*, 2d ed., Coimbra: Universidade, 1934.

          Sachs, Curt, *World History of the Dance*, trans. Bessie Schönberg, New York: W. W. Norton, 1937.

          Sacristán, Fermín, *Doctrinal de Juan del Pueblo*, 2 vols., Madrid: Murillo, 1907–1911.

Sage, Jack, "Early Spanish Ballad Music: Tradition or metamorphosis?," *Medieval Hispanic Studies Presented to Rita Hamilton*, ed. Alan D. Deyermond (London: Tamesis, 1976), pp. 195–214.

Sala, Marius, *Phonétique et phonologie du judéo-espagnol de Bucarest*, The Hague–Paris: Mouton, 1971.

Salazar, Flor, and Ana Valenciano, "El Romancero aún vive: Trabajo de campo de la CSMP: «Encuesta Norte 77»," *RH: Fronteras*, pp. 361–421.

Saldoni y Remendo, Baltasar, *Diccionario biográfico-bibliográfico de efemérides de músicos españoles*, 4 vols., Madrid: Antonio Pérez Dubrull, 1868–1881.

Salillas, Rafael, *El delincuente español: El lenguaje*, Madrid: Victoriano Suárez, 1896.

Salinas, Francisco, *De musica libri septem,* Salamanca: Mathias Gastius, 1577.

Salinas, Francisco, *De Musica*, ed. Macario Santiago Kastner, Kassel–Basel: Bärenreiter, 1958.

Salinas, Francisco, *Siete libros sobre la música*, trans. Ismael Fernández de la Cuesta, Madrid: Alpuerto, 1983.

Sánchez de Badajoz, Diego, *Recopilación en metro* (Sevilla, 1554), ed. Frida Weber de Kurlat, Buenos Aires: Universidad de Buenos Aires, 1968.

Sánchez de Vercial, Clemente, *Libro de los exemplos por A.B.C.*, ed. John E. Keller, Madrid: C.S.I.C., 1961.

Sánchez Pérez, José A., *Supersticiones españolas*, Madrid: S.A.E.T.A., 1948.

Santamaría, Francisco J., *Diccionario general de americanismos*, 3 vols., Mexico City: Pedro Robredo, 1942.

Santamaría, Francisco J., *Diccionario general de mejicanismos*, 4th ed., Mexico City: Porrúa, 1983.

Santos Neves, Guilherme, "Presença do Romancero Peninsular na Tradição Oral do Brasil," *RBFo*, 1 (1961), 44–62.

Saporta y Beja, Enrique, *Refranero sefardí*, Madrid–Barcelona: Instituto Arias Montano, 1957.

Sas, Louis F., *Vocabulario del Libro de Alexandre*, Madrid: Real Academia Española, 1976.

Sastre, Alfonso, *Lumpen, marginación y jerigonça*, Madrid: Legasa, 1980.

Saulnier, Verdun-Louis, "Étude sur Pernette du Guillet et ses *Rymes*," *BHR*, 4 (1944), 7–119.

Saulnier, Verdun-Louis, "Mellin de Saint-Gelais, Pernette du Guillet et l'air «Conde Claros»," *BHR*, 32 (1970), 526–537.

Scarborough, Dorothy, *A Song Catcher in Southern Mountains: American Folk Songs of British Ancestry*, New York: Columbia University Press, 1937.

Schewe, Harry, "Die 'Wette': Ein neu aufgefundene alte Ballade," *Volkskundliche Gaben: John Meier zum siebzigsten Geburtstage dargebracht*, ed. Erich Seemann and Harry Schewe (Berlin–Leipzig: Walter de Gruyter, 1934), pp. 176–186.

Schindler, Kurt, *Folk Music and Poetry of Spain and Portugal (Música y poesía popular de España y Portugal)*, New York: Hispanic Institute, 1941.

Schindler, Kurt, *Música y poesía popular de España y Portugal*, 2d ed., ed. Israel J. Katz and Miguel Manzano Alonso, with the collaboration of Samuel G. Armistead, Salamanca: Diputación de Salamanca, 1991.

Schirmunski, Viktor, "Die Ballade vom 'König aus Mailand' in den Wolga-Kolonien," *JVF*, 1 (1928), 160–169.

Schirmunski, Viktor, *Vergleichende Epenforschung*, I, Berlin: Akademie–Verlag, 1961.

Schlauch, Margaret, *Chaucer's Constance and Accused Queens*, New York: New York University Press, 1927.

Schmid, Walter, *Der Wortschatz des Cancionero de Baena*, Bern: Francke, 1951.

Schneider, Marius, "¿Existen elementos de música popular en el «Cancionero musical de Palacio»?," *AnM*, 8 (1953), 177–192.

Scholem, Gershom, *Sabbatai Şevi: The Mystical Messiah: 1626–1676,* trans. R. J. Zwi Werblowsky, Princeton: Princeton University Press, 1975.

SCHS = Albert B. Lord (and David Bynum) (ed. and trans.), *Serbocroatian Heroic Songs*, 6 vols., Cambridge, Massachusetts: Harvard University Press, 1954–1980.

Schubarth, Dorothé, and Antón Santamarina, *Escolma de cántigas do Cancioneiro Popular de Galicia*, La Coruña: Fundación «Pedro Barrié de la Maza Conde de Fenosa», 1991.

Schwartzbaum, Haim, *Studies in Jewish and World Folklore*, Berlin: Walter De Gruyter, 1968.

Seeger, Judith, "The Curious Case of *Conde Claros*: A Ballad in Four Traditions," *JHPh*, 12 (1988), 221–237.

Seeger, Judith, "El «Conde Claros de Montalbán» en el siglo XVI: Evidencia de la vitalidad de tres tradiciones: la juglaresca, la tradicional y la escrita," *El Romancero: Tradición y pervivencia a fines del siglo XX: Actas del IV Coloquio Internacional del Romancero (Sevilla–Puerto de Santa María–Cádiz, 23–26 de junio de 1987)*, ed. Pedro M. Piñero et al. (Cádiz: Fundación Machado–Universidad de Cádiz, 1989), pp. 237–242.

Seeger, Judith, *Count Claros: Study of a Ballad Tradition*, New York: Garland, 1990.

Seeger, Judith, "Can a Traditional Ballad be Myth? An Exploration of Heroism in *Count Claros*," *La Corónica*, 20:1 (1991–1992), 72–77.

Seeger, Judith, "Genre and the Ballad," *JFR*, 31 (1994), 151–176.

Seeger, Judith, "Just How Bounded is the Ballad? Two Brazilian Examples," *Ballads and Boundaries: Narrative Singing in an Intercultural Context: Proceedings of the 23rd International Ballad Conference of the Commission for Folk Poetry (Société Internationale d'Ethnologie et de Folklore): University of California, Los Angeles, June 21–24, 1993*, ed. James Porter (Los Angeles: Department of Ethnomusicology & Systemic Musicology, 1995), pp. 265–273.

Seemann, Erich, "Deutsch-litauische Volksliedbeziehungen," *JVF*, 7 (1941), 142–211.

Seis romancerillos = Samuel G. Armistead, Joseph H. Silverman, and Iacob M. Hassán, *Seis romancerillos de cordel sefardíes*, Madrid: Castalia, 1981.

Senabre Sempere, Ricardo, "La fuente de una novela de doña María de Zayas," *RFE*, 46 (1963), 164–172.

Senny, Edouard, *Chansons populaires de l'Ardenne Septentrionale (Lorce et Filot)*, 2 vols., ed. Roger Pinon, Brussels: Schott, 1961–1962.

Sephiha, Haïm Vidal, *Le Ladino: Judéo-espagnol calque: Deutéronome, versions de Constantinople (1547) et de Ferrare (1553)*, Paris: Centre de Recherches Hispaniques, 1973.

Sepúlveda, Lorenzo de, *Romances nuevamente sacados de historias antiguas dela Cronica de España*, Antwerp: Philippo Nucio, 1566; facsimile ed. Archer M. Huntington, New York: Hispanic Society, 1903.

Serra i Vilaró, J., *El Cançoner del Calic*, Barcelona: «L'Avenç», 1913.

Serrano Poncela, S., "Dos «Werther» del Renacimiento español," *Asomante*, 5 (1946), 87–103.

Servois, G. (ed.), *Le Roman de la rose ou de Guillaume de Dole*, Paris: Firmin Didot, 1893 (S.A.T.F., Vol. 33).

Shalian, Artin K. (trans.), *David of Sassoon*, Athens, Ohio: Ohio University Press, 1964.

Sharp, Cecil, and Maud Karpeles, *English Folk Songs of the Southern Appalachians*, 2 vols., Oxford: Oxford University Press, 1932.

Sholod, Barton (ed.), *Charlemagne in Spain: The Cultural Legacy of "Roncesvalles,"* Geneva: Droz, 1966.

Silva (1550) = Antonio Rodríguez-Moñino (ed.), *Silva de romances* (Zaragoza, 1550–1551), Zaragoza: Cátedra Zaragoza, 1970.

Silva (1561) = Antonio Rodríguez-Moñino (ed.), *Silva de varios romances* (Barcelona, 1561), Valencia: Castalia, 1953.

Silva Lima, Jackson da, "Achegas ao Romanceiro Tradicional em Sergipe," *Estudos de Folclore em Homenagem a Manuel Diégues Júnior* (Maceió: «Antropologia e Folclore», 1991), pp. 119–147.

Silva recopilada = *Silva de varios romances recopilados, y con diligencia escogidos los mejores Romances de los tres libros de la Silua*, Barcelona: Jayme Sendrat, 1582.

Silva Soromenho, Alda da, and Paulo Caratão Soromenho, *Contos Populares Portugueses*, Vol. I, Lisbon: Centro de Estudos Geográficos, 1984.

Silveira, Pedro da, "Materiais para um Romanceiro da Ilha das Flores," *Boletim do Núcleo Cultural da Horta* (Azores), 2:3 (1961), 471–490.

Silveira, Pedro da, "Mais alguns Romances da Ilha das Flores," *BCEHE*, 1 (1986), 25–42.

Silverman, Joseph H., "La contaminación como arte en un romance sefardí de Tánger," *RH: Poética*, pp. 29–37.

Siméon, Rémi, *Diccionario de la lengua nahuatl o mexicana . . .*, Mexico City: Siglo XXI, 1983.

Simon, Walter, "Charakteristik des judenspanischen Dialekts von Saloniki," *ZRPh*, 40 (1920), 655–689.

[Sintes Pros, Jorge], *Diccionario de aforismos, proverbios y refranes,* 4th ed., Barcelona: Editorial Sintes, 1967.

Škaljić, Abdulah, *Turcizmi u srpskohrvatskom jeziku*, 5th ed., Sarajevo: «Svjetlost», 1985.

Skeat, Walter W., *An Etymological Dictionary of the English Language*, Oxford: Clarendon, 1893.

Skok, Petar, *Etimologijski rječnik hrvatskoga ili srpskoga jezika,* ed. Mirko Deanović, Ljudevit Jonke, and Valentin Putanec, 4 vols., Zagreb: Jugoslavenska Akademija Znanosti Umjetnosti, 1971–1974.

Slim, H. Colin, "Francesco da Milano (1947–1953/44): A Bio-Bibliographical Study," *MDisciplina*, 18 (1964), 63–84; 19 (1965), 109–128.

Smith-Dampier, E. M., *A Book of Danish Ballads*, Princeton: Princeton University Press, 1939.

Smith, Victor, "Chants de quêtes," *Romania*, 2 (1873), 59–71.

Smyser, Hamilton Martin, "The Engulfed Lucerna of the *Pseudo-Turpin*," *HSNPhL*, 15 (1933), 49–73.

Sobelman, Harvey, and Richard S. Harrell, *A Dictionary of Moroccan Arabic: English-Arabic*, Washington, D.C.: Georgetown University Press, 1963.

Solomon, Andrew, *The Noonday Demon: An Atlas of Depression*, New York: Scribner, 2001.

Spiro Bey, Socrates, *Arabic-English Dictionary of the Modern Arabic of Egypt*, 2d ed., Cairo: Elias, 1923.

Spyridakis, Georges C., et al., *Anthologie des chansons populaires grecques*, Paris: Gallimard, 1967.

Stachowski, Stanislaw, "Die osmanisch-türkischen Lehnwörter im Serbokroatischen und ihre Bedeutung für die historische Phonetik des Osmanisch-türkischen," *Folia Orientalia*, 4 (1962), 143–170.

Stead, Ian M., J. B. Bourke, and Don Brothwell, *Lindow Man: The Body in the Bog*, London: British Museum, 1986.

Steiger, Arnald, "Zur Sprache der Mozaraber," *Sache, Ort und Wort: Festschrift Jakob Jud* (Geneva–Zurich–Erlenbach: E. Droz–Eugen Rentsch, 1942), 624–723 (+ two maps).

Steingass, Francis Joseph, *A Comprehensive Persian-English Dictionary*, New Delhi: Cosmo, 1977 (orig. 1892).

Steingass, Francis Joseph, *English-Arabic Dictionary*, New Delhi: AES, 1993 (orig. London, 1882).

Stein, Helga (ed. and trans.), *Rumänische Volksballaden zusammengestellt und herausgegeben von Al. I. Amzulescu: Thematischer Index*, Freiburg im Breisgau: [Deutsches Volksliedarchiv], 1974.

Stein, Louise K., *Songs of Mortals, Dialogues of the Gods: Music and Theatre in Seventeenth-Century Spain*, Oxford: Clarendon, 1993.

Stevens, John, *A New Spanish and English Dictionary . . .*, London: George Sawbridge, 1706.

Stevenson, James A. C., *A Dictionary of Scots Words & Phrases in Current Use*, New York: Hippocrene, 1989.

Stevenson, Robert M., "Salinas, Francisco de," NGDMM, XVI, 420–421.

Stith Thompson =   Stith Thompson, *Motif-Index of Folk-Literature*, 2d ed., 6 vols., Bloomington: Indiana University Press, 1955–1958.

Stone, Donald Jr., *Mellin de Saint-Gelais and Literary History*, Lexington, Kentucky: French Forum, 1983.

Strausz, Adolf, *Bulgarische Volksdichtungen*, Vienna–Leipzig: Carl Graeser, 1895.

Strohmeyer, Fritz, "Das Schachspiel im Altfranzösischen: Beiträge zur Kenntnis der Bedeutung und Art des Schachspiels in der altfranzösischen Zeit," *Abhandlung Herrn Prof. Dr. Adolf Tobler* (Halle: Max Niemeyer, 1895), pp. 381–403.

Sturtevant, Edward H., *An Introduction to Linguistic Science*, New Haven: Yale University Press, 1956.

Suard, François, "Le développement de la *Geste de Montauban* en France jusqu'à la fin du Moyen Age," *Romance Epic: Essays on a Medieval Literary Genre*, ed. Hans-Erich Keller (Kalamazoo: Western Michigan University, 1987), pp. 141–161.

Suárez Avila, Luis, "El romancero de los gitanos bajoandaluces: Del romancero a las tonás," *Dos Siglos de Flamenco: Actas de la Conferencia Internacional, Jerez, 21–25 junio 1988*, ed. Antonio Gala (Jerez: Fundación Andaluza de Flamenco, 1989), pp. 29–129.

Suárez Avila, Luis, "Bernardo del Carpio y los gitanos bajoandaluces," *Actes del Col.loqui sobre Cançó Tradicional: Reus setembre 1990*, ed. Salvador Rebés (Barcelona: Abadia de Monserrat, 1994), pp. 225–267.

Subirá, José, *Historia de la música teatral en España*, Barcelona: Labor, 1945.

Sutherland, Madeline, "*La fratricida por amor*: A Sixteenth-Century Spanish Ballad in the Modern Oral Tradition," *OT*, 8:2 (1993), 289–323.

Tabla =   José J. Labrador Herraiz and Ralph A. DiFranco, *Tabla de los principios de la poesía española, siglos XVI–XVII*, Cleveland, Ohio: Cleveland State University, 1993.

Tamariz, Cristóbal de, *Novelas en verso*, ed. Donald McGrady, Charlottesville, Virginia: Biblioteca Siglo de Oro, 1974.

Tansillo, Luigi, *Capitoli giocosi e satirici*, ed. Scipione Volpicella, Naples: Libreria di Dura, 1870.

Tavares, José Augusto, "Romanceiro Trasmontano," *RL*, 8 (1903–1905), 71–80; 9 (1906), 277–323.

Tavares, José Augusto, "Folk-lore Trasmontano: Lizarda," *IT*, 1 (1908), 24, 88, 103–104, 143; 2 (1909), 28, 124; 3 (1910), 40–41, 76, 93–94, 128, 135–136.

Taylor, Archer, "Themes Common to English and German Balladry," *MLQ*, 1 (1940), 23–35.

Taylor, Archer, "Attila and Modern Riddles," *JAF*, 56 (1943), 164–166.

Ten Cate, J. P., *Poema de Alfonso XI: Estudio preliminar y vocabulario*, Amsterdam: Swets & Zeitlinger, 1942.

Tent. Dict. =   Lloyd A. Kasten and Florian J. Cody, *Tentative Dictionary of Medieval Spanish*, 2d ed., New York: H.S.M.S., 2001.

Terrasse, Henri, *Histoire du Maroc*, 2 vols., Casablanca: Atlantides, 1949.

Terrasse, Henri, *History of Morocco*, trans. Hilary Tee, Casablanca: Atlantides, 1952.

Terry, Patricia, and Nancy Vine Durling (trans.), *The Romance of the Rose or Guillame de Dole*, by Jean Renart, Philadelphia: University of Pennsylvania Press, 1993.

Theros, Agis, *Tà tragoúdia tōn hellénōn*, 2 vols., Athens: Ethnikè Aetós, 1951–1952.

Thiébaux, Marcelle, *The Stag of Love: The Chase in Medieval Literature*, Ithaca: Cornell University Press, 1974.

Thomaz Pires, A., "Lendas & Romances (Recolhidas da Tradição Oral na Provincia do Alemtejo)," *A Tradição*, 1 (1899), 71–74, 93–94, 119, 157, 182–184; 2 (1900), 28–29, 106–107; 3 (1901), 42–44, 91–92, 143–144, 148–150, 166–169; 4 (1902), 14–15, 32, 38–41, 58–60, 75–76, 90–92, 110–112, 127–128, 143–144, 159–160, 176; facsimile ed., 2 vols., Serpa: Câmara Municipal, 1982: Vol. 1 = *A Tradição*, 1:1 (1900)–3:12 (1901); Vol. 2 = 4:1 (1902).

Thompson, Stith, *The Folktale*, New York: Dryden, 1951.

Ticknor, George, *Geschichte der schönen Literatur in Spanien*, 2 vols., ed. N. H. Julius, Leipzig: F. A. Brockhaus, 1852.

Timoneda, Juan, *El patrañuelo*, ed. Federico Ruiz Morcuende, Madrid: Espasa-Calpe, 1958.

Timoneda, Juan, *Rosas de Romances* (Valencia, 1573), ed. Antonio Rodríguez-Moñino and Daniel Devoto, Valencia: Castalia, 1963.

Timoneda, Juan, *El patrañuelo*, ed. Rafael Ferreres, Madrid: Castalia, 1971.

TLEC =   Cristóbal Corrales Zumbado, Dolores Corbella Díaz, María Angeles Alvarez Martínez, *Tesoro lexicográfico del español de Canarias*, Madrid: Real Academia Española–Gobierno de Canarias, 1992.

Tolkien, J. R. R., and E. V. Gordon (ed.), *Sir Gawain and the Green Knight*, Oxford: Clarendon, 1952.

Tordera, Antonio, "Historia y mojiganga del teatro," *Actas de las jornadas sobre teatro popular en España,* ed. J. Álvarez Barrientos and A. Cea Gutiérrez (Madrid: C.S.I.C., 1987), pp. 249–287.

Torner, Eduardo M., "Indicaciones prácticas sobre la notación musical de los romances?," *RFE*, 10 (1923), 389–394.

Torner, Eduardo M., "La canción tradicional española," *Folklore y costumbres de España,* ed. F. Carreras y Candi (Barcelona: Alberto Martín, 1931), II, 7–166.

Torner, Eduardo M., "El cancionero asturiano," *Temas folklóricos* (Madrid: Faustino Fuentes, 1935), pp. 35–47.

Torner, Eduardo M., "Góngora y el folklore," *Temas folklóricos* (Madrid: Faustino Fuentes, 1935), pp. 71–83.

Torner, Eduardo M., "Ritmos," *Temas folklóricos* (Madrid: Faustino Fuentes, 1935), pp. 129–141.

Torner, Eduardo M[artínez], *Temas folklóricos: Música y poesía*, Madrid: Faustino Fuentes, 1935.

Torner, Eduardo M., "La rítmica en la música tradicional española," *Nuestra Música*, 3:9, Suplemento 3 (1948), 55–68.

Tortajada =   Damián López de Tortajada, *Floresta de varios romances* (Valencia, 1652), ed. Antonio Rodríguez-Moñino, Madrid: Castalia, 1970.

Trapero, Maximiano, with Lothar Siemens Hernández, *El romancero de Gran Canaria*, I: *Zona del Sureste*, Las Palmas: Mancomunidad de Cabildos, 1982.

Trapero, Maximiano, "Hunting for Rare *Romances* in the Canary Islands," *Hispanic Balladry Today*, ed. Ruth H. Webber (New York: Garland, 1989), pp. 116–148.

Trapero, Maximiano, *Romancero tradicional canario*, [Las Palmas de Gran Canaria]: Viceconsejería de Cultura y Deportes, 1989.

Trapero, Maximiano, with Lothar Siemens Hernández, *El romancero de Gran Canaria*, II, Las Palmas: Cabildo Insular, 1990.

Trapero, Maximiano, *El romancero de Virgilios en la tradición canaria e hispánica*, Las Palmas: El Museo Canario, 1992.

Trapero, Maximiano, and Martha Esquenazi Pérez, *Romancero tradicional y general de Cuba,* Madrid: Gobierno de Canarias–Centro de Investigación y Desarrollo de la Cultura Cubana «Juan Marinello», 2002.

Trapero, Maximiano (ed.), *Romancero de la Isla de La Gomera*, San Sebastián de la Gomera: Cabildo Insular de la Gomera, 1987.

Trapero, Maximiano (ed.), *Romancero General de La Gomera*, 2d ed., [La Gomera]: Cabildo Insular de la Gomera, 2000.

Trend, John Brande, *The Music of Spanish History to 1600*, Oxford: Oxford University Press, 1926.

Trend, John Brande, "Catalogue of the Music in the Biblioteca Medinaceli, Madrid," *RHi*, 71 (1927), 485–554.

Trend, John Brande, "Salinas: A Sixteenth-Century Collector of Folk Songs," *ML*, 8 (1927), 13–24.

Trend, John Brande, "Folk Music: Spanish," GDMM, III, 368–372.

Tres calas =   Samuel G. Armistead and Joseph H. Silverman, with Israel J. Katz, *Tres calas en el romancero sefardí (Rodas, Jerusalén, Estados Unidos)*, Madrid: Castalia, 1979.

Triwedi, Mitchell D., "Las citas romancísticas de Sebastián Covarrubias," *BICC*, 39 (1984), 321–329.

TRV (1924–1926) =   Marcelino Menéndez Pelayo, *Tratado de los romances viejos*, 2 vols., *Antología de poetas líricos castellanos*, XI–XII, Madrid: Sucesores de Hernando, 1924–1926.

TRV (1944) =   Marcelino Menéndez Pelayo, *Tratado de los romances viejos*, 2 vols., *Antología de poetas líricos castellanos*, VI–VII, "Ed. Nac.," XXII–XXIII, Santander: C.S.I.C., 1944.

TSB =   Bengt R. Jonsson, Svale Solheim, Eva Danielson, et al., *The Types of the Scandinavian Medieval Ballad*, Stockholm–Oslo: Svenskt visarkiv–Universitetsforlaget, 1978.

Tuchman, Barbara, *A Distant Mirror*, New York: Ballantine, 1979.

Twain, Mark, *Adventures of Huckleberry Finn*, ed. Walter Blair et al., Berkeley–Los Angeles University of California Press, 1988 (*Works of Mark Twain*, Vol. 8).

UR =   Baruch Uziel, "Ha-folklor shel ha-yĕhûdîm ha-sĕfārādîm," *Reshumoth*, 5 (1927), 324–337; 6 (1930), 359–397.

Utsyn =   Leiv Heggstad and Hakon H. Grüner Nielsen, *Utsyn yver gamall norsk folkevisedikting*, Oslo: Olaf Norli, 1912.

Väänänen, Veikko, *Étude sur le texte et la langue des Tablettes Albertini*, Helsinki: Suomalainen Tiedeakatemia, 1965.

Valderrábano, Enríquez de, *Libro de mvsica de vihvela, intitvlado Silva de sirenas*, Valladolid: Francisco Fernández de Córdova, 1547; ed. Emilio Pujol, 2 vols., Barcelona: C.S.I.C., 1965.

Vale Judeu =   Idália Farinho Custódio and Maria Aliete Farinho Dores Galhoz, *Memória Tradicional de Vale Judeu*, 2 vols., Loulé: Câmara Municipal, 1996–1997.

Valenciano, Ana, *Os Romances tradicionais de Galicia: Catálogo exemplificado dos seus temas*, (Vol. I of *Romanceiro Xeral de Galicia),* Madrid–Santiago de Compostela: Centro Ramón Pineiro–F.R.M.P., 1998.

Vaquero, Mercedes, "The Tradition of the *Cantar de Sancho II* in Fifteenth-Century Historiography," *HR*, 57 (1989), 137–154.

Vaquero, Mercedes, *Tradiciones orales en la historiografía de fines de la Edad Media*, Madison, Wisconsin: H.S.M.S., 1990.

Vargyas, Lajos, *Researches into the Mediaeval History of Folk Ballad*, Budapest: Akadémiai Kiadó, 1967.

Vargyas, Lajos, *Hungarian Ballads and the European Ballad Tradition*, 2 vols., Budapest: Akadémiai Kiadó, 1983.

Vega Carpio, Lope Félix de, *Seis comedias,* Lisbon: Pedro Crasbeeck, 1693.

Vega Carpio, Lope Félix de, *Obras de Lope de Vega,* 13 vols., Academia Nueva, Madrid: Real Academia Española, 1916–1930; reprinted, Madrid: Galo Saez, 1929 (*Obras dramáticas,* Vol. XI).

Vega Carpio, Lope Félix de, *Novelas a Marcia Leonarda,* ed. Francisco Rico, Madrid: Alianza, 1968.

Vega Carpio, Lope Félix de, *La noche de San Juan,* ed. Anita K. Stoll, Kassel: Reichenberger, 1988.

Vega, José Blas, *Los corridos o romances andaluces,* Madrid: José Blas Vega, 1982.

Vélez de Guevara, Luis, *El conde don Pedro Vélez y don Sancho el Deseado,* ed. William R. Manson and C. George Peale; introductory study by Thomas E. Case, Fullerton, California: Cal State Fullerton Press, 1997.

Vélez de Guevara, Luis, *El conde don Pedro Vélez y don Sancho el Deseado,* ed. William R. Manson and C. George Peale; introductory study by Thomas E. Case, Newark, Delaware: Juan de la Cuesta, 2002.

Velimirovic, Milos, "The Byzantine Musical Tradition," *Proceedings of the World Congress on Jewish Music (Jerusalem, 1978),* ed. Judith Cohen (Tel Aviv: Institute for the Translation of Hebrew Literature, 1982), pp. 119–126.

Venegas de Henestrosa, Luys, *Libro de cifra nueva para tecla, harpa y vihuela* (Alcalá de Henares: Joan de Broca, 1557), ed. Higinio Anglés, Barcelona: C.S.I.C., 1944.

Vernet, Juan (trans.), *Las mil y una noches,* 2 vols., Barcelona: Planeta, 1997.

Vesce, Thomas E. (trans.), *The Knight of the Parrot (Le Chevalier du Papegau),* New York: Garland, 1986.

Vettori, Giuseppe, *Canti popolari italiani,* 3rd ed., Rome: Newton Compton, 1978.

Viegas Guerreiro, Manuel, *Contos Populares Portugueses,* Lisbon: Fundação Nacional para a Alegria no Trabalho, 1955.

Vieli, Ramun, and Alexi Decurtins, *Vocabulari romontsch sursilvan-tudestg,* Mustér: Ligia Romontscha, 1962.

Vigón, Braulio, *Vocabulario dialectológico del Concejo de Colunga*, ed. Ana María Vigón Sánchez, Madrid: C.S.I.C., 1955.

Vilela, José Aloísio Brandão, *Romanceiro Alagoano*, ed. Maria Thereza Wucherer Braga et al., Maceió: Edufal, 1983.

Viudas Camarasa, Antonio, *Diccionario extremeño*, Cáceres: Anuario de Estudios Filológicos, 1980.

Voces nuevas =   Suzanne H. Petersen, Jesús Antonio Cid, Flor Salazar, and Ana Valenciano (ed.), *Voces nuevas del romancero castellano-leonés*, 2 vols., Madrid: Gredos–S.M.P., 1982.

Voragine, Jacobus de, *The Golden Legend*, trans. Granger Ryan and Helmut Ripperger, New York: Arno, 1969.

Voretzsch, Karl, *Altfranzösisches Lesebuch*, 2d ed., Halle (Saale): Max Niemeyer, 1932.

VRP =   José Leite de Vasconcellos, *Romanceiro Português*, 2 vols., Coimbra: Universidade, 1958–1960.

Vuk =   Vuk Stefanović Karadžić, *Srpske narodne pjesme*, 4 vols., [ed. Vladan Nedić], Belgrade: Nolit, 1977.

Waddell, L. Austine, *Tibetan Buddhism with its Mystic Cults, Symbolism and Mythology, and its Relation to Indian Buddhism*, New York: Dover, 1972.

Wagner, Max Leopold, *Beiträge zur Kenntnis des Judenspanischen von Konstantinopel*, Vienna: Alfred Hölder, 1914.

Wagner, Max Leopold, "Os Judeus Hispano-portugueses e a sua Língua na Oriente, na Holanda e na Alemanha," *Arquivo de História e Bibliografia* (Lisbon), 1 (1924), 3–18; reprinted M. L. Wagner, *Sondersprachen der Romania*, ed. Heinz Kroll, 4 vols. (Stuttgart: Franz Steiner, 1990), Vol. II, 40–55 (= pp. 256–272).

Wagner, Max Leopold, *Dizionario etimologico sardo*, 2 vols., Heidelberg: Carl Winter, 1960–1962.

Walde, Alois, *Lateinisches etymologisches Wörterbuch*, 2d ed., Heidelberg: Carl Winter, 1910.

Ward, John M., *The 'Vihuela de mano' and its Music (1536–1576)*, Ph.D. dissertation, New York University, New York, 1953.

Ward, John M., "Spanish Musicians in Sixteenth-Century England," *Essays in Musicology in Honor of Dragon Plamenac on his 70th Birthday*, ed. G. Reese and R. J. Snow (Pittsburgh: University of Pittsburgh Press, 1969), pp. 353–364.

Ward, John M., *Tablatures for Elizabethan Lutes*, 2 vols., Geneva: Minkoff, 1991.

Ward, John M., *Music for Elizabethan Lutes*, 2 vols., Oxford: Clarendon, 1992.

Warrack, Alexander, *The Scots Dialect Dictionary*, New Lanark, Scotland: Waverley, 2000.

Watkins, Calvert (ed.), *The American Heritage Dictionary of Indo-European Roots*, Boston: Houghton Mifflin, 1985.

Webber, Ruth House, *Formulistic Diction in the Spanish Ballad*, *UCPMPh*, 34 (1951), 175–278.

Webster, Wentworth, *Basque Legends*, 2d ed., London: Griffith and Farran, 1879.

Weever, Jacqueline de, *Chaucer Name Dictionary*, New York: Garland, 1988.

Wehr, Hans, and J. Milton Cowan, *A Dictionary of Modern Written Arabic*, Ithaca, N.Y.: Cornell University Press, 1961.

Wellesz, Egon, *A History of Byzantine Music and Hymnography*, 2d ed., Oxford: Clarendon, 1961.

Wesle, Carl, and Peter Wapnewski (ed.), *Das Rolandslied des Pfaffen Konrad*, Tübingen: Max Niemeyer, 1985.

Westermarck, Edward, *Ritual and Belief in Morocco*, 2 vols., New Hyde Park, N.Y.: University Books, 1968.

Wheeler, Howard T., *Tales from Jalisco, Mexico*, Philadelphia: American Folk-Lore Society, 1943.

Whinnom, Keith, *A Glossary of Spanish Bird-Names*, London: Tamesis, 1966.

Whinnom, Keith, *La poesía amatoria de la época de los Reyes Católicos*, Durham: University of Durham, 1966.

Whitehead, Frederick (ed.), *La Chanson de Roland*, Oxford: Basil Blackwell, 1970.

White, T. H., *The Bestiary: A Book of Beasts, being a translation from a Latin Bestiary of the Twelfth Century*, New York: Putnam, 1960.

Wimberly, Lowry C., *Folklore in the English and Scottish Ballads*, New York: Frederick Ungar, 1959.

Wiora, Walter, *European Folk Song: Common Forms in Characteristic Modifications*, trans. Robert Kolben, Cologne: Arno, 1966.

Wolf, Fernando J. (ed.), *Über eine Sammlung spanischer Romanzen in fliegenden Blättern auf der Universitäts-Bibliothek zu Prag*, Vienna: Braumüller, 1850.

Woodhouse, S. C., *English-Greek Dictionary: A Vocabulary of the Attic Language*, London–New York: Routledge, 2002 (orig. 1910).

Xarabanda =   Jorge Torres (ed.), *Recolhas Xarabanda, I: Romances Tradicionais e Cantigas Narrativas*, introduction by João David Pinto-Correia, Funchal: Xarabanda, 1995.

Ximenius de Rada, Rodericus, *Opera*, ed. Maria Desamparados Cabanes Pecourt, Valencia: Textos Medievales, 1968 (= PP. Toletanorum, vol. III, Madrid: Viuda de Joaquín Ibarra, 1793).

Yoná =   Samuel G. Armistead and Joseph H. Silverman, *The Judeo-Spanish Ballad Chapbooks of Yacob Abraham Yoná*, Berkeley–Los Angeles–London: University of California Press, 1971.

Yoná, Yacob A., *Pizmônîm de bĕrîth mîlāh*, Salonika, 1895–1896.

Yule, Henry, and A. C. Burnell, *Hobson-Jobson: A Glossary of Colloquial Anglo-Indian Words . . .*, ed. William Crooke, London: Routledge & Kegan Paul, 1969 (orig. 1886).

Zajączkowski, Włodzimierz, "Vocabulaire gagaouze-français," *Folia Orientalia* (Krakow), 7 (1965), 29–73.

Zamora Vicente, Alonso, *Dialectología española*, 2d ed., Madrid: Gredos, 1970.

Zayas, Rodrigo de (ed.), *Los vihuelistas: Luys de Narváez*, Madrid: Alpuerto, 1981.

Zayas, Rodrigo de, "La musica a Napoli durante il seicento," *Atti del Convegno Internazionale di Studi, Napoli, 11–14 aprile*

1985, ed. D. A. D'Alessandro and A. Ziino (Rome: Torre D'Orfeo, 1987), pp. 93–103.

Zayas y Sotomayor, María de, *Novelas amorosas y ejemplares*, ed. Agustín González de Amezúa, Madrid: Aldus, 1948.

Zeydel, Edwin H. (ed. and trans.), *Ruodlieb: The Earliest Courtly Novel (after 1050)*, New York: AMS, 1969.

Zingarelli, N., "Stratagemmi legendarii di città assediate," *ASTP*, 22 (1903), 310–312.

Zunzer, Helen, "A New Mexican Village," *JAF*, 48 (1935), 125–178.

C. Unedited Ballad Collections

Amira Collection = We acquired photographs of this beautiful, tastefully ornamented manuscript from Mr. Max Mintesh Amira (from Salonika), in Los Angeles, during the summer of 1958. Mr. Amira himself collected and transcribed the songs, perhaps sometime during the 1930s or 1940s. The MS, bearing the beautifully decorated title page, *Chansons Diverses*, plus Mr. Amira's initials, begins with 179 numbered *coplas*, followed by five *romances*, interspersed with other songs, in Spanish and Turkish, all transcribed in French orthography. Additional *coplas* (numbered 181–223), in Hebrew letters, follow (folios 46 vo.–47 vo.).

Bennaim MS = Collection of 143 texts of Judeo-Spanish traditional poems, including 108 *romances* and narrative songs (= 120 text-types), formed in Tetuán, by Luna Bennaim (1893–1958), between 1919 and 1950 (approximately). The MS was given to Iacob M. Hassán by Moisés Benolol, circa 1970.

Castro MSS = Collection of 62 different ballad types, 21 folktale texts, six wedding songs, and five dirges, as well as extensive linguistic materials and field notes (on index cards and *papeletas*), brought together by Américo Castro, in Tetuán, Xauen, and perhaps also Larache, during the winter and spring of 1922–1923. Concerning this collection, see Armistead and Silverman, "Un aspecto desatendido," p. 184, and updated information in Armistead, "Américo Castro in Morocco," p. 75; also "Seis cantos de boda" and "Una tradición romancística previamente desconocida."

CMP =
Collection of some 2,150 texts of *romances,* narrative and lyric songs, representing 298 different text-types, brought together by Ramón Menéndez Pidal, between 1896 and 1957, and housed at the Archivo Menéndez Pidal, in Madrid (see CMP, under Published Sources). These materials include the extensive unedited musical transcriptions of Manuel Manrique de Lara. See Israel J. Katz, "Manuel Manrique de Lara and the Tunes of the Moroccan Sephardic Ballad Tradition," *RH: Fronteras*, pp. 75–87.

Coello Collection =
Collection of 10 *romances,* in a MS sent to Marcelino Menéndez Pelayo, from Istanbul, by Carlos Coello y Pacheco, in 1885. The MS (Bibl. Nac. Madrid 18.575), in Italian orthography, was given to Coello by a Sephardi in Salonika and the texts represent the Salonikan tradition. Menéndez Pelayo edited these texts— not always correctly—in standard orthography and published them in ASW, pp. 395–404, together with Danon's versions, originally published in *REJ* (1896). Concerning Coello's collection, see ASW, p. 391, and our comments (pp. 29–30, n. 13).

Fereres Collection =
Collection of 20 *romances* transcribed by Samuel Fereres, in Larache (Morocco), before August 25, 1962, when a transcription of the MS (including also some typewritten texts) was acquired in Larache by S. G. A., J. H. S., and I. J. K. Mr. Fereres forwarded a few additional texts by mail in August 1966.

Guzofsky Collection =
Collection of some 125 ballads recorded by Rosalía Guzofsky, in Flushing (New York), Toronto (Canada), Deuil-la-Barre (Paris, France), Ashkelon and Yeruham (Israel), in 1979 and 1980, from informants from Tangier, Tetuán, and Larache. See S. G. Armistead et al., *La Corónica*, 9:1 (1980–1981), 32–33, and Guzofsky, *Mujeres heroicas.*

Hassán Collection =
Collection of some 200 ballads and other forms of traditional poetry recorded by Iacob M. Hassán, from Moroccan Sephardic informants, in Ceuta, August–October, 1981.

Librowicz (II) =
Collection of some 480 ballad texts, representing approximately 90 text-types, from the Moroccan tradition (Tangier, Tetuán, Larache, Alcazarquivir, Gibraltar), collected by Oro Anahory Librowicz, in Málaga, Marbella, Madrid, New York, Montreal, Toronto, Caracas, and Migdal ha-Emek, Afula, and Eilat (Israel), between 1971 and the present. For a partial listing of the content of this collection (now greatly amplified), see Librowicz,

Florilegio, pp. 10–11, n. 4. For the ballads from Gibraltar, see Librowicz, "Romances judeo-españoles de Gibraltar."

Materiales inéditos =   An inventory of field collections housed at the Instituto Español de Musicología (presently Institución «Milà i Fontanals»–Departamento de Musicología, C.S.I.C.), Barcelona.

Onís Collection =   Collection of Eastern and Moroccan Judeo-Spanish and Peninsular *romances*, recorded by Federico de Onís, at the Casa de las Españas, at Columbia University, between 1933 and 1942, from six Eastern Sephardic, one Moroccan Sephardic, and six Peninsular Spanish informants. The collection includes approximately 24 Eastern Judeo-Spanish, 19 Moroccan Judeo-Spanish, and 30 Peninsular ballads and songs. Franz Boas worked with Onís in recording the Moroccan songs and Kurt Schindler helped in collecting the Peninsular material. Only brief segments of each text, mostly the initial verses with the songs' music, were recorded in each case, but, even so, the collection as a whole is an invaluable document of three branches of Hispanic balladry, as they existed in the 1930s and early 1940s. Concerning the Moroccan texts, recorded in collaboration with Franz Boas, see our article, "Judeo-Spanish Folk Poetry from Morocco: The Boas-Nahón Collection."

Pinto Collection =   Collection of 26 *romances* and traditional songs from Morocco, tape-recorded by Abraham Pinto, before 1978, when a copy of the tape was acquired by J. H. S. See no. 13*L*.

Thematic Classification

INDICES

1. Informants

Salonika

1. Flor Tevet, 85 years, Beth Avoth Recanati, Kiryat Matalon (Petaḥ Tikva, Israel), I. J. K., August 25, 1971:

    Conde Claros y el emperador: 10A.

Tetuán

2. Luna Elaluf Farache, 78–79 years, Tetuán (Morocco), S. G. A.-I. J. K.-J. H. S., August 13, 1962; May 31, 1963; August 13, 1962; August 7, 1962; August 21, 1962:

    Conde Claros y el emperador + *Conde Claros insomne*: 10B.
    Conde Claros y la infanta: 11A, 11B, 11C.
    Nacimiento de Bernardo del Carpio + *Conde Claros y la infanta* + *Conde Claros fraile*: 11D, 11E.

Larache

3. Mesodi Castiel Oziel, 68 years, Larache (Morocco), S. G. A.-J. H. S.-I. J. K., August 25, 1962:

    Conde Claros y la infanta: 11F.

4. Sultana viuda de José Melul, 55 years (±), Larache (Morocco), S. G. A.-J. H. S.-I. J. K., September 1, 1962:

    Conde Claros y la infanta: 11G.

5. Unnamed informant, Larache (Morocco), Samuel Fereres, before August 25, 1962:

    Conde Claros y la infanta: 11H.

Rábano de Sanabria (Zamora)

6. Sofía Anta, 67 years, Rábano de Sanabria (Zamora), S. G. A., July 19, 1980:
    Conde Claros fraile (*Lisarda*): text *C* (pp. 217–218).

Casillas de Coria (Cáceres)

7.   María Gómez, 28 years, Casillas de Coria (Cáceres), S. G. A., Madrid, June 25, 1972:

      Conde Claros fraile (*Lisarda*): text *D* (pp. 217–218).

Arroyo de la Luz (Cáceres)

8.   Domitila Parra Molano, 40 years (±), Arroyo de la Luz (Cáceres), S. G. A., June 22, 1963:

      Conde Claros fraile (*Lisarda*): text *E* (pp. 218–219).

Zagra (Granada)

9.   Carmen Cervera, 78 years, Zagra (Granada), S. G. A. and José Manuel Pedrosa, Madrid (Vallecas), December 9, 1992:

      Conde Claros fraile (*Lisarda*): text *F* (pp. 219–220).

Alphabetical List:

Anta, Sofía 6.
Castiel Oziel, Mesodi 3.
Cervera, Carmen 9.
Farache, Luna Elaluf 2.
Gómez, María 7.
Melul, Sultana, viuda de José 4.
Parra Molano, Domitila 8.
Tevet, Flor 1.
Unnamed informant 5.

2. Ballad Titles (Hispanic and Pan-European)

A cauallo va Bernardo 452 n. 196, 453 n. 196, 455.

A caza va el emperador 9 n. 1, 10, 11, 12, 32, 37, 43, 48, 51, 54, 58 n. 37, 65, 122, 146, 198, 221, 222, 223, 224, 228, 229, 236-237, 246, 274, 385, 401 n. 29, 439 n. 78.

A cazar va don Rodrigo 325.

A misa va el emperador 9 n. 1, 10, 11, 12, 32, 42, 43, 48, 51, 54, 55 n. 32, 121, 397 n. 19, 401 n. 29, 403 n. 32, 437 n. 73.

A monte sale el amor 295 n. 172.

Abenámar 50.

Adúltera (ó): *See* Blancaniña.

Alabanza del conde Vélez 179, 410 n. 54.

Aliarda y el alabancioso vi n. 8, 13, 14 & n. 13, 178, 181, 200–211, 200 n. 42, 212, 213, 263 n. 122, 372.

Almenas de Toro 41 n. 17, 54 n. 30, 285, 408 n. 52, 448 n. 150.

Almerique de Narbona 407 n. 52.

Alterada esta Castilla iv n. 4.

Amante confessore 275, 440 n. 81.

Anelli 412 n. 59.

Anneaux de Marianson 412 n. 59.

Apuesta ganada vi n. 8, 13, 200 n. 42, 205–210, 212, 232, 255, 372, 412 n. 59.

Archie o Cawfield 438 n. 76.

Asentado está Gaiferos 163 n. 12, 253 n. 102, 256 n. 110.

Aveine 56 n. 33.

Bañando están las prisiones 279.

Barbera de Francia 399 n. 22.

Belerma y Durandarte 253.

Bella en misa 51, 89, 398 n. 19; *see also* Misa de amor.

Bernal Francés 439 n. 78.

Bernaldino 396 n. 18, 403 n. 31.

Bernardo 451 n. 157.

Bernardo del Carpio iv, 256, 451 n. 157.

Bien se pensaba la reina 163.

Blancaflor y Filomena 255, 446 n. 130.

Blancaniña 14, 41, 50, 205, 208, 356, 408 n. 52, 444 n. 121.

Boda estorbada: *See* Conde Sol.

Bodas de sangre 13, 181.

Bodas en Paris 15 n. 15, 407 n. 52.

Bonetero de la trapería 393 n. 16.

Boy and the Mantle 422 n. 73.

Brombeerbrockerin 445 n. 124.

Broomfield Hill 412 n. 59.

3. Epics, Sagas, Romances

4. Other Literary Works

5. First Verses

Verses followed by a number in parentheses refer to *Primavera*; numbers in parentheses preceded by NC remit to Frenk, *Nuevo Corpus*.

A caza va el emperador / a Sant Juan de la Montiña (191) 9 n. 1, 10, 11, 12, 32, 37, 51, 122, 146, 198, 221, 222, 223, 224, 228, 229, 236–237, 246, 274, 385, 401 n. 29, 439 n. 78.

A cazar va don Rodrigo / y aun don Rodrigo de Lara (26) 325.

A eso de la media noche, / cuando los gallos cantar 332.

A la huellita, huella, / ¡ay! que no puedo (NC 1656) 428 n. 28.

A las once de la noche, / empezó el gallo a cantar 182.

A misa va el emperador / a san Juan de la Montiña (192) 9 n. 1, 10, 11, 12, 32, 33, 42, 51, 55 n. 32, 121, 401 n. 29, 403 n. 32, 437 n. 73.

¿A quién contaré yo mis quexas, / mi lindo amor? (NC 380) 310.

A[l] rededor del collado 122, 395 n. 18.

Abenámar, Abenámar, / moro de la morería (78–78*a*) 50.

Águila que vas bolando, / lleva en el pico estas flores (NC 571) 432 n. 56.

Alabóse conde Félix, / alabóse el gran traidor 86, 90, 91, 410 n. 52.

Alabóse el conde Vélez, / en las cortes de León 71, 90, 91, 124.

Alabóse el conde Vélez, / en las cortes se alabó 72, 79, 90, 91, 116–119, 124.

Alavóse el conde Belo, / en sus cortes s'alavó 72, 90, 91.

¡Albo día este día, / día de al-ᶜAnṣara ḥaqqā! 283 n. 146.

Alterada esta Castilla / por vn caso desastrado iv n. 4, 409 n. 52.

Ante me beseys que me destoqueys, / que me tocó mi tía (NC 1685) 310 n. 198, 452, 456.

Apostado tengo, madre, / con el rey de Portugal 412 n. 59.

Aposté con mis hermanos / castillos de plata fina 412 n. 59.

Aquel conde y aquel conde / en la mar sea su fin 407–408 n. 52.

Aquel rey de Inglaterra / hijos no tenía, non 446 n. 125.

Aquel traydor, / aquel engañador, / aquel porfiado (NC 1647) 310 n. 198.

Arbolero, arbolero, / arbolero atan yentil 51.

Arrodeó por el castillo entero, / por ande entrar no topó 77.

Asentado está Gaiferose/ en el palacio real (173) 163 n. 12, 253 n. 102, 256 n. 110.

Atal anda don García / por una sala adelante (133) 48 n. 19.

¡Ay, que non oso / mirar ni hazer del ojo! (NC 1656) 428 n. 28.

¡Ay Valensia y ay Valensia, / Valensia la bien sercada! 50.

Bañando están las prisiones 279.

Bien se pensaba la reina / que buena hija tenía (159) 163.

Blancaniña, Blancaniña 50.

Caminad, señora, / si queréys caminar (NC 1010) 310.

Canta tu Christiana Musa 310 n. 198, 452, 453, 455.

Casóme mi padre / con vn caballero (NC 233) 310, 316 n. 210.

Con cartas y mensajeros / el rey al Carpio envió (13*a*) iv n. 5, 278 n. 141, 280 n. 144, 448 n. 144.

Conde Claros, com amores, / não podia descançar 31.

Conde Claros con amores / no podía reposar 45, 294–295, 307, 310 n. 198, 453, 456, 312, 349, 395 n. 18, 396 n. 18.

Conde Claros con amores / non podiera reposare 40, 45, 122.

Conde Claros, / no podia reposar 395 n. 18.

Conde Claros, por amores, / não podia repoisar 331, 334.

Conde Montalvar não dorme, / não pára no cabeçal 30.

Conuiene mal dormir / por bien velar (NC 2019) 310 n. 198, 452, 455.

¿Cuándo acabarás, ventura? / ¿Cuándo tienes de acabar? 62 n. 44.

Cuando Carlos por amores / no podía sosegar 371.

Cuando el Mostadí partiera / de Constantina a la mar 404 n. 32.

De día era, de día, / de día y no de noche 51.

De Mérida sale el palmero, / de Mérida, esa ciudad (195) 256 n. 110.

De mi alma / de mi ánima 322 & n. 223.

De rosas y flores 316 n. 210.

Del rosal vengo, mi madre, / vengo del rosale (NC 306) 425 n. 5.

Dentro en el vergel / moriré (NC 3088) 425 n. 5.

Dexaldos mi madre, / mis ojos llorar (NC 596) 316 n. 210.

Día era de Sant Jorge, / día de gran festividad (187) 391 n. 1.

Días de mayo, días de mayo, / días de la rica calor 50.

Don Carlos, por amores, / no podía sosegar 215.

Don Claros con la infantita / está bailando en palacio 427 n. 28.

Donde vindes, filha, / branca e colorida? (NC 307) 425 n. 5.

Dormiendo está el conde Claros / la siesta por descansar 10, 11, 33, 42, 45, 55 n. 32, 122, 403 n. 32.

Dueñas entran, dueñas salen: / Todas dicen qu'es verdad 221.

Dulce érais, la mi siñora, / y a tan dulce en el hablar 142.

Dulce sox, la mi señora, / atan dulce en el hablar 143.

Dulse érax, la mi madre, / i atan dulse en el avlar 144.

Durmiendo esta el conde Claros / la siesta por descansar 396 n. 18.

Durmiendo está el conde Flore / la siesta por descansar 64.

Durmiendo estaua el cuydado / q*ue*l pesar lo adormescia 396 n. 18.

¡Ea, judíos, a enfardelar! / que mandan los reyes (NC 900) 310.

El cielo estaua nublado, / la luna no parecia 436 n. 67.

En Castilla y en León / el casto Alfonso reinaba 276, 386.

En el mes de Sanjiguale, / cuando las ovejas paren 400 n. 29.

En el nombre de Jesus / que todo el mundo ha formado (167) 421 n. 72.

En el reino de Aragón, / el casto Alfonso reinaba 278.

En el reyno de León, / quando el casto rey Alfonso reynaba 276, 386.

En la ciudad de Toledo, / donde los hidalgos son 452 n. 196, 456.

En las salas de París, / en un palacio sagrado (177–177*a*) 407 n. 52.

En los reynos de Leon / el casto Alfonso reynaua 276, 386.

Mandã tomar a Uirgili*us* / 7 a buẽ recaudo poner (cf. 111) 166 n. 15.

Manhanas de S. João, / pela manhã de alvorada 284.

Mañanita era mañana, / al tiempo que alboreaba 280, 378.

Mañanita, mañanita, / mañanita de oración 51.

Mañanita, mañanita, / mañanita de San Juan 51.

Más arriba y más arriba, / más arriba de Sofía 51.

Más envidia he de vos, conde / que mancilla ni pesar 11 & n. 2, 172–173, 392–393 n. 2, 394 n. 18.

Me levay un domatin / matinet denant l'alba 432 n. 56.

Media cena era por filo 330 n. 234.

Media noche era por filo, / los gallos querían cantar (174) (*Gaiferos*) 168, 172, 174, 182, 276, 311, 329–330, 382, 392 n. 2, 394 n. 16, 394 n. 18, 437 n. 73.

Media noche era por filo / los gallos querían cantar (190) (*Claros*) 9 n. 1, 10, 11, 12, 32, 38, 40, 41, 42, 43 & n. 18, 54, 55, 122, 146, 311.

Media noche era por filo, poco más o menos (*Don Quijote*) 394 n. 18.

Media noche era (va) por hilo / los gallos quieren cantar 29, 333, 394 n. 18.

Meia noite já é dada, / os gallos querem cantar 30.

Mes de mayo, mes de mayo, / mes de mayo, primavera 50.

Mi abuelo tenía un huerto / todo sembrado de nabos 304–305 & n. 185.

Mi grave pena crece de congoxa 309 n. 197.

Milagro bien sería, / si vos señora mía 252, 255, 310 n. 198.

Milagro no hazeys, / dama si me prendeys 310 n. 198, 452, 455.

Mira, Zaide, que te aviso, / que no pases por mi calle 448 n. 150.

Mitja nit era y passava, / els galls ja havian cantat 31, 331.

Mongica en religion / me quiero entrar / por no mal maridar (NC 215A) 310 n. 198 452, 455.

M'y levay par ung matin, / plus matin que ne souloye 432 n. 56.

No me digáys, madre, mal / del padre fray Antón (NC 1840*B*) 310.

Nochebuena y nochebuena, / noche de la Navidad 50.

Noches buenas, noches buenas, / noches son de enamorar 50.

¡Oh Belerma! ¡oh Belerma! / por mi mal fuiste engendrada (181) 253.

Oit'a noite a media noite, / antes do galo cantar 185.

Oydme vn poco, señora, / lo que yo quiero dezir 310 n. 198.

¡Padre santo, Padre santo, / señor, humíllome a ti! 394 n. 18.

Papagayos, ruyseñores, / que cantáys al alborada (NC 570) 432 n. 56.

Paseaba Griseldilla / por sus altos corredores 368.

Paseábase Lisarda / por sus altos corredores 354.

Paseando anda don Carlos, / por su palacio real 356.

Paseándose estaba [el rey], / el buen rey de la Mantilla 29.

Pensó el mal villano / que me adormecía 309 n. 197.

Per a ser filla d'un rey, / ne so ben desgraciada 353.

Perricos de mi señora, / no me mordades agora (NC 1670) 310 n. 198, 453, 457, 458.

Pésame de vos, el conde / porque así os quieren matar 11 & n. 2, 294 & n. 169, 296 & n. 175, 297–298.

6. Ballad Tunes

References are to ballad numbers (10*A*) or to page numbers (125). References to schematic arrangements and rhythmic notations are marked with an asterisk (*). This index can be used in conjunction with the indices of musical transcriptions in CMP, III, 225–238.

10. *Conde Claros y el emperador* (CMP B9)

> **Salonika** *10*A*.

Conde Claros y el emperador + *Conde Claros insomne* (B9 + B11)

> **Tetuán** 10*B*.

Jactancia del conde Vélez

> **commentary**: pp. 115–119.

11. *Conde Claros y la infanta* (B10)

> **Tetuán** 11*A*, *11*B* (music & rhythmic), *11*C*.

Nacimiento de Bernardo del Carpio + *Conde Claros y la infanta* + *Conde Claros fraile* (A1 + B10 + B12)

> **Tetuán** *11*E*.

Conde Claros y la infanta (B10)

> **Tetuán** 11*F*, 11*G*.

Lisarda

> **commentary**: pp. 352–375.

For the music of our previously unedited versions *D* and *F*, see the commentary:

> *D*. **Casillas de Coria** (Cáceres): text, pp. 217–218; music: p. 364 (text *b*).

> *F*. **Zagra** (Granada): text, pp. 219–220; music: p. 362.

For additional ballad transcriptions and studies, see Ch. 10, pp. 115–119 and Ch. 11, pp. 293–379.

7. Motifs and Tale-Types

Motifs listed here are from Stith Thompson, *Motif-Index of Folk-Literature*, 2d ed., 6 vols., Bloomington: Indiana University Press, 1955–1958. Tale types, listed at the end of this index, are from Antti Aarne and Stith Thompson, *The Types of the Folktale*, 2d revision, Helsinki: Academia Scientiarum Fennica, 1961. Compare now also Hans-Jörg Uther, *The Types of International Folktales: A Classification and Bibliography*, 3 vols., Helsinki: Academia Scientiarum Fennica, 2004, which had not yet been published when the text of the present volume was already in final form. References are to pages and footnotes.

B. ANIMALS

B211.1.2.	Speaking goat 420 n. 70.
B211.3.	Speaking bird 420 n. 70, 423 n. 74.
B211.3.4.	Speaking parrot 423 n. 74.
B211.6.1.	Speaking snake (serpent) 420 n. 70.
B540.	Animal rescuer 420 n. 70.

C. TABU

C12.5.	Devil's name used in curse. Appears 433 n. 60.

D. MAGIC

D100.	Transformation: man to animal 419 n. 70.
D791.1.8.	Disenchantment at midnight after owl hoots three times 397 n. 18.
D965.16.	Magic Rue 8.
D1071.	Magic jewel (jewels) 8.
D117.1.	Transformation: man to mouse 419 n. 70.
D1275.1.	Magic music 437 n. 72.
D1355.1.3.	Magic love-producing horn 94 n. 58.
D1385.2.2.	Rue, when burned, keeps evil spirits at a distance 8.
D1523.2.7.1.	Self-guiding rudderless boat 416 n. 68.
D1791.	Magic power of circumambulation 409 n. 52, 435 n. 61.
D2122.	Journey with magic speed 141.

E. The Dead

E587.1.	Ghosts walk at midday 397 n. 18.
E587.5.	Ghosts walk at midnight 397 n. 18.
E631.0.1.	Twining branches grow from graves of lovers 448 n. 135.

F. Marvel

F564.1.	Person of diabolical origin never sleeps 436 n. 67.
F567.	Wildman 8.
F771.1.	Castle of unusual material 141.
F771.1.6.	Crystal castle 141.
F771.1.6.1.	Castle with glass wall 141.
F823.1.	Golden shoes 420 n. 70.
F823.4.	Silver shoes 420 n. 70.
F826.	Extraordinary jewels 8.
F1041.21.1.1.	Tears of blood from excessive grief 436 n. 67.

G. Ogres

G303.6.1.1.	Devil appears at midnight 397 n. 18.
G303.6.1.2.	Devil comes when called upon 433 n. 60.

H. Tests

H51.1.	Recognition by birthmark 9, 419 n. 70.
H71.2.	Golden (silver) hairs as sign of royalty 413 n. 60, 415 n. 67.
H75.	Recognition by hair 419 n. 70.
H75.4.	Recognition by golden hair 419 n. 70.
H80.	Recognition by tokens 419 n. 70.
H86.2.	Articles of clothing with name embroidered on them taken as tokens 419 n. 70.
H86.3.	Ring with names inscribed on it 419 n. 70.
H86.4.	Handkerchief with name on it 419 n. 70.
H93.	Identification by jewel 419 n. 70.
H94.	Recognition by ring 9, 419 n. 70.
H110.	Identification by cloth or clothing 419 n. 70.
H111.	Identification by garment 419 n. 70.
H113.	Identification by handkerchief 419 n. 70.
H117.	Identification by cut garment 419 n. 70.
H125.	Identification by weapons 419 n. 70.
H217.2.	Decision by single combat of who is to marry girl 8.
H430.	Chastity index 414 n. 61, 421 n. 73, 422 n. 73.

H432.	Flower as chastity index 414 n. 61.
H432.1.	Rose as chastity index 414 n. 61.
H434.1.	Apple as chastity index: shines as long as woman is chaste 414 n. 61.
H439.1.	Picture as chastity index: indicates by its color 422 n. 73.
H461.	Test of wife's patience 255 n. 109.
H931.1.	Prince envious of hero's wife assigns hero tasks 418 n. 70.
H1385.7.	Quest for lost father 290 n. 161.
H1578.1.	Test of sex of girl masking as man 416 n. 68.
H1578.1.3.	Test of sex of girl masking as man: choosing flowers 416 n. 68.

J. THE WISE AND THE FOOLISH

J1141.	Confession obtained by a ruse 440 n. 81.
J1154.1	Parrot unable to tell husband details as to wife's infidelity 423 n. 74.
J1545.2.	Four men's mistress: A husband disguises as a priest to hear his wife's confession 440 n. 81.

K. DECEPTIONS

K52.4.1.1.	Girl escapes in male disguise 420 n. 70.
K442.	False claim of reward 9.
K512.	Compassionate executioner 415 n. 67.
K512.	Compassionate executioner: A servant charged with killing hero (heroine) arranges escape of the latter 420 n. 70.
K512.2.	Compassionate executioner: substituted heart 420 n. 70.
K512.2.0.2.	Eyes of animal substituted as proof for eyes of children 420 n. 70.
K527.	Escape by substituting another person in place of the intended victim 412 n. 59.
K534.1.	Escape by reversing horse's (ox's) shoes 438 n. 76.
K1210.	Humiliated or baffled lovers 9.
K1223.5.	King's daughter deceives king by substituting her maid 412 n. 59.
K1227.1.	Lover put off till girl bathes and dresses 162 n. 10.
K1271.	Amorous intrigue observed and exposed 141.
K1310.	Seduction by disguise 232.
K1344.	Tunnel entrance to guarded maiden's chamber 426 n. 20.
K1512.1.	Cut-off finger proves wife's chastity 413 n. 59.
K1513.	The wife's equivocal oath 440 n. 81.
K1523.	Underground passage to paramour's house 426 n. 20.
K1528.	Wife confesses to disguised husband 440 n. 81.
K1578.	Test of sex: to discover person masking as of other sex 420 n. 70.
K1587.	Adulteress uses public baths as a meeting-place with her lover 427 n. 20.
K1817.2.	Disguise as palmer (pilgrim) 413 n. 60.
K1817.3.	Disguise as harper (minstrel) 415 n. 62.
K1817.3.1.	Disguise as poet 415 n. 62.

L. REVERSAL OF FORTUNE

M. ORDAINING THE FUTURE

N. CHANCE AND FATE

N825.3. Old woman helper 227 n. 60, 267 n. 126, 419 n. 70.

P. SOCIETY

P171. Branding person makes him one's slave for life 417 n. 70.
P297. Nephew 8.
P365. Faithless servant 141.

Q. REWARDS AND PUNISHMENTS

Q243. Incontinence punished 140, 141.
Q243.2.1. Attempted seduction punished 9.
Q254. Girl punished for becoming pregnant 140, 141.
Q261. Treachery punished 141.
Q411. Death as punishment 141.
Q413. Punishment: hanging 420 n. 70.
Q413.3. Hanging as punishment for imposture 420 n. 70.
Q414. Punishment: burning alive 141, 420 n. 70, 441 n. 83.
Q414.0.3. Burning as punishment for incest (incontinence) 441 n. 83.
Q414.0.6. Burning as punishment for impostor 420 n. 70.
Q414.1.1. Punishment: being boiled alive 421 n. 72.
Q414.1.1. Punishment: boiling in oil (lead, tar) 420 n. 70.
Q416. Punishment: drawing asunder by horses 420 n. 70.
Q416.0.1. Quartering by horses as punishment for impostor 420 n. 70.
Q416.2. Punishment: dragging to death by a horse 413 n. 60, 420 n. 70.
Q416.2.1. Punishment: drawing at the tails of horses 413 n. 60, 420 n. 70.
Q421. Punishment: beheading 420 n. 70.
Q428.3. Drowning as punishment for adultery 420 n. 70.
Q431. Punishment: banishment (exile) 420 n. 70.
Q433. Punishment: imprisonment 140, 141, 420 n. 70.
Q433.4. Imprisonment for imposture 420 n. 70.
Q464. Covering with honey and exposing to flies 100–101 n. 67, 415 n. 67.
Q465.3. Punishment: pushing into well 420 n. 70.
Q466.0.2. Punishment: setting adrift in boat 420 n. 70.
Q466.0.1. Embarkation in rudderless boat as punishment 416 n. 68.
Q469.6. Heart and liver of murderer torn out 9.

R. CAPTIVES AND FUGITIVES

R41. Captivity in tower (castle, prison) 140.
R41.1. Captivity in castle 141.
R41.3. Captivity in dungeon 141.
R41.3.2. Prison with stream of water in it 141.

S. UNNATURAL CRUELTY

T. SEX

V. RELIGION

Z. MISCELLANEOUS

TALE-TYPES

Aarne-Thompson:

243.	The Parrot Pretends to be God 423 n. 74.
546.	The Clever Parrot 423 n. 74.
851.	The Princess who Cannot Solve the Riddle 424 n. 78.
851A.	Turandot 424 n. 78.
882.	The Wager on the Wife's Chastity 417–419 n. 70.
887.	Griselda 255 n. 109.
888.	The Faithful Wife 421–422 n. 73.
891B.	The King's Glove 419 n. 70.
1352A.	Seventy Tales of a Parrot Prevent Wife's Adultery 423 n. 74.
1422.	Parrot Unable to Tell Husband Details of Wife's Infidelity 423 n. 74.

Uther:

243 > 1422.	Parrot Reports Wife's Adultery.
546.	The Clever Parrot.
851 > 851A.	The Princess who Cannot Solve the Riddle.
882.	The Wager on the Wife's Chastity.
887.	Griselda.
888.	The Faithful Wife
891B.	The King's Glove.
1352A.	The Tale-Telling Parrot.
1422.	Parrot Reports Wife's Adultery.

8. Topoi

References to FLSJ, V, remit to the index of Topoi, pp. 518–522.

Abandoned wife 416 n. 68: *See* **Wife**.

^cAbīd: *See* **Slave soldiers**.

Adventures in the East 416 n. 68.

Arbor: lovers meet in arbor (garden) 262, 273.

Ballad endings: diversity of endings 291 & n. 163; FLSJ, V, 519.
    variable ballad endings; poetic creativity 238–254 & nn. 84–103.

Bathing excuse 162, 169 (vv. 41–42), 175, 176, 183, 185–186, 188, 193–194, 195.

Baths: opportunity for amorous encounter 426 n. 20; FLSJ, V, 519.
    sinfulness of baths 426–427 n. 20.

Bawd: aged bawd 416 n. 69.

Bed of rose petals (lemon leaves) 429 n. 38.

Bells: on horse's harness (breast strap) 6, 21, 29, 30, 32, 35, 39, 43, 46, 54 & n. 31, 55,
    57, 66, 67, 70, 114–115, 122, 168, 200, 300, 395 n. 184, 401–403 n. 31.

Belts, sashes, girdles: symbols of woman's chastity 411 n. 55.

Bestiary tradition 446 n. 124.

Bird: messenger 230, 261, 273, 274, 432 n. 56, 447 n. 131.
    talking bird 106, 432 n. 56.
    talking bird reveals false friend's treachery 106.
    buried lovers transformed into birds 261–262 and n. 121.

Birthmark 97, 414 n. 61. *See also* **Token(s)**.

Black mule: riding black mule ominous portent 408 n. 52.

Black servants 8, 79, 80, 84.

Blood: *See* **Letter written in blood; Tears of blood**.

Boast of wife's fidelity 101.

Brother: cruel brother 217, 218.
    friendly brother 268 n. 128.
    hostile brother 257, 267 & n. 127, 273.

Calf gorged with grain sent to the besiegers' camp 398 n. 19.

Candomblé 433 n. 60.

Charlemagne: C. Claros visits Charlemagne 236 & n. 79.

Chastity index 421 n. 73; *see also* **Rose**.

Chastity wager: *See* **Wager**.

Chest: hiding in chest, box 100, 417 n. 70.

Circumambulation: magic circumambulation 76, 77, 213, 227 n. 61, 229, 409 n. 52, 434
    n. 61, 442 n. 96.

'*Ēšeth ḥayil*: *See* **Woman**.

Evasive answers 444 n. 121.

Executioner: compassionate executioner 100, 102.

Exhaustion of steeds on a heroic ride 447 n. 133; *see also* **Rapid journey**.

Fainting: protagonist faints on hearing bad news 66 n. 49, 67, 85.

False friend (rival) 106.

False tokens: *see* **Token(s)**.

Fifteen days' ride accomplished in seven 77, 79, 447–448 n. 133; *see also* **Rapid journey**.

Food sent to enemy gives appearance of plenty 398–399 n. 19; *see also* **Calf, Grain, Hero, Women**.

Gallant: arrogant, boastful gallant 7–8.

Girl, claiming to be leprous, convinces knight she will blight any grass she steps on 437 n. 72.

Girl does not know identity of her confessor 440 n. 81.

Girl, who attempted to seduce her traveling companion, blights green forest 437 n. 72.

Goat: talking goat 106.

Going to mass: occasion for ballad action 51 n. 23.

Golden hairs 96, 413 n. 60, 415 n. 67, 417 n. 70; *see also* **Token(s)**.

Golden staff 87–88.

Goodbye to flowers 448 n. 135.

Grain poured onto street gives appearance of surfeit of food 398 n. 19; *see also* **Calf, Food, Grain, Hero, Women**.

Gypsies: ballad tradition of Andalusian Gypsies 448 n. 144.

Gypsy woman 105.

Hannah, "la buena judía" 400 n. 29.

Happy ending formula 66–69 & n. 50, 148, 158, 237 & n. 82, 238–254 & nn. 84–103, 291 & n. 163; FLSJ, V, 519.

Hawk: lost hawk 171, 176 n. 24.
> swiftness of hawk (falcon) 233 & n. 71.

Heart: Cutting out heart 7–8, 71–75, 80–81, 82, 85, 86, 89–90, 93, 408–409 n. 52.

Henna: staining beard with henna 286 n. 152.

Hermes fastens brushwood to tail of each cow to wipe out its footmarks 438 n. 76.

Heroic deed to attract princess 8.

Hero of illegitimate birth 290 n. 161.

Hero throws last remaining loaf into enemy camp 398 n. 19; *see also* **Food**.

High towers 405 n. 43.

Horn: magic horn 94 n. 58.

Horse as wager 94 n. 58.

Horse: chestnut horse 15 n. 15.
> chestnut horse has extraordinary speed 409 n. 52.
> horses (mules) die of exhaustion during rapid journey 272, 273, 447–448 n. 133.
> sorrel horse (*alazán*) 7.
> sorrel horse has extraordinary speed 7.

Neighbor: betrays wife 105.
Neo-Individualism 431 n. 49.
Nephew 17, 22; FLSJ, V, 521.
Nightingale 7 (*see also* Glossary).
　　　　as messenger 432 n. 56.
　　　　singing 250 & n. 97.
　　　　sings at the ear of sleeping person 407 n. 52.
Numbers: magic numbers 247; FLSJ, V, 520.
　　　　three: magic or formulaic number 258–259.
　　　　three ladies, ritualistically embroidering on St. John's morning 53.
　　　　three times a day 407 n. 52.
　　　　seven: magic or formulaic number 214, 252 n. 100, 253 & n. 102, 258–259, 442 n. 96, 426 n. 15.
　　　　seven years 214.
　　　　seven years imprisonment 426 n. 15.
　　　　eight: magic number 252 n. 100, 442 n. 96.
　　　　twelve 260.
　　　　twelve daughters 266 & n. 125.
　　　　fifteen days' ride in seven 77, 79, 447–448 n. 133.
　　　　two hundred bells 29, 57, 395 n. 18.
　　　　three hundred bells 21, 39, 46, 57, 122.
　　　　three hundred precious stones 39.
　　　　four hundred bells 32.
　　　　one hundred thousand 32.
Oath: equivocal, deceptive oath 440 n. 81.
Oaths 26 n. 11.
Oath taken on prayer book 162 n. 11 (*see also* Appendix).
Obscene insults 442 n. 91.
Old man hidden in chest 105.
Ostentatious display 95, 410–411 n. 54.
Page: faithful page (or bird, angel, cousin, brother, servant, etc.) 147, 158, 164–165, 167, 198, 213, 214, 225–227 & nn. 55–61, 257–258, 270–271 & n. 131, 274. *See also*: **Bird messenger.**
　　　　treacherous page 177, 197.
Parrot: talking parrot 7, 73, 78 (for real-life instance: *NYT*, Jan. 18, 2006, p. A4).
Partridges: female birds become pregnant if wind blows toward them from males 446 n. 124; *see also* **Conception.**
Pawning weapons 54.
Penance: going on pilgrimage 257–258 & nn. 116–117.
Picking flowers: prelude to abduction or seduction 425 n. 5.
Pilgrim disguise: *see* **Disguise.**
Plants: plants from graves entwine 258, 261.
Poludnica **'midday spirit'** 397 n. 18.
Predatory animals: Fear and disdain for predatory animals 434 n. 60.
Pregnancy from drinking from spring or lake 445 n. 124; *see also* **Conception.**

Priceless golden sash 411 n. 55.

Priest disguise: *see* **Disguise.**

Priest: lecherous priest 237 & n. 80, 278 & n. 138.

Prison: flooded dungeon 217, 218, 220, 222–223 & n. 53; *see also* **Punishment.**

Prosification: of Spanish epics in medieval historiography 449 n. 151.

Punishment: Abu Ghraib 432 n. 53; FLSJ, V, 521.

 beheading 106, 259, 260, 441 n. 83.

 boiling alive 102, 106, 109 & n. 72.

 burned to death 106.

 burning at the stake 97, 109, 237, 257, 266, 441 n. 83.

 death 99, 100, 105.

 deportation 106.

 dragging behind horse(s) 96, 97, 102, 106, 109.

 dungeon filled with snakes, scorpions, water up to knees 431–432 n. 53.

 exile 97, 102, 106, 109.

 Guantánamo 432 n. 53.

 hand squeezed in vise 106.

 hanging 96, 97, 99, 102, 106, 259, 269, 441 n. 83.

 imprisonment 106.

 mutilation 102.

 nose and ears are cut off 96.

 set adrift in rudderless boat 416 n. 68.

 shot 106.

 stabbed to death 106.

 taken into custody 106.

 tearing apart by wild horses 106, 109 & n. 72.

 throwing into sea 101.

 tied to stake, covered with honey, devoured by flies and wasps 102, 109.

 water pit 431 n. 53.

Rapid journey 77, 79, 147, 155, 158, 159, 199, 227 n. 61, 229, 232–235 & nn. 70, 71, 73, 74; 236, 257, 261, 272, 408–409 n. 52, 434 n. 61, 447–448 n. 133.

 exhaustion of steeds on a heroic ride 447 n. 133.

 fifteen days' ride accomplished in seven 447–448 n. 133.

 horse's hooves strike sparks 434 n. 61.

 horses (mules) die during rapid ride 447–448 n. 133.

 three days' ride accomplished in one (etc.) 434 n. 61.

Repetition: incremental repetition 259.

Retinue of numerous ladies 175 & n. 21.

Reversing horse's shoes: *See* **Horseshoes.**

Riches: ostentatious display to attract princess 8.

Ride: earth-shaking ride 434 n. 61.

Ring composition 167, 410 n. 54.

Rose arbor 145 & n. 5, 150, 158, 159, 169, 171, 173, 176, 188, 193–194, 214, 425 n. 5.

Rose: index of wife's chastity 414 n. 61.

Rudderless boat: set adrift 416 n. 68; *see* **Punishment.**

ring-finger 94.

slipper 409 n. 52.

wedding ring 96.

Torture: *see* **Punishment.**

Transformation to goat (and other magical retributions) 441–442 n. 89.

Traveling by night, hiding by day 147, 227 n. 61, 434 n. 61; *see also* FLSJ, V, 521.

Treacherous hunter: 182–190.

Treacherous old woman (witch) 105.

Treacherous servants: *See* **Servants.**

Treacherous wagerer 102.

Triadic patterns 399 n. 22.

Tunnel: digging tunnel to reach beloved 426 n. 20.

Turkish garb: dressed in Turkish fashion 8, 80, 404–405 n. 32.

Twining branches (plants) grow from lovers' graves 274 n. 135, 448 n. 135.

Uncle-nephew motif 391 n. 1, 399 n. 19; FLSJ, V, 521.

Valiant woman: *See* **Woman.**

Value: worth as much as a city 31, 39, 41.

Vergel de amor: See **Rose arbor.**

Voyage completed at supernatural speed: fifteen-day trip in seven; mules or horses die 408–409 n. 52; *see also* **Rapid journey.**

Wagers 69–115.

Wager: beheading 104.

chastity wager 7, 93 & n. 56, 95 & n. 59, 96, 97, 98 & n. 63, 100, 101, 104, 109 n. 73, 411 n. 59, 413–414 nn. 60–61, 416 n. 68, 421 n. 73; FLSJ, V, 521.

hanging 104.

heart as wager 7–8, 94.

his own head 100.

horse as wager 94 n. 58.

lands 97, 98, 99.

life 94, 104.

money 101.

property against life 104.

Weapons: pledged for loan 5, 15.

Wedding: interrupted wedding 413 n. 60.

Wedding ring as token: *See* **Token(s).**

Wife: abandoned wife 416 n. 68.

praising fidelity of wife 96–102.

Wife's chaperone 105.

Wildmen 6; see extensive treatment in FLSJ, VI.

Witches: good witch 106.

witch as helper 412 n. 59.

witch becomes mouse to enter wife's bedroom 105.

witches' spell 106.

Woman: old woman 226–227 & n. 60.

old woman helper 95.

9. Proverbs, Proverbial Phrases, and Traditional Expressions

Amor primero, el único verdadero 442 n. 96.

Amor primero, nunca olvidado, pero no postrero 442 n. 96.

Amores, los primeros los mejores 442 n. 96.

Antes envidia que manzilla 392 n. 2.

Antes envidiado que compadecido 392–393 nn. 2, 16.

Como quem semea na area 64 n. 47.

Como quien se mea en la arena 64 n. 47.

Culebra. ¡Lagarto, lagarto! 433 n. 60.

El amor primero xamás se olvida, pepita le keda por toda la vida 442 n. 96.

El diablo es el que no se cansa 436 n. 67.

El diablo no duerme 231 n. 67, 436 n. 67.

El diablo no duerme, pero se hace el dormido cuando le conviene 436 n. 67.

El diablo no duerme, y todo lo añasca 436 n. 67.

El lovo y la oveja, todos dos una negra conseja 434 n. 60.

En nombrando el ruín de Roma, luego (se) asoma 433 n. 60.

En San Xoan, a sardiña molla o pan 400 n. 29.

Envidia me ayáys y no piedad 392 n. 2.

Háganme envidia y no mancilla 392 n. 2.

Mejor es ser envidiado que amancillado 392 n. 2.

Mujer en la ventana, más pierde que gana 52 n. 28.

Mujer en la ventana, parra en el camino real 52 n. 28.

Mujer en ventana, o puta o enamorada 52 n. 28.

Mujer ventanera, ni para dentro ni para fuera 52 n. 28.

Mujer ventanera, o enamorada o ramera 52 n. 28.

Mujer ventanera, uva de calle 52 n. 28.

Nombrar la bicha 434 n. 60.

O diabo não tem sono 436 n. 67.

Oxos ke le vieron ir, no le verán mas en Franzia 253–254 & n. 103.

Que los yerros por amores / dignos son de perdonar 396 n. 18.

Que yo juraré sobre la hostia consagrada que es tan buena mujer como vive dentro de las puertas de Toledo (*Lazarillo*) 440–441 n. 81.

Sacar el pie del lodo (*Corbacho*, II, Chap. I) 215 & n. 44.

Siempre lo he oído decir / y ahora veo que es verdad 442 n. 96.

Siete vueltas dio al palacio, / por ver si podía entrar 442 n. 96.

Sopa y amores, los primeros, los mejores 442 n. 96.

Speak of the Devil and he appears 433 n. 60.

Tenho feito juramento, / na folhinha do missal 439 n. 81.

The devil never sleeps 231 n. 67.
Where the Turk's (Attila's) horse has trod, grass never grows 437 n. 72.

10. Motes

Avnque de contino arden / no se acaban de quemar 35 (v. 67).

Es mi dolor desigual 43 (v. 16*b*).

Es tan alto mi desseo / que no ay mas que dessear 35 (v. 72), 43 (v. 19).

Es vn dolor desigual 35 (v. 69*b*).

Estas arden sin quemar 42 (v. 14*b*).

Gran dolor es dessear 34 (v. 61*b*), 42 (v. 9*b*).

Más amargo es esperar 35 (v. 83*b*), 43 (v. 25*b*).

No tiene nombre mi mal 35 (v. 63*b*).

No tiene precio mi mal 42 (v. 11*b*).

11. Songs and Ballads from Salinas, *De Musica.*

Page numbers in Salinas are referenced in parentheses after each citation; all citations are from Book VI, unless otherwise indicated (VII). With a few exceptions, we list no Latin citations here, but only verses (or phrases) in Spanish or in other languages (Arabic, French, German, Italian).

A cauallo va Bernardo (307) 452–453 n. 196, 455.

A quien contare yo mis quexas mi lindo amor (326) 456.

Aficion grande me haze por ti sola padescer (355) 453 n. 196, 458.

Al muy prepotente don Iuan el segundo (and variations) (329, 331, 332).

Amigo si me bien queredes (319) 458.

Amor amargo mas que hiel amarga (VII: 437; *read* 435).

Amores me dieron corona (de amores) (331) 459.

Amores que quieren que muera amador (331) 459.

Ante me beseys que me destoqueys, / Que me toco mi tia (321) 310 n. 198, 452 n. 196, 456.

Aquel porfiado / Que en toda aquesta noche (330) 452–453 n. 196, 456.

Aquel traydor u / Aquel engañador (330) 310 n. 198.

Aquella Morica garrida / sus amores dan pena a mi vida (327) 452 n. 196, 456.

A quien contare yo mis quexas mi lindo amor / A quien contare yo mis quexas si a vos no (326) 456.

Aue maris stella Dei mater alma (VII: 397) 454 n. 196.

Aunque me abraso y quemo suffro y callo (354) 453 n. 196, 457.

Aunque soy morenica y prieta a mi que se me da (325) 452 n. 196, 456.

Aus hertzen grondt schrey ich zu dir (350) 457.

Ay amor como soys puntoso / la darga dandeta (321) 452 n. 196, 456.

Bella citella de la magiorana (348).

Calui vi calui / Calui araui (339).

Caminad señora si quereys caminar (308) 452 n. 196, 456.

Canta tu Christiana Musa (307) 310 n. 198, 452 n. 196, 453 n. 196, 455.

Caso me mi padre con vn cauallero (338) 453 n. 196, 456.

Cata el lobo do va, (Iuanica, / Cata el lobo do va) (343–344) 453 n. 196, 456, 458.

Conde Claros (con amores) / No podia reposar (342, 346) 312, 453 n. 196, 456, 457.

Contemplando, Tan callando (305) 454 n. 196, 458.

Conuiene mal dormir / por bien velar (300) (NC 2019) 310 n. 198, 452 n. 196, 455.

Dali dali dali (305).

Dama si quereys amor, amad (307) 454 n. 196, 458.

De las honduras llamo a ti, oye me señor mio (350) 453 n. 196, 457.

De rosas y flores que cria el verano (337) 454 n. 196, 459.

Dexaldos mi madre mis ojos llorar (338) 453 n. 196, 456.

Digades la casada cuerpo garrido (301) 452 n. 196, 455.

Diste qu'aues vous fay mal aux genoux (305) 458.

Donde son estas serranas del pinar de Auila son (333) 453 n. 196, 456.

Ea Iudios a enfardelar / Que mandan los Reyes que passeys la mar (312) 452 n. 196, 456.

En la ciudad de Toledo, / Donde los hidalgos son (309) 452 n. 196, 456.

En lo que mas valgo menos merezco (332).

En lo que valgo mas, menos merezco (332).

Fasta que al tiempo de agora vengamos (331).

Fe me condena, / amor me maltrata (362) 453 n. 196, 457.

Ferire el cabello (*sic*; *read* caballo?) ferirelo (324) 454 n. 196, 459.

Guarda me las vacas / Carillejo y besar te (348) 453 n. 196, 457.

Las mañanas de Abril / dulces eran de dormir (363, VII: 398) 453–454 n. 196, 457, 458.

La villana non pare bella se nõ la domenica (355).

Llamais me villana y yo no lo soy (338) 454 n. 196.

Lo que yo quiero dezir: *See* Oyd me vn poco señora.

Mal aya quien a vos caso, / (La de Pedro borreguero) (318, 321) 310 n. 198, 452 n. 196, 456.

Mal vezino es el amor: *See* Que mal vezino es el amor amargo.

Mas me querria vn çatico de pan que no tu saludar (320) 452 n. 196.

Meteros quiero monja / hija mia de mi coraçon, / Que no quiero yo ser monja non (302) 455.

Mi graue pena, / Cre(s)ce de congoxa (316, 362) 453–454 n. 196, 457.

Milagro bien sería, / Si vos señora mia (299) 252, 255, 310 n. 198.

Milagro no hazeys, / Dama si me prendeys (298) 310 n. 198, 452, 455.

Mongica en religion me quiero entrar / Por no mal maridar (300) (NC 215A) 310 n. 198, 452 n. 196, 455.

No me digays madre mal del padre fray Anton (309) 452 n. 196, 456.

Ombrosa valle di bei fior diinta / Dintorno cinta di cipressi e lauri (362).

Oyd me vn poco señora / Lo que yo quiero dezir(os) (354–355) 310 n. 198, 453–454 n. 196, 457.

Penso el mal villano / Que yo dormia (306) 452 n. 196, 455.

Perricos de mi señora, / No me mordades agora (356) 453 n. 196, 457, 458.

Por amor de mi alma, / Por amor de mi anima (324).

Prendiome el amor (330).

Quan bien auenturado / Aquel puede llamarse (VII: 437; *read* 435).

Que amor tengo que me seruira (326) 452 n. 196, 456.

Que auedes que U mal de amores he (305) 458.

Que con lagrimas te tiene (356) 453 n. 196, 456.

Que era mala la vsança (324) 454 n. 196, 459.

Que hare adonde yre (VII: 437; *read* 435) 457.

Que hare, / Que dire (323).

(Que) mal vezino es el amor (amargo) (VII: 437; *read* 435).

Que me quereys el cauallero / Casada me soy, marido tengo (325) 452 n. 196, 456.

Que pueden doblar por el (356) 453 n. 196, 457.

Quien te me enojo Ysabel / [Que con lagrimas te tiene] (356) 453 n. 196, 457.

GLOSSARY

Glossary

The Glossary lists Arabic, Hebrew, Persian, Turkish, and pan-Balkan loan words, Old Spanish, Judeo-Spanish and Pan-Hispanic archaisms and dialect forms in the texts edited in the present volume, as well as words in these and various other languages referred to in the commentary. Unless otherwise specified, Arabic words are glossed according to Wehr and Cowan; Moroccan Arabic, usually according to Mercier, Sobelman and Harrell, or Colin; Turkish, according to the *New Redhouse Turkish-English Dictionary* or occasionally also to Hony and İz; Persian follows Steingass; Urdu follows Platts; Eastern Judeo-Spanish forms glossed in French are from Nehama. Full citations of dictionaries, glossaries, and other works referenced in the Glossary are included in the Bibliography. References in the Glossary are to ballad number + version + verse + hemistich (e.g. 1A.1a) or to page number + note number or verse number, in this latter case placed in parentheses (e.g. 1 n. 1 or 1 (v. 1)).

Abbreviations

Alb. = Albanian.
Alg. Ar. = Algerian Arabic.
Am. Sp. = American Spanish.
Ar. = Arabic.
Arag. = Aragonese.
Arch. Sp. = Archaic Spanish.
Bulg. = Bulgarian.
Cl. Ar. = Classical Arabic.
Cat. = Catalan.
Du. = Dutch.
E. J.-Sp. = Eastern Judeo-Spanish.
Egypt. Ar. = Egyptian Colloquial Arabic.
Eng. = English.
Fr. = French.
Gal. = Galician.
Ger. = German.
Gk. = Greek.
H. = Hebrew.
Hisp.-Ar. = Hispano-Arabic.
I. E. = *Indo-European.
It. = Italian.

Maced.-Rum. = Macedo-Rumanian.
Med. Lat. = Medieval Latin.
Mex. Sp. = Mexican Spanish.
M. H. Ger. = Middle High German.
M. J.-Sp. = Moroccan Judeo-Spanish.
Mod. Gk. = Greek.
Moroc. Ar. = Moroccan Colloquial Arabic.
O. Alb. = Old Albanian.
O. E. = Old English.
O. Fr. = Old French.
O. H. Ger. = Old High German.
O. Ir. = Old Irish.
O. N. = Old Norse.
O. Port. = Old Portuguese.
O. Prov. = Old Provençal.
O. Sp. = Old Spanish.
Pers. = Persian (Farsi).
Port. = Portuguese.
Rum. = Rumanian.
Serb. = Serbian.
Serb.-Cr. = Serbo-Croatian.
Skt. = Sanskrit.
So. Sl. = South Slavic.
Sp. = Standard Spanish.
T. = Turkish.
Toch. = Tocharian.
Ukr. = Ukranian.
Venet. = Venetian.
Vulg. Lat. = Vulgar Latin.

abroches (M. J.-Sp.) '(shoe) buckles' 21 (v. 54*b*) (on Sp. *abrochar*).

abujitas (M. J.-Sp.) 'small needles' 27 (v. 45*b*) (Sp. *agujitas*).

ačetar (E. J.-Sp.) 'to accept'; *accettar* 17 (vv. 9*b*, 11*b*) (It. *accettare*; Sp. *aceptar*).

achófar (M. J.-Sp.) 'pearl' 84 (v. 24*a*) (Sp. *aljófar*; assimilated to Moroc. Ar. *žuhar*).

adamar (Arch. Sp.) 'to adore, love intensely'; *adama* 40 (v. 402); *adamaua* 71 (v. 6*b*), 92 (v. 6*b*); *adaméla* 61 (v. 4*a*); DCECH, I, 232; from L. *adamare* (= Sp. *amar*).

adolerse (M. J.-Sp.) 'compadecerse'; *aduela* 155 (v. 36*b*); *adueliéndose* 157 (v. 54*b*), *s'adueliera* 155 (v. 36*b*); but *aduelándose* 157 (v. 54*b*), supposing a nonexistent (to my knowledge) *adolarse (on Sp. *doler*).

afrechos (M. J.-Sp.) 'afflictions, misfortunes, troubles' 25 (v. 23*a*). This form is interesting. I have not found it in any *hakitía* dictionary (Benoliel, Bendayán, Benharroch), but E. J.-Sp. has *afriír* 'infligir des privations', together with a semi-popular *afrito* 'privé de nourriture, de plaisirs' (Nehama), and Corominas refers us to a semi-popular *afreír* in Jewish Bibles (DCECH, I, s.v. *afligir*; from Lat. *affligĕre*).

Note also Sephiha, *Deutéronome*, p. 248 (s.v. *afreír*). Now the M. J.-Sp. *Romancero* brings us a completely popular form: *afrecho* (< Lat. *afflictus*).

aína (M. J.-Sp.) 'quickly' 24 (v. 14*a*), 281 (v. 37a), 291 (v. 34a) (O. Sp. *aína*; Vulg. Lat. *agīna*). For survivals in modern Hispanic and Romance dialects, see DCECH, I, 88–89; Garrote, *Leonés*, p. 121.

aksak (T.) 'a rhythmic pattern of nine beats with a signature of 9/8', but also 'a rhythmic pattern of ten beats with a signature of 10/8' (*New Redhouse*, s.v.); pp. 316–317 nn. 211–212.

alazare (E. J.-Sp.) 'sorrel (horse)' 73 (v. 10*a*), 77 (v. 4*a*). See our studies in *En torno*, pp. 118–123, and earlier in *RPh*, 21 (1966–1967), 510–512. DCECH, I, s.v. *alazán*, overlooks both studies, which document the hypothetical **alazar* earlier proposed by Corominas. Ultimately the Hispano-Arabic etymon is *al-'az^c ár* 'rubio, rojizo' (Cl. Ar. *'áz^c ar*), influenced by *ruán* (DCECH, I, 111), "otro pelaje de caballo." Cf. Port. *alazão*; O. Cat. *alatzà*. In DECLIC, I, 137*a*, our *RPh* note is indeed finally taken into account, but in a skeptical tone, as if our various citations were not abundant, were poorly documented, or somehow at fault: "sembla estar documentada." Let the reader be the judge.

alcastá (E. J.-Sp.) 'chestnut colored (horse)' 18 (v. 21*b*). This would seem to be a false Arabism, under the influence of *alazare*, perhaps also reflecting the idea of an excellent breed of horse (*caballo de casta*) (on Sp. *castaño*).

alcotán (Sp.) a species of falcon (*Falco subbuteo*) 233 & n. 71. See DCECH, I, s.v.; Corriente, *Arabismos*, p. 143; Whinnom, *Glossary*, p. 49 (no. 137). Corriente alludes to the swiftness of the *alcotán* (Hisp.-Ar. *al-quṭán*; Cl. Ar. *qaṭām*).

alcotrar (Leonese) meaning?; origin? 29 (v. 3*b*).

Alemane: *See* **Alimár(e)**.

alfamares (= **alfaremes**) (O. Sp.) 'man's headdress' 398 n. 19; DCECH, I, s.v. *alfareme*; Corriente, *Arabismos*, p. 157, s.v. *alfarém* (Hisp. Ar. *alharám*) = Cl. Ar. *ḥirām*. Compare also Hebrew *ḥāram* and *ḥērem* (Brown et al., pp. 355–356); also E. J.-Sp. and related words: *un enḥēremado* 'an anathemized person' (expelled from the community, pronounced dead, etc.); Nehama: s.vv. *enjeremar; enjeremado*; (M. J.-Sp.) *ḥarmear* 'prohibir rabínicamente, vedar, impedir' (Bendayán, p. 345; Benharroch, p. 373; Benoliel, p. 202), but this latter form would seem to be based on the Arabic. Bendayán lists various traditional expressions involving *ḥarmear* and *ḥarmeado*, including the terrible curse: *te vayas ḥarmeado* 'te mueras solo, excomulgado, rechazado por todos'. Compare Moroc. Ar. *ḥram* (Mercier, p. 71).

alḥadrarse (M. J.-Sp.) 'to appear; to put in an appearance'; *se alḥadró* 10*B*.16*a*, 21 (v. 37*a*), 46, 82 (v. 6*a*), 132 (v. 28*a*), 134 (v. 17*a*), 147 (vv. 36*a*, 42*a*), 154 (v. 36*a*), 225; *alhadre* 26 (v. 37*a*). The context is, in most cases, formulaic: *ahí se alḥadró . . .*; *aḥadró* 154 (v. 36*a*) perhaps supposes an infinitive **aḥadrarse* which is closer to the Moroc. Ar. word in lacking the definite article *al-* (Moroc. Ar. *ḥder* 'comparaître, figurer, assister'; Cl. Ar. *ḥadara* 'to be present'). See also FLSJ, V, 529.

aḥadró: *See* **alḥadrarse**.

aligornar (E. J.-Sp.) 'from Livorno'; *aligornés* 400–401 n. 29.

Alimá(r)(e) (E. J.-Sp.) 'German'; also *Alemane* 400–401 n. 29 (Sp. *alemán*).

alvisia, alvisias (M. J.-Sp.) 'good news' 132 (vv. 20*b* & variants, 21*a*), 154 (v. 34+); DCECH, I, 121–123, s.v. *albricias*; DECLIC, I, *albíxeres*; DELP, I, 220, s.v. *alvíssaras*; Corriente, *Arabismos*, p. 124, s.v. *albíxeres*; CMC, III, 443 (*albricia*); and especially Malkiel, *StPh*, 43 (1946), 498–521. Compare also Yehuda ha-Levi's *kharja* about *meu Çidiello*: "tan bona al-bišāra" (García Gómez, *Las jarchas*, no. 3, p. 382; Heger, no. 3, pp. 61–64). None of the *hakitía* dictionaries carry the word, which, I suspect, must (recently?) have become an unused archaism, only characteristic of the poetic language of ballads; E. J.-Sp., however, knew the form *albrisiyás* (note here the accent on final syllable?) 'cadeau offert à celui qui apporte le premier une bonne nouvelle; remerciments'; *dar las albrisias* 'remercier pour l'annonce d'une nouvelle agréable'; also *alverísyas*; *alverisyár*; *alvisiyárse* (Nehama, pp. 24, 32, s.vv.). Arabic *bašara* 'to announce [as good news]; to bring good news'; *bišāra* 'good news, glad tidings'; and cognates: Wehr-Cowan, p. 59; *bišāra* 'buena noticia, recompensa que se daba al que la traía' (DCECH); as Corriente rightly suggests, the Sp. plural probably reflects the influence of *noticias*; note also both male and female personal names: *Bašarat, Bashīr, Baššar, Bashīra*: Ahmed, pp. 35–36, 247; compare H. *bāšar* 'to bear tidings'; *bĕšrāh* 'tidings; news; reward for good tidings' (Brown et al., pp. 142–143). Obviously this is an ancient Semitic root (BŠR), which also shows up in various modern South Arabic languages, as well as in early Sabaean inscriptions (Leslau, p. 99; Copland Biella, p. 61).

andar (E. J.-Sp.) 'to walk; to go'; *andó* 75 (v. 10*b*), 77 (v. 7*b*) (Sp. *anduvo*).

ankalsar (E. J.-Sp.) 'to reach, catch up with'; *ankalsí* 417 n. 70 (Sp. *alcanzar*).

anxugare (E. J.-Sp.) 'trousseau' (usually *axugar, axuguar*) 53 (v. 21*b*) (Sp. *ajuar*).

aqueste (M. J.-Sp.) 'this': *aquestas* 156 (v. 52*a*).

arrevolar (M. J.-Sp.) 'fly away' 127 (v. 16*b*) (on Sp. *volar*).

arronjar, arronjare (M. J.-Sp.) 'to throw, to hurl'; *arronjá, arronjara* 163 (v. 25*b*) (Sp. *arrojar*).

atafal (Port.) 'girth, saddle strap' 437 n. 73; DCECH, I, 387, s.v. *ataharre*; DECLIC, VIII, 205, s.v. *tafarra*; DELP, I, 342, s.v. *atafal*; Corriente, *Arabismos*, pp. 235–236, s.v. *atafal* (Ar. *thafar*; Hisp. Ar. *aththafar*).

atorgar (E. J.-Sp.) 'to grant, allow, agree to' 14 (v. 11*b*), 17 (v. 9*b*) (Sp. *otorgar*; O. Sp. *atorgar*). See DCECH, I, 416 (s.v. *autor*).

atristarse (M. J.-Sp.) 'to become sad' 154 (v. 33); *me atristo* 160 (v. 24*b*) (Sp. *entristecerse*).

avagar(e) (a –; de –) (M. J.-Sp.) 'slowly, at leisure' 10A.2*b*, 15 (v. 24*b*) 19 (v. 25*b*). I suspect that the verb had survived in M. J.-Sp. only as a formula. (I do not find it in Benoliel, Bendayán, or Benharroch.) Compare O. Sp. *vagar* 'descanso, reposo'. See CMC, II, 872, Lat. *vacare*. Compare survivals in Andalucía, Salamanca, and Extremadura: *vaga*: "En las frases *Me vaga* o *No me vaga*, 'tener tiempo u ocasión de ejecutar algo'" (Alcalá Venceslada, p. 637); *vagar* 'disponer de tiempo libre y desocupado' (Lamano, p. 656); *no me bága; no me bagan* 'no tengo tiempo; no he tenido tiempo' (Cummins, *Coria*, ¶35*e*), as I have also personally heard in Coria (1963+). See also DCECH, V, 728–729; DECLIC, IX, 15–18; DELP, V, 372.

*avolar (E. J.-Sp.) 'to run (at great speed)'; *avola* 75 (v. 11*b*) (on Sp. *volar* 'to fly').

ayás, hallar, hallás, halláz, la yas (and other variant readings) 'hope'; *no te cortaré el ayás* 'I will not make you give up hope'; based on Moroc. Ar. *qte^c* 'cut' and *iyas* 'hope' 25 (v. 28*b*). For more J.-Sp. variants and further discussion, see Appendix, Chap. 10, p. 393 n. 16. Note Cl. Ar. *iyâs* 'hopelessness'(!) 21 (v. 28*b*).

azofar (16th-cent. Sp.): "hice azofar a una mujer" (read *azófar?*) 284 n. 147; Ar. *sakhira* 'to mock, ridicule, deride, make fun of; to subject, exploit' (Wehr-Cowan, p. 401). See DCECH, I, 435, s.v. *azofra*; Corriente, *Arabismos*, p. 248, s.v. *azofra* (1).

barabar (E. J.-Sp.) 'together' 10A.1*b*, 14 & 16 (vv. 4*b*, 6*b*), 50 (v. 4*b*), 143 (v. 8*b*); *barabbar* 16 (v. 4*b*), 17 (v. 7*b*) (T. *beraber*; Pers. *barabar*; Urdu *barābar* [Platts, p. 143]).

barama (Ar.) 'twist, twine (a rope)' 393 n. 16; *see* **maroma**.

biá, bidrial *See* **brial**.

bint ^camm, ibn ^camm (Ar.) 'father's brother's offspring' 406–407 n. 51; as opposed to Ar. *ḥāl* (mother's brother). See Steingass, *Arabic*, pp. 83, 427; Badger, pp. 190, 1143 (s.v. *cousin, uncle*).

bon (Leonese) 'good' 88 (v. 18*b*). Certainly *ĕ* and *ŏ* diphthongize in León or are preserved "as is," depending on chronological and geographical considerations. In the present case, it is crucial that the adjective is a rhyme word, a consideration that may (or may not) have led the singer to opt for a borrowing from Galician. For a historical perspective on the *ĕ* and *ŏ* in Leonese, see Blake, "Sobre las vocales *ĕ* and *ŏ*." Compare also **bonhora** 'in an auspicious hour' 142 (vv. 9*a*, 13*a*).

brial (Gal., Cat., O. Sp., M. J.-Sp.) 'sayo o vestidura antigua'; *bidrial* 30 (v. 12*b*); *biá* 143 (v. 11*b*); *brial(e)* 196 & nn. 37, 39, 429–430 n. 39; *brillal(e)* (M. J.-Sp.) 429–430 n. 39; *brillar* 429 n. 38.

ca (M. J.-Sp.) 'casa' 158 (v. 61), in set phrases, such as: *en ca del rey* 'en casa del rey'; for example: *en cá de fulano* (Cepas, *Vocab. popular malagueño*, p. 49, or rather *en cá fulano*); the form is probably universal in colloquial or non-standard Spanish, as well as in various regional dialects on the Peninsula and in Canarias: "en ca don Valeriano" (Andalucía: Alcalá Venceslada, p. 105); "en câ la coja" (Aragonese: Moneva y Puyol, p. 115); "en ká'l mayístru" (Penny, *Habla pasiega*, p. 146; simplified transcription); "pa ca Monzón" (Canarias: TLEC, s.v. *ca*).

cabacero (M. J.-Sp.) 'pillow'(?) 151 (v. 11*b*); *cabasera, cabecerón*(?) 151 (v. 11*b*) (Sp. *cabecera* 'headboard; pillow, bolster').

caer 'to fall': **caigó** (M. J.-Sp.) 'he fell' 68 (text 10*B*); patterned on the "irregular" first person singular pres. ind. stem, as in *caigo* (Sp. *caer, cayó*).

cansiyería (E. J.-Sp.): *en cansiyería* 'in an official, public place; or in a tribunal' 72 (v. 9*b*) (Sp. *cancillería* + Fr. *chancellerie*?).

caporal (E. J.-Sp.) 'the leader, the most important, most active person' 143 (v. 17*b*); *kaporál* 'chef d'un group de joueurs, de soldats' (Nehama, p. 269); antiquated in Sp.: *caporal* 'capital o principal; el que hace de cabeza de alguna gente y la manda' (It. *caporale*; DCECH, I, 836, s.v. *caporal*).

çarçahán (Arch. Sp.) 'especie de seda delgada, como tafatán y vareteada, tela morisca' 394 n. 16; *zarzahán* 168 (v. 11*b*); DCECH, VI, 103, s.v. (Ar. *zardakhān; zardakhānī*);

Corriente, *Arabismos*, p. 477, s.v. *zarzagania* (Port.), suggests an Indic original, but gives no further data; DELP, s.v., documents the first(?) occurrence in 1511, but goes no further ("de origem obscura"). I find nothing immediately suggestive in Platts.

carcel, carceles (M. J.-Sp.) 'prison(s)' 154 (v. 30); *carseles* 157 (v. 56*a*), 158 (v. 61), 161 (v. 8*b*) (Sp. *cárcel, cárceles*). See DCECH, I, 862, s.v.

carditas (M. J.-Sp.) 'small carding instruments'(?) 21 & 27 (v. 41*b*), 56 (v. 29*b*); *cartaron* 24 (v. 21+) meaning?; DCECH, I, 866, s.v. *cardo* (on Sp. *cardar* 'to card, comb wool'). I suspect the verb may be losing currency in popular speech and especially in some regional dialects, where sheepherding does not carry much weight: *cardar* > *cargar*. See my *Spanish Tradition*, pp. 135–136; 2d. ed., pp. 197–198.

cartaron: *See* **carditas.**

catar (O. Sp.) 'to look'; **catido**, pret.; on *estido* 'estuvo' 445 n. 124; *catar* derives from Lat. *captāre* (REW, p. 157, no. 1661), as one might say in English: 'to *catch* sight of'. Note, however, St. Isidore's amusing false etymology concerning the word for *cat*: "Common people call it cat (*catus*) because it *catches* (*captat*) [mice]. Others say, because it sees (*catat*)" (Brehaut, *Encyclopedist*, p. 226, ¶38). For *catar* and *gato*, see CMC, I, 565; DCECH, I, 920–921; III, 123–124; DECLIC, IV, 416–419; DELP, III, 135. I believe that the word *cat*, and its European relatives, may—like the animal itself—ultimately be of Near Eastern origin (Onions, p. 151; Skeat, p. 98); note Ar. *qiṭṭ* 'tomcat'; Moroc Ar. *qeṭṭ* (*Colin*, IV, 1586; Mercier, p. 163); Alg. Ar. *qaṭṭ* (Cherbonneau, p. 59); Egypt. Ar. *quṭṭ* or *qiṭṭ* (Spiro, p. 357; Cameron, p. 222); Iraqi *qiṭṭ* (Clarity, p. 32). Gulf Ar. surprisingly has *gaṭu* (*g* corresponds to *q*) (Qafisheh, p. 426); Libyan Ar. *gaṭṭûs* (Griffini, p. 130) and Maltese *qattus* (Bugeja, p. 68; Busuttil, p. 173) must involve Latin. In Hisp. Ar., as attested to by Ibn Quzmān, both forms, *qaṭṭ* and *qaṭṭus,* were known (García Gómez, *Todo Ben Quzmān,* III, 420). See also DAA, p. 433. Walde, rather than from the Near East, would derive *cattus* from Celtic (p. 141), on the highly uncertain basis, it would seem, that Celtic languages provide some of the earliest documentation. Recent DNA studies place the origins of domestic cats in the Near East (Carlos A. Driscoll, et al., "The Near Eastern Origin of Cat Domestication," *Science,* 317 [27 July 2007], 519; Pat Bailey, "Tracing the Cat Family Tree," *UC Davis Magazine,* 25:3 [Spring 2008], 5).

çatico (O. Sp.; 16th-cent. Sp.) 'small piece' 452 n. 196, 459 (Basque *zati* 'piece, part, bit, fragment'); *-ko* may be diminutive or augmentative. See DCECH, VI, 103–104 (s.v. *zatico*); Morris, s.v.; Aulestia-White, s.v.; Larramendi, II, 244 (*zatia*).

cawker, calker, calkin (Scots) 'the turned-down ends of a horseshoe which raise the horse's heels from the ground; a turned edge under the front of the shoe'; *cauker* 'the hind-part of a horseshoe sharpened and turned down' 437–438 n. 76.

cenclina, centlinna (Mex. Sp.) 'una planta de tierra caliente . . ., que los indios emplean como febrífugo' 399 n. 19 (Santamaría, *Americanismos*, I, 345*b*; Id., *Mejicanismos*, p. 235*a*).

centli (Nahuatl) 'cured and dried ear of corn' 399 n. 19 (Molina, p. 18: "maçorca de mayz curada y seca"; Campbell, p. 59*a*; Andrews, p. 428; Bierhorst, p. 70; Karttunen, p. 31; Siméon, p. 87).

charcal (M. J.-Sp.) usually a 'ditch, pond, puddle'; *charcale* 156 (vv. 47*a*, 49+). Here, incongruously, *charcal(e)* has sometimes come to be associated with *šaral* 'undergrowth, thickets'. Though *charcal* 'sitio donde abundan charcos' exists in Sp., M. J.-Sp. *charcal* has changed meaning in some cases. The form's position as a rhyme word is, I believe, significant, as is the fact that it is not listed in any of the three glossaries I have at hand (Benoliel, Bendayán, Benharroch). This is now, I would suggest, not part of the everyday language, but rather reflects the *Romancero*'s specialized formulaic vocabulary, devoted here to the description of the grave discomforts and privations of the lover (or his messenger), hungry and thirsty, wandering in vain through uninhabited forests. Compare the M. J.-Sp. versions of *Moriana y Galván* (CMP B21), where the original meaning is preserved, as the lover, who now looks like a wildman (*salvaje*), is searching for Moriana, and has spent seven years "comiendo la hierba verde / y bebiendo agua de charcales" (Larrea 80, vv. 23–24) or "comiendo la carne curuda / y bebiendo agua d'un charcale" (uned.). The *romance* will be studied in detail in Vol. VII of the present collection. For now, see also the entry under **salvaje** (*infra*).

cloot (Scots) 'a division of the hoof of cattle, sheep, pigs' 433 n. 60. Since the devil is supposed to have a deformed foot, he is called in Scots *Auld Clootie* or *Cloots* (Kynoch, p. 17), so as not to bring about his suddenly appearing before us by calling him by his real name: *En nombrando el rey de Roma (ruín de Roma), luego se asoma. Clootie's craft* 'the devil's croft' (a *craft* or *croft* being a small garden) is a small plot of ground set aside to appease the devil. Such is also the *goodman's field* 'a small portion of land set apart for the devil and left untilled' (433 n. 60). In this case, we have a typical flattering name (*Schmeichelname*), such as also the apotropaic term *la buena ǧente* or *los mejores de mozotros* applied by Eastern Sephardim to the mischievous, small, subterranean people (we might call them *leprechauns*) or to the supposedly dangerous weasels (Fr. *belette*; Ger. dialect *Schöntierle*) to stave off their hostility. In Salonika, it was frowned upon to throw hot water from a window without warning: "Apartá la buena ǧente, que vo echar agua caente," was the formulaic call to avoid offending the little people. For more, see below s.v. **donezinha**. Emilio Montero's massively documented linguistic study of "El demonio y los espíritus diabólicos" in *El eufemismo en Galicia*, pp. 100–114, is indispensable. *Dickens* is another euphemistic substitute for the devil in American English, as in: *What the dickens are you doing?* etc. (DARE, II, 46; under *devil and Tom Walker*). The pig's cloven hoof, seemingly kosher, in contrast to all its other overwhelmingly *trēf* characteristics, entered Yiddish folk-speech in a phrase used to designate the superfluous opinion of an ignorant, totally unqualified individual who interrupts an otherwise coherent discussion: *Oh, oh, oh! De hazer hept zain koishere fisl oif* ('The pig lifts up its little kosher foot').

cobertón (M. J.-Sp.) 'blanket' 151 (v. 12*a*) (Sp. *cobertor* 'manta o cobertura de abrigo para la cama').

condeñar (Extremeño) 'to condemn' 219 (v. 39*a*) (Sp. *condenar*).

cordobán 'tanned goat skin' 168 (v. 10*b*), 393 n. 16; DCECH, II, 197 (Sp. *cordobán*).

cortaré: *See* **hallar.**

cravos (Leonese) 'nails' 30 (v. 8*b*) (Sp. *clavos*).

cuae (M. J.-Sp.) 'it falls' 152 (v. 17*a*); which reads "caza que en mi mano cae," but Luna Farache's pronunciation of the -*o* in *mano* must have been closer to -*u* than to -*o*. In both Moroccan and Eastern J.-Sp., a preceding -*u* tends to reappear after the first consonant in the following word: *el su puadre, un su guato* (= *gato*), etc. Other examples show up in the present volume: *la su cuara* 148 (v. 2*a*); *a su cuaẓa* 160 (v. 16*b*) (our text 11*F*, from Larache).

cuento: *See* **quento**.

dar 'to give': **daldeš** (E. J.-Sp.) 'give him' (2d pers. pl. imperative) 18 (v. 19*a*): This form derives from the well known metathesized imperatives *dalde* = *dad* + *le* (compare innumerable Golden Age examples: *decilde, matalde*, etc., etc.); to which has then been added the 2d pers. pl. suffix -*eš* (= Sp. -*eis*), since, for E. J.-Sp.-speakers, the -*d*- had clearly ceased to impart the 2d pers. pl. meaning of this form; (M. J.-Sp.) *daste* 'you gave' 23 (v. 4*a*) (= Sp. *diste*); suggested by regular -*ar* preterites (*hablaste, contaste*, etc.).

desfortunado (M. J.-Sp.) 'unfortunate' 131 (v. 13*a*) (Sp. *desafortunado*); perhaps suggested by *desgrasiado* or possibly a semantic calque of *desmazalado*, which would then lead to the omission of -*a*- in Sp. *desafortunado*. Both the J.-Sp. words were often pronounced, for special emphasis, with geminated -*ss*- or -*zz*-, patterned on Arabic emphatic pronunciation: *desgrassiado, desmazzalado*.

desherdar (M. J.-Sp.) 393 n. 16 'to disinherit' (Port. *deserdar*; Sp. *desheredar*). Rather than an authentic survival of the Luso-Spanish *Mischsprache* that was, in fact, current earlier on among Moroccan Sephardim, this particular word is probably a slip-up, reflecting José Benoliel's fluent knowledge of standard Portuguese. Compare **lidar** *infra*.

desotro (Zamora) 'the very next (day)' (= *de* + *ese* + *otro*) 216 (v. 8*a*); *essotro* 431 n. 45 (v. 8). Here colloquial non-standard Spanish is striving for clarification and linguistic efficacy, by bringing additional prefixes into play, just as did Vulgar Latin: not just *post*, but **de-ex-post* or **de-in-post* > *después* and E. J.-Sp. *dimpués* (Sp. *ese otro*).

desposicas (M. J.-Sp.) 'handcuffs' 164 (Sp. *esposas*).

despozar (E. J.-Sp.) 'to betroth': *desposí* 'I betrothed'; *despozada* 17 (v. 13*a*). See Nehama: *despozada, despozar, despozorio* (p. 131).

dían (Gal.) = *iban* (185, v. 12). I have not found *dir* = *ir* elsewhere in Galician, but it is widely distributed in other Hispanic languages, dialects, and non-standard regional variants. For example: Asturian, Leonese, Extremeño, Andalusian, Canarian, Louisiana, Panamanian, etc. (Vigón, p. 165; Millán Urdiales, p. 271; Cummins, p. 56, ¶8*g*, *díl*; Viudas Camarasa, p. 63; Alcalá Venceslada, p. 228; *TLEC*, s.v. *dir*; my *Spanish Tradition*, s.v. *dir*; Robe, *Rural Panama*, p. 196: *dir, diendo, diba, dibas*; among many other possible references).

dijís (M. J.-Sp.) 'you said' 22 (v. 4*a*). The standard Sp. 2d pers. sing. and pl. pret. and the 3rd pers. sing. pret. of *decir* (*dijiste, dijísteis, dijo*) have apparently combined to create this form.

diñeiro (Leonese) 'money' 88 (v. 15*a*) (text *e*) (Gal. *diñeiro*, Port. *dinheiro*). See García et al., s.v.; Navaza Blanco, p. 215; DCECH, II, 497–498; DELP, II, 341.

doblas (E. J.-Sp.) 'doubloons' 17 (v. 12+); *dobles* 10*A*.6*b*, 17 (v. 13*b*) (Sp. *dobla*).

donezinha (Old Gal.) 'weasel' 434 n. 60; Modern Gal. *denociña, doniña, donicela, donosiña, durmicela, dunicela, garridiña*, and numerous additional variants; s.v.

comadreja (Buschmann, p. 242; Crespo Pozo, p. 194; García et al., p. 432; Navaza Blanco, p. 221; Pensado, I, 441); Port. *doninha*; Algarve *doinina, doininha, dònina* (Brezão Gonçalves, p. 83). It goes without saying that a great many beliefs, superstitions, taboos, and fears have surrounded the weasel (*comadreja*), probably since time immemorial. Opie and Tatem cite a text from Theophrastus (c. 319 B.C.E.). However, the weasel has acquired, it would seem, an exclusively negative "press" in modern times. We need only recall our modern American slang words, some of which have now been accepted as part of the "standard" lexicon: a *weasel* is an 'informer, a police spy, a *fink*, a hypocrite'; a *weasel word* dishonestly changes the meaning of a word or statement; *to weasel out* of a compromising situation; a *weaselism* signifies 'mean or contemptible conduct' (M. M. Mathews, p. 1847; Deak and Deak, p. 802). But medievals knew nature much better than moderns. For all the superstitions and fears that have surrounded this small and graceful animal, Alfonso X's *donezinha* was obviously a beloved pet, whose life, indeed, was to be miraculously spared by none other than the blessed Virgin Mary. Medievals admired the weasel's lithesome grace. Chaucer's astoundingly seductive Alisoun—further on to attract various other significant animal comparisons—is first of all described in the following terms: "Fair was this yonge wyf and therwithal / As any wesele hir body gent and smal" (vv. 3233–3234, ed. Ross, pp. 141–143; ed. Robinson, p. 58). (*Gent* means 'refined, exquisite; genteel; slender, graceful'.) Of course, the positive, complimentary terms often applied to the weasel also had an apotropaic purpose, calculated to win the weasel's favor and stave off any mischief that it might otherwise commit (*Schmeichelnamen* 'flattering names'): Bavarian *Schöntierle*, Fr. *belette* (HDA, IX, 580). See also **cloot**, *supra*. For more on weasel lore, see especially Ross's splendid notes: pp. 141–144. Add to our references on p. 434, first of all: HDA, IX, 578–600; also Gili Gaya, *Tesoro*, I, 590; Leach and Fried, II, 1168–1169; Opie and Tatem, p. 431; Pickering, p. 278; Radford and Radford, p. 353. See also DCECH, III, 754 (s.v. *madre*); II, 515a, lines 45–49 (s.v. *donar*; Gal. *donosiña*); Pensado, p. 441 (s.v. *donicela*); DECLIC, V, 813–814 (s.v. *mostela*); Bloch-von Wartburg, p. 62 (s.v. *beau*, concerning *belette*); and Iordan's far-reaching and richly documented survey of lexical taboos and euphemistic apotropaic designations for (supposedly) dangerous and predatory animals: *Lingüística*, pp. 549–550 & n. 54; and Iordan-Orr, p. 306 & n. 1. See also **medved'** and ***ulkuos** (*infra*).

drento (de) (Leonese) 'inside' 88 (v. 16b); for the Leonese form: Alonso Garrote, p. 205; the metathesis is present in numerous Luso-Hispanic dialects: Aragonese: *drentro* (Andolz, p. 160); Villar del Arzobispo (Aragonese): *drento* (Llatas, I, 219); Pasiego: *dréntu* (Penny, p. 410); Salamanca: *drento* (Lamano, p. 398); Extremeño: *dréntu* (Cummins, pp. 76, 101); Isleño (Louisiana): *drento* (Alvar, *Sur de Estados Unidos*, p. 327, n. 545); Galician (dialectal): *drento* (C. García, p. 7); Algarvio: *drento* (Brazão Gonçalves, p. 83); Macaísta (Macao): *drento* (Nogueira Batalha, p. 167); note also Papiamentu: *drenta* 'to enter'; *drentada* 'entrance' (Dijkhoff, p. 48; Jansen, p. 35).

dulap (E. J.-Sp.) 'armoire' 417 n. 70 (T. *dolab* 'cupboard,' but also 'trick, plot,' so the storyteller may be playing with the word's semantics).

embinear (E. J.-Sp.) 'to ride (horseback)'; *enbineava* 448 n. 133 (< T. *binmek* 'to ride').

emprendadas (E. J.-Sp.) 'pledged (against a loan)' 18 (v. 15*a*); *empeñar* and *empeñadas* (E. J.-Sp. and Sp.) have been conflated with *prender* and/or perhaps also *prenda*.

endonar (E. J.-Sp.) 'to give (a gift)'; here, as a feudal boon (from a lord to a vassal) 22 (v. 11*b*); **endoñar** 10*B*.7*b*; Benharroch, p. 295 (Sp. *endonar*; *donar*; DCECH, II, 514–516: s.v. *donar*; DELP, II, 351: s.v. *doar*).

ermuera (E. J.-Sp.) 'daughter-in-law' 79 (v. 13*b*); unchanged, the Sp. form *nuera* continued in use in various modalities of E. J.-Sp.: Salonika: Nehama, p. 386 (who lists various sayings reflecting the implacable hostility between *suegras* and *nueras*); Sala, *Bucarest*, pp. 150, 179; Chérézli, II, 149: *nu'era* 'bru, belle-fille'. Wagner, *Beiträge*, p. 43, and Crews, no. 41, reasonably suggest that *ermuera* may reflect the influence of *hermana*, but as Crews also convincingly proposes, another factor may well have come into play in this case. As is well known, numerous words beginning with *nu*- were changed to *mu*- in E. J.-Sp.: *muevo, mueve, muestro, mues* (note also *mos, mozotros*). In line with such developments, *nuera* would have developed into **muera* (a form actually documented in Salonika: Simon, "Charakeristik," ¶15.2), but the word is very obviously taboo, especially given the traditional hatred between mothers- and daughters-in-law and the accretion of the initial *er*- (probably from *hermana*, as we have seen) thus acquired a very special urgency. (Among Rhodes speakers, I have also heard *elmuera*.) On the proverbial hatred between *suegras* and *nueras*, see our DRH, no. 7.8, and *J.-Sp. Ballads from New York*, pp. 100–102. I take this opportunity to cite an example from M. J.-Sp., remembered from the as yet unedited field notes of Américo Castro: "Mi nuera la garrida, discués de barrer, esfoyina" ('My elegant daughter-in-law, after sweeping the floor, she cleans the chimney'); *esfoyina* is related to Sp. *hollín* 'soot' (DCECH, III, 377–379). For *nuera* (from Vulg. Lat. *nŏra*), see DCECH, IV, 245.

escontrar (E. J.-Sp.) 'to meet, to encounter'; *escontró* 79 (v. 11*b*) from Salonika; compare Chérézli's and Luria's evidence from Jerusalem and Monastir: *'esku'entra* (*kontra, delantre*), 'contre, devant' (Chérézli, I, 36); *iscuntrar*, pp. 171, 175, 208, 217. Note also Asturian *escontrar* 'ir al encuentro de alguno que viene' (DCECH, II, 183*b*). The prepositions *escontra* and *escuentra* abound in O. Sp.: Sas, *Alexandre*, p. 253; De Gorog, *Fernán González*, p. 143; Id., *Arcipreste de Talavera*, p. 141; Schmid, *Baena*, p. 78; Ten Cate, *Alfonso XI*, p. 51. Note the rich documentation in Kasten and Cody, *Tent. Dict.*, II, 305; Kasten and Nitti, *Alfonso X*, I, 485–486. Clearly, the alternation *en*- against *es*- in *encontrar* vs. *escontrar* already has its origins in Vulg. Lat. and its ongoing struggle to achieve clarity and dominance in an ever-expanding and complexly multilingual Roman Empire. Compare E. J.-Sp. *después* and *dimpues* < **de-ex-post* vs. **de-in-post*, above: s.v. **desotro**.

escudero (Sp.) 'squire' 197 & nn. 40–41; 430 n. 40; the popular-etymological *escuchero parlero* attests to the semantic decline of a medieval concept: 427 n. 27. For the etymology: DCECH, II, 714, s.v. *escudo*; DECLlC, III, 570, s.v. *escut*.

essotro: *See* **desotro**.

estantigua (Sp.) 'a grotesque figure' 433 n. 60; Lat. *hŏstis antīquus* originally 'the devil'; O. Sp. *huest antigua* (DCECH, II, 775–776). The term will take on a variety of meanings and connotations in Hispanic folklore, including that of the Wild Hunt, riders condemned forever to pursue, unsuccessfully, some enchanted animal across the sky, or again, a ghostly—and ghastly—procession of *almas en pena*, sometimes led by four robed skeletons bearing a coffin (Carreras y Candi, *Folklore y costumbres*, I, 189–204; Castroviejo, *Apariciones*, pp. 163–165: "La Santa Compaña"). For extra-Hispanic traditions: Leach and Fried, II, 1177, s.v. *Wild Hunt*; Pickering, pp. 315–316; Erich and Beitl, pp. 888–890, s.v. *wilde Jagd*; HDA, X, 400–401 (cross references). Within living memory, the venerable tradition, which echoes ancient Germanic memories of Wotan (Odin, etc.), was genially reworked as an American popular song: *Ghost Riders in the Sky*.

estare (M. J.-Sp.) '*está, estuvo* or *estaba*', adjusted to the ballad's *á-e* assonance: "la dama con el conde estare; la dama en sintas estare" 161 (vv. 6*b*, 7*b*).

estormía (M. J.-Sp.) 'pillow' 288 n. 155 (Moroc. Ar. *sṭormiya* 'throw pillow; round cushion'); *estormía* 'cojín de forma redonda' (Benoliel, p. 61); 'cojín de forma redonda; almohadón, almohada' (Bendayán, p. 258); *estornía* (*sic*) 'almohadón, cojín redondo' (Benharroch, p. 317). See also FLSJ, II, 348.

folgar (M. J.-Sp.; O. Sp.; 16th-cent. Sp.) 'to rest; to have sex' 10*B*.9*b*, 14*b*, 20 (vv. 12*b*, 20*b*), 21 (v. 50*b*), 23 (v. 12*b*), 24 (v. 20*b*), 44 (*M*20), 56 (v. 38*b*), 57 (vv. 7*b*, 12*b*) (16th-cent. Sp.) 38 (v. 13*b*), 44 (*Caza* 13). E. J.-Sp. knows *folgar* in the sense of 'donner de l'ampleur, élargir; se détendre, se reposer' (Nehama, p. 214). For the word's history: DCECH, III, 375–376: s.v. *holgar*; DECLlC, IV, 72–73, s.v. *folgar*; DELP, III, 69: s.v. *folgar*; for late Lat. *follicāre* 'se gonfler et se remuer comme une soufflet' (Maigne d'Arnis, p. 947; Blaise, p. 358).

foyones (E. J.-Sp.) 'holes, potholes' 15 n. 15 (Sp. *hoyo*; O. Sp. *foyo*); see DCECH, III, 405–407, s.v. *hoya*: "probablemente del lat. *fŏvĕa* 'hoyo, excavación'"; DELP, III, 69, s.v. *fojo* 'cueva'; compare E. J.-Sp. *foya* 'fossé, fosse' (Nehama, p. 216).

franco (E. J.-Sp.) 'foreign, European'; *moro franco* 'a foreign, European Moor' 19 (v. 24*a*), 401 n. 29. Here Sp. *franco* is certainly calqued on T. *frenk* and its many compounds (Redhouse, p. 378); Pers. *farang, firing, farangī, firingī* 'Frank, Italian, European, Christian' (Steingass, *Persian*, pp. 922–923); Ar. *al-ifranj, ifranjī* 'Europeans' (Wehr-Cowan, p. 710); Hindi *farangī* (Platts, p. 780); and from T. then to most major Balkan languages: Alb., Bulg., Gk., Maced.-Rum., Rum., Serb.-Cr.: Knežević, p. 126; G. Meyer, p. 110; Boretzky, p. 51; Miklosich, p. 297, and *Nachtrag*, p. 116; Papahagi, p. 468; Pascu, II, 134; Škaljić, p. 285. See also **moro franco**.

frontal (M. J.-Sp.) '(horse's) chest' or 'breast' 21 (v. 56*b*), 28 (v. 48*b*) (Sp. *frontal* does not have this meaning; Sp. *pecho* [*del caballo*]).

fundir (E. J.-Sp.) 'to sink, to destroy' 15 (vv. 28–29). E. J.-Sp. seems to have limited or specialized the meaning to a certain degree: 'couler, faire périr en mer, naufrager' (Nehama, p. 219). M. J.-Sp. does not conserve the *f-*, but changes the conjugation: *hunder* 'hundir' (Benoliel, p. 199); *ḥunder* 'hundir, arruinarse' (Benharroch, p. 363). Benharroch explains that the *ḥ* is pronounced like the *he* in Hebrew, like a "*j* muy, muy suave" (p. 81).

fusito[s] (M. J.-Sp.) 'small spindles, bobbins' 27 (v. 42*b*), 56 (v. 30*b*) (Sp. *huso*); DCECH, III, 434–435, s.v. *huso*; DECLlC, IV, 238–241, s.v. *fus*; DELP, III, 106, s.v. *fuso*.

fustar (M. J.-Sp.) 'heavy cotton cloth' 27 (v. 42*b*), 56 (v. 30*b*). Benharroch lists *fustal* 'tela gruesa de algodón' as a "creación" of the dialect ("creación ḥaq."), but the word, with relatively little variation (*fustán, fustal, fustão*, etc.) has a long history in all the major Romance languages: Fr. *futaine*; Prov. *fustani* (E. Levy, p. 199), It. *fustagno* (with numerous regional manifestations), including also Sardinian *fustániu* 'fustagno' (Wagner, p. 562), Romantsch Sursilvan *fustagn* 'Zwilch' ('blouse or frock of coarse cotton cloth') (Vieli and Decurtins, p. 287), Rum. *fustă* 'skirt' (Cioranescu, p. 349). Note also Eng. *fustian* 'thick twilled cotton cloth; coarse cloth' (Onions, p. 383). The word is known in both dialects of J.-Sp. Note E. J.-Sp. *fostán* 'robe de femme', as in one of our traditional *romances*: *La pedigüeña*, where, among many other items, the importunate girl asks for a pretty dress: "Le demanda fostán bueno, / kundurias ačik maví" ('She asks him for a pretty dress and light blue shoes') ("Tres calas," p. 139). The word occurs in most major Balkan languages, including, undoubtedly, some minor ones as well: e.g. Gagaúz *fistan* 'dress' (Zajączkowski, p. 43). Note the following: Alb. *fustan, fëstan, fistan, fistan* 'Weiberrock' (Boretzky, pp. 50, 51, 200); Bulg. *fistàn* and *fustàn* 'sleeveless dress' (the first may be from T. and the second perhaps from It.); Serb.-Cr. *fistān* 'Art Frauenrock' is certainly from T., while *fùstān* is probably an Italianism (Knežević, p. 126; Škaljić, p. 284; Skok, I, 519). Greek, on the other hand, would definitely seem to derive from It.: *foústa* 'skirt'; *foustanélla* 'kilt'; *foustáni* 'dress, gown, frock' (Crighton, I, 1617; Andriōtēs, p. 284; Koulákēs, p. 970). Forms like Egyptian *fustán* or *fistán* (Spiro, p. 333; Cameron, p. 204) are known in many modern Colloquial Arabic dialects (DCECH, II, 982), as well as in Palestinian Yiddish: *fuste, fustan, fustn* (Kosover, no. 413). Returning to the origin of the Hispano-Lusitanian words, neither Corominas, nor Machado, nor again Corriente (*Arabismos*, p. 324) are satisfied with the etymology deriving *fustán* from the Egyptian city, al-Fusṭāṭ (Old Cairo), despite that city's having been a crucially important center for the Near Eastern textile trade, including that of cotton (Lombard, pp. 62, 154; Goitein, IV, 170–171, et alibi; Id., *Letters*, p. 349 et alibi), though cotton (*al-quṭn*) was far from being an esteemed textile in the Near Eastern trade (Goitein, III, 304–305). On the supposed etymology and attendant doubts or, in the case of Corriente, negation, see DCECH, II, 981–983, s.v. *fustán*; DECLIC, IV, 245, s.v. *fustani* ("d'origen incert"); DELP, III, 106: s.v. *fustão*. Dozy discusses Ar. *fuṣṭān* briefly in his *Vêtements*, p. 337. The city name, al-Fusṭāṭ, is, incidentally, a Latinism: from *fossatum*, like O. Sp. *fonsado* (CMC, II, 694; REW, no. 3461; DCECH, II, 982; Orel, p. 104, s.v. *fshat*).

ǧanfés al (E. J.-Sp.) 'red taffeta' 15 n. 15 (v. 21*b*), 46; *yanfés* 'taffeta' 18 (v. 21*b*) (T. *canfes* 'fine taffeta'; *al* 'red'); also Serb. *džàmfez*; Gk. *tsamfesi*; Miklosich, p. 107; Škaljić, pp. 233–234.

García = 'the bear' (?) 433 n. 60. Compare Gaulish *artos*, Middle Irish *art*, Welsh *arth* 'bear' (also Gk. *'árktos*); but *García* is also the wolf. For more data on bears in England and Wales, see Dent, pp. 35–37; see also **medved'** *infra*.

garrero (E. J.-Sp.) 'warrior' 17 (v. 14*a*); the usual form is *guerrero* (Sp. *guerrero*).

Ǧenar (E. J.-Sp.) 15 (v. 20*b*), 18 (v. 20*b*), 400 n. 29: Can this somehow reflect a memory of one of the two martyred saints *Januarius*? An intermediate form, *Iannarius*, lacking the *waw* and thus heralding subsequent developments in Romance, is documented in the early 5th-century *Tablettes Albertini*, from either Algeria or Tunisia (Tébessa or Qafṣa; Väänänen, pp. 12, 52).

goodman's field (Scots) 'a small portion of land set apart for the devil and left untilled' 433 n. 60. See also **cloot**.

gorgorán (M. J-Sp.) 'tela de seda con cordoncillo' (*Dicc. Autoridades*) 28 (v. 52*b*); variants: *gorgomán, gorgorá* 393 n. 16. Compare O. Fr. *grograin* and Eng. *grogram* 'a coarse fabric of silk' (OED, s.v.; Onions, p. 415, s.v.).

guila (Galician): *medianoche y guila* 'after midnight; midnight and somewhat later' 184 (v. 1); Arch. Sp. (16th-cent.) *guilla* 'abundancia en las cosechas'; *guilla de aceite* 'a good harvest' (= 'abundance') (*DQ*, ed. Lathrop, I, Ch. 12, p. 85); from Hisp. Ar. *ghīlla* 'cosecha; abundancia en los productos de la tierra' (DCECH, III, 263–264, s.v. *guilla*; Port. *guilha* 'colheita'; DELP, III, s.v.). Compare Cl. Ar. *ghallah*, pl. *-at*, *ghilāl* 'yield, produce, crops; grain, cereals; corn; fruits' (Wehr-Cowan, p. 679; Corriente, *Arabismos*, p. 337, s.vv. *guilha, guilla*, 'cosecha'; Id., *Andalusian Arabic*, p. 382, s.r. *GHLL*. I have found no other Galician documentation, but the present definition seems altogether convincing.

guillarda (M. J-Sp.) 'parade, gaudy spectacle'(?) 291 (v. 34*b*); *guiñarda* 281 (v. 37*b*); 282 n. 145 (etym.?).

haberchís (E. J.-Sp.) 'messengers' 144 (v. 8*b*) (T. *haberci*; on Ar. *khabar* 'news').

haber (de) (E. J.-Sp.) 'to have' (as an auxiliary verb expressing future obligation) *hadex de* 17 (v. 9*b*); (M. J-Sp.) *hais de*; *ha, hay, hei de* 25 (v. 27*b*), 26 (v. 30*b*); 26 (v. 30+) (Sp. *ha de*).

hallar, hallás, halláz, hayás: *See* **ayás**.

hermano, hermana (M. J-Sp.) 'beloved' 406 n. 51.

hezmét (E. J.-Sp.) 'service' 417 n. 70 (T. *hismet* 'service, duty, employment'; Ar. *khidmat*; Pers. *khedmat*; Urdu *khidmat*).

hi (M. J-Sp.) 'there' 82 (v. 6*a*). This is not any direct descendant of O. Sp. *hi, y* (< Lat. *hīc*), but simply a rapid or slurred pronunciation of *ahí* (Sp. *ahí*).

hobero (O. Sp.) 'white and red spotted horse; a peach colored horse' 402 n. 31(Sp. *overo*). See DCECH, IV, 325–327 (< Lat. *falvus*).

holanda (M. J-Sp.) 'Holland cloth; fine linen' 24 (v. 18+), 28 (v. 51*a*) (Sp. *holanda*). See DCECH, III, 374–375.

imá (M. J-Sp.) 'in regard to, as far as *X* is concerned' 11D.15*a* (p. 131); also *umá* (Moroc. Ar. *wa-amma, wamma* 'quant à'). See FLSJ, III, 409, s.v. *umá*; also **umá** *infra*.

infalta (E. J.-Sp.) 'princess' 78 (v. 16*a*) (Sp. *infanta*).

ir 'to go, depart': **vai** (Leonese: Zamora) 'she goes' 216 (v. 38*a*); **veis** 'go' (2d pers. pl. imperative) 216 (v. 18); 431 n. 45 (vv. 18, 38) (Sp. *va*; *id*); **vai** (E. J.-Sp.) *vare* (= *va* + *r* to accomodate a following paragogic *-e*) 216 (v. 38*a*); FLSJ, V, 535.

izyara: fazer izyara (E. J.-Sp.) 'to go on a pilgrimage' 417 n. 70 (T. *ziyaret* 'visit'; Ar., Pers., Urdu *ziyārat*; Alb. *zijaret* 'freundschaftlicher Besuch' (Boretzky, p. 145).

Januarius: *See* **Ğenar**.

jugón (M. J.-Sp.) 'jacket' 21 (v. 52*a*); *jubón, jugor* (Sp. *jubón*); *jugón* enoys wide currency in various regions of Spain (DCECH, III, 532–533, s.v. *jubón*; Corriente, *Arabismos*, p. 180: Ar. *jubba*). Seemingly, the word has been repeatedly borrowed over the centuries from different modalities of Arabic, Romance, and also from intermediate languages: DECLIC, IV, 501–504, s.v. *gipó*. The resultant word history is astoundingly complex. The repeated (?) impact of Colloquial Arabic *ǧibba* seems to have been crucial: e.g. Egypt. *gibba* 'outer robe or gown' (though here, of course, *g-* is pronounced as a velar stop; Spiro, p. 111; or *jubba*, Cameron, p. 39); Algerian *djebba* 'jupe, robe' (DeBussy, p. 384). Dozy's detailed study is indispensable (*Vêtements*, pp. 107–117). The Fr. Arabism *jupe* (Bloch-von Wartburg, p. 22) has even come over, as a *Rückwanderer*, into Mod. Arabic: *jūb* 'skirt' (Wehr-Cowan, p. 145). E. J.-Sp. adds yet another complexity to the adventures of Ar. *jubba*. Turkish has *cübbe* or *cüppe* 'robe worn by imams, judges, barristers and professors' from Arabic (Redhouse, pp. 233, 234; Iraqi Ar. *jubba*: Clarity, p. 66). E. J.-Sp. also has *ǧiboy* or *šiboy* (Attias, *Romancero*, p. 266: Salonika; also Rhodes); the latter, at least apparently, has been superficially associated with the Turkish botanical term *şebboy* 'wallflower' (Redhouse, p. 1051), which, in its turn, has also entered E. J.-Sp.: *šiboy* 'giroflée' (Nehama, p. 534).

la yas: *See* **ayás**.

labre (M. J-Sp.) 'hand work; embroidery'; *lagre* 27 (v. 47*a*) (on Sp. *labrar* 'to do needlework; embroider').

lear (M. J-Sp.) 'leal; real' 25 (v. 29*b*), 65 (v. 18*b*) (Sp. *leal*).

libro de rezar: *See* **misal**.

libro misal: *See* **misal**.

lidar (M. J.-Sp.) 'to fight, combat' 149 (v. 4*b*) (Port. *lidar*). See DCECH, III, s.v. *lidiar*; DELP, III, s.v. *lidar*. Is this perhaps an authentic survival of the earlier mixed Spanish-Portuguese dialect that we know was spoken and written during the 16th–18th centuries by Sephardic Jews in Morocco and which, to a certain degree, left its very slight impact even on *romances* recorded in the early years of the 20th century? For an example of such language, see the Jewish doctor's narrative in my *Don Sebastián* article (1990). This mixed language was analogous to that spoken in Amsterdam from the 17th century on down even to the early 20th. See, for example, M. L. Wagner's richly documented 1924 publication (pp. 259–269 = 42–52), K. Adams' important article, and now, of course, Harm den Boer's magnificent work. Note also my "Judeo-Spanish Traditional Poetry," pp. 357–358 and nn. 3–5. But another factor comes into play in regard to text *a* (= CMP B10.1), which forces us to view such an intriguing hypothesis negatively, or at very least with very strong doubts. The *lidar* reading is unique. I know of no other instances and text B10.1 was collected or transcribed by José Benoliel, who spoke fluent Portuguese (along with many other languages). I very much suspect—and regret—that this is probably, if not certainly, just Benoliel's *lapsus calami* and has nothing to do with the earlier mixed language. See also **desherdar** (*supra*). As to authentic survivals, I recall a *romance* verse (at the moment I do not remember which *romance*!): "Asomóse a una ventana /

y también a una janela." I am also reminded of a disguised and Hispanized Portuguese saying, which did survive at least until Benoliel's time and perhaps even later, to designate some totally useless activity: "Eso es como mearse en la arena," which corresponds to Port. "Isso é como semear na areia." Compare Benoliel, p. 212, no. 2. I also note that an identical expression, surely brought in by one of the many Moroccan Sephardim who emigrated to Algeria, was also current in the richly eclectic French *patois* spoken in the city of Algiers: *Pisser dans le sable* 'perte seche complètement': "C'est comme si j'pissais dans l'sable" (Bacri, pp. 142–143). Again, the expression only makes sense if seen through a J.-Sp. misinterpretation of a traditional Portuguese saying: *semear na areia.*

lustre (M. J.-Sp.) 'irradiance, brightness, brilliance' 136 (v. 2*a*); Benharroch, p. 1442 (Sp. *lustre*).

máis (M. J.-Sp.) 'more' 138 (v. 5*b*), 150 (v. 7*b*) (Sp. *más*; Port. *mais*). Is this possibly another authentic survival of a time when Sephardic language in Morocco was basically Spanish, but had a significant admixture of Portuguese? (See commentary, s.v. *lidar.*) For whatever stylistic effect, the formulistic phrase *más y más* (or *mad y made*) could have been expressed by a combination of Spanish and Portuguese: *más y mais.* For me, such a combination is a total *hapax*; I have seen it only here. All the same, its authenticity as a Portuguese survival suggests itself at very least as a possibility.

mancillar (M. J.-Sp.) 'to take pity (on someone)' 147 (v. 33*a*); *nos mansiyamos* 161 (v. 11*a*), 223; *vos mansiyéis* 161 (v. 12*a*). Compare O. Sp. *manziella* 'mancha, ensuciamiento moral' (*Tent. Dict.*, s.v.; *Dicc. de la prosa*, s.v. *amancillar*; Mod. Sp. *amancillar* 'manchar, deslustrar la fama o linaje'). The word's emotional implications have, it would seem, almost inevitably, occasioned an astoundingly wide range of semantic—and perhaps also morphological—diversity. Albeit, Golden Age sources attest to the same meaning, which has survived in M. J.-Sp.: "Decíalo con lágrimas, . . . los qu'estábamos presentes tuvimos mancilla" (Bernal Díaz, Chap. 46; *apud* DCECH, III, 797, with additional examples). Malkiel's richly documented monographic investigation is, as we would expect, indispensable: *Three Hispanic Word Studies*, pp. 227–243, especially 240–241.

maroma (M. J.-Sp.) 'métier à broder'; also 'rope', as in Spanish; Moroc. Ar. *mremma* 393 n. 16. DCECH, III, 856–857, cites Vulg. Ar. *mabrūm* 'wire rope, cable', on *bárama* 'to twist, twine (a rope)'; also Steingass, *Arabic*, p. 424.

mazal (E. J.-Sp.) 'luck; good fortune' 143 (vv. 13*b*, 15*b*) (H. *mazāl* 'luck, fortune, fate, destiny)'; also FLSJ, V, 536.

medved', mèdvjed, medved (Pan-Slavic) 'bear' = 'the one who eats (knows about or sees) the honey' (*mëd*) 433 n. 60; reflecting a linguistic taboo for names of dangerous or destructive animals (Entwistle and Morison, p. 19). See Skok, II, 398; also **García** (above).

mexeriqueiro (Port.) 'informer' (= Sp. *chivato*) 428 n. 30, 430 n. 40; on L. *mĭscēre*; Port. *mexer* (DELP, IV, 125; and cognates). For more details, see DCECH, IV, 9–10, s.v. *mecer*. Note how the same concept of 'mixing' denotes the Cid's defamation by evil *mestureros* ('cizañeros, malsines') (< L. *mĭsturāriu*; on *mĭstūra*), who betray the hero

in the eyes of King Alfonso, leading to his subsequent exile: "et los ricos omnes ...,
auiendo muy grand enuidia al Çid, trabiaronse de *mezclarle* otra uez con el rey don
Alfonso" (PCG, II, Chap. 850, p. 523*a*.37–40; CRC, pp. 94–95; C1344, III, 418–419;
Ocampiana, fol. cccij*b*); so also in the *Libro de buen amor*: "mescláronme con ella"
(con la dueña) 93*d*. For *mestureros*, see CMC, III, 757: "Por malos mestureros / de
tierra sodes echado" (v. 267). Compare O. Prov. *mesclar* 'soulever (une querelle)'
(Levy; Hackett, III, 795).

misal (M. J.-Sp.) 'Christian missal, prayer-book' 132 (v. 39*b*), 157 (v. 59*b*), 439 n. 81;
de-Christianized as *anisal, anisar, lisal, lissal, misar, nisar, a rezar*; *nisar* is
influenced by *Nîṣān* (first religious month and 7th civil month of the Jewish
calendar); *anisar* 127, 129 (v. 15*b*), 132 (v. 37*b*), 134 (vv. 26*b*, 28*b*), 151 (v. 15+),
162, 425 n. 11; *libro de rezar, libro misal* 425 n. 11; *lisal* 151 (v. 15+); *resal* 151 (v.
15+), 152 (v. 16+).

mor (M. J.-Sp.): *por mor de ti* (< *por amor de ti*) 'because of you; on your account' 89
(v. 21*a*). See Bendayán, p. 357*b*; Benharroch, p. 536. The same construction is well
known in Andalucía, Salamanca, and León (I suppose also in Extremadura and
probably in many other areas, though, at the moment, I have no documentation):
Alcalá Venceslada, pp. 412*b*–413*a*; Lamano, p. 543; Millán Urdiales, p. 335*a*. E. J.-
Sp. used the expression *por modre de ti* (Nehama, p. 366*c*). *Por mor de* is well
documented in Golden Age texts: "¿Vos cómo os llamáis? —Elvira. ¿Y vos? —Yo,
Elvirote; por mordella" (Correas, *Vocabulario*, ed. Infantes, p. 510*b*; ed. Combet, p.
524*a*); other early documentation: Lamano, p. 543; DCECH, I, 232*b*.

moro franco (E. J.-Sp.) 'European or foreign Moor' 401 n. 29; in E. J.-Sp. one said
vestirse a la franca 's'habiller à la manière occidentale'; *los frankos* were Europeans
(Nehama, p. 216, s.vv. *franka, frankito, franko*). I would suspect the usage goes back,
at least, to Crusader times. Near Eastern languages attest to multiple cognates: e.g. Ar.
al-ifranj 'the Europeans' (Wehr-Cowan, p. 710); *lafarnag* 'to adopt European habits
or manners' (Spiro, p. 332); compare T. *frenk, frengi* 'European' (Hony and İz, s.v.);
Pers. *farang, farangī* 'a Frank, European; a Christian' (Steingass, *Persian*, pp.
922–923; Palmer, p. 452); as also do various Balkan languages: compare Miklosich,
p. 297, s.v. *firénk*; Knežević, p. 126; Škaljić, p. 285, s.vv. *frèndija, frèngi*; Maced.-
Rum. *fréngu, frîncu* (Papahagi, pp. 468, 471, s.vv.); Alb. *freng* 'französisch'; *frenk*
'(West)europäer' (Boretzky, p. 51); For more data, see **franco** (above). Regarding
Palestinian Yiddish *frenk,* in the context of rivalries (if not hatred) between
Sephardim and *Yidishim* in Old Jerusalem, Kosover's detailed discussion is crucial:
pp. 212–219 (especially ¶233–235). Similar tensions and unfortunate scenarios were
again to arise and be replayed in the U.S., especially in New York and Seattle. See
Papo, "Sephardim in North America," pp. 270–276.

mocedad, mosedade 'virginity' 152 (v. 20*b*), 161 (v. 5*b*); see *En torno*, pp. 203–207.

moto 35 (v. 70*b*): read *mote*, as in texts *BC*.

nisán (M. J.-Sp.): first month of Jewish religious calendar; 7th month of civil calendar
(*Nîṣân*) 425 n. 11. See also above: **misal**.

palabrada (M. J.-Sp.) 'pledged (in marriage); engaged' 25 (v. 26*a*) (Sp. *apalabrada*).

perro moro (E. & M. J.-Sp.) 'Moorish dog' 19 (vv. 28*a*, 29*a*). This is patterned on the classic Arabic insult, *kalb bin-al-kalb*, a seriously aggravated imprecation, given the "unclean" nature of dogs (pigs, donkeys, etc.), according to Muslim criteria, which reject the concept of dogs as house pets or as outdoor companions. Note also *yā ibn al-kalb* 'you son of a bitch!' (Spiro, p. 380, s.v. *kalb*); identically, in Moroccan Arabic: *ā-wuld-el-kalb* 'oh, enfant de salaud!'. The splendid *Colin* dictionary expatiates—in delicious detail—upon the negative implications of *kelb*: not only 'chien', but also: 'individu vil et impudique, sans pudeur, sans vergogne; vaurien, salopard; individu sans moralité, sans honneur; salaud; canaille, homme débauché, de mauvaise vie, sans dignité'(!) (ed. Iraqui Sinaceur, VII, 1689). *Kelba* gets similar, though less detailed, treatment. I am reminded, finally, of a proverb, learned many years ago in Morocco: *ᶜasel fe-jeld el kelb* 'There is honey [even] in a dog's skin', which would seem to go, though it be only a short way, toward vindicating the species. Compare the Yiddish expression, which acknowledges a miserly, useless and valueless gift: *A sheynen dank fir aich! Afilu a hor fun a hazer is vert mer fun gornit!* ('Thank you so very much! Even a pig's bristle is worth more than nothing at all'). James Matisoff records a close and indeed even more gravely insulting variant, since it seems to equate the person addressed with the pig: "*A sheynem dank fir aykh—fun a khazer a hor iz oykh epes*" ('Thanks loads—coming from a pig, even a hair is something') (Matisoff, *Blessings, Curses*, 1st ed., p. 12; 2d ed., p. 15). This saying, which, I suggest, may have reached Eastern Europe by means of a Turkish intermediary, has an Arabic source (or analogue), that, at the moment, I cannot document. I can only cite from memory: "*Šaᶜr min ist al-ḥinzīr ḥairun ktīr*" ('A hair from a pig's arse is a great good thing'). For Ar. *kalb ibn kalb* and similar, though not quite so insulting, abusive expressions in Palestinian Yiddish, see Kosover, pp. 302–304 (especially ¶¶493 and 493 [*bis*]). For more data, see also FLSJ, V, 265, n. 109. Note too the dog insults documented by Nehama (p. 430). I seem to remember reading (though I cannot now specify the source) that, on being informed that the king of England had just made a treaty with the king of France, one of the Turkish sultans exclaimed: "How could it possibly be of interest to me that a pig had made friends with a dog?" Cats, on the other hand, were vindicated and greatly esteemed, because Muḥammad's good friend, Abū Huraira,—'the father (or owner) of the kitten'—an early convert to Islam, convinced the Prophet of the cat's cleanliness and value and always took a kitten with him while he watched his herd of goats (*Encyclopédie de l'Islam*, new ed., Vol. I, J. Robson, pp. 132–133).

plumo (M. J.-Sp.) 'eiderdown' 11*H*.7, 136 (v. 2*a*), 150 (v. 11*a*) (Sp. *plumón*).

polidad: *See* **poridad**.

poner 'to put': **pusió** (M. J.-Sp.) 'he put' 84 (v. 35*b*). The regular (or "weak") preterite ending -*ió* has been combined with the strong preterite *puso* (Sp. *puso*).

poridad (M. J.-Sp.) 'secrecy' 146, 177; *polidad, puridad* 152 (v. 20*b*) (O. Sp. *poridat, poridad*). *Poridad*, as in *Poridat de las poridades* (= *Secretum secretorum*), is a semantic calque, perhaps based on *khalaṣa* 'to be pure'; compare Ar. *khāliṣ* 'pure'; *khulūṣ* 'purity' (A. Castro, *Structure*, p. 100; Steingass, *Arabic*, p. 312). There can be no doubt that Don Américo was altogether correct in seeing an Arabic-based semantic calque in O. Sp. *poridad, poridat*, but, in this case, there is an even more convincing, closer, and more obvious origin. The Old Spanish *Poridat de las poridades* (ed. Kasten) is a translation of the Arabic treatise *Sirr al-asrār* ('Secret of Secrets'). Ar. *sirr* does, of course, primarily mean 'secret,' but also among its many connotations are 'the pure, or choice, or best part of anything; the pure, or genuine, quality of race or lineage' (Lane, IV, 1338*b*); *sarārat* 'pureté, perfection, le meilleur état d'une chose' (Biberstein Kazimirski, I, 1075*a*); *sarārat* 'optima rei conditio; puritas' (Freitag, II, 304*b*). So the medieval Spanish translator(s) would not have had to look beyond the very title of the work they were translating to discover a proper designation for their Castilian version. I suspect, indeed, that *poridat*, modeled on *sirr*, may already have gone over into the spoken language.

primo, prima (Sp.; M. J.-Sp.) 'beloved': Is there a possible relationship to tribal endogamy? See pp. 406–407 n. 51.

puerpo (M. J.-Sp.) 'body' 132 (v. 27*b*); the form is much more characteristic of E. J.-Sp. Neither Benoliel, nor Bendayán, nor yet Benharroch list it. See Nehama's extensive entry (s.v. *pwerpo*, p. 459). The labial articulation of *-u-* (= *w*) might have assimilated *k* to *p*. On the other hand, Wagner (*Beiträge*, p. 118) points to the assimilation of the initial *k* to the second *p*: *Fernassimilation*. See also Crews, p. 270, ¶1339. An opposite tendency is also evident in both major dialects of J.-Sp., where *puerco* gives *cuerco* in Morocco and *quierco* in Salonika (Attias, no. 50, p. 144, vv. 42–43; Attias translates: *khazîr*). So Wagner may very well be right. Note also M. J.-Sp. *encuerco* (= *empuerco*), *cuedo* (= *puedo*), *cuesto* (= *puesto*) (Benoliel, Vol. XIII, 355, 358).

puerta(s) de (los) reyes, puerta del rey (M. J.-Sp.; E. J.-Sp.) '(at) the king's court' 182 (v. 13*a*), 216 (v. 34*a*), 246 (v. 58*a*). The Sp. expression, already documented in O. Sp. (*Calila e Dimna*), is a semantic calque based on Ar. *bāb al-malik* (or *bāb al-sulṭān*) or, in E. J.-Sp., on T. *kapı*. The same formulation comes over into English when referring to the Ottoman government as the *Sublime Porte* (< Turkish-Arabic *Babiâlî*). The concept is expressed in various Near Eastern and South Asian languages and probably can already be documented many centuries earlier: *Babylon* being possibly the 'court (= door) of God'. For more details, see S. G. A. and James T. Monroe, "J.-Sp. *puertas de rey(es)* 'royal courts'." Note also Anglo-Indian *durbar, darbar* 'the court or hall of audience (of a king or chief)' (Yule and Burnell, p. 331; I. Lewis, p. 106*b*); from Pers. *darbār* 'a court area; a court or levee of a prince; an audience chamber'; on *dar* 'door, gate, passage, doorway, gateway' (Steingass, *Persian*, pp. 506, 508). This is the same I. E. root *dhuĕr- (dhwer-)* that will give us Eng. *door*, Gk. *thúra*, Skt. *dvārah*, O. Ir. *dorus*, Alb. *derë*, Toch. B *twere*, etc. (Pokorny, I, 278–279; C. Watkins, p. 15; Orel, p. 60; Meyer, p. 63).

quento (16th-cent. Sp.; Mod. Sp.) 'a large sum of money' 71 (v. 12*b*); *quētos* 72 (v. 14*b*) (Sp. *cuento* 'a million; a million millions; a billion').

raina (Granada) 'queen' 220 (v. 9*b*) (Sp. *reina*).

resal (M. J.-Sp.) 'prayer (book)' 151 (v. 15+), 152 (v. 16+) (Sp. *rezar* + *-al*, as in *misal*). See **misal**.

revolar (M. J.-Sp.) 'to fly away (again)' 129 (v. 16*b*) (Sp. *volar, revolar*). See also **arrevolar** (above).

roçagante (16th-cent. Sp.) 'extravagant, ostentatious; trailing (as a garment)'; *roçegante* 35 (v. 68*a*), 42 (v. 15*a*), 402 n. 31 (see DCECH, V, 48, 79: s.vv. *rocín, rozar*; DECLlC, VII, 475–480: s.v. *rossegar*).

rosillo (Argentina) 'light red, roan' 182 (v. 5*a*); possibly translates *alazán*.

rosiñol 'nightingale' 73 (v. 19*b*), 79 (v. 20*b*) (= Attias 3.4, pp. 119–120, v. 40; *La jactancia del Conde Vélez*, from Salonika or Larissa). In Crews' text (no. 10), also from Salonika, the form *rušiñó* (75, v. 19*b*), though better preserved, heralds an initial step toward the more aberrant forms we find in Coello's text of *Conde Vélez*: *rusción* 77 (v. 18*b*) and sparsely documented also in Eastern versions of *El conde Niño*: *rošió* (or *rušió*) (FLSJ, I, no. 12 v. 3), *rujiol* (Attias, no. 16, v. 6), *ruxión* (CMP J1.12) and *rusiyó* (CMP J1.13), all from Salonika (except Attias, in which case, as we have just seen, we don't know whether from Salonika or from Larissa). In both his texts, Attias correctly translates: *zāmîr* 'nightingale', which, of course, also embodies the Hebrew root *ZMR* 'song, sing' (Gesenius, p. 248; Brown et al., p. 278). For Moroccan J.-Sp., Bendayán lists only the academic form *ruiseñor* (pp. 625, 1167) and I do not remember any instances in M. J.-Sp. *romances*. In their origins, the Classical and Germanic languages have rightly and persistently associated the names for the nightingale with singing: Lat. *lŭscĭnĭa* may well derive from **lucs-cinia* 'dem dämmernden Lichte (Tage) entgegensingend' (among other possibilities, all involving singing) (Walde, p. 448); in Ancient and Modern Greek, *nightingale* is *'aēdón* or *'aēdoni*, which is related to *'aeídō* 'to sing' and other cognates (Boisacq, p. 15; Woodhouse, p. 558; Liddell and Scott, p. 29; Kontopoulos, II, 337; Pring, p. 211); and in our Germanic languages, the *-gal(l)(e)* in English *nightingale* and German *Nachtigall* goes back to an Ancient Germanic **galan* 'to sing' (also related to Eng. *yell*), as in O. H. Ger. *galan* and O. N. *gala*, so the nightingale, true to its name, is the 'night singer' (Skeat, p. 393; Onions, pp. 610, 1019; Kluge, p. 408; Noreen, p. 224, ¶427; compare also De Vries and Tollenaere, p. 261: *nachtegale*; Falk and Torp, I, 757: *nattergal*). So whether they be learned or unknown traditional poets, all have been overcome by the nightingale's superb singing: Keats' *Ode to a Nightingale* ("now more than ever seems it rich to die . . ."), or Marius Barbeau's classic collection of French-Canadian traditional poetry, *Le rossignol y chante*, or again, the unknown Catalan singers who crafted the deliciously nostalgic *Lo rossinyol*: "Rossinyol, que vas a França, rossinyol, / encomana'm a la mare, rossinyol" (Capmany, no. XXXIX). In the E. J.-Sp. tradition, the Hispano-Romance word(s) for 'nightingale' was (were), we can be sure, definitively regressive, if not at the final point of disappearing. Much more familiar now was its Turkish counterpart, *bülbül*, which is pan-Balkan in distribution (Miklosich, p. 270, s.v.) and known also to modern Sephardim from the popular song: *Los bilbilicos cantan* (see Nehama, pp. 87, 89; s.vv. *berbíl, bilbíl*). *Bulbul* is also known in Arabic, which is the probable source of the Turkish word. Compare also Pers. *bulbul* and *bulbulistān* 'a place abounding in nightingales' (Steingass, *Persian*, p. 197). Turning again to Spanish *ruiseñor*, the word attests, even in its academic form, to the repeated impact of popular etymology: *Ruy + señor = Rodrigo + señor*. Another popular-etymological solution occurs in a beautiful version of *El prisionero*, which I collected in San Ciprián de Sanabria, in 1963, where the single little bird (*avecica*) of the 16th-cent. renditions has been transformed into three birds, in line with the modern version's genial tripartite structure: "Si no son tres pasarcitos, / que me cantan el albor: // Uno era la calandra, / otro era el *reyseñor*, // otro era la golondrina, / la que lo hacía mejor" (Armistead, "Los siglos," p. xix). The same combination is widely known in Galician: *reiseñor* or *reisiñor* (Crespo Pozo, p. 576; *Irmandades da Fala*, p. 231; Carré Alvarellos, p. 640; García et al., p. 1005 [here *rousinol* is cited as an alternative]; Navaza Blanco, p. 495). Essentially all the Western Romance languages have unanimously adopted variations on an undocumented masculine diminutive of Lat. *lŭscĭnĭus*: **lŭscĭnĭŏlus*: Fr. *rossignol*, O. Prov. *rosinhol*, Cat. *rossinyol*, Port. *rouxinal*, It. *usignuolo* (REW, p. 421, no. 5180), Sardinian *rosiñólu* (Wagner, II, 363). A feminine **lŭscĭnĭŏla* 'a little nightingale' is, however, documented in Latin (Glare, p. 1052). There are many conservative Italian regional variations: *rossignolo, russignòl* (Venetian: Boerio, p. 584; Durante and Turato, p. 167); *riscignuolu* (et al.) (Calabrese: Rohlfs, III, 90): *rusign(u)olu* (Sicilian: Mortillaro, II, 221). It would seem very likely that Provence, with its famous poetic heritage, may have played a crucial role in exporting its particular rendition of **lŭscĭnĭŏlus* to other Romance linguistic domains; certainly to northern France and probably to other regions as well: "Le mot prov[ençal] doit sans doute sa diffusion au rôle du rossignol dans la poésie des troubadours" (Bloch-von Wartburg, p. 561). See also Rohlfs, *Léxico románico*, p. 40. Only a few outlying, conservative, lateral areas have opted for different solutions: Romantsch has derivatives of *lŭscĭnĭus*: *luscheina* (Sursilvan: Vieli and Decurtins, p. 357; other variants: REW, p. 421, no. 5179). Rumanian, however, chose a totally different and somewhat less romantic solution: The nightingale becomes a night watchman! Or again a "night watch woman," attending a wake: *priveghetor* 'ruiseñor macho'; or the academically accepted feminine term *privighetoáre*: "Mică pasăre, . . . care cîntă foarte frumos" (Macrea, *Dicţionarul*, p. 665; Cioranescu, p. 669, s.v. *priveghia*: < Lat. *pervĭgĭlare*). Macedo-Rumanian, on the other hand, chooses the Gk. word *aĭdóna, aĭdone* 'rossignol', also listing two synonyms: the pan-Balkan *bilbiliu* (from Turkish) and *viglitoare*, which echoes the Daco-Rumanian 'watchman' (Papahagi, p. 75). For detailed discussions of *ruiseñor* and *rossinyol* and their relatives, see DCECH, V, 93–94; DECLIC, VII, 480–482; DELP, V, 122, s.v. *rouxinol*. Yet another variant, *rosinól*, originates in Valle de Benasque, on the French border, in the boundary region of Ribagorza, at the linguistic frontier between Aragonese and Catalan: "Cante be el rosinól" (Ballarín Cornel, p. 193); on the region, see Alvar, *El dialecto aragonés*, pp. 11–12; Zamora Vicente, *Dialectología*, pp. 160–226; 2d ed., 211–286.

rublas 'ruble (Russian coin)' 17 (v. 12+) (Sp. *rublo*; here probably combined with J.-Sp. *dublas* 'doubloons').

Sacarrial = *Sacra Real* as in *Sacra Real Magestad* (Am. Sp.) 427 n. 28. Note also **Sara Real Majestad** 183 (v. 21*b*).

sakağí de agwa 'porteur d'eau' 417 n. 70 (Crews, p. 271, n. 1356; T. *saka* 'water carrier'; Crews attributes the T. suffix *-cι* in this J.-Sp. word to the Sephardim's occasionally imperfect knowledge of Turkish). I suppose that T. *saka* may be related to Vulg. Ar. *zaqq*; Cl. Ar. *ziqq* 'skin (as a receptacle)'; compare Pers. *ziqq* 'a skin used as a bottle (for wine)'; the colloquial Hispano-Arabic form gave Sp. *zaque* 'odre' (DCECH, VI, 81; Corriente, *Arabismos*, p. 476). A Sp. curse, from the late stages of the Reconquest, warned of the dangers of becoming a *cautivo*: "¡Que te mueras en Ronda, jalando zaques!"

salir 'to go out': **saldrís** (M. J.-Sp.) 'you will go out' 25 (v. 29*a*) (Sp. *saldréis*).

salvajes (M. J.-Sp.) 'wildmen' 25 (v. 23*a*). Wildmen were indeed sometimes represented as servants in Golden Age Spanish narrative. The wildman will be studied in detail in FLSJ, VII, in regard to the *romance* of *Moriana y Galván*. We may mention beforehand that a vigorous wildman tradition is still alive and well in parts of northern Europe, as I had the delightful opportunity to observe at first hand, during a recent trip to Basel (Switzerland): On a yearly basis, an immediately recognizable wildman appears, accompanied by a lion and a griffin and carrying an uprooted pine tree as his weapon. The three figures, representatives of three medieval guilds, parade through Kleinbasel (on the north bank of the Rhine), to the acclaim of enthusiastic crowds. For now, see Knuchel, *Vogel Gryff*, and E. A. Meier's richly illustrated and amply documented book of the same title. The short *Wild Ma-Gässli* 'wildman's alley', more like a tunnel under one of the buildings facing the Rhine, still leads to the pedestrian walkway that follows the Rhine (a modern photograph and 19th-cent. representation: Meier, pp. 20–21, 48–49).

sandá (E. J.-Sp.) 'sendal, a thin silk or linen'; *enforada* ('*forrada*') *con sandá* 'lined with silk' 18 (v. 21*b*). For modern E. J.-Sp. singers, the word *sandá* would be a meaningless fossil. O. Sp. *çendal* 'tela de seda muy delgada' (CMC, III, 571–572; DCECH, II, 28–29 ["de origen incierto"]); compare also FLSJ, III, 408–409, s.v. *sedale;* O. Fr. *cendaus*; O. Prov. *cendal, cendat, cendai* (Levy, p. 75; Hackett, III, 654).

San Ǧenar: *See* **Ǧenar.**

Sanǧeruán, Sanǧiguare, Sanjiguale, San Xuan: *See* **San Juan.**

San Juan (M. J.-Sp.) 'June'; Gal. *San Xoan*; Port. *São João* 400 n. 29. See FLSJ, V, 563; also D. Alonso, "Junio y Julio"; my "Portuguesismos"; note also *Santiago* 'July' (FLSJ, V, 390 n. 20; 563).

šarales (M. J.-Sp.) 'thickets, undergrowth' 132 (v. 32*a*), 134 (v. 21*a*), 156 (v. 47*a*) (Sp. *jaral, jara*; Hisp. Ar. *šáᶜra*; Cl. Ar. *šaᶜrā*; Wehr-Cowan, p. 473, s.v. *šaᶜrā* 'scrub country'); DCECH, III, 492*b*–493; Dozy, *Suppl.*, I, 763*a*; DAA, pp. 283–284; *Tent. Dict.*, p. 739, s.vv. *xara, xaral*; toponymy: *La Jara*, in numerous Peninsular locations; the M. J.-Sp. word is, I believe, clearly of ancient Peninsular origin, seemingly unaffected by subsequent contact with Arabic, and, to my knowledge, *šaᶜra* seems not to be used in Morocco. For more specifics: Corriente, *Arabismos*, pp. 307–308 (s.vv. *(en)xara; jara*); Asín Palacios, *Toponimia*, p. 114. Note also extensive treatment of the narrative formula: "de noche por los caminos, / de día por los xarales" (FLSJ, V, 119–124 & n. 122; 521).

Sara Real Majestad: *See* **Sacarrial.**

se (Leonese; Asturian) 'if' 431 n. 45 (v. 27) (Sp. *si*; Port. *se*).

setí probably 'satin', but possibly influenced by *ceptí* (< *Cepta* 'Ceuta') 31 (v. 8*b*). See DECLIC, VII, s.v. *setí* (pp. 877–879); Moroc. Ar. *Sebta*; or phonetically [*sébtsa*] = Ceuta.

sirma (E. J.-Sp.) 'silver thread' 15 (v. 21*a*), 18 (v. 19*b*), 53 (v. 22*b*) (T. *sırma*). See Nehama, p. 15, s.v.; FLSJ, I, 638; V, 564; also Maced.-Rum. *sirmă* 'soie; fil metallique' (Papahagi, p. 952).

slap (Scots) 'a narrow pass between two hills' 273, 447 n. 133.

sobrial (M. J.-Sp.) = Sp. *su brial* 182 (v. 4*b*); see **brial**.

soler 'to be accustomed': **suelgo** (non-standard Sp.; Leonese: Zamora) 'I am accustomed to' 216 (vv. 16*b*, 18*b*), 431 n. 45 (vv. 17, 19).

syne (Scots) 'then, afterward; thereupon' (= Eng. *since*) 273. See Warrack, p. 574, s.vv. *syn, syne*; Child, V, 381*b*; Kynoch, p. 91: as in *lang syne*: J. A. C. Stevenson, p. 207.

tafetán (M. J.-Sp.) 'taffeta, cloth of thick-woven silk' 28 (v. 52*b*), 393 n. 16; *tafetal* 27 (v. 38*b*) (Sp. *tafetán*); from Pers. *tāftan* 'to twist, bend; shine'; *tāfta* 'twisted, woven; shining' (Steingass, *Persian*, p. 276; Palmer, p. 124, Corriente, *Arabismos*, p. 446). The Persian word reaches Castilian by way of Italian and/or Catalan mediation (Migliorini, p. 566, s.v. *taffettà*); DCECH, V, 373–374; DECLIC, VIII, 205–206 (s.v. *tafetà*); DELP, V, 257 (s.v. *tafetà*; also Galician: Navaza Blanco, p. 555); Skeat, p. 621 (s.vv. *taffeta, taffety*); Onions, p. 899.

tefter (E. J.-Sp.) 'notebook' 142 (v. 12*a*); Nehama, p. 545 *a–b* (T. *defter* 'register; account-book, notebook; list, catalogue'). Derived from Ar. *daftar* 'booklet, notebook, copybook' etc. (Wehr-Cowan, p. 285); also Pers., Urdu, and Hindi *daftar* (Steingass, *Persian*, pp. 528–529; Platts, p. 519*b*). The word is essentially pan-Balkan: Miklosich (p. 172) lists Bulgarian, Serbian, Albanian, Greek forms; see also Škaljić, p. 208; Skok, III, 451–452; it is also known in Rum.: *defter* (Cioranescu, p. 280) and is, in addition, common to most Turkic languages (Öztopçu, p. 101), including also Gagaúz (Zajączkowski, p. 69). Concerning Serbo-Croatian forms, see also Stachowski, p. 162; for Albanian: *defter, tefter* (Boretzky, p. 40). The Ar. word is a borrowing from Greek: *difthera* 'Fell, Art Pergament' (Miklosich), which is also the origin of Eng. *diphtheria* (Onions, p. 27; Skeat, p. 168). From Hindi, by way of Persian, *daftar* was taken over by Anglo-Indian: *defter, dufter* (Yule and Burnell, p. 329; I. Lewis, p. 106). In Hindi, *daftar* has greatly expanded semantically — recalling, one might suppose, British plus Indian administrative practice — and, in addition to a 'list, roll, volume (of documents)', it may also denote 'a record-office, an archive, an office, a place of business, a report' (McGregor, p. 476).

tener 'to have': **tengoy** (M. J.-Sp.) 'I have' 155 (v. 43*b*); in M. J.-Sp. some verbs acquire the standard Sp. irregular 1st pers. sing. suffix, as in *soy, estoy, doy, voy* (Sp. *tengo*). According to Benoliel, this was a relatively recent development (p. 352).

torneo (M. J.-Sp.) 'celebration, spectacle, pageant'(?) 281 (v. 38), 282 n. 145 (v. 38); see FLSJ, III, 136, n. 12: *El sueño de doña Alda* (Sp. *torneo* 'tourney, tournament').

traer 'to bring': **trougera** (Leonese-Galician) "si no me lo trougera" 89 (v. 19*a*) (Sp. *trajera*; non-standard *trujera*; O. Sp. *truxera*; Port. and Gal. *trouxera*). See Navaza Blanco, p. xxxiii.

u (non-standard Sp.: Zamora) 'or' 217 (v. 43*a*), 431 n. 45; not exclusively before word-initial *o-*, as in standard Sp.; a widely distributed vulgarism (Bénichou, "Observaciones," p. 256*c*) (Sp. *o, u*).

*ulkuos, *ulp- (I. E.) 'wolf'; "Raubtierbezeichnungen" (taboo words referring to predatory canine animals) 434 n. 60; Pokorny (pp. 1178–1179) suggests that the abundant Indoeuropean evidence has, in many cases, already been altered or transformed because of traditional taboos concerning the wolf ("vielfach tabuistisch entstellt . . . es handelt sich zweifellos um verschiedene tabuistische Umbildungen"). Note also Alb. *ujk*, O. Alb. *ulk* (Orel, p. 484; Meyer, p. 457); Lith. *vĩlkas* (Bender, p. 293).

umá (M. J.-Sp.) 'in regard to, as far as *X* is concerned' 147 (v. 24*a*), 153 (v. 24), 158 (v. 61+), 163 (v. 24*a*), 177 (Moroc. Ar. *wa-amma, wamma* 'quant à'; *Colin*, I, p. 28; also Spiro, p. 32). See FLSJ, III, 409, s.v. *umá*; also **imá** *supra*.

vai, veis: *See* **ir.**

veluntad (E. J.-Sp.) 'will'; *lágrimas de veluntad* 'heartfelt tears' 144 (vv. 7*b*, 9*b*). See FLSJ, I, 639; Nehama, p. 583 (Sp. *voluntad*).

verdugo (M. J.-Sp.) meaning? 281 (v. 33*a*), 282 n. 145; *verdugo* has various meanings in Sp., none of which fit in the present context; one is a type of sword, but would the girl, no matter how brave, take a sword in hand when asking a favor of a king?

vidro (M. J.-Sp.) 'glass' 281 (v. 10+*a*). Latin knew both *vĭtrĕum* and *vĭtrum* and, in O. Sp., *vidro* exists side-by-side with *vidrio* (*Tent. Dict.*, p. 731; Kasten and Nitti, *Alfonso X*, III, 1878–1879, s.vv. *vidrio* and *vidro*), the former being "una forma vulgar . . . [que] tiene gran extensión" (DCECH, V, 804–805). There is no need, in this case, to think of a Portuguesism, despite Cynthia Crews' as always perceptive observations (*Recherches*, pp. 212–213, ¶478). See Benoliel, p. 279; Bendayán, p. 733; Benharroch, p. 629.

vosté (Leonese: Zamora) 'you' 216 (v. 4*b*), 430 n. 45; see Corominas' extensive discussion (DCECH, V, 843–845, s.v. *vos*; DECLlC, IX, 399–403, s.v. *vós*); DELP, V, 407, s.v. *vossemecê* or *vossamercê*; Galician: *vostede*: Navaza Blanco, p. 611.

whin (Scots) 'furze' 267 n. 126; Warrack, p. 647 (with cognates).
wile (Scots) 'wild; vile' 269 n. 129; Warrack, p. 653.

xaral: *See* **šarales.**
xarav (M. J.-Sp.) 'hill, elevation' 164 & n. 14 (v. 35) (Moroc. Ar. *šaraf* 'élevation [dans le caractère]'; Mercier, p. 197; *Colin*, IV, 930–931; Cl. Ar. 'elevated place'; Wehr-Cowan, p. 467; Corriente, *Arabismos*, p. 104, s.vv. *ajarafe* and *aljarafe* 'terreno elevado'; Hisp. Ar. ŠRF, Corriente, p. 280*b*). Most Arabic references are abstract concepts, abstractions implying 'nobility, illustrious rank, exalted status, age, honor, descent from the Prophet,' etc. (*Colin*, IV, 930–931), but note also such Peninsular toponyms as *Aljarafe* (Sevilla) 'el otero'; *Aljorf* or *Alchorf* (Valencia) 'el alto' (Asín Palacios, *Toponimia*, p. 65). The *Šorfa* (*Chorfa*) are the reigning *ᶜAlawīya* dynasty of Morocco.

yanfés: *See* **ǧanfés al.**

yelikos (E. J.-Sp.): I do not know the meaning or the origin of this form: 143 (v. 1*a*). In the context in which it is used, it might seem to be a rhythmic filler word, such as *hey nonny no, dydeedée* and the like, but I may well be wrong (?).

Yenar: *See* Ǧenar.

yolǧís (E. J.-Sp.) 'travelers' 417 n. 70 (T. *yolcu* 'traveler, passenger'; on T. *yol* 'road, path'; see Miklosich, p. 136; Škaljić, p. 372). Note also Alb. *jollxhi* 'Wanderer' (< *yolcu* 'Reisender'; Boretzky, p. 70).

zarzahán: *See* çarçahán.

PLATES

PLATES

1. Francisco Salinas cites the second verse, with music, of *Conde Claros insomne* (*De Musica*, p. 342).
2. Francisco Salinas again cites the second verse, with music, of *Conde Claros insomne* (*De Musica*, p. 346), omitting the crucial words *con amores*.
3. Yacob Yoná prints *Conde Claros y el emperador* (*Livriko de romansas*, Sofia, Bulgaria, 1908).
4. A 15th-century MS of *La jactancia del conde Vélez* (Bibl. Nacional, Madrid).
5. *Conde Claros y el emperador*: A Gothic-letter *pliego suelto* (Bibl. Nacional, Madrid).
6. *Conde Claros insomne*: A 16th-century pen trial from the binding of a Morisco MS (Almonacid papers, Escuela de Estudios Árabes, Madrid).
7. A modern interpretation of *Conde Claros fraile* (according to Joan G. Junceda, in Marian Aguiló i Fuster, *Romancer popular de la terra catalana*, Barcelona: La Llumenera, 1947, p. 179).
8. A modern interpretation of *Conde Claros fraile* (Joan G. Junceda, in Marian Aguiló i Fuster, *Romancer popular*, p. 181).
9. Luna Elaluf Farache, from Tetuán, sang for us all four of the Conde Claros ballads current in Morocco.

Cuius cantus apud Hifpanos talis eft.

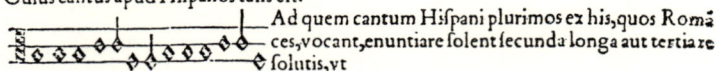

Ad quem cantum Hifpani plurimos ex his,quos Romã ces,vocant,enuntiare folent fecunda longa aut tertia re folutis,vt

Conde Claros con amores nopodia repofar.

Poteft etiam cum dipodia iambica hic pes coniunctus inueniri,vt in hoc metro

Virtus eft benignitas.

Si moloffus percutiatur in vltima,vt dijambus etiam in vltima feriatnr,quod iambi natura poftulat,cuius cantu ab Hifpanis accepto vtuntur Itali ad faltationis genus, quam Gallardam appellant,& optimi modulatores ad difcantandum,vt dicunt;qui talis eft

Super quem tenorem ego Romæ modulantem audiui coram Paulo 3. Pont.Max.Francifcum Mediolanenfem, qui fuit fui temporis Citharœdorum facilè princeps,&mihi valde familiaris.Pétametrum autem, quod vnicũ diximus inueniri,illud eft,quod Victorinus Laconicum appellatũ fuiffe dicit

Ite ò parcæ primores nunc fauftæ parcas ducentes.

Cui fyllabam fi adijcias,fiet te trametrum difpondaicũ.Octo metrum vero, quod in verbis nullum inueniffe me dixi,in fonis tale apud Italos ad eiufdē faltationis,genus inftitutũ eft

Et de molofsico quidem in tro hæc dixiffe fatis fit. Nunc ad reliqua metra fenorum tē porum explicanda pergamus, in quibus eundem ordinem, quem in fuperioribus tenuimus,fequemur,vt illud primum ftatuamus,aliud ex quo per epiplocas reliqua,aliud ex alio nafcentur;quod rationi congruit antifpafticum effe;deinde ionicum à maiori; poftea choriambicum:poftremo ionicum à minori;quoniam antifpafticum incipit à breui,quæ longa prior eft,vt vnitas binario:reliqua verò tria vel à duabus longis, vel à longa, vel à duabus breuibus incipiunt.Exempla in quibus hæ demõftrantur epiplocæ,hæc effe poffunt, nam affumpto Horatianæ odes initio

Miferarum eft,neque amori dare ludum.

Quod ionicis à minori conftat,fi præponas illi has tres fyllabas. Et, o, quam,fiet metrum antifpafticum hoc modo

Et o quam miferarum eft nec.

A quo detracta prima fyllaba fiet ionicum à maiori fic

O quam miferarum eft neque amori dare.

Et ab hoc eodem modo proueniet choriambicum fic

Quam miferarum eft neque amori dare lu.

Et detracta,quam,quæ reliqua erat ex tribus præpofitis;remanebit ionicum à minori

Miferarum eft neque amori dare ludum.

Quæ,cum ita fe habeant,iure de metris antifpafticis primus habendus eft fermo.Antifpaftica ergo metra pedem principaliter habent antifpaftum, fed tamen cùm antifpaftus ex duobus fimplicibus,iambo videlicet & trochæo,compofitus fit,à principio pro ea parte, qua iambum habet,fpondæum apud poëtas fæpenumero,& quemlibet etiam alium ex dif fyllabis,vt Hephestio ait,recipiunt,medijs autem regionibus, fi pura fuerint, antifpaftũ, & in fine iambicam fyzygiam habent;vt in hoc Horatij carmine

Illi robur & æs triplex,circa pectus erat qui fragilem truci.

Apud

---

1.   Francisco Salinas cites the second verse of *Conde Claros insomne*, together with its music, in his *De Musica Libri Septem* (Salamanca: Mathias Gastius, 1577), p. 342 (facsim. ed. Mario Santiago Kastener, Kassel and Basel: Bärenreiter, 1958) (reproduced with permission).

iori ionico in fine, minori verò intra initia ponamus: quoniam fi moloffus ionicum à maiori præcedat, tres eius longas cum duabus ionici neceffe erit continuari, & fi colloce-tur poft eum, duæ breues ionici quinque longas difgregabunt: & contra fiet, fi præcedat ionicum à minori, quoniam incipit à duabus breuibus, quæ tres longas mololsi ab ipfius duabus feparabunt. Conficitur autem hoc metrum varijs modis: nam aut fit ex fuis pedi-bus, hoc eft ionicis puris, aut ex ijs cum trochaicis dipodijs eiufdem quantitatis admiftis, aut ex anapæftis & tribrachis, atque alijs pedibus, qui per longarum refolutiones varij pro creantur. Quorum exempla inter numerandas eius fpecies fuis quæque locis afferentur: quas vt enumerare iam incipiamus, minimum huius generis metrum, quemadmodum in fuperioribus, monometrum hypercataleɕicum effe dicimus, conftans pede fimplici & fyllaba, vt eft hoc apud Viɕorinum

              Per Leucadiam.

Vel illud apud Senecam   *Quidquid patimur.*

      Quod ab anapæftica dipodia plaufus mefura difcernitur: quoniam in hoc arfis & thefis non in æqualitatis, fed in dupli ratione confiftunt: illa verò di podia æqualitatis ratione côftat, vnde per quaterna tempora, hoc verò per fena plaudendum eft. Præterea in illa fpondæus percutitur in fecunda longa, quia pro ana pæfto pofitus eft, in hoc autem in prima, vt lex huius ionici poftulat. Alterum eft dime-trum brachicataleɕicum ex pede fimplici & fpondæo, quale eft hoc

           Veris coma florens.

Et hoc   *Palmam cape viɕor.*

      Tertium eft dimetrum cataleɕicum ex pede fimplici & minimo metro trochaico, qualia funt hæc

Virtute para viam ∪   *Qui tendis ad æthera.*

      Et epodi, quibus vtuntur Hifpani in canticis earum compofitionum, quas, Romances, appellant, quale eft hoc illius, quæ dicitur

Conde Claros,   *No podia repofar.*

Cuius cantus notifsimus eft.   Quartum eft dimetrum acataleɕicum conftans plerunque hoc ionico & dipo dia trochaica, quæ totidem eft tempo-rum, qualia funt illa

      Nemo volet impudico   *Seruire diu tyranno.*

Quæ admodos illius cantionis, cuius modò mentionem fecimus optimè quadrant: ad quos omnes compofitiones Hifpanæ, quibus hiftoriæ feu fabulæ narrantur, ab antiquis noftris canebantur, qualia funt hæc

      Retrayda eſta la Infanta,   *Bien aſsi como ſolia.*

Quorum cantus antiquifsimus & fimplicifsimus hic erat.

      Quintum dimetrum hypercataleɕicum conftans duobus pedibus & fyllaba, quale eft hoc

Fortis iuuenis ſume roſas.   In cuius repetitione quatuor tempo-ra filentur. Sextum eft trimetrũ bra-chicataleɕicum ex duobus pedibus

& fpondæo, vt hoc

                                      For-

2.   Francisco Salinas again cites verse 2 of *Conde Claros insomne*, together with its music, in his treatise, *De Musica Libri Septem* (1577) p. 346. The crucial words *con amores* are omitted (facsim. ed. Mario Santiago Kastener, Kassel and Basel: Bärenreiter, 1958) (reproduced with permission).

.רומאנסה 10

לו ריל דיאס אי קלאירידאד, קי איל דיאס מוס דאס איל סול,
אי לה גוז' קלאירו לונאר:

אי לה גוז' קלאירו לונאר, לאס מאטייאניקאס לאס מיסטריאס,
קואנדו קירי אלבוריאר:

אי קואנדו קירי אלבוריאר, סי סאסיאס טיזו אי סולדינו, ג'ונטוס
לאן אה און במרחבאר:

אי ג'ונטוס לאן אה און במרחבאר, קי קמבאיום ייזאן די און
פריסייו, אי סור ליר קונאל קוריזאס מאס:

אי סור ליר קונאל קוריזאס מאס, קי קורי אונו אי קורי אוטרו,
ג'ונטוס לאן אה און במרחבאר:

אי ג'ונטוס זאן אה און במרחבאר, אלבאנדו לאן אי פלאטיקאנדו,
לוקי ליס אימפורטס מאס:

אי לוקי ליס אימפורטס מאס, אונס מירכיל לי רונו טיזו,
קונאל מי לה אלים די אטורנאר:

אי קונאל מי לה אלים די אטורנאר, קי מי דים אה בלאנקה
נינייה, סור מוזיר אי סור מינוזל:

אי סור מוזיר אי סור מינוזל, איסטס מירסיד איל מי סולדינו,
נון לו לס פומידו אלצטאר:

אי נון לו לס פומידו אלצטאר, קואנדו לו לס אלזאס דאדו,
נון לס קיזיטים טומאר:

אי נון לס קיזיטים טומאר, קידאדס לה טיננו אין פראנסייה,
סור סיין דובלאס אי אלנו מאס:

אי סור סיין דובלאס אי אלנו מאס, קי דיספוזאדס לה טיננו
אין פראנסייס, אי קון איל קונדי אלינורנאל:

אי קון איל קונדי אלינורנאל, ג'יריבו סוס איל מי סולדינו,
אי לס פוזידים מויי ביין גאנאר:

3.   Yacob Yoná prints *Conde Claros y el emperador* (*Livriko de romansas 'importantes* (Sofia, Bulgaria, 1908), no. 10 (See FLSJ, I, 448).

4. A 15th-century MS of *La jactancia del conde Vélez* (Biblioteca Nacional [Madrid], MS 1317, fol. 454) (reproduced with permission).

¶ Aqui se contienen quatro romãces

viejos. Y este primero es de don Claros de Montalua n; el qual trata de las differencias q̃ huuo cõ el empe= rador, por los amores dela princesa su hija.

A Missa va el emperador
a sant Juan de la mõtiña.
con el yua el conde Claros
por le tener compañia
contando le yua contándo
el menester que auia
dize le desta manera
desta manera dezía
vos me distes emperador
el castillo de Montaluan
distes me lo por mi bien
yo tomelo por mi mal
los moros me lo han cercado
la mañana de sant Juan
tienen lo tambien cercado
que no lo basto a descercar

por mi grán desauentura
y mi gran necessidad
mis armas tẽgo empeñadas
por mil doblas de oro y mas
otras tantas deuo en francia
sobre mi buena verdad
mis caualleros el rey
nò he con que los gouernar
y vna hermana que tengo
no he con que la casar
que en todos mis palacios
no entiendo que ay vn pan
si yo me le como el rey
los mios que comeran
si vuestra alteza no socorre
yo me yre moro a tornar

5.   *Conde Claros y el emperador*: A Gothic-letter *pliego suelto* (Biblioteca Nacional, Madrid: R-9482; *Nuevo Diccionario,* ed. Askins and Infantes, no. 729) (reproduced with permission).

6. *Conde Claros insomne*: "conde claros con amo . . . ," A 16th-century pen trial on a parchment sheet found in the binding of a Morisco MS (Almonacid papers; Escuela de Estudios Árabes, Madrid, *carpeta* 66, *pliego* 1). (See Armistead, "Existió un romancero de tradición oral entre los moriscos?," pp. 224–227.)

— A mi no em reca el morir
ni tampoc d'esser cremada,
me reca la criatura
que és filla de tan bon pare.
Si tengués paper i ploma
jo n'escriuria una carta,
que l'anessen a portar
an el castell de don Carles.
   Les monges són piadoses,
paper i·ploma li daven:
—Paper i ploma tenim,
de tinta no n'hem portada.
   Amb sang de les sues venes
ella n'escriu una carta.
Quan la carta va esser feta

no saben per qui enviar-la.
   —¡Qui tingués un bon correu
que anés volant a entregar-la
i una anada de tres dies
la fes en una jornada!
   Mentre està dient això
un petit vailet entrava,
vol esser patge del Rei
i fa tot lo que li manen.
   —Jo la hi portaré, Senyora,
jo la hi portaré, la carta.
   —No la mostres a ningú,
a ses mans has d'entregar-la.
   Ja ha trobat un bon cavall,
ja l'ensella i l'embridava.

7.   A modern interpretation of *Conde Claros fraile* (according to Joan G. Junceda, in Marian Aguiló i Fuster, *Romancer popular de la terra catalana*, Barcelona: La Llumenera, 1947, p. 179).

8. A modern interpretation of *Conde Claros fraile* (Joan G. Junceda, *Romancer popular,* p. 181). The confession in a prison cell is suggested by the Catalan version, over against typical Castilian texts, where the "*fraile*" is already riding his horse and is preparing to depart with the girl.

9. Our peerless informant from Tetuán, Luna Elaluf Farache (August 1962), knew all four of the Conde Claros ballads current in Morocco: *Emperador, Insomne, Infante,* and *Fraile* (photo: J. H. S.).

Printed in the United States
205626BV00002B/124/P